The Six Wives
of Henry VIII

The Six Wives of Henry VIII

Alison Weir

GROVE WEIDENFELD
New York

Published by Grove Weidenfeld
A division of Grove Press, Inc.
841 Broadway
New York, NY 10003-4793

First published in Great Britain in 1991
by The Bodley Head, London

Due to limitations of space, permissions and acknowledgments appear
on page 644, which constitutes an extension of this copyright page.

Library of Congress Cataloging-in-Publication Date

Weir, Alison.
The six wives of Henry VIII / Alison Weir.—1st American ed.
p.   cm.
Includes bibliographical references and index.
ISBN 0-8021-1497-0
1. Henry VIII, King of England, 1491–1547—Marriage.   2. Great
Britain—History—Henry VIII, 1509–1547.   3. Great Britain—
Queens—Biography.   4. Wives—Great Britain—Biography.
I. Title.   II. Title: 6 wives of Henry VIII.
DA333.A2W45   1992
942.05′2′092—dc20   91-29522
[B]   CIP

Manufactured in the United States of America

Printed on acid-free paper

First American Edition 1992

10 9 8 7 6 5 4 3 2 1

This book is dedicated to
my parents,
Doreen and James Cullen,
my mother-in-law,
Margaret Weir,
and in loving memory of
William Blackwood Weir

Contents

Chronology

1485	22 August	Battle of Bosworth. Henry Tudor usurps the English throne as Henry VII and founds the Tudor dynasty.
	16 December	Birth of Katherine of Aragon.
1486	19/20 September	Birth of Prince Arthur, eldest son of Henry VII.
1489	27 March	Treaty of Medina del Campo: Katherine and Arthur betrothed.
1491	28 June	Birth of Prince Henry, second son of Henry VII.
1499	19 May	Katherine and Arthur married by proxy.
c. 1500/1		Birth of Anne Boleyn.
1501	19 May	Katherine and Arthur married for a second time by proxy.
	27 September	Katherine arrives in England.
	12 November	Katherine enters London in state.
	14 November	Marriage of Katherine of Aragon and Arthur, Prince of Wales.
1502	2 April	Death of Prince Arthur.
1503	25 June	Katherine betrothed to Prince Henry.
1504	18 February	Prince Henry created Prince of Wales.
	26 November	Death of Isabella of Castile.
1505	27 June	Prince Henry secretly repudiates his betrothal.
c. 1507/8		Birth of Jane Seymour.
1509	22 April	Death of Henry VII and accession of Henry VIII.
	11 June	Marriage of Henry VIII and Katherine of Aragon.
	23 June	Henry and Katherine enter London in state.
	24 June	Coronation of Henry VIII and Katherine of Aragon.
1510	31 January	Birth of a stillborn daughter to Katherine of Aragon.
1511	1 January	Birth of Prince Henry, son of Henry VIII and Katherine of Aragon.
	22 February	Death of Prince Henry.
c. 1512		Birth of Katherine Parr.
1513	30 June–22 October	Katherine rules as regent while Henry VIII campaigns in France.

	16 August	Battle of the Spurs.
	9 September	Battle of Flodden.
	October	Birth of a son, who died soon after birth, to Katherine of Aragon.
1514	November	Birth of a son, who died soon after birth, to Katherine of Aragon.
1515	22 September	Birth of Anne of Cleves.
1516	January	Death of Ferdinand of Aragon.
	18 February	Birth of the Princess Mary, daughter of Henry VIII and Katherine of Aragon.
1518	10 November	Birth of a daughter, who died soon after birth, to Katherine of Aragon.
1519	February	Death of the Holy Roman Emperor, Maximilian, followed by the election of Charles of Castile, Katherine of Aragon's nephew, in his stead.
	June	Birth of Henry FitzRoy, bastard son of Henry VIII by Elizabeth Blount.
1520	3–23 June	The Field of Cloth of Gold, summit meeting between Henry VIII and Francis I of France.
1524		Katherine of Aragon known to be past the age for bearing children. Cessation of sexual relations between her and Henry VIII.
c. 1525		Birth of Katherine Howard.
1525	August	Princess Mary's household established at Ludlow.
1526	February	First indication that Henry VIII courting Anne Boleyn.
1527	6 May	Sack of Rome by the Emperor's troops.
	17 May	Proceedings to annul Henry VIII's marriage to Katherine of Aragon instituted in an ecclesiastical court at Westminster.
	22 June	Katherine informed by Henry of his doubts concerning the validity of their marriage.
	September	Henry VIII asks the Pope to help him gain an annulment of his marriage.
1528	29 September	Cardinal Campeggio, sent by the Pope to try the King's case, arrives in England.
1529	31 May	The legatine court opens at Black Friars, London.
	23 July	Campeggio adjourns the case indefinitely to Rome.
1530	November	Death of Cardinal Wolsey.

1531	11 February	The Reformation Parliament acknowledges Henry VIII as Supreme Head of the Church of England under Christ.
	14 July	Henry separates from Katherine and she is banished from court.
1532	1 September	Anne Boleyn created Lady Marquess of Pembroke.
1533	25 January	Secret marriage of Henry VIII and Anne Boleyn.
	12 April	Anne Boleyn first appears in public as Queen of England.
	23 May	Archbishop Cranmer declares the marriage of Henry VIII and Katherine of Aragon to be invalid and unlawful.
	28 May	Archbishop Cranmer declares the marriage of Henry VIII and Anne Boleyn to be good and valid.
	31 May	Anne Boleyn enters London in state.
	1 June	Coronation of Anne Boleyn.
	7 September	Birth of the Princess Elizabeth, daughter of Henry VIII and Anne Boleyn.
1534	23 March	Parliament passes the Act of Succession vesting the succession in Anne Boleyn's children by the King.
	23 March	Pope Clement VII pronounces the marriage of Henry VIII and Katherine of Aragon to be lawful and canonical.
	c. July	Birth of a child, sex not known, either still-born or dead soon after birth, to Henry VIII and Anne Boleyn.
1535	22 June	Execution of John Fisher, Bishop of Rochester.
	late June	Birth of a stillborn child to Anne Boleyn.
	6 July	Execution of Sir Thomas More.
	November	First mention of Henry VIII's courtship of Jane Seymour.
1536	7 January	Death of Katherine of Aragon.
	29 January	Birth of a stillborn son to Anne Boleyn.
	2 May	Anne Boleyn arrested and taken to the Tower of London.
	15 May	Trial of Anne Boleyn.
	19 May	Execution of Anne Boleyn.
	20 May	Henry VIII betrothed to Jane Seymour.
	30 May	Marriage of Henry VIII and Jane Seymour.
	7 June	Jane Seymour enters London in state.

	June	Parliament passes the Act of Succession vesting the succession in Jane Seymour's children by the King.
	13 June	Henry's daughter Mary offers him her submission.
	September 1536– March 1537	Pilgrimage of Grace.
1537	12 October	Birth of Prince Edward, son of Henry VIII and Jane Seymour.
	24 October	Death of Jane Seymour.
1539	4 September	Henry VIII betrothed to Anne of Cleves.
	27 December	Anne of Cleves arrives in England.
1540	6 January	Marriage of Henry VIII and Anne of Cleves.
	4 February	Anne of Cleves enters London in state.
	April	First mention of Henry VIII's courtship of Katherine Howard.
	9 July	Henry VIII's marriage to Anne of Cleves annulled.
	28 July	Execution of Thomas Cromwell.
		Marriage of Henry VIII and Katherine Howard.
1541	1 November	Henry VIII informed by Archbishop Cranmer of Katherine Howard's misconduct.
1542	7 February	Parliament passes the Act of Attainder condemning Katherine Howard to death.
	13 February	Execution of Katherine Howard.
1543	12 July	Marriage of Henry VIII and Katherine Parr.
1544	14 July– 30 September	Katherine Parr rules as regent while Henry VIII campaigns in France.
1547	28 January	Death of Henry VIII; accession of Edward VI.
	c. April	Marriage of Katherine Parr and Thomas Seymour.
1548	30 August	Birth of Mary, daughter of Katherine Parr and Thomas Seymour.
	7 September	Death of Katherine Parr.
1553	6 July	Death of Edward VI.
	10 July	Lady Jane Grey proclaimed Queen of England.
	19 July	Queen Jane deposed; accession of Mary I, daughter of Henry VIII and Katherine of Aragon.
1557	16 July	Death of Anne of Cleves.
1558	17 November	Death of Mary I; accession of Elizabeth I, daughter of Henry VIII and Anne Boleyn.

Introduction

The reign of Henry VIII is one of the most fascinating in English history. Not only was it a time of revolutionary political and social change, but it was also dominated by one of the most extraordinary and charismatic men to emerge in the history of the British Isles – the King's contemporaries thought him 'the greatest man in the world' and 'such a king as never before'. He ruled England in unprecedented splendour, surrounded by some of the most intriguing personalities of the age, men and women who have left behind such vivid memorials of themselves that we can almost reach out across the centuries and feel we know them personally.

Six of these people were the King's wives. It is – and was then – a remarkable fact in itself that a man should have six wives, yet what makes it especially fascinating to us is that these wives were interesting people in their own right. We are fortunate that we know so much about them – not only the major events and minutiae of their public lives, but also something of their thoughts and feelings, even the intimate details of their private lives. Henry VIII's marital affairs brought the royal marriage into public focus for the first time in our history; prior to his reign, the conjugal relationships of English sovereigns were rarely chronicled, and there remain only fragmentary details of the intimate lives of earlier kings and queens. Yet, thanks to Henry VIII, such details became a matter of public interest, and no snippet of information was thought too insignificant to be recorded and analysed, a trend that has continued unabated for 450 years, and which has burgeoned in the twentieth century with the expansion of the media.

Thanks to the wealth of written material that has survived in the form of early biographies, letters, memoirs, account books and diplomatic reports, unprecedented in any preceding reign, we know a great deal about, and are able to make sense of, the lives of these six long-dead women. That such material was for the first time available to any sizeable extent was thanks to the humanism of the Renaissance and the widening interest in learning it engendered. There was a dramatic expansion of educational facilities, with the founding of many new colleges and schools, and literacy was now seen as being of prime importance, not only for men, but – to an increasing degree as the Tudor period progressed – for women also. The development of printing gave rise to a growth industry in popular works and tracts, which coincided with a renewed interest in history, leading to a succession of books by a new generation of chroniclers. Greater care was taken, both in England and abroad, to maintain public records, and with the evolution of intelligence systems, such as that established by Thomas Cromwell, more detailed information than ever before was accumulated.

Much of the source material for the reign of Henry VIII was collated by historians and published in the late nineteenth and early twentieth centuries, giving rise to a succession of biographies, learned and otherwise, of the King, his courtiers and his wives. Yet while there have been several excellent recent individual biographies of the wives (see *Bibliography*), there has been no serious collective biography since 1905 when M.A.S. Hume's scholarly book, *The Wives of Henry VIII* was published. This present book aims to fill that gap for the general reader, with information drawn from only the most reliable of the original sources.

What were they really like, those six wives? Because of the nature of the source material for the reign, nearly all of which has a political or religious bias, a writer could come up with very different assessments of each of them, all of which might be equally valid. But this would be abdicating some of the responsibilities of an historian, whose function is to piece together the surviving evidence and arrive at a workable conclusion. What follows are the conclusions I have reached after many years of research into the subject, conclusions that, on the weight of the evidence, must be as realistic as anything can be after a lapse of 450 years.

Thus, we will see that Katherine of Aragon was a staunch but misguided woman of principle; Anne Boleyn an ambitious adventuress with a penchant for vengeance; Jane Seymour a strong-minded matriarch in the making; Anne of Cleves a good-humoured woman who jumped at the chance of independence; Katherine Howard an empty-headed wanton; and Katherine Parr a godly matron who was nevertheless all too human when it came to a handsome rogue. They were fascinating women, both because of who they were and what happened to them; yet we should not lose sight of the fact that, while they were queens and therefore, nominally at least, in a position of power, they were also bound to a great degree by the constraints that restricted the lives of all women at that time. We should therefore, before proceeding with their story, pause to consider those constraints.

'Woman in her greatest perfection was made to serve and obey man,' wrote the Scots reformer John Knox in his treatise *First Blast of the Trumpet against the Monstrous Regiment of Women*, published in 1558. In Tudor England, as in the Middle Ages, women were brought up to believe that they were vastly inferior to men. Even a queen was subordinate to the will of her husband, and – like all wives – was required to learn in silence from him 'in all subjection'. Two of Henry VIII's wives – Anne Boleyn and Katherine Parr – being highly intelligent and outspoken women, found this particularly hard, and consequently both clashed with the King on numerous occasions. Naturally, Henry won. The concept of female inferiority was older than Christianity, but centuries of Christian teaching had rigidly enforced it. Woman was an instrument of the devil, the author of original sin who would lure man away from the path to salvation – in short, the only imperfection in God's creation.

Henry VIII's wives would all have learned very early in life that, as women, they had very little personal freedom. Brought up to obey their parents without question, they found that, once married to the King, they were expected to render the same unquestioning obedience to a husband – indeed, more so than ordinary wives, for this husband also happened to be the King of England. Even widowhood brought its constraints, as Katherine of Aragon found after her first husband died and she was left to the tender mercies of her father and father-in-law until she remarried. Only during courtship might a woman briefly gain the upper hand, as both Anne Boleyn and Jane Seymour did, but woe betide her if she did not quickly learn to conform once the wedding-ring was on her finger.

The notion that women could be equal to men would have been totally foreign to the King and most of his male contemporaries. Thus women, single or married, possessed very few legal rights. A woman's body and her worldly goods both became her husband's property on marriage, and the law allowed him to do exactly as he pleased with them. Infidelity in a wife was not tolerated, but for queens Henry VIII made it a treasonable offence punishable by death, because it threatened the succession. Two of Henry's wives died on the scaffold after being found guilty of criminal intercourse, and the wife of a peer could face the same penalty if her adultery was proved and her husband petitioned the King to have her executed. A wife who murdered her husband was guilty, not of murder, but of petty treason, and the penalty for this until the eighteenth century was death by burning. Even if a wife merely displeased her husband, justifiably or not, the law allowed him to turn her out of the house with just a shift to cover her, and she had no right of redress. Wife-beating was common and, instead of provoking the horrified reaction it arouses today, 450 years ago it would have been regarded as a righteous punishment for an erring or disobedient wife, although there is no evidence that Henry VIII ever beat any of his wives.

From the cradle to the grave, the lives of Henry's queens – and of all women – were lived according to prescribed rules and conventions. Only four of the six received any formal education; Jane Seymour and Katherine Howard appear to have been barely literate. Many people in the first half of the sixteenth century still did not believe that women should be educated, holding to the medieval view that girls taught to write would only waste their skill on love-letters. But thanks to men such as the Spanish educationist Juan Luis Vives, and Sir Thomas More, whose daughters were renowned examples of womanly erudition, as well as the shining examples of both Katherine of Aragon and Katherine Parr who proved that women could be both learned and virtuous, the Renaissance concept of female education gradually became accepted and even applauded. Nevertheless, the Elizabethan bluestocking was not yet born; in Henry VIII's time, the education of girls was the privilege of the royal and the rich, and its chief aim was to produce future wives schooled in godly and moral precepts. It was not intended to promote independent thinking; indeed, it tended to the opposite.

When it came to choosing a marriage partner, high-born girls – and princesses in particular – were at the mercy of their fathers, for it was almost unheard of for them to select their own husbands. One married for political reasons, to cement alliances, to gain wealth, land and status, and to forge bonds between families; marrying for love was merely wayward and foolish. Royal marriages, of course, were largely matters of political expediency: it was not unknown for a king to see his bride's face for the first time on their wedding day, and it was still thought unusual for a king to marry one of his own subjects. Kings were expected to ally themselves with foreign powers for political and trading advantages, and had done so until 1464 when Henry's grandfather, Edward IV, had married Elizabeth Woodville, a commoner, for love alone, and caused a furore. Half a century later, a burgeoning sense of English nationalism meant that Henry VIII's marriages to four commoners passed without anyone complaining that they were not of royal blood. What did excite comment was that he had married them for love, a sensational departure from tradition. In a sense, however, these were political marriages too, since the political and religious factions at Henry's court were continually trying to manoeuvre their master in and out of wedlock.

Negotiations for marriages between royal houses could be – and often were – very protracted. It took thirteen years to arrange the marriage of Katherine of Aragon and Arthur Tudor; fortunately – as so often happened – negotiations began when both were toddlers. Royal courtship in such cases consisted of formal letters containing fulsome declarations of love, and symbolic gifts, usually rings or jewels. Unless a bride was being reared at her future husband's court, geographical barriers often prevented the couple from meeting. Kings had to rely on the accuracy of descriptions sent by ambassadors, and also on the artistry of court painters, though there were notable mishaps: Holbein painted Anne of Cleves, but in doing so unduly flattered the lady, and a distraught Henry was driven to complain that it was 'the fate of princes to take as is brought them by others, while poor men be commonly at their own choice'.

There was no legal age for marriage in the sixteenth century. Marriage between children was not unknown, but the usual age of both partners was around fourteen or fifteen, old enough for cohabitation. No one questioned whether young people were mature enough to marry and procreate at such an early age: life expectancy was short, and the average woman could not expect to live much beyond thirty. In this context, therefore, all of Henry's wives except Katherine Howard married him at quite a late age. Katherine of Aragon was twenty-four (it was her second marriage), Anne Boleyn around thirty-two, Jane Seymour twenty-eight, Anne of Cleves twenty-four, and Katherine Parr thirty-one (her third marriage). By contrast, Katherine Howard was only fifteen or thereabouts when Henry, at the age of forty-nine, took her to wife, and the bride's youth excited much comment.

A formal betrothal was called a precontract; in the case of a royal union, its terms and conditions were set out in a formal marriage treaty. A precontract could be in written form, or consist of a verbal promise to marry made before witnesses. Once it had been made, only sexual intercourse was necessary to transform it into marriage, and many couples lived together quite respectably after having conformed to this custom. Some, of course, went on to take their vows in church, but this was not a necessity except in the case of a royal or noble union, such as that between Henry VIII and Anne Boleyn, which came about in this way, but which was later regularised by a ceremony of marriage.

The dowry, or marriage portion, was always the chief issue in any betrothal contract. A dowry could consist of lands, money, jewellery, plate, even household goods, and a girl's chances of marriage depended more upon her father's financial and social status than upon her face and form, although these sometimes helped. Even the plainest girl, if she had a rich dowry, would never lack for suitors. The contract would also feature the terms of the bride's jointure, settled upon her by her husband-to-be or his father, for her maintenance after marriage and during widowhood. Yet it was never hers to control directly unless her husband permitted it, or unless she was widowed and did not remarry.

Without a precontract, sex before marriage was forbidden, although, of course, it was a frequent occurrence that was not just confined to the lower orders of society. As Katherine Howard's experiences prove, lax morality could prevail among the nobility also. Men, however, were encouraged to sow their wild oats, but a woman who did so became a social outcast and ruined her chances of making a good marriage. For this reason, Henry VIII conducted his courtships of Katherine Howard and Jane Seymour in the presence of their relatives, in order to preserve the good reputation of his future wives.

Weddings themselves were performed according to ancient Roman Catholic rites, with vows being exchanged in the church porch, followed by a nuptial mass at the high altar. Two witnesses had to be present. The old form of the service then in use required the bride to vow to be 'bonair and buxom [amiable] in bed and at board'. Henry VIII's weddings were all solemnised in private ceremonies, with only a few selected courtiers present. Only three were marked by public celebrations afterwards: those to Katherine of Aragon, Jane Seymour and Anne of Cleves. The date and place of the King's marriage to Anne Boleyn were kept so secret that even Archbishop Cranmer could not be certain about them. This is not to say, however, that the modern concept of a royal wedding, with all its attendant pageantry, was unknown. Public royal weddings had been the rule up until the reign of Henry VIII, and that of his parents, Henry VII and Elizabeth of York, in 1486 at Westminster Abbey was a very public affair, as was the wedding of Katherine of Aragon and Arthur Tudor at St Paul's Cathedral in 1501. Indeed, the ceremonies observed, the procession through the streets, and the cheering crowds, were not so very different from those that a worldwide television audience saw when the present Prince of Wales married Lady Diana Spencer on the same site 480 years later.

The English had a fondness for traditional customs, and celebrated their weddings with feasting and a good deal of bawdy revelry. Dancing would follow the nuptial banquet, and then the bride and groom would be ceremoniously put to bed by the guests, the marriage bed being blessed by a priest before the couple were left alone to consummate their marriage. There is, however, no record of Henry VIII being publicly put to bed with any of his wives, although Katherine of Aragon was with Prince Arthur, in front of many witnesses.

Once the marriage had been consummated, the couple were literally viewed as one flesh, and Sir Thomas More advised them to regard their sexual union as being similar to 'God's coupling with their souls'. Theological doctrine inclined to the view that all carnal relationships were of a base and sinful nature; only the sacrament of marriage made the 'damnable act' 'pure, clean, and without spot of sin'. However, although instances of marital sex did not have to be mentioned in the confessional, the marriage ceremony was not intended as a gateway to self-indulgent lust. The Church taught that sex was only for the procreation of children, that the Word of God might be handed down to future generations; sex was therefore a sacred duty in marriage. 'Who does not tremble when he considers how to deal with his wife?' asked Henry VIII in his treatise *A Defence of the Seven Sacraments*; 'for not only is he bound to love her, but so to live with her that he may return her to God pure and without stain, when God who gave shall demand His own again.'

Marriage brought with it further constraints for women. Matrimony was essential to the Tudor concept of the divine order of the world: the husband ruled his family, as the King ruled his realm, and as God ruled the universe, and – like subjects – wives were bound in obedience to their husbands and masters. In 1537, Sir Thomas Wyatt advised his son to 'rule his wife well' so that she would love and reverence him 'as her head'. 'I am utterly of the opinion,' wrote Thomas Lupset in *An Exhortation to Young Men* (1535), 'that the man may make, shape and form the woman as he will.' Certainly this was what Henry VIII expected to do as a husband. In his eyes, and in those of other men of his era, a loving, virtuous and obedient wife was a blessing direct from God. But for women, even queens, marriage often brought with it total subjection to and domination by a domestic tyrant.

Marriage was therefore a period of great upheaval and adjustment for young women, and even more so for those born royal, for a princess often had to face a perilous journey to a new land and a stranger she had never before set eyes on, as well as a heart-wrenching parting from parents, siblings, friends, home and native land, all of which she might never see again. If she were clever, however, a royal bride could come to enjoy considerable power and influence, as did both Katherine of Aragon and Anne Boleyn. Yet such status and power emanated solely from her husband. She enjoyed no freedoms but those he permitted her. Without him, she was nothing.

Queens of England were housewives on a grand scale, with nominal charge of vast households and far-flung estates from which they derived huge revenues. In fact, they had an army of officials to administer these for them, and only controlled their own income to the degree permitted them by the King; no major transactions would be conducted without his consent. Any decisions they made concerning finances, patronage, benefactions, estate management and household matters were subject to his approval; their privy council was an advisory body appointed by him to oversee their affairs on his behalf. There is evidence that Henry VIII was in fact happy to leave a good many domestic decisions to his wives' discretion, and was certainly generous with money when the mood took him. He could also be callous when he felt the need, and was not above reminding Anne Boleyn that he had the power to lower her more than he had raised her, leaving her in no doubt as to who held the upper hand.

What was really required of a queen was that she produce heirs for the succession and set a high moral standard for court and kingdom by being a model of wifely dignity and virtue. To depart from this role could spell disaster, as both Anne Boleyn and Katherine Howard found to their cost. Katherine was certainly promiscuous, but Anne merely lacked the necessary modesty, circumspection and humility of manner; thus it was easy for her contemporaries to believe her guilty of moral laxity.

A queen's formal dignity was reinforced by the clothes and jewels she wore, and nowhere were the constraints upon women as obvious as when it came to the rules governing their attire. The everyday dress of a married woman was preordained by convention. Hair that had been worn loose before marriage must now be hidden under a hood and veil; only queens might have their hair flowing after marriage, and then only on state occasions when it was necessary to

9

wear a crown. Women only cut their hair to enter a cloister; most wore it long – Anne Boleyn and Katherine of Aragon both had hair so long they could sit on it. Widows were required to wear a nun-like wimple and chin-barbe, familiar on portraits of the Lady Margaret Beaufort, Henry VII's mother. This practice was dying out by the time of the Reformation, although for some time afterwards widows would wear severe white caps or hoods.

Even in summer, sleeves were required to reach the wrist, and gowns were worn long, sweeping the floor. Such were the dictates of modesty, which also required a woman to suffer agonising constriction within a corset of stiff leather or even wood. Yet it was not thought indecent to wear gowns with a square neckline low enough to expose most of the upper breasts; in an age when hand-reared babies rarely survived, the sight of a female breast was a common one and excited little censure.

The sumptuous attire of queens provided yet further limitation; the heavy velvets and damasks used, the long court trains, the elaborate head-dresses, and the cumbersome oversleeves, all had the effect of severely restricting movement. Queens walked slowly, danced slowly, and moved with regal bearing, not just because they were born to it, but because their clothes constrained them to it. Yet they did not complain – like many women in all periods of history, they were willing to suffer in the cause of fashion.

The chief function of a queen – and of the wives of lesser men, for that matter – was to bear her husband male heirs to ensure the continuity of his dynasty. Pregnancy could be, and often was, an annual event – from the male point of view, a highly satisfactory state, although not so satisfactory for those wives who were worn out with frequent childbearing, or for the high proportion of women and babies who died in childbed. Pregnancy and childbirth were extremely hazardous. As well as preparing a layette and a nursery, an expectant mother would, as a matter of routine, make provision for someone to care for her child in the event of her dying at its birth. And even if she survived the birth, she might be physically scarred for life. This is not the place to discuss the truly horrific things that could happen to a woman in childbed – suffice it to say that lack of medical knowledge (only midwives attended confinements, doctors were rarely called in unless it was to deal with severe complications) and the absence of any real understanding of hygiene were what really killed women.

A woman who bore ten children could expect to see less than half grow to full maturity if she were lucky. Katherine of Aragon and Anne Boleyn had ten pregnancies between them: two children survived. Caesarian section and forceps were unknown, and many babies died at birth. Given the problems with the feeding and management of babies that prevailed at the time, it is surprising that any survived at all. Many were given unsuitable foods, and there were no antibiotics; any chance infection could carry an infant off with hardly a warning. A mother could herself be at risk, even after the birth was successfully over, for at any time during her lying-in period, puerperal fever could strike; Jane Seymour died of this, probably because a tear in her perineum became infected. In this respect, marriage brought no real security to women; in all too many cases, they died as a result of it.

In an age of arranged marriages, a wife could not expect her husband to be faithful. Marriages were business arrangements, pleasure could be found elsewhere. Adultery in men was common, and Henry VIII is known to have strayed frequently during his first two marriages. Nor did he expect to be censured for it: he once brutally advised Anne Boleyn to shut her eyes as her betters had done when she dared to upbraid him for being unfaithful.

The medieval tradition of courtly love still flourished at the Tudor court. It was a code of behaviour by which the chivalrous knight paid court to the lady of his heart, who was usually older, married and of higher rank – and thus conveniently unattainable. A man could refer to his 'mistress' in the noblest sense, without implying that there was any sexual relationship, yet all too often the courtly ideal was merely an excuse for adultery. We shall see that Henry VIII was a great exponent of this chivalric cult, a concept inbred in him from infancy, and which inspired the courtship of all of his wives as well as the pursuit of his mistresses.

Marriage, however, was as far removed from courtly love as night from day. Once married, couples had to make the best of things, however bad, for there was rarely a way out. Divorce was very rare, and was only granted by Act of Parliament in exceptional cases, usually involving adultery among the nobility. Annulment by an ecclesiastical court, or even by the Pope, was more common, but the only grounds permissible were non-consummation of the marriage, discovery of a near degree of affinity, insanity, or the discovery of a previous precontract to someone else. Where a couple were within the forbidden degrees of affinity, the Pope was usually happy to issue a dispensation before the marriage took place. The validity of such a dispensation was accepted without question in Europe until Henry VIII brought his suit against Katherine of Aragon in 1527, claiming that the Pope had contravened Levitical law by issuing a dispensation allowing him to marry his brother's widow. Such a stand, taken at a crucial time in the history of the Church, was enough to rend Christendom asunder.

To today's liberated women and 'new men', the lives of Henry VIII's wives appear to have been shockingly narrow and hemmed by intolerable constraints. Yet, having experienced nothing else, they did not think to question these, and accepted their inferior status as part of the divine order of things. Katherine Parr even applauded it; in her book, *The Lamentations of a Sinner*, published in 1548, she exhorted wives to wear 'such apparel as becometh holiness and comely usage with soberness', and warned them against the evils of overeating and drinking wine. Young women, she said, must be 'sober minded, love their husbands and children, and be discreet, housewifely, and good'. Henry VIII was dead when these words were written, but we may certainly read in them a reflection of his own views. Jane Seymour took as her motto the legend 'Bound to obey and serve', while Katherine Howard's was 'No other will than his'. They, like the King's other wives, accepted their subjugation; it was the price of their queenship and of marriage.

Part I
Katherine of Aragon

I
The princess from Spain

The child, thought the ambassadors, was delightful, 'singularly beautiful'. Seated upon the lap of her mother, the Queen of Castile, she was gravely surveying the important yet deferential men who were taking such polite and fulsome interest in her. Only two years old in the spring of 1488, the Infanta Katherine of Aragon was already displaying the plump prettiness that was to enchant her two future husbands. Her wide blue eyes gazed from a round, firm-chinned face, which was framed by wavy, red-gold hair, worn loose as was the custom for princesses at that time. She sat with her mother on a dais in the midst of the court of Castile and Aragon, which had gathered for a brief respite in the wars against the Infidel to enjoy a tournament. And, during the interval, when the contesting knights had withdrawn to their tents, the English ambassadors, sent by King Henry VII, came to pay their respects.

Queen Isabella, sovereign of Castile in her own right, and her husband Ferdinand of Aragon were well aware of their purpose. They came from a king whose title to his crown was dubious, to say the least. Although three years had now elapsed since Henry Tudor had usurped the throne of England after defeating Richard III, the last Plantagenet king, at the battle of Bosworth, he was still working hard to consolidate his position. He had, in fact, no title at all to the crown by descent; therefore he professed to claim it by right of conquest and through a questionable descent from the early British kings – not for nothing did he name his eldest son, born in 1486, Arthur. Nevertheless, there were still living at least six male members of the House of Plantagenet with a better lineal claim to the throne than Henry VII, and he knew it. Ferdinand and Isabella knew it too, and they were sensible of the fact that a marriage alliance between England and one of the great European powers would imply recognition of Henry VII's title and immeasurably strengthen his position both in his own kingdom and in the eyes of the world at large.

There were, at that time, two major powers in Europe: France and Spain. English distrust of the French, engendered by nearly 200 years of war, forced Henry VII to consider a more congenial alliance for his son with Spain, then a new political entity. Until 1479, Spain had been made up of a group of minor kingdoms ruled by interrelated monarchs, and since the eighth century, much of the Spanish peninsula had been held by the Moors. Slowly, the Christian rulers had reclaimed the land. The 'Reconquest' had been going on for centuries, an internal crusade that absorbed Spanish energies and kept her to a large extent out of European politics. This long struggle against the Moors was in fact the greatest source of a sense of national identity, and the biggest single unifying factor, more so even than the marriage between Ferdinand of Aragon and Isabella of Castile that brought the Spanish kingdoms together under a single monarchy. No Spanish rulers were more zealous in eliminating the Moors than Ferdinand and Isabella, and by 1488 only the Moorish kingdom of Granada remained unconquered by the Christians. The sovereigns were rulers of the rest of the Iberian peninsula, save for the kingdom of Portugal, and it would only be a matter of time before Granada too came under their dominion. Spain was therefore taking its place as a major European power.

Ferdinand and Isabella represented everything that seemed desirable to Henry VII: they were the descendants of ancient monarchies, their position was strong, and their reputation glorious. If they could be persuaded to agree to a marriage alliance between Prince Arthur and one of their four daughters, then the Tudor dynasty would be far more secure than hitherto. Moreover, Spain and France were hereditary enemies, and therefore a joint pact between England and Spain would benefit both sides. The Spanish sovereigns were well aware of the potential advantages to themselves of such an alliance, but they were in no hurry to make a commitment. Ferdinand was as wily a politician as Henry Tudor, and was not prepared to sign any treaties until he could be sure that the English King was firmly established on his throne. Given England's susceptibility to dynastic warfare, it seemed more than likely that Henry VII might not long enjoy his regal dignity.

There was, however, something that Ferdinand desired very much, and that was military assistance against the French. In March 1488, the Spanish ambassador at the English court was Dr Roderigo de Puebla, an unscrupulous diplomat of Jewish origins. Ferdinand had instructed him to offer Henry an infanta for his son in return for an undertaking on Henry's part to declare war on France. The King of England had reacted enthusiastically to the proposal, and promptly despatched his ambassadors to Spain to view the sovereigns' youngest daughter, Katherine.

A Spanish herald, Ruy Machado, was moved to comment on the charming impression made on the envoys by both the little girl and her mother, the Queen. At the same time, in England, Henry VII was welcoming Ferdinand's representatives and enthusiastically showing off his nineteen-month-old son, first dressed in cloth of gold and then stripped naked, so they could see he had no deformity. The Spaniards saw an auburn-haired, fair-skinned child who was tall for his age, and thought him both beautiful and graceful, with 'many excellent qualities'.

Ferdinand and Isabella were impressed by their reports, but still not happy about sending their daughter to a realm whose king might be deposed at any time. As Puebla told Henry VII quite candidly in July, 'Bearing in mind what happens every day to the kings of England, it is surprising that Ferdinand and Isabella should dare think of giving their daughter at all.' But at last Ferdinand decided that assistance against France was more important to him than his daughter's future security, and instructed his ambassadors to draw up a treaty of marriage. There was some haggling between the representatives of both sides over the financial settlement to be made on the bride, but this was settled amicably and it was agreed that the Infanta should bring with her a dowry of 200,000 crowns (equivalent to about £5 million today). The alliance was ratified, and the dowry confirmed, by the Treaty of Medina del Campo, which was signed by the Spanish sovereigns on 27 March 1489. Thus Katherine's matrimonial future was decided when she was three years old, a common fate of princesses at that time.

Katherine of Aragon was named after her English great-grandmother, Katherine of Lancaster, a daughter of John of Gaunt (a younger son of Edward III), who had married Henry III of Castile in 1388 and died in 1418. Her son by Henry succeeded his father as John I, and married his cousin, Isabella of Portugal; they were the parents of Isabella of Castile. Isabella had been born into a land ravaged by war, both dynastic and holy. Her brother, Henry IV, was a spineless weakling, and her mother went insane when she was a girl. Fortunately, in 1469 a marriage was arranged for Isabella with her cousin, Ferdinand of Aragon, a vigorous youth eleven months her junior. In 1474, Henry IV died childless, and Isabella became Queen of Castile in her own right.

The new Queen was of middle height with a good figure that would soon be ruined by ten pregnancies in quick succession. She had skin so fair it looked white, and her eyes were a greeny blue. She was graceful, beautiful, modest and pious, but was also blessed with a sense of humour and boundless energy. She was both clever and sensible, and turned a blind eye to her husband's many infidelities, although she loved him dearly. Her only fault, as noted by her contemporaries, was her love of ostentation in dress, for, like her daughter Katherine in later years, she was 'a ceremonious woman in her attire', favouring the rich velvets and cloth of gold so typical of the period.

In 1479, the King of Aragon died and Ferdinand succeeded him. Thus, for the first time in her history, Spain became united under centralised rule, with only the Moorish Kingdom of Granada refusing allegiance to the sovereigns. The reconquest of this Infidel bastion was to be the great enterprise of their reign, to which they would devote most of their time and resources. Campaign followed campaign, with the ever growing family of the King and Queen being trailed after them in the wake of their army, from city to city, through inhospitable and hostile territory, the monarchs themselves sometimes suffering gruelling privation in their quest for a holy victory.

This left the Queen with little time to devote to her children. Her first child, Isabella, was born in 1470, and was followed in rapid succession over the next fifteen years by nine others. Sadly, all the campaigning took its toll: five babies died young. However, the rest grew to maturity. An heir to the throne, the Infante John, was born in 1478; then there was Juana, born in 1479, Maria in 1482, and Katherine (who was called Catalina in her native land), born on the night of 15–16 December 1485 in the palace of the Bishop of Toledo at Alcala de Henares, in the midst of war. The Queen had been in the saddle all day, and rose from her bed the day after the birth to go back on the march, consigning her youngest daughter to the care of nurses. Nevertheless, she cared deeply for all her children, and personally supervised their education. They, in turn, all loved and respected her, especially Katherine, who grew up to be the most like her in looks and character.

While Isabella lived, Katherine had a champion who would consider her welfare and security before all else. Yet Katherine was Ferdinand's daughter as well, and he was very different from her mother. In appearance he was of medium height with a well-proportioned body, and had long dark hair and a good complexion. He was genial, charismatic and a good conversationalist. Like his wife, he possessed great energy which he put to good use on military campaigns but also expended on women. His contemporaries thought him compassionate, yet this did not always extend to his own family; he later abandoned one daughter to penury and had another declared insane in order to seize her kingdom. He was notorious as a great dissimulator, and for being fond of political intrigue. Yet for all his failings, he loved his wife, and theirs was a dynamic and successful partnership.

The only glimpse we have of Katherine of Aragon during her childhood is at the tournament where she was presented to the English ambassadors. Yet she was an innocent witness to most of the great landmarks of her parents' reign: the fall of Granada in 1492, the discovery of America by Christopher Columbus, and the establishment of the notorious Spanish Inquisition. All of these things served to enhance the reputation of Ferdinand and Isabella as champions of the Catholic Church; Spain's prestige in the world had never been higher.

After the conquest of Granada, the four infantas were sent there to live in the Moorish palace of the Alhambra. There they grew to maturity and were educated among the arched courtyards and splashing fountains where once the caliphs had kept their harem. The Christian princesses rarely left their sunny home, except for the great occasions of state at which their presence was required. Katherine's tutor, appointed by her mother, was a clerk in holy orders, Alessandro Geraldini, who would later accompany her to England as her chaplain. Her education was very much in the medieval tradition, although Erasmus, the celebrated Dutch humanist, who met Katherine in England, tells us that she was 'imbued with learning, by the care of her illustrious mother'. She learned to write with a graceful hand, and improved her mind with devotional reading, but she was also taught the traditional feminine skills of needlework and dancing, lacemaking, and embroidery in the Spanish 'black-work' style, which she would later popularise in England. Before her eyes was the image of her pious mother as the supreme example of Christian queenship, an example that Katherine would try to emulate all her life.

Ferdinand and Isabella arranged advantageous marriages for all their children, although none turned out as successfully as they had hoped. Isabella was married in 1490 to the Infante Alfonso of Portugal. Although it was an arranged marriage, the young couple quickly fell in love, but their happiness was shattered when, only seven months later, Alfonso was killed after a fall from his horse. His widow returned to Spain declaring it was her intention to enter a nunnery, but Ferdinand was having none of this, and after protracted negotiations sent her back to Portugal in 1497 to marry Alfonso's cousin, King Manuel I. In 1498, Isabella died giving birth to a son, the Infante Miguel, who only lived two years. Manuel would later remarry, and his bride would be Isabella's younger sister Maria.

Juana, the second daughter of the sovereigns, was volatile and highly unstable, yet her parents arranged for her an even more glorious marriage. Their fame had led many princes to seek alliance with them, one such being the Holy Roman Emperor, Maximilian I, Hapsburg ruler of vast territories, including Austria, parts of Germany, Burgundy and the Low Countries. He had two gifted children, Philip and Margaret, and Ferdinand and Isabella were happy to ally themselves with Maximilian by marriages between

Philip and Juana and Margaret of Austria and the Infante John, the heir to Spain.

Juana and Philip were married in 1496. Philip was not for nothing nicknamed 'the Handsome', and Juana fell violently and possessively in love with him, with the predictable result that he soon tired of her and took mistresses. This provoked his wife to terrible rages, and her behaviour became a public scandal both in Flanders and Spain. Reports of it reached Queen Isabella, who was deeply troubled by them, yet powerless to do very much to alter the situation. However, Juana's mental instability did not affect her fertility, and she produced six children, her eldest son Charles being born in 1500 at Ghent.

Her brother John fared rather better in his marriage, which took place in 1497. He was a pleasant youth who excelled in all the knightly virtues and who had captured the hearts of his future subjects. His constitution, however, was delicate, and Ferdinand and Isabella were concerned that his spirited and robust bride would wear him out. Their fears were well founded, too, for the Infante died only six months after his marriage, leaving Margaret of Austria pregnant with a child that was later stillborn. This meant that the Infanta Isabella was now the heiress to the Spanish throne, and when she bore her son Miguel in 1498, there were great celebrations, in spite of her death in childbirth, for Spain once more had a male heir. Yet when Miguel succumbed to a childish illness in 1500, the unstable Juana became heiress to the sovereigns, which was naturally a matter of concern to them, though at least she had a healthy son of her own.

Queen Isabella grieved deeply for the loss of her children and grandchildren, which made her remaining unmarried daughter, Katherine, seem all the more precious to her. Throughout these years of marriages and tragedy, negotiations had dragged on for Katherine's wedding to Prince Arthur, and Isabella was now determined to ensure that her daughter's future would be as secure and happy as she could make it. In 1493, when Katherine was seven years old, it had been decided that she would go to England in 1498, when she was twelve. In 1497, Henry VII sent her 'a blessed ring' as a token of his fatherly affection. She could not remember a time when she had not been referred to as the Princess of Wales, and from the

21

age of two she had been schooled for her destiny as Queen of England. She had been brought up in the knowledge that one day she must leave Spain and her parents for ever, being told that such was the fate of all princesses like her. As she had been reared to absolute obedience to the will of her parents, she did not question this.

In August 1497, Katherine and Arthur were formally betrothed at the ancient palace of Woodstock in Oxfordshire, Dr de Puebla standing proxy for the bride. Katherine did not go to England in 1498; the date of her arrival was postponed until September 1500, when Prince Arthur would be fourteen and capable of consummating the marriage. There was concern at the English court that the bride would find it difficult to make herself understood when she arrived there, and both Queen Elizabeth and the Lady Margaret Beaufort, the King's mother, requested the sovereigns of Spain to ensure that Katherine always spoke French – the diplomatic language of Europe – with her sister-in-law Margaret of Austria, as they themselves did not understand Latin or Spanish. They also suggested that Katherine accustom herself to drink wine, as the water of England was not drinkable. In December 1497, Queen Elizabeth wrote to Queen Isabella asking to be kept informed of the health and safety of her future daughter-in-law 'whom we think of and esteem as our own daughter'.

The Spanish marriage alliance was popular in England, and Henry VII and his subjects were impatient to see the girl who would one day be Queen Consort of England. Spain's second ambassador at the English court, Don Pedro de Ayala, boldly suggested to the sovereigns that it would be a good thing if Katherine came to England soon in order to accustom herself to the way of life and learn the language. He thought she could only lead a happy life by 'not remembering those things which would make her less enjoy what she would find here'. However, considering the manners and way of life of the English, he thought it best if she did not come until she was of marriageable age. Ferdinand was in no hurry: the recent appearance of a new pretender to the English throne, Perkin Warbeck – an imposter – and the continued existence of the Earl of Warwick, who had a very good claim to it, had made him cautious, and if another, better match had presented itself for his daughter at that time he would have accepted it. However, he did agree to a proxy wedding taking place on 19 May 1499 at Prince Arthur's manor house at Bewdley near Worcester. Again Dr de Puebla acted as proxy for the bride, and the Prince declared to him in a loud clear voice that he much rejoiced to contract the marriage because of his deep and sincere love for the Princess his wife, whom of course he had never seen. Such courtesies were the order of the day, however superficial.

Prince Arthur wrote several letters to his bride, of which only one survives, dated October 1499 and written in Latin to 'my dearest spouse'. In it he acknowledges the 'sweet letters' sent to him by her (none of which are extant), which so delighted him that he fancied he conversed with and embraced her. 'I cannot tell you what an earnest desire I feel to see your Highness, and how vexatious to me is this procrastination about your coming. Let [it] be hastened, [that] the love conceived between us and the wished-for joys may reap their proper fruit.' Such florid and adult sentiments from the pen of a thirteen-year-old boy hint at the assistance of a tutor, yet nevertheless it must have been a comfort to Katherine to receive encouragement from her future husband.

There remained only one obstacle to Katherine's departure for England, and that was the young Earl of Warwick, the nephew of Edward IV and Richard III, who was then a prisoner in the Tower. Ferdinand now made it very clear to Henry VII that unless Warwick were eliminated Katherine would never set foot in England, and Henry, anxious to preserve at all costs his friendship with Spain and the benefits the marriage alliance would bring, acted at once. Warwick was arraigned on a charge of conspiring with the pretender Perkin Warbeck; the simple-minded youth, beguiled by an *agent provocateur*, pleaded guilty, but was sentenced to death for his co-operation and beheaded on Tower Hill in November 1499. There was now nothing to stand in the way of Katherine's wedding to Arthur. Yet not for nothing would she one day say that her marriage had been made in blood, nor would she ever cease to feel an irrational sense of responsibility for the young Earl's death.

In 1500, assured by Dr de Puebla that 'not a doubtful drop of royal blood remains in England', the sovereigns began to prepare for their daughter's departure from Spain. Henry VII, in turn, was commanding the Mayor and aldermen of the City of London to arrange a lavish reception for his son's bride. He also requested that only beautiful women be sent in the Princess's train, stipulating that 'at least, none of them should be ugly.' We do not know if Queen Isabella took this into account when appointing the ladies of her daughter's household; for her, the main criterion was that they should come from the noblest and most ancient families of Spain. There was also a trousseau to be assembled. Katherine was to take with her many fine gowns of velvet and cloth of gold and silver, cut in the Spanish fashion, as well as undergarments edged with fine black-work lace, and hoods of velvet braided with gold, silver or pearls. The latter she would need after her marriage, when convention required a wife to cover her hair; only on state occasions would she wear it loose. Then there were night robes edged with lace for summer and fur for winter, cloth stockings and wooden stays, as well as the stiff Spanish farthingales that belled out the skirts of her gowns. Also in the trousseau was the gold and silver plate which was part of Katherine's dowry, and her jewellery, some of which was very fine and included heavy collar chains and crucifixes, and large brooches to be pinned to the centre of Katherine's bodices beneath the square necklines that would stay fashionable, and plunge ever lower, for the next sixty years. Lastly, a reminder to the Princess of where her duty lay, the Queen packed a beautifully embroidered christening robe.

When Isabella heard of Henry VII's extravagant plans for Katherine's reception, she was quick to write and tell him that she and Ferdinand would prefer it if 'expenses were moderate', as they did not want their daughter to be the cause of any loss to England; 'on the contrary, we desire that she will be the source of all kinds of happiness.' Isabella hoped, she said, that 'the substantial part of the festival should be his love'. But Henry was determined that this, the first major state occasion since his coronation, should be celebrated on a lavish scale in order to underline the splendour of the Tudor dynasty. In March 1501, he paid £14,000 for jewels alone for the wedding, and the City of London was sparing no expense in its plans for a magnificent reception for the Infanta. Already, workmen were building a great platform outside St Paul's Cathedral so that the crowds might witness the young couple taking their vows, and as this was a popular marriage there was mounting excitement in London.

In April 1501, Queen Isabella announced that her daughter was ready. Accordingly, on 19 May, another proxy wedding ceremony took place at Bewdley, just to make sure that nothing could be found lacking in the first. Two days later, Katherine left the Alhambra for ever, and began the first stage of her journey to the port of Corunna, whence she was to take ship for England. She took her final leave of her parents in Granada, knowing full well that she might never see them again. Isabella had carefully chosen a duenna for her, Doña Elvira Manuel, a noblewoman of mature years, who would act as chief lady-in-waiting, governess, chaperon, and general mother substitute. Doña Elvira was stern and proud, yet she was zealous in protecting her charge and concerned for her welfare. Only in later years, when Katherine began to resent the strict etiquette she imposed, did a rift develop between them.

The Infanta's household was headed by the Count and Countess de Cabra. It included the Commander Mayor Cardenas, Don Pedro Manuel (the duenna's husband), a chamberlain, Juan de Diero, Katherine's chaplain Alessandro Geraldini, three bishops and a host of ladies, gentlemen and servants. Travel in those days was by litter or on horseback; the strict conventions of the Spanish court demanded that Katherine's face be veiled in public, and that she travel behind the closed curtains of a litter, even during the hot summer months.

Katherine and her suite arrived at Corunna on 20 July, but could not embark for England until 17 August because of unfavourable winds. The sea crossing was terrible: a violent storm blew up in the Bay of Biscay, and the ship was tossed for four days in rough seas. Katherine was very sea-sick and later wrote to her mother to say 'it was impossible not to be terrified by the storm'. The captain was forced to return to Spain, and docked at Laredo on the Castilian coast for a month while the tempests raged. At last, on 27 September, the winds died down, and Katherine once more stepped on board the ship that would take her to England. Five days later, it arrived at Plymouth in Devon.

2

A true and loving husband

As Katherine walked down the gangway, followed by her retinue, the first thing she saw through her veil was the Mayor of Plymouth and his aldermen, come to welcome her to England. The townsfolk were there too, cheering and waving, and there were banners in the streets. Señor Alcares, a gentleman in the Infanta's train, wrote to Queen Isabella that Katherine 'could not have been received with greater joy if she had been the saviour of the world'. After being served a great feast by the citizens of Plymouth, Katherine heard mass and gave thanks for her safe arrival in her adoptive land. Meanwhile, a royal messenger was speeding away to the King, to tell him that the Princess whose arrival he had awaited for thirteen years was actually in his kingdom.

From Plymouth, Katherine travelled eastwards on the road to London. Along the way, people who had heard of her coming lined the roads to see the mysterious veiled lady who would one day be their queen. When Henry VII received news of her arrival, it was already November, and he set off at once from the royal manor at Easthampstead, Berkshire, with Prince Arthur. In Hampshire, word reached the King that Katherine was lodged at the bishop's palace at Dogmersfield; Henry, Arthur and the lords of the Privy Council arrived there on the evening of 4 November, eager to see her.

The Count de Cabra and Doña Elvira met Henry at the door and politely informed him that Katherine had retired for the night and could see no one. Henry was first astonished and then, typically, suspicious. Why would they not let him see his daughter-in-law? What was wrong with her? Was she deformed or ugly? His temper rose; he insisted he would see her, even if she were in bed. After some argument, the Spaniards had to agree to his demand and admit him to the Princess's rooms. Here, a mute and outraged Doña Elvira presented the Infanta, heavily veiled, to King Henry, who, with a marked lack of patience, lifted the veil. His relief was evident, for the ambassador had not lied: Katherine was a very pretty girl, with no sign of any blemish or deformity.

There are still in existence several portraits of Katherine of Aragon, painted at different stages of her life. Two early ones, said with good reason to portray her, were painted by the Spanish artist, Miguel Sittow. The earlier, thought to be Katherine posing as Mary Magdalene, is in the Berg Collection, and shows a plump, heavy-featured girl with loose wavy golden hair, aged perhaps around fifteen years. The other portrait, now in the Kunsthistorisches Museum, Vienna, was executed around 1505, and shows what must be the same young woman, with round face and golden hair, eyes demurely lowered, wearing a brown velvet dress and a black velvet hood called a béguine. The sitter wears a heavy gold collar decorated with Ks and pomegranates; this fruit, symbol of fertility, was Katherine's personal badge. On this, and the strong resemblance to Isabella of Castile, rests the identification of the sitter with Katherine of Aragon.

These two portraits give us a good idea of what Henry VII saw when he lifted Katherine's veil on that November evening in 1501, a girl with a fair complexion, rich reddish-gold hair that fell below hip level, and blue eyes. It would be interesting to know Katherine's first impression of her father-in-law, that unknown Welshman who had usurped the Plantagenet throne sixteen years earlier.

Henry Tudor came from bastard stock. His mother, Margaret Beaufort, was his only link by blood to the Plantagenets, and she herself was descended from the bastards born to John of Gaunt, Duke of Lancaster, fourth son of Edward III, and his mistress Katherine Swynford. These children, all surnamed Beaufort, were legitimised by statute of Richard II in 1397, after Gaunt married their mother; however, ten years later, Henry IV, confirming this, added a rider to the statute which barred the Beauforts and their heirs from ever inheriting the crown. Thus Henry Tudor could claim only a disputed title to it through his mother. His father, Edmund Tudor, who died before he was born, was one of the offspring of Henry V's widow, Katherine of Valois, by her liaison with the Welsh groom of her wardrobe, Owen Tudor; there is no proof that they ever married. Henry VII therefore had an extremely dubious claim to his throne, and was well aware of the fact that every single surviving member of the Plantagenet House of York had more right to occupy it than he. Nevertheless, after half a century of civil war, what England needed was firm, stable government, and this Henry VII had provided. He had also eliminated his most dangerous rivals for the crown. His marriage to the Plantagenet heiress, Elizabeth of York, had in the eyes of many gone a long way towards cloaking his usurpation with the mantle of legitimacy, although Henry himself insisted he occupied his throne by right of conquest, and not as Elizabeth's husband. Now, after sixteen years, he had obtained recognition by one of the greatest monarchies in the known world, and this in itself did much to consolidate his position.

According to the description of the King given by the Tudor chronicler, Edward Hall, Henry VII was tall and lean, his seeming fragility concealing a sinewy strength. He had gaunt, aquiline features, with thinning, greying hair and grey eyes. He presented to the world a genial, smiling countenance, yet beneath it he was suspicious, devious and parsimonious. He had grown to manhood in an environment of treachery and intrigue, and as a result never knew security. For all this, he ruled wisely and well, overcame plots to depose him, and put an end to the dynastic warfare that had blighted England during the second half of the fifteenth century.

Henry was miserly by nature, but he was also highly sensitive about the dubious validity of his claim to the throne, and therefore took much care to emphasise his majesty on as grand a scale as possible, thus setting a precedent for his Tudor successors. He was prepared to spend huge sums to impress the world with the splendour of his welcome to his daughter-in-law.

When, through an interpreter, pleasantries had been exchanged between the King and the Infanta, Katherine was presented to her future husband, the Prince of Wales, who later informed his parents that he 'had never felt so much joy in his life as when he beheld the sweet face of his bride'. The only portrait to survive of Prince Arthur is in the Royal Collection at Windsor, and shows a marked resemblance to youthful likenesses of Henry VIII. Arthur had reddish hair, small eyes and a high-bridged nose. In November 1501, he was fifteen years and two months old, while his bride was a month short of sixteen. He was well educated, thanks to his tutors, Dr Thomas Linacre and the poet Bernard André, and much beloved by the English because he so resembled his maternal grandfather, the popular Edward IV. Much of his childhood had been spent at Tickenhill, his manor house at Bewdley, which still survives camouflaged by a Georgian façade; the King favoured this thirteenth-century, oak-beamed house because it was near the Welsh marches, a suitable place for a Prince of Wales to live, particularly this one, who had more Welsh blood in him than any of his predecessors since the native line of Welsh princes died out.

Katherine and Arthur conversed together in Latin; later that evening, Katherine entertained the King and his son in her chamber with music and dancing. She and her ladies danced the slow, stately pavan that permitted two beats to a step; when Arthur joined in, Katherine and one of her ladies taught him a dignified Spanish dance, after which he danced with Lady Guildford in the English style 'right pleasantly and honourably'. In the morning, Henry and Arthur took their leave of Katherine and returned to London to prepare for the wedding, due to take place in ten days' time. The Infanta and her household followed at a more leisurely pace, arriving on 9 November by river at Deptford, where they were received by the Lord Mayor, aldermen and guildsmen of the City, who saluted her from their barges before escorting her to the landing stage at Lambeth. Here, Katherine was welcomed by Edward Stafford, third Duke of Buckingham, one of the few remaining members of the older nobility and a descendant of Edward III, and by the King's younger son, Henry Tudor, Duke of York, a big robust boy of ten with red-gold hair and glowing skin, who was there as his father's representative. These two conducted Katherine to her lodging in Lambeth Palace, where there awaited a letter from the King, expressing his great 'pleasure, joy and consolation' at her coming, and telling her that he and the Queen intended to treat her 'like our own daughter'. These were doubtless heartening words to a girl who had weathered a long and terrible journey to a strange land, with the prospect ahead of marriage to a virtual stranger. It says much for Katherine's strength of character that she was coping so well; beneath her docile, demure manner, there was an inner toughness and a strong will to succeed that sustained her.

Katherine made her state entry into London on 12 November, two days before her wedding. The streets were lined with expectant citizens jostling for a good view of the procession. The Infanta entered London from Southwark, passing over London Bridge with its huddle of shops and houses and its chapel dedicated to St Thomas à Becket, with her Spanish retinue following her. One person who saw her that day was the young Thomas More, future Lord Chancellor of England, who was then a lawyer at the London Charterhouse. He later wrote of the 'tremendous ovation' Katherine had received from the people: 'She thrilled the hearts of everyone; there is nothing wanting in her that the most beautiful girl should have. Everyone is singing her praises.' About her household, however, he was less than complimentary: 'Good heavens! What a sight! You would have burst out laughing if you had seen them, for they looked so ridiculous: tattered, barefoot, pygmy Ethiopians, like devils out of hell!' The chronicler Edward Hall, relying on the accounts of other eyewitnesses, later described the costly garments of the Princess and her ladies as 'strange fashions adorned with goldsmiths' work and embroidery'.

Katherine had on a wide gown with a gathered skirt over a farthingale with bell-shaped sleeves. The English had never before seen a lady thus attired, and, since she was small in stature, thought the hooped skirt made her look as broad as she was high. She also wore a little hat with a flat crown and wide brim, like a cardinal's, held in place with a gold lace under her chin. Beneath it she wore a Venetian coif covering her ears. Gone was the veil, gone also the litter; instead the Princess showed her face to the world and rode a gaily caparisoned horse. She was accompanied by a retinue of prelates, dignitaries, nobles and knights, all richly dressed in her honour.

The procession wound its way over the bridge, along Fenchurch Street to Cornhill, and then to Cheapside where Katherine was formally welcomed to London by the Lord Mayor. At six places on her route she stopped to watch elaborate pageants that had been prepared for her entertainment, and on which vast sums of money had been spent, tableaux depicting heraldic, Christian or mythical figures whose purpose it was to laud and praise the future Queen with music and verse. There was even a prefabricated castle surmounted by a fierce Welsh dragon representing the King. In another pageant, the 'Archangel Gabriel' reminded Katherine that her chief duty was 'the procreation of childer', and that this was why the deity had given mankind the capacity for 'sensual lust and appetite'. Later, 'God' himself appeared to her, saying 'Blessed be the fruit of your belly; your substance and fruits I shall increase and multiply.'

When the Lord Mayor and civic dignitaries had presented their loyal address beneath the Eleanor Cross at Cheapside, Katherine and her train passed on to St Paul's Cathedral, where a magnificent service of thanksgiving was the climax to the day's celebrations. Katherine had been the centre of it all, for the King, the Queen and Prince Arthur had watched the procession from the window of Master William Geffrey the haberdasher's house in Cheapside. When the service was over, Katherine rode back to Lambeth through the crowds who shouted acclaim from every street corner.

Two days later those same crowds were back in force for the royal wedding itself. The King and Queen, wearing their crowns and velvet robes trimmed with ermine, sat enthroned on the temporary platform erected outside St Paul's. Elizabeth of York was then thirty-five, and still retained something of her former beauty. Polydore Vergil, Henry VII's official historian, described her as a woman of great character whose chief qualities were wisdom and moderation, and the Venetian ambassador spoke of her great beauty and ability. Yet for all that, she had no political influence, and very little authority in her own household even, which was ordered by the King's mother, the learned and pious Margaret Beaufort.

Elizabeth had borne her husband seven children; three had died young, one, the Princess Mary, was still in the nursery, and the rest now sat with their parents, waiting for the marriage ceremony to begin: Prince Arthur, clad in white satin for the occasion, twelve-year-old Margaret, a headstrong girl who was shortly to marry James IV of Scotland, and Prince Henry, whose duty it was to give the bride away. Katherine also wore white satin, in the Spanish style, with bell sleeves and a full pleated skirt over a farthingale. On her head she had a huge white-silk coif edged with a border of gold, pearls and precious stones 1½" wide; the coif overshadowed her face, and its lappets hung to her waist. Her ladies, following behind, were similarly attired.

The marriage ceremony was conducted by Henry Deane, Archbishop of Canterbury, assisted by William Warham, Bishop of London. Prince Arthur and his bride made their vows in full view of the crowds before proceeding into the Cathedral for the nuptial mass, which the whole court attended. Then the Prince and Princess of Wales emerged into the November daylight, man and wife at last after thirteen years of hard bargaining; they nodded and bowed to the cheering throng, then rode off in procession to the riverside mansion known as Baynard's Castle, where the wedding banquet was to take place in the great hall. Here, where Richard Plantagenet, Duke of York, Edward IV and Richard III had once held court, the couple were entertained by 'the best voiced children of the King's chapel, who sang right sweetly with quaint harmony'. Later, after the feast, doves and rabbits were let loose into the hall, giving much 'mirth and disport' to the company.

Marriage feasts at that time were occasions for hilarity and bawdiness, and this one was no exception. In the evening there was dancing. Whilst Katherine danced in very stately manner, clicking castanets, the young Duke of York threw off his gown and whirled his sister Margaret around the floor, leaping and twirling to the music. The King and Queen were much amused, and watched their son with evident pleasure. Katherine, too, delighted them, dancing gracefully with her new husband; she looked, said an onlooker, 'delectable'.

It was now time for the bride and groom publicly to be put to bed. Arthur, we hear, was feeling 'lusty and amorous', and was anxious to be alone with his pretty wife. The young couple were undressed by their attendants, then brought to the nuptial chamber where they sat side by side in the great tester bed whilst the Archbishop of Canterbury and the Bishop of London blessed the bed and prayed that their union might be fruitful. The guests departed amidst much mirth and ribaldry, leaving Arthur and Katherine alone behind the

33

closed curtains. Thus began one of the most controversial wedding nights in history.

What happened? According to Katherine, testifying on oath twenty-seven years later, nothing. To the end of her life, she maintained that her marriage to Prince Arthur was never consummated. The Prince was fifteen at the time of his marriage, and afflicted with a weak constitution. It is doubtful that he was capable of achieving full intercourse. Certainly, according to later reports by eyewitnesses, he bragged about feeling 'lusty', and on the morning after the wedding he boasted that he 'had been in Spain', saying that marriage was 'thirsty work', but these were probably the self-conscious boasts of a boy who had failed in his duty and wanted no one to guess it. It was automatically assumed at the time that the union had been consummated, although when Katherine was widowed she immediately declared that she was still a virgin and that she had only shared a bed with her husband for six or seven nights. At her coronation in 1509, when she was newly married to Henry VIII, she dressed herself in virginal white, and in 1529, she publicly affirmed that, when she married for the second time, 'I was a true maid, without touch of man.' She also swore as much on her deathbed, believing that she was about to meet her Maker. Although she had her own interests to protect, she was a religious woman of sound principles; it is far less likely therefore that she was guilty of deception than that she was telling the truth.

As Princess of Wales, Katherine ranked second lady at court after the Queen, taking precedence even over the King's mother, the formidable Lady Margaret Beaufort, whose word was law on domestic matters until her death in June 1509. For her personal motto, Katherine adopted the device 'Not for my crown', and her badge was the pomegranate. For many days after her wedding there were banquets and revels at court, interspersed with pageants and a tournament.

Outwardly, all was well with the marriage. Arthur wrote to Ferdinand and Isabella, telling them how happy he was and assuring them he would be 'a true and loving husband all of his days'. At the end of November, the Spaniards delivered to King Henry the sum of 100,000 crowns, the first instalment of the Princess's dowry, whereupon he immediately sent a letter to the sovereigns in which he praised the 'beauty and dignified manners' of their daughter. In himself, he declared, 'you may be sure that she has found a second father who will ever watch over her happiness.'

That night, the wedding celebrations ended with another pageant, acrobats, and singing by the children of the King's chapel. On the following day, those Spaniards who were not to remain in England with Katherine departed for Spain, laden with costly gifts from King Henry. This breaking of yet another link with her homeland was upsetting for the Princess, but the King diverted her by showing her his library and allowing her to choose a ring from a selection presented by his jeweller. Yet this untypical generosity was only one side of the picture. In reality, Henry had his eye on the remaining portion of Katherine's dowry, which was not yet due, and he was well aware that part of it comprised the plate and jewels she had brought with her from Spain, which were not for her personal use but to be given to the King when Ferdinand so directed. Henry, however, preferred hard cash so, with the assistance of the unscrupulous Dr de Puebla, he conceived a plan whereby Katherine would be forced to use the plate and jewels; then, when the time came, he could refuse to accept them, and could ask for their value in money. Puebla had already tried to involve Katherine in this duplicity, but Henry VII told her that, although such an arrangement would be of advantage to them both, he would not consent to it. He would be content with what the treaties stipulated, he told her, and advised her to warn her parents of Dr de Puebla's treachery. Thus, when matters came to a head, they would blame the doctor and not Henry for what had happened.

The King had the ideal opportunity in December to put his plan into action. It had been arranged that after their marriage the Prince and Princess would go to live at Ludlow Castle on the Welsh marches, so that Arthur could learn how to govern his principality and so prepare himself for eventual kingship. But there was concern about the Prince's delicate health. He seems to have been consumptive, and had grown weaker since his wedding. The King believed, as did most other people, that Arthur had been over-exerting himself in the marriage bed. Fate was playing into Henry's hands in this, because it gave him the ideal opportunity to pretend that he did not

35

want Katherine to accompany her husband to Ludlow. However, he did not wish to risk offending her parents, so he consulted the Spanish envoy, Ayala, who advised that Katherine remain with the court. The King, making a great pretence of deliberation, then asked Katherine herself if she thought it wise to go with Arthur to Ludlow whilst he was in such poor health; Katherine would only say that she would be 'content with what he decided'. Prince Arthur, on the King's instruction, tried to persuade her to go with him, but she was frightened of going against the King's wishes, and in the end Henry, with a great show of reluctance, commanded her to accompany her husband.

Because of all this procrastination, nothing was ready for the Princess's departure, nor had any provision been made for her at Ludlow. All that had been decided was the number of Spanish servants who would accompany her. Prince Arthur, the King had decreed, would pay their salaries out of his own privy purse. Ferdinand was informed by Pedro de Ayala, who had by this time realised what the King planned to do, that Henry had given nothing to Arthur with which to furnish his house, nor any 'table service'; this was a significant omission, for it meant that Katherine would be obliged to use her plate.

Seemingly, Henry VII cared more for money than for the welfare of his son and heir. However, if Henry had shut his eyes to the possible consequences of allowing the Prince and Princess to live together, Ayala and Doña Elvira had not. Both pleaded with the King to let Katherine stay at court, saying the sovereigns would prefer it. Henry replied that Dr Puebla had told him, on the contrary, that Ferdinand and Isabella did not wish the young couple to be separated on any account, and this view had already been endorsed by Alessandro Geraldini, the Princess's chaplain. Defeated, Ayala wrote again to Ferdinand, urging him to command that the plate and jewels be given to Henry at once, to avoid further trouble.

On Tuesday, 21 December 1501, the Prince and Princess left Baynard's Castle for the Welsh marches and Ludlow. It was the middle of winter, and the landscape bare and unforgiving, with skeletal trees blowing in the bitter winds. Katherine travelled by litter, wrapped in furs and accompanied by her duenna; everyone else was on horseback, the Prince included, which cannot have done much to improve his state of health.

Ludlow Castle was an eleventh-century fortress that had been transformed into a palatial residence of imposing grandeur during the thirteenth and fourteenth centuries. It had once been the seat of the powerful Mortimer family and their descendants, the Yorkist Plantagenets. Edward IV had sent his young son, the future Edward V, to be educated here in the 1470s, and it was from Ludlow that the boy king Edward V had set out in 1483 on the road that was to take him to London, the Tower and death. No royal person had lived in Ludlow Castle since then, but a staff had been maintained, and the royal apartments kept in good repair. When the Prince and Princess arrived in January 1502, their servants quickly transformed these rooms with tapestries, roaring fires, personal belongings and the controversial plate. With Prince Arthur was his council, whose members were there to help him learn the art of government; not a hard task, as the Welsh border was quiet now after many centuries of warfare. A Welsh-born king occupied the throne, and his son enjoyed great popularity locally.

Henry VII told Ferdinand and Isabella that Alessandro Geraldini, Katherine's chaplain, 'a venerable man for whom we have the greatest regard', would be keeping him informed of her welfare and Arthur's. It is unfortunate that none of Geraldini's letters survive, as they would have provided us with much valuable information about Katherine's early married life. We can only surmise that hers was the conventional routine of a lady of rank: taking responsibility for the smooth running of her household, entertaining local worthies, and attending to religious and charitable duties. Doubtless she did embroidery and occasionally went hunting. What is certain from her own testimony, is that she did not share a bed with her husband.

In late March, both Katherine and Arthur were struck down with a virus, 'a malign vapour which proceeded from the air'. People died frequently from such illnesses then, but Katherine was lucky, for she was basically healthy and made a quick recovery, although she would suffer unpleasant after-effects. Not so Arthur, who succumbed to the virus on 2 April, leaving his bride of six months a widow in what was still to her a strange land.

At once, a messenger was despatched to the King, who was then at Richmond Palace in Surrey. He had to be roused from sleep by his confessor, who said in Latin: 'If we receive good things at the hands of God, why may we not endure evil things?' The King was puzzled, wondering why his confessor should be quoting Job to him at this time of night. Then the friar said gently, 'Your dearest son hath departed to God.' Henry burst into harsh sobbing, whereupon the Queen, laying her own grief aside, came to comfort him, reminding him that God had left him three other children, 'and God is still where he was, and we are both young enough'. Then she too broke down, and it was Henry's turn to comfort her.

The Prince's body was embalmed, and conveyed on a chariot to the Abbey of St Wulfstan in Worcester, now the cathedral, where it was interred in its own chantry chapel, later to be adorned with the statues of saints and of the wife with whom Arthur had shared such a brief time. Katherine, conforming to royal tradition, did not attend the funeral. Much sympathy was felt for her; barely out of her sick bed, she was a wan figure in her widow's black and mourning barbe, which swathed her chin and face like a nun's wimple. There was also great grief in the country for the popular Prince who had been cut down in his youth. The new heir to the throne, Henry, Duke of York, was not well known, having been kept out of the public eye for most of his life.

A question mark hovered now over Katherine's future. As soon as she was well enough, she travelled back to London, shrouded in black and hidden from public view by the curtains of a closed litter. When she reached Richmond, she was conducted at once to the Queen, with whom she shared a mutual sorrow. Elizabeth of York would play a mother's part until such time as Katherine's future was decided.

3

Our daughter remains as she was here

On 10 May 1502, Ayala having been recalled, King Ferdinand instructed his new ambassador in England, Hernan Duque de Estrada, to demand the immediate return to Spain of the Princess Katherine and repayment of the first instalment of her dowry. This was intended to frighten Henry VII into agreeing to a new proposition Ferdinand was about to make, that a marriage be arranged between Katherine and the new heir to the English throne, Prince Henry. Ferdinand could foresee only two objections to such a union: first, Katherine, at sixteen, was five and a half years older than the Prince; and second, the Bible forbade a man to marry his brother's widow. Age was deemed to be of little account: in that period, the marriage of children was not unknown, and it was not that long since an octogenarian Duchess of Norfolk had married a man sixty years her junior. Nor would the age gap seem too great when young Henry was of an age to be married.

That left the delicate matter of the couple being within the forbidden degrees of affinity. Ferdinand was certain that the Pope would be only too happy to provide a dispensation if it could be shown that Katherine's marriage to Arthur had not been consummated – and immediately the intimate details of their short-lived union became a matter of international importance. 'Be careful to get the truth as regards whether the Prince and Princess of Wales consummated the marriage,' Queen Isabella instructed Estrada, who, prevented by decorum from asking Katherine outright, was

39

driven to making discreet enquiries of the ladies of her household and even of her laundresses.

Henry VII was not so delicate, and bluntly asked Katherine if she were still a virgin. He, too, had seen the advantages of her marrying Prince Henry, but he was also hopeful that she might be pregnant with Arthur's child. She replied, quite candidly, that although she had slept with Arthur for six nights, she remained a virgin, and had confided as much to her duenna. Henry told her he was thinking of suggesting that she be betrothed to Prince Henry, but that he would prefer it if the matter was first broached by her parents. Whatever happened, he wanted to preserve the Anglo-Spanish alliance intact.

Gossip travelled fast in the court, and it was not long before the proposed betrothal was common knowledge. Reaction was swift, especially among some churchmen. William Warham, Bishop of London, who had officiated at Katherine's wedding, thought the idea 'not only inconsistent with propriety, but the will of God Himself is against it. It is declared in His law that if a man shall take his brother's wife, it is an unclean thing. It is not lawful.' This was one of the finer points of canon law, and a heated debate ensued which resulted in the King being assured by learned divines that the Pope would almost certainly grant a dispensation, since the Princess was still a virgin. Even if she were not, the Pope, were he so inclined (and persuaded with financial incentives), still had the power to dispense in such a case: there were precedents. Nevertheless, although their voices were muted, Warham and several other churchmen still maintained their stand.

Henry VII and Ferdinand and Isabella were now agreed on the match; Henry had written to Isabella, recounting his conversation with Katherine, and the Queen pronounced herself satisfied that 'our daughter remains as she was here' – that is, a virgin. The sovereigns made the signing of the new marriage treaty a priority, as there were rumours of a proposed French marriage for Prince Henry; Louis XII of France was said to be trying to block the betrothal to Katherine. Estrada was given full powers to draw up the treaty; Henry VII would be allowed to keep the first instalment of Katherine's dowry, and the final payment would be handed over when the Princess's marriage to Prince Henry was consummated. Isabella instructed Estrada to ensure that King Henry provided Katherine in the interim with whatever was necessary for her maintenance; in return, he should have the final say in how her household should be constituted, provided Doña Elvira remained as duenna. If Henry proved difficult, the ambassador was to make immediate arrangements for Katherine's return to Spain with her dowry intact. 'The one object of this business is to bring the betrothal to a conclusion as soon as you are able,' wrote the Queen.

Several weeks passed in negotiation. Naturally, no one saw fit to consult the two people most closely concerned: Henry was a boy of eleven, Katherine not yet seventeen, and both were drilled in strict obedience to their elders. The prospect of betrothal to a mere child cannot have been welcome to the Princess, deferring as it did her prospects of motherhood, yet she had been told that her destiny was to be Queen of England, and that she very much wished to be. At present, her life was humdrum, filled with religious observances, needlework, and quiet sociability in the Queen's apartments. As a widow, it was not thought fitting for her to dance in public or take part in court entertainments. A betrothal to Prince Henry would end all that, however, and thus Katherine may well have come to view it as a desirable escape from her present situation.

But there was to be further delay. Just as Estrada proceeded to draw up the marriage contract, Queen Elizabeth, who had conceived her eighth child after Prince Arthur's death, bore a daughter in the royal apartments in the Tower of London, and died soon afterwards on her thirty-seventh birthday, 11 February 1503. 'Her departing was as heavy and dolorous to the King as ever was seen or heard of,' and the court was plunged into mourning. Katherine, keeping vigil by the Queen's body with the other ladies of her court in the Norman chapel of St John the Evangelist within the Tower, sincerely mourned her gentle mother-in-law, and no doubt felt lonelier than ever. Prince Henry, too, felt the loss of his mother deeply. It has been suggested that his future matrimonial career reflected his subconscious efforts to replace her; it cannot be doubted that Elizabeth's memory always held a special place in his heart, and in time to come he would name one of his daughters after her.

No sooner had the Queen been buried in Westminster Abbey than the matter of the King's own remarriage was broached. Only the life of Prince Henry stood between stable Tudor government and bloody civil war, and it was thought imperative that the King remarry and provide his realm with more male heirs, especially as he was 'but a weak man and sickly'. It was at this juncture that the odious Dr de Puebla stepped in and suggested to the King that, rather than marry Katherine to his son, he marry her himself. The idea appealed to Henry, but it left Isabella and Ferdinand shocked and furious. The Queen wrote to Puebla, severely censuring him for his meddling, but her anger was provoked not so much by sensitivity about a middle-aged widower of eight weeks proposing himself as a groom for a young girl, as by her fears for Katherine's status. Henry VII was known to be ailing, and was probably in the first stages of the consumption that was eventually to kill him; the best Katherine could hope for from such a marriage was a brief reign as queen consort, then a long widowhood, commencing perhaps in her twenties, with no political influence. Marriage to Prince Henry would assure her of a far more stable and glorious future.

The practical Isabella suggested an alternative bride for the King, the widowed Joan of Naples, a relative of King Ferdinand, who was young and beautiful, as her portrait by Raphael shows. At the same time, Isabella commanded Estrada to tell Henry VII that a marriage between him and Katherine was 'a thing not to be endured'. Estrada played his part well: Henry, not wishing to offend Spain, and realising that he stood to lose not only Katherine but her dowry if he did so, immediately abandoned any notion of marrying her himself, and proceeded at once to conclude the treaty of betrothal between the Princess and his son. There was further haggling over the dowry, but eventually it was agreed that the remaining 100,000 crowns would be paid as soon as the marriage was consummated, and would be made up of 65,000 crowns in gold, 15,000 crowns in plate of gold and silver, and 20,000 crowns in jewellery, the plate and jewellery already being in the possession of the Princess.

The marriage itself was to take place in 1505, when Prince Henry reached his fourteenth birthday. In the meantime, Ferdinand and Isabella and Henry VII would request the Pope for a dispensation that would resolve all canonical difficulties. The treaty was signed by Henry VII on 23 June 1503, and two days later the Duke of York and Katherine of Aragon were formally betrothed in the Bishop of Salisbury's house in London's Fleet Street. Mourning weeds discarded,

Katherine appeared once more garbed in virginal white, her golden hair unbound and falling loose as a token of purity, with her future assured and her status at court preserved.

Prince Henry, who was not quite twelve, had conceived for her from the first both affection and respect. She aroused the chivalrous instincts of a boy who had been bred on knightly precepts, and who was already manifesting the charm and charisma that would in time attract people of both sexes to him. Katherine, for all her five and a half years' seniority, was beginning to fall under the spell. There was in her a strong maternal streak, and this boy had just lost his mother. She would be the one to comfort and console him, perhaps even guide him. Thus was set, early on, a pattern for the future.

The future Henry VIII had been born on 28 June 1491 at the Palace of Greenwich, which remained a favourite residence to the end of his life. In 1492, when he was less than nine months old, his father appointed him Lord Warden of the Cinque Ports and Constable of Dover Castle, and in that same year a sister, Elizabeth, joined him in the nursery; unfortunately, she died at the age of three. Later, there were other siblings, Mary, Edmund, Edward and Katherine (the baby born in the Tower), but only Mary survived infancy. Henry was particularly fond of Mary, much more so than of his elder sister Margaret, who married the King of Scots in 1503.

The young Prince was made Lord Lieutenant of Ireland at the age of three, as well as being admitted to the Order of the Bath. He was then created Duke of York, following the precedent set by Edward IV, and continued to this day, whereby the second son of the monarch is always given this title. To celebrate the event, the King held a joust and set his son on a table so that he could see properly. A portrait sketch of Henry at two shows him to have been a chubby, solidly made toddler with wide, intelligent eyes and a straight fringe of Tudor red hair; he wears a gown with a square neck and a wide-brimmed bonnet with a coif beneath, tied under the chin; altogether a child to be proud of.

The young Duke was made a Knight of the Garter in 1495, just before his fourth birthday. Shortly afterwards, he commenced his formal education, with the poet laureate John Skelton as his first tutor, who taught him reading, writing and spelling. Later, a more

43

classical curriculum was introduced, and Henry would study the works of Homer, Virgil, Plautus, Ovid, Thucydides, Livy, Julius Caesar, Pliny, and other Greek and Roman authors. He was taught to write a sprawling Italic script, and received instruction in mathematics, French and music, a subject at which he would excel. The growing Prince found an outlet for his energy in the coaching that was given him daily in horsemanship, archery, fencing, jousting, wrestling, swordsmanship and royal (real) tennis. Erasmus, who saw Henry in 1499, when he was eight, called him a 'prodigy of precocious scholarship'. At only seven years old, he had performed his first public duty, attending a meeting of the City of London trade guilds to be presented by the Lord Mayor with a pair of gilt goblets. The Prince thanked them in a clear high voice for their 'great and kind remembrance', and told them he would not forget their kindness. Nor did he, for to the end of his life Henry VIII enjoyed a relationship of mutual liking with the City of London.

He was maturing fast. At eight, according to Erasmus, he already had 'something of royalty in his demeanour, in which there was a certain dignity combined with singular courtesy'. The death of Prince Arthur in 1502 brought about a cataclysmic change in Henry's life, since it made him the heir to his father's kingdom and immeasurably increased his importance. Yet for all that he enjoyed no greater freedom. His father, who had already lost three sons, insisted that the Prince lead an almost cloistered life with his tutors, avoiding the public eye, and Henry's bedchamber was only accessible from a door in his father's room. His contact with his future wife was to be strictly limited for the present.

In August 1503, Ferdinand instructed his ambassador in Rome to procure the necessary dispensation from the Pope, saying that while it was 'well known in England that the Princess is still a virgin', he thought it 'more prudent to provide for the case as though the marriage had been consummated'. A watertight dispensation was vital because 'the right of succession depends on the undoubted legitimacy of the marriage'. The Pope, Julius II, was disposed to prevaricate, saying he did not know if he was competent to grant it. Moreover, there were conflicting texts in the Bible: Leviticus forbade a man to marry his brother's wife and warned that such unions would be cursed with childlessness, while Deuteronomy positively encouraged them. There had, however, been precedents, which proved that other Popes had had fewer qualms. In the end, ambassadorial pressure persuaded Julius to relent, and on 26 December 1503, he issued the desired Bull of Dispensation permitting Henry and Katherine to marry, notwithstanding the fact that she had 'perhaps' consummated her first marriage 'by carnal knowledge'. The young couple were now free to marry when Henry was fourteen in June 1505. On 18 February 1504, he was formally created Prince of Wales.

During 1504 Katherine suffered a period of poor health, with intermittent attacks of a mysterious sickness that has been attributed to her inability to adapt to the English climate and food. The illness seems to have been gastric, producing symptoms of shivering and fever, and it was at its worst during the summer, when the Princess was unable to eat very much. She grew alarmingly pale, and there were fears that she would die. For weeks she lay ill at Greenwich, until she was well enough to travel to Fulham Palace, a country house owned by the Bishop of London which had been placed at her disposal. The move did her little good, for in August she was reported to be 'rather worse' and in a serious condition. The King sent every day to ask after her health, offering many times to visit her, though she was too ill to receive him. Perturbed, Henry wrote to inform her parents of her illness. The news could not have reached them at a worse time, for Queen Isabella herself was mortally sick. Katherine, of course, had no knowledge of this, yet as her condition improved, so her mother's deteriorated, and by November Isabella herself realised she was about to die. On her deathbed, she voiced her inner doubts about the validity of the dispensation issued by the Pope, but these were unresolved and largely ignored when she died on 26 November 1504.

There was great mourning in Spain for the death of a queen who had been a legend in her lifetime, but it was not only because of her passing. The kingdom would once more be divided, if only for the lifetime of King Ferdinand. He, not being Isabella's heir, could no longer hold sovereignty over Castile: that kingdom would pass to the Queen's eldest daughter, Juana, and Ferdinand – who had for thirty years ruled a united Spain – now found his authority confined

45

solely to the minor kingdom of Aragon. It would not be long before this situation had repercussions for Katherine.

Katherine wrote to her father on the very day Isabella died, chiding him for not having written to her for some time. Weakened by her illness, she may well have been suffering from depression, for she felt there was something ominous about Ferdinand's silence. 'I cannot be comforted or cheerful until I see a letter from you,' she wrote; 'I have no other hope or comfort in this world than that which comes from knowing my mother and father are well.'

Any depression Katherine felt was not just the result of her illness, however. Since arriving in England, she had come to know a freedom she had never dreamed of in Spain, where women were kept in seclusion and observed an almost conventual style of life. They wore clothes that camouflaged their bodies and veiled their faces in public. Etiquette at the Spanish court was rigid, and even smiling was frowned upon. But in England, women enjoyed much more freedom: their gowns were designed to attract, and when they were introduced to gentlemen they kissed them full upon the lips in greeting. They sang and danced when they pleased, went out in public as the fancy took them, and laughed when they felt merry. Of course, there were rules of behaviour governing their conduct at court, which was expected to be decorous and formal, but this bore favourable comparison with the conventions then existing in Katherine's native land. To the maturing Princess, exposure to these unfamiliar freedoms brought with it a desire for some measure of independence and liberation from the restrictions hitherto imposed upon her. Several courtiers had told her that she 'ought to enjoy greater freedom', and, indeed, since her betrothal to Prince Henry, she had by degrees entered into the wider life of the court whenever her illness permitted. She had danced and sung, gone riding, taken part in the chase, and generally begun to enjoy herself.

Doña Elvira had been scandalised by such behaviour on the part of her charge, and was concerned that Katherine might cheapen herself in the eyes of the English. So concerned was the duenna that she complained both to King Henry and King Ferdinand. Ferdinand replied that Katherine must behave 'as was fitting for her honour and dignity', and commanded his daughter to observe the same rules at court as Doña Elvira insisted upon in her own house, and Henry VII endorsed this, saying the Princess must obey her father's orders. Katherine therefore had no choice but to do so, but from that time on relations between her and Doña Elvira were merely civil at best.

Katherine's spirits, therefore, were at a low ebb: she was debilitated by a lengthy illness, depressed by the lack of news from Spain, and chafing at the unwelcome restrictions imposed upon her, feeling very much that she was kept apart from the normal mainstream of life. And then came the news that her mother was dead.

There is no record of how Isabella's death affected Katherine on a personal level. We do know that politically it affected her a great deal, because, when news of it reached England in December 1504, and Henry VII had had time to think about its implications, he realised that he had concluded a marriage alliance, not with a strong, united Spain, but with the kingdom of Aragon, to which far less prestige was attached. This fact devalued Katherine's importance overnight and diminished her status in the world. Henry VII was the first to perceive that she was no longer the personification of a great Spanish alliance. Other, more advantageous marriages might be considered more appropriate for his son and, with this in mind, Henry VII now acted: he stopped Katherine's allowance.

By February 1505, Katherine was beginning to feel the pinch. Although she was living with the court at Richmond and did not lack for daily comforts and food, she had no money with which to pay her servants, and this was very embarrassing for her. She had also noticed a certain coolness in the King's attitude towards her, which troubled her, for she did not understand how she had offended him. She asked Dr de Puebla to remind Henry 'of the misery in which she lives, and to tell him, in plain language, that it will reflect dishonour upon his character if he should entirely abandon his daughter,' but Puebla did nothing except write to King Ferdinand asking him to clarify the position concerning financial provision for Katherine. In the meantime, Katherine's circumstances worsened. The clothes she had brought from Spain were now growing shabby, and she could not afford to replace them. Her attendants made no complaints, but she could sense their concern over the non-payment of their salaries. Then there was Doña Elvira clucking about decorum and propriety and the correct behaviour to be observed by a princess of Spain.

47

Katherine, still grieving for her mother, was nearly at breaking-point.

Ferdinand did not reply to Puebla until the end of June, and when he did it was to say, quite correctly, that it was King Henry's responsibility to 'provide abundantly for the Princess and her household'. This was little help to Katherine: etiquette prevented her from asking the King of England outright for money, and Puebla would not do it for her, so she was obliged literally to tighten her belt and endure what could not be remedied. Nor was there any end to her plight in view. On 28 June 1505, Prince Henry reached his fourteenth birthday, and by the terms of the marriage treaty should have been married to Katherine soon afterwards. However, it was becoming increasingly obvious that no immediate plans for a wedding were being laid. Henry VII had decided that, if a better match presented itself for the Prince, he would take it, but at the same time he was reluctant to forgo Katherine's dowry. Hence his policy was to delay the marriage for as long as possible to see what transpired.

Katherine, of course, did not know this, and could only guess at the reason for her marriage being postponed. Fortunately for her peace of mind, she was unaware that on the day before the Prince's birthday, the King had marched him before the Bishop of Winchester and made the boy solemnly revoke the promises made at his betrothal, on the grounds that they were made when he was a minor and incapable under the law of deciding such things for himself. The purpose of this little drama, which took place in secret, was to ensure that, if a better match presented itself, there would be no difficulty in breaking his precontract to Katherine.

4

Pain and annoyance

In October 1505, Henry VII entered into secret negotiations with the new King and Queen of Castile for the marriage of the newly created Prince of Wales to Philip's and Juana's six-year-old daughter Eleanor. Philip, antagonistic towards his father-in-law because of Ferdinand's interference in Castilian affairs, saw this marriage as a means of exacting revenge. At the same time, it was widely believed in diplomatic circles that King Henry was having doubts as to the validity of a union between his son and Katherine of Aragon, despite the Pope's dispensation: it was said to weigh 'much on his conscience'. However, the main reason for his change of direction was that Eleanor was a far greater matrimonial prize than Katherine: not only was her mother Queen Regnant of Castile and heir to Aragon, but her father was heir to all the Hapsburg territories and might one day be Holy Roman Emperor as well.

It is clear that Katherine herself had not yet understood how her mother's death had led to her own devaluation in the marriage market; it was some time before she thought she knew why Henry VII was treating her so shabbily, and why the Prince, whom she saw sometimes about the court, was dutifully ignoring her. Eventually, it occurred to her that perhaps her father's failure to hand over the second instalment of her dowry might be the cause of the problem, and in December she asked Ferdinand to substitute a payment of gold for the jewels and plate in her possession, as she felt certain that the King of England would refuse to receive them as part of the instalment. Ferdinand promised to do as she asked, but failed to keep his word. By April 1506, Henry VII – who had been led by Katherine to expect prompt payment of the second instalment – complained bitterly about the delay, and began to cast doubt upon Ferdinand's good intentions.

By the terms of the marriage treaty, Ferdinand was well within his rights to withhold the remainder of the dowry until the union between the Prince and Princess was consummated, but he did not stand on this and chose instead to prevaricate, make excuses, and offer promises he did not keep, primarily because he needed to retain the friendship of Henry VII. According to Katherine, this provoked rage and fury in Henry VII, and she bore the brunt of it. In March 1507, he granted Ferdinand a further six months' grace in which to hand over payment, although he sanctimoniously reminded him at the time that 'punctual payment' was a 'sacred duty', and warned him that 'many other princesses have been offered in marriage to the Prince of Wales with greater marriage portions'. For Katherine, it was vital that her father complied with King Henry's wishes in order to 'prevent these people from telling me that they have reduced me to nothingness'. Yet when October arrived, Henry magnanimously extended the term of grace until March 1508. Katherine, rightly, saw this as ominous, for while the dowry remained unpaid, 'he regards me as bound and his son as free.'

In December, Ferdinand was in Castile, doing his best to raise the enormous sum required to complete the dowry, and promising Henry VII to deliver it before March. But when March came, and Ferdinand had still not paid up, Henry VII lost patience and reopened negotiations for a marriage between the Prince and Eleanor of Austria.

During the summer of 1508, Ferdinand, fearing for Katherine's future, insisted Henry VII keep faith with the terms of the treaty. But Henry, whose health was failing, was determined to have the dowry before committing his son to the marriage. 'Your King has many crowns,' he sneered to the Spanish ambassador, 'but he hasn't 100,000 to pay his daughter's dowry!' The ambassador, a tactless man named Fuensalida, retorted that his master did not 'lock away his gold in chests' – a direct reference to Henry VII's legendary miserliness – 'but pays it to the brave soldiers at whose head he has always been victorious'. The obvious insult stung Henry to fury, and he marched the ambassador along to Katherine's apartments, saying, 'The Princess shall see how you handle her affairs!' In front of an astonished and distressed Katherine, he accused Fuensalida of jeopardising her marriage by his failure to press her father for the dowry, and warned her that he was not obliged in the circumstances to honour his part of the treaty.

In April 1509, at last, the final instalment of the dowry, 100,000 crowns in gold – Ferdinand had graciously consented to make good the value of the used plate and jewels – was ready to be delivered. Furthermore, a new ambassador, Don Luis Caroz, was to be sent to England empowered to inform Henry VII that it would be paid as soon as the King agreed to proceed with the marriage. However, when Caroz arrived in England, he found the King too ill to see him: Henry VII was dying, and the political situation was about to change dramatically.

During those four years of tortuous negotiations over Katherine's dowry, she herself suffered untold misery and humiliation. Her marriage to Prince Henry was never a certainty, and this placed her in a highly invidious position at the English court. At best, she was regarded there as a possible but ill-advised bride for the Prince, at worst as an unwanted dependant. Throughout this time she was very much the pawn of ambitious men, her happiness subject to the shifting vicissitudes of European politics.

Katherine's domestic life during her widowhood was anything but tranquil. In 1505, Durham House on London's Strand was placed at her disposal by the Bishop of Ely, whose town residence it was. Hitherto, she had lived either at court or at Fulham Palace, a house belonging to the Bishop of London. Durham House was sited to the east of Charing Cross, just beyond the City boundary and in an area populated mainly by the nobility and gentry, whose houses lined the Strand. Here, in peaceful and attractive surroundings, Katherine's household was briefly established. The house was built around a courtyard, and had two towers, one at each extremity. There were lawns and gardens leading down to the River Thames, where there was a jetty and landing stage. In those days persons of rank rarely travelled through London's noisome and congested streets, preferring to go by barge along the river.

In November 1505, Katherine was deprived of this peaceful refuge. Her duenna had to go abroad for a time, and Henry VII summoned Katherine to live at court, in order to save the cost of maintaining a separate establishment for her. Reluctantly, and with a depleted household, she obeyed the King's command, but she was extremely unhappy about doing so, knowing that there was little privacy to be had at court and that she would doubtless be the object of much speculation and gossip. Nevertheless, she was obliged to remain there for the next year.

Her lack of money brought further problems, especially concerning her household. In 1505 she employed mostly Spaniards on her staff, the majority of whom had come from Spain with her. Many were girls from noble families who had come to England in the hope of attracting aristocratic husbands, and Katherine knew she was obliged to provide dowries for them, when the time came, out of the income due to her from the King, which of course had ceased in the summer of 1505.

A case in point was that of Doña Maria de Salinas, who had once been a maid of honour to Queen Isabella. Her family had arranged her marriage to a noble Fleming, whom she was anxious to marry. Katherine, having no money at all, begged her father to provide a dowry, 'as Maria has served me well', but Ferdinand ignored her request. As a result, plans for the marriage had to be abandoned, to Katherine's great embarrassment and sorrow. Yet such was her ability to inspire devotion in others that Maria de Salinas remained close to her for three more decades until death severed the friendship.

Lack of money affected Katherine personally too. By December 1505, nearly a year after Henry VII had stopped her allowance, her financial situation was grave. Her father had failed to send her any money, despite repeated requests, and all King Henry had given her was a small pittance for food – she was often reduced to eating yesterday's fish from the market. She was also in debt to some London merchants for household necessities, and the gowns she had brought from Spain four years before were so shabby that she felt, as she told her father, 'nearly naked'. At Christmas, she had a humiliating interview with King Henry, who refused to pay her even a small allowance. An argument ensued, which resulted in Katherine bursting into tears, something her rigid training had schooled her not to do in public. But even this did not move Henry.

Katherine wrote again and again to her father, but Ferdinand was adamant that Henry VII should honour his undertaking to defray Katherine's living expenses, and would not help her. In Spain, her suffering aroused indignation and sympathy. It was generally felt that it was Henry VII's duty to support her and that, in failing to do this, he was guilty of a serious breach of his sacred oaths of knighthood and kingship, by which he was bound to protect defenceless maidens such as his daughter-in-law.

By the end of 1505, Katherine had come to realise that the King no longer desired her marriage to his son, and warned her father that she would 'be lost if I am not assisted from Spain'. Alas for Katherine, Ferdinand had no knowledge of Henry VII's secret negotiations with Philip of Castile, and consequently had no reason to believe that the English King wanted to break the alliance; nor did he himself wish to prejudice it, for he now needed Henry more than Henry needed him. As a result, he chose to ignore his daughter's complaints.

It was unfortunate that Katherine was ill-served throughout her widowhood by the men who should have championed her: her father's ambassador, Dr de Puebla, was more interested in ingratiating himself with Henry VII and serving his own ends than in carrying out his master's wishes. In December 1505, Katherine decided that all her troubles were 'on account of the Doctor', and begged Ferdinand to consider 'how I am your daughter' and help by sending another ambassador, 'who would be a true servant of your Highness', since Dr de Puebla had caused her so much 'pain and annoyance that I have lost my health in a great measure', and might 'soon die'.

There was, at that time, another Spanish envoy in England, Hernan Duque de Estrada, who was sympathetic towards Katherine and tried to offer her some comfort. For a time she confided in him, and he, highly indignant on her behalf, wrote to King Ferdinand endorsing her requests, but to no avail. Later, however, Katherine was to say that he had not done as much as he could have done to assist her when she most needed it. Certainly his pleas, like hers, fell on deaf ears. Ferdinand was in no hurry to replace Puebla, and instructed Katherine to make use of him before another ambassador could be selected, which would not happen for more than a year.

All of these problems had indeed, as Katherine complained, taken a severe toll on her health. She had been unwell since shortly after her arrival in England, when she suffered a viral infection at Ludlow in 1502. Since then, she had continued to be susceptible to fevers and stomach upsets, which may be attributed in part to the changes in climate and diet to which she had had to accustom herself. She does not seem to have suffered one long illness, but a succession of ailments following one upon the other, and from April 1502 until early in 1507 was constantly unwell.

The likelihood is that much of her ill health was the result of stress. She herself attributed the 'severe tertian fevers' she suffered during the autumn of 1505 to all the aggravation to which she was being subjected. She wrote to tell her father that she had been 'at death's door for months', but this may have been an exaggeration born of depression, for she was 'in the deepest anguish'. Again, in March 1506 she informed Ferdinand she had been 'near death' for six months, although she was then 'somewhat better, but not entirely well'.

Her partial recovery may have been due in some measure to a brief reunion with her sister Juana. In January 1506, Juana and Philip were sailing from the Low Countries to Spain when they were shipwrecked off the English coast and welcomed at Windsor Castle as guests of the King. Although Juana was Queen Regnant of Castile, she was mentally unstable, and real power lay in the hands of her husband, King Philip. Because of the hostility between Philip and Ferdinand, Philip was anxious to conclude the betrothal of his daughter Eleanor to the Prince of Wales, thereby driving a wedge between Henry VII and his own father-in-law, and he welcomed this opportunity of a meeting with the English King.

Katherine, who knew nothing of these negotiations, was at Windsor for the visit, and was naturally elated at the prospect of seeing her sister, being hopeful also that Juana would use her influence with their father to improve her own situation. Henry VII made sure that Katherine had a prominent role in the festivities. Wearing Spanish dress, she danced for her good-looking brother-in-law, or sat with the King's daughter Mary Tudor at table or around the fire while the Kings talked. She may have wondered whether her inclusion really signified her return to favour or whether the King merely intended that Philip should return to Spain with the impression that she was being well treated and was accorded all the dignities and privileges appropriate to her status. Nevertheless, it would not have escaped Philip's shrewd eyes that all his meetings with Katherine took place under Henry VII's watchful supervision, thus preventing her from airing her grievances to her brother-in-law. Nor was Katherine allowed more than half an hour alone with her sister.

Katherine's expectations of Juana proved greatly overestimated; the sisters had not met for ten years and had very little in common. Juana was sunk in depression, obsessed with jealousy of her wayward husband, and not in the slightest interested in the problems of her younger sister. Katherine did not even attempt to ask for her help.

The two Kings spent several hours closeted together discussing the possible betrothal between their children, but nothing was finally concluded. Philip and Juana left England in April 1506, with Katherine in no doubt that they were completely unaware of her suffering. She never saw her sister again, even though Juana was to outlive her by nearly twenty years.

Philip and Juana returned to Spain, where only six months later Philip fell ill and died at the early age of twenty-eight. Queen Juana's mind, never very stable, became unhinged, and she suffered a complete nervous collapse. This gave her father the chance he had been hoping for to take over the reins of government in Castile on his daughter's behalf, and since it was obvious to everyone there that Juana was incapable of ruling for herself, there was little dissent. The widowed Queen seemed to be under the impression that her husband was not dead, and would not surrender his corpse for burial. Her attendants were horrified when she insisted upon opening the coffin and embracing and kissing what lay within, even though the body was rapidly decomposing; only with difficulty could she be parted from it and persuaded to allow it to be laid to rest.

Ferdinand had had long years of experience of governing Castile, and once he regained power there he was determined never again to relinquish it. After two years, he declared his daughter mad and unfit to reign, and had her shut up in the grim castle of Tordesillas, where she remained until her death fifty years later. She was deemed to have abdicated in favour of her son, now Charles I of Castile, but as the boy was only eight real power remained in the hands of his grandfather, who would govern both Castile and Aragon until his death.

Katherine's health might have been slightly improved when her sister left England, but her financial situation was worse than ever. In April 1506 she was deeply in debt, 'and this not for extravagant things', but for food. She had no decent clothes to wear, and not even enough money to buy a new chemise. Since arriving in England she had had only two new gowns, and the only serviceable ones left from her trousseau were two made of damask. It would be seventeen months, however, before she was able to afford to buy herself some decent clothes, and in that time she would appear ever shabbier. Mindful that she should maintain the standards suitable to her rank in an age when appearances counted for a lot, she felt she 'dared not neglect my own person', and consequently had to sell or pawn other items from her dower plate and jewels just for necessities. By the summer of 1506, she could no longer pay her servants their salaries, and told King Ferdinand that her people were 'ready to ask for alms', which caused her more anguish than Maria de Salinas's dowry. Predictably, she fell ill again at this time, suffering recurrent bouts of fever, doubtless exacerbated by anxiety over her situation.

In the autumn, however, she was somewhat better, thanks to the King allowing her to spend more time with the Prince of Wales. Young Henry, ever obedient to his father, had never hinted of his secret repudiation of his betrothal to Katherine, and in 1506 was still referring to her as 'my most dear and well-beloved consort, the Princess my wife'. When they were together during the late summer and autumn, a bond of affection began to develop between them, and the gap between their ages to seem narrower. The King, realising what was happening, deemed it prudent to separate them, as it now seemed unlikely that their marriage would ever take place. Saying he was concerned for her health, he sent Katherine to live at Fulham Palace once more; it was still unoccupied, having been put at the disposal of the Castilian ambassadors, who had not used it. The King told Katherine that 'if she preferred any other house, she had only to say so, and it would be kept for her'. She told him she was content to go to Fulham, but she does not appear to have lived there long, and was soon reinstalled in apartments at court, where she remained for the rest of her widowhood. Henry VII took care to keep her apart from the Prince, and from January to April 1507 she did not see him. This distressed her, and she thought it ominous. She told Ferdinand that the hardest thing she had to bear was to see her betrothed 'so seldom. As we all live in the same house, it seems to me a great cruelty.'

In 1507, Henry VII negotiated with the Emperor Maximilian a betrothal between the Princess Mary Tudor and Maximilian's grandson, Charles of Castile, an alliance that would be highly advantageous to England with her trade links through the wool-cloth trade with the Low Countries, of which Charles – as Archduke of Austria – was heir; it would also counterbalance a recent political alliance between Ferdinand and Louis XII of France. Henry VII had decided he no longer needed Ferdinand, and Katherine was made aware of this by what she described as his 'want of love'; she told her father it was 'impossible for me any longer to endure what I have gone through and am still suffering'.

By April 1507, Katherine's servants were walking about 'in rags' and existing 'in such misery it is shameful to think on it'. She begged her father to succour them, as there were 'no persons to whom your Highness is more indebted'. They had served her with unfailing goodwill through prosperity and increasing adversity. Now, however, their patience was, like their clothes, becoming rather frayed at the edges.

During the sixteenth century, servants were treated far more familiarly than, for example, they were in Victorian times. Friendships could flourish between royal personages and those who served them, since 'condescension' was expected and not resented. Servants often performed the most intimate tasks: ladies of rank were always given assistance with dressing, coiffure and even bathing. Ladies-in-waiting and maids of honour would keep their mistress company for hours, sewing, reading aloud, chatting or making music in the intimate panelled rooms of the period. They would take it in turns to sleep on a pallet at the foot of her bed when she was alone at night. Indeed, there would be no time of the day when she was unattended, no bodily function that did not have its rituals, and no private emotion that went unwitnessed.

In return, a lady of rank was responsible for her servants' physical, moral and spiritual welfare, for housing, clothing and feeding them, and in some cases for arranging marriages for them and providing dowries. The strong bonds that developed between Katherine of Aragon and many of those who served her were no doubt forged not only from her innate kindness but also the shared experience of being foreigners together in a strange and hostile land, almost the only people there who spoke their native Spanish. There were in her household, however, some who took advantage of her kindness, or let self-interest stand in the way of their duty. Certainly intrigue was rife among the Princess's servants.

Katherine's patience and forbearance were by now little short of saintly. Trained from the cradle to be submissive to the men of her family, she did not venture to criticise, but contented herself with pitiful pleas for assistance, which were calculated to flatter the powerful men with whom she had to treat. Honest and sincere to a fault, and perhaps lacking humour, her humility and self-effacement were at odds with her staunch pride in her royal blood and lineage. Yet it was her pride that helped her to cope with the many tribulations laid upon her, not the least of which was being besieged daily by creditors demanding payment.

Yet some relief was at hand. In April 1507, Ferdinand wrote to ask Katherine for her views as to the kind of ambassador who should be sent to replace Dr de Puebla. She replied that he should be someone 'who dared to speak an honest word at the right time'. Ferdinand had suggested Don Guitier Gomez de Fuensalida, Knight Commander of the Order of Membrilla, a high-minded Spanish aristocrat who had already spent some time in England, and although he was not Katherine's first choice – she preferred Pedro de Ayala, who had visited England with Philip and Juana in 1506 – she made no objections to Fuensalida, as she believed him to be 'a man of great experience, knowledge and high status'. Meanwhile, she told her father that, when the new ambassador came to England and made his first report, Ferdinand would be 'frightened at that which I have passed through'. If Puebla were any kind of man, he would not have consented to her being treated as 'never knight's daughter was in the kingdoms of your Highness'. This alarmed Ferdinand, who, prompted by 'royal and paternal solicitude', and impressed by the way in which Katherine was handling a very difficult situation, took the unprecedented step, on 19 May 1507, of appointing his daughter to act as his ambassador in England until a replacement could be found. Never before in Europe had a woman acted in such a capacity, and the appointment naturally enhanced Katherine's status at the court of Henry VII. It was also a timely appointment, as Puebla was ill and having to be carried from his house to the palace in a litter. Henry VII, hearing the news, 'rejoiced', although it is obvious that he and his advisers believed Katherine to be a lightweight who could easily be manipulated. To some extent she would confound them.

In her role as ambassador, Katherine grew more confident in her dealings with the King, disputing with him, flattering him, even telling him she was 'very well treated and very well contented'. She never used the Doctor as an intermediary, for she feared the 'injurious consequences'; Puebla was still playing a double game, and she viewed him with jaundiced eye as 'the adviser to the King' whose chief interest was to make his own life in England as comfortable as possible. Staunchly moral herself, she was finally beginning to appreciate the lack of scruple in the men with whom she was dealing, and slowly, painfully, she was learning to play the game of power politics their way. Nevertheless, she realised that she now was getting nowhere with Henry VII on the main issues, and continued to press her father for a new ambassador.

Acting as her father's ambassador certainly had a beneficial effect on Katherine's health, however. In May 1507, her physician, Dr Johannes, reported to Ferdinand that she was entirely recovered 'from the long malady which she has suffered ever since her arrival in England', and had regained 'her natural healthy colour. The only pains she now suffers are moral afflictions beyond the reach of the physician.' Money was still a problem, yet worry over it did not affect Katherine as badly as previously, and her health remained stable for the next eighteen months. Being allowed once more to see the Prince doubtless helped.

During May and June, Katherine was present at the tournaments held to celebrate young Henry's sixteenth birthday, and delighting to watch him showing off his prowess in the lists. Already he was a skilful horseman and jouster, being very tall and of strong build, 'most comely of his personage', and so amiable that he was perfectly happy discussing warfare with 'gentlemen of low degree', something his contemporaries marvelled at. Prince Henry was popular with his future subjects for his common touch, something his father had never had. He dreamed of war and glory and chivalry, and since he was openly pro-Spanish and anti-French the prospect of marriage to the Princess Katherine was very attractive to him. For the present, however, he was bound to obey his father, and could only exchange pleasantries with his betrothed. The King had seen to it that his life was sheltered and secluded during his formative years, and Henry had learned to keep his own counsel.

The age gap between Henry and Katherine seemed to be narrowing as Henry grew to manhood. The time was now ripe for their marriage, and yet, in July 1507, it still seemed to be a long way off. 'Nothing has changed,' Katherine told Ferdinand then. She herself was now twenty-one, old by Tudor standards for marriage, and to her the delay was extremely distressing. An indication of her true feelings was given in September, when she overheard speculation that her marriage would never take place and told Henry VII 'she could not bear to have such a thing said'. Prince Henry was the husband she wanted. 'There is no finer youth in the world,' wrote Dr de Puebla at this time; 'he is already taller than his father and his limbs are of gigantic size. He is as prudent as is to be expected for a son of Henry VII.'

By the autumn of 1507, Ferdinand had firmly established himself as ruler of Castile and Henry VII began to look upon Katherine in a more favourable light, something that substantially increased the esteem in which she was generally held at court. Katherine herself believed that her marriage to Prince Henry might now go ahead as planned if only her father would comply with Henry VII's demands for payment of her dowry. Yet while Ferdinand prevaricated, he instructed her to 'always speak of your marriage as a thing beyond all doubt', as though 'God alone could undo what has been undone'.

But it was not just Ferdinand's extended power that provoked Henry VII to a change of heart; since January 1507, the English King had cherished a desire to marry Queen Juana and thereby rule Castile himself, and to do so now he needed Ferdinand's goodwill and his permission. It was this that precluded him from breaking off his son's betrothal to Katherine, and this that influenced his dealings with Ferdinand throughout the year.

It was to Katherine that Henry had first disclosed his intentions, telling her he did not care about Juana's mental derangement; he had seen for himself her sultry, almost oriental beauty, and knew she was capable of producing healthy children. From the first, Katherine favoured an alliance between the King and her sister. Family feeling apart, she saw it as a surety for her own marriage taking place. She did not perceive that Ferdinand would never allow Henry VII to marry Juana, and that he meant to continue ruling Castile himself without foreign interference. Yet at the same time, he did not wish to alienate his ally, and therefore, when the King's proposal was put to him by Katherine, he instructed her to tell Henry that it was 'not yet known whether Queen Juana be inclined to marry again', although it was certain that if she became so inclined, 'it shall be with no other person than the King of England'. Ferdinand continued to dangle the carrot of Juana, believing that this was the best way to induce Henry VII to proceed with the marriage of his son to Katherine, but by September 1507 Henry was chafing at the delay and looking elsewhere for a wife, telling Katherine that the whole business had 'occasioned him great perplexity', and begging her to urge her father to think again. She did her best to bring negotiations for the marriage to a successful conclusion, which resulted in Ferdinand promising, in October, to persuade Juana 'by degrees' to it.

Katherine took advantage of this situation, and her authority as ambassador, by asking both her father and King Henry to redress the wrong done to her servants, who were still 'in absolute misery'. At long last, Ferdinand's conscience pricked him, and in September he sent her 2,000 ducats, not a large sum but enough to clear some of her debts, although she was somewhat perplexed as to which should have priority. Her creditors must be satisfied, her servants paid, her depleted plate needed replacing, and she herself needed new clothes. Then Henry VII, eager to ingratiate himself with her father, stepped in, telling her he loved her so much he could not bear the idea of her being in poverty, and would give her, without delay, 'as much money as you want for your person and servants'.

61

For the present, it seemed that Katherine's troubles would soon be over. She had also achieved tranquillity in her spiritual life with the advent of a new confessor. Early in 1507, she had been forced to apply to the General of the Order of the Franciscan Friars Observant in Spain for a new confessor, as Alessandro Geraldini had gone home a year earlier, leaving her virtually without spiritual comfort. She still could not speak English, and her father had failed to send a replacement, despite repeated requests. The confessor sent by the Order, who arrived later in the year, was in Katherine's opinion 'very good': he was a young Spanish friar called Fray Diego Fernandez, a man of magnetic charm and forceful personality, who rapidly gained a powerful influence over the Princess, to whom he offered the kind of devoted friendship and support she had so often found lacking in England. Moreover, he was a learned young man, and had about him an air of authority that commanded respect.

Before long, Katherine was showing herself reluctant to take any step without the friar's advice and blessing. She was a deeply pious person, but also a woman of twenty-one who had for long lacked a male figure – father, lover or husband – in her restricted life. It is perhaps no coincidence that she recovered her health shortly after Fray Diego's arrival. The friar certainly knew his power over her, and soon capitalised on it. He told her there was no need to suffer any more humiliating delay in waiting for her marriage to take place; the marriage treaty had been concluded conditionally, Henry VII had defaulted on its terms, and she was free to renounce it. But King Ferdinand was unimpressed by this view, and ignored the letter in which Katherine set it forth.

Katherine's marriage prospects received a major setback early in 1508 when Henry VII finally lost patience with Ferdinand over the delay in arranging his marriage to Juana. When he was informed that she was completely deranged, he retorted that he did not believe it. In fact, though, he now realised only too well that Juana was not in the marriage market, and the matter of their betrothal was quietly dropped without further recriminations. But the damage had already been done. By March 1508 relations between Henry and Ferdinand had deteriorated badly, and that month saw the King re-entering into negotiations with the Emperor Maximilian for the marriage of the Prince to Eleanor of Austria. Young Henry himself was behaving as if he was 'hardly much inclined' towards marrying Katherine; it was what his father expected of him, especially as Henry VII was becoming convinced that their union would be of questionable validity anyway.

In the spring of 1508, Ferdinand finally granted Katherine's request for another ambassador and sent Fuensalida to England. Unfortunately, the new ambassador proved to be as proud, pompous and dogmatic as only a Spanish grandee could be; the first thing he did was ruffle King Henry's feathers over the sensitive matter of Juana, thus setting a pattern for diplomatic relations over the next year. Katherine took an instant dislike to Fuensalida, and accused him of behaving with 'too great rigour towards the King'. She did not trust him, and she resented the fact that the respect formerly shown to her as her father's official ambassador had diminished with the Knight Commander's arrival in England. Fuensalida, for his part, immediately assessed how matters stood between Katherine and Fray Diego, and decided that the friar was a bad influence and should be removed at the earliest opportunity. In this he had Katherine's best interests at heart, since he could foresee a scandal brewing; Katherine, however, resented his animosity towards the friar, and preferred to heed the vitriol poured in her ears by Fray Diego about Fuensalida than Fuensalida's warnings about the integrity of Fray Diego.

Negotiations for the betrothal of Prince Henry to Eleanor of Austria broke down early in the summer of 1508, and before long Henry VII was scouring the courts of Europe for another possible bride for his son. At seventeen, the Prince was approaching manhood and should be fathering heirs to safeguard the dynasty and the peace of the realm. Unfortunately, Ferdinand's spies told him what was afoot, and he wrote heatedly to Fuensalida, saying, 'The King of England must keep faith in this matter!' He also threatened war if Henry VII broke the treaty. Fuensalida was further instructed to ingratiate himself with the Prince of Wales, and 'use all the means in his power for bringing the marriage to a speedy conclusion'. Fortunately, many of the English nobility were eager for it to take place. In January 1509, when the King was trying to negotiate a French match for his son, a deputation of them confronted him and pressed him to marry the Prince to Katherine, as they had heard that her dowry was ready for payment and, more important, they had noted the sickness of their sovereign and feared for the succession. The King, who was indeed ill with consumption, agreed to consider their request, but Katherine was not hopeful of his agreeing to it, and there was even talk of her returning to Spain to await another acceptable marriage.

During the early months of 1509 she was 'in deep despair', feeling herself unable to endure much more. She told Ferdinand that her sufferings continued to increase, and that she felt so depressed that life seemed not worth living. She feared, she said, that she 'might do something which neither the King of England nor your Highness would be able to prevent'. In Lent, she was physically unwell again, which commonly happened to her at that season, perhaps because she was confined to a diet of mainly fish, which may not always have been fresh or agreed with her. She was not seen about the court, and was probably still unwell in April, when an event occurred that would dramatically change her life. It is significant that, when her circumstances improved, as they did within two months, her illnesses disappeared for good.

Money had again become a problem during the early months of 1509, and had been since September 1508, for Henry VII, piqued by Ferdinand's duplicity, had once again ceased paying Katherine's allowance. In March she told her father that 'my necessities have risen so high that I do not know how to maintain myself'. She had sold all her household goods and most of her dower plate – 'it was impossible to avoid it' – and had since spent the money thus raised. Once again, she was driven to begging King Henry for help, though he told her he was not bound to give it; nevertheless, he added that the love he bore her would not allow him to do otherwise, and grudgingly gave her enough to defray the expenses of her table. She found this humiliating, and wrote to Ferdinand: 'From this your Highness will see to what a state I am reduced, when I am warned that even my food is given me almost as alms.'

To add to Katherine's woes, there was a good deal of tension within her household, due not only to the uncertainty overshadowing her future, but also to petty disputes and jealousies. Early in the year, Katherine quarrelled with Doña Elvira over the latter's constant intrigues and dismissed her, leaving no suitable person to supervise her servants and protect her reputation. Katherine was now twenty-three and mature enough to order her own affairs, and circumstances would shortly dictate that the duenna would never be replaced. Her desperate lack of money meant that her servants were once more facing destitution, for again they had not been paid, 'which hurts me and weighs on my conscience'. This time, they were not so forbearing. The Princess's chamberlain, Juan de Diero, responded by treating her with great 'audaciousness' and failing to order her household properly, and because she could not pay him the arrears of salary due to him, she could neither reprimand nor dismiss him.

Much of the tension in Katherine's household was generated by Fray Diego. The friar had already acquired a reputation as a womaniser, and most of the ladies in the Princess's household, not to mention some about the court, were a little in love with him. His hold over Katherine was stronger than ever, and the relationship between them intense. Fuensalida had watched the Princess and marked her complete dependence on Fray Diego, and by March 1509 was so alarmed about it that he confided his fears to his master, alleging that the friar was 'unworthy' to hold his office. Katherine was 'full of goodness' and 'conscientious', but her confessor was making her 'commit many faults'. The ambassador did not elaborate, but sent his servant to Spain to inform Ferdinand in person 'of the things which for two months past have happened'.

Fuensalida called Fray Diego 'light, haughty, and scandalous in an extreme manner'. Even Henry VII had heard of his promiscuity and had spoken to Katherine 'in very strong words' about her confessor's behaviour. But the friar, perceiving that Fuensalida was hostile to him, 'put me out of favour with the Princess, so that if I had committed some treason she could not have treated me worse'. Fuensalida accordingly begged Ferdinand to recall the friar and replace him with 'an old and honest confessor'.

The implication was clear: Katherine was placing herself in moral danger and risked ruining her reputation by associating with Fray Diego, a confessor who was stressing the avoidance of sin on one hand and fornicating with women on the other. Fuensalida feared that Katherine too would succumb, for if this had not been the issue at stake, then the nature of the complaints against the friar would have been stated more specifically by the ambassador.

Today, it is hard to assess the precise nature of the relationship between Katherine and Fray Diego. In view of Katherine's character, and her repeated later assertions that she had come to Henry VIII 'a true maid, without touch of man', it was certainly not a sexual one – Henry VIII's retention of the friar in his office after his marriage to Katherine is sufficient proof of this. Katherine's respect for the friar's vows and for her own rank and person were enough to deter her from overstepping the bounds of accepted morality, but the men around her were hardened realists, and saw life in basic terms; they well knew what could develop from such a potentially explosive situation. To them, the removal of Fray Diego was therefore imperative for the sake of Katherine's as yet unblemished reputation and her future marriage prospects.

Katherine, meanwhile, could see no wrong in her confessor; in her view, he was 'the best that ever woman in my position had'. She reacted with passionate anger to Fuensalida's criticism, not perhaps fully comprehending why he should be so concerned, and wrote to inform Ferdinand 'how badly the ambassador has behaved' towards the friar. By March 1509, she would have nothing to do with him, and was demanding that her father replace him with someone else. 'Things here become daily worse,' she wrote, 'and my life more and more insupportable. I can no longer bear this.' Fuensalida, she went on, had 'crippled your service'; Henry VII did not want him, and would undoubtedly welcome a replacement. Whatever Fuensalida wrote in his reports, she warned, 'might not be true'. Because of this, Ferdinand immediately ordered the recall of Fuensalida: Luis Caroz could take his place. Later on, after the accession of Henry VIII, Fuensalida did make his peace with Katherine, thanks to the intercession of the new King, before leaving England in May 1509. At the same time, Katherine also bade farewell to Dr de Puebla, who was likewise returning to Spain, where he died a few months later.

By defending her confessor to her father, Katherine had provided a credible reason for her rift with Fuensalida, but at the same time she had exposed her emotional and spiritual dependence on the friar. By now, she would do nothing without the friar's consent. When the court moved to Richmond and he told her to remain behind, for no apparent reason, she obeyed him without protest, even though no provision had been made for her to stay. When the King heard, he was 'very much vexed', and when Katherine did arrive at Richmond the next day, after a comfortless night, she met with a very chilly reception. The King did not speak to her for three weeks after the incident.

The friar had also managed to alienate most of the senior members of Katherine's household, including the chamberlain, Juan de Diero, and when Katherine wished to sell her remaining plate 'to satisfy the follies of the friar', Diero spoke out against it, with the result that the Princess behaved towards him as though he had 'committed the greatest treason in the world'. Fuensalida, seeing this, continued to press Ferdinand for the removal of the friar, whom he referred to as 'this pestiferous person'. He was writing, he said, 'not so openly as I would desire'; instead, he was sending one of Katherine's devoted servants who would disclose more sensitive information. Katherine, learning of her servant's departure and guessing what was afoot, warned Ferdinand not to credit anything that was written or said to him about 'my confessor, who serves me well and loyally'. She herself refused to believe the rumours then circulating about the friar, nor could she see the damage he was causing. In fact, he had brought about a rift between Katherine and Henry VII, and when it became obvious in April 1509 that Henry was dying, Katherine's fortunes were at a low ebb. She was ill and depressed, even suicidal, and once more in grave financial difficulty.

Nevertheless, an end to her troubles was in sight. That month, Luis Caroz arrived to replace Fuensalida as ambassador, and brought with him the reassuring news that her dowry was ready for payment. This was comfort indeed, but Katherine was anxious about what would become of her once the King was dead. Already the courtiers were behaving towards her with a new respect, believing she might shortly be Queen of England, but she had as yet heard no word from Prince Henry, who was so distraught at the prospect of losing his father that all other matters had temporarily been banished from his mind.

Henry VII died a hard, difficult death from tuberculosis on 22 April 1509. On his deathbed, he admitted to his son that his conscience was troubling him over his poor treatment of the Princess Katherine, and commanded young Henry to do the honourable thing and marry her, something that was much in accord with the Prince's own inclinations.

When Henry VII died, England's reputation in Europe was so impressive that it was said that all Christian nations were eager to forge alliances with her. Much of Henry's power lay in the wealth he had accumulated over the years; there was well over £1 million in the treasury at his death, a fantastic sum in those days. In this wealth lay England's strength and security. Yet when Henry VII was buried in the chapel named after him in Westminster Abbey early in May, few mourned his passing. The English had always underestimated his greatness, seeing him as a parsimonious schemer who was not to be trusted, rather than the wise founder of a strong dynasty and the guardian of a precarious peace.

There was little doubt in anyone's mind that the new King, Henry VIII, had already chosen the lady who would share his life and his throne. The Princess had always been on close and affectionate terms with the young Henry before his father's death, even though the old King had kept them apart for much of their five-year engagement. Although the Prince had secretly renounced his vows on his father's orders in 1505, few knew of it, and in the eyes of the world Henry and Katherine were still betrothed. As a result, Katherine found herself treated with a new and gratifying deference by courtiers. It was, of course, a matter of absolute necessity that the King marry and get himself an heir as soon as possible: there were still living some members of the House of York who thought they had a better claim to the throne than he, and the spectre of civil war still loomed large.

After the funeral of Henry VII, the court moved to Greenwich, the red-brick hilltop palace on the Thames where Henry had been born. Here, where the windows afforded magnificent, panoramic views of London, the new King made it clear that he intended to pursue traditional foreign policy and revive Edward III's ancient claim to the throne of France and have himself crowned at Rheims. The possibility of war with France, England's hereditary enemy, made an alliance with Spain all the more desirable. King Ferdinand was urging him to marry Katherine without delay, and was promising him 'all the advantages which were denied to his father, on the sole condition that the marriage is immediately consummated'. The dowry, he promised, would be 'punctually paid'.

But, briefly, Henry VIII hesitated: his councillors told Fuensalida that, unexpectedly, he was suffering 'certain scruples of conscience' and wondering whether he would 'commit a sin by marrying the widow of his deceased brother', as such unions were forbidden in the Bible. It seemed that certain churchmen had been whispering in Henry's ear, Warham amongst them; and the King's conscience was a rather tender organ, as many would later find to their cost. Informed of Henry's doubts by Fuensalida, Ferdinand hastened to reassure the young King that 'such a marriage is perfectly lawful, as the Pope has given a dispensation for it, while the consequence of it will be peace between England and Spain'. He drew Henry's attention to the King of Portugal, who had married two of Katherine's sisters in succession and was 'blessed with numerous offspring, and lives very cheerfully and happily'. Ferdinand felt certain that 'the same happiness is reserved for the King of England, who will enjoy the greatest felicity in his union with the Princess of Wales, and leave numerous children behind him'. Fuensalida told Katherine that Ferdinand loved her 'the most of his children and looks on the King of England like a son'. It was Ferdinand's intention to give advice about everything to Henry VIII, 'like a true father'; Katherine's duty would be to foster an understanding between the two men and ensure that her future husband would heed Ferdinand's guidance in all matters of state.

Early in June 1509, the Privy Council urged the King to marry Katherine and fulfil the terms of the betrothal treaty. They did not have to spell out why the matter was urgent, as Henry was more than cognizant of the insecurity of his dynasty. Instead, they extolled Katherine's virtues, saying she was 'the image of her mother, (and) like her possesses that wisdom and greatness of mind which win the respect of nations'. As for Henry's scruples about the canonical legality of the marriage, 'we have the Pope's dispensation,' they said; 'will you be more scrupulous than he is?'

The King could only agree that there were many good reasons for the marriage; above all, he told them, 'he desired her above all women; he loved her and longed to wed her.' Most of the Councillors knew this: since the age of ten, Henry had looked up to and admired his pretty sister-in-law; and, as he had grown to manhood, and had seen how well Katherine had coped with the adversity and humiliations she had suffered, his admiration had deepened, not to passion – it would never be that – but to love in its most chivalrous form, blended with deep respect. This apart, honour demanded that Henry should marry her, as by so doing he would rescue her from penury and dishonour, like a knight errant of old, and win her unending gratitude. It was a plan that appealed vastly to the King's youthful conceit. Indeed, there was even a certain smugness in his approach to his marriage, for he was later to inform King Ferdinand that he had 'rejected all the other ladies in the world that have been offered to us', which, in his view, proved beyond doubt the depth of the 'singular love' he bore to his 'very beloved' Katherine. Undoubtedly he found her attractive, with her long golden hair and fair skin; he was impressed by her maturity, her dignity, her lineage and her graciousness. Everything about her proclaimed her a fit mate for the King of England, and Henry, who was no fool, realised this.

Yet in some ways she was an unwise choice. Doubts that the marriage might be uncanonical were well founded in the opinion of some churchmen of the time, though they, knowing the King's will in the matter, kept silent for the most part. Then there was the matter of the five-and-a-half-year age gap, and the fact that Katherine, at twenty-three, was well past her first youth by the standards of her day, and rather old to be contemplating motherhood for the first time. Many girls married at fourteen and bore a child the following year, while the average age at death for women in Tudor times was around thirty. Henry VIII could have had his pick of the young princesses of Europe, but he needed the alliance with Spain, he wanted Katherine's dowry to add to his already rich inheritance, and, above all, he wanted Katherine herself.

And what Henry VIII wanted, he usually got.

5
Sir Loyal Heart
and the Tudor court

One day in early June 1509 Henry, in a buoyant mood, made his
way from the Council Chamber at Greenwich to Katherine's
apartments. He came alone, and dismissed her attendants. Then he
raised the Princess from her curtsy with a courtly gesture, declared
his love for her, and asked her to be his wife. Without any hesitation,
she joyfully agreed, relief and happiness evident in her face and
voice.

This was the culmination of all Katherine's hopes during the last
six years: God had now seen fit to answer her prayers, and she was
filled with thankfulness. She would be Queen of England, raised by
this magnificent young man to be the bride of his heart and the
mother of his heirs. Those courtiers who had scorned her and tried to
humiliate her would now have to defer to her, and she would not
have been human if she did not relish the prospect. The days of want
were gone for good, for very shortly she would be the wife of the
richest monarch ever to reign in England.

Fray Diego was all but forgotten now, as Katherine gave her heart
unreservedly to her future husband. That she fell quickly in love
with him we may easily believe as she had long ago responded to his
charm and good looks, and he, now that the matter had been
decided, saw no need to wait much longer before they could legally
share a bed. His coronation was planned for midsummer, and he
wanted Katherine to share it with him as queen.

Henry VIII and Katherine of Aragon were married privately on

71

11 June 1509, the feast day of St Barnabas, in her closet at Greenwich, by William Warham, who was now Archbishop of Canterbury, and had once spoken out against their union. Katherine wore virginal white with her long hair flowing free under a gold circlet, and vowed to be 'bonair and buxom in bed and at board' as was laid down in the more robust form of the marriage service then in use.

The Archbishop pronounced the young pair man and wife, then the small wedding party proceeded to the Chapel of the Observant Friars within the palace precincts to hear mass.

There is no record of the King and his new Queen being publicly put to bed together; their wedding was private, therefore it is likely that they were accorded some privacy afterwards. However, there was never any doubt that Katherine's second marriage was ardently consummated that night.

To his contemporaries, Katherine's bridegroom was the true heir in blood to both Lancaster and York, and the reincarnation of his magnificent maternal grandfather, Edward IV. He was a man of great physical beauty, above the usual height, being around 6′3″ tall (his skeleton, discovered at Windsor in the early nineteenth century, measured 6′2″ in length, whilst his armour, preserved in the Tower of London, would fit a man of nearly 6′4″). He was magnificent to look at, being lean and muscular, with an extremely fine calf to his leg of which he was inordinately proud, and had skin so fair that it was almost translucent; we are told that it glowed, flushing a rosy pink after the King had exercised. All were agreed that he was extremely handsome, and the ambassadors who visited Henry VIII's court during the early years of his reign were united in their praise of his personal endowments: 'His Majesty is the handsomest potentate I ever set eyes on,' wrote the Venetian Sebastian Giustinian in 1514, adding that Henry had 'a round face so beautiful that it would become a pretty woman'. Five years later, that same ambassador was still singing the King's praises: 'Nature could not have done more for him. He is very fair, his whole frame admirably proportioned.' He had strong features, with piercing blue eyes, a high-bridged nose, and a small but sensual mouth. His voice was slightly high-pitched. He had 'auburn hair combed straight and short in the French fashion', and until 1518 he was clean-shaven. He then grew a beard, saying he would not shave it off until he had met with and embraced his ally, the King of France. Queen Katherine protested, for she did not like this new bearded Henry, but the beard remained until 1519. Many thought it attractive – 'it is reddish and looks like gold' – but Katherine continued to complain about it, and by November that year the King had given in to her entreaties and shaved it off. An international catastrophe was only narrowly averted by Henry's ambassador to France, who told King Francis the truth, whereupon the French courtiers, far from being indignant, were amused to learn that the mighty sovereign of England had capitulated to his usually complacent and meek wife. Thus, peace was preserved, and the Queen was kept happy.

Henry VIII had boundless energy and a strong constitution. When, in 1514, he contracted smallpox, his doctors were afraid for his life, yet within days he was up, having 'risen from his bed to plan a military campaign'. However, throughout his life he had a pathological hatred of anything to do with illness and death, and he was as terrified as a child of the plague that troubled his kingdom during hot summers.

Giustinian thought Henry 'the best dressed sovereign in the world; his robes are the richest and most superb that can be imagined, and he puts on new clothes every holy day.' As the calendar was full of saints' days and religious festivals, that meant a lot of new clothes. There were outfits of cloth of gold, Florentine velvet, silver tissue, damask and satin, mantles lined with ermine, heavy gold collars with diamonds the size of walnuts suspended from them, ceremonial robes with trains four yards long, and jewelled rings worn on fingers and thumbs. Some clothes were cut in 'Hungarian' or 'Turkish' fashion, and many had raised embroidery in gold or silver thread. It was an age in which men strutted like peacocks in their finery, although none was finer than the King, who looked upon costume as a visual art.

Henry's contemporaries thought he was 'the most gentle and affable prince in the world'. He was quick to laugh and 'intelligent, with a merry look'. He had great charisma and a strong personality that won golden opinions. In 1509, Katherine's future chamberlain, Lord Mountjoy, told the Dutch humanist scholar Erasmus that the

King, 'our Octavius', had an 'extraordinary and almost divine character. What a hero he now shows himself, how wisely he behaves, what a lover he is of goodness and justice! Our King does not desire gold or gems, but virtue, glory, immortality!' As Henry himself declared in one of his songs, idleness was the chief mistress of all vice, and he meant to follow the path of virtue, something by which he set great store throughout his life. That his expectations often related to others rather than himself he did not regard as inconsistent, for in his opinion his own deeds and behaviour were always morally justified. He was bursting with confidence, 'prudent, sage, and free from every vice'.

On the debit side, he was quick-tempered, headstrong, immature and vain. In 1515, he asked the Venetian ambassador if the King of France was as tall as he: 'Is he as stout? What sort of legs has he?' 'Spare,' he was told. 'Look here!' crowed Henry, 'I also have a good calf to show!' And he opened his doublet to display his shapely, muscular legs. He 'could not abide to have any man stare in his face' when in conversation, yet he himself would often turn a steely gaze on people, and Sir Thomas More was not the only one to stammer under the 'quick and penetrable eyes' of his sovereign.

As the years passed, Henry continued to attract praise and acclaim. He was well aware of his glorious reputation, and on occasions boasted about it. Yet as early as 1514 there were indications of the kind of ruler he would one day become, and the Spanish ambassador was moved to warn his master, King Ferdinand, that if a bridle was not put on 'this colt, it will afterwards be found impossible to control him'. His words were echoed seven years later by Sir Thomas More, who advised Thomas Cromwell, then newly admitted to the King's service, that he should handle Henry with caution: 'For, if the lion knew his strength, hard were it to rule him.'

Henry was gifted with acute powers of reasoning and observation, as well as the ability to evaluate a person or situation almost immediately. He had a vast store of general knowledge that he used to good effect. Above all, he was an intellectual with 'most piercing talents'. According to Sir Thomas More, he had 'cultivated all the liberal arts' and possessed 'greater erudition and judgement than any previous monarch'. From infancy, he had been imbued with a passion for learning, thanks to the good offices of his grandmother, the austere Lady Margaret Beaufort and was the most learned king yet to have ascended the throne of England. He was 'so gifted and adorned with mental accomplishments of every sort' that the Venetian ambassadors 'believed him to have few equals in the world'. 'What affection he bears to the learned!' wrote Lord Mountjoy in 1509, informing Erasmus of Henry's intention to establish a haven for scholars at his court. Europe was then on the brink of a period of cultural flux, when men were beginning in earnest to question and rationalise in matters of religion or philosophy. During Henry's own lifetime, two great movements would affect his realm: the Renaissance, which would have a profound effect upon England's cultural life; and the Reformation, which was to overthrow the traditional conception of a Christian Republic of Europe for ever.

Henry's education had been extremely thorough. He could speak and write fluent French and Latin, understood Italian well and spoke it a little, and by 1520 was conversant with Spanish. He loved reading, and his favourite books during his younger years were the works of St Thomas Aquinas and Duns Scotus. However, in 1519, he began to suffer from recurring headaches and migraines, which made reading and writing 'somewhat tedious and painful'. The headaches continued to plague him for the rest of his life, and may well account to some extent for his later irascibility.

The King wrote several treatises during his life, and his letters to the Vatican were said to have been the most eloquent received there, for which reason they were exhibited in the consistory. His literary talents extended to passionate love letters, as well as poetry. His chief interest was theology; he was a master of doctrinal debate, of which he was 'very fond', and would hear others out with 'remarkable courtesy and unruffled temper'. He was good at mathematics, and also keenly interested in astronomy, a passion he shared with Sir Thomas More, who would often join him on the leads above Greenwich Palace to look at the night sky.

Henry VIII professed all his life a deep and sincere faith in God, and for many years regarded himself as a true son of the Church of Rome. He was known to attend as many as six masses in a single day, and at least three on days when he hunted. Every evening, at 6.0 p.m. and 9.0 p.m., he went to the Queen's chamber to hear the offices of vespers and compline. At Easter, he 'crept to the Cross' on

75

his knees, with all due humility. He also held himself up as an authority on doctrine, and was acknowledged as such by his contemporaries because 'he is very religious'.

In 1521, while convalescing after a fever, the King added the finishing pages to a Latin treatise he had been working on for some time with assistance from others, notably Sir Thomas More. It was entitled *A Defence of the Seven Sacraments against Martin Luther*, and was an attack upon the heresies propagated since 1517 by a former monk of Wittenburg in Germany, who would – thirty years later – be hailed in England as the founder of the Protestant religion. Henry was well aware that information about Luther's controversial teachings was already filtering through to England, and had gained hold in Germany. Yet although he himself enjoyed disputing points of doctrine, heresy was another matter entirely, and he was appalled that any credence should be given to the corrupt teachings of 'this weed, this dilapidated, sick and evil-minded sheep'.

Henry VIII, like most of his contemporaries, was well aware that there were certain abuses within the established Church that needed reforming, but he was a religious conservative at heart, and would not countenance heresy as a means of achieving this. To Henry, and men like him, heresy was a poison that threatened the very foundations of the superstructure of Church and State as one body politic. It encouraged disaffection among the lower classes, challenged the divinely appointed order of things, and – worst of all – meant eternal damnation for those who succumbed to its lure. In sum, it represented every evil that could be manifested in a well-ordered world, and must therefore be eradicated.

In his book, the King's central argument was for the retention of the seven sacraments – Luther had rejected all but two. Marriage, in particular, was upheld by Henry, for it turned 'the water of concupiscence' into 'wine of the finest flavour. Whom God hath joined together, let no man put asunder.' Luther had also rejected the authority of the Pope, but the King exhorted all faithful souls to 'honour and acknowledge the sacred Roman See for their supreme mother'. When Thomas More suggested that this was a little extravagant, Henry protested that he was so 'bounden' to the See of Rome that he could not do enough to honour it: 'We will set forth the Pope's authority to the uttermost,' he declared – words he was later to regret.

Although Luther himself accused Henry VIII of raving 'like a strumpet in a tantrum' in the book, and spoke of 'stuffing such impudent falsehoods down his throat', the Pope received the treatise with rapturous praise, and in the autumn of 1521 rewarded Henry with the title *Fidei Defensor* (Defender of the Faith) in gratitude. Elizabeth II still bears this title today, though Britain has been an independent Protestant state for more than four centuries.

Apart from religion, Henry loved gambling, good food, and dancing, in which he did 'marvellous things, both in dancing and jumping, proving himself indefatigable'. He was obsessive about hunting, which he preferred above all else. The 'grease season' was traditionally in the autumn, but Henry also hunted at other times of the year, both for pleasure and to provide for his table. In the autumn, however, he would take a rest from state duties and go on a progress through parts of his kingdom, chiefly for the purpose of discovering the delights of different chases. 'He never takes his diversion without tiring eight or ten horses,' wrote the Venetian ambassador in 1519; 'when he gets home, they are all exhausted.' In fact, he exhausted most of his male companions too by 'converting the sport of hunting into a martyrdom'. And, after a successful day, it was not unknown for him to boast about his success for three or four hours at a time. Queen Katherine enjoyed hunting too, and sometimes accompanied her husband.

Being an excellent horseman and an expert in the martial arts, Henry was also passionately fond of that other great medieval sport, the jousting tournament, which was almost a weekly event during the early years of his reign. He was a fine jouster who was conspicuous in the combats, both on horseback and on foot, excelling everyone else 'as much in agility at breaking spears as in nobleness of stature'. At one tournament in 1518, Henry performed 'supernatural feats', causing his magnificent charger to 'jump and execute other acts of horsemanship'. Then, changing mounts, he made his fresh steed 'fly rather than leap, to the delight and ecstasy of everybody'. The Queen would never miss a joust if she could help it, and watched with her ladies from specially erected pavilions at the side of the lists.

Another sport at which he excelled was tennis, not the game played at Wimbledon today, but 'royal' (real) tennis played on a hard, enclosed court – Henry's court is preserved at Hampton Court – an altogether tougher and more dangerous game. The Household Accounts for the year 1519 record a payment for 3¼ yards of black velvet for a 'tennis coat for his Grace'. 'It is the prettiest thing in the world to see him play, his fair skin glowing through a shirt of the finest texture,' reported the Venetian ambassador.

Henry enjoyed hawking, 'running the ring', 'casting the bar', wrestling, and archery. He practised daily at the archery butts and passed a law requiring every man in England to spend an hour doing the same on Saturday afternoons, such was his faith in the reputation of the longbow as the traditional instrument of English military success; he himself could 'draw the bow with greater strength than any man in England'. He also wished to ensure that the young men of his court were expert in the martial skills, and on one occasion in 1510 arranged for a fight with battle axes to take place in the presence of the Queen and her ladies in Greenwich Park, thus mixing military exercise with pleasure.

Henry had a lifelong love of the sea and all things maritime. He ordered the building of several great ships – including the *Henry-Grace-à-Dieu* and the *Mary Rose* – and has been rightly acclaimed as the founder of Britain's modern navy. In 1515, he went with the Queen to review his fleet at Southampton, wearing a 'sailor's coat and trousers of frieze cloth of gold' and carrying 'a large whistle with which he whistled almost as loud as a trumpet'. He was in his element that day, on board his flagship, where for a couple of hours he enjoyed himself immensely, acting as pilot.

His pleasures were not always so boisterous. He inherited from his Welsh forbears an abiding love of music, and could play a number of instruments, sing and compose. He was particularly accomplished on the lute, harpsichord, recorder, flute and virginals, and would often entertain the court by singing and playing his own compositions. He could 'sing from the book at sight', often set his own verses to music, and composed anthems and hymns. One, 'O Lord, the maker of all things', is still sung in churches today. Yet Henry preferred writing secular songs, mostly in the courtly tradition, with English or French lyrics. The most famous were 'Green groweth the holly' (probably written for Katherine of Aragon), '*Adieu Madame et ma maîstresse*' (written much later for Anne Boleyn), and 'Pastime with good company', which vividly portrays his mood at the commencement of his reign.

In these early years, Henry VIII's pleasures took precedence. His attitude to kingship and the duties of state he was required to perform was a different matter entirely. He had had a cloistered upbringing before suddenly finding himself in a position of power, honour and wealth, a heady experience for a youth of eighteen. Perhaps it was not surprising that he spent his days in pursuit of amusement rather than learning statecraft. Matters of state, he felt, could safely be left in the hands of his Privy Council; in fact, 'he did not care to occupy himself with anything but the pleasures of his age'.

The mature men appointed to advise him were so slow that they caused him 'much disgust': Henry preferred the company of the young men of the court with whom he had shared his boyhood. His councillors were alarmed to see him squandering his father's carefully amassed wealth on expensive and frivolous pastimes when he should have been learning about the government of his kingdom, and they were at pains to persuade him – not without difficulty – to sit in on meetings of the Privy Council, 'with which at first he could not endure to be troubled'. As the French ambassador observed, 'Henry is a youngling, cares for nothing but girls and hunting, and wastes his father's patrimony.'

His councillors hoped that, given time to mature, he would settle down and fulfil their expectations. Yet it was a slow process. In 1514, the Milanese ambassador complained that the King had put off their discussion about politics to another time, 'as he was then in a hurry to go and dine and dance afterwards'. Affairs of state, even after five years on the throne, were still ranking fairly low on Henry's scale of priorities. Even as late as 1519, the Papal nuncio reported that he was 'devoting himself to accomplishments and amusements day and night, being intent on nothing else'. All business was left to Cardinal Wolsey, 'who rules everything'. This was the situation that endured until the late 1520s, when Henry began to take the reins of government into his own hands.

It was the outward trappings of kingship that were important to Henry VIII during these early years: the pageantry, the ceremonial, the gorgeous robes, the priceless jewels, and the glittering court, and he passionately believed that they all served to enhance the image of royalty. It was Henry who was the first English King to express a preference to be styled 'Your Majesty' rather than the customary 'Your Grace'. He saw himself, indeed, as a hallowed being set apart from the ordinary species of men, and it was a persona he consciously cultivated, so confident did he become of his own divinity. No King of England before him enjoyed such power, nor ever would after him.

A man of contrasts, he personified for the average Englishman all the strengths and virtues of his race, and it was this that lay at the root of his vast popularity. As Prince of Wales his charm had won the hearts of his people, and now, exalted to kingship, he was fêted as the herald of a new age, a golden epoch that would witness a return to England's former glory, the revival of the days of chivalry, and the ultimate conquest of France – the new King's ambitions were well-publicised. The English loved Henry for his youth, his beauty, his high courage, his accomplishments, and above all for having identified their interests as his own. He was very knowledgeable about most of the issues that touched their lives, having been born with a talent for absorbing information, and there was 'no necessary kind of knowledge, from King's degree to carter's, but he had an honest sight of it'. He was fond, in his younger years, of mingling incognito among his subjects, in order to learn their views on the issues of the day.

In 1509, it was said that the whole world was 'rejoicing in the possession of such a King'. The passing of years did not dampen this enthusiasm, for in 1513 we are told that 'love for the King is universal with all who see him, as his Highness does not seem a person of this world but one descended from Heaven'. Erasmus, later still, described Henry as 'more of a companion than a King', a view that would have earned the hearty agreement of those courtiers with whom the King hunted, tilted, and otherwise amused himself. This common touch came naturally to him, and would serve to hold the love and loyalty of his subjects until he died.

In an era of arranged marriages, men were not censured for taking their pleasure when they found it. In his youth, the King was commendably discreet about such matters, so much so that we know absolutely nothing about his sexual activities, if any, before his accession. As Prince of Wales, he had led a cloistered life and had cultivated a chivalrous attitude towards the opposite sex, seeing himself as the knight errant whose role it was to flirt, offer elegant compliments, and profess undying love. When he came to the throne, women were waiting for him in droves, and freed from the confines of his princely existence, he made the most of his position and took what they offered. In this respect, though he was far from virtuous by modern standards of morality, by the standards of his time, and compared to other princes of the age, he was quite circumspect. Thanks to his discretion, Queen Katherine never knew of these early infidelities, which were fleeting anyway, and as far as Henry was concerned, they had nothing to do with her. His love for her was on a different plane completely.

Having sex was one thing, talking about it quite another. The King was very prudish, and was known to blush at bawdy remarks. He abhorred lightness in married women, even though he was not above pursuing them himself. And from his wife, he expected total fidelity and absolute obedience.

Katherine of Aragon first appeared at court as Queen of England on the day her marriage to the King was proclaimed, 15 June 1509. Henceforth, she would be at Henry's side at all state and court functions. She had already adopted the pomegranate, symbol of fertility, as her personal badge, and now she took the motto 'Humble and Loyal' for her personal device. In the royal palaces of England, an army of carpenters, stonemasons and embroiderers were already carving, chiselling and stitching her initials and Henry's, 'H' and 'K', on every available surface, and her throne was set beside the King's under the rich canopy of estate.

In 1509, Fray Diego described Katherine as 'the most beautiful creature in the world'. Marriage certainly made her seem so. She was twenty-three, and had kept her looks thus far. She was plump, pretty, and still had beautiful red-gold hair that hung below her hips when loose. Yet, within six years, she had lost her youthful bloom and her figure, and in 1515 was described by the Venetian ambassador as 'rather ugly than otherwise'. Sadly, he spoke the truth. By 1515, Katherine had suffered several bitter disappointments and five pregnancies, and these had aged her considerably. A miniature of her painted by Lucas Hornebolte (now in the National Portrait Gallery) survives from this time, and shows with cruel clarity that the pretty girl depicted in Miguel Sittow's portrait of 1505 had in fact aged almost beyond recognition in ten years. Hornebolte's portrait is of a stout, mature woman with a face overshadowed by anxiety and sadness. The red-gold hair seems to have darkened (although this may be due to pigment in the paint), and is gathered into a bun or plait on the nape of the neck, being surmounted by a Juliet cap, a rare fashion in England at that time.

This miniature should be compared with a portrait painted about five years later, which has been attributed to Johannes Corvus. Several versions exist, the most famous being in the National Portrait Gallery in London. Katherine is here shown wearing the gable hood traditionally associated with her, with long frontlets that would shortly become unfashionable. She is in a rich brown velvet gown with a low square neckline and furred sleeves, and is portly in build, with no pretensions to beauty, having a pale face in which the mouth has a slightly disdainful look and the firm chin juts out. A similar portrait, probably painted from a lost original during the reign of Mary I and until recently in the possession of the Royal Academy of Arts, is kinder, and shows the Queen smiling graciously. Yet the face is the same, that of a woman no longer young, obviously well-bred, with the marks of sadness etched upon it. And the figure, camouflaged in dark velvet furred with ermine with ropes of gold chains slung across the bodice, has likewise gone to ruin, spoiled by frequent childbearing. Perhaps the best existing likeness of Katherine in her later years is the fine miniature in the collection of the Duke of Buccleuch, which shows a stout woman, with large attractive blue eyes, holding a monkey.

Katherine's gradually fading looks were brought increasingly into contrast by the maturing beauty of her younger husband. She selected her ladies for their looks as well as their background, which showed up even more her own ageing face. To compensate for this, she took care to dress herself as magnificently as she could, being, like her mother, 'a ceremonious woman in her attire'. On marrying the King, she had been provided with a sumptuous new wardrobe, most of it in the English fashion. After her marriage, she rarely wore the farthingale, although she did very occasionally appear in Spanish dress. Her new gowns would have had court trains several yards in length, and were of rich materials such as satin, velvet – often with raised gold embroidery – or cloth of gold. If one had wealth, it was not considered vulgar to display it.

Katherine did not dictate fashion, like Anne Boleyn who came after her, but she had a lifelong love of rich clothes and jewellery. In fact, her jewellery was magnificent, and comprised two sets: the crown jewels, pieces that had been worn by former queens of England, and which were not her own but public property; and those items that the King had given her personally, which alone were worth a fortune. She favoured ropes of pearls from which hung suspended pendants made of diamonds in the form of a cross or a St George medal or religious symbols such as the IHS, representing Christ. Like many people at that time, the Queen wore several rings at once, and her corsage was rarely without a jewelled brooch pinned in the centre. On her head, she would usually wear the English gable hood and black veil made popular twenty years before by Elizabeth of York, although on occasion she would wear a different head-dress such as the Flemish hood which 'gave her additional grace', or the Juliet cap already mentioned. Her crown, which was melted down in the time of the Commonwealth, was worn only occasionally, for the great occasions of state; then she would wear her hair loose.

Katherine had all the personal qualities needed for a Queen of England. She had adapted to the customs of her new land, although she would continue actively to further Spanish interests for several years to come. She had strong principles, and set a high moral tone for her household. Beneath her outward air of meekness and submissiveness to her husband, she concealed a tough and tenacious character that would help her to bear the blows later dealt her with calm dignity. Those who served her invariably became devoted to her, for she was both kind and unfailingly courteous. In 1514, she was described by a Flemish diplomat as 'a lady of a lively, kind and gracious disposition, and of quite different complexion and manner from the Queen her sister.' Unlike Juana, Katherine was neither given to tantrums, hysteria or bouts of melancholia, nor was her love for her husband as obsessive as Juana's had been. Yet it was a deep love and would

83

survive until death; in this, as in everything else, the Queen displayed singlemindedness and a trusting naïvety.

Katherine had received a good education, comparable to or better than that given to most girls of her rank. Erasmus called her 'a miracle of learning', and while this was probably an exaggeration in the best courtly tradition, there is every indication that there was some truth in it. The Queen was literate, well read and thoroughly conversant with the Scriptures, although her intelligence and her powers of perception were somewhat limited. Nevertheless she was far more erudite than most women at the court, and her qualities were justly recognised by the scholars who gathered there at the King's invitation. Katherine herself thrived in this cultural atmosphere, for she was interested in humanism and matters of religious doctrine and, as she grew older, she turned to intellectual pleasures more and more, finding little to stimulate her mind in the daily round of courtly revels. In 1526, she was very impressed by Erasmus's new book, *The Institution of Christian Marriage*, which was shown to her by Sir Thomas More. More himself warmly praised the work, and remarked that 'her Majesty the Queen correctly regards it as being of supreme importance'.

Katherine also took an interest in the universities. When she visited Merton College, Oxford, in 1518, she was welcomed by the students with 'as many demonstrations of joy and love as if she had been Juno or Minerva'. She also lent her support to Wolsey's foundation at Oxford, Cardinal College (now Christ Church), and when, in 1523, the King brought his confessor, Dr Longland, to show her the plans for it, she showed herself 'joyous and glad' to learn that she herself was 'particularly prayed for' in the chapel of the new establishment.

Since her arrival in England, when she spoke only Spanish, Katherine had laboured to learn English. It was a long process, for languages were not a strong point with her, but by the time of her marriage to the King she was able to speak English passably well, and her command of it would increase considerably over the following years. Yet she still spoke with a Spanish accent which never left her; this is evident from the phonetic spelling in her letters, in which, for example, Hampton Court becomes 'Antoncurt.'

According to Erasmus, Katherine was 'more pious than learned', and 'as religious and virtuous as words can express'. The great humanist praised her warmly to Henry VIII, saying: 'Your wife spends that time in reading the sacred volume which other princesses occupy in cards and dice.' From her youth, Katherine spent a considerable part of each day at her devotions, hearing mass, kneeling privately at prayer at the prie-dieu in her chamber, reading the Bible (then in Latin, which she understood to a degree) and other religious works, and hearing the Divine Offices of the day, which her chaplains performed in her private apartments. As she grew older, her faith deepened and, since her philosophy was a passive one, she faced up to and accepted what she understood to be the will of God without question or complaint.

By 1519–20, the Queen was leading an almost conventual existence. She withheld herself to some extent from the mainstream of court life, preferring to devote her time to her religious observances, and there are frequent references in the sources for the period to her being in her chapel, or 'just come from hearing mass', or on pilgrimage, our Lady of Walsingham being a favourite shrine of hers. From now on, religion would be the mainstay of her life and her chief consolation.

Her life was nevertheless lived under the public gaze. Nearly everything she did was attended by ceremony and performed according to strict rules of courtly etiquette. She was never alone. As Queen of England, she was given a household of 160 servants, and several of these – usually ladies-in-waiting, maids of honour and pages – were always in attendance upon her. Her meals were frequently taken in public, in full view of the court (and, on occasion, the common people, when they were admitted to watch their betters at meat); sometimes they were served in her apartments, where she was waited on by pages, her ladies standing in attendance behind her.

There were many demands on the Queen's time: charitable enterprises, religious observances, ambassadors come to pay their respects, domestic matters to be discussed and acted upon, and meetings with her own council. Such leisure time as she had she spent mainly at needlework, embroidering tapestries, altar-cloths, vestments, rich gowns and head-dresses for herself, shirts for her husband worked with the Spanish black-work lace that she herself had popularised, linen shifts to wear beneath her gowns, infant layettes on occasion, and clothing for the poor. Sometimes she and her ladies would entertain themselves with music – although there is no record of Katherine herself being able to play any instrument, she certainly enjoyed hearing others – with dancing – she herself would sometimes partner her ladies in the privacy of her chamber – in discussion, or even gambling with cards, dice, backgammon or other table games.

Even her sex life was surrounded by ritual. Traditionally, kings and queens had separate apartments in the royal palaces. If the King wished to sleep with his wife at night – a matter of public interest, since the succession must be assured – he went in procession, escorted to her chamber door by members of his guard and gentlemen of his privy chamber. Katherine, in turn, having been undressed by her ladies, would be sitting up in the great tester bed waiting for him. On the nights the King did not honour her with his company, a maid would occupy a truckle bed at the foot of her bed, but she was banished whenever the King arrived unannounced, as he often did. Then his guards would be posted outside the doors to the Queen's apartments. Henry VIII was very sensitive about security, and any bed he slept in was always made up by his servants according to an elaborate ritual which involved a sword being thrust between the mattress and the feather bed, just in case an intruder had secreted himself there.

As queen, Katherine was more often than not an observer, rather than a participant, in the pageants and entertainments performed at court, even though she had in her teens been a good dancer. But dignity and gravity now sat heavily upon her in public, and probably in private also, and as she grew older, pageants and court balls lost their appeal. Nevertheless, she was always at Henry's side on state occasions or whenever foreign dignitaries visited the court. Indeed, we know very little else of her activities during the middle years of her marriage to the King; in the foreign dispatches and the chronicles of the period, she is very much a background figure, gracing these state occasions but doing little else of note.

Katherine was always an extremely popular queen, partly because her marriage had strengthened the vital commercial links between England and the Low Countries. This, however, was only one reason for the affection in which she was held. The main reason for it lay in her personal qualities, her unfailing graciousness and dignity, and her kindness. Not for nothing was it said of her that she was 'more beloved than any queen who ever reigned'. The English had taken her to their hearts; they rejoiced on her marriage, grieved with her in her sorrows, and – much later – were ready to champion her cause in the face of the King's displeasure.

Henry VIII established the first Renaissance court in England, using a large portion of his father's fortune to finance it and to refurbish the palaces in which it would be housed. The court in those days was a nomadic institution, moving between Greenwich, Richmond, Windsor, Westminster (until the royal apartments were destroyed in the fire of 1512), the Tower of London in the early years of the reign, Eltham Palace, Hampton Court after 1514 and a host of smaller palaces and manor houses. It comprised noblemen, churchmen of every degree, privy councillors, officers of the King's household, gentlemen of the Privy Chamber, the Queen's household, ladies, servants and menials, and could on occasions number several thousand people, especially when most of the aristocracy were in residence with their attendants.

It was a very splendid court; the King was extremely liberal, and enjoyed displaying the riches at his disposal. Following in his father's footsteps, he insisted on the observance of elaborate ceremonial on state occasions, though at other times he preferred to be more relaxed. Venetian envoys visiting the English court in 1515 were astonished at the lack of formality, and delighted when the King himself, while walking in the gardens, actually stopped under their windows and called up to them, then stayed there some time chatting and laughing with them, 'to our very great honour'. These same ambassadors reported to the Venetian Senate that the whole of Henry's court 'glittered with jewels and gold and silver, the pomp being unprecedented'. It was noticed that the Queen's ladies in particular were of 'sumptuous appearance', being very handsome.

Scholars, notably those from Italy, then the hub of European culture, were particularly welcome at the English court. The King wished to surround himself with learned men and bask in their reflected glory, preferring them – according to Erasmus – to the 'young men lost in luxury, or women, or gold-chained nobles'. Sir Thomas More applauded Henry VIII for cultivating all the 'liberal arts', and Erasmus thought that 'under such a King, it may not seem a court, but a temple of the Muses'. When Henry dined, he was attended by writers, divines, humanists, poets and artists, with whom he eagerly conversed and exchanged ideas.

One of the scholars who ranked highest in the King's estimation was Thomas More, a friend of Erasmus and a fellow humanist. A man of upright character with a gentle, dry wit, More was also a brilliant lawyer and well read in theology. In 1516, he published a book entitled *Utopia*, which described the ideal political state and earned him a generous measure of fame. He was also renowned for his exemplary family life and for his learned daughters, the products of his advanced views on female education. His eldest daughter, Margaret, the future wife of the Protestant writer William Roper, could speak both Latin and Greek. Henry and Katherine admired More, and the King invited him to court, though he only accepted with great reluctance, being unhappy about leaving the peace of his Chelsea home for public life; in later years, Henry would often throw up More's lack of enthusiasm for the court 'in a joke in my face'.

As he had feared, he hated it. 'I am as uncomfortable there as a bad rider is in the saddle,' he wrote. However, the King was 'so courteous and kindly' and did all in his power to make More welcome, singling him out for special friendship and showing he realised what a sacrifice More had made to humour him. 'I should not like to think that my presence had in any way interfered with your domestic pleasures,' he told him, intrigued by this rare, unworldly man who seemed content with his family, his books and his animals.

More's integrity, and his conservatism in matters of religion – he advocated the burning of heretics – appealed to Queen Katherine, and theirs was a friendship that would remain untarnished by events. 'He is an upright and learned man,' the Spanish ambassador would one day say of More, 'and a good servant of the Queen.' When the King and Queen dined privately, they would often send for Thomas More to be 'merry with them', and so much did they enjoy his company that, according to his son-in-law, William Roper, 'he could not once in a month get leave to go home to his wife and children'. The King would frequently summon More to his private study, where the two men would sit for hours discussing astronomy, geometry and divinity.

All of this brought its rewards, of course. In 1518, More was admitted to the Privy Council; three years later he was knighted. Yet he himself had few illusions about his standing at court. When William Roper congratulated his father-in-law on his advancement. More replied: 'Son Roper, I may tell you I have no cause to be proud thereof, for if my head would win the King a castle in France, it should not fail to go off!'

By 1517, Henry VIII's court had a magnificent reputation. 'The wealth and civilisation of the world are here,' enthused the Venetian ambassador; 'I here perceive very elegant manners, extreme decorum and great politeness.' Yet it all had to be paid for, and by 1518, Henry had dug so deep into the fortune left by his father to finance his pleasures and his court that his treasury was emptying at an alarming rate. This meant that for a time there would have to be fewer pageants, fewer tournaments, fewer entertainments than in earlier years. It is even possible that the King had grown a little bored with these things. He seems also to have got into bad company at this time, and whereas previously he had won praise for 'putting a silence on all brawlers', in 1519 he was attracting criticism for preferring the company of 'youths of evil counsel, intent on their own benefit, to the detriment, hurt and discredit of his Majesty' rather than seeking the society of 'demure, sober and sad' persons. In the eyes of many, these young bloods were bringing scandal on the throne by encouraging their young master to go amongst his people in disguise and behave in 'a foolish manner'. Their habits were scathingly described as 'French', and they were said to indulge in 'French vices'. They poked fun at 'all the estates of England, even the ladies and gentlemen of the court'. The King was for a time coming increasingly under their influence, and his Council was resolved to put an end to his associating with them. Fortunately, the Council prevailed, and Henry agreed to banish the offenders from court, having been convinced that his hitherto glorious reputation was at stake.

The court itself was an extravagant, wasteful institution. It moved from palace to palace so that each royal residence it had occupied could be cleansed. There were carpets on the floors of the royal apartments only; elsewhere there were rushes, which were anything but sweet-smelling when the court had been in residence for a few weeks. Gentlemen did not always bother to use the privies, which were primitive anyway; they sometimes urinated on the rushes, as did the many pets owned by the courtiers. The food waste from the kitchens mounted up; in the summer, it stank, and the stench from the privies on hot days was terrible indeed. Thus the court had to move on, so that the palace might be cleansed. This arrangement meant that a skeleton staff had to be maintained in all the palaces.

Cardinal Wolsey, the King's chief minister, was concerned about the way in which the royal household was run, and anxious to make economies, especially after the crippling of the Exchequer by the Field of Cloth of Gold in 1520, when the courts of England and France met amid scenes of unprecedented splendour. Thus, in 1526, after much research, the Cardinal drew up the Eltham Ordinances. The Ordinances, which were strictly enforced, rid the court of hangers-on and laid down rules of etiquette and practice, streamlining finances and cutting back on expenditure. Restrictions were placed on the number of retainers allowed those visiting the court, and also on the number of pets permitted (not only dogs but birds and monkeys were favoured by the courtiers); scullions were forbidden to go about the kitchens naked, and were given new clothes. The King's servants were to wear the Tudor livery of green and white at all times. Even the food was rationed, although fairly generously: from this time on, the Queen's maids would each breakfast on two small loaves and a gallon of ale. The result was a far more efficiently run household and a saving of both money and resources.

During the early years of the reign, when the young King and Queen passed their time in 'disports', there were hunts, tournaments, banquets, balls, sporting events, and 'disguisings'. The latter were elaborate masquerades in which the King and his gentlemen would dress up and disguise themselves – sometimes in the strange costumes of other lands – and then come upon the Queen and her ladies unawares, dance for her, or perform other scintillating feats, and then disclose their identity, 'whereat the Queen and her ladies were greatly amazed'. It afforded Henry great amusement to come thus attired upon Katherine and see her astonishment. It was a game of which, in his youth, he never tired; and she, for her part, never spoilt his pleasure by disclosing that she knew who it was, even when these 'disguisings' had been going on for several years.

But perhaps the most popular and spectacular of the entertainments staged for the pleasure of the Tudor court was the pageant, an early dramatic form. Pageants followed a set pattern: the male participants would enter the hall clad in matching costumes with a certain significance; then the ladies, in complementary attire, would emerge from a kind of stage on wheels, which could be made to resemble a castle, a forest, a mountain, the sea, or anything else that the King's Master of the Revels could devise. Pageants usually followed allegorical or classical themes, such as 'The Garden of Hope', or they could be based on English legends such as Robin Hood. When the ladies had appeared, the gentlemen would invariably show off their prowess in a mock fight, then the ladies would descend and dance with them as a reward. Often the participants were disguised. The King frequently took part in these pageants, partnering his sister Mary since the Queen preferred to watch rather than join in.

The pageants give us some idea of the opulence of the Tudor court: the materials used for the costumes were all of the richest quality, and purpose-made; the gold and jewels were all genuine. The King's intent was not entirely frivolous. Visiting princes, ambassadors, and other foreigners watching them would quickly gain the impression that the King of England was extremely wealthy and that his court was the most splendid in Christendom. Wealth and its trappings were evidence of political and military strength, and Henry used pageantry to build up the reputation of the Tudor monarchy in Europe.

The first pageant to be staged in Henry VIII's reign took place at Christmas 1509, when twelve men, dressed as Robin Hood and his Merry Men danced with the Queen's ladies in Katherine's chamber to the music of a consort of minstrels – Robin Hood later turned out to be the King in disguise. From then on, pageants were held whenever there was something to celebrate at court, and often when there was not. Sometimes the male dancers wore masks, which would be removed after the dancing by the ladies to the accompaniment of much laughter and flirtation.

The pageants to celebrate the birth of a son to Henry and

Katherine in 1511 were particularly elaborate: one took the form of 'a mountain glistening at night' with a golden tree adorned with Tudor roses and pomegranates. The celebrations for the birth of the prince continued for well over a month, culminating in the day when the palace doors were thrown open to the common people, so that they could watch the pageants. Unfortunately, matters got rather out of hand when they rushed into the hall and 'rent, tore and spoiled' the stage and its props. Pandemonium reigned as the courtiers ran for the shelter of the thrones on the dais, but the King was enjoying himself enormously, playing the role of a benevolent prince indulging his subjects. Laughing, he stood unresisting as they stripped him down to his hose and doublet, carrying off his clothes as souvenirs. The other courtiers had no choice but to follow their monarch's example, and they too were forced to suffer the indignity of losing their clothes and jewels; the unfortunate Sir Thomas Knyvet was stripped stark naked, and had to climb a pillar for safety! But when the mob began to despoil the ladies' costumes, the King called a halt. Fortunately, the people obeyed him, and the day ended in 'mirth and gladness', with Henry's popularity greater than ever.

Pageants were staged frequently during the early years of the King's reign. Perhaps the most original was that which took place on May Day 1515, for the benefit of the Venetian ambassadors, when Henry and Katherine, who was richly robed in the Spanish fashion, entertained their guests to a woodland picnic in Greenwich park, which had been made to resemble Robin Hood's hideout in Sherwood Forest. Henry and his nobles appeared dressed in Lincoln green as Robin and his men, and carried bows. Yet this was not a simple rustic idyll, for no detail had been left to chance: singing birds in cages had been hidden in the trees, and 'carolled most sweetly'; the court musicians sat in a bower, and the tables set beneath the trees groaned with a feast of gastronomic splendour; an archery contest took place for the visitors' entertainment. Afterwards, a procession formed and the May Queen and the court were brought back to the palace in triumphal cars adorned with figures of giants, escorted by the King's guard. Music played, courtiers sang, and the King and Queen brought up the rear with an estimated crowd of '25,000 persons' (a slight exaggeration, perhaps).

After 1518, there were fewer pageants, due to the depleted state of the King's finances and also to his growing preference for Italian masques. The last opulent court pageant of these years took place in May 1527, to celebrate a new treaty between England and France. On this occasion, a banqueting house was set up in the tiltyard at Greenwich, where the King and Queen sat under canopies of estate. A masque was performed first, after which a pageant in the form of an artificial mountain was performed in the great hall of the palace. One of the participants was the King's daughter, the Princess Mary, who, like her ladies, was dressed in Roman fashion with robes of 'cloth of gold, and so many precious stones that the splendour and radiance dazzled the sight'.

Masques differed from pageants in that there was more plot to them; whereas a pageant was merely a tableau with music and dancing, a masque incorporated a story, and was the forerunner of the modern musical. The first masque ever seen in England was performed at court in January 1512, and greatly impressed the King: in it, the participants were disguised by visors and caps of gold and told their tale with singing and dancing. In 1517, he and Katherine watched a masque entitled 'Troilus and Cryseide', based on an old tale made popular by Geoffrey Chaucer, at Eltham Palace as part of the Christmas festivities. After that masques were staged more frequently at court, and eventually replaced pageants as its chief form of dramatic entertainment.

Pageants and masques were often used to entertain foreign guests. Henry VIII always extended a magnificent welcome to visiting princes, ambassadors and churchmen, and was anxious to impress them with the splendour of his court. The Queen was always present, unless she was in an advanced state of pregnancy, and played her part as hostess, being particularly skilled at the courteous conversation required in diplomatic circles. In 1515, when she received the Venetian ambassadors, who had come to present to her the Doge's compliments, they spoke to her, they reported home, 'in good Spanish, which pleased her more than I can tell you'. Katherine spent some time discussing Spanish affairs with them, and was happy to share her memories of her mother, Queen Isabella.

Central to this lavish entertaining was the court banquet, the first of which took place in February 1510, when Henry and Katherine entertained all the foreign ambassadors then in England at the Palace of Westminster. The King led the Queen in procession into the great hall, followed by her ladies, the ambassadors, and all the nobility. Henry himself showed the ambassadors to their seats, then sat down beside Katherine at the high table on the dais, beneath the canopy of estate. However, he would not remain seated for long, for he was soon walking around the tables, chatting to his wife and guests. He then disappeared and came back wearing Turkish robes with a troupe of mummers in tow, who proceeded to perform for the assembled company.

The food at such banquets would have consisted of several courses, each with several dishes. Meat was served throughout the year, except in Lent, when fish was the main entrée. The meat or fish would be spiced and served in a sauce, and accompanied by bread soaked in gravy. There were few vegetables; however, Queen Katherine would sometimes have a salad in season, which she had introduced into England from Spain; her salad, however, would have been served hot, as raw vegetables were considered dangerous. Desserts were elaborate: fruit pies with decorated crusts, 'subtleties' of sugar resembling castles or coats of arms, and marchpane comfits. Wine flowed freely throughout the meal, as well as ale or mead for the lower tables. After the banquet had ended, the guests chatted as the tables were cleared for the pageant which usually followed. When the entertainment had ended, there was dancing for up to two hours, to the music of a consort of flute, harp, fife and violette, then spiced wine or hippocras was served, after which the King and Queen would retire to bed. Sometimes, the King himself would serve the food at a banquet, and at other times, when the Queen was heavily pregnant, he would bring the guests into her private apartments after dinner, to be entertained with music, conversation, 'disguisings' and dancing. Katherine never forgot to praise Henry's munificence on such occasions.

No effort was spared to make guests feel welcome. When Henry's sister, Queen Margaret of Scotland, visited London in 1515, Katherine sent a white palfrey to her for her state entry into the capital. The Queen of Scots had her own London residence at Scotland Yard near Westminster, but it was not ready for her, so Baynard's Castle was placed at her disposal. The King organised jousts in her honour, and a lavish banquet in the Queen's chamber at Greenwich.

In 1518 the French ambassadors were entertained to a banquet consisting of 260 dishes, followed by a 'very sumptuous' pageant. In 1519, Katherine herself hosted a banquet for the Duke of Longueville at her manor house at Havering-atte-Bower in Essex, a house once owned by several medieval queens. The King was present at this 'sumptuous' feast, which the Queen had arranged in 'the liberallest manner'. When it ended, Henry thanked her 'heartily', and the French guests were full of praise. Six weeks later Henry himself hosted a banquet at Newhall in Essex for these same envoys; afterwards, the Queen unmasked eight dancers, who all turned out to be 'somewhat aged; the youngest was at least fifty!' On the following day, Katherine again acted as hostess at yet another banquet.

Tournaments, too, were often staged in honour of specific events, and they could go on for some considerable time. One joust in November 1510 lasted for several days, during which 'the King broke more staves than any other'. In 1511, the Queen watched the jousts, held at Westminster to celebrate the birth of her son, from a pavilion hung with cloth of gold and purple velvet and embroidered with the letters 'H' and 'K' in fine gold. Her young husband appeared in the lists as 'Coeur Loyal' (Sir Loyal Heart), being her champion, and this device was emblazoned for all the world to see on his armour and his horse's accoutrements.

Thereafter, the King held tournaments frequently, being an active participant at every one. Usually they were staged in the spring, to celebrate May Day, but they also took place in winter and at other times of the year. Jousts were usually held 'in honour of the ladies', who often followed medieval tradition and gave their favours to their chosen knights. At one joust, Queen Katherine and her ladies received the men's jousting apparel as 'largesse'. In December 1524, the Queen took part in a pageant that heralded the commencement of a tournament at Greenwich, sitting in a prefabricated castle in the tiltyard. Two elderly knights then appeared and craved her leave 'to break spears'; however, when Katherine 'praised their courage' and gave her consent, they threw off their robes to reveal a laughing Henry and his friend and brother-in-law, the Duke of Suffolk.

Tournaments took place mainly in the spring, Easter was spent at Windsor, followed by the feast of St George with its attendant Garter ceremonies, then there were more jousts on May Day. In the autumn came the King's customary progress, which combined a break from court routine with the opportunity to see his realm and meet his subjects, as well as to avail himself of the hunting to be had in other parts. In 1511, the King and Queen made the first of these progresses, visiting the West Midlands, where they saw 'a goodly stage play', a mystery play performed by guildsmen at Coventry.

The annual routine of the court culminated in the twelve days of merrymaking that constituted a Tudor Christmas. Henry VIII usually kept the festival at Greenwich Palace. Christmas Day itself was then a holy day, devoted to acts of worship, but the days after it were given over to feasting and 'disports', the King celebrating Christ's birth with 'much nobleness and open court'. The festivities reached their climax on Twelfth Night, the Feast of the Epiphany, when they were usually brought to an end with a sumptuous banquet.

Gifts were exchangd on New Year's Day, not on Christmas Day. On New Year's Day 1510, Katherine's first Yuletide gift from Henry was a beautifully illuminated missal inscribed in his own hand: 'If your remembrance be according to my affection, I shall not be forgotten in your daily prayers, for I am yours, Henry R., forever.' Touched by this, Katherine immediately added a further inscription of her own beneath: 'By daily proof you shall me find to be to you both loving and kind.'

At Christmas, the court was usually thrown open to the public, who were allowed in to watch the 'goodly and gorgeous mummeries'; festive fare was distributed, boar's head and roast peacock served in its feathers being the chief meats at this season. There were pageants, disguisings and feasts, and carols danced and sung in the great hall while the Yule log crackled on the hearth, 'to the great rejoicing of the Queen and the nobles'.

Unusually at Christmas 1517, the court was closed, but there was a very good reason for it. Plague was a notorious killer, and during an epidemic drastic measures had to be taken to avoid the spread of infection, for it was no respecter of persons. And plague struck often, particularly in sixteenth-century summers. The plague that had hit London in the July of 1517 was of a type known to be extremely deadly – the sweating sickness, a scourge prevalent only in Tudor times, having first appeared in England in 1485; some saw it as a judgement of God upon the usurping dynasty.

Illness in any form horrified and disgusted Henry VIII, but the sweating sickness reduced him to a state of abject fear. It was a loathsome disease: the victim would suddenly feel unwell, break out into a profuse sweat, and continue to sweat until a crisis was reached, at which point death usually occurred. This could happen with frightening speed, taking only three to four hours from first symptoms to last breath. Recovery was rare, and those that did recover were often weakened for life. Above all, the sweating sickness was highly infectious, and spread with terrifying rapidity.

At the first sign of plague in July, the King had given orders for the court to leave the capital and move into the country, which he much preferred anyway, leaving behind him strict instructions that those people who had been in contact with the disease were under no circumstances to approach him. There were fears for a time that Queen Katherine had contracted the dreaded plague, as she complained of feeling unwell for a few days, though she soon recovered. By September, the plague was spreading further still, and the death toll was rising. Henry, fearful for the succession, as he still had no son to succeed him, and petrified of catching the disease, took himself and the Queen, with only a few attendants, off to a 'remote and unusual habitation' that has not been identified, and there he remained, whilst the sweating sickness continued to ravage his kingdom. By December, however, it was on the wane, although it was deemed prudent of the King to keep 'no solemn Christmas' that year because there was still some risk of infection.

As well as presiding over a glittering, cultivated court, Katherine of Aragon also administered her own household. This numbered some 160 persons, many of them Spaniards who had come to England with her in 1501. There were also some English officers and servants in her entourage, because the King preferred her to be served by English people, and on her marriage several members of her former household had returned to Spain, including the chamberlain, Juan de Diero. This was not so much the King's doing as the Queen's, for many of those dismissed her service at that point had in the days of her widowhood grown insolent, not treating her with the respect she should have been shown. Nevertheless, at Katherine's command they were all paid the arrears of salary due to them, though she did ask her father to administer a mild rebuke in certain cases.

After her marriage to the King, the chief officer in the Queen's household was Lord Mountjoy, the celebrated humanist, who became her chamberlain. The King was indulgent enough to allow her to retain most of her Spanish ladies, although they were now supplemented by the wives of some of the great English nobles. Katherine had grown very attached to a number of her Spanish attendants, several of whom would remain with her until she died, but the one she favoured the most, 'whom she loves more than any other mortal', was Maria de Salinas, who had once been a maid of honour to Queen Isabella. Maria was the daughter of a Castilian grandee, Don Martin de Salinas, by Doña Josepha Gonzalez de Salas. She had come to England with Katherine in 1501, and the two girls had quickly struck up a lasting friendship, which was cemented by sharing the enforced privations of Katherine's long widowhood. In 1509 Katherine told her new husband that she wished to keep Maria as 'the girl desires of all things to remain with me'. Henry VIII agreed to Maria staying on, and never resented the influence she had upon his wife, who treated her as her chief confidante.

In 1516, Maria de Salinas became a naturalised subject of the King of England as a preliminary to her marriage in June that year to William, Lord Willoughby d'Eresby, who had been courting her for some time. After her wedding, she left the court, but it was gratifying for the Queen to know that her friend, whose earlier betrothal had been broken because she could not give the girl a dowry, had at last made a good marriage. The Queen may have attended the christening of Maria's son Henry in 1517, and it is probable that she was godmother to the daughter born two years later and named Katherine in her honour. Sadly, Lord Willoughby died in 1526, leaving his widow with two young children to rear. She was still close to the Queen, and probably visited Katherine at court during her widowhood. Later still, she would brave the King's wrath for the sake of her friendship with the Queen.

When Maria de Salinas left court upon her marriage, Katherine turned to another lady with whom she had formed a close friendship, Margaret Pole, the niece of Edward IV and Richard III, and, some said, the rightful heiress of the Plantagenets. In 1513 the King had restored to Margaret Pole part of the inheritance forfeited under the Act of Attainder passed on her father the Duke of Clarence in 1478, prior to his death in the Tower – by drowning in a butt of malmsey, it was said. Henry obviously had no reservations about Margaret Pole's loyalty to the Crown at that point, for he created her Countess of Salisbury, a title she should have inherited in 1499 on the execution of her brother, the Earl of Warwick. Katherine had always felt a sense of guilt because Warwick's death had paved the way for her coming to England, and she had singled out his sister for special friendship. This was warmly reciprocated, and in later years the two women would cherish a shared hope that their children would marry and thus further cement the bond between Tudor and Plantagenet.

In 1513, Margaret Pole was forty, and had been a widow since 1505. She had several children, of whom the most gifted was Reginald Pole, who also benefitted from the King's generosity when Henry arranged for, and funded out of his own privy purse, the boy's education at Oxford, where Reginald justified the faith of his royal patron by obtaining an honours degree after only two years of study. His mother was a learned woman, whose erudition was much respected by the Queen, and, in later years, Katherine would choose Lady Salisbury as her daughter Mary's state governess, knowing that her many qualities made her eminently suitable for such a post.

In 1513, Katherine had to enlist the aid of the King's chief minister Thomas Wolsey when she wished to rid herself of a former lady-in-waiting, Francesca de Caceres, who had been in her entourage prior to her marriage to the King, and was now asking to be readmitted to her service. Francesca had once intrigued with Fuensalida to get rid of Fray Diego, and had been privy to most of Fuensalida's information about the time when Katherine had foolishly succumbed, to whatever degree, to the charms of the friar. Much of what Francesca knew was mere supposition, but the Queen felt that nevertheless it would be 'perilous and dangerous' to employ her, or even to send her abroad with a reference recommending her to a foreign princess. She dared not risk having her former maid of honour gossiping about that unhappy episode with Fray Diego at foreign courts. Happily, Wolsey, who was probably unaware of the real reason for the Queen's concern, arranged for Francesca to return to Spain, where she could do least harm.

Fray Diego himself remained in the Queen's service for five years after her marriage to the King. 'I hope to keep him all the time I shall be able,' she told her father. However, it was not long before he began to cause trouble once more. He did not trust Ferdinand's ambassador, Luis Caroz, believing that Caroz had come to England with the prime objective of having him removed from the court. As a result, though he behaved towards the ambassador with elaborate courtesy, he did not deceive Caroz, who rightly deduced that the friar was 'very suspicious and fearful of me'. Undoubtedly, he concluded, 'his mind is not quite right.'

Fray Diego still retained considerable influence over the Queen, but this was nowadays confined mainly to spiritual matters. However, he kept her 'engaged' to such an extent that it was difficult for Caroz and others to obtain an audience with her and, so the friar believed, criticise him to her face. Lesser members of her new household went in fear of Fray Diego, and dared not cross him, as they knew he could have them dismissed if he so pleased. Caroz saw what was going on, and informed Ferdinand's secretary of state that he had 'never seen a more wicked person in my life'. He had tried to warn the Queen about him, he said, but Katherine would not listen.

This state of affairs continued until 1514, when several members of the Queen's household went to the King with complaints about Fray Diego, accusing him of fornicating with women of the court. Henry at once confronted the friar, and warned him that such behaviour would not be tolerated in one so close to the Queen. Fray Diego was highly indignant: 'If I am badly used, the Queen is still more badly used!' he retorted, pointedly referring to Henry's latest mistress. At this, the King's anger erupted, and it was not long before the friar was summarily dismissed from the Queen's service and ordered to return to Spain. Shocked and angry, he left in November, but not before he had written a letter to the King, reminding him how he had served Katherine faithfully for seven years, 'enduring evil for her sake, even lack of meat and drink, of clothes and fire'. He swore he was no fornicator: 'Never, within your kingdom, have I had to do with women.' He had been 'condemned unheard', and those who had accused him were 'disreputable rogues'. But Henry was implacable, and the friar's protestations only served to confirm his belief that Fray Diego was a liar as well as a womaniser.

As for the Queen, she lifted no finger to save her confessor. She too must have been shocked by what she had heard about him, and her submission to the King's will was absolute; from henceforth she would suffer no man but her husband to rule her.

6

A chaste and concordant wedlock

On Friday, 22 June 1509, the King and Queen went by royal barge from Greenwich to the Tower of London, where custom decreed the King must spend the night before his coronation. Henry had ordered the refurbishment of the old royal apartments in the Norman keep, and here, that same afternoon, he created twenty-four Knights of the Bath. On the following morning, the grand procession formed within the Tower precincts. Henry rode on horseback, Katherine in a litter through cheering crowds via Cheapside, Temple Bar and the Strand to the Palace of Westminster, through streets hung with rich tapestries, where on every corner stood priests swinging censers.

Crowds had turned out to see them, Henry in a robe of crimson velvet trimmed with ermine over a coat of 'raised gold', which was embroidered with diamonds, rubies, emeralds, great pearls and other rich stones, and Katherine in virginal white satin. At Westminster, there was a lavish banquet, after which the King and Queen retired to the chapel of St Stephen to pray.

The 24th of June was midsummer day. A long scarlet runner had been laid from the Palace doors to the great west door of the Abbey of Westminster and, at the appointed time, the King and Queen went in procession along it, Henry walking beneath a canopy of estate borne by the five barons of the Cinque Ports, and Katherine riding in a litter of rich cloth drawn by two white palfreys. She was dressed like a bride, in an embroidered gown of white satin, with her hair – 'of a very great length, beautiful and goodly to behold' – falling loose down her back beneath a coronet set 'with many rich Orient stones'. Her officers and ladies followed her, in chariots and on palfreys. 'There were few women who could compete with the Queen in her prime,' wrote Sir Thomas More, many years later. Katherine might have been past her first youth by Tudor standards, yet marriage, and the knowledge that the King loved her, had enhanced her buxom charm and her still-pretty face.

The coronation ritual followed the form laid down by St Dunstan in AD 973, which in turn had been modelled on the ceremony devised for Charlemagne in AD 800. Now it was the turn of Henry VIII to sit in Edward I's coronation chair and receive the Crown of St Edward the Confessor, whose shrine lay only a few feet away in the Abbey; and when he had been accepted and acclaimed as England's King by the assembled lords spiritual and temporal, and due homage had been paid by all who owed him fealty, Queen Katherine received from the Archbishop of Canterbury the smaller crown of the Queen Consorts of England. For her, this was a sacred moment in which she would dedicate her life to God and to the service of her husband's realm.

Outside the Abbey, however, behaviour was anything but sacred, for the crowds had descended like vultures upon the scarlet runner along which the King had walked and ripped it to shreds, each person carrying off a piece as a souvenir of the day. So elated were the King and Queen when they at last emerged from the Abbey that they did not notice its removal, and proceeded to Westminster Hall to the acclaim of the crowds. There, in the vaulted edifice built by William Rufus and beautified by Richard II, Henry and Katherine sat down to their coronation banquet, where 'sumptuous, fine and delicate' food was served in abundance. Half-way through the proceedings, the King's champion entered and dared anyone to challenge his master's right to the throne. There was, of course, no response, and the champion was presented with a golden cup before he withdrew. This little ceremony had been performed at coronation banquets since the early Middle Ages, and always provided excitement at what was usually a very long and ceremonious occasion.

Several days of celebrations followed the coronation, with

tournaments in the gardens of the old Palace of Westminster, where a timber pavilion had been erected so that the King and Queen could watch the proceedings in comfort. There were pageants and banquets, all paid for out of the vast wealth that Henry VIII had inherited from his father. Queen Katherine was present at every festivity, and presided over the jousts with her ladies in true courtly fashion. To some extent she shared Henry's love of hunting, and was not squeamish about it. When the bloody bodies of deer killed in a hunting pageant were laid at her feet as trophies, the Queen did not flinch at the sight, but thanked the hunters and commanded that the venison be served at yet another court banquet. Blood sports were a pleasurable way of providing entertainment as well as meat for the table.

Henry VIII spoke openly of the 'joy and felicity' he had found with Katherine. According to Fray Diego, he adored her, and she him. Yet his love for her was no grand passion; it epitomised rather all his ideals about women and chivalry. Throughout their marriage, he would treat Katherine with the respect due to his wife and queen, and with genuine affection, long after love and desire had died. Her gratitude for his rescue of her from penury and humiliation was flattering to his highly inflated ego, which was further gratified by her submissiveness. She happily conceded that Henry was intellectually her superior, and deferred to him accordingly, as a wife was expected to. This, to Henry, was a most satisfactory state of affairs, and he congratulated himself on having chosen such an amiable bride. Because he was young and inexperienced, he did not perceive the steel beneath the meek exterior, and he certainly underestimated Katherine's tenacity. It is possible that he regarded Katherine almost as a mother figure. The loss of his own mother when he was eleven had affected him deeply, and Katherine, to a degree, was a substitute. She was older than he, more mature, and was always ready with advice when he needed it, and sometimes when he did not.

Katherine herself had always been solemn, with a gravity beyond her years, but for a time now her Spanish training was forgotten and she was able to laugh with the pure happiness of being in love with her young husband and free at last from care. She was, according to her confessor, Fray Diego, 'in high health, with the greatest gaiety and contentment that ever there was'. Gone were her traumatic ailments, gone her depression. She was rational enough in love to realise that Henry was in many ways immature, and sensible enough not to let him know it. She seems to have had a good insight into the youthful mind of the King, and common sense cautioned her to treat him with due respect. This came naturally from years of long training, and it was not difficult, for she was in love.

Henry wrote to Ferdinand that summer: 'My wife and I be in good and perfect love as any two creatures can be,' and Katherine also wrote to her father, thanking him for seeing her 'so well married' to a husband she loved 'so much more than myself'. Ferdinand answered that he 'rejoiced to find you love each other so supremely, and hope you may be happy to the end of your life; a good marriage being not only for the blessing of the man and woman who take each other, but also to the world outside.' It must have seemed to Katherine that her marriage was built upon a sure foundation of love, respect, desire and good political sense. How could it fail to succeed?

Within a year, however, matters were to deteriorate significantly.

In August 1509, Katherine informed the King with delight that she was to bear a child in the spring. In November, the baby stirred for the first time, and a proud Henry informed King Ferdinand of the fact, to signify to him 'the great joy thereat that we take, and the exultation of our whole realm'. The public announcement of the Queen's pregnancy had given rise to great rejoicing in England, for the birth of an heir to the throne would stabilise the dynasty and remove the ever present threat of civil war.

The court was in residence in Henry VIII's great gothic palace at Westminster when, on 31 January 1510, the Queen went into labour prematurely. Her infant, a daughter, was stillborn, which, although considered a calamity, was not an uncommon misfortune with first babies at that time. But Katherine suffered a strong sense of failure, compounded by guilt, because 'she had desired to gladden the King and the people with a Prince'. Henry, however, was philosophical, but even his reassurances and attempts to comfort his wife were to little avail, for she was profoundly shaken by her loss and remained depressed for several weeks, tormented by irrational feelings of guilt. When she wrote to break the news to her father, she begged him: 'Do not storm against me. It is not my fault, it is the will of God. The King, my lord, took it cheerfully, and I thank God that you have given me such a husband.' Again, she repeated, as if to reassure herself, 'It is the will of God.'

The King wasted no time in fathering another child, believing that it was the only thing that would cure Katherine of her depression, and in May 1510, Fray Diego was able to inform King Ferdinand that 'it has pleased our Lord to be her physician, and by His infinite mercy He has again permitted her to be with child'. She was already 'very large', which indicates that the baby was almost certainly conceived during February and that Katherine was one of those women who 'shows' early. The friar hoped this would be 'the beginning of a hundred grandsons' for King Ferdinand.

There are hints in diplomatic records that the young King had been pursuing other women at the time of his accession; whether these adventures continued after his marriage is not recorded, but in 1510, when Katherine was pregnant with her second child, Henry strayed. He had become a complacent husband, secure in his wife's devotion, and Katherine had changed from a young woman 'who cannot be without novelties' into a grave, sedate matron, who had to adjust to a second pregnancy coming hard on the heels of the first. Henry felt he had done his duty by the Queen, and now he was going to enjoy himself. By the standards of his day, his attitude was not unusual.

Henry's first known mistress was his second cousin Lady Elizabeth FitzWalter, sister of the Duke of Buckingham. In her late twenties, she had recently arrived at court with her sister, Lady Anne Herbert. The King immediately pursued her, while his friend, Sir William Compton (who had been close to Henry since being appointed a royal page in 1493) provided a front for his master by pretending to carry on an intrigue with Lady Elizabeth himself. Thus, for a time, Henry was able to make love to his mistress in secrecy.

It was not long, however, before Lady Anne noticed the attention Compton was paying to her sister, who was after all a married woman; in some agitation Lady Anne called a family conference, at which she confided her suspicions to her brother the Duke and to Sir Robert FitzWalter, Elizabeth's husband. As a result, a furious row broke out between the Duke and Compton when the Duke shortly afterwards found Compton in his sister's rooms at court. Buckingham used 'many hard words' and 'severely reproached' Compton, who slunk off to the King and warned him what was happening. Henry, in a simmering rage at the prospect of being deprived of his pleasures, summoned Buckingham and reprimanded the Duke angrily, whereupon Buckingham left the court in a fury. Meanwhile, Lady Elizabeth had confessed to her incensed husband the truth of the matter, and had been forcibly removed by him from the court and immured in a convent sixty miles away. By then, the real identity of her lover was known to the whole Stafford family, Lady Anne included.

Deprived of his mistress, Henry VIII cast his eye about to see where blame could be laid, and guessed that the prime mover in the matter had been Lady Anne Herbert, whom he knew to be one of the Queen's closest friends. Exacting revenge, he banished Lady Anne and her husband from the court, and had a mind to turn out a lot of other ladies also, believing that they had been set by Lady Anne to spy on him. However, he could not quite face the scandal such drastic action would give rise to and, moreover, the worst had already happened: someone, probably Lady Anne, had told the Queen. This resulted in a stormy confrontation between husband and wife, in which Katherine reproached Henry for his infidelity, and he upbraided her for daring to censure him for it. They both ended up 'very vexed' with each other, and the whole court knew it.

Luis Caroz, the Spanish ambassador, feared that Katherine might prejudice her considerable influence with the King by being so openly hostile about what was, after all, a common failing amongst men of rank whose marriages were arranged for them. Yet, to Caroz's dismay, she continued to berate Henry for betraying her, and made matters worse by her evident ill will towards Compton. She was now suffering as countless other queens before her had suffered, having found themselves neglected for the less dignified charms of the ladies of the court, and although she was behaving badly, she could not help herself. The honeymoon was undoubtedly over, and Katherine was shattered by the realisation.

Henry himself could not see what all the fuss was about. In fact, he saw himself as the injured party, Katherine having dared to challenge his right to do as he pleased. He had been discreet, had not intended publicly to humiliate her, and he felt he was being unfairly treated. Of course, in the end, Katherine capitulated, and faced the fact that it was a wife's duty to turn a blind eye to her husband's extra-marital affairs. The onus was on her to adapt to circumstances. It was a hard lesson to learn, but she learnt it well. Never again would she publicly call Henry to account for his behaviour, even under the most extreme provocation. She had emerged from this affair without dignity or pride – even her friend Caroz had criticised her behaviour. Now she resolved to accept what could not be altered with as much grace as she could muster, and on the surface the relationship between the royal couple reverted to its former happy state. It would never, however, be quite the same.

Late in 1510, the Queen 'took to her chamber' at Richmond in readiness for the birth of her baby. Strict regulations, laid down by the Lady Margaret Beaufort in the preceding reign, governed the correct procedures to be observed when a queen was confined. The appointed chamber must be hung with tapestries which covered the walls, ceiling, windows and doors, and these tapestries must depict scenes of light romance only, so that neither the Queen nor the newborn infant should be 'affrighted by figures which gloomily stare'. Fresh air was not considered necessary, indeed it was thought to be dangerous, but one window was left uncovered to admit light to the chamber.

The rich tester bed in which the royal infant was to be born was truly magnificent. It was made up with sheets of fine lawn, a counterpane of scarlet velvet edged with ermine and a border of cloth of gold, with curtains and hangings of crimson satin embroidered with crowns of gold and the Queen's coat of arms. Four silver damask cushions were provided for the royal head to rest upon. When her labour was over, the Queen would put on a circular mantle of crimson velvet trimmed with ermine, in which she would receive visitors while still in bed.

Men were not admitted to the Queen's presence during the last weeks of her pregnancy; even the King stayed away. Her chamberlain, Lord Mountjoy, arranged for the duties of all male officers within her household to be taken over by her ladies and gentlewomen, who became, for a few weeks, 'butlers, servers and pages', receiving all 'needful things' at the door to the Queen's apartments. When the Queen 'took to her chamber', she bade her chamberlain and other male retainers a formal farewell, and Mountjoy in return desired all her people, in her name, to pray 'that God would send her a good hour'.

Katherine's labour began on 31 December 1510, and on New Year's Day 1511, she was at last 'delivered of a Prince, to the great gladness of the realm'. In honour of the occasion, a jubilant Henry ordered beacons to be lit in London and the distribution of free wine to the citizens. Churchmen went in procession through the streets, and in the churches the *Te Deum* was sung. The child was given his father's name, Henry.

The little Prince was christened at Richmond before he was a week old, his godparents being the Archbishop of Canterbury, the Earl of Surrey, and the Countess of Devon, who was the daughter of Edward IV and the King's aunt. Katherine's happiness was now complete, for she had done her duty by providing England with an heir, and the King could not do enough to honour or praise her. Messages of congratulation were arriving hourly at the palace, and in the streets, people were chanting, 'Long live Katherine and the noble Henry! Long live the Prince!' After the birth, Henry went to the shrine of our Lady of Walsingham, the special patron of mothers and babies, to give thanks for his boy, and, on his return, the court moved to Westminster. Katherine had now been churched and had resumed public life; her child had been left at Richmond in the care of nurses, and if this caused her any qualms she did not show it, but immersed herself wholeheartedly in the celebrations arranged by the King in honour of his son's birth.

Then tragedy struck, and the festivities were brought to an abrupt halt when the King and Queen were informed that the little prince had died on 22 February at Richmond. The chronicler Edward Hall says that Henry, 'like a wise Prince', was deeply grieved yet still philosophical; his concern was mainly for Katherine, who, 'like a natural woman', was devastated by the news and 'made much lamentation'. However, her husband comforted her 'wondrous wisely', and in time she came to accept the death of her baby as the will of God. The King 'made no great mourning outwardly', but spent a lavish sum on a funeral for Prince Henry, who was buried in Westminster Abbey, and the daily routine of the court was very quiet for the next two months, during which time Katherine remained mostly in seclusion, regretting no doubt that she had spent so little time with her child during his short life, and also facing up to the fact that England still needed an heir. In September that year she was rumoured to be pregnant again, but nothing more is heard of it, and it may have been a false hope.

By 1511, there was a new power in the ascendant at court. Thomas Wolsey was then thirty-six, and had been born the son of an Ipswich butcher. He had had the good fortune to be educated at Oxford, and after that had taken holy orders, becoming chaplain to Henry VII in 1507, and Dean of Lincoln in 1509. When Henry VII died, Wolsey, ever industrious in his own interests, had quickly ingratiated himself with Henry VIII, proving his abilities by sheer hard work and well-timed, sound advice. The young King liked this affable cleric, and by 1511 Wolsey was already enjoying considerable influence, besides being honoured with the friendship of the King, who was coming increasingly to rely upon him. Wolsey would shoulder the matters of state that Henry hated, and never let the King guess that it was Wolsey, and not Henry Tudor, who was, in effect, taking over the government of England. Yet this was what happened, with Wolsey becoming the real power behind the throne to a greater degree as the years passed, while his young master rode in the lists, planned glorious but impractical campaigns, and wrote love songs.

Wolsey was resented at court by the older nobility, who were jealous of his power which they felt should be theirs by right; nor did his increasingly lavish lifestyle endear him to his colleagues. The King's favour had brought with it a string of lucrative honours: Wolsey was made Bishop of Lincoln, and then Archbishop of York, in 1514, and in 1515 the Pope made him a cardinal. He was then supporting a household that rivalled that of his master for luxury, and he had his own palace, Hampton Court, built in 1514 on the site of an old priory by the Thames. When completed, it far exceeded any of the King's palaces for luxury and grandeur. Wolsey's private rooms were lined with linenfold panelling and wall paintings by Italian masters, and his ceilings were carved, moulded and painted in gold leaf. There was space for thousands of retainers. Wolsey could well afford such extravagance, for the King had been generous to him on a grand scale. By 1515 he was virtually running the country; the King was content to leave everything to the capable

Cardinal, who was the most powerful man in England after himself. At Christmas 1515, Wolsey was appointed Lord Chancellor of England, an office he would hold for the next fourteen years, and in 1518, the Pope made him Papal Legate in England.

Katherine of Aragon did not like or trust Wolsey for several reasons. She felt that he was ousting her from her rightful place in the King's counsels, and she thought him insincere and lacking in the humility desirable in a prince of the Church. She also deplored his pro-French foreign policies, and the fact that he was working against the interests of Spain. In fact, after 1521, the Cardinal became ever more antagonistic towards Spain, because the Emperor had lifted not a finger to help Wolsey achieve his greatest ambition, that of being Pope; there had been two papal elections in 1521, and Wolsey – a candidate at both – had been overlooked, which he blamed upon Charles V's influence.

As the years went by, Wolsey's arrogance grew as, simultaneously, did his unpopularity. There was criticism from both nobility and commons, some of it calculated to make the King jealous. For a time, Henry resisted: Wolsey was an able and efficient statesman, whose grasp of European affairs was second to none. But, by 1526, heavy hints about the Cardinal's excessive power and riches were beginning to have an effect, and the King started to make meaningful comments about how much richer than his sovereign he was. Wolsey, seeing that some sacrifice was expedient, took the hint, and promptly surrendered to the King the deeds of Hampton Court. It was a magnificent gesture that had the desired effect and, through it, the Cardinal hoped to reap greater benefits in the future. Besides, he did have another residence, York Place by Westminster, the London house of the Archbishops of York, which had been refurbished by him to almost the same degree of luxury as Hampton Court.

From the first, Katherine of Aragon was mindful of the fact that she was in England to represent her father's interests, and in the early days of their marriage her influence over the young Henry VIII was very strong indeed. Henry would do nothing without her approval; even when it came to matters of state, he would say to his councillors, or to visiting ambassadors, 'The Queen must hear this,' or 'This will please the Queen.' And his advisers, dismayed though they were at their master's reliance on his foreign wife's judgement, were powerless to do anything about it. Nevertheless, there was a good deal of head shaking and muttering that, at this rate, England would shortly be ruled at one remove by Spain.

This, of course, was what Ferdinand of Aragon intended should happen, and he was duly gratified when Katherine spoke of her husband as being 'the true son of your Highness, with desire of greater obedience and love to serve you than ever son had to his father'. She would have done well at this stage to have studied the example of certain queen consorts in the past, who had put the interests of their own families before those of the kingdom into which they had married. Such queens had at best courted vilification, and at worst been suspected of treason. Already the King's councillors were complaining about the extent of the Queen's influence, and they had cause, for Katherine, reared to obey her father in every respect, and not really understanding the attitude of the English towards foreign interference in their politics, saw nothing amiss with manipulating Henry. 'These kingdoms of your Highness,' she wrote to Ferdinand, forgetting that her husband owed no allegiance whatsoever to his father-in-law, 'are in great peace, and entertain much love towards the King my lord and me. His Highness and I are very hearty towards the service of your Highness.'

It was easy to foresee, as Henry's councillors did, that the Queen would soon be prevailing upon the King to favour Spain's interests above those of England; already she viewed her husband's realm as an extension of her father's, and never ceased reminding the King of the virtues of King Ferdinand, whom he was coming to regard as the fount of all wisdom. Henry would take no step without first discussing it with Katherine, Katherine would not approve anything without her father's sanction, and unfortunately Henry was too inexperienced to realise what was happening.

With her father's warm approval, Katherine set about turning Henry's mind against France, the traditional enemy of England and Spain. This was not difficult; Henry detested the French anyway, and was intent on making war on France in the not too distant future, the conquest of that realm and the fulfilment of England's ancient claims to its throne being his ultimate goal. In November

1511, Ferdinand's scheming, and Katherine's, reached a successful conclusion with the signing of the Treaty of Westminster, whereby Henry and Ferdinand pledged to help each other against France, their mutual enemy. Katherine had done her work well, and Ferdinand was proud of her.

Henry VIII sent an army under Lord Dorset into France in 1512, but the campaign ended in inglorious failure. It was therefore relatively easy for Katherine to persuade the King to mount a second campaign in 1513, which he would lead himself. By doing this, the Queen was rendering a signal service to her father, who was also planning to take the offensive against the French. Henry was excited and enthusiastic about the coming campaign, even though his councillors tried to talk him out of it. As the Venetian ambassador put it, 'the King is bent on war, the Council is averse to it; the Queen will have it, and the wisest councillors in England cannot stand against the Queen.' Katherine had assured Henry of the full co-operation of his allies, King Ferdinand and the Emperor Maximilian, and Henry seems to have persuaded himself that those two wily old self-seekers would support him in his bid to take the French throne. For the young King the glorious adventure was about to begin, and he saw himself returning victorious from his righteous war, crowned with laurel wreaths and the ultimate prize, the crown of France.

By June 1513, all was ready for the King's departure. Katherine was to be Regent in his absence, and due precautions had been taken to guard the northern border against an attack by the unpredictable Scots, France's traditional allies. At last, on 30 June, Henry rode from London to Dover at the head of 11,000 men, with Katherine by his side. In Dover Castle, he formally invested his wife with the regency, and commanded the Archbishop of Canterbury and the seventy-year-old veteran Thomas Howard, Earl of Surrey, to act as her advisers. The Earl was to escort the Queen back to London and then travel north to be at hand in the event of trouble with the Scots. Katherine cried when the King bade her farewell, being fearful for his safety, but Surrey gallantly comforted her on the ride back to London, and she rose to the occasion with courage, remembering that, if only for a short while, she was now the effective custodian of her husband's kingdom.

Henry and his magnificent fighting force created a sensation when they arrived in France – 'you will never have seen anything so gorgeous!', reported an imperial envoy. Yet, in reality, his presence was anything but welcome to Ferdinand and Maximilian when they discovered that his ultimate purpose was to depose Louis XII and have himself crowned King of France. Alarmed, they resolved to pack him off home as soon as possible, and wasted no time in drawing up a secret treaty with Louis XII whereby the young King of England would be permitted one or two inconsequential victories, which would hopefully satisfy his craving for military glory before the advent of winter forced him to return to England. On 24 July, Henry and Maximilian laid siege to the town of Thérouanne, and on 16 August an Anglo-Imperial army routed the French at what became known as the Battle of the Spurs, so called because the French army took one look at the superior forces of England and the Empire and fled. It was not a decisive victory, but it sufficed for the present.

Wolsey, who had gone with the King to France, had arranged to keep the Queen regularly informed of Henry's progress, but letters were sometimes held up, and then her fears grew. 'I shall be never in rest until I see letters from you,' she wrote to Henry. Accounts of the risks he was taking filled her with alarm, especially when she learned that he insisted on being present in the ranks before Thérouanne, well within range of enemy cannon, and she begged Wolsey to remind the King 'to avoid all manner of dangers'. As for herself, she was 'encumbered' with matters arising from the war. 'My heart is very good to it,' declared the daughter of Ferdinand and Isabella, 'and I am horribly busy with making standards, banners and badges.'

Not all of these were destined for France, for in the midst of this activity, news reached Katherine at Richmond that the Scots were planning an invasion of England, and were mobilising their forces. Not for nothing was Katherine her mother's daughter, and she threw herself with courage and zeal into preparations for defence, informing Wolsey that the King's subjects were 'very glad, I thank God, to be busy with the Scots'. On 22 August, the 80,000-strong army of Henry VIII's brother-in-law, the 'false and perjured' James IV, invaded England, advancing into Northumberland. At the same time, an English force led by the Earl of Surrey was moving north to meet them.

Three days later, the Queen received news of the fall of Thérouanne to Henry VIII and the King's triumphant entry into the town; immediately, she dashed off a letter of congratulation, opining that 'the victory hath been so great that I think none such hath been seen before. All England hath cause to thank God for it, and I specially.' In early September the Queen travelled north to Buckingham, where she would await news from Surrey. Here she made a speech to the reserve forces camped outside the town, urging them to victory in a just cause. But there was to be no need for their services, for on Friday, 9 September 1513, the Earl of Surrey scored a resounding victory over the Scots at the Battle of Flodden, one of the bloodiest combats ever seen in Britain, and at the end of the day, ten thousand Scotsmen lay dead on the moor, among them their King and the flower of his nobility. Scotland would now be ruled by a council of regency, for the new King, James V, was only a baby; the war with England would of necessity have to be shelved.

The impact of Flodden and its consequences was immediately felt in England. Surrey wrote at once to the Queen, informing her of the victory, and sent her James's banner and the bloody coat he had died in as trophies; Katherine duly sent them on to Henry by a herald. Then she gave devout thanks to God for Surrey's success, and returned in triumph to Richmond. On the way, she stayed the night at Woburn Abbey, and it was here that she took time to write to her husband, referring, perhaps rather tactlessly, to 'the great victory that our Lord hath sent to your subjects in your absence. To my thinking, this battle hath been more than should you win all the crown of France.' Not that Katherine intended any offence; indeed, she was praying that God would 'send you home shortly, for without no joy can here be accomplished'.

If Henry felt somewhat disgruntled by the implication of Katherine's words, he was soon to forget it, for on 21 September he captured another town, Tournai. He had thoroughly enjoyed his first taste of warfare, and was disappointed that it was now autumn and time to return to England, for no commander ever campaigned through the winter months by choice. It was agreed between the allies that they should launch a combined invasion of France before June 1514, and also that the marriage of Henry's sister Mary to Charles of Castile should take place in the spring. After a short sojourn in Lille, the court of Maximilian's daughter and Katherine's former sister-in-law, the Archduchess Margaret, Henry returned to England, landing at Dover on 22 October after an absence of four months. With only a small company, he rode at full speed to Richmond to see his wife, and when he arrived, 'there was such a loving meeting that everyone rejoiced who witnessed it'.

Katherine had been pregnant for the third time during the Flodden campaign, and after the victory celebrations were over, she went to Our Lady of Walsingham to pray for the safe delivery of a son. The war had drained her energies, and there were fears that she might miscarry: 'If the Queen be with child, we owe very much to God,' wrote Sir Brian Tuke, Henry's secretary, to Wolsey. Yet in October, just prior to the King's homecoming, Katherine was delivered of a premature son, who died shortly after his birth. It was a bitter disappointment, but mitigated to some extent by her joyful reunion with her husband later that month. Both Henry and Katherine were becoming increasingly anxious about the succession and the King's lack of a male heir. Nevertheless, time was still on their side, and in June 1514, the Queen was visibly pregnant once more.

This was not, however, to be a happy pregnancy, for by that time, the King had been forced to the realisation that he had been duped by his so-called allies, Ferdinand and Maximilian, who had made it very clear that they had not the slightest intention now of pursuing the war with France. Nor would the Council of Flanders accept Mary Tudor as a bride for the Archduke Charles. This was an insult, which, together with his humiliation over Ferdinand's betrayal, inspired Henry to an outburst of righteous anger against his father-in-law and the Emperor, calling down the wrath of Heaven upon them for having deceived him. The person who suffered most was Katherine, who had for years urged Henry to heed the advice of her father. This would now cease, he warned her icily, 'upbraiding the innocent Queen for her father's desertion', and informing her that 'the Kings of England had never taken place to anyone but God', according to the chronicler Peter Martyr. In future, he would govern his kingdom by himself, with the aid of Wolsey, and without any outside interference. One after the other, 'he spat out his complaints against her'. Katherine was distressed at the realisation that her husband and her father were now enemies, and that her own role as

Henry's confidential adviser would in consequence be much diminished, and all at a time when Wolsey's influence was growing ever more powerful. It was doubtful if the King would ever listen to her again to the same extent, or trust her advice.

Katherine's friends, notably Fray Diego before his dismissal and Maria de Salinas, now urged her to forget the interests of Spain and render her loyalty wholly to her adopted land, for only by doing this could she hope to avoid further censure by the King. Katherine accepted that this was the wisest option, for she dared not antagonise her husband further. Luis Caroz, however, felt that it would be catastrophic for Spain if her remaining link with England was severed. 'The Queen has the best of intentions,' he reported, 'but there is no one to show her how she may become serviceable to her father.' Maria de Salinas realised that Katherine's services on her father's behalf had brought her to this impasse, and she effectively blocked all Caroz's attempts to persuade Katherine to place Ferdinand's interests before those of her husband. As for the King, he behaved 'in a most discourteous manner' whenever King Ferdinand's name was mentioned.

What Katherine, Caroz and Ferdinand had failed to take into account was the growing effect of regal responsibility upon Henry VIII, and his developing egocentricity; nor did they allow for the ever increasing influence of Thomas Wolsey, who was even now urging the King towards a French alliance. In October 1514, Henry married his sister Mary to the King of France, who now became his friend and ally, peace between the two kingdoms having been proclaimed with the signing of a new treaty in August. This was all Wolsey's doing, and naturally it was unwelcome to Queen Katherine, not only because of her inbred distrust of the French, but also because it meant that Wolsey's influence was unlikely to be dislodged, which could only be detrimental to her own interests and Spain's.

It was essential that she regain the King's confidence, yet Henry never came to her now for advice on political matters, and she was obliged to retire into the background and settle for a purely domestic and decorative role. For someone who had, for several years, been at the centre of events, this was hard to take, yet take it she did, with patience and humility, never betraying her sense of isolation or her distaste for her husband's new allies. If she could bring him an heir, she might yet win him back, but in November 1514 her latest pregnancy ended with the birth of yet another prince who died within hours of his birth. In Spain, it was the general opinion that this tragedy had occurred 'on account of the discord between the two kings, her husband and father; because of her excessive grief, she ejected an immature foetus.' It was a bitter blow, and Katherine herself commented that the Almighty must love her to confer upon her 'the privilege of so much sorrow'.

She was destined, however, to bear a living child. A fifth pregnancy was confirmed in the summer of 1515, and at four o'clock in the morning of 18 February 1516, Katherine gave birth to a healthy daughter. Although the baby was the wrong sex, the King was delighted with her, for she was 'a right lusty princess', and he named her Mary. Katherine's emotions when she beheld her 'beauteous babe' may well be imagined – even the news of the death of her father, King Ferdinand, which had been kept from her until after her confinement, could not dampen her joy. God, it seemed, had spoken at last, and – as Henry confidently said – 'if it is a daughter this time, by the grace of God, boys will follow. We are both still young.' The Princess Mary was christened with 'great solemnity' three days after her birth in the chapel of the Observant Friars at Greenwich. In accordance with tradition, neither parent attended the ceremony, and the infant was borne to the font by her sponsors, or godparents, under a canopy of estate.

In August 1517, Queen Katherine was again supposed to be pregnant, but it was either a rumour or a false hope. Her sixth and last child was conceived in February 1518, when she was thirty-two, well past her youth by contemporary standards, and possibly aware that this might be her last chance to present Henry with an heir. 'I pray God heartily that it may be a prince, to the universal comfort and security of the realm,' wrote Richard Pace, the King's secretary, to Wolsey; sentiments echoed by the Venetian ambassador, who hoped God would grant the Queen a son, 'in order that his Highness, having a male heir to follow him, may not be hindered, as at present, from engaging in affairs of the moment'. This was a veiled reference to Henry's reluctance to lead an army against the Turks, who were encroaching upon Eastern Europe.

The forthcoming birth was announced in June as 'an event most earnestly desired by the whole kingdom', and in churches throughout the land prayers were said for Katherine's safe delivery. She herself was then at the old palace of Woodstock, and could there take the air in gardens where Henry II had once courted his mistress, 'Fair Rosamund' Clifford, and perhaps see traces of the maze built for that lady. Here, too, in 1330, another beloved queen, Philippa of Hainault, had borne a son, the Black Prince. All seemed well when, in July, the King visited Woodstock; Katherine greeted him at the door of her chamber, proud to show him 'for his welcome home her belly something great'. Then before all the courtiers, she told him that the child had stirred in her womb; Henry was so delighted that he gave a great banquet to celebrate, and fussed around his wife to ensure that she took good care of herself, for – as he wrote to Wolsey – he knew by now that a happy outcome to her pregnancies was 'not an ensured thing, but a thing wherein I have great hope and likelihood'.

Tragically, his hopes were to come to nothing yet again, for on 10 November Katherine had a daughter, 'to the vexation of as many as knew it. Never had the kingdom desired anything so anxiously as it did a prince.' The baby was very weak, and died before she could be christened. The Queen found this latest disappointment almost too much to bear, and openly wondered if the loss of her children was a judgement of God 'for that her former marriage was made in blood'.

The Queen had conceived six, possibly eight, times, yet all she had to show for it was one daughter. She had borne her losses with amiability, resignation and good humour, yet the burden of failure was great. In the patriarchal society of Tudor England, blame for stillbirths and neonatal deaths was always apportioned to the woman, and some were of the opinion that Henry had made a grave mistake in marrying a wife older than himself. 'My good brother of England has no son because, although young and handsome, he keeps an old and deformed wife,' was the King of France's cruel comment at this time. It was true that Katherine had begun to show her age, and that her figure had been ruined by her pregnancies. Her youthful prettiness had gone for ever, while Henry, at twenty-seven, was approaching his physical peak. Yet, to his credit, he did not once reproach Katherine for his lack of a male heir, although he was himself desperate for a son, and beginning to wonder why this one crucial gift should be denied him.

By 1519, with no sign of another child on the way, the succession had become the King's most critical problem. Although his throne was based on firmer foundations than his father's had been, he still had to contend with a legacy of stray Plantagenets, and, though at present these descendants of the House of York appeared to be behaving themselves, one could never anticipate what they would do if the King died suddenly, leaving a three-year-old girl on the throne. There would, without doubt, be factions formed and a return to civil war; Mary's very life might well be threatened. Of course, the Queen might yet conceive, but that was a possibility which seemed more remote with each passing year. Henry later hinted that she suffered from some gynaecological trouble, possibly as a result of her last confinement, and that this made intercourse with her distasteful to him. At any rate, he ceased to have sexual relations with her in 1524, by his own admission, made seven years later, and by the spring of 1525, it was well known that Katherine was 'past that age in which women most commonly are wont to be fruitful'. There would be no more children.

For the King, this was a bitter pill to swallow; it was galling in the extreme for a robust and virile man of thirty-four to face the fact that he would have no more legitimate issue of his body. It was almost a slur on his manhood. Sex with Katherine had long become just a means to an end, and when the Queen's menopause came upon her, it became glaringly apparent that Henry's desire for her had long since died; nevertheless, he would still visit her bed for some years to come, if only for appearances' sake.

In August 1514, a curious rumour had been reported in Rome, to the effect that 'the King of England means to repudiate his present wife because he is unable to have children by her, and intends to marry a daughter of the French Duke of Bourbon.' Then in England, in September, it was being said that 'the King wishes to dissolve his marriage.'

Did Henry, as early as 1514, seriously consider divorce? The main argument against these reports having any basis in fact is that Katherine was pregnant when they were written, and it is unthinkable that the King would have contemplated putting her away when he was hopeful of her bearing him an heir. Rome, however, was a long way from England, and a report of something Henry had said in June, when he was furious with Katherine because of her father's treachery, would not have reached Italy for several weeks, and may well have been embroidered in the process, as nowhere else do we hear this tale of a French marriage for the King. It is therefore, on balance, highly improbable that he seriously thought of divorce at this stage.

He was, however, at that time enjoying a flirtation with fourteen-year-old Elizabeth (Bessie) Blount, a distant relative of the Queen's chamberlain, Lord Mountjoy. Her name was first mentioned in connection with the King's in October 1514, in a letter written to Henry by Charles Brandon, Duke of Suffolk, which implies that the King and Brandon were partners in flirtations with Elizabeth and another girl, Elizabeth Carew. The King was discreet about his love affairs, so we know very little about this one, except that it was what Fray Diego was referring to when he accused Henry of having 'badly used' the Queen in the autumn of 1514. Katherine, however, was by then growing used to her husband's infidelities, writing resignedly in one letter that 'young men be wrapped in sensual love'. Hence she kept her peace. The King's affair with Bessie Blount would last for the next five years at least, but it was conducted well out of sight of his wife. Thus, in 1519, Erasmus would still feel moved to extol Henry's virtues as a husband: 'What house among all your subjects presents such an example of a chaste and concordant wedlock as your own? There, you find a wife emulous to resemble the best of husbands!'

Of course, unknown to Erasmus, Henry had been anything but chaste. He was rumoured to be still in love with Elizabeth Blount, who shared with him a passion for singing, dancing and 'goodly pastimes'. In 1519 Elizabeth disappeared from court for several months; Henry had arranged for her to go to 'Jericho', a house he leased from St Lawrence's Priory at Blackmore in Essex; it was a house with a poor reputation, where the King maintained a private suite. When he visited, he took with him only a few attendants. No one was allowed to approach him during his stay, and pages and grooms of the privy chamber were warned 'not to hearken and enquire where the King is or goeth, be it early or late', and to refrain from 'talking of the King's pastime' or 'his late or early going to bed'. Obviously Jericho was a trysting place where Henry could pursue his affair with Elizabeth Blount, and perhaps other women whose names are lost to history. Elizabeth certainly lived there for a time, for in 1519 she gave birth to the King's bastard son in the house. Henry was delighted to have a boy at last: here was proof indeed that he himself was not responsible for the lack of a male heir, though it must have seemed to him ironical that his only son should be born out of wedlock. He named the child Henry, and bestowed upon him the old Norman-French surname FitzRoy, which means 'son of the King'. News of the birth soon leaked out at court, and in due course the Queen learned of it, to her sorrow and humiliation.

Henry's affair with Elizabeth Blount seems to have ended with the birth of her child, and he arranged through Wolsey to have her honourably bestowed in marriage as a reward for services rendered. Late in 1519 she married Lord Tailboys, although Wolsey was savagely criticised for his part in this, and accused of encouraging young women to indulge in fornication as a means of finding a husband above their station. Yet Elizabeth Blount would go on to make an even more impressive second marriage after her husband's death, to Lord Clinton, later Earl of Lincoln. She died in 1539. Her son by the King, Henry FitzRoy, was sent at a young age to live with a tutor, Richard Croke, at King's College, Cambridge, where he would receive part of his education.

Although she could not approve of the Princess Mary's marriage to King Louis of France, Katherine – wearing a gown and Venetian cap of ash-coloured satin – attended the banquet given after the proxy wedding ceremony at Greenwich in August 1514, and shortly afterwards rode with the court to Dover to say goodbye to her sister-in-law, of whom she seems to have been fond.

The 'amorous marriage' of Louis XII and Mary Tudor lasted less than three months; worn out with making love to his beautiful, giddy bride, the middle-aged Louis died of exhaustion at the beginning of January 1515, to Mary's great relief, and was succeeded by his distant cousin, Francis, Count of Angoulême. Francis I was just three years younger than Henry VIII, and already had a dire reputation where women were concerned. Henry was immediately distrustful of him, and not a little jealous. In fact, the strong sense of rivalry between the two monarchs would endure until their deaths, which occurred within weeks of each other. Henry's jealousy was rooted in the awareness that, until Francis's accession, he had been the youngest, most charismatic and most good-looking sovereign in Europe – all were agreed on that. But this new King of France might now be about to send Henry's star into eclipse, and Henry was determined that should not happen.

Francis, who played a significant role in the history of Henry VIII's marital adventures, was far from handsome, being dark and saturnine with an over-long pointed nose, which gave him the look of a satyr and earned him the nickname 'Foxnose'. Living up to this epithet, he could be as devious as any of his predecessors when it came to politics. Yet he was also a true prince of the Renaissance, a lover of the arts, and the patron of Leonardo da Vinci. His court was at once a school of culture and elegance and a cesspit of vice and debauchery, his palaces without peer in northern Europe.

Francis made ineffectual attempts to seduce Queen Mary during her brief widowhood, but he was pre-empted by Charles Brandon, newly created Duke of Suffolk, whom Henry had sent to convey her back to England. Unknown to the King, Mary had long cherished a secret love for Brandon, and the effect of his arrival in Paris was cataclysmic. She wanted no more arranged marriages, she told him, and begged him to marry her himself. Such was the pressure she brought to bear upon him that Brandon capitulated, and secretly made her his wife.

Charles Brandon had since childhood been very close to the King. Born in 1485, he was the son of Henry VII's standard bearer, Sir William Brandon, who had been killed at the Battle of Bosworth. Young Charles had then been taken into the royal household to be brought up with Prince Henry, whom he much resembled in looks, build and colouring. A great favourite with the ladies, Brandon had already disentangled himself from two disadvantageous marriages. Now, realising the enormity of what he had done, he wrote at once to Wolsey, confessing that he had married Mary 'heartily, and lain with her'. When he heard, the King was furious – so furious he wanted Brandon's head. But thanks to Wolsey's intervention and his suggestion that the Suffolks make reparation by payment of a crippling fine, Henry forgave them, and allowed them to return to England, where he arranged a splendid public wedding for them at Greenwich. Afterwards, the couple retired to live somewhat frugally for a time in the country, where Mary bore three children, one of whom, Frances, would later become the mother of Lady Jane Grey.

By the autumn of 1515, Henry VIII's anger against Ferdinand of Aragon had burnt itself out, and there was a renewal of friendship between them before Ferdinand's death in January 1516. He was succeeded in Aragon by his grandson, Charles of Castile, who was from now on effective ruler of a reunited Spain. Henry and Katherine welcomed Charles's ambassadors to England in March 1516, and entertained them with a banquet lasting seven hours, and a joust in which the King gave a practised display of horsemanship, 'making a thousand jumps in the air'.

Peace now existed between the great European powers. By 1517, many foreigners had come to London to set up businesses or to see the sights; many were Spaniards. This created a certain amount of tension, for the English disliked the 'strangers', as they called them, and on May Day 1517, this resentment bubbled into hatred and boiled over, as fighting broke out between mobs of London apprentices and any foreigners who were unlucky enough to cross their paths. What made these riots so ugly was the fact that they were almost certainly premeditated.

The King was picnicking with Katherine at Greenwich when news reached him of the disturbances in his capital, and he left for the City at once, sending his guards ahead, who swiftly brought the rioters under control. The youths who had caused the violence were all arrested and brought to Westminster Hall, where the King, determined to avenge the outrage committed against the foreigners under his protection, wasted no time in condemning them all to the gallows. At this, the wives and mothers of the apprentices, who had gathered at the back of the hall, burst out into pitiful weeping and wailing. Queen Katherine, seated on her throne behind the King, heard them, and her heart was touched. Without hesitation, she rose from her place and knelt before her husband, begging him with tears in her eyes: 'Spare the apprentices!' Wolsey added his pleas to hers, rightly judging that such an act of mercy would greatly enhance his own and the King's popularity with the people. Henry could resist neither his wife, nor his minister, nor could he turn down this opportunity of winning golden opinions. He therefore pardoned the prisoners and gave them back their liberty, thus turning this 'Evil May Day' into a day of rejoicing, as the apprentices threw their halters into the air and hastened to be reunited with their families. Some of the mothers went up to the Queen and thanked her for her intervention, praising her for championing Englishmen above the Spaniards who had suffered injury and loss in the riots. Katherine answered them 'gently' and then departed, more beloved than ever.

The French alliance held good for six years. In 1518, it was agreed that Henry's daughter, the two-year-old Princess Mary, should one day marry the Dauphin, Francis I's heir. Henry, still hopeful of a son to succeed him, was enthusiastic about the match, as it would guarantee Mary a glorious future as Queen of France. Katherine, however, was not happy at all at the prospect of her only child being given to France, though she did not venture to criticise.

In February 1519, the Emperor Maximilian died. His death was to have far-reaching consequences for the whole of Europe. His grandson Charles was elected Holy Roman Emperor in his place, at the age of nineteen. The new Emperor Charles V now ruled Germany, Austria, the Low Countries, parts of Italy and, from 1526, Hungary also, as well as Spain: half of Europe, in fact. Such unity had not featured in the Holy Roman Empire since the days of Charlemagne. However, Charles's title was based on tradition rather than fact: the Empire was no longer based in Rome, neither was it particularly holy. Not only were the Emperors often at loggerheads with the Popes, but the Empire itself was shortly to be divided by schism as Luther's doctrines gained currency. The 'Christian republic' of the European Middle Ages was about to become a thing of the past, although in due course Charles V would follow in the steps of Charlemagne to Rome, there to be crowned by the Pope.

The election of Charles V had the immediate effect of improving Katherine of Aragon's status in England. She was his aunt, and could command greater respect as such than as Henry VIII's barren consort. In England, she now represented the combined might, and reflected glory, of Spain and the Empire, a formidable heritage. Yet, for all this, her life continued as quietly as before. The gulf between her and the King was widening all the time; her influence was still minimal, and her function now merely ceremonial. She had failed in every way that mattered, and beside this her considerable personal qualities paled into insignificance.

Katherine's two consolations were her religion and the emotional fulfilment she found in her daughter Mary. The Queen was a very maternal woman, and fiercely protective of her child, who was a pretty little girl. 'This child never cries!' the King proudly told the French ambassador when Mary was two. She had inherited her father's colouring and her mother's air of gravity, and was 'decorous in manners', having been schooled rigidly to good behaviour from the cradle. In time, she would display a profound piety that would even exceed Katherine's, and her first recorded words – 'Priest! Priest!' – were strangely prophetic.

The Princess was brought up in an atmosphere of domestic harmony. A lady governess, Lady Margaret Bryan, looked after her daily needs from an early age. Any tension between her parents was concealed by the fact that they both doted upon her. Henry was fond of showing her off to visiting dignitaries, and when Katherine had led her by the hand into his presence, he would sweep her up in his arms and carry her round, bursting with pride. She, in turn, adored him. 'See how she jumps forward in her nurse's lap when she catches sight of her father!' exclaimed the Bishop of Durham, an entranced observer. As she grew older, she was allowed to take part in court festivities and pageants, and at four she was receiving foreign envoys and entertaining them with music played rather shakily on the virginals. At seven, she was an expert dancer, and – according to a Spanish envoy – twirled 'so prettily that no woman could do better'.

Mary's formal education began in 1523. The King and Queen wished it to be a classic grounding in all the subjects appropriate to a Renaissance princess, with sound religious teaching at its core. They had taken advice from Juan Luis Vives, a Spanish educationist with a reputation for advanced views on female education, and with his approval the King appointed Richard Fetherston, who had been chaplain to Queen Katherine and was a gentle, devout man, to be Mary's first tutor. Vives himself drew up a plan for her formal curriculum, which would later be the basis for his treatise *The*

Institution of a Christian Woman, which was dedicated to Queen Katherine. He also taught Mary Latin, while Katherine herself helped the child with her translations.

Vives's curriculum was, by modern standards, severe for a child of seven, and involved much learning of the Scriptures, the works of the early Fathers of the Church, as well as the study of ancient classics and history. Light reading was forbidden, in case it encouraged light behaviour.

In August 1525, the King sent Mary with her own household to live at Ludlow Castle. Although she was her father's heiress, she had never been formally invested with the principality of Wales, but Henry now decided to follow tradition and send her with 'an honourable, sad, discreet and expert council' to the castle on the Welsh marches where Katherine had spent most of her brief married life with Prince Arthur nearly a quarter of a century before. Here, Mary would learn something of the art of government. Lady Salisbury, her mother's close friend, was appointed state governess, and the Queen and Wolsey worked together on a plan for the regime to be followed by the Princess at Ludlow, giving 'most tender regard' to her age, education and moral training. She was to enjoy plenty of fresh air walking in the gardens, to practise her music, and continue learning Latin and French. Her lessons were not to fatigue her, and her diet was to be 'pure, well-dressed, and served with merry communication'. Her private apartments and her clothes must be kept 'pure, sweet, clean and wholesome', and those in attendance on her must treat her with 'humility and reverence'. It is not difficult to read into this remarkable document a mother's anxiety that her child should suffer no diminishment of care while they were apart.

Katherine bore the separation with stoicism, although she wrote to Mary that it troubled her. Mary's own letters were the chief joy in her life during the long months apart, as was the finished written work that the Princess sent her; 'it was a great comfort to me to see you keep your Latin and fair writing and all,' replied her mother. Katherine did not see Mary again until the Princess came to Greenwich for the Christmas festivities of 1526, when Henry led her out with him to dance before the court. After Twelfth Night, she returned to Ludlow, but was back at court in April 1527, when it was noted that, at eleven, she was 'the most accomplished person for her

age'. Thereafter, Mary remained at court, where she completed her
education – as she had begun it – under her mother's supervision.

In February 1520, preparations for the long-awaited summit meeting
between Henry VIII and Francis I began. After discussion between
Wolsey and the French ambassador, it was agreed that the English
court should cross to France in May, and stay at Henry's own castle at
Guisnes in the Pale of Calais, then in English hands. The French visit
was Wolsey's brainchild, and he was in charge of all the arrangements, drawing up a code of etiquette which cleverly solved all
questions of precedence and courtesy that might vex 'the King of
England and the Queen his bedfellow'. The Cardinal then set about
planning what was to be one of the most expensive charades ever
staged in history, the Field of Cloth of Gold, so called because no
expense would be spared in displaying the wealth of England and
France to each other.

Katherine had been against the French visit from the first, and
spoke out against it to her council, who were surprised she had dared
be so bold. However, Henry VIII himself was having second
thoughts about his alliance with Francis I, and was beginning to find
the prospect of friendship with the new Emperor more appealing.
He therefore paid some heed to his wife's protests, for once, and thus
Katherine found herself 'held in greater esteem by the King and his
Council than ever'. Nevertheless, Wolsey was so far forward with
plans for the visit that it was too late to cancel it, and Henry never
could resist an opportunity to show off. Katherine recognised that it
was expedient to go to France with as much grace as she could
muster.

Charles V himself was eager to form a tie of friendship with
England, and in May 1520 he paid Henry and Katherine a visit. The
King spent lavishly on new clothes for himself and his wife
in honour of his 'well beloved nephew', while Katherine was
elated at the prospect of coming face to face with Juana's son, whom
she had never seen and of whom she had such high hopes. 'I thank
God I shall see his face,' she said; 'it will be the greatest good that I
can have on earth.' The meeting took place at Canterbury at
Whitsun, with Emperor and King embracing 'right lovingly'.
Charles greeted his aunt in his customary distant and correct manner,

with little outward warmth, but she did not seem to mind, and 'most joyfully received and welcomed him'. He was not the most prepossessing figure, being graced with a pronounced version of the heavy Hapsburg jaw, which made it impossible for him to close his mouth, and gave him a somewhat vacuous look. For all this, and his inbred reticence, Charles was a hard-headed realist, already evincing something of the strength and single-mindedness with which he would rule his vast dominions for the next third of a century.

Charles's purpose in coming to England was to persuade Henry not to attend the proposed meeting with Francis I. However, Henry explained why the meeting must go ahead, and arranged to meet with Charles afterwards in Flanders. After attending mass together in the Cathedral on Whitsunday, the two monarchs presided over a banquet; Katherine was there, resplendent in a gown of cloth of gold and violet velvet embroidered with Tudor roses. Four days of feasting followed, then Charles left England, on the same day that Henry and Katherine, with a huge retinue – Katherine's train alone numbered 3,000 persons – travelled to Dover and there took ship for Calais, where they would stay briefly at the Palace of the Exchequer before moving to Guisnes on 3 June. Here, in a temporary palace erected to Wolsey's specifications, the Queen found herself occupying rooms of unsurpassed magnificence. Her closet was hung with cloth of gold and jewels; it had an altar adorned with pearls and precious stones, with twelve golden statuettes; even the ceiling was lined with cloth of gold and precious stones.

The Field of Cloth of Gold would for ever after be remembered for the riches and splendour witnessed there. On 7 June, the two kings met in the Vale of Ardres, in what is now a turnip field, but was then dotted with silken pavilions and thronged with the members of the English and French courts. It was a most satisfactory encounter; after saluting and embracing each other, Henry and Francis exchanged gifts and signed a new treaty of friendship; Henry then spoke to Francis about his hopes for a reconciliation between France and the Empire. However, as the Venetian ambassador observed, 'these sovereigns are not at peace. They hate each other cordially.' Nevertheless, this did not prevent them from indulging in three weeks of festivities to celebrate their meeting, an empty charade that would cost a fortune and achieve virtually nothing, except to cement the rivalry between them, and drive Henry directly into the arms of the Emperor. Thus what should have been a politically advantageous meeting quickly degenerated into a mere masque for the prodigal entertainment of two extravagant courts, whose sovereigns postured in new outfits of increasing splendour every day and ended up barely able to conceal their jealousy of each other.

Both their queens did what they could to calm the troubled waters. Katherine and Claude liked each other immediately; at mass, after arguing in the friendliest manner over who should kiss the Bible first, each indicating the other, they compromised by kissing each other instead. And both intervened at a wrestling match between their lords, when Francis threw Henry and Henry, red with fury, was about to retaliate.

On 11 June, the two kings tilted in their wives' honour; Katherine arrived in a crimson satin litter embroidered with gold, and sat to watch the jousts under a canopy of estate lined entirely with pearls. She wore a Spanish head-dress, with her long hair loose beneath it, and a gown of cloth of gold. Three days later, she entertained King Francis at Guisnes 'with all honour', while Henry went to Ardres as the guest of Queen Claude. Katherine sat beside Francis at a 'right honourably served' banquet, and afterwards her ladies danced for his pleasure. Later, she would call him 'the greatest Turk that ever was', for she had seen with her own eyes the effect he had on the opposite sex.

And still the extravagant festivities continued, to the ruin of both the English and French treasuries. Jousts, sporting events, banquets, balls all followed in quick succession, and at every event Queen Katherine appeared superbly dressed and displayed exquisite courtesy. At last, on 23 June, the great charade came to an end when Wolsey celebrated mass before the assembled courts; then there was a farewell banquet, and fireworks to end the day. On 25 June 1520, the English court returned to Calais, where it remained at the Exchequer. Two weeks later, Henry rode to Gravelines to meet the Emperor, and conducted him back to Calais where he and the Queen hosted an impressive banquet for their nephew before bidding him farewell and returning to England. When news of this meeting reached King Francis, he was not best pleased, and the already tense relationship between France and England was dealt a death blow on 14 July when Henry concluded a new treaty with Charles in which each agreed not to make any new alliance with France during the next two years.

Wolsey quietly arranged the breaking of Mary's betrothal to the Dauphin, to the great relief and joy of the Queen, and in the spring of 1521 Katherine's happiness was further compounded when Charles asked for Mary's hand in marriage; she had always hoped for a Spanish match for her child. Charles was undoubtedly the greatest matrimonial prize in Europe, and Mary would be assured of a brilliant future. The marriage treaty was signed in August, and Katherine found herself feeling unusually cordial towards Wolsey, who had helped arrange it. In May 1522, Charles returned to England for the betrothal ceremony, and three days after his arrival England declared war on France. Katherine had dreamed of and prayed for a Spanish alliance for the past eight years: it was now a fact.

The Emperor was met by King Henry, who brought him in the royal barge to Greenwich, where they were met at the doorway of the great hall by the Queen and her daughter. Charles knelt for his aunt's blessing and expressed great joy at seeing her, then greeted his future bride, who was still small for her age, but promised to be 'a handsome lady'. During the visit there were the usual banquets and jousts, as well as a masque, then the whole court rode to Windsor for the formal ceremony of betrothal on 19 June. Mary was due to go to Spain when she was twelve, but Charles asked if she might come earlier, to be educated as befitted a future Empress and Queen of Spain. Henry told him that if he should search all Christendom for 'a mistress to bring her up after the manner of Spain, then he could not find one more meet than the Queen's Grace, her mother, who, for the affection she beareth to the Emperor, will nurture her and bring her up to his satisfaction'. Katherine felt that Mary was not strong enough for 'the pains of the sea' or 'the air of another country', remembering her own voyage to England and how ill she had been for six years after her arrival.

Nevertheless, although Charles left England without his bride, relations between England and the Empire were never better than at this time. Charles declared war on France, and in February 1525 scored a resounding victory at Pavia in Italy, where King Francis was taken prisoner; later, he was sent to Madrid. Henry VIII was jubilant when he heard the news, and told the messenger he was 'like the Angel Gabriel announcing the birth of Jesus Christ'. In April, he sent Charles an emerald ring on Mary's behalf, with a loving message; Charles replied he would wear it for her sake. He continued to press for her to be sent to Spain, but Henry was adamant that she should not go until the appointed time, and would not budge on this point. Charles then demanded payment of her dowry as an act of good faith, but again Henry refused: it was not due for another three years. This wrangling went on until August 1525, when Charles suddenly announced that, as he had received neither his bride nor her dowry, he considered his betrothal null and void. He had, in fact, found a richer bride, Isabella of Portugal, another of Katherine's nieces, who had a dowry of one million crowns, was very beautiful, and also of an age to bear children.

Even before Henry had learned of Charles's perfidy, Wolsey had begun to edge him back into the open arms of the French, who needed a strong ally. This new alliance was Wolsey's project from start to finish: he had not forgiven or forgotten being ousted from the contest for the papacy. Of course, these events caused Queen Katherine great distress, and when, in September, Henry formally released Charles from his promise and ratified the treaty with France, her dream of a united England and Spain was finally shattered. Politically she would once more be a nonentity in her husband's realm, and for this she blamed Wolsey.

Nor was her domestic life particularly congenial. She could not have failed to guess the reason for the promotion of Sir Thomas Boleyn to the peerage as Viscount Rochford in 1525, just the latest in a string of honours accorded to a man who had been one of Henry's favourite courtiers since 1511. Yet this latest honour had undoubtedly been bestowed as a reward for services rendered to the King by Boleyn's elder daughter Mary, who had for some time been Henry's mistress. As usual, the affair was conducted discreetly, and for this reason it is impossible to pinpoint when it began or ended. Mary Boleyn had married William Carey, a gentleman of the King's household, in February 1520; the King attended their wedding, offering 6s. 8d. in the chapel. Mary accompanied Queen Katherine to the Field of Cloth of Gold later that year. Henry had just discarded

Elizabeth Blount, and it would not be fanciful to conclude that Mary Boleyn was the reason why he did so. In 1533, Mary's son, Henry Carey, who had been born around 1524, would claim he was 'our sovereign lord the King's son', but Henry never acknowledged him as such, which should be taken as conclusive evidence that the boy was William Carey's, for the King had been eager enough to acknowledge Henry FitzRoy as his own.

Mary Boleyn had spent some time at the French court, which was far more licentious than Henry's, in the train of Henry's sister the Duchess of Suffolk and had succumbed early on to the temptations there, becoming so easy with her favours that the papal nuncio called her 'a very great and infamous whore'. King Francis himself boasted of having 'ridden her', and fondly referred to her as 'my hackney'. This may have been the reason why her father removed her from the French court and brought her back to England. It seems likely that her affair with Henry VIII began around 1519–20, and that it was still continuing in 1523, when Henry named one of his ships the *Mary Boleyn*. The relationship seems to have ended in 1525, or thereabouts.

By then, the Queen was known to be incapable of having any more children and, while Henry still displayed affection for her and there was no obvious breach between them, he had reached the stage where he was prepared to go to any lengths to have an heir. Of course, he already had a son, Henry FitzRoy, who was now six years old and much resembled his father in looks. It was therefore in Henry's mind to have the boy declared legitimate by Act of Parliament and name him his heir; he even contemplated marrying him to his half-sister Mary. There was, of course, no precedent in English history for the succession devolving upon a bastard son, and no way of knowing if the King's subjects would accept FitzRoy as the lawful successor to his father, but Henry was desperate. It is highly significant that, as soon as it was confirmed that the Queen was 'past the ways of women', FitzRoy was brought to court to receive a host of honours, having the royal dukedoms of Richmond and Somerset conferred upon him in 1525, being admitted to the Order of the Garter and appointed Lord High Admiral. From then on, he was 'well brought up like a prince's child' and 'furnished to keep the state of a great prince', and it was quickly understood that he might 'easily, and by the King's means, be exalted to higher things'.

Queen Katherine was deeply offended by FitzRoy's ennoblement, which amounted, in her view, to a public snub on Henry's part. For once, she could not hide her disapproval, and the Venetian ambassador clearly perceived she was resentful and 'dissatisfied'. However, she was in no position to complain, and was 'obliged to submit and have patience', a virtue of which she was to need vast reserves in the years to come.

In the summer of 1526, Francis I, released from captivity, offered himself as a husband for the Princess Mary, Queen Claude having died in 1524. Henry was enthusiastic, as was Wolsey, who expected some hostility from the Queen but discounted it as unimportant, not rating her influence very highly. Yet from December 1526, Katherine was not to be entirely isolated in England, for in that month there arrived at court the new Spanish ambassador, Don Diego Hurtado de Mendoza, a man of very astute judgement and deep integrity, who was to prove a loyal and gallant friend to Queen Katherine. He quickly summed up the situation in England, and guessed that the Queen was very unhappy. In his opinion, 'the principal cause of her misfortune is that she identifies herself entirely with the Emperor's interests.' After the arrival of Mendoza, Katherine's life is better documented, and from this date the Calendar of State Papers relating to Spain is full of information about her life.

What was immediately apparent to Mendoza was that Katherine was kept in isolation on purpose, and that Wolsey was taking care to be present whenever the new ambassador had an audience with the Queen, having no desire to let her unburden her troubles into the ear of a Spaniard. Hence Katherine found it very difficult to pass any messages or information to Charles V, although one letter did reach him, in which she bewailed the fact that she had not heard from him in two years; 'such are my affection and readiness for your service that I deserve better treatment.' Yet Wolsey's spies were everywhere, and letters were intercepted; Charles might not after all have been at fault.

In the spring of 1527, Francis sent an embassy to England headed by Gabriel de Grammont, Bishop of Tarbes, to discuss the forthcoming betrothal of the Princess Mary to Francis himself or one of his sons. There were the usual jousts and banquets in honour of the visitors, then the two parties settled down to business. It came as something of a bombshell when the Bishop of Tarbes suddenly began questioning the legitimacy of the Princess and 'whether the marriage between the King and her mother, being his brother's wife, were good or no'. As a result of the Bishop's queries, negotiations were suspended for a short while, during which time Wolsey apparently managed to reassure him that Mary had indeed been born in lawful wedlock. Then talks resumed without further complications.

The envoys also saw the Queen, who made some pointed and rather hostile remarks about King Francis, and they left with the correct impression that there was only one alliance that would satisfy Katherine, and that would not be with France. She would, they felt, have done 'anything in her power to preserve the old alliance between Spain and England', but however strong her desire to do so, 'her means for carrying it out are small'.

The new marriage treaty, which provided for the marriage of Mary Tudor to Francis I or his second son the Duke of Orléans, was ratified by Henry VIII in May 1527 – Francis shortly afterwards became betrothed to the Emperor's sister Eleanor, and Henry of Orléans was substituted as the bridegroom. At the banquet and ball which followed, Queen Katherine put on a brave face, watching her husband and daughter dancing together. At one point, Henry, anxious to display Mary's charms to the Frenchmen, pulled off the jewelled garland she wore on her head and let fall 'a profusion of fair tresses, as beautiful as ever seen on human head'.

The festivities were brought to an abrupt end, however, by news of the sacking of Rome on 6 May by the unfed and unpaid mercenary troops of the Emperor, who was then campaigning in Italy. Lacking a commander, they surged into the eternal city and unleashed an orgy of violence and murder that went on for several days; details of the atrocities they committed shocked even that brutal age. The Pope was forced to take refuge in the Castel St Angelo, where he soon afterwards found himself a virtual prisoner of the Emperor. Charles had not been personally responsible for the sack of Rome, and was as appalled as anyone else by it, but he was not averse to having the Pope in his power.

The sack of Rome was to have far-reaching consequences for Henry and Katherine. Their marriage had failed, for many reasons. On a personal level, the age gap seemed wider than ever, and there had long ago been a divergence of interests. With the French alliance newly signed, it no longer seemed desirable for the King to have a Spanish queen. More importantly, Katherine had failed in her crucial duty, that of bearing an heir. But, above all, the King, for some years past – or so he later claimed – had, when reading the Bible, turned again and again to the passage in chapter 20 of the Book of Leviticus, which warned of the severe penalty inflicted by God on a man who married his brother's widow: 'And if a man shall take his brother's wife, it is an unclean thing: he hath uncovered his brother's nakedness; they shall be childless.' To Henry's mind he was as good as childless, lacking a male heir, and years of worrying whether the prohibition in Leviticus applied to his own marriage had by now crystallised into the conviction that indeed it did. He and Katherine had offended against the law of God by their incestuous marriage and, because of this, God, in His wrath, had denied them sons. By the spring of 1527, the King was 'troubled in his conscience' about this; the more he studied the matter, the more clearly it appeared to him that he had broken a divine law, and that something must be done to rectify the situation.

Just how long the King's conscience had been troubling him we do not know. In 1527, he declared he had had doubts about his marriage 'for some years past', though there is no mention of the matter in contemporary records before May of that year. It is likely that these doubts first became serious around 1524, when Katherine went through the menopause and Henry ceased to have sexual relations with her; but they could have been in the King's mind as far back as 1521, for in that year he quoted the critical verses from Leviticus in his treatise against Luther, an indication that he was already aware of a possible impediment to his marriage. At the same time, Dr John Longland, Bishop of Lincoln, became the King's lord almoner (or confessor), and it was to him that Henry first confided his doubts; Wolsey's secretary, George Cavendish, confirms this in his biography of his master, quoting Henry as saying he himself 'moved first in the matter, in confession to my lord of Lincoln, my ghostly father'. Longland later bore this out, revealing that for a time he and Henry had waged a spiritual battle over the issue. 'The King never left urging me until he had won me to give my consent,' declared the Bishop in later years.

By 1524, Henry's conscience had become tender as far as his marriage was concerned; although he no longer desired his wife, and may have found sex distasteful because of the mysterious female ailment she suffered, these were not the only reasons why he decided to cease having intercourse with her. He had persuaded himself that their marriage was incestuous, and that any sexual congress would be a sin. Nevertheless, it was not until three years later that he resolved to act upon his doubts and seek an annulment of his marriage.

Two separate factors combined in the spring of 1527 to provoke the King to action. One was the questioning by the Bishop of Tarbes of the Princess Mary's legitimacy, which only served to compound Henry's own doubts. Nor was this the first time that the validity of his union with Katherine had been questioned. Others, among them his own father and the conservative William Warham, now Archbishop of Canterbury, had spoken out about it as far back as 1502. Henry VII, however, had inclined to the view that the law as laid down in Leviticus only applied where the first marriage had been consummated, and he had been satisfied that Arthur had left Katherine a virgin. However, as a precaution, Ferdinand and Isabella had insisted that the Bull of Dispensation issued by Pope Julius II in 1503 provided for the marriage of Katherine and Henry, even in the event of her first marriage having been consummated.

For Henry VIII, Katherine's virgin state when she came to his bed was not the issue to be disputed, although he did his best to cast doubts upon it. Katherine, on the other hand, would come to see it as the crux of the matter, for, to her understanding, Leviticus only applied when the first marriage had been consummated, and hers had not. Henry, of course, must have known this, and realised that for his case to succeed he had to take his stand on the Levitical law applying whether the marriage had been consummated or not. Here he was treading on dangerous ground, for of course the dispensation of 1503 permitting his marriage to Katherine had had precedents, notably in the case of Katherine's own sisters, Isabella and Maria, who were married in turn to the same King of Portugal. What Henry VIII was really questioning, therefore, was the power of the Pope to dispense at all in such a case as his. This was not immediately apparent as the central issue in the affair, but it would soon become so, and then the shock waves would reverberate around Europe, for to question the Pope's authority, which all good Catholics believed was invested in him by Christ, was tantamount to heresy. Yet the European climate was ripe for it: for two centuries the papacy had been recognised as corrupt, and was held in disrepute by those who argued the need for reform of a church riddled with abuses, not all of them followers of Luther. Given this, it is not perhaps surprising to find a devout Catholic, as Henry undoubtedly then was, calling the Pope's authority into question over a matter of canon law.

The other factor spurring the King into action in the spring of 1527 was that he was, by a fortuitious coincidence, passionately in love for the first time in his life, and wished to remarry. This has often – and erroneously – been understood to have been the real basis for the King's doubts of conscience, which has tended to trivialise the whole issue. In fact, Henry VIII did, desperately, need a male heir; his wife of eighteen years was now barren. His concern for the succession and the future of his kingdom was sincere and genuine. He had been questioning the validity of his marriage for several years, long before he had fallen in love with this latest mistress. Moreover, he and the Queen had had little in common for years. It was a sensible decision, therefore, to consider applying for the annulment of his marriage and taking another wife who could bear him children. Falling in love was merely the final spur to action.

Like all the others, this latest affair was conducted in the strictest secrecy, yet Henry was hinting at it in courtly fashion from the beginning of 1526, when, on Shrove Tuesday, at a joust held at Greenwich, he appeared in the lists decked in a splendid outfit of cloth of gold and silver, on which was embroidered in gold the device *Declare je nos* ('Declare I dare not'), which was surmounted by a man's heart engulfed in flames, typical of the symbolism so beloved by the Tudor court. The King's affair with Mary Boleyn had ended, probably in the previous year, so this pretty conceit could only mean that he had found someone else. The Queen was by now used to his infidelities, and probably attached little significance to this evidence of a new one.

In May 1527, the affair was still going on, although the identity of the chosen lady was still a well-kept secret. Yet Henry could not resist dropping hints, for he was now completely enslaved by her, and wanted the world to know it. One evening, he entertained the court with a poignant song he had written that told of the heart's torment when spurned by the beloved:

> The eagle's force subdues each bird that flies;
> What metal can resist the flaming fire?
> Doth not the sun dazzle the clearest eyes,
> And melt the ice, and make the frost retire?
> The hardest stones are pierced through with tools,
> The wisest are with princes made but fools.

Few present were aware to whom the song was addressed, nor guessed that she was probably present at the banquet in her official capacity as one of the Queen's maids of honour. Nor did anyone realise that this love affair, which had now been gathering momentum for more than fifteen months, was to be the most significant of them all. For the King was passionately, abjectly in love, a novel experience for him. Even more novel was the fact that the object of his desire was holding herself tantalisingly aloof, and would not even agree to being named his mistress in the courtly sense. This was surprising indeed in an age when it was considered almost honourable, and was at least lucrative, to become the mistress – in the sexual sense even – of a king. Yet this lady was keeping him firmly at arm's length and loudly proclaiming her virtue, which of course only served further to inflame the King's passion. She would have marriage, and the crown of England, or nothing.

Her name was Anne Boleyn.

Part II
The 'great matter'

7
Mistress Anne

The story of Henry VIII and Anne Boleyn began with passion and ended with a bloody death. At its outset, Henry VIII was still a youthful ruler much praised by his contemporaries; by the time it ended he had degenerated into a ruthless tyrant, feared by his subjects, vilified throughout most of Europe, and capable of sending the woman he had so passionately loved to her execution.

Throughout those years, Henry's motives remained clear, even though he was fast gaining a reputation for keeping his own counsel and being excessively secretive. Anne Boleyn, conversely, is an enigma. Her biographers, both before and after her death, were never impartial. On the one hand, we have the Jezebel portrayed by hostile Catholic writers, the 'Concubine' who would use any means at her disposal to ensnare a king and be rid of his wife and child, and who would not stop at adultery or incest to provide her husband with a son and so save her own skin. This violent hostility towards Anne Boleyn began in her own lifetime, and when she was beheaded in 1536 there were few who did not believe her to be guilty of at least some of the crimes attributed to her. The Spanish ambassador, who detested her, referred to her at this time as 'the English Messalina or Agrippina', and Reginald Pole, the son of the Princess Mary's former governess, openly called Anne 'a Jezebel and a sorceress'. In many ways, Anne was her own worst enemy: she attracted the enmity of Catholics because she openly espoused the cause of church reform, and was widely, but erroneously, reputed to be a Lutheran. She was also indiscreet, arrogant, vindictive in her treatment of her enemies, and given to abrupt mood swings. Although there is very little evidence that she was ever promiscuous, she was regarded as immoral from the first simply because she was the 'other woman' in the King's life. Her enemies, and they were many, thought her a she-devil, a tigress, and – according to a later Catholic source – the 'author of all the mischief that was befalling the realm'.

On the other hand, we have the saintly queen of the Protestant writers, who did so much to further true religion in England, gave her protection to the followers of Luther, and produced the great Queen Elizabeth. These writers saw Anne as a veritable saint. 'Was not Queen Anne, the mother of the blessed woman, the chief, first and only cause of banishing the beast of Rome with all his beggarly baggage?' asked John Aylmer, the renowned Protestant scholar, in the reign of Anne's daughter. Likewise George Wyatt, grandson of the poet Thomas Wyatt and Anne's first biographer, who compiled his work at the end of the sixteenth century from the reminiscences of his family and those who had known her, such as her former maid of honour, Anne Gainsford; he concluded that 'this princely lady was elect of God'.

Both these conflicting portraits of Anne Boleyn have in them some degree of truth; and both are partially inaccurate. Anne was no saint, but neither was she an adulteress nor guilty of incest. She was however, ruthless and insensitive, and if she was not as black as the Catholics tried to paint her, it is likely they were nearer the truth. Nevertheless, she was a remarkable woman of considerable courage and audacity, who knew exactly what she wanted, and made sure she got it. Once she had achieved her goal, and was expected to conform to conventional ideals of queenship, disaster overtook her, for she was demonstrably unsuited to her role, and incapable of playing the part of a docile, submissive wife.

Much is known about Anne, but there are also vital gaps. Her date of birth was not recorded, and even the date and place of her marriage to the King were kept secret. The best-documented period of her life is the last seventeen days of it, which were spent in the Tower of London, when her courageous bearing at her trial and execution were in stark contrast to her hysterical fits on her arrest, and a world away from the days when she held sway over the court with such hauteur as the King's mistress.

Anne Boleyn was only the second commoner to be elevated to the consort's throne in England – the first had been Elizabeth Woodville, wife of Edward IV. Anne's origins were uninspiring, although, like all Henry VIII's wives, she could trace her descent from Edward I. She was well-connected on her mother's side, but her father's origins were in trade. The Boleyn family came from Norfolk, where there are no records of them before 1402. Anne's forbears lived at Salle, near Aylsham, which was then a thriving community grown prosperous as a result of the profitable wool trade with the Low Countries. Salle is now a deserted hamlet, and the only trace remaining of its former prosperity is its incongruously large church where several early Boleyns are buried.

Geoffrey Boleyn, who died in 1471, was the first member of the family to make a name for himself. A mercer by trade, he became an alderman of the City of London in 1452, and Lord Mayor in 1457. By then he was a wealthy man, having purchased the manor of Blickling in Norfolk from Sir John Fastolf in 1452, and a 200-year-old castle at Hever in Kent in 1462. His wife, Anne, was the daughter of Lord Hoo and Hastings, and his marriage to her was of great social value; he now mixed with the local gentry – such as the Paston family – and the lesser nobility, and even with the much more exalted Howard family. It was probably through their influence that Geoffrey was knighted by Henry VI.

Sir Geoffrey's son, Sir William Boleyn, made an even more impressive marriage, to Margaret Butler, daughter of the Irish Earl of Ormonde. Lady Margaret bore four sons: Thomas, James, William and Edward. Thomas was the eldest, being born around 1477, when his mother was only twelve years old. When he was twenty, he fought with his father for the King, Henry VII, against the men of Cornwall, who had risen in protest against high taxation. The Boleyn family was loyal to the Crown, and came early on to the favourable notice of the Tudor kings, who preferred 'new men' of merchant stock to members of the old nobility.

At around the turn of the century, Thomas Boleyn was married to Elizabeth, the daughter of Thomas Howard, Earl of Surrey. It was fortunate for Thomas that the Howard fortunes had suffered a reversal after the Battle of Bosworth, when Surrey's father had fought on the losing side, otherwise Elizabeth might have been considered too grand for him. Yet it was still in every way a brilliant match: Elizabeth's brother, Lord Thomas Howard, was then married to the Queen's sister, Anne Plantagenet, and as the Howard family was gradually received back into favour, Thomas Boleyn's status increased accordingly.

Elizabeth Howard proved a fertile bride. 'She brought me every year a child,' Thomas recorded later, remembering what a struggle it had been to provide for them all on an income of only £50.00 per annum. But only three of the children grew to maturity: Mary, Anne and George. Of those who died in infancy, Thomas was buried in Penshurst Church in Kent, and Henry in Hever Church. There has been some dispute as to which of the surviving Boleyn children was the eldest, but it seems clear that Mary was. In 1597, her grandson, George Carey, Lord Hunsdon, referred to her in a letter to Lord Burleigh as 'the eldest daughter' of Sir Thomas Boleyn. This is supported by the wording of the Letters Patent creating Anne Boleyn Marquess of Pembroke in 1532, which refers to Anne as 'one of the daughters' of Sir Thomas Boleyn. Had Anne been the elder, the Patent would surely have said so.

Even more controversy surrounds the dates of birth of Anne and her siblings. Their parents married around the turn of the century, and thus the earliest date for Mary's birth would have been around 1499–1500. George was the youngest of the three: he was not more than twenty-seven when he was preferred to the Privy Council in 1529, and therefore cannot have been born before 1502. It is likely also that his dead brother Thomas was the eldest son, and that George was actually born after 1502, probably in 1503–4.

Until recently, it was accepted that Anne Boleyn was born in 1507; this was the date noted by William Camden in the margin of his manuscript copy of his biography of Elizabeth I, printed in 1615; another late source, Henry Clifford's *Life of Jane Dormer, Duchess of Feria*, based on the reminiscences of one of Mary Tudor's maids of honour as told to her secretary in old age, published in 1645, also gives Anne's date of birth as 1507, stating that she was 'not 29 years of age when she was executed'. However, if Anne was born in 1507, she could not have been more than six years old when she entered the service of Margaret of Austria in 1513, an impossibly early age. For a more realistic date we must turn to Lord Herbert of Cherbury's biography of Henry VIII, written during the early seventeenth century and based on many contemporary sources now lost to us. Herbert states that Anne was twenty when she returned from France in 1522; this would place her date of birth in 1501–2, and make her around eleven or twelve when she entered the Archduchess's household. Two other late sources support an even earlier date of birth: Gregorio Leti's suppressed life of Elizabeth I, which suggests 1499–1500, and William Rastell's biography of Sir Thomas More, both written in the late sixteenth century.

If Anne Boleyn was born in 1500–1501, she would have been around thirty-five when she died, middle-aged by Tudor standards. Life had not been kind to her, and stress had aged her prematurely. In 1536, the Spanish ambassador referred to her as 'that thin old woman', and there is other evidence that Anne was ageing visibly: the portrait of her (in a private collection) painted at this time is in striking contrast to earlier portraits, which show her as youthful and vivacious. None of this evidence is conclusive, but it all points to an earlier date of birth than 1507, probably 1501.

Finally, there is conflicting archaeological evidence. In 1876, during restoration work in the Chapel of St Peter ad Vincula within the Tower of London, workmen found Anne Boleyn's bones beneath the altar pavement. Victorian archaeologists described the bones as those of a woman of delicate frame; the neck vertebrae, which had been severed, were very small. They estimated that Anne had been aged between twenty-five and thirty at her death. It is a fact, however, that the science of pathology was then in its infancy, and this estimate may easily have been inaccurate.

If we date Anne's birth to around 1501, we are able to establish exactly where she was born, for – prior to Sir William's death in 1505 – Thomas Boleyn and his family lived at the manor house at Blickling in Norfolk. Anne's chaplain, Matthew Parker, confirmed her birth here in later years when he referred to himself as her 'countryman', in the sense that he came from the same part of the country that she did; he, too, was born in Norfolk. It has sometimes been claimed that Anne was born at Hever Castle, but her father did not move his family there until after Sir William Boleyn's death. As the eldest son, Thomas inherited both properties, but made over Blickling to his brother James, preferring to settle at Hever which was more convenient for the court.

Here, in the moated castle amid the Kentish countryside, Anne Boleyn spent most of her childhood. If we are to believe Lord Herbert, Thomas noticed early on that Anne was an exceptionally bright and 'toward' girl, and 'took all possible care for her good education'. As well as receiving the usual 'virtuous instruction', Anne was taught to play on various musical instruments, to sing and to dance. She quickly became accomplished in all these things, excelling on the lute and virginals, and soon learned to carry herself with grace and dignity. Her academic education was limited to the teaching of literary skills, including a fine Italianate hand and – achieved after some struggle – French. Under her mother's guidance, she became expert at embroidery, and also learned to enjoy poetry, perhaps as a result of associating with the young poet Thomas Wyatt, who lived nearby at Allington Castle. Anne, too, had a talent for composing verse. In sum, her education was similar to that enjoyed by many girls of her class, its purpose being to perfect those feminine accomplishments that were so prized, both in the marriage market and at court. With this behind her, and her undoubted charm and vivacity, she would not fail to attract the right kind of husband.

During Anne's childhood, her father's career traced an upward curve. After the accession of Henry VIII in 1509, he was often at court, and by 1511 already figured prominently in the King's circle of intimates. He was an affable man and highly cultivated, if at times somewhat brusque, and he was a natural diplomat, sent by the King on a succession of embassies to foreign courts. Henry's favour also brought a string of honours his way, and with them came increasing wealth and status. Some attributed this to sexual favours bestowed upon the King by Lady Boleyn, but this was categorically denied by Thomas Cromwell, in Henry's presence, in 1537. Thomas Boleyn was nothing if not ambitious; when sent on an embassy to the court of Margaret of Austria, Regent of the Netherlands, at Mechelen in Brabant, he quickly ingratiated himself with his hostess and wasted no time in extolling to her the virtues and accomplishments of his daughter Anne, the brightest of his children. Margaret responded by offering to take Anne into her household as one of her eighteen maids of honour, and when Thomas returned to England in the spring of 1513, Anne was despatched immediately to the Low Countries in the care of a knight surnamed Broughton.

The Regent was delighted with her new maid of honour, and wrote to thank Sir Thomas for sending her, for Anne was

> a present more than welcome in my sight. I hope to treat her in such a way that you shall be quite satisfied with me. I find in her so fine a spirit, and so perfect an address for a lady of her years, that I am more beholden to you for sending her than you can be to me for receiving her.

To improve Anne's command of the French language, Margaret appointed a governess called Simonette to tutor her, and insisted that Anne's letters to her father be written in French, so that Sir Thomas, who spoke that language fluently, would be suitably impressed. Anne herself later wrote and confessed to him that these early letters were dictated by Simonette but 'the work of my hands alone'. By then, however, she would be as proficient in French as if it were her native tongue.

Anne stayed at the court of Brabant for about eighteen months, until her father found a better position for her as maid of honour to Mary Tudor, who was betrothed to Louis XII of France in August 1514. There was the usual rush to obtain places in the future Queen of France's household, and Sir Thomas was influential enough to secure two, for both his daughters. Yet only one 'Mistress Boleyn' was listed amongst her attendants when she sailed to France in October 1514; this was probably Mary, for it appears that Anne travelled to France direct from Mechelen. Anne's position in Brabant had latterly become slightly uncomfortable due to the deteriorating relationship between England and the Empire, though the Regent recorded in a letter that she was sad to lose her. Anne herself was delighted at the prospect of serving Mary Tudor, and wrote to her father:

> Sir, I find by your letter that you wish me to appear at court in a manner becoming a respectable female, and likewise that the Queen will condescend to enter into conversation with me. At this

I rejoice, as I do think that conversing with so sensible and eloquent a princess will make me even more desirous of continuing to speak and to write good French.

The transition to Mary Tudor's service could only be to her advantage, she reasoned. She and her father were kindred spirits in their desire for advancement, their ambition, and their self-interest. Even at this age Anne had a shrewd eye to the future.

Once in France, Anne was reunited with her sister Mary, and they were among the six young girls permitted to remain at the French court by King Louis XII after he had dismissed all Mary's other English attendants. When Louis died in 1515, Anne and Mary remained in the service of his young widow until she married Suffolk and returned to England. They were then invited to serve Queen Claude, the long-suffering wife of the new King, Francis I – perhaps because both of them by this time spoke French so well.

Claude of Valois was a virtuous woman, crippled from birth by lameness; her household resembled nothing so much as a nunnery. Places in it were much sought after, and the Boleyn girls were honoured to be accorded them. They would now be expected to follow the Queen's example and conduct themselves with modesty and decorum by observing an almost conventual routine based upon prayers, good works and chastity. Claude's marriage had brought her little happiness; she was constantly pregnant, while her philandering husband entertained scores of mistresses and set the tone for one of the most licentious courts of the period. Because Claude was ill at ease in such an environment, she lived mainly at the châteaux of Amboise and Blois in the lush countryside of the Loire valley. On the occasions when her presence was required at court, the Queen was extremely watchful over her female attendants, knowing full well that they were morally at risk from Francis and his courtiers.

In such contrasting worlds did Mary and Anne Boleyn grow to maturity. The experience would shape their characters in strikingly different ways. Mary succumbed early on to the temptations so feared by Queen Claude, briefly shared her favours with Francis I, and then went on to become Henry VIII's mistress. Anne, however, was more discreet, and learned from the example set by her sister. She benefited from the regime observed in Claude's household in that she learned dignity and poise. 'She became so graceful that you would never have taken her for an Englishwoman, but for a Frenchwoman born,' wrote the French poet, Lancelot de Carles. She adopted becoming French fashions, and the French courtier Brantôme tells us in his memoirs that she dressed with marvellous taste and devised new modes which were copied by all the fashionable ladies at court; Anne wore them all with a 'gracefulness that rivalled Venus'. Later, she would be responsible for introducing the French hood into England, a fashion that would last for sixty years. Even the Jesuit historian, Nicholas Sanders – who was responsible for some of the wilder inaccuracies that later gained currency about Anne Boleyn, such as the tale that she was raped by one of her father's household officials at the age of seven – felt moved to praise her inventiveness, saying she was regarded in France as 'the glass of fashion'.

Brantôme remembered Anne Boleyn in his later years as 'the fairest and most bewitching of all the lovely dames of the French court'. According to Lancelot de Carles, her most attractive feature was 'her eyes, which she well knew how to use. In truth, such was their power that many a man paid his allegiance.' She used her eyes, he tells us, to invite conversation, and to convey the promise of hidden passion. It was a trick that enslaved several men. Even King Francis was smitten by the fascinating Anne, and wrote:

> *Venus était blonde, on m'a dit:*
> *L'on voit bien, qu'elle est brunette.*

Anne's charm lay not so much in her physical appearance as in her vivacious personality, her gracefulness, her quick wit and other accomplishments. She was petite in stature, and had an appealing fragility about her. Her eyes were black and her hair dark brown and of great length; often, she would wear it interlaced with jewels, loose down her back. But she was not pretty, nor did her looks conform to the fashionable ideals of her time. She had small breasts when it was fashionable to have a voluptuous figure, and in a period when pale complexions were much admired, she was sallow, even swarthy, with small moles on her body. George Wyatt says she had a large Adam's apple, 'like a man's'. This was described by the hostile

Nicholas Sanders as 'a large wen under her chin', which Anne always concealed by wearing 'a high dress under her throat'. Nowhere is this borne out by other contemporary writers, or by portraits. Anne did, however, have a small deformity, which her enemies sometimes delighted in describing as a devil's teat. Wyatt tells us she had a second nail 'upon the side of her nail upon one of her fingers', about which she was rather self-conscious, for she took pains to hide it with long hanging oversleeves, another of her fashionable innovations. Sanders described it as a sixth finger, as did Margaret Roper, the daughter of Sir Thomas More.

Even Sanders, however, conceded that Anne was 'handsome to look at, amusing in her way, and a good dancer', while John Barlow, a divine who was later in Anne's service, thought her 'very eloquent and gracious', but less beautiful than Elizabeth Blount, Henry VIII's former mistress. Anne Boleyn undoubtedly had charm and personality in great measure, as well as that indefinable quality, sex appeal. It was this that made her appealing to so many men. Though not beautiful in the conventional sense, she had the gift of making men think she was.

Her portraits – and there are several extant – show in nearly every case a dark-haired woman with a thin face, high cheekbones and a pointed chin – facial characteristics all inherited by her daughter, Elizabeth I, who resembled her in everything but colouring. Portraits claiming to be of Anne Boleyn as a young woman at the French court are all spurious. The most famous portrait of her is that in the National Portrait Gallery, a copy of a lost original, painted between 1533 and 1536. The Gallery portrait, as well as other versions (notably at Windsor Castle, Hever Castle, and the Deanery at Ripon), once formed part of a long gallery set of royal portraits, popular in Elizabethan and Jacobean times. This portrait type still has something of the charm and vivacity that made Anne so attractive. She wears a black velvet gown with furred sleeves, a French hood edged with pearls, and a rope of pearls with a 'B' pendant. Anne was fond of initial pendants, and had at least two others – an 'A' and an 'AB', both of which were inherited and worn by her daughter. Some versions of the portrait show Anne wearing a golden filet and carrying a red rose in her hands. The miniaturist John Hoskins made a fine copy of the lost original of the National

Portrait Gallery picture in the seventeenth century; now in the collection of the Duke of Buccleuch, its quality is striking, reflecting the artist's great skill in this medium.

Other authentic representations of Anne Boleyn are little known. Her features were faithfully depicted on a medal struck in 1534 bearing the legend 'A.R. The Moost Happi'; Henry may have intended to issue it when Anne presented him with a son, for she was pregnant with her second child that year. Now it is defaced, but, in spite of this, the image is clear, in essence the same as the portraits already discussed, and the face depicted on an enamelled ring now at Chequers, the Prime Minister's country house. This was made in 1575 for Elizabeth I by an artist who had perhaps seen Anne Boleyn, or copied a lost portrait.

Some portraits said to be of Anne are of doubtful authenticity, such as the Holbein sketch at Weston Park. The sitter wears an English gable hood of the 1530s, and has dark hair, large eyes, a long nose and full, sensual lips; her face is fuller than shown in authentic portraits, and her chin not so pointed. Copies in oils exist; one is at Hever Castle, and one was at Warwick Castle until recently. (At Hever, there is a companion portrait of Mary Boleyn, of doubtful authenticity.) Yet is this Anne? Because the sitter is shown from a different angle, it is hard to tell. Holbein was a far better artist than any of the workshop limners who produced copies of authentic portraits, and his portraits are stunningly realistic when compared with the flat portrait panels produced in the studios of the age. Moreover, the portrait was first identified as Anne Boleyn in 1649, not too late to be accepted as proof of a reliable tradition of authenticity.

Anne Boleyn was highly accomplished, intelligent and witty, and in her younger years, according to George Wyatt, 'passing sweet and cheerful'. She loved gambling, played both cards and dice, had a taste for wine, and enjoyed a joke. She was also fond of hunting and the occasional game of bowls. At the glittering French court, she shone at singing, making music, dancing and conversation, and became friendly with the King's sister, the blue-stocking Margaret of Alençon, a lady of great talent and humour, who encouraged Anne's interest in poetry and literature.

Not surprisingly, the young men of the court swarmed round her.

Francis I was impressed by the way she handled them, and told her father in a letter that she was discreet and modest. He had heard a rumour that she desired to be a nun; 'This I should regret,' he wrote. It is highly unlikely that Anne Boleyn had any inclination whatsoever towards the religious life; perhaps she used it as a weapon with which to ward off unwelcome suitors, or whet the appetites of those men she found attractive. There is some later evidence that she was perhaps not so virtuous during her years in France as has hitherto been supposed. Brantôme tells us that 'rarely, or never, did any maid or wife leave that court chaste', and in 1533, Francis I confided to the Duke of Norfolk, Anne's uncle, that she 'had not always lived virtuously'. More tellingly, Henry VIII told the Spanish ambassador in 1536 that Anne had been 'corrupted' in France, and that he had discovered this when sexually experimenting with her. Whatever the extent of Anne's sexual experience in France, however, she was certainly much more discreet than her sister Mary, for no breath of scandal attached itself to her at the time. Nor would this have been in her interests, for she was eager to make a good marriage. One slip, and that ambition would be finished.

Anne's prospects of marriage came under discussion while she was still in France. In 1515, her great-grandfather, James Butler, Earl of Ormonde, died without any male heir of his body to succeed him. The earldom was claimed both by his cousin, Sir Piers Butler, and by Sir Thomas Boleyn, his grandson. It was a contest that would drag on for fourteen years before a solution was reached, although in 1520 Sir Thomas saw a way of resolving the dispute. He proposed a marriage between his daughter Anne and James Butler, the son of Sir Piers. James was described by Cardinal Wolsey as 'right active, discreet and wise', and Thomas was agreeable to the earldom devolving upon him if he married Anne. Boleyn's brother-in-law, the Earl of Surrey, agreed to lay the proposal before the King, whose consent was necessary in such matters. Anne, of course, was not consulted, and no one thought to question whether she would be happy to exchange the sophistication of the French court for a primitive castle in Ireland.

Henry VIII told Surrey he would consult Wolsey on the matter, and Surrey immediately wrote to the Cardinal, hoping to enlist his support, for James Butler was at that time a member of Wolsey's household, one of many young artistocrats who were sent to him to complete their education and gain experience of the court.

Wolsey took his time. It was not until November 1521 that he informed the King that he intended to 'devise with your Grace how the marriage betwixt [James Butler] and Sir Thomas Boleyn's daughter may be brought to pass'. However, although negotiations dragged on, they were mysteriously abandoned in the autumn of 1522. It may be that Sir Thomas Boleyn had had second thoughts, and decided to pursue his own claim to the earldom of Ormonde after all. Whatever the reason, at the end of 1522 Anne Boleyn was no nearer to being betrothed than she had ever been.

Anne had left France early that year. The recent pact between Henry VIII and Charles V had brought England and France to the brink of war, and English subjects living in France were advised to return home. Anne left Paris around January 1522, when English scholars were curtailing their studies at the Sorbonne. Queen Claude regretted losing a valued attendant, and King Francis, in a letter to Wolsey, expressed himself saddened by the 'strange' departure of the fascinating Boleyn.

The Anne Boleyn who returned home to Hever was a very different person from the girl who had left it more than eight years before. Everything about her was now very French: her mode of dress, her manners, her speech, her behaviour. Having lived at the most civilised court in the world, she stood out by reason of her wit, her grace and her accomplishments. It was no time at all before Sir Thomas had secured her a place in the household of Katherine of Aragon, which she entered around February.

At the English court, Anne's social skills brought her instant admiration from all quarters, and she was immediately chosen by the Master of the Revels to take part in one of the pageants planned for Lent. On 4 March Cardinal Wolsey gave a great banquet for the King and Queen at York Place, his London palace near Westminster. After dinner, the hall was cleared and a model of a castle called the *Château Vert* was wheeled in; from it issued five ladies and five gentlemen, who danced together before the court, the King, as Ardent Desire, being one of the dancers. However, he had eyes for no one but his partner, Mary Boleyn, who was then his mistress. The other ladies were the King's sister, Mary Tudor, his aunt the

Countess of Devon, Jane Parker, daughter of Lord Morley, who was betrothed to Anne's brother George, and Anne. All wore gowns of white satin embroidered with gold thread.

In April 1522, Sir Thomas was appointed Treasurer of the royal household. Rather than deploring his daughter Mary's immorality, he was in fact capitalising on it, and hoping for greater rewards to come. Nor did he have to wait long, for in 1525 he was elevated to the peerage as Viscount Rochford. But by that time, Henry's interest in Mary Boleyn had waned: if Wolsey's secretary and biographer, George Cavendish, is to be believed, he was casting amorous eyes in her sister Anne's direction, and had in fact been doing so since 1523. However, he had refrained from actively pursuing her, and had not disclosed his secret inclinations to anyone, least of all to the lady herself. Cavendish's information was probably correct; he was an eyewitness of the events of the period who was often taken into Wolsey's confidence, and Wolsey, of course, knew nearly all his master's secrets and made it his business to learn about the private intrigues of the court.

In 1523, Anne Boleyn's life revolved around her duties within the Queen's household. Katherine liked to surround herself with attractive young women, often to her own detriment, and was a benevolent mistress to those who served her, never failing in courtesy towards them, and taking an almost maternal interest in their lives. Young men were made welcome in the Queen's apartments, and there were plenty of opportunities for flirtation. Anne had attracted a number of suitors, and one young man who was smitten with her charms was Henry Percy, the 21-year-old heir to the earldom of Northumberland. Percy had served on the Council of the North in 1522 before joining the household of Cardinal Wolsey, hoping like many other young men of similar rank to find preferment. Percy was the Cardinal's servitor at table; whenever Wolsey went to court, Percy would go with him, but as soon as he had been excused from his duties, he would resort to the Queen's apartments, there to chat and flirt with the maids of honour. Thus he had met Anne Boleyn, and before very long he had eyes for no one else.

Anne Boleyn was not for nothing her father's daughter; she saw in Henry Percy not only an ardent suitor to whom she was attracted, but also the heir to one of the greatest and most ancient earldoms in England. The prospect of becoming Countess of Northumberland and chatelaine of Alnwick Castle, was a glorious one, and falling in love with Henry Percy was consequently very easy. He was quick to declare his feelings for her, and that summer he proposed marriage and secretly contracted himself to marry Anne before witnesses. But although their betrothal was to be kept a secret for the time being, the lovers could not conceal their feelings, and there was talk. It reached the ears of Cardinal Wolsey and alarmed him, for he was aware that Percy had been betrothed since 1516 to Lady Mary Talbot, daughter of the Earl of Shrewsbury. Percy had been very rash to involve himself with Anne Boleyn, a precontract being then as legally binding as a marriage. Anyway, in Wolsey's opinion, Anne Boleyn was no fit bride for a Percy, and it was unlikely that the Earl of Northumberland would ever have agreed to such a match.

Wolsey wasted no time in laying the matter before the King, without whose permission no aristocratic marriage could be contracted and who was angry at not being consulted. According to Cavendish, who relates the whole episode as one with inside knowledge of it, the thought of Anne Boleyn betrothed to another man disturbed him, so much so that he reluctantly confessed to the Cardinal the 'secret affection' he had been nurturing for her, and ordered Wolsey to break the engagement. This Wolsey agreed was the best course, and when he arrived back at York Place, he summoned Percy and proceeded to lecture him sternly over his folly in involving himself with 'that foolish girl yonder in the court, Anne Boleyn'. In front of Cavendish and other onlookers, the Cardinal accused the young man of having offended his father and his sovereign; Anne was 'one such as neither of them will be agreeable with the matter', and anyway, 'His Highness intended to have preferred Anne Boleyn unto another person, although she knoweth it not'. Henry, of course, had done no such thing: he was reserving Anne for himself.

Percy was dismayed at his master's words, but he outfaced the Cardinal and argued that he was 'old enough to choose a wife as my fancy served me best', emphasising Anne's 'right noble parentage, whose descent is equivalent with mine'. But Wolsey was not to be swayed, and called Percy a 'wilful boy'. Percy retorted that he had 'gone so far, before so many worthy witnesses', that he knew no way of extricating himself from his engagement without offending his conscience. Too late, he realised his error, for the Cardinal, well-versed in canon law, swooped. 'Think ye that the King and I know not what we have to do in as weighty a matter as this?' he interrupted smoothly. Percy was beaten, and he knew it. His father was sent for, and he was commanded in the King's name not to resort to Anne's company again. When the Earl of Northumberland arrived, he soundly berated his son, threatening to disinherit him if he did not do his duty. Then he had a long talk with the King and Wolsey, which resulted in a decision that Percy should marry Lady Mary Talbot as soon as it could be arranged. After that, Wolsey put in hand the legal process whereby Percy's contract with Anne Boleyn was 'clearly undone'.

Forbidden to see Anne, Percy was frantic with worry about her, having no means of knowing what she had heard. In desperation, he sent her a message via his friend, James Melton, begging that she would never allow herself to be married to another man: 'Bid her remember her promise, which none can loose but God only.' But Percy's hopes were futile. In September 1523, he married Lady Mary Talbot, and went home to Northumberland. His marriage would prove a very unhappy one, blighted not only by incompatibility but by his own advancing ill health.

Anne's first reaction, upon hearing that her betrothal to Percy had been broken, was not sorrow but anger. The Cardinal had ruined her life, the upstart butcher's son had dared to dismiss her as a 'hasty folly', and had had the effrontery to refer to her as 'a foolish girl'. Worst of all, he had proclaimed her unfit to mate with a Percy. Of the King's involvement in the affair, she suspected nothing; it was Wolsey with whom she was 'greatly offended'. If ever it lay in her power, she openly declared, 'she would work the Cardinal as much displeasure as he had done her.' However, it seemed she would have little opportunity to do so, for an order arrived almost immediately for her to return to her father's castle at Hever for a time. This made her so angry, says Cavendish, that 'she smoked'!

Anne was left to simmer and sorrow at Hever for a year or more. As for the King's interest in her, this would seem to have been a case of out of sight out of mind; he was still preoccupied with her sister anyway, although his interest in Mary dwindled as the months went by. Anne's life during her exile is not documented. She may have attended the wedding of her brother George to Jane Parker in 1524; as a wedding present, the King granted George the manor of Grimston in Norfolk, which proves that any displeasure he may have felt towards the Boleyns on account of the Percy affair was transitory.

Anne returned to court some time in 1524 or 1525, and resumed her duties in the Queen's household. In the months of her absence she had learned the hard way to be wary of men, although she still attracted them and once more established herself as one of the brightest young women at court.

In 1525, the King's interest in Anne reawakened. He was intrigued by her grace and her sharp wit, while her sophistication and sexual allure were in delightful contrast to Queen Katherine's piety and grave dignity. Anne was twenty-four, Katherine approaching forty: in every way Anne was in direct contrast to his ageing wife. He himself was still magnificent, larger than life, in his middle thirties, and ripe for an affair. When he looked at Anne, he found himself drawn to her as he had been to no woman before her; and in view of the ease with which he had made his past conquests, he did not doubt that he would succeed in seducing her.

He was destined to be quickly disillusioned, for no sooner was the object of his desire firmly established back at court than she seemed to be encouraging the advances of the poet Thomas Wyatt, a married man whose wife's adulteries were notorious. In reality, Anne's participation in this affair was at best half-hearted, for she knew there was no brilliant future in it. She did not see any more in Wyatt's attentions than the polite conventions of the courtly affair, nor did she have any intention of granting sexual favours to the poet, for all his fervent protestations of love. For her it was an enjoyable flirtation, but the King, of course, did not know this and, suspecting the worst, grew tense with jealousy.

Wyatt's grandson, George Wyatt, later recounted how the poet had been taken with Anne's beauty and her witty and graceful speech, and tells us that Wyatt was supposed to have expressed his feelings for her in some of his verses. In fact, his poems tell us very little about the affair, as few of them can be proved to relate to it, while one or two of those once accepted as referring to Anne Boleyn are now thought not to have been composed by Wyatt at all. One verse, which is in the form of a riddle about a disdainful lover, has as its answer the name 'Anna'; but which Anna cannot be proved. What is clear, though, is that Wyatt was far more interested in Anne Boleyn than she was in him, and before his courtship went too far she 'rejected all his speech of love' as kindly as she could, encouraging friendship rather than amorous advances. Wyatt went on hoping and dreaming, writing of 'the lively sparks that issue from those eyes, sunbeams to daze men's sight', and seeking her company. What he failed to realise was that it had dawned at last upon Anne Boleyn that other, more august eyes were upon her.

In February 1526, Henry VIII appeared in the tiltyard wearing the jousting dress embroidered with the words 'Declare I dare not'. This was the first indication that he had begun paying court to Anne Boleyn in secret, and doubtless his courtiers assumed that once more their sovereign had taken a new mistress. They would have been wrong: Henry had asked Anne to become his mistress, but – to his astonishment – she had refused. She would not be his mistress in the courtly sense nor in the physical sense. She had seen what had happened to her sister, who had been cast off without so much as a pension, and she told the King (according to George Wyatt):

> I think your Majesty speaks these words in mirth to prove me, but without any intent of degrading your princely self. To ease you of the labour of asking me any such question hereafter, I beseech your Highness most earnestly to desist, and to take this my answer in good part. I would rather lose my life than my honesty, which will be the greatest and best part of the dowry I shall have to bring my husband.

Henry, who was used to women surrendering the instant he beckoned, was intrigued. It was new for him to be placed in the position of having to beg for sexual favours; far from being angry or irritated, he was captivated, and Anne at once became infinitely more desirable. 'Well, Madam,' he told her, 'I shall live in hope.' But then it was Anne's turn to express astonishment: 'I understand not, most mighty King, how you should retain such hope! Your wife I cannot be, both in respect of mine own unworthiness, and also because you have a queen already. Your mistress I will not be.' Besides, she added, referring to the Queen, 'how could I injure a princess of such great virtue?'

Whether these were Anne's actual words is really immaterial; she must have said something of the sort, for she made it very clear to Henry VIII that she would only surrender her virginity after marriage. The only way that Henry would ever enjoy her would be by making her his wife, and that, as she pointed out, was impossible. It may be that he had told her already of his doubts about the validity of his marriage; if not, he would soon do so. Nor was it long for the seed once sown to take root in Henry's mind. Wyatt says the King told Wolsey he had spoken with a young lady with the soul of an angel and a spirit worthy of a crown who would not sleep with him. Wolsey, who failed to see the significance of what the King was really saying, observed in his worldly-wise way that if Henry considered Anne worthy of such an honour, then she should do as he wished. 'She is not of ordinary clay,' sighed the royal lover, 'and I fear she will never condescend in that way.' 'Great princes,' Wolsey insisted, 'if they choose to play the lover, have means of softening hearts of steel.'

Henry chose to play the lover. He sent Anne expensive gifts as tokens of his affection; these she accepted, which led him to hope that she might come to relent, given time. Yet already Anne was playing for the highest prize of all. As soon as she learned from the King of his doubts about his marriage, she saw her advantage. If he obtained an annulment, which might not be very difficult in the circumstances, then he would be free to marry again and father the heirs he so desperately needed. A Percy had considered her worthy, and a strain of Plantagenet blood ran in her veins. Why should she not become Queen of England?

Anne was setting out on a dangerous path, which she would have to tread with the utmost care. Whatever happened, she must not surrender to the King: his interest cooled too quickly. For the moment, she contented herself with dropping subtle hints, intimating that in the right circumstances she was ready to give heart, body and soul to him, and Henry, like any man kept at bay, grew daily more intent upon having her. Her studied aloofness only added to his torment lest she was harbouring some secret passion for Wyatt.

161

Anne was on friendly terms with the poet, who, blithely unaware of his sovereign's interest, was still paying court to her. One day, he playfully snatched a small jewel hanging by a lace out of her pocket, and thrust it into his doublet. Anne begged for its return, but Wyatt kept it, and wore it round his neck under his shirt. Presently, Anne forgot all about it, the jewel being of little value. However, not long afterwards, Wyatt was the King's opponent at a game of bowls; Henry thought the winning cast was his, and pointing to it with a finger on which a ring Wyatt recognised as Anne's was displayed, said, 'Wyatt, I tell thee, it is mine!' Thomas, not to be outdone, rashly produced Anne's trinket from about his neck, and taking the chain, said, 'If Your Majesty will give me leave to measure it, I hope it will be mine!' The winning cast was indeed his own, but he had not been referring to that, and the King, to whom his meaning had been clear, lost his temper. 'It may be so, but then I am deceived!' he snapped, and broke up the game.

Henry was not only jealous, he was hurt, because the ring he wore had been given to him by Anne, under some pressure, as a token of her affection. It was not, as has sometimes been supposed, a betrothal ring, because Anne had not received one in return. Nevertheless, it was not long before Henry did make up his mind to 'win her by treaty of marriage'; in his mind, he was a free man, having convinced himself that his marriage was uncanonical, and that for the Pope to declare it so would be a mere formality. He now wanted Anne more than anything else in the world, except, perhaps, a son, and he could see no reason why he should not enjoy lawfully what she would not permit him illicitly. His proposal to her was made in the latter part of 1526 or early in 1527, yet there was a delay of some months before he sought Wolsey's advice about obtaining an annulment. This delay was caused by Anne's reluctance to commit herself, a ploy calculated to banish any regrets the King might have had after asking her to become his wife. She had cleverly manoeuvred him into proposing marriage; now she would make him play a guessing game, while she affected to consider whether she would accept him.

Anne had assured the King that Wyatt meant nothing to her, and that the poet had taken her trinket without her permission. She had also made it clear to Wyatt that his courtship of her must end. Henry was taking no chances, however, and sent Wyatt off on a diplomatic mission to Italy, from which he would not return until May 1527, when it was becoming obvious to everyone just how serious the affair between the King and Anne Boleyn was. Wyatt accepted defeat with good grace, and drowned his sorrows in some very apt verse:

> Who list her hunt, I put him out of doubt;
> As well as I may spend his time in vain.
> And graven with diamonds, in letters plain,
> There is written her fair neck round about:
> *Noli me tangere*, for Caesar's I am,
> And wild for to hold, though I seem tame.

Wyatt soon recovered from his loss and shortly afterwards found a new love, Elizabeth Darrell, who remained his mistress until his death in 1542. Soon, he was celebrating her in a new poem:

> Then do I love again;
> If thou ask whom, sure since I did refrain
> Her, that did set our country in a roar;
> The unfeigned cheer of Phyllis hath the place
> That Brunette had.

Later, Thomas amended the third line of this verse to 'Brunette, that set my wealth in such a roar,' deeming it wiser to delete all references to his affair with Anne Boleyn, which is perhaps why very few of his poems about it survive today.

Having eliminated his rival, the King may now have hoped that his way was clear to ecstasy with his sweetheart. Anne found his ardour hard to deal with, and retaliated by withdrawing from the court to Hever Castle. This only inflamed the King more, and he began sending her passionate love-letters, of which this is one of the first:

My mistress and my friend,
I and my heart commit ourselves into your hands, beseeching you to hold us recommended to your good favour, and that your affection to us may not be by absence diminished. For great pity it were to increase our pain, seeing that absence makes enough of it,

and indeed more than I could ever have thought; remembering us of a point in astronomy, that the longer the days are, the farther off is the sun, and yet, notwithstanding, the hotter; so it is with our love, for we by absence are far sundered, yet it nevertheless keeps its fervency, at the least on my part, holding in hope the like on yours. Ensuring you that for myself the annoy of absence doth already too much vex me; it is almost intolerable to me, were it not for the firm hope that I have of your ever during affection towards me. And sometimes, to put you in mind of this, and seeing that in person I cannot be in your presence, I send you my picture set in a bracelet. Wishing myself in their place, when it should please you. This by the hand of your loyal servant and friend,

  H.R.

Anne was better able to cope with separation than Henry, for she was not so deeply involved emotionally. Seven years in France had taught her skill in the game of courtship, and she sent the King the gift of a jewel fashioned as a solitary damsel in a boat tossed by a tempest. The allusion was clear. At the same time, she wrote her lover a warm letter, hinting at her inner turmoil, but implying that she might, with some reassurance from him, see her way to accepting him as her future husband. Sadly, this letter, and all the others written to the King by Anne, have not survived. His to her, however, she kept, but they were stolen by a papal servant in 1529, and today rest in the Vatican archives.

Anne's letter and love-token provoked a passionate reaction from Henry, who wrote:

For so beautiful a gift, I thank you right cordially, chiefly for the good intent and too-humble submission vouchsafed by your kindness. To merit it would not a little perplex me, if I were not aided therein by your great benevolence and goodwill. The proofs of your affection are such that they constrain me ever truly to love, honour and serve you, praying that you will continue in this same firm and constant purpose, ensuring you, for my part, that I will the rather go beyond than make reciprocal, if loyalty of heart, the desire to do you pleasure, even with my whole heart root, may serve to advance it. Henceforth, my heart shall be dedicate to you alone, greatly desirous that my body could be as well, as God can bring it to pass if it pleaseth Him, Whom I entreat once each day for the accomplishment thereof, trusting that at length my prayer will be heard, wishing the time brief, and thinking it but long until we shall see each other again.

Written with the hand of the secretary who in heart, body and will is your loyal and most ensured servant.

H. autre ne cherche R.

'Henry the King seeks no other than Anne Boleyn.' And around Anne's initials the King drew a heart, as lovers have done from time immemorial. Anne may have been flattered, yet her resolve remained firm, and she stayed tantalisingly out of reach. When Henry, driven to desperation, made a brief visit to see her at Hever, she told him she was returning to court. Then, when he had gone, she changed her mind, and sent a message to say she could not come after all, even in her mother's company, which Henry had suggested as a means of preserving her good name. Frantic in case her feelings had cooled, he complained bitterly in his next letter that she had not written often enough and that she was being unduly hard on him:

To my mistress,

Because the time seems to me very long since I have heard of your good health and of you, the great affection that I bear you has prevailed with me to send to you, to be the better ascertained of your health and pleasure, because since I parted with you I have been advised that the opinion in which I left you has now altogether changed, and that you will not come to court, neither with my lady your mother, nor yet any other way. I cannot enough marvel, seeing I am well assured I have never since that time committed fault; methinks it is but small recompense for the great love I bear you to keep me thus distanced from the person of that she which of all the world I most do esteem. And if you love me with such settled affection as I trust, I assure me that this sundering of our two persons should be to you some small vexation. Bethink you well, my mistress, that your absence doth not a little grieve me, trusting that by your will it should not be so;

but if I knew in truth that of your will you desired it, I could do none other than lament me of my ill-fortune, abating by little and little my so great folly.

Unknown to Anne, the King had already made the decision to test the validity of his marriage in the ecclesiastical courts; this was a matter too sensitive to be written of in his letter, so he entrusted the bearer with a message for Anne, 'praying you to give credence to that which he will tell you from me'. The news had the desired effect, and elicited a prompt reply, in which Anne, as his humble subject, professed her love and devotion to a gracious sovereign. This was not quite what Henry had hoped for, but it was enough to provoke him into a fervent declaration of his intentions towards her in his next letter, written in the spring of 1527. He was in great distress, he said, because he did not know how to interpret her last letter, and he prayed her,

with all my heart, you will expressly certify me of your whole mind concerning the love between us two. . . . . If it shall please you to do me the office of a true loyal mistress and friend, and to give yourself up, heart, body and soul to me, who will be and have been your very loyal servant, I promise you that not only shall the name be given you, but that also I will take you for my only mistress, rejecting from thought and affection all others save yourself, to serve you only.

He ended by beseeching her for an answer, if not in writing, then in person.

It is clear from this letter that the King was using the word 'mistress' in its honourable, courtly context, yet equally clear that he meant Anne to interpret it in its fullest sense. But there is more to the letter than that. She was to be placed above all others, including, presumably, the Queen herself. Henry was not yet free to marry her, and saw no reason why they could not be lovers while he was waiting for his freedom: he wanted Anne to commit herself publicly to the relationship. For her, this was a prospect fraught with danger and insecurity, and therefore not to be considered. If she became the King's mistress now, she might never become Queen of England.

Nevertheless, she could not go on absenting herself from Henry for ever, and it was at this stage that she consented to return to court. It was the right psychological moment, for Henry was ready to do whatever she asked, and was adamant that their futures lay together. Almost immediately, Anne found herself in a position of unparalleled influence: even Queen Katherine had never held such sway over the King. But Anne had an old score to settle, and she was now in a position to exact vengeance. Since 1523 she had blamed Cardinal Wolsey for publicly humiliating her, and her burning desire since then had been to teach him that one did not mishandle members of the Boleyn family with impunity. She had never guessed that it had been the King, and not Wolsey, who was the prime mover in the affair, and Henry had not seen fit to enlighten her.

When Anne returned to court, the King made no secret of his love for her, nor that she was from henceforth to play a prominent role in affairs. He began showering her with fine jewellery and clothes, and saw that she was lodged in splendid apartments. The courtiers made much of her, using her as an intermediary between themselves and the King, and she was soon revelling in her growing influence and power. According to George Wyatt, she began to look 'very haughty and proud'.

The Queen had both heard by report and seen with her own eyes what was going on between her husband and her maid of honour, yet she showed neither of them any grudge or displeasure, but accepted the affair with good grace and commendable patience, openly declaring herself to be a 'Patient Grizelda', and telling her ladies, according to George Cavendish, that she held Anne Boleyn 'in more estimation for the King's sake than she had before'. Had she known just what her husband's intentions were towards Anne, she might not have accepted the situation with such equanimity, but as far as she was concerned, Anne was merely the latest in a line of royal mistresses and would be discarded in due course.

Others at court were more perceptive, and correctly assessed the intensity of the King's passion for Anne Boleyn. One was Anne's maternal uncle, Thomas Howard, third Duke of Norfolk, son of the victor of Flodden, who had died in 1524. In 1527, Norfolk was a hardened soldier and statesman of fifty-four, who would retain his position as premier duke of the realm and one of the most prominent members of the Privy Council until his disgrace in 1546. After the death of his first wife, Anne Plantagenet, Henry VIII's aunt, Howard had married Elizabeth Stafford, daughter of the Duke of Buckingham who had been executed for treason in 1521, and by her had three children, the eldest being Henry, Earl of Surrey, who would become one of the greatest poets of the Tudor age. The Duke and Duchess were not happily married; he had taken for his mistress the low-born Elizabeth Holland, whom his wife described as 'a churl's daughter, who was but a washer in my nursery eight years'. Norfolk's involvement with his laundress lasted more than twenty years and in 1539 the Duchess was still complaining about him keeping 'that harlot' and other whores also, vindictive women who had bound and restrained the Duchess while one sat on her breast 'till I spat blood'. By that time, the ducal couple had long since gone their separate ways, and the Duchess reckoned that 'if I come home, I shall be poisoned'.

Thomas Howard might have been brutal and callous in his domestic life, but his male contemporaries considered him to be a man of the utmost wisdom, solid worth and loyalty. His portrait by Holbein shows a granite-faced martinet, and it is difficult to imagine him being the prudent, liberal, astute and affable man he was reputed to be. Nevertheless he had the common touch, and associated with everybody regardless of rank. What made Norfolk valuable to Henry VIII was his astute judgement and his ruthless expediency. He had great experience in the administration of the kingdom, and could discuss affairs of state in depth. Like all his clan, he was ambitious.

Norfolk, like most of the older nobility, hated Wolsey. Because he and several other lords believed the Cardinal was preventing them from enjoying the power that should rightly be theirs, they meant to use Anne Boleyn as 'a sufficient and apt instrument' to bring what Cavendish calls 'their malicious purpose' to fruition. To this end, they very often consulted with her as to what was to be done, and she, 'having a very good wit, and also an inward desire to be revenged upon the Cardinal, was as agreeable to their requests as they were themselves'. Thus Anne began her long campaign to discredit Wolsey in the King's eyes, and then bring about his ruin, not only for the sake of her pride but also in the interests of her family.

Wolsey was at first unaware of her enmity. He had virtually forgotten the Percy affair and the furious girl he had dismissed so lightly four years earlier. Now, to please his master and ingratiate himself with the new favourite, the Cardinal entertained them both to sumptuous banquets at York Place. Then, wrote Cavendish, 'the world began to be full of wonderful rumours' because 'the love between the King and this gorgeous lady grew to such a perfection that divers imaginations were imagined'. Nor were the rumours without foundation, for in the late spring of 1527, Anne finally accepted the King's proposal of marriage and agreed to become his wife as soon as he was free.

She was well aware of the domestic politics of the court and the struggle between factions for power, but she was not afraid. With the King at her side, an ardent lover, she had no cause to be. Her hardest task, as she viewed it, was to keep his love and maintain his desire at its present pitch without giving way to it. It was this that would test her resolve to the utmost during the years to come, and this that lay at the root of the chronic insecurity she later manifested.

As soon as he had Anne's consent, the King took her father, now Viscount Rochford, into his confidence, 'to whom we may be sure that the news was not a little joyful', observed George Wyatt with exquisite understatement. Rochford was no less ambitious than his daughter, yet the prospect of being the father of the next Queen of England, and possibly grandfather to a future monarch, was more than he had ever dreamed of. Such a position automatically brought with it not only wealth, power, fame and honour such as he had always craved and worked so hard to obtain, but also a considerable amount of influence in public affairs. From the first, he would be his daughter's greatest supporter. Like her he was also an enemy of the Cardinal. Rochford was bitter because when, in 1525, he had been created a Viscount, he had been forced to resign his post as Treasurer without any financial compensation. For this, he blamed Wolsey.

It did not take long for the Cardinal to realise what was happening: a faction was forming around Anne Boleyn, and he knew it to be hostile towards himself. For the present he could afford to be sanguine about this, for the King had not acquainted him with his true intentions towards Anne. Like the Queen, Wolsey saw her as just another mistress, who could go the way of the others. Yet to keep the King happy he paid court to the lady, sending her gifts – she had in particular expressed a desire for carps, shrimps and other delicacies from his famous ponds – and putting on entertainments for her. On the surface, cordial relations existed between Anne and Wolsey, and no doubt he was privately of the opinion that she was as light-minded and foolish as he had thought her four years earlier, having no great opinion of the intelligence of women. This particular young woman, however, did have brains, and was determined to use them to good effect when it came to manipulating Wolsey's downfall. First, however, she would make use of the Cardinal, for Henry had made it clear that he was the one man who could effectively negotiate the annulment of his marriage. Then she would do her best to discredit him in the King's eyes, and take her revenge.

Anne was now constantly in the King's company. She ate with him, prayed with him, hunted with him, and danced with him, but she did not sleep with him. Henry had no leisure to ponder his thraldom, however, for he was about to embark on the greatest enterprise of his life: the annulment of his marriage to Katherine of Aragon, which would come to be known as the King's 'great matter'. When Henry set out to obtain what has often, but erroneously, been called his 'divorce', he little dreamed it would take him six years, nor envisaged the far-reaching effects it would have on himself, the woman he loved, or his kingdom and people.

8
A thousand Wolseys
for one Anne Boleyn

In the spring of 1527, Henry VIII finally set in motion the
ecclesiastical machinery that he hoped would bring about the
dissolution of his marriage to Katherine of Aragon; what he desired
was a declaration that their union had been invalid and unlawful
from the first. When news of his intentions leaked out, several people
believed that Anne Boleyn had been the cause of his doubts about his
marriage. In fact, she was merely a catalyst, and the indications are
that Henry would have pursued an annulment at some stage anyway,
for overriding all other considerations was his desperate need for a
male heir.

Throughout the course of the 'great matter', Henry behaved like a
man possessed, on two counts. One was his conviction that he was
right, the other was his passion for Anne Boleyn: the French
ambassador thought him 'so much in love that God alone can abate
his madness'. Under Anne's influence, he was beginning to display
the character traits that would govern his later behaviour, and this
period of his life saw the beginning of the transition from knight
errant to tyrant. It was a slow metamorphosis, however, and would
only be accomplished once the King had thrown off first the tutelage
of Wolsey, and afterwards the influence of Anne Boleyn. Then he
would at last be his own master.

Once the King had made his decision to take proceedings, and
because she was the butt of so much speculation at court, Anne
Boleyn resolved to return to Hever again. Hever Castle has changed

immeasurably since Anne's day. By the eighteenth century it was a ruin, and it was gutted and refurbished at the beginning of the twentieth century, when the present gardens were laid out and the lake dug. Apart from the stone fabric of the building and the moat very little remains from the sixteenth century; yet the restoration has been so harmonious that it is easy to picture Henry and Anne there, in formal gardens very like the present ones.

Anne was rarely at court between May 1527 and the summer of 1529. She joined the King at his manor of Beaulieu in Essex in August 1527, and spent the greater part of a month hunting with him and supping each evening in his privy chamber. From Beaulieu, Anne returned to Hever. She paid a brief visit to court at the end of September, but spent most of the winter at Hever. In March 1528, she and her mother, who acted as chaperon, were the King's guests at Windsor, whither Henry had gone with only a handful of attendants. It was a brief idyll: when the weather was fair, Henry and Anne would ride out hunting or hawking every afternoon, not returning until late in the evening, or would go walking in Windsor Great Park. At other times they occupied themselves with the pastimes they both enjoyed: cards and dice, music, poetry, and dancing. Anne and her mother were again at court during July and August 1528, but by September the political situation was such that Henry sent them back to Hever.

Throughout these long absences, the King found himself once more playing the role of scribe, and his letters to Anne, whom he referred to as 'mine own sweetheart' or 'darling', were written with increasing intensity. He would often abase himself as a courtly suitor should, thanking her 'right heartily for that it pleaseth you still to hold me in some remembrance'. Occasionally, he would end his letters in a code that has never been deciphered, or sign himself 'by the hand which fain would be yours, and so is the heart', or 'by the hand of him which desires as much to be yours as you do to have him'. He needed to see her

more than any earthly thing; for what joy in the world can be greater than to have the company of her who is the most dearly loved, knowing likewise that she, by her choice, holds the same, which greatly delights me.

172

He spoke often of his 'fervency of love', and told Anne that their frequent separations 'had so grieved my heart that neither tongue nor pen can express the hurt'; she could not begin to imagine 'the sufferings that I, by your absence, have sustained', nor 'the great loneliness that I find since your departing'.

There is a strong sexual tone to these letters. The King spoke often of his need to be 'private' with Anne, and wished he was, 'specially an evening, in my sweetheart's arms, whose pretty dugs [breasts] I trust shortly to kiss'. 'Mine own darling,' he wrote on another occasion, 'I would you were in mine arms, and I in yours, for I think it long since I kissed you.' It would not be long, he assured her, before 'you and I shall have our desired end, which shall be more to my heart's ease than any other thing in this world'. There is no evidence, however – despite rumours to the contrary – that Anne Boleyn surrendered to the King before the autumn of 1532. Even the imperial ambassador, who would become her sworn enemy, had to admit that there was no positive proof of adultery. Some intimacies she may have permitted, but never full intercourse. This is substantiated, not only by the King's repeated denials that she was his mistress in the sexual sense, but also by the fact that, once the affair was consummated, Anne became pregnant immediately and conceived regularly thereafter. Of course, there were rumours that she had borne children in secret before then, but they were without foundation, for it is certain that if Anne had conceived during these early years, the King would have moved heaven and earth to have the child born in wedlock, and many people would have known about it. Above all, Anne's surrender was her trump card, and she would have been a fool to play it with the future so uncertain and with the memory of her sister ever before her.

Anne's biographer, George Wyatt, asserted that she was not in love with the King and had hoped for a future husband who was 'more agreeable to her'. He also says she resented the loss of freedom she had suffered as a result of the King's courtship. There was probably an element of truth in these statements. Certainly her feelings for Henry were less intense than his for her; she handled him with such calculated cleverness that there is no doubt that the crown of England meant more to her than the man through whom she would wear it. Nor was she a good correspondent. She often failed to reply to the King's letters, probably deliberately, for everything she did, or omitted to do, in relation to Henry was calculated to increase his ardour. In this respect she never failed. He always wrote again, chiding her for her 'tardiness', begging her 'to advertise me of your well-being', and sending gifts of venison or jewels to please her. If she detected a hint of irritation in his letters, she dealt with it by quickly reverting from the unattainable to the affectionate, and sending a loving reply.

It was Wolsey to whom the King had turned for help and advice about his doubts concerning his marriage. When the Cardinal learned that his master was seeking an annulment, he was horrified, and fell to his knees, begging Henry to proceed no further since the matter would be fraught with difficulties. The King ignored this, insisting the Cardinal take steps to instigate proceedings and, with grave misgivings, Wolsey, as papal legate, convened in secret an ecclesiastical court, which opened on 17 May 1527 at Westminster, its purpose being to consider the King's collusive suit. William Warham, Archbishop of Canterbury, presided, assisted by Wolsey and a host of bishops and canon lawyers. The King was summoned, and asked to account 'to the tranquillity of his conscience and the health of his soul, for having knowingly taken to wife his brother's widow'. He admitted the charge, confessed his doubt, and asked for judgement to be given upon his case. Thereafter, the court reconvened for two further sessions and debated the matter, yet on 31 May the commissioners announced that the case was so obscure and doubtful that they were not competent to judge it. The King then consulted his Privy Council, who agreed there was good cause for scruple, and advised him to apply to the Holy See in Rome for an annulment, the Pope being the only authority qualified to pronounce on the matter.

Elaborate precautions had been taken to keep what was going on a secret, especially from the Queen, but these were not proof against the perception of the Spanish ambassador, who, only the day after proceedings started, was writing to inform Charles V that 'the Cardinal, to crown his iniquities, is working to separate the King and Queen'. That same day, Mendoza sent a secret message to Katherine, informing her of the convening of the Westminster court, and requesting an urgent audience. She sent word that she 'was so afraid she has not dared to speak with me'. The Cardinal's spies were watching.

Mendoza's note shattered the Queen's peace of mind, though she very quickly convinced herself that the proceedings were all Wolsey's doing since they could not be her husband's. Mendoza, fearful that the court and, subsequently, the Pope would be provided with false statements purportedly from the Queen, wanted Katherine to be on her guard. She was grateful for the warning, and acted quickly, asking Vives to represent her at Warham's court. However, not wishing to offend the King, he refused, and the Queen, whose moral courage was never in doubt, withdrew his pension. Nevertheless, events were in her favour. At the beginning of June, news reached England of the sack of Rome, and not only was the King shocked and outraged at reports of the atrocities, but also sensible of the fact that, with the Pope now a prisoner of the Emperor, Katherine's nephew, a favourable decision on his nullity suit was unlikely to be forthcoming for the time being. Wolsey now suggested that he himself should go to France to enlist the support of King Francis, who might prevail upon the Pope to extend Wolsey's legatine powers and thereby enable him to adjudicate on the King's case. Henry agreed that this might be the best solution, and Wolsey began to prepare for his journey.

By late June, events were moving at such a pace, and rumours proliferating so alarmingly, that it was impossible to keep the 'great matter' from the Queen any longer. Henry, of course, was unaware that she had already found out about it from Mendoza, and thus, when he went to her apartments on 22 June 1527, he was feeling distinctly uncomfortable. As soon as Katherine had risen from her curtsey, he blurted out that he was much troubled in his conscience about their marriage, and had resolved to separate himself from her at bed and at board. All he asked was her co-operation, and that she choose a house to retire to, at least until the matter was settled.

As Mendoza reported later, Katherine was 'in great grief' when she heard this. Her usual self-control deserted her, and she wept uncontrollably. The King hastened to pacify her, saying he hoped he might be allowed to return to her, and that he only wished to find out the truth about their marriage. All would be done for the best, he assured her, begging her at the same time not to speak of the matter to anyone – he feared that news of his collusive suit would provoke a hostile reaction from Charles V. But Katherine was beyond comprehension, and continued to sob her heart out. Unable to do anything with her, Henry fled.

After she had pulled herself together, Katherine was able to assess her situation. She was alone and without counsel, far from her friends in Spain, with spies watching her every move. Yet she was not for nothing the daughter of Isabella of Castile: her principles were firm, her moral courage undoubted, and she believed her marriage was good and valid. Pope Julius had permitted it, and that was enough for her. She was the King's true wife, and the Princess Mary his legitimate heir, and on these premises she would take her stand. She was convinced that both Wolsey and Anne Boleyn had led the King astray and planted doubts in his mind, and she saw it as her sacred duty to rectify the situation and persuade her husband that he was in error.

To Katherine, what Henry was contemplating was morally reprehensible: the casting off of a blameless and devoted wife after eighteen years of honourable wedlock, and the setting aside of an innocent child. She was at a loss to understand how he could countenance such a thing, though this was a somewhat blinkered view, which did not take into account England's desperate need for a male heir. Henry himself came to feel that Katherine was allowing her earthly pride in her rank to stand in the way of his moral scruples, but it was not so much this as the fact that her pride would never allow her for a minute to acknowledge that she had been, not his wife, but his harlot for eighteen years. That pride, the abiding love she bore him, and the deep conviction that right was on her side would enable her to stand firm in her resolution until the day she died.

In every respect other than that which touched her conscience, Katherine was ready to obey her husband, but in the event her conscience was to prove every bit as formidable as Henry's. Both were strong-willed people, and beneath the Queen's apparent meekness there was a layer of steely determination. The battle once engaged, neither would give any quarter. As Katherine told the Pope's legate in 1528:

Neither the whole kingdom on one hand, nor any great punishment on the other, although she might be torn limb from limb, could compel her to alter her opinion; and if, after death, she should return to life, rather than change her opinion, she would prefer to die over again.

She failed to appreciate that by taking her stand upon the power of the papacy to dispense in a case such as hers, she was in fact doing as much as the King to place its position in jeopardy.

Throughout the course of the 'great matter', Katherine rarely reproached Henry. She could not accept, and never would accept, that his love for her was dead. Affection and respect remained, he observed all the courtesies when they were together, and this led her to believe that all was not lost. If Anne Boleyn's influence were to be removed, she was certain he would return to her and abandon all ideas of annulment. She therefore ignored his initial suggestion that she retire from court, and continued with her daily routine as if nothing amiss had occurred. He wanted no more scenes, and was happy for the present to maintain the pretence that all was well; above all, he wanted to be judged in a favourable light by the Pope when the time came, and Wolsey had warned him to handle Katherine 'both gently and docilely'. He therefore kept her at his side for state functions and visits to their daughter, who had been sent to live at Hunsdon where she owned a manor house. Henry and Katherine were together to welcome the French ambassadors to court in September 1527, and three days later sat side by side to watch a tragic masque in Latin, played by children. In public, the Queen would appear smiling and cheerful. Even the Duke of Norfolk, a man of little feeling and the uncle of Katherine's rival, was able to find words to praise her fortitude in showing such a brave face to the world: 'It was wonderful to see her courage,' he said; 'nothing seems to frighten her.'

Sexual relations between Henry and Katherine had ceased in 1524; since then, they had occasionally shared a bed for form's sake. Now, Henry's confessor advised him not to do even this until a decision had been given on his case. However, Henry chose to ignore this advice, and as late as 2 December 1528, the Spanish ambassador was reporting that the King and Queen were sleeping together at

Greenwich, though on that very day Henry declared himself 'utterly resolved and determined never to use the Queen's body again', and thereafter left her to sleep alone.

Towards Anne Boleyn Katherine never betrayed any sign of jealousy, even though she believed – and continued to believe even after Henry's outright denial of the fact in November 1529 – that he and Anne were lovers. As for Anne, George Wyatt says she had been reluctant to accept the King's advances because of the great love she bore the Queen. This may have been so at the beginning of the affair, but her love for her mistress quickly turned into antipathy and then into hatred as she realised that Katherine meant to fight back.

The Queen sought guidance in prayer before making up her mind to ask her nephew, the Emperor, to intercede with the Pope for her. She realised this would not be easy, because of Wolsey's spies about her, but had thought of a plan to outwit the Cardinal. She announced that one of her servants, Francisco Felipez, was to visit his widowed mother in Spain, and obtained for him a safe conduct from the King. In fact Felipez was to carry a message from the Queen to Charles V, and knowing how suspicious Henry could be, Katherine pretended that she did not want him to go. Unfortunately, this did not deceive the King, and Felipez was arrested at Calais and sent back to England. The episode proved to Henry that his wife was not going to submit meekly to having her marriage annulled.

Later in 1527, Katherine did succeed in sending Felipez to the Emperor, and her physician Vittorio also slipped unnoticed out of England to acquaint Charles with further details of her plight. The Emperor had already heard from Mendoza of her situation; in May, the ambassador had told him that 'all her hope rests, after God, upon your Imperial Highness,' and advised him to put pressure on the Pope to tie the hands of the papal legate, Wolsey, and have the case referred to Rome for a decision. Charles V knew perfectly well that Clement VII, a weak and vacillating man, would not dare to give a decision in Henry's favour while he was the Emperor's prisoner, and was perfectly willing to let Henry apply for an annulment if he wished. The Queen, had she known it, was in a very strong position indeed. Nevertheless, in July 1527, Charles expressed to Mendoza his indignation at 'so strange a determination. We do not believe it possible. For the honour and service of God, put an end to this scandalous affair.' And in August, he wrote to Katherine:

> You may well imagine the pain this intelligence caused me, and how much I felt for you . . . I have immediately set about taking the necessary steps for a remedy, and you may be certain that nothing shall be omitted on my part to help you.

Mendoza, Charles's ambassador, was a true friend to Queen Katherine during this period, and did his best in a difficult situation. It was almost impossible to communicate directly with the Queen, but he too had his spies, and with their help he tirelessly gathered together every scrap of information he could discover, and kept his master extraordinarily well-informed. It was Mendoza who predicted, correctly, in May 1527, that 'there will be many more voices in her favour than against her, both because she is beloved here, as because the Cardinal, who is suspected to be at the bottom of all this, is universally hated.'

The King's 'great matter' first became public knowledge beyond the confines of the court in the early summer of 1527; by July, it was as notorious as if it had been proclaimed by the public crier. Rumour had it that the King was planning to marry the French King's sister, Margaret of Alençon. Henry was irritated by the rumours, and commanded the Lord Mayor of London to ensure that the people ceased such communications upon pain of his high displeasure. This achieved absolutely nothing, and the rumours became, if anything, more widespread. In June 1527, Wolsey informed all the English ambassadors abroad of the situation, and by the spring of 1528 the 'great matter' was common knowledge throughout the courts of Europe, thanks to the diplomatic network. Outside the dominions of the Emperor, there was a good deal of support for Henry VIII, it being generally felt that his marriage was of doubtful validity.

As Mendoza had reported, Katherine was indeed very popular, both at court and in the kingdom at large, so much so that the King feared demonstrations within her household, once her staff learned what was afoot. Mendoza too had contemplated the possibility of 'some great popular disturbance', but observed that the English 'will probably content themselves with grumbling only'. Nevertheless, from the beginning, Henry believed that Katherine was quite capable of inciting a war with the Emperor or a rebellion of his subjects against him, and had her watched closely.

When Katherine appeared in public, crowds would gather and cry: 'Victory over your enemies!' Women, in particular, spoke out in her favour, believing that the King only sought to be rid of her for his own pleasure, and the French ambassador drily commented that 'if the matter were decided by women, the King would lose the battle'. Nevertheless, those at court and those who looked for preferment tended to support the King, though there were honourable exceptions. In the summer of 1527, Sir Thomas More told the King he believed his marriage to be good and valid. Though disappointed, Henry accepted this in good part, for he respected More. John Fisher, Bishop of Rochester, a man with a reputation for wisdom and sanctity, told Wolsey in June 1527 that it could by no means be proved to be prohibited by any divine law that a brother may marry his wife of his deceased brother, and said he had been powerfully moved to declare himself in favour of the validity of the royal marriage.

Another staunch supporter of the Queen was Reginald Pole, the son of the Princess Mary's governess, Lady Salisbury; he had been studying in Italy at the King's expense and planned to enter the Church. Pole later expressed the belief that Anne Boleyn was responsible for 'the whole lying affair', and became quite outspoken in his views. Later still, when his opposition to the King had made his position in England too uncomfortable and unsafe, Pole fled abroad, remaining a continual thorn in the King's side. Nor did the King enjoy the full support of Archbishop Warham. Warham had been one of those who had advised Henry VII against marrying Katherine to Prince Henry, though the Pope's dispensation had at the time set his mind at rest. He was King's man enough to support his master's pursuit of the truth concerning the validity of his marriage, and told Wolsey in 1527 that 'however displeasantly the Queen might take it, yet the truth and judgement of the law must be followed'. Yet when it came down to basics, Warham was a traditional churchman who would not countenance any attack on the authority of the Holy See. As for Vives, he was reconciled to the Queen in 1528, when she confided to him her profound distress, saying her grief was the greater because she loved Henry so much. Later, Vives wrote: 'Can anyone blame me for consoling her? Who will not praise her moderation?' Even the King's sister Mary supported the Queen, of whom she was very fond, and she hated Anne Boleyn so much that she refused to come to court while she was there.

Some of Katherine's supporters she could have done without. Symbolic of widespread public feeling was the appearance in Kent of a nun, Dame Elizabeth Barton, who suffered from epileptic fits but was reputed to have the gift of prophecy and to have had holy visions. In the summer of 1528, the Nun would prophesy that if the King put away his lawful wife, God would ensure that he should no longer be King in England, and he would die a villain's death. Although it was not yet treason to foretell the King's death, Elizabeth Barton would be fortunate in that for the time being the authorities were prepared to dismiss her as a harmless lunatic; nor did they molest her when she persisted in repeating her prophecies and threats. However, Queen Katherine wisely refused to have anything to do with her.

Wolsey left for France in July 1527. Apart from enlisting the support of King Francis, he hoped also to discuss the possibility of a French marriage for the King, being still unaware that Henry had already decided to marry Anne Boleyn as soon as he was free. However, by August 1527, rumours were circulating in England to the effect that, when Henry had set aside his lawful queen, he would marry his mistress. Such rumours gathered momentum with alarming speed, and provoked a highly undesirable reaction, for if the Londoners as a body had looked unfavourably upon the news that the King intended to put away Queen Katherine, they were scandalised at the reports that he intended to replace her with Anne Boleyn, who was considered an upstart who was no better than she should be. From the first Anne was openly called a whore and a sorceress; nor was there anything the King could do to stop this. Anne might pretend it did not bother her, but her flippancy concealed anger and disappointment.

Before very long, the rumours spread across the Channel to France and beyond. Mendoza told the Emperor that Henry was 'so swayed by his passions, that if he can obtain a divorce, he will end by marrying a daughter of Master [*sic*] Boleyn'. Some foreign governments recognised that Henry was acting in the interests of his kingdom, but most were scandalised. In France, Wolsey heard the rumours with mounting dismay, and a letter from the King forbidding him to mention to Francis I the question of remarriage only served to confirm his worst fears. He knew Anne to be his enemy now, and he realised that he would in future be working to bring about a marriage that would almost certainly be his own downfall. He had no choice: his loyalty to his master as well as his sense of self-preservation were such that he would continue to spare no efforts to have Henry's marriage annulled, whatever the consequences. He told the King that he was occupied with solving his problems as if it were his only means of obtaining Heaven, and Henry, in turn, made it clear that 'we trust, by your diligence, shortly to be eased out of that trouble'.

Anne Boleyn and her supporters took advantage of Wolsey's absence by doing their best to poison the King's mind against him. Word soon reached him of what was going on, and he was dismayed to learn that Anne, Rochford, Norfolk and Suffolk had all spent the greater part of August at Beaulieu with the King, doubtless undermining his influence and criticising him to his master. He was right to be concerned. The Boleyn faction repeatedly warned Henry that, far from working to secure an annulment, Wolsey was actually doing his best to prevent the Pope from ever granting one. And once this doubt was planted in Henry's mind, the first breach in his friendship with the Cardinal had been successfully made.

To make matters worse, Wolsey had failed to elicit King Francis's support. His mission a failure, he returned home on 17 September; Anne and her supporters were waiting for him. If he thought he was going to be joyfully received by the King, he was very much mistaken.

It was customary for the Cardinal to send a messenger to Henry upon his return from trips overseas; this was the signal for the King to join him in his closet for a briefing. This time, the King was relaxing after dinner with Anne and his courtiers when the messenger arrived and informed him that the Cardinal waited outside and wished to know where he should speak with him. Before Henry could answer, Anne exclaimed, 'Where else should the Cardinal come? Tell him he may come here, where the King is!'

Henry, somewhat taken aback, merely nodded at the messenger. Thus the Cardinal was received like any other courtier, with Mistress Anne looking on triumphantly.

It now occurred belatedly to the King that his former relationship with Mary Boleyn placed him in exactly the same degree of affinity to Anne as he insisted that Katherine was to him. Yet while he saw this as an impediment to his union with Katherine, when it came to the prospect of marrying Anne, he still believed a papal dispensation – like the one he was doing his best to have declared invalid – would put matters to rights as far as Mary was concerned. In September 1527, Henry sent his secretary, Dr William Knight, on a secret mission to Rome with instructions to obtain such a dispensation and apply to the Pope for a general commission which would give Wolsey, as papal legate, the authority to examine the King's marriage. His findings could then be submitted to Clement, who would hopefully act upon them, and Katherine would have no right of appeal. What Henry did not know was that, soon after Knight left England, Charles V told the Pope that he was 'determined to preserve the Queen's rights', and commanded Clement not to take any steps preparatory to annulling her marriage, and not to allow the case to be tried in England.

Knight was joined in Italy by Gregory Casale, an English diplomat who had been sent by Wolsey formally to request Clement for a dispensation annulling Henry VIII's marriage to Katherine of Aragon on the grounds that the dispensation of Pope Julius was founded on 'certain false suggestions'. Wolsey was hoping that, out of consideration for the King's services to the Church, the Pope would find a way to ease his conscience and, to this end, Casale was to stress 'the vehement desire of the whole nation and nobility that the King should have an heir'. He was also to assure Clement that, if he granted what the King was asking for, Henry was ready to declare war on the Emperor to procure the freedom of the Holy Father.

Knight and Casale saw Pope Clement in December 1527, and implored his 'prompt kindness', but were told it was not at present possible for him to grant a dispensation annulling the King's marriage. However, he was willing to grant one enabling Henry to remarry within certain prohibited degrees should his first marriage ever be declared unlawful – this was issued on 1 January 1528 – and he also granted Cardinal Wolsey a general commission to try the King's case, though not to pass judgement.

Clement was aware of the constraints placed upon him and terrified of the Emperor. Secretly, he urged Casale to advise Henry to take matters into his own hands and remarry without involving the Holy See, something that would not appeal to the King, who had the future stability of the succession to consider.

Wolsey, meanwhile, had written to Rome to request the appointment of a fellow legate with power to pronounce judgement on the King's case. He suggested Cardinal Lorenzo Campeggio, who had begun his career as a lawyer and, after the death of his wife, had entered the Church and quickly risen to the rank of cardinal. He had visited England and been ordained Bishop of Salisbury on the King's recommendation. Clement said he could not spare Campeggio, and hinted that Wolsey should 'pronounce the divorce' himself and afterwards seek the confirmation of the papal consistory, another course too fraught with uncertainty to meet with Henry's approval.

By December 1527, Wolsey was aware that Anne Boleyn and her faction had undermined his influence with the King to such an extent that Henry was now growing resentful of his power and wealth. He had already handed Hampton Court over to the King in 1526, but now Anne was constantly urging Henry to assert his own authority. Yet he still needed Wolsey, whom he knew to be the most able of his ministers and the only man capable of securing an annulment. Wolsey was bombarding the envoys in Rome with instructions, promises, threats and inducements. Of his own anxiety, he made no secret: 'If the Pope is not compliant,' he wrote, 'my own life will be shortened, and I dread to anticipate the consequences.' At the same time, he was spending large sums on banquets for the entertainment of the King and Anne Boleyn, and doing his best to counteract the slanders heard by the Pope about Anne by praising her for her

> excellent virtues, the purity of her life, her constant virginity, her maidenly and womanly pudacity, her soberness, chasteness, meekness, humility, wisdom, descent of right noble regal blood, education in all good and laudable manners, and apparent aptness to procreation of children.

On 22 January 1528, England and France together declared war on the Emperor, an unpopular move in England, since it threatened trade links with the Low Countries. A month after this, a committee of canon lawyers assembled by Wolsey at Hampton Court reached the conclusion that the King should press the Pope to grant a decretal commission, which would empower Wolsey to pronounce a definitive sentence on Henry's case. In February, the King sent to Rome Edward Fox, a doctor of divinity who was well versed in canon law, and Stephen Gardiner, a doctor of both civil and canon law and a religious conservative with a ruthless streak whose loyalty to the King was unswerving. Both he and Fox were advocates of an annulment, and could be relied upon to present Henry's case with conviction.

Gardiner and Fox saw the Pope in March 1528, when Clement told them that he had heard that the King wanted an annulment for private reasons only, being driven by 'vain affection and undue love' for a lady far from worthy of him. Gardiner sprang to Henry's defence, pointing out his dire need of a male heir and declaring that Anne Boleyn was 'animated by the noblest sentiments; the Cardinal of York and all England do homage to her virtues'. He also pointed out that the Queen suffered from 'certain diseases' which meant that Henry would never again live with her as his wife. Then he presented the Pope with a treatise that Henry had written on the case, which Clement later pronounced to be 'excellent'. Gardiner and Fox wheedled, begged and bullied over a period of several weeks, but Clement only dithered and procrastinated. In the end, he agreed to send Campeggio to England to try the case with Wolsey, but refused to grant either of them a decretal commission. This was not quite what the King wanted, but it was a start, and the envoys felt reasonably optimistic when they left Rome in April 1528. Fox wrote to Gardiner that Henry heard the news with 'marvellous demonstrations of joy', and Anne Boleyn was so elated that she confused Fox with Gardiner and kept calling him 'Master Stephen'! Yet Wolsey was sceptical about the Pope's intentions. 'I would obtain the decretal bull with my own blood if I could,' he told Casale privately. However, on 4 May, he told the King he was satisfied with the general commission granted to him and Campeggio. It was as well to let Henry believe there was cause for optimism.

In June 1528, the sweating sickness returned to plague London and, later on, the rest of the country. This was a particularly virulent outbreak, and the King, learning with horror that some members of his household had succumbed to the disease, fled with the Queen and Anne and a small retinue to another house, and then another after that, until he was sleeping in a different place each night. Finally, he arrived at Tittenhanger, the Hertfordshire residence of the Abbot of St Albans, where he decided he was far enough from the contagion to stay put for a time. Fearfully, he wondered whether this plague was a visitation from an angry God who was displeased with him for having remained married incestuously to Katherine for so long, or whether the Almighty was wrathful because he was thinking of putting her away. For a time, he believed it might be the latter, and spent the months of May and June almost exclusively in the Queen's company, though as his fear of the sweating sickness abated, so did his doubts.

In the middle of June, one of the ladies assigned to wait on Anne Boleyn caught the plague. A petrified Henry uprooted his decimated court and hastened to an unidentified house twelve miles from Tittenhanger, while Anne was ordered home to her father at Hever. Henry would not have her near him in case she had contracted the deadly virus – his fear of illness and death was stronger than his love for any woman. His anxiety for her was nevertheless acute; 'I implore you, my entirely beloved, to have no fear at all,' he wrote. 'Wheresoever I may be, I am yours.' Wolsey, fearful of a wrathful God, wrote to Henry at this time and begged him to abandon his nullity suit. The French ambassador was present when the King opened the letter, and saw him explode with rage. 'The King used terrible words, saying he would have given a thousand Wolseys for one Anne Boleyn. . . . No other than God shall take her from me,' he had cried.

No sooner had these words been spoken, it seemed, than news reached the King in the night that Anne had fallen ill of the sweating sickness. She had taken to her bed on 22 June, the same day that her sister Mary's husband William Carey, died of the disease. The King was thrown into a frenzy of agitation. He sent for his chief physician, Dr John Chambers, only to be told that he was away from the house attending the sick. However, Dr William Butts, Chambers's second-in-command, was at hand, and Henry dispatched him immediately to Hever, bearing a hastily scribbled letter for Anne. He told her he would willingly bear half her malady to have her well again, and lamented the fact that her illness would lengthen the time they would have to be apart. Dr Butts would 'soon restore your health', he told her, and he himself would then 'obtain one of my chief joys in this world, which is to have my mistress healed'. Anne was to 'be governed by Butts's advice in all things concerning your malady'.

As it happened, when Butts arrived at Hever, he found his patient already recovering, having been visited with only a mild attack of the plague. In fact, she was showing much of her old spirit, declaring that she would have died content if she could die a queen. The King, when he heard the news, was enormously relieved, and sent letters and gifts to aid his sweetheart's recovery, while Wolsey did likewise, knowing it would please Henry. And knowing that Anne was concerned about her sister, who had been left destitute with one child of three and another on the way, the King commanded that Lord Rochford make necessary provision for her, Rochford having hitherto shown himself impervious to his elder daughter's appeals for succour. He then wrote to Anne, telling her what he had done, and, 'seeing my darling is absent', sending her a haunch of venison, 'which is hart flesh for Henry, prognosticating that hereafter, God willing, you must enjoy some of mine . . . I would we were together an evening.'

By the end of July, the plague had died out in London, and both Henry and Anne returned to court. The Queen knew very well that Anne was hoping to supplant her, yet she still maintained her attitude of placid forbearance, although she did make one gentle thrust during a game of cards – Henry saw nothing unusual in including both wife and sweetheart in such pastimes – when Anne won by drawing a king. Katherine, with a dry smile, observed, 'My Lady Anne, you have the good hap ever to stop at a king, but you are like the others: you will have all or none.' History does not record the reactions of Anne or the King to this remark.

Cardinal Campeggio left Rome at the end of July 1528. It took him two months to travel to England because he was prone to agonising attacks of gout, something Clement may well have taken into account when appointing him legate, for Clement was playing for time, hoping that the Emperor might set him at liberty, or that Henry would tire of Anne Boleyn and forget about an annulment. In his luggage, Campeggio carried a decretal bull which had been secretly issued on 18 June; the legate had strict instructions not to divulge its existence to Wolsey unless authorised by the Pope, something which would only happen if Charles V relaxed his grip on affairs.

The King and Anne Boleyn were much elated at the prospect of the legate's arrival; 'I trust within a while after [Campeggio's arrival] to enjoy that which I have so longed for, mine own darling,' wrote Henry. They would not have been pleased to learn that Campeggio had in fact been instructed to do his best 'to restore mutual affection between the King and Queen', and, if this was not feasible, 'to protract the matter for as long as possible'. Suffolk, in France to welcome the legate, warned Wolsey that Campeggio's mission to England 'will be mere mockery', but the King did not believe him.

Meanwhile, Anne and her faction had continued their efforts to bring about the destruction of the Cardinal, Anne's malice all the more deadly because it was concealed under a cloak of friendship. When, in 1528, Wolsey brought the long-standing dispute over the earldom of Ormonde to an end by pronouncing in favour of Anne's father, she wrote him a letter couched in the warmest of terms, and promised that, when she was raised to queenship, if there was 'any thing in this world I can imagine to do you pleasure, you shall find me the gladdest woman in the world to do it'. She also assured him of her 'hearty love unfeignedly through my life'. In another letter, she acknowledged that Wolsey was doing everything possible 'to bring to pass honourably the greatest wealth that it is possible to come to any creature living'. And in June 1528, she wrote: 'I do know the great pains and troubles you take for me are never likely to be recompensed, but only in loving you next unto the King's Grace, above all creatures living.'

In April 1528, Anne challenged Wolsey on a new front. The abbess of the ancient and rich foundation at Wilton had just died, and there was fierce competition for the vacant position. Anne's candidate was Dame Eleanor Carey, sister of Mary Boleyn's husband William, and Anne recommended her warmly to the King, knowing that Wolsey favoured the election of the prioress, Dame Isabel Jordan. But Wolsey had heard unsavoury rumours about Eleanor Carey – who had not only had two children by different fathers, both priests, but had also left her convent and lived for a time as the mistress of a servant of Lord Willoughby de Broke – and when Anne was absent from court, he seized his advantage and appointed Isabel Jordan abbess. This earned him a public reproof from the King, who had concluded that Wolsey had gone out of his way to offend Anne, and prompted an abject apology from the Cardinal. Later, when Henry learned the reasons why Eleanor Carey had been passed over, he arranged that neither she nor Dame Isabel should be abbess, writing to Anne to explain the situation and telling her he would not 'for all the gold in the world, clog your conscience nor mine to make her ruler of a house which is of so ungodly demeanour', and that 'the house shall be better reformed, and God the much better served' if someone else were appointed. To mollify Anne, Wolsey sent her an expensive gift, for which she thanked him in a letter in which she begged him never to doubt that she would vary from her loyalty to him. On the surface all was well again.

In the autumn of 1528, though, the Boleyn faction was busy spreading rumours that the Cardinal was working in secret in the Queen's favour. Even the Spanish ambassador believed this, as did many other people, and although Wolsey was in reality as anxious as the King to have the royal marriage annulled, he was powerless to stop this damaging gossip. At present, Henry was disposed to treat it as malicious talk, but if the Pope's sentence ultimately went against him, he might take a very different view, which, observed the Boleyns and their adherents with satisfaction, would mean the end of the Cardinal.

Campeggio arrived at Dover on 29 September 1528. The King had offered him a state welcome to London, but he refused it, remembering that the Pope desired him to execute his commission with as little publicity as possible. Nor did he wish to provoke any public demonstrations, so he travelled quietly by barge to Bath Place, the London house of the bishops of Salisbury by Temple Bar – and took straight to his bed.

The next day, 9 October, he spent three or four hours discussing the 'great matter' with Wolsey, and told him that the best solution would be a reconciliation between the King and Queen. However, as he told the Pope later, he had 'no more success in persuading the Cardinal than if I had spoken to a rock'. Wolsey urged the expediting of the business with 'all possible despatch', alleging that 'the affairs of the kingdom are at a standstill'. If he had not known it before, Campeggio realised then that his sojourn in England would be fraught with difficulties.

The legate first saw the King on 22 October at Bridewell Palace by the Thames, near the monastery of the Black Friars. The interview did not begin well, for Henry was angered by Campeggio's suggestion that he return to the Queen. To pacify the King, and because the Pope had just authorised him to do so, Campeggio produced the decretal bull, saying the Pope had granted it 'not to be used, but kept secret; he desired to show the King the good feeling by which he was animated.' Henry visibly relaxed. The discussion then continued more amicably, although it was clear to the legate that the King wanted nothing less than a declaration that his marriage was invalid. Campeggio realised that, 'if an angel was to descend from Heaven, he would not be able to persuade him to the contrary.'

The legate put forward a suggestion made by the Pope, that Katherine be persuaded to enter a nunnery. If she could be assured that her daughter's rights would not be prejudiced, it might be in her best interests to make a graceful exit and so save everyone a lot of trouble. There were precedents, and her piety was renowned. The Pope could issue a dispensation allowing the King to remarry, and the Emperor could not possibly object. Henry could then make Anne his wife, and England, God willing, would in due course get its heir. Most important of all, the peace of Europe and the stability of the Holy See would no longer be threatened. This sensible idea met with the King's wholehearted approval; he hastened to assure Campeggio that Katherine would only lose 'the use of his person' by entering religion; as matters stood in the convents of the age, she could still enjoy any other worldly comforts she desired.

The two legates waited upon the Queen two days later in her apartments at Bridewell Palace. She was on her guard and very tense, and when Campeggio suggested that entering a nunnery was the ideal solution to her troubles, she refused out of hand on the grounds that she was the King's wife. 'Although she is very religious and extremely patient, she will not accede in the least,' the legate told the Pope. Katherine then swore on her conscience that Prince Arthur had never consummated their marriage, and declared that 'she intended to live and die in the estate of matrimony to which God had called her.' None of Campeggio's arguments could persuade her to change her mind, and when Wolsey warned her it might be better to yield to the King's displeasure, she turned on him, retorting that

> Of this trouble, I thank only you, my lord of York! Of malice you have kindled this fire, especially for the great grudge you bear to my nephew the Emperor, because he would not gratify your ambition by making you Pope by force!

Wolsey excused himself, saying it had been 'sore against his will that ever the marriage should come in question', and promised, as legate, to be impartial; Katherine, knowing him to be first and foremost the King's servant, did not believe him. Afterwards, Campeggio wrote to Clement to say he had 'always thought her to be a prudent lady, and now more than ever'.

On 26 October, the legate heard Katherine's confession, at her request, in which she affirmed, upon the salvation of her soul, that she had never been carnally known by Prince Arthur. Campeggio did not doubt she was telling the truth, but he still did his best to persuade her to take the veil, begging, cajoling and bullying in turn. None of it had the slightest effect. She declared she would abide by no sentence save that of the Pope himself, and that she did not recognise the authority of the legatine commission to try the case since she believed it to be biased in Henry's favour.

With Katherine proving obdurate, Henry pressed Wolsey to wrest the decretal bull from Campeggio, but the legate stood firm, and refused to hand it over, saying he could only do what the Pope instructed. It seemed that matters were still weighted strongly in the Queen's favour.

Outwardly, relations between the King and Queen were still cordial, although there was a good deal of tension below the surface. Henry resented the fact that Katherine was able to ignore what was staring her in the face; he also was irritated by the way in which she seemed able to rise above her misery, and in October 1528 he complained to the Privy Council about her behaviour. She was too merry, too richly dressed; she should be praying for a good end to her case rather than gracing courtly entertainments with her presence. Worst of all, by riding out and acknowledging the cheers of the crowds, she was inciting the King's subjects to rebellion. It seemed to Henry that she did not care for him, and he felt she might at least show some sorrow at the prospect of losing him. He even inferred that she was involved in a mysterious plot to kill himself and Wolsey, which can only have been the product of his imagination. Nevertheless, the Council wrote to the Queen, warning her that 'if it could be proved she had any hand in it, she must not expect to be spared.' She was also informed of the King's other complaints about her, and advised that the Privy Council, who thought 'in their consciences that his life was in danger', had urged him to separate from her entirely and take the Princess Mary from her. She was told bluntly that she was 'a fool to resist the King's will'.

The letter was devastating indeed to Katherine, realising as she did that the Council's censure proceeded directly from the King himself. Yet even this did not make her less conscientious regarding her duty to obey him, and she obeyed him now, by taking care to dress more soberly, spending more time at her devotions, adopting a more solemn and grave demeanour, and not venturing out of the palace so often, nor going where she might excite public interest. For all this, she was well aware that she was still under constant observation by the Cardinal's spies, who were usually women in her service who had been bribed with money, gifts and – according to the reformer William Tynedale – sex, in order to get them to betray anything of interest their mistress might have said or done. At least one of these ladies left court because she could no longer injure the Queen in such a way. All of this placed Katherine under an intolerable strain, and when Campeggio saw the Queen in October 1528, he thought she was fifty, when in fact she was just forty-three.

Henry rarely visited her now. When he did, he never stayed long, fearing Anne Boleyn's jealousy, though in public he was anxious to appear as the afflicted husband pining for a wife barred from him by canon law. Few were deceived by this charade – Anne Boleyn being too much in evidence – but Henry persisted with his role-playing, and made sure he was seen in public with Katherine as often as possible. When he saw her in private, they often quarrelled. In November 1528, he told her it would be better for her if she went of her own volition to a nunnery, but she cried out that it was against her soul, her conscience and her honour. 'There will be no judge unjust enough to condemn me!' she said hotly, whereupon Henry, in a very bad temper, left without answering her.

From the autumn of 1528 courtiers left Katherine to herself while they flocked in droves to pay court to Anne Boleyn. Anne was not easily carried away by the great events that had overtaken her, but she was now beginning to enjoy the trappings of power and the adulation that went with them. In July 1528, the King had placed an apartment off the tiltyard at Greenwich at her disposal; at around the same time, she had left the Queen's service. However, her anomalous position, both as an unmarried woman with a reputation to protect and as the future Queen of England, presented a problem. Wolsey thought it more in keeping with propriety for her to have an establishment of her own, and ordered the refurbishment of a London house for her. This was either Durham House on the Strand, where Katherine had once briefly stayed years before, or Suffolk House near Westminster; she would have preferred a house near Greenwich, but one could not be found.

Anne's new residence was made ready for her by her father in his capacity as comptroller of the King's household, and he ensured that it was renovated to a standard fit for a royal bride-to-be. When work was completed, an army of servants and ladies-in-waiting were engaged to serve Anne, and she moved into her new home, where she would keep as much state as if she were queen already. 'Greater court is now paid to Mistress Anne than has been to the Queen for a long time,' observed the French ambassador in November 1528. 'I see they mean to accustom the people by degrees to endure her.'

In December 1528, Mendoza noticed that Wolsey 'was no longer received at court as graciously as before', and reported that 'the King had uttered angry words respecting him'. Nevertheless, when Christmas that year was held at Greenwich, Wolsey and Campeggio were the guests of honour. The King arranged jousts, banquets, masques and disguisings for their entertainment, but the Queen, who was present, took no pleasure in them and hardly smiled. Anne Boleyn was also at Greenwich, lodged separately, attended by a host of servants, and being treated as if she were queen. She kept open house throughout the season, and people flocked to visit her, but she held aloof from the main festivities because, as the French ambassador correctly surmised, 'she does not like to meet the Queen'.

During the first months of 1529, Henry was showering Anne with jewels. His account with his goldsmith, Cornelius Hayes, settled at the end of March, records gifts of diamonds, rubies, bracelets, borders of gold set with gems, pearls for edging sleeves, heart-shaped head ornaments and diamond brooches. In April, Anne took it upon herself to perform a duty normally reserved for anointed queens, that of blessing rings for distribution amongst those afflicted with severe cramps.

By May 1529, she was making headway. With the help of Norfolk, Rochford, Suffolk and their supporters, she had begun to convince Henry that Wolsey had not advanced his nullity suit as energetically as he might have done. When Wolsey denied this, Henry would not listen, and the Cardinal was driven to pleading with the French ambassador to urge Francis I to use his influence in Rome to 'forward the divorce'.

Campeggio, seeing Anne with the King, thought Henry's passion 'an extraordinary thing', and told the Pope: 'He sees nothing, he thinks of nothing but Anne. He cannot do without her for an hour, and it moves me to see how the King's life, the stability and downfall of the whole country, may hang on this.' The King was constantly 'kissing her, and treating her as if she were his wife'. In spite of this, Campeggio was nevertheless almost certain that the lovers 'had not proceeded to any ultimate conjunction'.

Future queen she might be, yet Anne remained exceedingly unpopular with the King's subjects. The notoriety of his 'great matter' and the public enmity displayed towards Anne Boleyn had for some time been a matter of concern to the King. He was horrified to learn that the main topic of discussion among all classes of society was his private life. 'Lack of discreet handling must needs be the cause of it,' he told Anne. Katherine's supporters also felt that such public exposure could only be injurious to her cause. In November

1528, the King had invited his subjects to Bridewell Palace, and, standing before the throne, resplendent in his robes of estate, he had done his best to justify his need for an annulment of his marriage, reminding his audience how peace had prevailed during his reign, and confiding to them his fear of dying without a male heir to succeed him, when, 'for want of a legitimate King, England should again be plunged into the horrors of civil war'. This, he had assured them, was his only motive, and, as touching the Queen, if it was judged that she was his lawful wife,

> nothing will be more pleasant or acceptable to me, for I assure you she is a woman of most gentleness, humility and buxomness – she is without comparison. So that if I were to marry again, I would choose her above all women.

When he had gone, many Londoners expressed compassion for him, some said nothing, and others were of the opinion that he should never have raised the matter in public. Nevertheless it had been a shrewd move: it had enlisted the sympathy of a section of the public who had hitherto been hostile, and who would now be more aware of the wider issues involved in the 'great matter' and perhaps not be so eager to listen to wild gossip.

Henry's speech had failed in one respect: it had made no impact on the hatred felt by the public for Anne Boleyn. Not only did they see her as a whore and an adulteress, but also, latterly, as a heretic who had succumbed to the lure of Martin Luther's teachings. Anne herself was to some degree responsible for this, although she was not, and never would be, guilty of heresy. She had been brought up in the traditional Catholic faith, and would continue to observe its rites faithfully until her death. Not until the final week of her life would she display the kind of religious devotion exhibited by Katherine of Aragon, yet she was sincere in her beliefs, and became more interested in religious matters as she grew older.

Anne was never a Lutheran – a term not invented until 1529. She was, however, like her father and brother, a fervent champion of the movement for reform within the Church, and she took an enlightened view of so-called heretical literature. She was so interested in it, and presumed upon her influence with the King to such an extent, that she openly read books that he had banned in

England, and even asked Henry for his opinions on them. One such book, *The Supplication of Beggars* by Simon Fish, argued the case for translating the Scriptures into English so that all could read them. Anne was sent this from abroad in 1528 and showed it to Henry, telling him that Fish had fled from England for fear of persecution by Wolsey. The King read the book, which also argued an early form of communism, and decided it should remain on the banned list, but he did not censure Anne, and allowed her to continue reading works like it unchecked.

In 1529, Anne's copy of another forbidden book, William Tynedale's *The Obedience of a Christian Man, and how Christian Kings ought to Govern,* found its way into Wolsey's hands. Discovering this, Anne went straight to the King, begging him on her knees to help her retrieve it. At Henry's command, the Cardinal returned it personally to Anne, knowing he could not touch her in spite of the heresy laws. Anne then lent Henry the book, which challenged the authority of the Pope and his cardinals; he expressed approval, being impressed by some of the arguments it contained, and declared it 'a book for me and all kings to read'.

Thanks to Anne's influence over him, Henry, increasingly disillusioned with the Church of Rome, was becoming more interested in the subject of reform and more liberal in his views, although his observance of his faith was as conventional as ever. It was apparent that if Anne became queen, there might be radical changes in the Church, and while this prospect elated some people, others trembled at it.

In January 1529, Queen Katherine lodged an appeal in Rome against the authority of the legatine court. During the previous months, she had not been idle, but had marshalled her defences to the best of her ability. In October, she had announced that she had in her possession a copy of a brief of dispensation purportedly issued by Julius II in 1503 at the request of Queen Isabella, which provided for Katherine's marriage to Prince Henry while assuming that her first marriage with his brother had been consummated. If genuine, the existence of this document would demolish the King's argument that his marriage was uncanonical because Katherine had been his brother's wife in the fullest sense. The brief differed from the original bull of dispensation in that it omitted the word 'perhaps' when referring to whether or not the first marriage had been consummated. Yet as no one until now had ever heard of the brief's existence, the King and his councillors concluded that it must be a forgery given to the Queen by Mendoza. Mendoza had indeed given Katherine the copy, but he insisted that the original, in the possession of the Emperor, was genuine. The Council therefore decided that it must be removed, by fair means or foul, from the imperial archives and destroyed. Katherine was duly instructed to send to Spain for it, and had no alternative but to comply, although she guessed that once it was in England the brief, genuine or not, would conveniently disappear.

The original brief was filed among the papers of the late Dr de Puebla, but the Emperor, no fool, would not part with it. Wolsey insisted that a search be made for the copy that should be in the Vatican archives, and sent a five-man embassy to Rome for the purpose. As well as finding the brief and checking its authenticity, they were also to ask the Pope if the King could follow Old Testament precedents and have two wives, the issue of both being legitimate!

Meanwhile, the Emperor sent yet another copy of the brief to London with a subscription attesting it to be genuine, signed by the most eminent Spanish bishops in his presence. Nevertheless, both Wolsey and Henry suspected trickery, and Wolsey asked the Pope to declare the brief a forgery, knowing that, if Clement agreed to do so, the Queen's case would founder. Clement, however, refused. The English envoys could find no record of the brief at the Vatican, and two English divines sent to Spain to see the Emperor's copy wrote to Wolsey in April 1529 to say that it was undoubtedly a forgery. After that, Katherine realised that it would be useless to produce her copy as evidence at the legatine court; her case would have to stand on its own merits.

That April, Henry ordered her to choose the lawyers who would act as her counsel; she could pick from the best in the realm, he said. She chose Archbishop Warham, the Bishops of Ely and St Asaph, and her staunch supporter, John Fisher, Bishop of Rochester. In naming them, she had shown herself to be an obedient wife, though she still refused to acknowledge the authority of the court. Staunch as her counsellors were, they remained her husband's subjects, and if the verdict should go in her favour, the King's anger, and Anne Boleyn's, might be visited upon them. She did not therefore expect them to give her totally disinterested advice. If the case was heard in Rome, however, she would have more chance of receiving an impartial judgement, and on 16 June, she made yet another formal protest against the legatine court at Baynard's Castle and again appealed to the Pope to hear the case in Rome.

Very little was accomplished with regard to the 'great matter' during the early months of 1529, mainly due to the illness of the Pope, but by March Clement had recovered, and the judicial machinery began to grind slowly into action. Henry was warned by his ambassador in Rome that 'the Pope will do nothing for your Grace'; Clement's hands were well and truly tied by the Emperor, and he told Stephen Gardiner that it would be better 'for the wealth of Christendom if the Queen were in her grave'. Henry, hearing rumours that the Pope was about to revoke the legatine commission, tackled Campeggio, but was assured that Clement was, in fact, 'extremely well disposed' towards him, and that the Emperor 'had not moved him by a hair's breadth from whatever he could rightly do in your Grace's favour'. Charles, however, recalled his ambassador, Mendoza, to Spain in May 1529, and did not replace him until August, wishing to demonstrate his disapproval of the King's case by not being represented in England while it was being heard.

As the date for the hearing approached, Anne Boleyn grew pessimistic and even panicky. The French ambassador reported her as being so agitated about the outcome of the case that she could not conceal her anxiety. She was now twenty-eight, almost middle-aged by the standards of her time, and the likelihood of her producing a healthy child grew less with each passing year. She distrusted Wolsey, believing he was secretly conspiring with the Pope to get rid of her, and she was well aware of how poor her reputation was both in England and abroad. Such power and influence as she had had no basis in law. She knew that, once the King's case came before the legates, she would have to leave London, but where once she would have welcomed a separation, she now dreaded it, and remained in the capital until the last possible moment. Then in June she went to Hever, there to await the outcome of the hearing.

At last, on 30 May 1529, Henry VIII formally authorised the legates to convene their court and hear his case. The court was to sit in the great hall of the monastery of the Black Friars in London, where Parliament sometimes met. Bridewell Palace, where the King and Queen would stay for the duration of the case, was adjacent.

Great care was taken in preparing the courtroom: two chairs upholstered in cloth of gold were placed ready for the legates behind railings on a dais at the end of the hall opposite the door; before them was a table covered with a Turkey carpet for their papers. To the right, in the body of the court, stood the King's throne beneath a cloth of estate, and to the left was a similar seat for the Queen. The court was officially opened on 31 May, but because the workmen were still busy preparing the hall, the actual proceedings did not commence until 18 June, when crowds gathered to see the King and Queen arrive.

It was unheard of for an English sovereign to be summoned to appear in a court of law, still less to await the judgement of a subject, and in the courtroom, where nobility, lawyers, theologians and prelates had gathered, the atmosphere was tense. The day's business opened with the legatine commission being read, followed by a brief summary of the case. To the great disappointment of the crowds waiting outside, the King did not appear but sent two proctors instead. Queen Katherine made a brief appearance, with the four bishops appointed as her counsellors and a great train of attendants. She walked up to the legates, curtsied to them, and reiterated her formal appeal against them as judges not competent to try the case, asking that it be referred to Rome. Then she left. Her appeal was ignored, and a further citation to attend the court three days hence was issued to her. This made her very angry – 'I be no Englishwoman but a Spaniard born!' she cried. If she was not the King's wife, then she was not his subject. Nevertheless, when the three days were up, she was in her place, opposite her husband, before a packed court.

At the appointed time, the crier demanded silence, then called: 'King Harry of England, come into the court!' The King answered in a loud firm voice: 'Here, my lords!' The crier than called: 'Katherine, Queen of England, come into the court!' The Queen did not answer. There was an uncomfortable pause, and then the King turned to the legates and told them he wished to have his doubts resolved for the discharge of his conscience. All he asked was that they determine whether or not his marriage was lawful; he had had doubts about that, he said, from the beginning. Katherine interrupted at this point, saying that this was not the time to say so after so long a silence, but Henry excused himself by reason of the great love he had had, and still had, for her, avowing that he desired, above everything else, that their marriage should be declared valid. Katherine's request to have the case referred to Rome he dismissed as unreasonable, due to the Emperor having the Pope in his power. 'This country is perfectly secure for her, and she has the choice of prelates and lawyers,' he told the court.

Katherine was again called when the King had finished speaking, and all eyes turned to the small stout figure attired in a gown of crimson velvet edged with sable, its skirt open at the front to display a petticoat of yellow brocade. The Queen made no answer to the crier; instead, she rose and walked over to where the King sat on his throne, weaving around the crowded benches and tables. Then she fell on her knees before him, and made a dramatic plea for justice. Several versions of what she said survive, but what follows is extracted from the account given by Wolsey's secretary, George Cavendish, an eyewitness. Speaking in broken English, with a heavy Spanish accent, the Queen's voice echoed in the hushed courtroom:

Sir, I beseech you, for all the loves that hath been between us, and for the love of God, let me have justice and right. Take of me some pity and compassion, for I am a poor woman and a stranger born out of your dominion. I have here no assured friend, and much less indifferent counsel. I flee to you as the head of justice within this realm.

Alas, Sir, where have I offended you? Or what occasion have you of displeasure, that you intend to put me from you? I take God and all the world to witness that I have been to you a true, humble and obedient wife, ever conformable to your will and pleasure. I have been pleased and contented with all things wherein you had delight and dalliance. I never grudged a word or countenance, or showed a spark of discontent. I loved all those whom ye loved only for your sake, whether I had cause or no, and whether they were my friends or enemies. This twenty years and more I have been your true wife, and by me ye have had divers children, though it hath pleased God to call them out of this world, which hath been no fault in me. And when ye had me at the first, I take God to be my judge, I was a true maid, without touch of man; and whether it be true or no, I put it to your conscience.

[A pause. Then:] If there be any just cause by the law that you can allege against me, either of dishonesty or any other impediment, to put me from you, I am well content to depart, to my shame and dishonour. If there be none, I must lowly beseech you, let me remain in my former estate and receive justice at your princely hands.

The King your father was accounted in his day as a second Solomon for wisdom, and my father Ferdinand was esteemed one of the wisest kings that had ever reigned in Spain. It is not therefore to be doubted but that they gathered such wise counsel about them as was thought fit by their high discretions. Also, there were in those days as wise, as learned men, as there are at this present time in both realms, who thought then the marriage between you and me good and lawful.

It is a wonder to hear what new inventions are invented against me, who never intended but honesty, that cause me to stand to the order and judgement of this new court, wherein you may do me much wrong, if you intend any cruelty. For ye may condemn me for lack of sufficient answer, having no indifferent counsel. Ye must understand that they cannot be indifferent counsellors which be your subjects, and taken out of your Council beforehand, and dare not, for your displeasure, disobey your will and intent.

Therefore, most humbly do I require you, in the way of charity and for the love of God, to spare me the extremity of this court, until I may be advertised what way and order my friends in Spain will advise me to take. And if ye will not extend to me so much favour, your pleasure then be fulfilled, and to God I commit my cause.

Throughout Katherine's speech, Henry said nothing, but sat staring past his wife. Nor did he make any comment when she had finished. After a few moments, the Queen rose, curtsied, and made her way out of the hall on the arm of her receiver-general, Griffin

Richards. The King commanded the crier to call her back, but she paid no heed, commenting to Richards: 'It is no indifferent court to me, therefore I will not tarry.' Outside the monastery she was greeted by crowds of Londoners, many of them women, who shouted words of encouragement. She acknowledged their support with nods and smiles, and briefly addressed them, requesting their prayers, before returning to Bridewell Palace.

Back in the courtroom, Henry was declaring that Katherine had been to him 'as true, as obedient, and as conformable a wife as I could in my fantasy wish or desire'. He had been fortunate to be blessed with such a queen. 'As God is my witness, no fault in Katherine moved me!' he cried. Then, as his listeners were trying to equate what he was saying about his love for the Queen with what they knew of his passionate pursuit of Anne Boleyn, he reminded them how all his legitimate sons had 'died incontinent after they were born'. That, he believed, had been a punishment from God. His concern was chiefly for the succession; he had not brought these proceedings 'for any carnal concupiscence or mislike of the Queen's person or age, with whom I could be well content to continue during my life if our marriage might stand within God's laws'.

The King then produced a parchment on which was set forth the case his bishops had agreed he had to answer, saying that every bishop in England had set his hand and seal to it. He was interrupted, however, by John Fisher, Bishop of Rochester, one of the Queen's counsellors, who denied he had ever signed or sealed such a document. 'Is this not your hand and seal?' asked the King. 'No, Sire,' answered the Bishop, in a rage. 'Well, well, it shall make no matter,' said Henry testily, 'you are but one man.' Fisher reluctantly sat down, but he had in effect scored a minor victory for the Queen, since he had exposed what was obviously a forged signature and seal and had thereby cast doubts in the mind of Campeggio at least upon the integrity of the King's advisers.

The court sat again on many successive days. Katherine did not appear, despite several citations, and Henry was absent from most of the sessions. Both, however, were represented by their counsel, who spent much of the time arguing about whether the Queen's first marriage had been consummated. They even quarrelled among themselves – Warham and Fisher had a heated dispute over the validity of the royal marriage, and Nicholas Ridley, acting for the Queen, expressed disgust that her private life had ever come under scrutiny in open court.

Meanwhile, Wolsey was doing his best to gain possession of Campeggio's decretal bull, but on 24 June the legate told him that the Pope had written expressly to forbid its use. Wolsey paled. 'That will be my ruin!' he lamented. The King would not be pleased when he found out.

The hearings continued, as did the arguments. At the end of June, the legates were no nearer a conclusion than when the court first sat, notwithstanding a visitation from the King, who begged them to reach a 'final end' as he was so troubled and could not attend to 'anything which should be profitable for my realm and people'. Thereafter, the court met daily without the principal parties. The general consensus of opinion was that the King and Queen's marriage could only be lawful if Katherine had been left virgo intacta by Prince Arthur. Katherine had sworn on the Blessed Sacrament, and in open court, that she had, but the King – who was the only other person who knew the truth of the matter – alleged otherwise, and had gone to great lengths to seek out witnesses to that first wedding night. Nineteen of them gave evidence at the end of June, much of it deeply embarrassing to the Queen, and all of it inconclusive. Prince Arthur's boastful remarks on the day after his wedding were recalled, and several elderly peers were happy to attest that they had been sexually active at Arthur's age and even younger. A few of the witnesses, such as Rochford and Norfolk, belonged to the Boleyn faction.

The King's 'inconceivable anxiety' about the case prompted him, at the beginning of July, to send Wolsey to the Queen in an attempt to persuade her to be reasonable and accept the authority of the court. But she asked the Cardinal to stop and think: 'Will any Englishman counsel or be friendly unto me against the King's pleasure? Nay, my lord. I am a poor woman, lacking in wit and understanding.'

Henry, whose patience was almost at breaking-point, now heard that Campeggio had said he meant to prorogue the court until October, as the papal curia enjoyed a holiday during the summer months, and since the legatine court was an extension of the court of

Rome, the same rules must apply to it. This meant that judgement was unlikely to be given this side of the summer recess. On 13 July, Campeggio informed the Pope that some people were expecting a sentence within ten days, but assured him: 'I will not fail in my duty. When giving sentence I will have only God before my eyes, and the Holy See.' Four days later, Clement gave way to imperial pressure and revoked the general commission granted to Campeggio and Wolsey, thus invalidating any further proceedings at the Black Friars court, which was still going ponderously about its business.

In England, rumour had it that Campeggio would pass sentence on 23 July. On that day, the King himself attended the court, sitting with the Duke of Suffolk in a gallery above the door, facing the legates. But it was only to hear Campeggio announce that he would give no hasty judgement in the case until he had discussed the proceedings with the Pope. So saying, he adjourned the court indefinitely.

The effect of his words was tumultuous. The King rose and walked out, his face thunderous, whereupon uproar broke out in the court. The Duke of Suffolk shouted from the gallery: 'By the mass, it was never merry in England whilst we had cardinals amongst us!' Wolsey retorted loudly that 'If I, a simple cardinal, had not been, you should have had at this present time no head upon your shoulders wherein you should have a tongue to make any such report in despite of us!' Suffolk did not answer, and stalked off in search of the King. The legates were left sitting looking at each other.

It might well be a matter of years, and not months, now before the Pope reached a decision. Worse still, the waiting might be in vain: Wolsey knew with bitter certainty that, if the case were heard in Rome, judgement would go in the Queen's favour. If the King went to Rome, he warned the English ambassadors at the Vatican, it would be at the head of a formidable army, and not as a supplicant for justice. And the King, when letters citing him to appear before the papal curia arrived in August, was speechless with rage: 'I, the King of England, summoned before an Italian tribunal?' he cried. But that same month, Charles V and Francis I made peace, which left Henry isolated in Europe. Even now, it was being rumoured at court that the King would take matters into his own hands and force

Parliament to grant him an annulment, and although this was not his immediate intention, his anger with the Holy See was mounting, and he was already casting about for another solution.

The referral of the case to Rome had been a consolation to Queen Katherine: the Pope had listened to her, and she was still confident that her husband would eventually return to her. But the King, as if to underline his determination to have his way, left her behind when he went on progress that August, and took Anne Boleyn instead. When he returned, matters were very strained between the royal couple, and at the beginning of October a heated exchange took place, when Katherine told Henry that she knew she had right on her side, and that as she had never been a true wife to his brother, their marriage must be legal.

Katherine now had a new champion in England. In the autumn of 1529 the new Spanish ambassador arrived. Eustache Chapuys was a cultured attorney from Savoy, a man of great ability and astuteness. Never afraid of speaking his mind, he was devoted to the service of the Emperor and those connected with him. He had been well briefed about the treatment meted out to Queen Katherine by her husband, and when he arrived in London he was already committed to her cause. Nor would it be long before, having come to know her, he conceived the deepest admiration and respect, and a very sincere affection, for the Queen.

From the first, Chapuys carried out his duties with more zeal than any of his predecessors, even Mendoza. His initial brief was to bring about a reconciliation between the King and Queen by using 'gentleness and friendship'. But it would only be a matter of time before Chapuys had far exceeded these instructions and became a continual thorn in the side of Henry VIII. He was distrusted by the King's courtiers and advisers, and hated by the Boleyn faction, who feared his influence. The enmity was mutual. Chapuys would never refer to Anne Boleyn as anything other than 'the Concubine' or 'the Lady'. Sir William Paget, one of the King's secretaries, did not consider Chapuys to be a wise man, but a liar, a tale-teller and a flatterer, who had no regard for honesty or truth. Paget, it must be said, was biased, but his comments should be borne in mind, for the dispatches of Chapuys form a major proportion of the source material for this period.

By October 1529, Chapuys had met the King, the Queen, Cardinal Wolsey, and the Privy Council, and had assessed the situation in England. 'The Lady is all powerful here, and the Queen will have no peace until her case is tried and decided at Rome,' he told Charles V. He was right. Henry could not do enough to make up for the disappointment Anne had suffered at the prorogation of the legatine court. In October 1529, the ambassador reported: 'The King's affection for La Boleyn increases daily. It is so great just now that it can hardly be greater, such is the intimacy and familiarity in which they live at present.' In October 1529, Lord Rochford boasted to the French ambassador that the peers of the realm had no influence except what it pleased his daughter to allow them.

It now pleased her to urge them to seek revenge on the man whom she considered to be responsible for her present position, Cardinal Wolsey. After the legatine court had been formally closed on 31 July, this was brought home to Wolsey himself by a letter Anne sent him, in which she accused him of abandoning her interests in favour of those of the Queen. In future, she said, she would rely 'on nothing but the protection of Heaven and the love of my dear King, which alone will be able to set right again those plans which you have broken and spoiled'. There would be no more need for hypocrisy.

For the moment Henry was still reluctant to proceed judicially against Wolsey. Nevertheless, it was soon obvious to the court that the Cardinal had fallen from favour. In August, Henry and Anne went on progress, visiting Waltham Abbey, Barnet, Tittenhanger, Holborn, Windsor, Reading, Woodstock, Langley, Buckingham and Grafton before returning to Greenwich in October. When they were at Grafton in the old royal hunting lodge deep in the Northamptonshire countryside, Campeggio, accompanied by Wolsey, arrived to take formal leave of the King before returning to Rome. No accommodation had been prepared for Wolsey, and he was left standing at a loss in the courtyard until Sir Henry Norris, the King's Groom of the Stole, came and offered him his own room. Norris also advised the King of his arrival, and later brought a summons from Henry, requiring the Cardinal to attend him in his presence chamber with Campeggio.

Wolsey approached the packed room with trepidation, fearing

public humiliation, and seeing Norfolk, Suffolk, Rochford and their supporters waiting like birds of prey for the kill. But when the King entered, he greeted Wolsey warmly and helped him up from his knees, gripping him on both arms. Then he led him to a window embrasure where he chatted affectionately to him until dinner was announced. Meanwhile, Norfolk and Rochford had gone straight to Anne Boleyn and warned her what was going on. Consequently, when Henry dined with her that evening, she was in a dangerous mood, showing herself – according to George Cavendish – 'much offended' with him, and reminding him that 'there is never a nobleman within this realm that if he had done but half so much as the Cardinal had done, he were well worthy to lose his head.' 'Why then, I perceive that you are not the Cardinal's friend,' said Henry, with devastating naïvety. 'Forsooth, Sir,' cried Anne, 'I have no cause, nor any other that loves your Grace, if ye consider well his doings.'

She was still sulking when, later in the evening, Henry resumed his talk with Wolsey, but the next morning, knowing that the King had planned to sit in council with the Cardinal, she seized her opportunity and persuaded Henry to go hunting with her instead. Thus, when the Cardinal appeared, he found the King, dressed for riding, already mounted in the courtyard. Henry ordered him to return south with Campeggio, and bade him a fond farewell with the whole court looking on. They would never meet again.

Campeggio left England on 5 October. He took with him Henry's love letters to Anne Boleyn, which had been stolen from Anne's London house by one of his agents. Nor were they ever returned, for they are still in Rome today in the Vatican archives. The King's officials searched Campeggio's luggage at Dover, in the hope of securing the decretal bull. They never found it, or the letters.

Anne and her faction did their work thoroughly. In October 1529, the King stripped Wolsey of his office of Lord Chancellor of England and demanded that he surrender the Great Seal. He also commanded his attorney general to prepare a bill of indictment against the Cardinal. In a desperate attempt to placate the King, Wolsey surrendered to him York Place and most of his other property, before retiring to his more modest house at Esher in Surrey. The

King was elated at the acquisition of York Place, and in October 1529 he announced it was to be renamed Whitehall and renovated as a palace for Anne Boleyn. That same month, he took Anne and her mother to inspect it, and notwithstanding the presence of a great army of workmen, all engaged upon refurbishment, Anne moved in at once. Whitehall boasted no lodging suitable for Queen Katherine, and Anne was tired of giving precedence to her rival. Now she had her own court and was queen in all but name.

In November, Wolsey, in an agony of anxiety over his future, sent the King a message begging for mercy, and Henry, whose anger had to a great extent been dispelled by the acquisition of his property, placed the Cardinal under his own protection, graciously permitting him to retain the archbishopric of York. And when, thanks to Anne's adherents, Parliament presented the King on 1 December with a list of forty-four articles or charges against Wolsey, Henry declined to punish him further. Anne must perforce wait.

Henry VIII met the man who would present him with a solution to his marital problems in the autumn of 1529. When Stephen Gardiner and Edward Fox were returning from Rome in September, they lodged in a house belonging to Waltham Abbey in Essex. There they met a cleric called Thomas Cranmer, who had sought hospitality in the same house because there was plague in Cambridge, where he was resident in the university.

Cranmer was then forty. Cambridge educated, he had gained a degree in divinity, but soon ruined his career by marrying a barmaid called Black Joan. Marriage was then an impediment to any career in the Church; however, when Joan died in childbirth, the university readmitted Cranmer, who shortly afterwards took holy orders and devoted himself to a lifetime of study. Fox and Gardiner had been fellow students of Cranmer's in their youth, so their meeting turned out to be a friendly reunion, the envoys treating Cranmer to a good dinner. Over the meal, they asked him his opinion on the King's nullity suit. He had not really studied the matter, he said, but he ventured the opinion that the King's case should be judged by doctors of divinity within the universities, and not by the papal courts. 'There is one truth in it,' said Cranmer, and the Scriptures would soon declare it if they were correctly interpreted by learned men trained for such a task; 'and that may be as well done in the universities here as at Rome. You might this way have made an end of the matter long since.' The case, so his argument ran, should be decided according to divine law, not canon law, therefore the Pope's intervention was unnecessary. If the divines in the universities gave it as their opinion that the King's marriage was invalid, then invalid it must be, and all that was required was an official pronouncement by the Archbishop of Canterbury to that effect, leaving the King free to remarry.

This was a radical solution, but to Gardiner and Fox it made sense, and when the King returned to Greenwich in October after his progress they told him about Dr Cranmer's suggestion. 'Marry!' exclaimed Henry, 'This man hath the sow by the right ear!' Cranmer was duly sent for, and came to Greenwich, where Henry was impressed with the sober, quietly spoken, rather timid cleric. He ordered Cranmer to set all other business aside, and 'take pains to see my cause furthered according to your device'. He could begin by writing a treatise expounding his views.

Lord Rochford, Anne's father, was asked to prepare accommodation for Dr Cranmer at his London house, so that he could write in comfort. Rochford gladly complied, and seeing the admiration Dr Cranmer conceived from the first for Anne, he made much of his guest. Not only was Cranmer learned and reassuring, but he was also interested in the new learning and in the arguments for Church reform that were so often aired in the Boleyn household. In no time at all Rochford made Cranmer his family chaplain, and he stayed in that capacity for some time, being allowed frequent access to the King.

Henry VIII's acceptance of Cranmer's suggestion to sound out the universities marks the beginning of a new phase in the 'great matter'. Hitherto, the King's main concern had been to have his marriage declared invalid by the Pope, but now he began to take cognizance of the wider issues involved. He was politically isolated in Europe, and, disillusioned with the Holy See, he perceived himself also as an outcast from a corrupt Church of Rome. Even before the advent of Cranmer, Henry had contemplated severing the Church of England from that of Rome. Now, this seemed a very real possibility for the future if the King wanted his marriage dissolved, for it was almost certain that the Pope would not help him. In this way what began as a matrimonial suit became transformed, very gradually, into a political, theological and ultimately a social revolution. The period of Wolsey's tutelage was over; the lion was at last discovering the full extent of his strength and power. The King was now intent on becoming absolute ruler in his own realm, and More's prophecy, made eight years earlier, would soon be fulfilled.

9
It is my affair!

In November 1529, Henry VIII was as much in love with Anne Boleyn as ever, and still showering her with gifts; although these were now more in the way of peace offerings, for the relationship between them was by then often a stormy one. Anne felt that time was passing her by. She accused the King of having kept her waiting; she might, in the meantime, have contracted some advantageous marriage, she said, and had children – a pointed barb, this. Peace was bought with a length of purple velvet for a gown, linen cloth for under-clothes, a French saddle of black velvet fringed with silk and gold with a matching footstool, and a black velvet pillion saddle and harness so that Anne could ride in intimate proximity to her royal lover.

Often, she would threaten to leave Henry, as in January 1531, when they quarrelled violently. At the prospect of losing her, Henry went hotfoot to Norfolk and Anne's father, and begged them with tears in his eyes to act as mediators. When the quarrel was made up, he placated Anne with yet more gifts: furs and rich embroideries. This charade was repeated on several occasions, with Anne lament-ing her lost time and honour, and Henry weeping, begging her to desist and speak no more of leaving him. And, always, there were the peace offerings.

As the months, and then the years, went by, Anne became increasingly difficult to deal with. The long delays and the resultant stress, coupled with the constant strain of holding Henry at arm's length, tested her endurance to the limit. Her position was insecure, and she knew it. Yet she seemed unable to avoid friction with her royal lover. She was furious to discover that the Queen was still mending Henry's shirts. She herself was an expert needlewoman, and the King's admission that the shirts had been sent to Katherine on his orders did little to sweeten her temper. After such quarrels, however, Anne would soon be fervently assuring Henry how much she loved him. 'Even if I were to suffer a thousand deaths,' she told him – referring to an old prophecy that a queen would be burned at this time – 'my love for you will not abate one jot!' Chapuys drily observed that, 'As usual in these cases, their mutual love will be greater than before.'

Once installed at Whitehall Palace, Anne was attended like a queen and courted like one. In December 1529, her father was formally created Earl of Wiltshire which meant that she herself would from henceforth be styled the Lady Anne Boleyn, and her brother be known as Viscount Rochford. To celebrate Wiltshire's elevation, the King gave a banquet at Whitehall, at which Anne took precedence over all the ladies of the court and sat by the King's side on the Queen's throne. Chapuys was present and, after seeing the lavish feast, the dancing and the 'carousing', came away with the impression he had just witnessed a marriage feast: 'It seemed as if nothing were wanting but the priest to give away the nuptial ring and pronounce the blessing.' Anne also presided over a magnificent ball hosted by the King on 12 January in honour of the departing French ambassador, who was sympathetic to her cause.

For all Anne's prominence in the life of the court, the King was at pains to convince everyone that he and the Queen were still on good terms, and kept Katherine constantly with him. She even followed the hunt each day. The Venetian ambassador observed that 'so much reciprocal courtesy is being displayed in public that any one acquainted with the controversy cannot but consider their conduct more than human'. Both were good at concealing the tensions that lay below the surface.

In private, however, it was a different story. On 30 November 1529, when Henry paid a rare visit to her after dinner, Katherine blurted out that she had been suffering the pangs of purgatory on earth, and that she was very badly treated by his refusing to dine with her and visit her in her apartments. He told her she had no cause to complain, for she was mistress in her own household, where she could do as she pleased. He had not dined with her as he was so much engaged with business of all kinds, the Cardinal having left the affairs of government in great confusion. As to his visiting her in her apartments, and sharing her bed, she ought to know that he was not her legitimate husband. He had been assured of this by many learned doctors.

'Doctors!' retorted Katherine, in a passion. 'You know yourself, without the help of any doctors, that you are my husband and that your case has no foundation! I care not a straw for your doctors!' For every doctor or lawyer who upheld Henry's case, she went on, she could find a thousand to hold their marriage good and valid.

But she was getting nowhere. Henry was immovable on that issue, and the quarrel ended with him leaving to seek comfort from Anne Boleyn. Yet she, knowing he had been with Katherine, was decidedly unsympathetic. 'Did I not tell you that whenever you argue with the Queen she is sure to have the upper hand?' she scolded. 'I see that some fine morning you will succumb to her reasoning, and cast me off!' With this, Henry had had enough, and fled back to his own apartments in search of peace.

Gradually the concept of radical change had become firmly rooted in Henry Tudor's mind, and on Christmas Eve he told the Queen that if the Pope pronounced sentence against him, he would not heed it, adding that 'he prized and valued the Church of Canterbury as much as the people across the sea did the Roman'. Severing the Church of England from the main body of Christendom was an idea entirely repugnant to Katherine, and she had difficulty in believing that this was what the King really intended. But, as far as his own case was concerned, Henry was being realistic. The long silence from the Vatican was proof that his suit was being deliberately shelved, and it seemed inevitable that he would soon have to take matters into his own hands.

In February 1530, Charles V went to Bologna to be crowned by the Pope, and Henry, resolving to turn the situation to his own advantage, sent an embassy headed by Cranmer and Wiltshire – newly appointed Lord Privy Seal – to stress to the Emperor that the King had pressed for an annulment only 'for the discharge of his conscience and for the quietness of his realm'. The embassy was not a success, due partly to the aggressive and provocative attitude of Wiltshire, an ardent reformist, and although Charles told the ambassadors that he would abide by whatever decision the Pope reached, he added that he thought Julius II's dispensation was 'as strong as God's law'. It was painfully obvious that Clement would not dare gainsay him, and in April Henry told the French ambassador that he intended to settle the matter within his own kingdom by the advice of his Council and Parliament, so as not to have recourse to the Pope, 'whom he regards as ignorant and no good father'. Katherine, conversely, was relying entirely on the Pope. In April, she wrote to Dr Pedro Ortiz, whom the Emperor had sent to represent her interests in Rome, and begged him to put pressure on Clement to give a ruling in her case. 'I fear that God's vicar on earth does not wish to remedy these evils,' she wrote. 'I do not know what to think of his Holiness.' Throughout the summer months, she sent letter after letter to Clement, beseeching him to take pity on her and pass sentence, but he ignored them, fearing that a decision in the Queen's favour might provoke Henry into creating a schism within the Church.

Henry's subjects were as supportive as ever of Katherine, and in the spring of 1530 a rumour was circulating widely that the King had separated the Queen from her daughter out of spite. This was not true, and to prove it Henry summoned the Princess to Windsor to be with her mother, and left them there together when the court moved on elsewhere. Mary was now fourteen, old enough to realise what the presence of Anne Boleyn at court betokened. Hitherto, she had been studiously sheltered from her parents' troubles, thanks to the diligence of her mother and her governess, Lady Salisbury. When Katherine left Windsor to rejoin the court, Mary went back to Hunsdon, where her father visited her on 7 July. He had seen very little of her in recent years, and one purpose of his visit was to reassure himself that she had not been infected by what he was pleased to call Katherine's obstinacy. Yet when he left Hunsdon, he almost certainly carried with him the realisation that both Mary and her governess were already staunch supporters of the Queen.

In July 1530, a petition was sent to the Pope from all the lords spiritual and temporal of England – including Wolsey – beseeching

His Holiness to decide the case in Henry's favour. Clement peevishly accused them of having troubled him for little cause, and warned them that he had to consider all the interested parties. Nor could he deny the Queen's right of appeal to Rome.

Meanwhile, Henry's agents had canvassed most of the European universities on the issue of the validity of the King's marriage, and where it was felt necessary, bribes were issued to the learned divines in order to obtain the opinions the King hoped to hear. In July 1530, Henry tested his Council's reaction to the prospect of him declaring himself a free man and marrying Anne Boleyn without the Pope's sanction. One councillor threw himself on his knees, and begged his master to wait at least until winter to see what transpired, and Henry, seeing the others to be of like mind, reluctantly agreed. Even the Emperor, however, was certain that the King would marry Anne with or without the Pope's permission. After three years of tortuous negotiations to end his marriage, Henry was still obsessed with her, and more than ever convinced that God was guiding his actions. He described his flexible conscience as 'the highest and most supreme court for judgement and justice', and – according to Chapuys – told the Queen he 'kept her [Anne] in his company only to learn her character, as he had made up his mind to marry her. And marry her he would, whatever the Pope might say.' He was, in truth, no longer the same man who had lodged a plea in Archbishop Warham's ecclesiastical court in 1527. The despot was emerging, determined to have his own way, and even if necessary to alter the process of law to get it.

Throughout 1530, the Emperor pressed Clement VII to pronounce in 'the sainted Queen's' favour, and he urged him to order Henry to separate from Anne Boleyn until judgement was given. In August, Charles granted Chapuys special powers to act on the Queen's behalf, and this gave the tireless ambassador the freedom he desired and needed; from that time on, he would be more zealous than ever in the Queen's cause. Katherine herself liked and trusted him implicitly, and her warm feelings were reciprocated. Years later, after his retirement in 1545, Chapuys would remember her as 'the most virtuous woman I have ever known, and the highest hearted, but too quick to trust that others were like herself, and too slow to do a little ill that much good might come of it'. Here, Chapuys was referring to Katherine's continual refusal during the 1530s to agree to an imperial invasion of England on her behalf. Chapuys would try again and again to convince her that this alone would put an end to her troubles, but such was her loyalty to the man she considered to be her husband that she consistently refused to have anything to do with the plan. Her attitude exasperated Chapuys, but it also increased his admiration for her.

In spite of the pressure from Charles V, Dr Ortiz and Chapuys, the Pope avoided giving a definitive sentence on the King's case. In March 1530, he issued a brief forbidding Henry to contract a new marriage before sentence was given; in May, another brief was issued forbidding anyone to express an opinion on the case if prompted by bribes or unworthy motives – even Clement had heard how Henry had bought off some of the universities. Then, in August, a papal encyclical forbade all persons to write anything against their consciences concerning the 'great matter'; this was a threat to the unity of the English government itself, as the new Lord Chancellor, Sir Thomas More, was known to be against annulment on moral grounds. Then, to add insult to injury, in September the Pope suggested that Henry 'might be allowed two wives', as he could permit this with less scandal than granting an annulment. The King's anger was further fuelled in December, when he was cited to appear in Rome to defend his case. He ignored this, and also a brief issued by Clement in January 1531, ordering him to 'put away one Anne whom he kept about him', and forbidding his subjects to meddle with his case.

Thanks to Clement's conduct, Henry was losing all respect for the Holy See, and paying greater heed to the clamour of Anne Boleyn's faction for reform of the Church in England. This prompted him to consider that the English Church might be better off with himself as its head than owing allegiance to a weak and vacillating Pope. It was a notion that appealed vastly to the King, and once it had taken root in his mind, a break with Rome was inevitable. Both he and Anne were anticipating that much would be accomplished in the new session of Parliament that was due to commence in January 1531, and that their marriage could not be far off. 'The Lady feels assured on it,' commented Chapuys.

By late 1530, Henry was beginning to feel a certain amount of resentment towards Anne Boleyn, and was not above reminding her on one occasion how much she owed to him and how many enemies he had made for her sake. She remained unimpressed. 'It matters not,' she shrugged, refusing to be baited. Nevertheless, according to the Venetian ambassador, her will was still law to him. This had been demonstrated clearly in what had happened to Wolsey.

Just after Christmas 1529, the Cardinal had fallen ill and was thought to be dying. The King sent Dr Butts to him with a message saying he 'would not lose him for £20,000', and bade Anne 'send the Cardinal a token with comfortable words'. Anne knew when not to oppose the King, and meekly detached a gold tablet from her girdle, which she handed to the physician. As a result of these signs of goodwill, Wolsey's health improved daily, though the longed-for summons back to court never arrived.

But while Anne was sending comforting messages to the sick man, she was still plotting his downfall. In February, she remarked in Chapuys's hearing that it would cost her a good 20,000 crowns in bribes 'before I have done with him'. She also made Henry promise not to see Wolsey, for, as she told him, 'I know you could not help but pity him.' Chapuys was convinced that 'to reinstate him in the King's favour would not be difficult, were it not for the Lady'. Because Henry would not order Wolsey's arrest, Anne sulked for several weeks, and was enraged when, on 12 February 1530, the King formally pardoned the Cardinal and confirmed him in his See, which meant he ranked second only to the Archbishop of Canterbury within the Church hierarchy. After that, Anne was 'incessantly crying after the King' for Wolsey's blood. Wolsey himself realised that 'there was this continual serpentine enemy about the King, the night crow, that possessed the royal ear against him.' She was, he told Cavendish, the enemy that never slept, 'but studied and continually imagined his utter destruction'.

At heart, Wolsey was a conventional churchman, and had never supported an annulment of the royal marriage. During the summer of 1530, he began taking an interest in the progress of the Queen's case, and in a letter to Chapuys urged strong and immediate action as the key to its success. In July, he supported Charles V's call for Clement to order Henry's separation from Anne Boleyn, and in August, he wrote to the Pope to urge a speedy conclusion to the

King's case, and to ask why the Queen's cause was 'not more energetically pushed'. In Chapuys's opinion, Wolsey was hoping for a return to power once the 'great matter' was settled, but this would only be possible if it were settled in Katherine's favour. With Anne Boleyn out of the way, and a grateful Queen Katherine exerting her influence upon a contrite husband, the path would be clear for him. But Wolsey, like many other people, underestimated the strength of the King's feelings for Anne Boleyn, and this time the miscalculation would be fatal.

Rumours of Wolsey's activities provoked Anne to fresh efforts. Her uncle, Norfolk, was a willing ally, and was not above bribing the Cardinal's physician into falsely accusing his master of having urged the Pope to excommunicate Henry VIII and lay England under an interdict in the hope of provoking an uprising on the Queen's behalf, perhaps dethroning the King and seizing power for himself. When this information was laid before him, Henry, who had recently been informing his councillors that Wolsey 'was a better man than any of you', was shocked and suspicious. For a while, images of the two Wolseys warred in his mind: the mentor of his youth who had devoted his energies to running the kingdom, the kindly avuncular man whom he had chosen as godfather to the Princess Mary; and the arch-traitor of Anne Boleyn's imagination and the evidence put forward by her party.

Anne won. On 1 November, a warrant was drawn up for the Cardinal's arrest and – in a form of poetic justice – was sent to Henry Percy, Earl of Northumberland, Anne's former suitor. Percy waited on Wolsey at his episcopal palace at Cawood in Yorkshire, and apprehended him on a charge of high treason. Then began the slow journey back to London, the Tower, and inevitable death. But Wolsey was a sick man, and on the way he succumbed to the ill health that had plagued him in recent months, dying at Leicester Abbey, where his escort had been obliged to find him shelter. 'If I had served God as diligently as I have done the King,' he said on his deathbed, 'he would not have given me over in my grey hairs.' He was buried next to Richard III in what Chapuys was pleased to call 'the tyrants' sepulchre'.

The King was saddened by news of his death: 'I wish he had lived,' he remarked. Anne Boleyn, however, was jubilant, and staged a masque for the edification of the court entitled 'The going to hell of Cardinal Wolsey'. Though Henry found this distasteful, Anne's temper was such these days that he dared not cross her. Early in 1531, Chapuys reported:

> She is becoming more arrogant every day, using words in authority towards the King of which he has several times complained to the Duke of Norfolk, saying that she was not like the Queen who never in her life used ill words to him.

Henry did not have the courage to say these things to Anne's face, for he was afraid of losing her, although she had no such qualms. Her thwarted ambition and repressed sexuality had turned her into a virago with a sharp tongue, with which she managed to alienate many of her former supporters. For all this, her power over the King remained, based as it was on sexual blackmail and shared aims.

With Cranmer's plan now being put into effect, Anne was preparing for queenship. In December 1530, she commissioned the College of Arms to draw up a family pedigree that invented a descent from a Norman lord who had supposedly settled in England in the twelfth century. 'The King is displeased with it, but he has to be patient,' Chapuys wryly commented. On the same day she ordered new liveries for her servants embroidered with the device: *Ainsi sera, groigne qui groigne* (Thus it will be, grudge who grudge). When the court rocked with suppressed mirth, Anne was at a loss to know why, until the King bade her get rid of the device, explaining that the motto was meant to read: *Groigne qui groigne, Vive Bourgogne!* (Grudge who grudge, long live Burgundy!), a device used by the Emperor.

Anne's attitude towards the Queen had by January 1531 deteriorated into outright hatred. Chapuys wrote:

> The Lady Anne is braver than a lion. . . . She said to one of the Queen's ladies that she wished all Spaniards were in the sea. The lady told her such language was disrespectful to her mistress. She said she cared nothing for the Queen, and would rather see her hang than acknowledge her as her mistress.

Because of Anne's attitude, and the King's resentment of the Queen's stand, Katherine's supporters were finding that their lives were becoming increasingly uncomfortable. There were also signs that the King was no longer prepared to tolerate any defiance on his wife's behalf. Late in 1530, the Duchess of Norfolk was smuggling letters received from Italy to the Queen concealed in oranges. Katherine passed them to Chapuys, who sent them on to the Emperor. The Duchess's actions were noticed, and she was warned not to help the Queen, Anne using 'high words' to her aunt in front of the courtiers. Katherine was of the opinion that the duchess had sent the letters 'out of the love she bears her' and because she loathed Anne Boleyn, but Chapuys suspected that she might have sent them at the behest of the Duke, who perhaps hoped to implicate the Queen in a conspiracy. His fears were without foundation, for, in 1531, the Duchess again acted as go-between for the Queen and the Spanish ambassador, and when the King found out, he banished her from court.

Then there was Thomas Abell, one of Katherine's chaplains. In 1530, he published a book in her defence, entitled *Invicta Veritas*, which argued that 'by no manner of law may it be lawful for King Henry the Eight [*sic*] to be divorced'. It was a very brave thing to do, for Abell incurred the King's severe displeasure, and the book went immediately on to the banned list, although not before some copies had been circulated. It would soon be apparent that one supported the Queen at one's peril.

On 21 January 1531, the Convocations of the clergy of Canterbury and York met at Westminster, and anyone with any grasp of English affairs would have reckoned this significant, for it was only with the assent of Convocation that important ecclesiastical reforms could be implemented. Something momentous was indeed at hand: the meeting marked the beginning of the English Reformation.

It was Thomas Cromwell who had finally convinced the King of the advantages of severing the Church of England from Rome. Cromwell's promotion to the King's service from Wolsey's had been arranged in 1521 by the Cardinal, when Cromwell was thirty-five. The son of a blacksmith, a thick-set bull of a man with black hair and small, porcine eyes, Cromwell had led a somewhat disreputable early life, and had soldiered as a mercenary in Italy, where he may have learned to admire the Machiavellian ideal of political expediency. Upon his return to England in 1513 he had taken up law, and in this capacity had attracted the attention of the Cardinal, to whose service he had been recruited the following year. To great intelligence and ability Cromwell added a complete lack of scruple, although he always professed to be a devout Christian. It was this facet of his unattractive personality that would in time make him essential to the King. Unscrupulous and efficient, his spy network, instituted after his rise to favour following the disgrace of Wolsey, was to become a model for future governments.

Henry was aware that England's relations with the papacy had often lacked harmony over the centuries: several medieval kings had come into conflict with the pontiffs, and the English had always resented paying the burdensome levy to Rome known as 'Peter's Pence'. In the late fourteenth century, John Wycliffe and his Lollards had spoken out against the wealth and corruption of churchmen, and now, in the more enlightened world of Renaissance Europe, there was even more cause for criticism. Henry was no heretic, but he was determined to govern his kingdom 'in concert with his lords and commons only', and even some supporters of the Queen were disillusioned with the Holy See, which had become an institution increasingly at odds with the burgeoning nationalism of the English people. It was in this climate that the English Reformation was planned.

On 7 February 1531, the King stood in Parliament and demanded that the Church of England recognise and acknowledge him from now on to be its 'sole protector and supreme head'. Neither Parliament nor Convocation dared defy the King, and on 11 February, Archbishop Warham announced that the clergy were prepared to acknowledge the King as supreme head of the Church of England 'as far as the law of Christ allows' – a qualification conceded by Henry after some heated negotiations. From henceforth the English Church would not recognise the Pope, who would be referred to as the Bishop of Rome, and he would not receive allegiance from the English bishops or enjoy any canonical jurisdiction in England.

Henry VIII's Church of England remained Catholic in its precepts. The only immediate change was in its leadership, which since that day has remained vested in the sovereign. Parliament at once passed an Act confirming the King's new title, and the news was conveyed to the people of England by proclamation. They learned that Henry VIII was now effectively King and Pope in his own realm, with complete jurisdiction over his subjects' material and spiritual welfare. There was little resistance. Anne Boleyn was ecstatic, and Chapuys wrote: 'The woman of the King made such demonstrations of joy as if she had actually gained Paradise.' Her father, sharing her enthusiasm, offered to prove from scripture that 'when God left this world He left no successor or vicar.' Like Wiltshire, most of the nobility supported the King, and the clergy had no choice. Even Chapuys conceded that the Pope's 'timidity and dissimulation' had been the cause of Henry's break with Rome, and had done much harm to the Catholic Church.

Yet one or two brave voices were raised against the King. John Fisher, Bishop of Rochester, made no secret of his opinion that it was against God's law for the King to be Head of the Church of England. Henry was becoming increasingly irritated by Fisher's resistance, and Anne Boleyn and her faction were so furious that they made plans to remove the Bishop from the scene. On 20 February 1531, Fisher's cook, Richard Rouse, added a white powder to the soup which was served to Fisher and his household. Several men died at table, others fell seriously ill, but Fisher himself ate only a little soup and, although he suffered terrible stomach pains, he escaped what was obviously an attempt on his life. Rouse was arrested, even though it was widely believed he had been acting on the instructions of Wiltshire who was said to have given him the poison, and that Anne herself was privy to the plot. However, the King refused to credit the rumours, and pressed Parliament into passing a new law providing for harsh treatment of poisoners: in future, they would be publicly boiled to death, a punishment meted out to the unfortunate Richard Rouse. Chapuys thought the King had been wise to deal so severely in this case; 'nevertheless, he cannot wholly avoid some suspicion, at least against the Lady and her father.' Anne's involvement was confirmed in October 1531, when she sent a message to Fisher warning him not to attend the next session of Parliament in case he should suffer again the sickness he had almost died of in February. If she had not actively intrigued for Fisher's death, she had at the very least condoned the attempt to murder him.

Thomas More was appalled by the break with Rome, the more so because, as Lord Chancellor, he could not do other than condone it. His reluctance to become involved in the 'great matter' was widely known, and he had made enemies because of it. His old friendship with the King had been strained to the limit, and Cromwell, recently appointed to the Privy Council, had taken his place as Henry's chief adviser. How long he could continue in his office was anybody's guess, but he feared it would not be long before he and the King came into open conflict, something he would have given much to avoid.

In July 1531, Chapuys was writing: 'The Lady allows only three or four months for the nuptials. She is preparing her royal state by degrees, and has just taken an almoner (Edward Fox) and other officers.' Visiting ambassadors were warned to 'appease the most illustrious and beloved Anne with presents'; she went about decked like a queen and dispensed favours as one. Save for the crown and the title, her reign had in effect begun.

Although Anne was not, as Chapuys alleged, 'more Lutheran that Luther himself', she certainly supported the idea of radical reform in the Church, while at the same time observing all the conventions of traditional Catholicism. One of the staunchest advocates of the royal supremacy, she was now openly flaunting her controversial views, and was still reading forbidden literature with the King's knowledge. She also had in her possession more conventional works: a volume of the letters of St Paul, as well as a beautifully bound edition of Lord Morley's translation of *The Epistles and Gospels for the LII Sundays in the Year*, presented to her at Christmas 1532, and several devotional and other works in the French language, among them the *Ecclesiaste* and a letter-writing treatise by Louis le Brun, the first book ever dedicated to her, as 'Madame Anne de Rochefort'.

One reason for Anne's strong anti-clericalism was because she felt there were too many priests supporting the Queen. When Henry put in a good word for an erring priest brought before his justices, Anne said loudly to her father that the King 'did wrong to speak for a priest, as there were too many of them already'. She had no love at all for the Church of Rome, and because she supported the newly established Church of England with such conviction it was widely believed that she would urge the King to do away with traditional forms of worship as well. At the end of 1532, Queen Katherine would warn the Emperor that, thanks to Anne Boleyn, Henry had already seized a great deal of Church property. Like Chapuys, Katherine believed Anne to be a heretic, and Anne's own behaviour tended to confirm this: in 1532, she obtained a reprieve from the stake for a noted Protestant, John Lambert, who had been examined and found guilty of heresy by Warham. Her patronage of such people suggested she was one of them, though in truth she was merely putting into effect her own views on religious enlightenment, which were revolutionary enough in her time.

Parliament had, as yet, done nothing about the King's nullity suit, but every day leave of absence was being granted to those Members who supported the Queen, which Chapuys thought ominous. From the pronouncements made by the universities – all of which had now been received – it was easy to see which way the wind was blowing. So confident was Henry of receiving favourable opinions, and of the effect of his bribes, that there was no room in his mind for the possibility of the body of learned opinion being against him. Nor was it. Of the sixteen European universities canvassed, only four supported the Queen. The majority of the finest and most learned minds in Europe – not all of them susceptible to bribes – pronounced the King's marriage to be incestuous and against the law of God; it was therefore null and void, and the papacy had had no business in the first place to dispense with it.

The verdicts of the universities were read out in Parliament at the end of March, and were later published. Most of the King's subjects accepted them, but women, who were, according to Hall, 'more wilful than wise or learned', spoke out and accused the King of having corrupted the learned doctors. A similar reaction was met with by Henry's own treatise on the 'great matter', entitled *A Glass of the Truth*, which was published that year.

In the spring of 1531, Henry tried again to force Katherine to withdraw her appeal to Rome. Again, she refused, and wrote to the Emperor, begging him to press Clement to give a ruling before October, when Parliament was due to reconvene. In April, a papal nuncio arrived in England, and told the King his case could only be tried in Rome and nowhere else. Henry told him he would never consent to such a thing, even if the Pope were to excommunicate him. 'I care not a fig for his excommunications!' he stormed.

It was Archbishop Warham who now stood in Henry's way. Warham was old and ailing, a staunch religious conservative who had already gone against his principles to acknowledge the King's supremacy, but without him there could be no annulment. Henry, knowing Warham to be near death, did not press the point. He could afford to wait a little longer, and when Warham was dead, Cranmer, who had already shown Henry the way out of his dilemma, could take his place.

Henry was now seeing as little of Katherine as possible, and when they did meet he only pestered her to retire to a convent or withdraw her appeal to Rome. She had been ill in November 1530, and he left her to recover at Richmond while he went to London with Anne. 'He has never been so long without visiting her now,' wrote Chapuys a few weeks later. However, the Queen was well enough to travel to Greenwich for the Christmas season, sitting enthroned with the King in the great hall on Twelfth Night to watch a masque and some dancing. Henry made a point of dining with her every night, and showed her every respect.

After Christmas, Katherine confided to the Pope that her complaint was

> not against the King, my lord, but against the instigators and abettors of this suit. I trust so much in my lord the King's natural virtues and goodness that if I could only have him with me two months, as he used to be, I alone would be powerful enough to make him forget the past. They know this is true, so they try to prevent his being with me.

This was a viewpoint from which Katherine never wavered, whatever the King might do to prove she was wrong: she could never accept that Anne Boleyn's influence was more powerful than hers could be, given the chance.

In March 1531, Henry was still playing the part of a man who had been forced to set aside a beloved wife against his will, and was visiting the Queen regularly, even though it was a charade he had grown heartily sick of. 'The Queen is now firmer than ever,' wrote

Chapuys in April, 'and believes the King will not dare to make the other marriage.' In fact Henry was doing his best to provoke Katherine into giving him grounds for a divorce by deserting him. When the Princess Mary fell seriously ill with a digestive disorder in March, Katherine, learning that her daughter had not kept any food down for eight days, wanted to go to her. Henry, seeing his advantage, replied meaningfully that 'she might go and see the Princess if she wanted, and also stop there.' The implication was ominous, but Katherine guessed his purpose and refused to leave his side, even though she was desperate to see her child. Throughout the course of her marital problems, her chief aim had been to protect her daughter's interests. According to canon law, a child conceived of a marriage made in good faith could not be declared illegitimate if that marriage were found to be invalid. Mary therefore had a lawful right to a place in the succession, either as Henry's heiress or after any legitimate sons born to the King. Yet Katherine feared that any issue of a marriage between Henry and Anne would oust Mary from her place in the succession. For this reason, she was determined to preserve Mary's rights, with her own life-blood if need be.

Mary's illness marks the beginning of the bouts of ill health that were to ruin her constitution and her life. At fifteen, she was fully aware of the rift between her parents and her ailments were almost certainly the products of anxiety. Her problems were further complicated by a difficult adolescence and the onset of painful and irregular periods and debilitating headaches. Mary loved her father, but, from the first, her sympathies had lain with her mother. She rarely saw either of them, and in her loneliness and grief she turned to her religion for solace: it would very soon become the dominant influence in her life.

Ten days after their confrontation, Henry and Katherine dined together in public. Chapuys was present, and heard the Queen, 'with supernatural courage', ask Henry once again to dismiss 'that shameless creature', Anne Boleyn. He angrily refused. Undeterred, Katherine again asked if she might visit the Princess Mary, who was still very poorly. 'Go if you wish and stop there!' he snapped, to which she replied quietly: 'I would not leave you for my daughter or for anyone else in the world.'

Henry now, belatedly, began to feel concerned about his child's health, and guilty for having deprived her of the comfort of her mother's presence. On 24 March, he arranged for Mary to be brought by litter to Richmond Palace, and for Katherine to join her there. By April, Mary was much better, well enough for Katherine to return to court and leave her in the care of Lady Salisbury. On 4 May, Katherine suggested that Mary visit the court, but Henry was in a cantankerous mood and refused, although a month later he arranged for the Princess to join her mother when the court moved to Windsor.

Henry was still trying to make Katherine withdraw her appeal to Rome. On 31 May 1531, he sent a deputation from the Privy Council to wait on her at Greenwich, its purpose being to ask her to 'be sensible'. She refused to do as the King asked. She denied his supremacy, declaring that the Pope was 'the only true sovereign and vicar of God who has power to judge in spiritual matters'. Then she said:

I love and have loved my lord the King as much as any woman can love a man, but I would not have borne him company as his wife for one moment against the voice of my conscience. I *am* his true wife. Go to Rome and argue with others than a lone woman!

Then, when the bishops attempted to prolong the dispute, she cut them short, saying, 'God grant my husband a quiet conscience, but I mean to abide by no decision save that of Rome'. Afterwards, Chapuys told Charles V that the deputation had been 'confounded by a single woman', and the Duke of Suffolk told Henry VIII that Katherine was ready to obey him in everything save for the obedience she owed to two higher powers. 'Which two?' Henry fumed. 'The Pope and the Emperor?' 'No, Sire,' replied Suffolk, 'God and her conscience.'

This incident provoked Henry's decision to separate from Katherine for good. The court was then at Windsor, but was due to move to Woodstock on 14 July. On that day, Henry left Windsor Castle early, without informing the Queen of his departure, and she, left behind with only her daughter and her attendants for company in the deserted royal apartments, was not immediately aware of the momentous step he had taken, nor that she would never see him again. Then she was informed by a messenger that it was the King's pleasure that she vacate the castle within a month, and in that moment everything fell into place. He had gone, had left her, without saying goodbye. Even in her distress, she remained calm. 'Go where I may, I remain his wife, and for him I will pray,' she told the messenger, and bade him convey a message of farewell, saying how sad she was that Henry had not said goodbye to her, and enquiring after his health as a good wife should. The King, hearing her message, fell into a violent rage, crying,

> Tell the Queen I do not want any of her goodbyes, and have no wish to afford her consolation! I do not care whether she asks after my health or not. Let her stop it and mind her own business. I want no more of her messages!

Nor did his spite end there. He wrote to Katherine warning her it would be better for her if she spent her time in seeking witnesses to prove her 'pretended virginity' at the time of their marriage than in talking about her cause to whoever would listen to her; she must cease complaining to the world about her imagined wrongs. To be fair to Henry, it is likely that, had she agreed to the annulment of their marriage, he would have treated Katherine generously and remained on good terms with her – his later treatment of Anne of Cleves argues this. Yet time and again she had opposed him, seemingly blind to the very real dilemma he was in with regard to the succession, and when thwarted Henry could, and frequently did, become cruel.

Katherine remained at Windsor until early August 1531, when she received a message from the King commanding her to leave court. Having seen Mary off to Richmond, she moved with her household to Easthampstead, where, on 13 October, she was visited by another deputation of the Council, come to explain to her what the determinations of the universities meant and to inform her that Julius II's dispensation was 'clearly void and of none effect'. Katherine remained unmoved, declaring on her knees that she was the King's true wife; he had succumbed, she said, to 'mere passion'. And when the lords warned her of what the King might do to her if she persisted in her defiance, she answered, 'I will go even to the fire if the King commands me'. A few days later, Henry sent her to The More in Hertfordshire, a manor house formerly owned by Wolsey, very well appointed and set in excellent parklands. Here, for a time, Katherine kept great state, being attended by 250 maids of honour. At the end of October, thirty Venetians were her guests and were impressed by her vast household and the splendour of their surroundings. On that day, they noticed, thirty maids of honour stood round the Queen while she dined, and a further fifty waited at table. As for Katherine herself, they found her of short stature, 'inclined to corpulence, of modest countenance; a handsome woman of good repute. She is neither disheartened nor depressed,' but 'virtuous, just, replete with goodness and religion, constant, resolute, prudent, good, and always smiling.' But while foreigners were happy to visit The More, Henry's courtiers stayed away.

When winter came, Katherine's mask slipped, and in November, she told the Emperor that

> what I suffer is enough to kill ten men, much more a shattered woman who has done no harm. I am the King's lawful wife, and while I live I will say no other. At The More, separated from my husband without having offended him in any way, Katherine the unhappy Queen.

In another letter written that month, she begged Charles, 'for the love of God, procure a final sentence from His Holiness as soon as possible. May God forgive him for the many delays!' The Emperor, touched to the heart by her pleas, summoned the papal nuncio and told him he thought it 'a very strange and abominable thing, that the lust of a foolish man and a foolish woman should hold up a law suit and inflict an outrageous burden upon such a good and blameless Queen'. Then he ordered the nuncio to press for Henry VIII's excommunication, in the hope that that would bring the King to his senses. The Pope, as usual, refused to do anything that might provoke Henry to further excesses against the Church: 'His conduct cuts me to the soul,' wrote Katherine of Clement.

On 10 November 1531, Henry and Katherine hosted two separate banquets for dignitaries of the City of London at Ely Place in Holborn, Henry in one hall and Katherine in another. They did not meet, and this was to be the last state occasion that Katherine would attend. On her way home to The More afterwards, crowds gathered to see her and to shout words of encouragement, which greatly displeased the King. He did not invite the Queen to court that Christmas, and the absence of mirth from the festivities at Greenwich was put down to her absence. Mary, too, was absent, being at Beaulieu in Essex. Nevertheless, Katherine sent Henry a gift of a gold cup, with a humble message, for they had always exchanged presents at Yuletide. Henry sent it back with a curt message commanding her not to send him such gifts in future, for he was not her husband, as she should know. 'He has not been so discourteous to the Lady,' observed Chapuys; Anne had given him 'darts of Biscayan fashion, richly ornamented', and in return he had given her a room hung with cloth of gold and silver and crimson satin heavily embroidered. And he even remembered Mary Boleyn, who received a shirt with a collar of black-work lace.

Anne was still as unpopular as ever. Her reputation throughout most of Christendom was dire, and she was openly called a whore, an adulteress, and sometimes even a heretic in the courts of Europe. At home public feeling made itself felt in an incident that occurred on 24 November 1531. On that day, Anne went with only a few attendants to dine with one of her friends at a house by the Thames. Word spread quickly through the City of London that she was there, and before very long a mob of seven or eight thousand women, or men dressed as women, were marching upon the house with intent to seize her, even lynch her. Fortunately for Anne, she received warning of their coming, and escaped by barge along the river. She was, however, badly shaken by this evidence of just how unpopular she was with her future subjects. Since Henry could not arrest every woman in London, he was powerless to do anything about it; all he could do was hush up the affair, so that word of it should not incite further incidents, though the Venetian ambassador learned what had happened, and recorded it for posterity.

News that Anne Boleyn had usurped the Queen's place at court during the Christmas season provoked an outcry in London, and in March 1532, the Abbot of Whitby made history by being the first man brought to justice for calling her a 'common stewed whore'. The Nun of Kent had continued to prophesy against the King, accusing him of wishing to remarry for his 'voluptuous and carnal appetite', and by the winter of 1531, the government had begun to view her as a threat to national security since she was inciting disaffection among the King's subjects, and was secretly believed by Cromwell to be in league with the Bishop of Rochester. From this time on, she would be watched by Cromwell's agents.

On Easter Sunday 1532, Friar William Peto preached before Henry and Anne at Greenwich, and warned the King that if he made 'an unlawful marriage' with the woman sitting next to him, he would be punished as God had punished Ahab, and the dogs would lick his blood. Henry, hearing this, went purple with rage and walked out, with Anne hard on his heels. A month later, one of his own priests, Dr Richard Curwen, delivered a sermon denouncing Peto as a 'dog, slanderer, base and beggarly rebel and [a] traitor. No subject should speak so audaciously to his prince!' Peto was then banished; he went to Antwerp, and later to Rome, where he was eventually made a Cardinal, dying in 1578.

Anne had not only made enemies of the people and Katherine's supporters, but she had also alienated some of her own supporters by her behaviour. By the summer of 1531, she was on increasingly bad terms with Norfolk, although he would for some time to come continue to promote her cause, seeing in her advancement future benefits for himself. Yet he could not approve of the way she treated the King. It was to Norfolk that Henry came running, often in tears, when Anne had been unkind to him, and the Duke's estranged wife told Chapuys that her husband had confided in her that Anne would be 'the ruin of all her family'. Anne had also managed to offend the Duke of Suffolk in the spring of 1530, and he had gone straight to Henry with lurid tales of her supposed affair with the poet Wyatt. Henry refused to listen, lost his temper, and temporarily banished Suffolk from court, but the rift upset him. Suffolk was a close friend and a staunch supporter, even in the face of opposition from his wife, Mary Tudor. Lastly, there was Sir Henry Guildford, the comptroller of the King's household, who in 1531 said complimentary things about Queen Katherine in Anne's hearing. Furious, she threatened him with the loss of his highly remunerative and prestigious office. 'You need not wait so long!' he retorted in anger, and immediately offered the King his resignation. Henry tried to talk him out of it, saying he should take no notice of women's talk, but Sir Henry was adamant: he would go.

On New Year's Day 1532, Anne returned to court after visiting her family at Hever, and was lodged by the King in the Queen's old apartments with almost as many female attendants as Katherine had had. Two weeks later, the King reconvened Parliament 'principally for the divorce [*sic*]'. In May, as a penalty for their past loyalty to the Pope, he exacted a heavy fine from Convocation. This open defiance of the Holy See was not without repercussions, for the next day Sir Thomas More resigned from his office of Lord Chancellor and surrendered the Great Seal of England to the King. He could no longer reconcile his conscience to Henry's reforms, and he wanted nothing to do with the King's plans to marry Anne Boleyn. The King was upset, disappointed, and rather angry, but he let More go, and Sir Thomas was grateful to retire to his house at Chelsea, his family, and his books. Sir Thomas Audley, a staunch King's man, was shortly afterwards appointed Lord Chancellor in his place.

In May 1532, Henry was busy spending a small fortune on providing Anne Boleyn with a wardrobe fit for a queen. One gown was made entirely of gold-embroidered velvet, and cost over £74. Then there was the glamorous nightgown, supplied in June, made of black satin lined with black velvet, which was not to be worn in bed, but to keep warm and to receive guests out of it. That same month, Henry granted Anne the manor of Hanworth, which boasted a fine house in which she frequently stayed.

Meanwhile, in Rome, the King's case still dragged on. A hearing had been set for November 1531, but then it was adjourned again until January 1532, when 'that devil of a Pope' (as the French ambassador described him to Chapuys) once more postponed it. It would not take place until after Christmas, even though Francis I had told Clement, at Henry's behest, that if he agreed to an annulment then Henry might forget all about his new-found supremacy and once more become a dutiful son of the Church. Clement was waiting for Henry to appear in Rome and answer for himself, which Henry dismissed as a foolish 'fantasy'. He would never go, he said. Then the Pope sent a solemn injunction to the King, ordering him to restore Queen Katherine to her rightful place at court and remove 'that diabolic woman' from his bed forthwith; whereupon Henry, who had waited so long and with such impatience to manoeuvre Anne into that bed, reacted with hot fury. 'It is my affair!' he cried. How dared the Pope interfere! But interfere Clement did, threatening excommunication, a threat that Henry ignored. And in May, he issued a brief ordering Henry to treat Katherine with more kindness. In July, in secret consistory, he decreed that if the King did not appear in Rome by 1 November, he would be declared contumacious, and the hearing would go ahead without him.

The Queen also received support from other quarters. In January, Reginald Pole, then studying in Paris, spoke out against the King, after having once used his influence to cause a division of opinion in Henry's favour in the Faculty of Theology at the Sorbonne over the question of the validity of the royal marriage. Henry ordered Pole to explain himself, which he wisely refused to do; later the King tried to gain Pole's support for his reforms, but again, Pole proved uncooperative. In June 1532, John Fisher, Bishop of Rochester, preached a sermon in favour of the rights of the Queen, thereby incurring the King's grave displeasure. And in February that year, Archbishop Warham, fearing an earthly king less than a celestial one, formally protested in Parliament against all legislation passed since November 1529 that was derogatory to the Pope's authority, thereby effectively denying the royal supremacy. This was a setback for the King, but he let it pass, for Warham could not live much longer. But he could not silence his own sister, the Duchess of Suffolk, who, in April 1532, used what Chapuys called 'opprobrious language' about Anne Boleyn, and who still stayed away from court on her account. Nevertheless, finally, Mary Tudor would be reconciled to the King before her tragic early death in June 1533, and would tell him in her last letter that 'the sight of your Grace is the greatest comfort to me that may be possible.' Lastly there was Chapuys, who was still as zealous as ever in the Queen's cause. He had even obtained an assurance from the Earl of Shrewsbury, Keeper of the Queen's Crown, that he would not allow it to be placed on any other head than Katherine's.

There were signs in 1532 that the government meant to deal harshly with those who persisted in supporting the Queen. In August, Maria de Salinas, Lady Willoughby, Katherine's closest friend, was ordered to leave her household and not communicate with her royal mistress. And in that same month, Thomas Abell was sent to the Tower of London for publicly upholding Katherine's cause. However, he was released at Christmas, with a stern warning not to meddle in the King's matrimonial affairs. Most ominous of all was Katherine's separation from her daughter. In January, Mary had made a much publicised visit to her mother at Enfield, Henry being anxious to placate his subjects. When the visit ended neither mother nor daughter realised that they would never be allowed to meet again. It suited the King to keep them apart; now that Mary was growing older, he feared they might well intrigue with the Emperor against him. Besides, keeping Katherine from seeing Mary was a good way of punishing her for her obstinacy.

And there were other ways, too. In May 1532, the King ordered Katherine to leave The More and move to the palace at Bishop's Hatfield in Hertfordshire, a red-brick edifice built in the late-medieval style by Henry VII's chief minister, Cardinal Morton, in 1497. Built around a courtyard – all that remains nowadays is one wing containing the great hall – it was a royal enough residence that would later be used as a nursery palace for the King's children. Katherine was installed there by the end of June, but she did not stay long, for on 13 September, Henry sent her to Enfield, where she would be less comfortably housed. She went meekly enough, still holding firmly to her conviction that she was right.

In June 1532, England and France signed a mutual treaty of alliance. Henry now expected to be able to count on Francis I's support when it came to dissolving his marriage and marrying Anne Boleyn, and the two Kings agreed to meet at Calais in the autumn to discuss those matters and to formulate their policy towards the Emperor. In the summer, Henry told Chapuys that he meant to marry Anne as soon as possible, and would celebrate their nuptials in 'the most solemn manner'. Yet for a while it seemed there might be an impediment to their union. The Countess of Northumberland was petitioning Parliament for a divorce from her husband, Anne's former suitor Henry Percy, on the grounds that there had been a precontract between him and Anne Boleyn. Henry had Percy closely questioned by the Archbishops of Canterbury and York, who made him swear solemnly on the Blessed Sacrament that there had never been such a precontract. Parliament, accordingly, threw out his wife's petition, and the unhappy marriage of the Percys had perforce to continue.

In August, Henry took Anne on a progress with him through the southern counties, but was forced to cut it short as a result of the hostility shown by the crowds who lined the roadsides and hurled abuse at her. Some cried out that he should take back the Queen, others that Anne was a whore and a heretic. 'The Lady is hated by all the world,' observed Chapuys with satisfaction. It was around this time that Anne found a book of prophecies in her apartments at Whitehall, obviously left by one of her enemies for her to find for one crude picture showed her with her head cut off. Anne was unperturbed, and told her maid of honour, Anne Saville, that she thought it 'a bauble', adding that she was resolved to marry the King 'that my issue may be royal, whatever will become of me'.

On 22 August 1532, Archbishop Warham died, and the King wasted no time in appointing Thomas Cranmer to the vacant See of Canterbury. Chapuys wondered if the Pope knew of 'the reputation Cranmer has here of being devoted heart and soul to the Lutheran sect', a reputation that was not undeserved, although the new Archbishop had to keep his heretical views a strict secret from Henry. 'He is a servant of the Lady's,' the ambassador informed his master, 'and should be required to take a special oath not to meddle with the divorce [*sic*]. It is suspected that the new Archbishop may authorise the marriage in this Parliament.'

Of course, Cranmer had every intention of meddling with the annulment, not only because he believed in it, but because his appointment was enthusiastically supported by the Boleyns, whose chaplain he had been; the new primate had a sincere affection for Anne Boleyn, and saw her as a means whereby he might push through the ecclesiastical reforms that were so dear to him. The Queen, like Chapuys, regarded his promotion as ominous, and was also concerned about her daughter, having heard that Anne Boleyn's enmity towards the Princess was as great as it was towards herself. It was said that the King dared not praise Mary in Anne's presence for fear of provoking her vicious temper, and that she had made spiteful remarks about the girl. By September 1532, Henry was having to keep his visits to Mary as brief as possible because Anne was so jealous, and not long afterwards she was boasting that she would have Mary in her own train and might one day 'give her too much dinner, or marry her to some varlet'. Chapuys, hearing her, was concerned, remembering the attempt on Bishop Fisher's life; he had no doubt that Anne was perfectly capable of putting her threats into effect.

Henry VIII took the first step towards making Anne Boleyn his queen on Sunday, 1 September 1532. On that day, at Windsor Castle, he bestowed upon her a peerage in her own right, something that had never before been granted in England to a woman. He created Anne Marquess – using the male style – of Pembroke, Pembroke being a title borne in the fifteenth century by Henry's great-uncle, Jasper Tudor. The ceremony of ennoblement was performed with great pomp, with the King enthroned in his vast presence chamber attended by the Dukes of Norfolk and Suffolk and the lords of his Council, while Anne was conducted into his presence by a great train of courtiers and ladies. She had on a surcoat of crimson velvet beneath a short-sleeved overgown trimmed with ermine – traditional robes of nobility of a style dating from the fourteenth century – and her hair hung loose down her back. She curtsied three times as she approached the King, then knelt, as the Letters Patent conferring her new title were read out. As the herald spoke, the King placed a crimson velvet mantle of estate about her shoulders and a golden coronet on her head. She then gave him humble thanks, and retired to the sound of trumpets. Afterwards, she and Henry heard mass in St George's Chapel, where a *Te Deum* was sung in honour of the occasion.

The wording of the patent of creation left some room for speculation, however, as the phrase 'lawfully begotten' had been omitted when referring to the male issue to whom the title might one day descend. Some thought this an indication that Henry had tired of Anne and was pensioning her off and providing for any bastard she might bear him, but this was not the case. Henry was enhancing Anne's status for the coming French visit, and the unusual wording of the patent was devised to ensure that any child conceived out of wedlock would be provided for in the event of the King dying before his marriage to Anne took place. This was highly significant: it could only mean that Anne had at last surrendered to the King.

Henry's and Anne's sexual relationship had begun only a short time before, probably during the previous week. The death of Archbishop Warham on 22 August had broken Anne's resolve to remain chaste, for she knew that it would now only be a matter of time before the King was free to marry her. Thus she took a final gamble, and it was this, not her imminent dismissal, as some courtiers speculated, that prompted her ennoblement. The ceremony on 1 September was arranged at very short notice, so that Anne would have rank and financial security if the King died suddenly.

Those who had predicted Anne's fall were soon to be speedily disappointed. The consummation had only enhanced Henry's passion, and the Venetian ambassador was amazed at his 'great appetite' for Anne. 'The King cannot leave her for an hour,' wrote Chapuys, and it was true: Henry was more infatuated than ever, if that were possible. Thereafter, he and Anne would live together quite openly; in December, the Venetian envoy reported that 'the King accompanies her to mass – and everywhere'.

Undoubtedly, the sexual relationship between Anne and Henry was to begin with a very satisfactory one. Henry was an attractive man. In the despatches of the Venetian ambassadors we find that 'in this eighth Henry, God has combined such corporeal and intellectual beauty as to astound all men! His face is angelic rather than handsome, his head imperial and bald, and he wears a beard, contrary to English custom.' He had a 'bold address', and still excelled with ease at

> manly exercise: he sits his horse well, jousts, wields the spear, throws the quoit, and draws the bow admirably. He plays at tennis most dextrously. He has an air of royal majesty such has not been witnessed in any other sovereign for many years.

Anne was certainly not immune to Henry's charm, and he found in her a bedmate at once loving and adventurous – perhaps too adventurous, in fact, for he would later declare with disgust that she had been 'corrupted' in France in her youth. The discovery that she had had some sexual experience after all, though it may be that she was still technically a virgin, was doubtless a disconcerting one for Henry, especially after Anne's constant protestations that she meant to preserve her virtue until she married. However, at this stage of their relationship he was too much in love to let it concern him overmuch; though in time to come this would undoubtedly be one of the grounds for his disillusionment with her.

With her marriage reported to be imminent, Anne had gathered her own court about her, and in its inner circle were young people with wit, charm and intelligence who could be guaranteed to ensure that life was never dull. Among them were Anne's brother, Lord Rochford, of whom she was very fond, his wife, the former Jane Parker – with whom he was not happily matched – Sir Francis Bryan – known, with good reason, as 'the Vicar of Hell' – Sir Francis Weston, William Brereton, Sir Thomas Wyatt, and various relations of the Boleyns and their supporters. The older nobility, who as a rule represented the more conservative element at court, were not welcome and resented their exclusion.

There were now only a few weeks to go before the French visit. Henry had expressed a desire for Anne to accompany him as his future queen, and she threw herself happily into preparations for the trip to Calais, confident that Francis I, once her admirer and now Henry's friend and ally, would surely support her forthcoming marriage. There was just one formality to be disposed of, and that was the vexing question of which royal lady would receive Anne in France. Queen Eleanor was the Emperor's sister, and refused to do so; besides, Henry was adamant that 'he would as soon see the devil as a lady in Spanish dress'. Nor would Francis's sister, now Queen of Navarre – whom Anne had known well and admired when she lived at the French court – agree to go to Calais; in fact she delivered a humiliating snub by refusing to have anything to do with one whose behaviour was the scandal of Christendom.

The bickering went on for weeks. Without any lady of rank to receive her, Anne could not go officially to France. King Francis was at pains to find a solution that pleased everybody and would soothe the ill feeling among all the ladies involved, and, at the last minute, suggested that his *maîtresse en titre*, the Duchess of Vendôme, do the honours. It never occurred to Henry that most people regarded Anne as his *maîtresse en titre*, and he angrily protested that this would be an insult to Anne and her ladies. At last, it was decided – with reluctance on both sides – that Anne would remain in Calais while Henry went to meet King Francis in French territory. There was no question of her being left behind in England – Henry wanted her with him, and many people thought they would secretly marry while in France, for which reason the trip was not popular at court. But Anne Boleyn, hearing the rumours, made it very clear that she would not consent to being married abroad; she wanted to enjoy the moment of her triumph in England.

She and Henry spent the weeks before their departure at Hanwell, where they hunted daily, and here Anne conceived the idea of further humiliating the Queen. She told Henry that she wished to take to France those jewels that were the official property of the queens of England which were still in Katherine's possession; some of them were centuries old, and of great historical importance. Henry dutifully sent a messenger to Katherine demanding that she deliver them to him. These jewels were of particular significance to Katherine; although they were Crown property, and not her own, she considered it her right, and hers alone, to wear them. She therefore refused to surrender them without the King's express command in writing, saying that to do so would 'weigh upon my conscience'. Nevertheless, she had no choice but to do so when the King's written order came.

Katherine was well aware that Anne Boleyn was behind Henry's harsh treatment of herself, and knew she would try to humiliate her at every turn. Proof of this was forthcoming that same month, when Anne appropriated the Queen's barge with Henry's knowledge and consent. Afterwards, without consulting him, Anne had Katherine's coat of arms deliberately defaced as belonging to a usurper before it was burnt off. When he learned of this, the King was 'very much grieved', and Chapuys commented: 'God grant that she may content herself with the said barge, the jewels, and the husband of the Queen!'

On 7 October, Henry and Anne, with a vast train, left Greenwich and began their journey to Dover. At Canterbury, the Nun of Kent was waiting for them. Anne had seen her two months earlier, when the Countess of Wiltshire had suggested she neutralise the Nun by making her one of her waiting women, but Elizabeth Barton made no secret of her distaste and turned down the position. In Canterbury she repeated her prophecies, though the King ignored her, and went on his way, but after he had gone to France, she continued to speak

239

out publicly in favour of the Queen, and large crowds came to hear her. Cromwell, whom Anne Boleyn called 'her man', now had her under surveillance, and was waiting to pounce.

Henry and Anne sailed to France in the *Swallow* on 10 October; the voyage took seven hours. They were welcomed in Calais by a deputation of civic dignitaries led by the Governor, and conducted in procession to the Church of St Nicholas, where they heard mass. They then took up residence in the Exchequer Palace, where they had interconnecting bedchambers. There followed a week of merry-making before, on 21 October, Henry rode out of Calais to meet Francis I and discuss with him his nullity suit. Francis showed himself sympathetic, and at Henry's invitation, he came to Calais on Friday, 25 October, as the King's guest. For two days, Anne Boleyn kept out of sight, but on the Sunday evening, when the supper table had been cleared, she made her entrance, accompanied by seven ladies in gorgeous gowns and masks; her own outfit was of cloth of gold slashed with crimson satin, puffed with cloth of silver and laced with gold cords. She advanced boldly to King Francis and led him out to dance, the other ladies following suit with King Henry and the other gentlemen present. Henry took great pleasure in removing the ladies' masks, and after the dancing Francis spent some time in conversation with Anne. Two days later, he left Calais. The English court stayed on at the Exchequer for another fortnight, while Henry and Anne enjoyed what was effectively their honeymoon. The Milanese ambassador to the French court, seeing them together, thought they had already married in secret, and referred to Anne as 'the King's beloved wife' in dispatches. The idyll came to an end at midnight on Tuesday, 11 November, when a convenient wind made departure for England imperative. The lovers took ship for Dover, and then made their way to Eltham Palace.

Now that she was the King's mistress, Anne realised that becoming pregnant would both consolidate her position and expedite her marriage. Her hopes of this were awakened during the Christmas festivities at Whitehall, and with the coming of the new year of 1533, hope turned to certainty: she was, indeed, pregnant. When the King learned of it, he made up his mind that they should be married at once. As far as he was concerned, he had never been lawfully married to Katherine, and was therefore a free man. The best scholars in Europe had said so.

Just before dawn, on the morning of 25 January 1533, a small group of people gathered in the King's private chapel in Whitehall Palace for the secret wedding of the King to Anne Boleyn. The officiating priest was either Dr Rowland Lee, one of the royal chaplains, or – according to Chapuys – Dr George Brown, Prior of the Austin Friars in London and later Archbishop of Dublin. As Lee was preferred to the bishopric of Coventry and Lichfield in 1534, he seems to have been the likelier choice. There were four, possibly five, witnesses, all sworn to secrecy: Henry Norris and Thomas Heneage of the King's privy chamber, and Anne Savage and Lady Berkeley, who attended Anne. William Brereton, a groom of the chamber, may also have been present. Thus, in a hushed ceremony quite unlike the one she had hoped for, Anne Boleyn become Henry VIII's second wife.

Although their marriage and Anne's pregnancy remained strictly guarded secrets for some time, neither Henry nor Anne could resist dropping hints about what had happened, and Chapuys took them so seriously that he was thoroughly alarmed. Anne Boleyn was going about in a mood of high elation and, in February, Chapuys heard her say to Thomas Wyatt, before a large crowd of courtiers, that she had

> an inestimable wild desire to eat apples, such as she has never had in her life before, and the King had told her it was a sign she was with child, but she had said it was nothing of the sort. Then she burst out laughing loudly.

Wyatt, whose desire for Anne was long since 'sprung and spent', told Chapuys afterwards that he was ashamed of her. A few days later, Anne told Norfolk that if she did not find herself pregnant by Easter, she would go on a pilgrimage to Our Lady of Walsingham. On 24 February, she and the King held a great banquet at Whitehall. Henry behaved like a bridegroom; Chapuys watched him fawning upon Anne and showing every sign of uxoriousness. By the end of the evening he was very drunk and roaring with laughter; much of what he said was incoherent, yet the Duchess of Norfolk heard him refer to Anne Boleyn's 'great dowry and a rich marriage' – waving his hand to indicate their sumptuous surroundings.

During that month, the Privy Council once again examined the facts of the King's case, and recommended that he proceed at once 'to his purpose by the authority of the Archbishop of Canterbury' and the Queen was officially informed of Henry's intentions.

Katherine had spent a wretched Christmas in isolation at Enfield, and the news filled her with dread. Little information reached her nowadays. She was forbidden to communicate with Chapuys, but both defied this order whenever possible, although it was difficult for Katherine, as she knew Cromwell's spies were watching her. In January, she had got a message through to the ambassador, begging him to press for a papal sentence on her case, and saying she took full responsibility for the consequences. Even if the King refused to return to her, she would 'die happy' if their marriage was decreed good and valid, knowing that the Princess Mary would not lose her place in the succession. Furthermore, she believed the people of England would support a papal decision in her favour.

In February, when the King had decided to proceed to the annulment of their marriage, Katherine was ordered to move to Ampthill. As this new abode was some way from London, the move amounted to virtual banishment, which Henry hoped would break the Queen's resistance. Built in the early-fifteenth century, Ampthill had hitherto been a favoured residence of the court while on progress. Nothing remains of it today, for it was demolished in 1616, and by the eighteenth century only traces of the gardens could be seen. Katherine had been there several times, and tried with good grace to make herself feel at home. Yet she would not be left untroubled in her new home for long, for in early March Henry sent a deputation to Ampthill in another vain attempt to make her withdraw her appeal to Rome.

The Pope had several times threatened Henry with excommunication, yet even the threat of this, the most dire sentence that could be meted out to a devout Christian, did not move the King. Nor did appeals to take back Katherine and dismiss Anne. When the papal nuncio ordered Henry, in the Pope's name, in January 1533, to recall Katherine to court, Henry refused 'for good reasons', notably 'her disobedience and her severity towards me'. In February, the Pope and the Emperor concluded a new alliance, and Clement promised Charles that the Queen's case would be heard in Rome and nowhere else. Yet no date was set.

Charles V was then fully occupied with driving back the Turks from the eastern borders of his Empire; he had for the present neither the leisure nor the resources to invade England on his aunt's behalf. This, and the knowledge of Anne Boleyn's advancing pregnancy, prompted Henry VIII to the decision that now was an opportune moment to resolve his marital problems. Moreover, it was essential that the succession of Anne's child be lawfully assured, for the infant's rights must be undisputed from the first. What Henry was planning was for a time kept entirely confidential. Anne's brother Rochford was sent to France on 13 March with a secret message for Francis I, but no one knew what it was. After his return on 7 April, the King summoned his Council and informed them that he had married Anne Boleyn two months ago, and that she was carrying in her womb the heir to England. On hearing this staggering news, the Council advised the King to inform Queen Katherine at once. Henry chose Norfolk and Suffolk to perform the unpleasant duty, and on 9 April they saw Katherine at Ampthill and warned her she must not attempt to return to the King, seeing that he was married. From henceforth, she was told, she was to abstain from the title of Queen and be referred to as the Princess Dowager of Wales. The King, in his generosity, would allow her to keep her property, although he would not pay her servants' wages or her household expenses after Easter. Katherine took the news quite calmly, although her inner turmoil must have been considerable. Afterwards, she told her chamberlain, Lord Mountjoy, that as long as she lived she would call herself Queen of England. Failing food for herself and her servants, she would go out and beg 'for the love of God'.

When Chapuys heard that Katherine had refused to allow her servants to address her as anything but Queen, he resolved never to refer to Anne Boleyn by that title, and he urged Charles V to declare war on Henry VIII, reminding him of

the great injury done to Madam your aunt. Forgive my boldness, but your Majesty ought not to hesitate. Your Majesty must root out the Lady and her adherents. When this accursed Anne has her

243

foot in the stirrup, she will do the Queen and the Princess all the hurt she can, which is what the Queen fears most.

Charles was in no position to act; he had enough to do in fending off the Turks. However, the English government had no means of knowing where his priorities lay, and even the King anticipated trouble with the Emperor, fearing that he might have brought England to the brink of war by marrying Anne. He knew also that public opinion was not with him.

None of these things deterred him. One by one he had removed all the obstacles in his way, and he would remove any others that presented themselves. When, on 11 April 1533, Archbishop Cranmer requested permission to proceed to the 'examination, final determination and judgement in the said great cause touching your Highness', Henry VIII wasted no time in granting his request.

10

Happiest of Women

The eve of Easter Sunday fell on the 12th of April in 1533. On that Saturday morning, Anne, dressed in robes of estate and laden with diamonds and other precious stones, proceeded as Queen of England to her closet to hear mass; sixty maids of honour followed her. At last she had achieved her chief ambition, and she had adopted for her motto the legend 'Happiest of Women'. Her success now seemed assured, and she was confident that the child she carried would be the son for which the King had always craved.

The court looked on with ill-concealed dismay. According to Chapuys, even some of Anne's own supporters felt that the King should have waited for his marriage to Katherine to be formally dissolved before taking another wife. The King, sensing that his nobility were less than enthusiastic about their new queen, commanded them to pay court to her, announcing that he would have her crowned on Whitsunday, 1 June. Within days, the Lord Mayor of London would have been ordered to prepare a lavish civic welcome, with pageants, for the occasion. Henry had taken an irrevocable step; he might have gained his heart's desire, but he now had to face the consequences to himself and his kingdom and the censure of most of Europe.

On the evening of 12 April, the King authorised Cranmer to pass judgment on his union with Katherine, believing, rather naïvely, that his marriage to Anne would put an end to any opposition from the former Queen. He also set about appointing the officers of the new Queen's household: Lord Burgh was to be chamberlain, Edward Baynton vice-chamberlain, Anne's uncle Sir James Boleyn of Blickling would be chancellor, and John Uvedale secretary. Another Boleyn relative, William Cosyn, was master of her horse. Her ladies included Anne Saville, Anne Gainsford (now Lady Zouche), Lady Berkeley, Jane Seymour (who had served Katherine of Aragon), Anne's cousin Madge Shelton, and Norfolk's mistress Elizabeth Holland. As soon as all these had sworn their oaths of allegiance, Queen Anne summoned them to attend the first meeting of her council, and exhorted them to be virtuous and discreet. Male servants were forbidden to frequent brothels, on pain of instant dismissal.

On 15 April, Chapuys saw the King and tackled him on the subject of his marriage to Anne. 'I cannot believe that a prince of your Majesty's great wisdom and virtue will consent to the putting away of the Queen,' he said. 'Since your Majesty has no regard for men, you should have some respect for God.' 'God and my conscience are on good terms!' retorted Henry. Chapuys tried further remonstration, but to no avail. 'You sting me!' cried the King, at which the ambassador apologised, knowing he would never be able to help Katherine if he fell foul of Henry. But he had already overstepped the mark, for in May he was summoned before the Privy Council and warned not to meddle further in the Queen's affairs, an order Chapuys chose to ignore.

News of the King's new marriage spread quickly; it was anything but well received. Courtiers and subjects alike resented Anne. Her elevation to queenship spelled disaster for Anglo-Flemish trade, and might well plunge the country into a war with the Emperor. Moreover, by her behaviour she had alienated many people who might have supported her.

In April, there was a spate of public protests against the marriage: a priest, Ralph Wendon, was hauled before the justices for saying that Anne was 'the scandal of Christendom, a whore and a harlot'; another priest in Salisbury, commending the King's new wife to his flock, suffered greatly at the hands of his female parishioners. When, at the end of the month, the order went out that Queen Anne was to be prayed for in churches, one London congregation walked out in disgust: the Lord Mayor later suffered a reprimand when the King learned of it. The Dean of Bristol lost his office for forbidding his priests to pray for Henry and Anne. Some people even suffered imprisonment for slandering the new Queen, such as Margaret Chancellor, who had not only cried out 'God save Queen Katherine!' but had also called Anne 'a goggle-eyed whore'.

The King was determined that those who spoke out against him would be silenced, and the government made strenuous efforts to eradicate seditious talk. In May, it issued the first of a series of propaganda tracts designed 'to inform his Grace's loving subjects of the truth'. His Grace's loving subjects were not impressed.

Abroad, news of Anne's elevation met with little enthusiasm. Cromwell's agents in Antwerp informed him that a cloth picture of the new Queen had been pinned obscenely to a portrait of Henry VIII; and in Louvain, students were scratching scurrilous slogans about Henry and Anne on the walls and doors.

On 15 April, Katherine's chamberlain, Lord Mountjoy, received a message from the King, bidding him warn the Princess Dowager that she would soon be retired to a smaller house, there to live on a reduced allowance which Chapuys feared would not be enough to cover the expenses of her household for three months. Chapuys was, in fact, very anxious about Katherine's future, having perceived that her very existence posed a threat to Anne Boleyn's security. The ambassador realised that the King's subjects were too frightened to intervene on Katherine's behalf, while he knew that Anne could be vindictive and that her influence over the King was enormous. If Chapuys was not mistaken, malignant forces were already at work against Katherine, and on 16 April he warned Charles V that the King was 'in great hope of the Queen's death. Since he was not ashamed to do such monstrous things, he might, one of these days, undertake some further outrage against her.' It was a well-founded conclusion, given Anne's rumoured involvement in the poison plot against Fisher. Katherine and Mary now posed the most serious threat to her future, and that of her unborn child. What might she not do to them? Katherine herself was aware of the danger threatening her and Mary, and from now on would keep a careful vigil, wary of anything that might be an attempt on her life.

Henry soon learned from Chapuys that the Emperor would neither recognise Anne Boleyn as Queen of England, nor accept any judgement of Cranmer's on his marriage to Katherine. The King remained unmoved, and told the ambassador he would 'pass such laws in my kingdom as I like'. Cranmer, meanwhile, had summoned various divines and canon lawyers to a specially convened ecclesiastical court in the twelfth-century priory at Dunstable, not far from Ampthill. At the end of April, Katherine was cited to appear before this court in May, but ignored the summons because she did not recognise Cranmer's competence to judge her case. Although the recently passed Act of Restraint of Appeals prevented any person from appealing to Rome for any cause whatsoever, Katherine maintained that she was Henry's wife, not his subject, and not bound by his laws. Cranmer declared her contumacious, and proceeded without her.

Six miles from where Katherine now lived the clergymen gathered on 10 May to decide her fate. Several days of debate followed, then – at last – on 23 May, the Archbishop finally reached his decision, and with the assent of the learned divines in the court, pronounced Henry VIII's union with Katherine of Aragon to be 'null and absolutely void' and 'contrary to divine law'. The Pope, said Cranmer, had no authority to dispense in such a case.

Cranmer then dealt with the King's marriage to Anne Boleyn, and on 28 May 1533, from a high gallery at Lambeth Palace, he announced that he had found it to be good and valid. The Dunstable court was then closed. After six long years, Henry finally had what he wanted: Anne was now legally his, and their child would be indisputably legitimate.

Cranmer's pronouncement had come not a moment too soon, for on that very day, Queen Anne was escorted by barge by the Lord Mayor of London and his brethren from Greenwich to the Tower, where she would spend the night before her civic reception and coronation. Norfolk, as Earl Marshal, had been put in charge of the arrangements, but so fraught was the relationship between himself and his niece that by the time Anne left Greenwich they were barely on speaking terms. On that day, the much tried Duke confided to Chapuys that he had always opposed the King's marriage to Anne – which was a lie – and had tried to persuade the King therefrom – an even bigger lie. He even went so far as to praise Katherine of Aragon for her 'great modesty, prudence and forbearance, the King having been at all times inclined to amours'. Anne, of course, was neither modest, prudent, nor forbearing, but she had arranged brilliant marriages for two of Norfolk's children – his heir, Surrey, married the daughter of the Earl of Oxford, and his daughter, Mary, married the King's natural son, Henry FitzRoy – and she had persuaded the King to waive a dowry in the case of his son's bride. This went a long way towards endearing her to Norfolk's estranged Duchess, who stopped plotting the restoration of Queen Katherine and returned to court.

In spite of the antipathy of the Earl Marshal towards the Queen, the coronation festivities went as planned. When Anne came to the Tower, the river was full of gaily decorated barges, many of them filled with musicians. Crowds lined the riverbanks to see the water pageants and the Queen's own barge, hung with cloth of gold and heraldic banners, making its stately way along the Thames. At the Tower, Anne was greeted by the King who displayed a 'loving countenance' and kissed her heartily before leading her into the newly refurbished royal apartments where they would spend the next two nights. On the Friday evening, Henry dubbed eighteen gentlemen Knights of the Bath, an ancient ritual normally performed only at the coronations of reigning monarchs.

On Saturday, 31 May, wearing a surcoat of white cloth of tissue and a matching mantle furred with ermine, with her hair loose beneath a coif and circlet set with precious stones, Anne rode in a litter of white cloth of gold drawn by two palfreys caparisoned in white damask through the City of London to Westminster. Before and behind her streamed a great procession of courtiers and ladies, said to have extended for half a mile, and over her head the Barons of the Cinque Ports held aloft a canopy of cloth of gold with gilded staves and silver bells.

Anne's civic reception and the route she followed were much the same as at Katherine of Aragon's welcome to London thirty-two years earlier, and the pageants – staged at great cost to the citizens – were on similar themes. As was customary, free wine ran in the conduits for the crowds lining the streets, children made speeches, and choirs raised their voices in honour of the new Queen. The verses recited in one pageant were composed by Nicholas Udall, Provost of Eton College from 1534 to 1541, and ended in the chorus:

'Honour and grace be to our Queen Anne!' She was wished 'hearty gladness, continual success and long fruition'. 'Queen Anne, prosper, go forward and reign!' she was told and in St Paul's Churchyard the choristers sang an anthem, 'Come, my love, thou shalt be crowned!' The City of London had spared no expense in honouring a queen who was not popular, even commissioning Hans Holbein to design triumphal arches for the processional route, and regilding the Eleanor Cross in Cheapside for the occasion. But although the crowds had turned out in their hundreds, perhaps thousands, their reception of their new queen was cold. They came to stare, not to cheer, and as Anne passed by, smiling and greeting the people on either side, she counted less than ten people who called out 'God save your Grace!' as they had once called to Queen Katherine. Anne's fool, who rode in the procession, was angered by the sparsity of uncovered heads in the crowds, and yelled, 'Ye all have scurvy heads and dare not uncover!' Worst of all, when the people saw the intertwined initials of the King and Queen amongst the decoration, they roared with laughter, crying out 'HA! HA!' When Anne finally arrived at Westminster Hall, to be greeted by Henry, she was upset at the hostility shown her by the crowds. 'How liked you the look of the City, sweetheart?' enquired the King. 'Sir, the City itself was well enow,' Anne answered, 'but I saw so many caps on heads and heard but few tongues.' Chapuys too had sensed the hostility, although he had not been part of the procession. 'All people here cry murder on the Pope for his procrastination in this affair,' he told the Emperor.

Sunday, 1 June 1533 was Anne's coronation day. Dressed in a gown of crimson velvet edged with ermine beneath a purple velvet mantle, and with her hair loose beneath a caul of pearls and a rich coronet, Anne walked in procession from Westminster Hall to Westminster Abbey beneath a glittering canopy of cloth of gold. Following her went a great train of lords and ladies, the yeomen of the King's Guard, the monks of Westminster, bishops and abbots richly coped and mitred, and, finally, the children of the Chapel Royal with the two archbishops. The red carpet along which they proceeded extended right up to the high altar of the abbey, where Anne sat enthroned upon a raised platform. Cranmer performed the ceremony of anointing, then he placed the crown of St Edward upon her head, a sceptre of gold in her right hand, and a rod of ivory in her left, thus effectively crowning her as queen regnant, as no other queen consort has been before or since.

A fanfare of trumpets announced the Queen's return to the Palace of Westminster. 'Now the noble Anna bears the sacred diadem!' enthused the future Bishop of Ely, Richard Cox, an eyewitness, but his enthusiasm was shared by few of his fellow Englishmen. Chapuys thought the coronation was 'a cold, meagre and uncomfortable thing', and the London crowds evidently agreed with him, for again they watched in silence, few bothering to cheer or uncover.

Anne's coronation banquet in Westminster Hall was a lavish affair that lasted several hours. She was seated alone at the centre of the top table, with two countesses behind her, ready with napkin and fingerbowl. She ate three dishes (out of twenty-eight served) at the first course, and twenty-three at the second. As the Knights of the Bath served the food, trumpeters played. When the feast ended, Anne was served wine, comfits and sweets, and gave the Lord Mayor of London her gold cup, thanking him and the citizens of London for their efforts on her behalf. The King also gave them his hearty thanks on the day following. Court festivities continued for some days after the coronation with tournaments, hunting expeditions, banquets and dancing, the courtiers falling over themselves to do honour to their new mistress. Yet, as the French ambassador observed, this was not because they approved of her, but because they wished to gain favour with the King.

Henry had done for Anne all he had promised to do: he had married her and had her crowned with as much pomp as if she were a reigning monarch. It was now up to her to seal her part of the bargain by presenting him with the son which Henry, at forty-two, now needed more desperately than ever, not only to ensure the succession, but also to justify the risks he had taken to marry Anne and break with Rome. The birth of a male heir would bring many waverers and dissidents over to his side, and, he was well aware, it would silence once and for all that infuriating woman at Ampthill.

On the day of Anne Boleyn's coronation, the Nun of Kent was publicly prophesying doom for the King and his new wife, something she had been doing effectively for the last two years. This time the authorities acted, and in July she was brought before Cranmer to be examined. He let her go with a warning not to incite the people with her so-called prophecies, but in August, the Privy Council received a report that she had ignored this, and she was brought before Cranmer again. This time, she admitted she had never had a vision in her life. In September, she and her associates were arrested, having confessed that their visitations and revelations were fraudulent, and in September, the Nun was sent to the Tower. Chapuys applauded Katherine's repeated refusals to see Elizabeth Barton: there could be no suspicion of collusion, although the Council was doing its best to unearth evidence of it, and so incriminate her in the Nun's treasonable activities. But there was nothing to find, and even Cromwell told Chapuys he admired Katherine's prudence: 'God must have given her her wit and senses,' he said. Yet Elizabeth Barton had now said enough to convince the Council that she and her associates were guilty of high treason, and they were made to do public penance at Paul's Cross before being sent back to the Tower.

Others had also expressed their disapproval of Anne Boleyn's coronation. The Marquess of Exeter, the King's cousin, and his wife stayed away, pleading sickness. Henry was not fooled: both were known to be supporters of the Princess Dowager and associates of the Nun of Kent. When the Nun was arrested, Lady Exeter wrote a grovelling letter to the King protesting that she had never meant to offend him, and the Exeters escaped Henry's wrath for the time being. Bishop Fisher had also believed in the Nun of Kent; he was now under house arrest, having been placed there on Palm Sunday, 'the real cause of his detention being his manly defence of the Queen's cause', according to Chapuys. In fact, Henry had wanted Fisher silenced when Cranmer came to pronounce judgement.

In Spain, the Emperor was outraged at the way in which his aunt had been treated, though Chapuys was forced to admit to the Council that his master had no intention of declaring war on Katherine's behalf. At this, Cromwell openly expressed his relief. It was as well the Princess Dowager was a woman, he reflected: 'Nature wronged her in not making her a man. But for her sex, she would have surpassed all the heroes of history.'

The Pope, meanwhile, having heard the shocking news from

England, was realising at last that he ought to act swiftly, and on 11 July, he declared the marriage between Henry and Anne null and void, and threatened Henry with excommunication if he did not get rid of Anne by September. He also annulled all the proceedings of the Dunstable court, and in August issued a brief of censure when he realised that Henry meant to ignore his decrees. Henry continued to take no notice. 'God, who knows my righteous heart, always prospers my affairs,' he told Chapuys loftily.

In May, the Princess Mary was officially informed by a deputation of the Privy Council of Cranmer's judgements. She bravely told them that she would accept no one for queen except her mother, whereupon the councillors forbade her to communicate in any way with Katherine, and would not allow even a note of farewell. For Mary, the long, sad years of trial had begun. Her defiance, inspired by Katherine's courage, had the effect of fanning Anne Boleyn's smouldering resentment into bitter hatred, and also caused an open rift between Mary and her father. Anne tried at first to bribe Mary into submission by sending cordial letters and inviting her to court, asking her to honour her as queen, and promising it would be a means of reconciliation with her father. Mary replied curtly that she knew of no queen of England save her mother, but if 'Madam Boleyn' would intercede for her with the King, she would be much obliged. Anne was furious, but she sent Mary another invitation. Again, Mary rebuffed her, so she moved to the next stage in her campaign, threats. These had no effect either, and from then on it was open war, with Anne publicly vowing to bring down the pride born of Mary's 'unbridled Spanish blood'.

Katherine was not officially informed of the Archbishop's two judgements until 3 July. On that day, another deputation of lords of the Council, headed by Lord Mountjoy, arrived at Ampthill and presented her with a parchment advising her that the King was lawfully divorced and married to the Lady Anne, who was now queen. 'As the King cannot have two wives, he cannot permit the Dowager to persist in calling herself queen,' she was informed. It would be better for her if she accepted this new marriage and recognised Anne as Queen of England – better for everyone, in fact. But Katherine took a pen and, to the horror of Mountjoy, scored through the words 'Princess Dowager' with such vehemence that the nib tore the parchment, which still survives today bearing the marks of its mutilation. 'I am not Princess Dowager but the Queen and the King's true wife!' she cried angrily. 'And since I have been crowned and anointed queen, so I will call myself during my lifetime.' When Mountjoy ventured to remind her that the rightful queen was now Queen Anne, Katherine retorted with scorn that 'all the world knoweth by what authority it was done,' and declared she would abide by no judgement save that of the Pope.

The lords, who had heard her out with growing irritation, then delivered an ultimatum from the King. If she persisted in her obstinacy, he might withdraw his fatherly love from their daughter. Katherine blanched at this, but remained resolute and said she would not yield for her daughter's sake or anyone else's, notwithstanding the King's displeasure. Warned that she was putting herself in danger of the King's anger and its consequences, she replied: 'Not for a thousand deaths will I consent to damn my soul or that of my husband the King.'

Henry was furious at the failure of Mountjoy's mission, and took his revenge by ordering, at the end of July, that Katherine be moved to the Bishop of Lincoln's thirteenth-century palace at Buckden in Huntingdonshire. Part of this building still survives today. When Katherine stayed there, the newer Great Tower assigned to her was already fifty years old, and rendered chilly and uncomfortable by the damp that rose from the Fens upon which it was situated. Katherine and her much reduced household were lodged in a corner turret of the three-storyed red-brick building, which was, by intention, more comfortless than the rest. Buckden was also very remote, and a long way from London and the court. It was surrounded by a secure moat, and located in a wild and desolate area, overlooking the Great Fen. Few people lived in the district, a fact that had not escaped Henry's attention. But if he had hoped to bring Katherine to submission by exiling her to such a place, he was destined to be disappointed. As the former queen's cortège wound its way to Buckden on 30 July, the country people ran after it in hordes, wishing Katherine comfort and prosperity, and professing themselves ready to serve her and, if need be, die for her.

At Buckden visitors were forbidden, by the King's express command, and there was very little money. What Katherine could spare she gave in alms to local poor folk. Nor was food plentiful, and she fasted often, usually for religious reasons. Beneath her clothes, she wore the hair shirt of the third order of St Francis, to remind her of the frailty of the flesh. Her leisure hours were spent on embroideries with her women, fashioning altar-cloths for the churches in the district, but the greater part of her days was devoted to prayer, and it was prayer that sustained her. At Buckden, a room with a window adjoined the chapel, and Katherine would kneel here, day and night, praying at the window. When she had gone, her ladies would find the sill wet with her tears, for she shed many for the loss of both husband and child. Yet her forbearance was remarkable. When one of her women began to curse Anne Boleyn, Anne's greatest rival bade her hold her peace and 'pray for her', for the time would come when 'you shall pity and lament her case'.

Chapuys relates how in August, Anne demanded that Katherine surrender the rich triumphal cloth and christening gown she had brought from Spain. These were in fact Katherine's personal property, and she refused to let Anne have them: 'God forbid I should ever give help in a case so horrible as this!' she exclaimed. Nor did the King press the point. The christening robe remained at Buckden.

In August, the Pope drew up a sentence of excommunication against Henry VIII. Katherine, appalled, wrote to Clement, begging him not to put it into effect, and Clement, for once, heeded her plea. But by September, she was feeling desperate about her predicament. The Pope must be made to give judgement, and soon.

> There is no justice for me or my daughter [she wrote to Chapuys]. It is withheld from us for political considerations. I did not ask His Holiness to declare war – a war I would rather die than provoke – but I have been appealing to the vicar of God for six years and I cannot have it! Write to the Emperor, bid him insist that judgement be pronounced!

She had also heard malicious gossip, designed to scare her, that the next Parliament would decide if she and her daughter were to 'suffer martyrdom'. Bravely, she declared she did not fear it, but what was

ominous to Chapuys was that Katherine's keepers had been instructed
to break her resistance with such threats.

The Queen's pregnancy progressed well. It was made public in May,
when her increasing girth obliged her to add a panel to her skirts.
Being Anne, she complained bitterly about the loss of her figure, but
her father told her bluntly to thank God she found herself in such a
condition. In July, she went with Henry to Hampton Court to rest,
and was reported to be in good health and spirits. Normally at that
time of year Henry would be preparing to go on progress, but in
1533 he stayed near London, hunting, so as to be on hand. He also
ordered prayers for her safe delivery to be said in churches.
Astrologers and seers were consulted by the future parents about the
baby's sex. Only one dared predict it would not be a boy: William
Glover, famous throughout the kingdom for foretelling the future,
told Anne he had had a vision of her bearing 'a woman child and a
prince of the land'. This was not well received.

   In August, the first cracks in the relationship between Henry and
Anne began to appear. With his wife fully occupied with preparations
for the coming child, and perhaps no longer inclined to want his
sexual attentions, the King, who had now settled down in his
marriage to a point where he could be complacent about it, had been
unfaithful. The identity of this fleeting inamorata is not known,
although Chapuys thought her 'very beautiful', and reported that
many nobles had promoted the affair, doubtless to spite Anne.
Whoever she was, the liaison was quickly over. However, Anne
found out. Unlike Katherine, she was not reticent about such
matters, and made a fuss. Henry was irritated to find her upbraiding
him for a passing infidelity; now that they were married, he expected
her to be as meek, docile and submissive as Katherine had been, and
he did not take kindly to her censure. Worse still, he was hurt, for he
had just presented her with a great French bed, part of the ransom for
the Duke de Longueville in 1515, and he made it clear that it was as
well it had already been delivered, for she would not have had it
now, having used displeasing words and shown herself so full of
jealousy. This only made Anne angrier, but Henry cut her short.
Chapuys says he told her she must shut her eyes, 'and endure as more
worthy persons. She ought to know that it was in his power to

humble her again in a moment, more than he had exalted her before.' After this, he avoided her for three days, and then there was much 'coldness and grumbling' between them. Chapuys dismissed this as a 'love quarrel, of which no great notice should be taken', but there was more to it than that. The wheel had come full circle: not a year before, Anne had been the mistress and Henry the servant. Eight months of marriage had changed all that. Henry was now dominant, and he expected Anne, as his wife, to play a subservient role, though, after seven years of having the upper hand, this did not come easily to her. It would be foolish to read into Henry's remarks much more than the bluster of a man caught straying, but all the same they are an indication that he was mentally comparing Anne with Katherine and finding her wanting. Anne had now been queen for five months, long enough for him to realise that she lacked the dignity and circumspection required for success in that capacity, and long enough for her arrogance to begin to irritate him. This is not to say that her spell was wearing thin, merely that marriage had altered the balance of their relationship. Henry was still in love with her, but that did not now preclude sex with other women when he felt the need.

In the middle of August, the King and Queen went to Windsor, then to Greenwich, where Anne took to her chamber to await the birth. 'I never saw the King merrier than he is now,' commented a courtier, Sir John Russell, as Henry occupied himself during the last tense weeks of waiting with his favourite sport, hunting. At last, on the morning of 7 September 1533, in a bedchamber hung with tapestries depicting St Ursula and her 11,000 virgins, Anne went into labour, just as the Duke of Suffolk, whose wife Mary Tudor had died in June, was being married in another part of the palace to thirteen-year-old Katherine Willoughby, daughter of Maria de Salinas, Katherine's close friend. On the face of it, the bride was a strange choice, but the 48-year-old Duke had wanted her when she had been betrothed to his son, and had broken the betrothal to marry her himself. He must have set out with every intention of avoiding his formidable mother-in-law whenever possible, for he had already suffered a conflict of loyalties during his first marriage. As it turned out, though, he forged a satisfactory friendship with Lady Willoughby. His young wife grew up to be an ardent reformist and one of the early luminaries of the Protestant faith.

Suffolk's marriage, however, was completely eclipsed by the events taking place in the Queen's apartments. All went well, the mother-to-be being sustained by the assurances of the physicians and astrologers that her child would be male. A vain fancy, as it turned out, for the infant born to her shortly after three o'clock that afternoon was a girl.

According to Chapuys, both Henry and Anne were disappointed at the child's sex, and Henry was angry that he had been so misled by those paid to make predictions about it. Yet his new daughter was strong and healthy, with Tudor red hair and her mother's features, and her arrival surely presaged a long line of sons. When Henry came to see his wife and child for the first time after the birth, he had had time to reflect on this, and was philosophical when Anne expressed regret at not having given him a boy. 'You and I are both young,' he told her, 'and by God's grace, boys will follow.' It was not perhaps the most tactful remark to make to a woman who had just experienced childbirth for the first time, particularly when he went on to assure her he would rather beg from door to door than forsake her. Their child, he announced, would be called Elizabeth, which by happy coincidence was the name of both his mother and Anne's.

Reaction to the birth was predictable. Chapuys spoke for the Emperor and the rest of Europe when he concluded that God, by sending a daughter, had entirely abandoned the King. The Princess Mary, who had been forced against her will to attend Anne's confinement, was secretly triumphant, knowing that as far as Catholic Europe was concerned Elizabeth would never be regarded as anything other than a bastard begotten and borne in sin by an infamous courtesan. In England too, there was unfavourable comment. The Bishop of Bath's secretary, John Erley, made insulting remarks about the King's apparent inability to sire male heirs. 'I would have gotten a boy,' he boasted, 'or else I would have so meddled with the Queen till my eyes did start out of my head!'

Letters announcing the birth of a prince had already been prepared; now, with an 's' added, they were dispatched abroad. The King ordered a *Te Deum* to be sung in churches, and went ahead with the splendid christening he had already planned for the hoped-for son. On the Wednesday after her birth, the Princess Elizabeth was wrapped in a purple mantle with a long train furred with ermine, and, escorted by the Dukes of Norfolk and Suffolk, was carried in the arms of the Dowager Duchess of Norfolk under a canopy of estate to her baptism in the chapel of the Observant Friars. Neither Henry nor Anne attended, and the central figures at the christening were the baby's godparents, Archbishop Cranmer, the Dowager Duchess of Norfolk, the Dowager Marchioness of Dorset, and the Marquess of Exeter – who, as a supporter of the former Queen, told Chapuys he really wanted to have nothing to do with the ceremony, but did not wish to displease the King.

Inside the chapel, a vast throng had gathered. The font was of solid silver, three steps high, and covered with a fine cloth. Around it stood many gentlemen with aprons on and towels over their shoulders, who received the baby when she was lifted, naked and dripping wet, out of the font by the Archbishop. A brazier burned in a nearby cubicle where she was dressed after the ceremony. Then Garter King of Arms cried: 'God, of His infinite goodness, send prosperous life and long to the high and mighty Princess of England, Elizabeth!' The trumpets blew a fanfare, and the child was brought to the altar, where the Archbishop confirmed her. Then refreshments were served to the guests, and the godparents presented the Princess with gifts, standing cups of gold and gilt bowls with covers.

Now, with the trumpets sounding before them, the procession re-formed and made its way back through corridors lit by 500 torches to the Queen's apartments, where Anne, robed and lying on her great French bed with the King at her side, received her daughter joyfully, and offered the guests more refreshments.

Elizabeth had been baptised with all possible ceremony, yet there were no attendant celebrations. The tournament planned by the King was cancelled, as were the fireworks, and no bonfires were lit in the City of London. Two friars were arrested for saying they had heard that the Princess had been christened in hot water, 'but it was not hot enough'. Chapuys thought 'the little bastard's' christening had been 'cold and disagreeable', but he was viewing it through prejudiced eyes. The fact remained, however, that although Elizabeth was Henry's recognised heir, she had not been welcomed like one.

Anne quickly conceived a deep and protective love for her child, and to begin with hated to let her out of her sight. When she returned to take her place at court, there, by her throne under the canopy of estate, lay her baby on a velvet cushion. She had wanted to breastfeed Elizabeth herself, but Henry was shocked at the notion: queens never suckled their own offspring. A wet-nurse was engaged, and Anne was forced to endure the first break in the bond between herself and her child. In December, when she was three months old, Henry assigned to Elizabeth her own household, and established it at Hatfield Palace, which was convenient for London yet well away from its unhealthy, plague-infested air. Lady Margaret Bryan, who had formerly cared for the Princess Mary, was appointed Lady Governess to Elizabeth, and had the command of a veritable army of nursemaids, laundresses, officials and servants. Chapuys noticed that the child was taken to Hatfield from Greenwich by a roundabout route, via Enfield, 'for the sake of pompous solemnity', and the better to impress upon the people the fact that she was the King's heiress.

The Princess Mary's trials began in earnest after Elizabeth was born. She was deprived of the title of princess, and her household was disbanded. Then, in December, she was sent to Hatfield – not without protest – to act as a maid of honour to her half-sister, whose title she refused to recognise. Her beloved Lady Salisbury was dismissed, and in her place were appointed Lady Anne Shelton and Lady Alice Clere, two female relatives of Anne Boleyn, who had been set to spy on her and generally make her life a misery. Anne, commented Chapuys, had alienated the King from his former humanity and was doing her utmost to break Mary's resolve.

She began her persecution by demanding Mary's jewels, on the grounds that the King's bastard daughter could not be permitted to wear what was meant for his heiress. Nor did Anne approve of the King visiting Mary, and would throw a tantrum whenever he suggested doing so. Once she even sent Cromwell after him to Hatfield, to dissuade him from seeing Mary, but when Henry was leaving, he chanced to look up and saw his daughter on a balcony, kneeling in supplication to him. Deeply moved, he bowed and touched his hat, at which all the members of his retinue followed suit; then he rode away, not daring to defy his wife by actually speaking to Mary. When Anne heard about the incident, she was not pleased.

By this time, Mary was perilously near to breaking-point, and her health had suffered, though four months of misery in Elizabeth's household had only strengthened her determination to defend her rights and those of her mother. This took courage, however, in such a hostile environment. She missed her mother intolerably, and thought of little but escaping from England, though Katherine forbade it, bidding her obey her father in all things save those that touched her conscience.

Henry strayed again sexually while Anne was lying-in after the birth of Elizabeth. At the same time, rumours were circulating in the court that he was beginning to tire of her. In November 1533, the French ambassador noticed that 'the King's regard for the Queen is less'. Disappointment in not having a son may have accounted for this; for all his brave words at Elizabeth's birth, Henry must have felt that Anne had failed him. In less than a year of marriage the magic had worn off to some degree and the King had leisure to wonder why he had risked so much for her, though he would not have admitted as much. He still maintained he had been right to put away Katherine and marry her, but he could see for himself how unpopular Anne was. 'There is little love for the one who is queen now, or any of her race,' reported the French ambassador in November, and in January 1534 there were more outbreaks of treasonous talk, with Henry accused of being a heretic living in adultery and Anne of being a mischievous whore who would one day be burned at the stake. Even the Duke of Northumberland, Anne's former admirer, was overheard by Chapuys saying to a friend that the Queen was a bad woman, which effectively demolishes the myth that he loved her to the end of his days. And when Lord Dacre was tried for treason, having long supported Katherine of Aragon and been one of Anne's most bitter enemies, twenty-four peers and twelve judges, having heard him speak for seven hours in his defence, unanimously acquitted him. The Queen's anger knew no bounds when she heard of this, yet both she and Henry were aware that Dacre's acquittal was symbolic of the general mood.

By Christmas 1533, all was well again on the surface between the royal couple. They exchanged gifts, Anne giving Henry a splendid gold basin encrusted with rubies and pearls and containing a diamond-studded fountain with real water issuing from the nipples

261

of three solid gold naked nymphs. Yet the same festive season saw quite a drama being acted out at Buckden. Early in December, the Princess Dowager had sent a message asking the King if she might move to a healthier house, as her present lodging was hopelessly damp and cold, and her health was beginning to suffer. Of course, this was what Anne Boleyn had intended should happen, and she suggested that her rival be moved to Somersham Castle, near Ely. Henry agreed to this, but when Chapuys protested that Somersham was 'the most unhealthy and pestilential house in England, surrounded by deep water and marshes', he changed his mind and said Katherine should go to the old Yorkist stronghold Fotheringhay Castle in Northamptonshire instead. Unknown to Chapuys, Fotheringhay was in an even worse condition than Somersham, and Henry knew it. Katherine knew it too, and when she was informed of the proposed move, she refused to go there. Henry, goaded by Anne, was equally adamant that she should, and dismissed yet more of her servants, insisting that those remaining must not address their mistress as queen, but as Princess Dowager, the title she refused to acknowledge. To enforce her obedience, the Duke of Suffolk was sent to Buckden with a detachment of the King's guards.

Suffolk did not relish his task. It was December, and he was reluctant to leave the warmth and splendour of a court preparing for Christmas and his bride of three months for a damp, lonely house on the Fens and a mission he found distasteful: harrying a sick woman. He told his mother-in-law, Lady Willoughby, that he hoped he would meet with an accident on the way that would prevent him from carrying out his orders. Unfortunately for the Duke, he arrived at Buckden on 18 December safe and sound, and entered almost immediately into a heated exchange with Katherine, who told him she would rather be torn in pieces than admit she was not the King's wife. This set the tone for the visit. Suffolk told her he had come to escort her to Fotheringhay, at which – without further argument – she withdrew to her chamber and locked herself in. 'If you wish to take me with you, you will have to break down the door!' she cried, and no threats or entreaties could persuade her to come out.

Suffolk dared not force the door, or seize Katherine by force: she was the Emperor's aunt, and there would be repercussions. So he proceeded to the business of dismissing her servants, leaving only a few to care for her needs. Those remaining were ordered in the King's name to refer to their mistress in future as the Princess Dowager, but her chaplains, Father Abell and Father Barker, insisted that as they had both sworn their oaths of service to Queen Katherine, they could not perjure themselves by calling her anything else. Suffolk placed the two priests in custody in the porter's lodge, and wrote to the King, asking what he should do with them.

While he waited for a reply, Suffolk was reduced once again to standing outside Katherine's door and pleading with her to come out. She would not listen, either to him, or to Lord Mountjoy, or to her almoner, Father Dymoke. Suffolk wrote again to the King, telling him her defiance was 'against all reason'; unless he bound her with ropes and 'virtually enforced her', there was no hope of her compliance. He was heartily sick of his mission, having seen for himself how the years of anxiety and sorrow had taken their toll of Katherine's health. Nevertheless, he thought her 'the most obstinate woman that may be'.

Meanwhile, word had reached the local people, via Katherine's departing servants, of what was going on in the castle, and men from the surrounding district began to gather silently outside the walls, armed with scythes, pitchforks and other implements. They did nothing, but watched and waited for any sign of ill-treatment of the woman they still held to be their queen. Suffolk grew uneasy, and wished he had never heard of Buckden. As it was, he was obliged to remain there until 31 December, when he received instructions from the King bidding him leave Katherine where she was and return to court. Henry would graciously allow the Bishop of Llandaff, who spoke Spanish, to remain as Katherine's chaplain. When Suffolk had gone, the labourers dispersed, and Katherine emerged from her chamber to find her rooms stripped of most of their furniture, and the majority of her servants gone.

Suffolk was not entirely an unfeeling man, and when he returned to Greenwich, he warned the King about Katherine's precarious health. Later, Henry told Chapuys she had dropsy, and would not live very much longer. 'I think he would be glad,' commented the ambassador. In fact, Katherine did not have dropsy, but Henry was right on one point: she was already in the first stages of the cancer that would eventually kill her. Henry, who could not have known

263

this, thought her environment was responsible for her ill health, and he callously left her at Buckden in the hope that she would soon succumb to her malady.

Queen Anne conceived again soon after the birth of Elizabeth. At the beginning of December 1533, her family knew she was pregnant for the second time, and her cousin, Lord William Howard, made the news public while on an embassy to Rome, for which he had left England early in December. Care was taken not to weary the Queen, and Archbishop Cranmer warned the reformist preacher Hugh Latimer not to make his sermons longer than an hour and a half, as Anne tired easily. Nor did disturbed sleep help the exhaustion of early pregnancy. Henry had just been presented with a peacock and a pelican, but unfortunately these birds made such a clamour outside Anne's windows from dawn onwards that she could not rest in the mornings. The King therefore found the birds another home at Sir Henry Norris's house in Greenwich – Lady Norris's broken nights were not a matter of state importance. Birds of a different sort found more favour with Anne when, in May 1534, Lady Lisle, wife of the Governor of Calais – who was anxious to ingratiate herself with the Queen as she had daughters she wished to place at court – sent her a brace of dotterels (a species of game bird) and a singing linnet in a cage. 'The Queen liked them very well,' reported Lady Lisle's London agent, especially the songbird, 'which doth not cease at no time to give her Grace rejoicing with her pleasant song'.

In April, Anne and Henry visited their daughter, who had moved to Eltham Palace, and there inspected the preparations that were in hand 'against the coming of the Prince'. That month, Anne's receiver-general reported that she was already showing 'a goodly belly', and she made it known that her chief desire was to present the King with a son who would be the living image of his father.

In March 1534, the King paid Anne the supreme compliment of providing for her to be regent and 'absolute governess of her children and kingdom' in the event of his early death. Then, on 23 March, Parliament passed one of the most controversial pieces of legislation of Henry's reign: the Act of Succession, which vested the succession to 'the imperial crown of England' in the children of Henry and Anne. On 1 May, the contents of this Act were proclaimed in all the shires of England, and the King's subjects were warned that anyone saying or writing anything 'to the prejudice, slander or derogation of the lawful matrimony' between the King and 'his most dear and entirely beloved wife Queen Anne', or against his lawful heirs, would be guilty of high treason, for which the penalty was death and forfeiture of lands and goods to the Crown. Furthermore, it was proclaimed that the new Act required all the King's subjects, if so commanded, to swear an oath 'that they shall truly, firmly, constantly, without fraud or guile, observe, fulfil, maintain, defend and keep the whole effect and contents of this Act'. The oath also required recognition of the King's supremacy. Those refusing to take it would be accounted guilty of misprision of treason and sent to prison. The Crown had thrown down the gauntlet, and it remained to be seen how the people of England would react to the challenge.

Nothing now could save the Nun of Kent. She had been attainted, with her accomplices, of high treason on 20 March, and on 20 April, all five were drawn on hurdles to the gallows at Tyburn and there hanged, cut down while still alive, and beheaded before great crowds. Theirs was the first blood spilt as a result of the 'great matter'. It would not be the last.

Most people, including members of the religious orders, took the oath required by the Act of Succession without demur. Although Anne Boleyn herself was unpopular, the new order in England was welcomed by many, and people flocked to the churches on Easter Day to hear, in the words of Chapuys, 'the most outrageous and abominable things in the world', which presumably included the bidding prayers for Anne and Elizabeth. On 5 May, Convocation met at York and formally renounced its allegiance to the Pope.

Thomas Cromwell, promoted in April to be Secretary to the King, was now in a position that involved him in increasingly confidential business; he was also able to advise Henry on decisions on policy. Though Henry never had the affection for Cromwell that he had had for Wolsey, nevertheless 'Mr Secretary' was to prove extremely useful to him, having successfully planned the break with Rome, and the King congratulated himself on having discovered the man's undoubted ability and potential. Most important of all was the fact that Cromwell was prepared to deal with those tasks that called for a certain flexibility of conscience, and that made him invaluable. Those who wanted to communicate with Henry generally had to go through Cromwell, and hence, though outwardly on good terms with most people, he became both envied and greatly resented. The old nobility despised him for his lowly origins, much as they despised Wolsey, and many feared him, knowing his lack of scruple. His spies were known to be everywhere, and with the King so touchy about his marriage and the royal supremacy, even chance remarks, heard by the wrong ears, might be construed as treason.

Some brave souls were defiant, and refused to take the oath to the Act of Succession. One was John Fisher who was still under house arrest, and had received letter after letter from the King containing 'terrible' words about his opposition to Henry's remarriage. In January 1534, Henry had deprived Fisher of his bishopric, and in March, he was attainted of misprision of treason for having supported the Nun of Kent, and sent to the Tower. Chapuys thought him to be 'in great danger of life', even though Fisher had written to the King protesting his loyalty. In April, Fisher refused to take the oath, and when, in May, Henry learned that the Pope had made the former bishop a cardinal, and was sending his red hat to England, he observed tartly that Fisher would have to wear it on his shoulders, for by the time it arrived he would not have a head to put it on.

Thomas Abell, Katherine's chaplain, was also attainted in March 1534, and sent to the Tower, where he would suffer dreadful privations during his imprisonment. And in April, the King's wrath reached Sir Thomas More, who had likewise refused to swear the oath. More, who had declared himself the King's loyal subject and had denied he had ever been against Anne Boleyn, 'this noble woman really anointed Queen', was arrested, and asked again if he would take the oath. For the second time he refused, and no amount of persuasion could make him reveal his objections. By then, Queen Anne was crying out for his blood, and on 17 April, he too was sent to the Tower, and lodged in a cell above Fisher's in the Bell Tower. His arrest shocked many, given his standing as lawyer, scholar and statesman, and his former friendship with the King. Finally, the Princess Mary's former tutor, Richard Fetherston, went to the Tower in December 1534.

In March 1534, the Pope gave judgement at last on Henry VIII's nullity suit, after seven years of procrastination. As a result of the pressure brought to bear upon him by the Emperor, Clement had reluctantly convened the consistory in January finally to resolve the problem. Katherine, hearing of this from Chapuys, wrote to the Emperor in February: 'Beg His Holiness to act as he ought for God's service. There is no need to tell you of our sufferings. As long as I live, I shall not fail to defend our rights.' For weeks, Clement dithered and prevaricated, until his cardinals lost patience with him and urged him to proceed to sentence. Finally, on 23 March, he pronounced that the marriage between Henry VIII and Katherine of Aragon 'always hath and still doth stand firm and canonical, and the issue proceeding standeth lawful and legitimate'. Henry was ordered to resume cohabitation at once with 'his lawful wife and Queen, to hold her and maintain her with such love and princely honour as becometh a loving husband and his kingly honour so to do'. If he refused, he would be excommunicated. As a final indignity, Henry was required to pay the costs of the case.

When Henry heard the sentence, from the French ambassador, he was visibly shaken, but undeterred. The Pope, he declared, no longer had any authority over English affairs. News of Clement's judgement spread rapidly, and here and there public celebrations were held to herald Katherine's expected return to favour. At Buckden, there was a loyal demonstration of goodwill towards her, and Katherine herself went down on her knees and thanked God. After seven long and bitter years, she was at last vindicated, and now trusted that the King would restore her to her lawful place. Patiently, she waited for a message from him, summoning her back to court, her heart brimming with forgiveness. But no such message ever came, and gradually the bitter truth dawned: nothing had changed so far as Henry was concerned, nor would change. In deep sorrow, Katherine wrote to Chapuys, and came as near as she ever would to urging the Emperor to use armed force to deal with her husband. 'She now realises that it is absolutely necessary to apply stronger remedies to the evil,' wrote the ambassador, but 'what they are to be, she durst not say.' When the Emperor realised that Henry meant to ignore the Pope's judgement, he told his advisers he would not fail 'in what is necessary for the execution of the sentence'. What was necessary, Chapuys told Katherine, was armed force, but Charles had not meant to imply this. He meant to compel the Pope to excommunicate Henry, in the hope that that would bring the English king to his senses. Charles also instructed Chapuys to advise Katherine and Mary to take the oath required by the King, protesting that they were taking it out of fear; 'it cannot prejudice their rights,' he wrote.

From April 1534, Chapuys's reports are full of unspecified dangers threatening Katherine and her daughter. Henry might not countenance the outright murder of his wife and child, but he was not above hounding them to their deaths by ill-treatment, and in this Anne Boleyn aided and abetted him. She also urged the King to put them to death by judicial process, but Henry was too concerned about the consequences to agree to that, although he made threats often enough. There remained poison, and many people, among them Chapuys, believed Anne to be quite capable of using it to achieve her end, while Dr Butts, Henry's physician, believed that unless the King fell ill – when he might be persuaded to listen to the advice of someone other than Anne – the lives of Katherine and Mary were in danger.

Anne's hostility was on a personal level. It was based on jealousy of Katherine's breeding and virtues, which showed up Anne herself in none too favourable a light, on rage that Katherine had dared defy Henry for so long, and on fear, because Katherine and her daughter appeared to be doing their best to oust her own daughter from the succession and herself from the throne. 'Neither the Queen nor the Princess will be safe for a moment while the Cuncubine still has power; she is desperate to get rid of them,' warned Chapuys. He alerted Katherine to the danger threatening her, and told her bluntly that he had heard Anne saying she 'would not be satisfied until both the Queen and her daughter had been done to death by poison or otherwise'.

Katherine exercised constant vigilance to ensure that her food was prepared only by those servants she trusted. At any time now the King's commissioners would come and demand that she take the oath. Failure to do so could mean imprisonment. But when the Archbishop of York arrived to administer the oath to her and her household, Katherine stood firm and, ignoring the Emperor's advice, refused to swear. The Archbishop, who had been briefed 'not to press very hard', was dismayed by the hostility shown him by Katherine's servants, who either refused to take the oath or pretended not to understand English, and in exasperation he dismissed those who proved obdurate.

Katherine's obstinacy provoked the King, at the end of April 1534, to order her removal to Kimbolton Castle in Huntingdonshire, a house built in 1522 of wood and stone. It was a secure residence, access being gained only through an archway on the western side, and would be, in effect, Katherine's prison. Today, the Tudor house is encased in a Georgian exterior, and Katherine's rooms have been entirely remodelled. Two officers of the Crown were appointed her governors, Sir Edmund Bedingfield and Sir Edward Chamberlayne. Her small household would accompany her, and would only remain subject to Bedingfield's approval. Katherine asked if she could be allowed to keep her confessor, her physician, her apothecary, two menservants, and 'as many women as it should please the King's Grace to appoint. I am often sickly,' she told Bedingfield, 'and I require their attendance for the preservation of my poor body.' Her request was granted; fortunately, most of her people were Spaniards who had not been naturalised and were therefore exempt from taking the oath.

Katherine was taken to Kimbolton early in May 1534, and found herself housed in two rooms on the opposite side of the courtyard to the governors' apartments and the great hall. Bedingfield and Chamberlayne kept very much to their side of the house, and Katherine's household of twenty servants had as little communication with them as possible. Bedingfield was not the kindest of gaolers, and he was later to report to Cromwell that 'my fidelity in executing the orders of the King renders me no favourite with the Princess Dowager, therefore she conceals everything from me'. In fact, he hardly ever saw her. A division was apparent in the household from the first, as Katherine refused to speak to anyone who did not address her as queen.

She had been at Kimbolton for three weeks when the Bishop of Durham was sent by the King in another attempt to make her swear the oath. She told him she would never relinquish the title of queen, but retain it till death. The Bishop then threatened her, as he had

269

been authorised to do, with the penalty required by the law for persons who refused the oath, but at this her anger flared. 'Hold thy peace, Bishop!' she cried. 'These are the wiles of the devil! I am Queen, and Queen I will die! By right, the King can have no other wife. Let this be your answer.' The Bishop warned her she might be sent to the scaffold if she persisted in her obstinacy. 'And who will be the hangman?' she retorted. 'If you have permission to execute this penalty on me, I am ready. I ask only that I be allowed to die in sight of the people.' At this, the Bishop backed down, for he had rather exceeded his brief. The penalty for refusing to swear the oath was imprisonment, not death, and Katherine could be said to be suffering that already.

When the Bishop came to administering the oath to Katherine's household, he was neatly outwitted, for the naturalised Spaniards readily swore, in their native tongue, as Katherine had bidden them: '*El Rey se ha heco cabeza de la Iglesia.*' The Bishop had expected considerable opposition, and was surprised at such co-operation. He did not know, however, that, instead of acknowledging the King to be head of the Church, they had merely acknowledged that he had made himself head of the Church!

When the King heard that Katherine had again refused to take the oath, he grumbled bitterly to Chapuys that 'the Lady Dowager is being well-treated in everything, but has very disobediently behaved herself to us'; although he had sent bishops to give her advice 'in the most loving fashion', she had disobediently and wilfully resisted and 'set at naught and condemned our laws and ordinances'. Chapuys, who had his own secret links with Katherine, knew that Henry was lying. It was an alarming situation, and Chapuys was not alone in his concern. He told the Emperor: 'Everybody fears some ill turn will be done to the Queen, seeing the rudeness to which she is daily subjected.' He considered her loyalty to Henry to be superhuman: 'She is so scrupulous, and has such great respect for him, that she would consider herself damned if she took any way tending to war.'

In the spring of 1534, Mary became very ill. Her sickness was undoubtedly the result of sorrow and stress. The ambassador begged the Council to allow Katherine to nurse Mary herself, but they refused. Henry trusted no one these days, and believed that together mother and daughter would hatch a plot with the Emperor to depose him. Cromwell told Chapuys that Mary's present predicament was her own fault, 'and that if it pleased God . . .'. He did not finish, and Chapuys concluded that the King 'really desires the Princess's death'.

In July 1534, recovered from her illness and fortified by a letter from her mother secretly conveyed by Chapuys, Mary refused to take the oath. Lady Shelton, who was present, shook the girl violently in front of the Earl of Wiltshire, who had been sent to administer the oath. 'If I were the King,' she cried, 'I would kick you out of the house! I would make you lose your head!' But Mary stood firm, and when Anne heard what had happened, she wrote suggesting Lady Shelton administer 'a good banging' to 'the cursed bastard'.

By this time, Anne was well advanced into her pregnancy. In June, she was reported to be in good health. The baby was due around the end of July, but before the Queen could take to her chamber, something went wrong and it was born prematurely; it was either stillborn, or died very soon after birth. Such was the secrecy surrounding the event that even the sex of the infant is not recorded – it was probably a girl, and Henry could not afford to lose face a second time. Anne made a quick recovery, but the loss of her child had been a bitter blow and she was very difficult to live with for a time. Late in July, the King and Queen went on their annual summer progress without any official announcement of the end of her pregnancy being made.

During that summer, Chapuys became increasingly concerned about Katherine's health. He had heard that her condition had deteriorated. In July, Henry agreed he might visit her, but had second thoughts about it and sent a messenger after the ambassador, commanding him to return to court, where he was informed by Cromwell that at no time in the future would he be permitted access to the Princess Dowager. In mid-September, when Katherine's illness grew worse, and it was thought for a time that she was dying, Lady Willoughby begged Cromwell for leave to see her, but it was likewise refused. Hearing of his aunt's illness, Charles V questioned the English ambassadors closely about reports that she had been badly treated. Henry personally instructed his envoys to say that the reports lied, and that the Lady Katherine had an honourable establishment with her own servants and money to meet her needs;

as for his daughter, he would deal with her 'as we think most expedient'. Charles was not deceived by all this; he had, after all, read the dispatches of Chapuys, which told an entirely different story.

In September 1534, Anne thought she was pregnant again. Yet her hopes were premature, for on 23 September, Chapuys informed the Emperor that 'the Lady is not to have a child after all.' Relations between the royal couple were not at all satisfactory just then. Once again, at the end of Anne's last pregnancy, the King had been unfaithful. Chapuys reported that the object of Henry's desire was 'a very beautiful and adroit young lady for whom his love is daily increasing'. She was probably one of the Queen's ladies, but her name is unknown. However, the ambassador had hopes that the affair would serve to diminish Anne's influence with Henry. The young lady was known to be sympathetic towards Katherine and Mary, and that could only be to their advantage. The course of the affair was interrupted by the summer progress, but when Henry returned, he renewed his attentions more ardently than before, and without bothering to conceal what was going on from the Queen, whose sexual attraction had begun to pale; Chapuys noted triumphantly that Henry was 'tired to satiety of her'. Thus, when Anne remonstrated with him, and threatened to send the girl away from court, he turned on her and angrily told her that she had good reason to be content with what he had done for her, which he would not do now if he were to begin again. Chapuys did not attach too much importance to these remarks, 'considering the changeable character of the King and the craft of the Lady, who well knows how to manage him'. But Anne did.

With the loss of her second child, she realised she had lost much of her influence, and some good measure of Henry's love. Her French ways of love-making were beginning to repel him and drove him into the arms of other women, while Anne was left facing the bitter fact that only by bearing a son could she revive her husband's love and respect. The diminishing of Anne's influence, noted Chapuys, 'has already abated a good deal of her insolence'. Her gradual fall from favour meant that some courtiers now deemed it safe to visit the Lady Mary; even Anne herself wrote her a conciliatory letter, telling Mary to be of good cheer for her troubles would soon be at an end. She perhaps feared she might one day be in need of Mary's clemency, given the insecurity of her own position.

Anne's discontent and unhappiness were made worse in the autumn of 1534 by the appearance of a pregnant Mary Boleyn at court. It transpired that Mary had secretly married – for love – a young man of little standing and no fortune called William Stafford. This was a highly unsuitable match for the Queen's sister; Wiltshire, learning of it, immediately cut off Mary's allowance, and Anne banished her and her husband from court. It was three months before Mary attempted a reconciliation, and when she did it was by means of a letter to Cromwell, in which she confessed that 'love overcame reason'. Yet while she begged Mr Secretary to help her recover the 'gracious favour of the King and Queen', her letter had a sting in its tail, which perhaps holds a clue as to the true nature of the relationship between the sisters, who had never been close, for it ended:

> For well I might a' had a greater man of birth, but I assure you I could never a' had one that loved me so well. I had rather beg my bread with him than be the greatest queen christened.

The letter, unfortunately, came into the hands of the Queen, and her reaction to it shattered any hopes of a reconciliation, for Anne, naturally, did not take kindly to the obvious comparison with herself. The taunt went too deep. Mary Stafford and her husband were never again received at court, and retired to William's modest house in the country, where they lived together in peaceful obscurity until Mary's death on 19 July 1543.

On 26 September 1534, Pope Clement died, and three weeks later the College of Cardinals elected his successor, Paul III. The new pontiff was infinitely more resolute than his predecessor, and one of his first acts was to threaten to put into effect the sentence of excommunication on Henry VIII drawn up by Clement but never published. Though Henry ignored this, there still remained the ever-present threat that Paul would publish his Bull and incite the Emperor to war: Henry, as an excommunicate ruler standing alone, could not expect aid from the other Christian princes of Europe.

The King tired of his unnamed mistress by the end of October 1534, although Anne knew by now that there were sure to be others. There are hints in contemporary letters that Henry kept several young girls for his pleasure at Farnham Castle, and Norfolk, who knew Henry well, told Chapuys that his master had always been 'continually inclined to amours'. A man called William Webbe was out on his horse near Eltham Palace one day, with his pretty sweetheart riding pillion, when he chanced to encounter his sovereign on the road. The King pulled the girl from the horse and kissed her in front of the aghast Webbe, then took her straight back to the palace with him. Such encounters were purely sexual and did not last, yet there was a strong anti–Boleyn faction at court that would dearly have loved to see Anne displaced, and who did their best to encourage any amorous intrigues of the King.

Anne was now ageing visibly. The portrait of her painted at around this time shows she had already lost her looks. Her once vivacious eyes now regard the world with suspicion, her smiling lips are pinched tight shut, and her cheeks are beginning to sag. The frustration, sadness and stress she had suffered had left their marks on her face, and Henry's desire for her had cooled, leaving him susceptible to the charms of younger women. Anne had bitterly resented Henry's last affair, and had conspired with her sister-in-law Lady Rochford to have the girl removed from court, but the King found out and banished Lady Rochford instead. When Chabot de Brion, the Admiral of France, came to England on a state visit in November 1534, the King made a point of inviting a number of beautiful ladies to court to take part in the festivities. 'He is more given to matters of dancing and ladies than he ever was,' observed Chapuys hopefully. A great banquet was given in the Admiral's honour. The Queen was present; she had for some time been trying to bring about a marriage between the Princess Elizabeth and the Duke of Angoulême, third son of Francis I. If the French were to agree to it, then Anne would have manoeuvred Francis I into recognising her as Queen – which, to her chagrin, he had never done – and her daughter as lawfully born.

Chapuys records that at the banquet, the Admiral sat talking to the Queen while they watched the dancing. Then the King arrived and told Anne he would fetch the Admiral's secretary and present him to her. Moments after his departure, de Brion realised that Anne was no longer taking part in their conversation: she was glancing about the hall furtively. Then, to his consternation, she suddenly burst out laughing. The Admiral, ever conscious of his dignity, asked if she were amusing herself at his expense, but she shook her head, still laughing, although tears were in her eyes as she pointed across to where the King was standing. 'He went to fetch your secretary,' she said, 'but he met a lady, who made him forget the matter!' And she laughed again, but without mirth.

Christmas 1534 was not a happy one. Anne's favourite dog Little Purkoy (from the French word *pourquoi*, presumably because of his enquiring expression), a gift from Lady Lisle, died. A great dog lover, the Queen had 'set much store' by him, and no one dared tell her the sad news until, in the end, the King broke it to her. Yet he was feeling less than sympathetic towards her at the time. She had quarrelled again with Norfolk, exercising her peculiar talent for alienating her supporters; Norfolk told the King she had used words to him that should not have been used to a dog; he, however, had retaliated by calling her 'a great whore'. Once upon a time, Anne might have expected Henry to avenge such a gross insult, but not any more. Henry's view was that she had provoked Norfolk beyond endurance, and he sympathised with the Duke.

Chabot de Brion's secretary, Palmedes Gontier, met Anne at a court banquet on 2 February 1535, and recorded his impressions in a letter to his master sent three days later. He perceived that all was not well. She seemed extremely apprehensive. Three days later he saw her again, and noted how her face fell when she saw that there was no reference in the letters he brought from the Admiral (who had returned to France) to her daughter's proposed betrothal. When the King was out of earshot, she complained to Gontier of the long delay in receiving word on this matter, saying it had 'caused and engendered in the King her spouse many strange thoughts, of which there was great need that a remedy should be thought of'. She could only conclude that King Francis intended her to be 'maddened and lost, for she found herself quite near to that, and more in pain and trouble than she had been since her espousals'. She dared not speak as openly as she would have liked, she went on, 'for fear of where she was and of the eyes that were watching her countenance'. She told

Gontier 'she could not write, could not see me, and could no longer talk with me.' She then left with the King, leaving Gontier to conclude that she was 'not at her ease' and that she had 'doubts and suspicions' of her husband.

It seems Henry had finally realised that marrying Anne had been a mistake. No longer did he see her through a lover's eyes: after two years of marriage, he was well able to regard her objectively, and could see little to impress him. Her arrogance, vanity and hauteur all proclaimed her inadequacy as a queen, and her public displays of emotion and temper were embarrassing. She had succeeded in making enemies of those who might have been her friends, and had displayed an unbecoming eagerness to wreak vengeance upon her enemies. She had probably lied about her virginity, and – worst of all – she had failed as yet to produce a son. Not only did Henry regret having married her, he had also brutally acquainted her with the fact. Yet, given any sign that he was contemplating her removal, the imperialists would be urging him to take Katherine back, something he could never contemplate. For the time being, therefore, Anne must remain; she might yet give him an heir. A son would still solve all her problems, as she well knew, but she told Henry early in 1535 that God had revealed to her in a dream that it would be impossible for her to conceive a child while Katherine and Mary lived. They were rebels and traitresses, she said, and deserved death. Henry failed to rise to her bait, another sign that her power was diminishing.

In February 1535, Mary fell gravely ill, and there were fears she might die. Even the King was alarmed, although he refused to heed his physicians' advice, and Chapuys's pleas, that she should go to her mother for whom she was pining. Katherine, in desperation, wrote to Cromwell, begging him to urge the King to let her nurse Mary herself at Kimbolton: 'A little comfort and mirth with me would be a half health to her.' She would 'care for her with my own hands and put her in my own bed and watch with her when needful'.

In March, Mary's condition worsened, and Katherine's anguish deepened, for she knew her own sickness to be mortal, and once again she begged Henry to let her see Mary. Yet still he refused. 'The Lady Katherine,' he told Chapuys, 'is a proud stubborn woman of very high courage. She could easily take the field, muster a great army, and wage against me a war as fierce as any her mother Isabella ever waged in Spain.' His remarks are proof that he knew very little about Katherine's illness. Fortunately, Mary recovered, and by April she was well enough to rejoin Elizabeth's household which was then at Eltham.

In February 1535, the King found a new mistress, thanks to his wife, who had now come to terms with the inevitable and reasoned that, if Henry had to have an affair, it should be with someone sympathetic to her, and not a member of the imperialist faction. She had therefore deliberately selected her cousin and lady-in-waiting Madge Shelton, who was the daughter of Lady Shelton; Anne persuaded Madge, who seems to have been quite amenable to the arrangement, to encourage Henry's advances. In no time at all, Madge was in the King's bed, where Anne hoped she would use her influence to make Henry a little kinder to his long-suffering wife. However, the short affair resulted, predictably, in Anne once more suffering pangs of jealousy; nor did it improve her situation at all.

By mid-March, though, she was in an altogether happier frame of mind, for she had discovered she was pregnant again. By 24 June, her condition was obvious, and Sir William Kingston remarked that 'she hath as fair a belly as I have seen'. But after that no more is heard of this pregnancy, and it is safe to assume it ended in a stillbirth at around the sixth month at the end of June. Again, details of the confinement were kept secret: Henry did not wish to parade another failure before the world. Nor was Anne's disappointment helped by news brought from France by her brother that Francis I would not agree to Elizabeth's betrothal to his son. Her mood now swung from hopeful anticipation to despair, and then to anger. 'She has been in a bad humour,' wrote Chapuys, 'and said a thousand shameful words of the King of France and the whole nation.' Sometimes she managed to hide her chagrin and grief under a façade of gaiety. Margaret More, visiting her father in prison, told him that there had been nothing else at court but sporting and dancing, and that the Queen 'never did better'.

Alas, it pitieth me to remember into what misery, poor soul, she will shortly come [mused More]. These dances of hers will prove such dances that she will spurn our heads off like footballs, but it will not be long ere her head will dance the like dance.

None knew better than he how easily the King's favour could turn to wrath.

Around this time, Cromwell, earning the approval of the reformists and the Queen, was preparing an enquiry into the abuses said to be rife within the religious houses. Closure of minor houses, or badly run ones, had been commonplace since the days of Henry V, and had accelerated under Wolsey, but this was something of quite a different order. Cromwell meant to have every monastery and convent visited and reported upon, with a view to its possible closure and the appropriation of its wealth by the Crown.

It was a masterful plan, and it had great appeal for a king who had long since squandered his father's fortune and was now desperately in need of funds, and who as its supreme head, was trying to divest the Church of England of the kind of abuses that had corrupted the Roman Church as well as any lingering allegiance to the papacy. It is doubtful if either Henry or Cromwell foresaw the far-reaching social consequences that would result from the closure of a large number of religious houses, nor that they envisaged much opposition from the English people, who had not protested overmuch about the break with Rome. Cromwell was made Vicar General in January 1535, and given permission to arrange for the visitation of every religious house in England. His report on the wealth of the Church – the *Valor Ecclesiasticus* – was compiled by July 1535, and in that month the King's commissioners began their visitations, starting with minor establishments.

Queen Anne vigorously supported the reforms. After she became queen, she had become the focus of all the hopes of those who had secretly embraced the Lutheran faith; they imagined she shared their views, which was not so, although she did constrain the King to be tolerant with heretics. One Protestant, Robert Barnes, who had once fled from England for fear of persecution, was able to return, thanks to Anne's protection, and preached openly in London, unmolested. In 1534, Anne secured the freedom of another convicted heretic, Richard Herman, whom Wolsey had sent into exile for having advocated the translation of the Bible into English, something of which Anne herself was strongly in favour. Not for nothing did Miles Coverdale, in 1536, dedicate his English translation of the Bible to both Henry VIII and 'your dearest wife and most virtuous Princess, Queen Anne': this book, with Anne's initials beautifully embossed on the cover, is now in the British Library. It is a fact that not a single heretic was burned while Anne was queen. Her tolerance was unusual in an age that favoured rigid religious practice. However, it also lent ammunition to her detractors, for, to many, it was proof that she was herself a heretic.

In 1533, Anne had tried to save Catesby Priory from closure at the request of the nuns, and even offered to buy it herself. However, when the King learned that the nuns were unable to support themselves, he was compelled to refuse her request. Two years later, Anne would not have been so anxious to help. In 1535, she sent her officers to examine the famous phial of the Holy Blood at Hayles Abbey in Gloucestershire, which had been revered for centuries; back came the report – it was the blood of a duck, renewed as necessary by the monks who charged pilgrims to see it. The Queen ordered it to be removed from public view, but as soon as her men had gone, the monks put it back, and people still flocked to see it. In December 1535, Anne visited Syon Abbey, and harangued the nuns about their popish forms of worship.

Of the ten bishops preferred to sees while she was queen, seven were of the reformist persuasion, and in this her influence was plain. 'What a zealous defender she was of Christ's Gospel!' John Foxe would write many years later; and the Scots reformer, Alexander Aless would one day tell Elizabeth I that 'true religion in England had its commencement and its end with your mother'. Elizabeth's first Archbishop of Canterbury, Matthew Parker, began his career as Anne Boleyn's chaplain, even though Anne knew he favoured the teachings of Luther.

She was also a patron of the new learning. In 1533, Erasmus dedicated two books to her father, and referred in each preface to 'the most gracious and virtuous Queen Anne'. She also assisted the French humanist Nicholas Bourbon, who had been imprisoned in France for his religious views – Anne earned his undying gratitude for securing his release, and even after her death, when her name was never uttered, he would boldly dedicate one of his treatises to her memory.

As she grew older, Anne consciously cultivated a new image for herself, that of godly matron. She rarely appeared in public without a book of devotions in her hands. She aided scholars, particularly poor ones, and provided money for their education, maintaining several at the University of Cambridge, and she entrusted her nephew and ward, Henry Carey, to the fine tutelage of Nicholas Bourbon. She also helped Wolsey's bastard son, Thomas Winter, when he returned penniless from his studies at the University of Padua, which had been paid for by the King.

Anne's charities were widespread, yet little publicised during her lifetime. She had begun them in 1532, when she had, among other good deeds, sent money and medicine for the relief of the mother of Richard Lyst, a lay brother in the convent of the Observant Friars at Greenwich. Lyst had at one time been much against her, but her kindness softened his heart, and he became such a staunch supporter that other members of the community scathingly referred to him as Anne's 'chaplain'.

Anne gave alms weekly to the poor to the value of 100 crowns, together with clothing sewn by herself and her ladies. Throughout her reign, she discreetly provided also for widows and poor householders, sometimes giving out £3 or £4 for cattle or other livestock. When visiting a town or village, she sent her almoner ahead to find out from the parish authorities if there were any needy families in the district. A list would be drawn up, and the Queen would make grants of money towards their support. After her death, there was found among her papers a list of grants she intended to use for the relief of poor artisans. At the end of the sixteenth century, George Wyatt estimated that her charities had amounted to at least £1,500 yearly for the poor alone. He also commended her work for the poor in providing them with garments she had sewn herself; he had seen with his own eyes examples of her needlework in the fine tapestries on display at Hampton Court; yet, in his opinion, far more precious in the sight of God 'were those works which she caused her maidens to execute in shirts and smocks for the poor'.

In the spring of 1535 the shadow of treason, real or imagined, and the King's wrath with those who opposed his marriage and his policies hung over England. In April, an Oxford midwife was jailed for calling the Queen a 'goggle-eyed whore and a bawd', and a priest, Robert Feron, was also imprisoned for saying that 'the King's wife in fornication, this matron Anne, be more stinking than a sow'. But these were just the little fish. To snare more influential traitors the King would unleash a minor reign of terror, as he demonstrated to his subjects just how terrible his justice – and his vengeance – could be.

In May, the Prior of the London Charterhouse and four Carthusian monks, having denied the royal supremacy, suffered traitors' deaths at Tyburn. Sir Thomas More watched the men being tied to hurdles at the Tower, and noticed that they were 'as joyful as bridegrooms going to their marriages'. Wearing their habits, they were dragged by horses through the streets of London, strung up on the gallows, and left to hang until half-choked. Then they were cut down and revived with vinegar, so that they might suffer the full horrors of the punishment required by the law for treason: castration, disembowelling, and decapitation. After their deaths, their bodies were cut into quarters, which were publicly exhibited. The monks died bravely, before a shocked audience, and news of their end was greeted with horror throughout Catholic Europe. Of course, it was Anne who was blamed for the atrocity. She herself considered that justice had been done, and remained unmoved: one of the condemned men had had the effrontery to allege that Henry had once had an affair with her mother.

On 7 May, for the last time, Fisher and More refused to take the oath. Anne was constantly urging the King to put them to death, and 'when the Lady wants anything, there is no one who dares contradict her, not even the King himself,' wrote Chapuys. Anne was then pregnant, and must be humoured, since when Henry 'does not want to do as she wishes, she behaves like someone in a frenzy'.

In June, more Carthusian monks were executed for refusing to acknowledge the King's supremacy. They were chained upright to stakes and left to die, without food or water, wallowing in their own filth – a slow, ghastly death that left Londoners appalled. In the King's view, such measures were necessary to bring his subjects to heel, and while the monks suffered, he feasted with Anne at Hanworth, and allowed himself to be persuaded that Fisher, too, ought to die for his obstinacy. Two days later, the former bishop was put on trial for treason and sentenced to death, and two days after that, three more monks of the Charterhouse suffered at Tyburn. Fisher himself was beheaded on 22 June 1535 on Tower Hill at the age of seventy-six. A shocked populace blamed Anne for his death, and it was partly for this reason that news of the stillbirth of her child was suppressed – people would very clearly have seen the hand of God in it. Anne herself suffered pangs of conscience on the day of Fisher's execution, and attended a mass for the repose of his soul, though by the evening of the next day she had composed herself sufficiently to stage for the King's entertainment a masque depicting divine approval of recent events in England. Henry was so pleased to see himself cutting off the heads of the clergy that he told Anne she must have the performance repeated on the Eve of St Peter, a day formerly dedicated to honouring the Pope.

The political executions of 1535 gave Chapuys fresh cause for concern over the future safety of Katherine and Mary, who had also refused to take the oaths or acknowledge the royal supremacy. One Monday in June the King sent a deputation of his Council to Kimbolton to search Katherine's rooms for anything incriminating that might be hidden there. The councillors made no secret of their anger at not finding what they were looking for, and at court the advantages her death would bring were spoken of quite openly. On 30 June, Cromwell told Chapuys that 'if God had taken to Himself the Queen, the whole dispute would have been ended, and no one would have doubted or opposed the King's second marriage or the succession.' Fortunately for Katherine, the fear of Charles V, bent upon vengeance, was enough to stay Henry's hand.

Others were not so fortunate. On 1 July, Sir Thomas More was tried for treason in Westminster Hall and condemned to death. He mounted the scaffold on Tower Hill on 6 July, and died bravely by the axe, saying he was 'the King's good servant, but God's first'. If there had been tremors of horror at Fisher's death, there were shock waves now, and they reverberated around Europe, where the consensus of opinion was that Henry had gone too far this time. Even Henry had serious doubts that he had been right, and characteristically he blamed Anne Boleyn for More's death.

Then there was Father John Forrest, a member of the Order of Observant Friars at Greenwich, and a former confessor to Katherine

of Aragon, who had been imprisoned for espousing her cause in
1533. In 1535, he was attainted and sentenced to be burned at the
stake. Katherine, hearing this news, wrote offering what comfort she
could to Forrest, signing herself 'your very sad and afflicted
daughter, Katherine'. He replied promptly, saying her words had
'infinitely comforted me', and asking for her prayers, 'that I may
fight the battle to which I am called. In justification of your cause, I
am content to suffer all things.' However, on the following day, the
King was graciously pleased to commute his sentence to life
imprisonment. For some years to come Forrest would continue to
assert that Katherine had been the King's true wife, and by May 1538
Henry had had enough, sending him to an agonising death at
Smithfield: he was suspended by chains about his arms and waist
above a slow-burning fire, and slowly roasted to death. His
execution provoked murmurs of protest, and the French ambassador
complained to Francis I that he had 'to deal with the most dangerous
and cruel man in the world'. Mary's former tutor, Richard
Fetherston, and Katherine's former chaplain, Thomas Abell, were
also condemned to death in July 1540, their crimes being described as
high treason. Even after both the women involved in it were dead,
his 'great matter' remained a sensitive issue with the King for the rest
of his life.

One person who escaped Henry's clutches was Reginald Pole,
who had condemned the King's marriage to Anne Boleyn in 1533
after choosing exile on the Continent. Still hoping to gain his
support, however, in February 1535 Henry asked Pole if he would
set out in writing his opinions on the King's marriages. It was an
invitation that Pole could not resist, and he spent several months
working on a reply. When it came, it would be so damning, so
offensive to the King, and so provocatively treasonous that Henry's
suppressed dislike of Pole grew overnight into pathological hatred,
and his reaction was ultimately so savage that Pole's friends knew he
would never be able to return to England while the King lived.

With the loss of Anne's child around the end of June, Henry ceased
playing the doting husband. In the summer of 1535 the Venetian
ambassador reported that he was 'tired to satiety' of Anne, and there

were rumours at court that he wished to put her away. Once he accused her of having been responsible for the recent executions, and for having been the cause of all the present troubles in his kingdom. Anne retaliated swiftly, reminding him he was more bound to her than man could be to woman. Had she not delivered him from a state of sin? Had she not helped to make him the richest prince in Christendom? Without her, he would not have reformed the Church, to his own great profit and that of all his subjects. Henry ignored her: Anne had done all these things and more, but she had failed to bear a living son.

Anne's chief consolation nowadays was her little daughter, and she often visited her at Eltham or Hatfield. Sir William Kingston thought Elizabeth to be 'as goodly a child as has been seen', and 'much in the King's favour, as should be, God save her!' Henry too was proud of his red-haired daughter, and liked to show her off to visiting ambassadors, sometimes dressed in rich clothes, and sometimes naked, so that they could see how well formed she was. Elizabeth had been weaned off breast milk at the age of one, at the King's express command, and with the Queen's assent. Orders were relayed from the royal parents through Cromwell to Lady Bryan, who had instructions to approach Mr Secretary on any matter relating to her charge. This meant that Cromwell's duties now ranged from overseeing the closure of the monasteries to approving nursery routines.

Anne was delighted when, in July 1535, King Francis at last agreed to enter negotiations for the marriage of Elizabeth to his third son. Yet it was Mary to whom people were looking when they considered the future. Elizabeth was not yet two, and if anything should happen to the King, Mary would have an infinitely better chance of holding the throne. Even Cromwell decided at this time to lend Mary his support, and discussed with Chapuys the possibility of altering the Act of Succession with a view to naming Mary the King's heir. The Queen got to hear of this, and her anger knew no bounds, but although she threatened Cromwell with execution, he paid little heed: 'She cannot do me any harm,' he told Chapuys.

Only five days after More's execution, Chapuys noted that his Majesty was happily dancing and flirting once again with the ladies of his court. When William Somers, Henry's fool, proclaimed to the court: 'Anne is a ribald, the child is a bastard!', Henry was angry – so angry, in fact, that Somers had to leave court for a while – but he did nothing more, whereas once he would have acted swiftly to punish anyone who slandered his wife.

In the summer of 1535, the King and Queen set off on a progress westwards towards Wales. There was, however, little of the usual holiday atmosphere, for Henry was troubled by news lately arrived from the Continent that the Emperor was about to take Tunis from the Turks, thereby depriving them of a great naval base and stemming the tide of their encroachment upon the eastern reaches of the Empire. What concerned Henry was that, if Charles were successful in this enterprise, his armies would be free to fight elsewhere, and England might be a prime target for invasion. Henry knew he was regarded as a schismatic rebel, and he feared Charles would make this the excuse to interfere on his aunt's behalf.

Late in July, the royal party arrived at Winchcombe; from thence they rode into Wales, and then back through the south-west of England, and so into the county of Wiltshire. On 4 September, Henry and Anne arrived at Wulfhall, a half-timbered manor house on the outskirts of Savernake Forest, where they were to stay for six days. Wulfhall was the home of the Seymour family, hereditary rangers of Savernake Forest, and its present owner was Sir John Seymour, whose daughter Jane was one of the Queen's maids of honour. There is no evidence that Henry VIII's courtship of Jane Seymour began during this visit, yet it is significant that mention was made of it in diplomatic reports within two months, and it may well be that the traditional assumption that it began at Wulfhall is the correct one.

Wulfhall has long since disappeared. In the sixteenth century, it was a substantial house that had already been standing for at least 300 years. The manor of Ulfhall (probably derived from 'Ulf's hall', after a Saxon or Danish thane) was recorded in the Domesday Book in 1086. The house Henry stayed in was built along traditional lines around a courtyard, with a chapel and a recently incorporated innovation, a long gallery, which was quite novel in the 1530s. Surrounding the house were three gardens.

Sir John Seymour was well known to his royal visitor. A man with a sound reputation for being a capable administrator, he had at

time carried out diplomatic missions abroad on the King's
half. He had been Sheriff of Wiltshire since 1508, and Sheriff of
Dorset and Somerset since 1518. He was also a Justice of the Peace
for Wiltshire, and an extensive landowner in that county. The
Wulfhall estate itself comprised 1,270 acres, most of which had been
converted to pasture for sheep, conforming to the prevailing
agricultural trend. For all this, however, Sir John ranked quite low
on the aristocratic scale, and for him this royal visit was a signal
honour.

Sir John, then nearing sixty, was the father of a large family. His
wife was Margaret, the daughter of Sir Henry Wentworth of
Nettlestead in Suffolk; as a young girl at Henry VII's court she had
been a celebrated beauty, and the poet laureate, John Skelton, had
written in her honour a poem entitled 'To Mistress Margery
Wentworth', praising her maidenly virtues and her 'benign, courteous
and meek' qualities. Mistress Margery had been married to Sir John
Seymour around 1500 and for him it was a brilliant match, for
although the Seymours were said to have been descended from one
of William the Conqueror's Norman knights, surnamed St Maur
after his birthplace in Touraine, they had never been more than
country gentry. Their first certain ancestor came from Monmouth-
shire; a branch of the family was already established in Wiltshire at
the end of the fourteenth century, and provided a Member of
Parliament for Bedwyn Magna, the village near Wulfhall. The
manor of Wulfhall had come to the Seymours by marriage to the
heiress of the Esturmi family in the early fifteenth century, through
which they also acquired the hereditary guardianship of Savernake.
Thereafter, they proudly displayed in the manor house the great
ivory hunting-horn, bound with silver, that was the symbol of their
office. Gradually, by lucrative and advantageous marriages, they
had, like the Boleyns, increased not only their land and wealth, but
also their social standing. The marriage of Sir John Seymour to Lady
Margaret Wentworth, however, was the most prestigious of them
all, for Lady Margaret was descended from Edward III and Henry
'Hotspur' Percy, the hero of Shrewsbury. She was, in all respects, a
most desirable wife for a man like Sir John, who was considered to
be one of the foremost in the rising class of gentry known as 'new
men', solid, respectable, loyal to the crown, and owing their status

to wealth rather than breeding. Such men were greatly favoured by Tudor monarchs distrustful of the ancient blood of the older nobility.

Of the ten children born of the marriage, four died young, probably of plague. Two of the surviving sons, Edward and Thomas, were to play prominent parts in English history. The other son, Henry, shunned public life and led the existence of a country gentleman. The eldest daughter, Elizabeth, was a widow in 1535, her husband having died the previous year. The other daughters were Dorothy, later the wife of Sir Clement Smith, and Jane.

Unhappily, there had been a rift in the Seymour family some five years before the royal visit, and the ensuing scandal had shocked even Henry VIII's courtiers. Young Edward Seymour had been sent to court at an early age, and had served as page to both Mary Tudor when she was Queen of France, and the King himself. When still quite young, he had been married to Katherine, the daughter of Sir Edward Fillol. Very little is known about the marriage apart from the fact that Katherine bore two sons, John and Edward, in 1528 and 1529. A year later, Edward was shattered to discover that his wife and his father had for some time been lovers, and that there was every possibility that Sir John had fathered Katherine's two children. Edward's retaliation was swift. Katherine was bundled into a nunnery, where she died within five years. For a time, Edward spoke of divorcing her, though he did not do so, but he disinherited her two boys, and would have nothing to do with them. After his wife's death, he remarried immediately, his bride being the formidable Anne Stanhope, a lady who would rule both her husband and her family with a will of steel, and whose pride would be notorious.

By the time Henry VIII arrived at Wulfhall in 1535, the scandal had died a natural death, and a truce had been called between Edward and his father; Edward's new marriage had done much to mellow his bitterness. The King certainly knew of the affair, but probably felt that the family had suffered enough without his censure. As for Sir John, he must have seen his sovereign's visit as a sign that the past was done with and forgotten.

Although royal visits to private subjects were at this date by no means as crippling financially as they were to become under Elizabeth I, entertaining one's king and queen of necessity called for a

287

substantial outlay to pay for the special fare provided for the royal table, for not only did the royal guests have to be accommodated but their retainers also, and that could mean a good many people. However, the King's charm and courtesy, especially towards the ladies, were well known; Henry VIII was invariably an appreciative and genial guest, laying aside formality and conversing with his host and the family as if they were his equals.

Despite the brooding presence of the Queen, Henry must have enjoyed his stay at Wulfhall, where the excellent hunting to be found in Savernake Forest provided a welcome respite from the cares of state. Sir John was a good host, and Lady Margaret typified all that the King thought a wife should be: meek, decorous, well bred, and, above all, fruitful – unlike Anne in every way.

Jane Seymour was probably the second daughter of Sir John and Lady Margaret. The date of her birth is nowhere recorded, and has until now been estimated as 1509–10. This calculation has been based on two things: a report of the Spanish ambassador, dated May 1536, stating that Jane was then more than twenty-five years old, and a miniature of her painted in the 1580s by Nicholas Hilliard, which gives her age as twenty-five in 1536. The miniature may be discounted as reliable evidence: it was based on one of Holbein's portraits of Jane Seymour, none of which give her age. A far more likely date of birth, based upon sound evidence, would be between October 1507 and October 1508. When Jane was buried with the full honours due to a queen of England in November 1537, twenty-nine ladies walked in he funeral procession: seemingly an odd number until one discovers that it was customary at medieval funerals to mark the age of the deceased in such a way, just as it was traditional to ring the passing bell once for every year the departed soul had spent on earth. On this assumption, Jane was twenty-nine when she died, and a birthdate of 1507–8 would accord with Chapuys's statement that she was over twenty-five in 1536.

This means that Jane was around twenty-seven when the King visited Wulfhall, a very late age to remain single in an era when most girls were married by fifteen or sixteen. There had, at an unspecified date, been talk of a betrothal between Jane and Sir Robert Dormer's son William; Sir Francis Bryan, who was connected by marriage to the Seymours, did his best to promote the match, but met with opposition from Lady Dormer, who seems to have felt that Jane was not a good enough match for her son. Eventually William Dormer was betrothed elsewhere, and it was probably this that precipitated Bryan into securing a position at court for Jane; thus she came to join the household of Katherine of Aragon as a maid of honour sometime during the 1520s.

Jane greatly admired Queen Katherine, and later used her as her own role model when she herself became queen. Katherine's court provided a kind of finishing school for young women of good family, and it was in this learned and pious atmosphere that Jane Seymour grew to maturity. Of her education, we know very little. During her childhood there had been a salaried priest, Father James, at Wulfhall, who may have given Jane some rudimentary lessons along with her brothers. As an adult, she could read and sign her name, but she was not learned as both Katherine of Aragon and Anne Boleyn were, nor was she as intelligent as they. For Jane, an education of a traditional sort had been provided, and it was doubtless her mother – as was customary – who taught her the usual feminine skills such as household management, needlework, and cookery. Jane's expertise as a needlewoman became legendary, and examples of her work still survived a century after her death to testify to her skill. Yet she also enjoyed outdoor sports, having been taught to ride at an early age, and as queen she would enjoy following the hunt.

Jane was just one of many aspiring young women in Queen Katherine's household. She grew to know and like the Princess Mary, eight years her junior, and she would also have known Anne Boleyn well, for she was a fellow maid of honour for a time. By virtue of her position, Jane would have been a witness to the events leading up to the legatine court hearing in 1529, and would have observed at first hand the downfall of the Queen and the rise to power of Anne Boleyn. She certainly saw enough of these things to make her decide that her sympathies lay with Katherine, and, later on, when Katherine was beyond all human help, Jane would extend her friendship to the Lady Mary, in an attempt to make up to her for what she and her mother had suffered.

When the Queen was exiled from the court in 1531, Jane may have been one of those who went with her to The More and ultimately to Ampthill. Yet it is more likely that she transferred to the household of Anne Boleyn at this time: she had certainly joined it by Christmas 1533, and Anne would hardly have accepted someone who had chosen to share Katherine's exile. Like Anne, Jane was ambitious; her family, too, were ambitious for her. To remain in the service of a fallen queen, however much admired, would not have done much for Jane's chances of making her way in the world and contracting an advantageous marriage. Anne Boleyn was at that time amassing a huge train of female attendants, and it would have been easy for Jane, with her experience of the court, to secure a place with her.

At Christmas 1533, Henry VIII presented gifts to several ladies in his wife's household, among them Jane Seymour, whom he had known since she first arrived at court; he would certainly have approved of her timely transfer to Anne's service. Yet it was not until September 1535 that he began to take particular notice of her. This probably came about as a result of the visit to her family home. Far from being in residence at Wulfhall at the time of the King's arrival, which is the traditional version of events, Jane was in the Queen's train and travelling on progress with her.

Henry was no longer the athletic young man who had married Katherine of Aragon. After 1533, he had begun to put on weight, and became less active than in his youth; he had also had recurrrent trouble with one leg after being wounded by a fall from his horse in 1528. Yet he continued to hunt regularly and rode with skill, and people still thought him handsome, in spite of the fact that his red hair had receded, leaving the crown of his head bald. Although in recent years his latent ruthlessness and cruelty had become more evident, and his subjects now feared rather than loved him, he could be charming when he pleased, and he was being charming now.

For her part, Jane presented a welcome contrast to the Queen. She concealed her ambition beneath a veneer of placid gravity, and where Anne's eyes had once flashed an invitation, Jane's were kept modestly lowered. Her manner was pleasing, her temperament calm. The King was very taken with her, and before long his courtiers were aware, as was his wife, that he was pursuing the plain Mistress Seymour, and that – as Anne had once done to great advantage – the lady was holding him off while protesting a chaste devotion for her king. There were those at court who had been waiting for an opportunity like this to unseat Anne from Henry's affections, not only because she was unpopular and had not borne a male heir, but also because they resented her promotion of the reformist cause. Foremost among them was Chapuys, who desired nothing more than Anne's fall, and who, at a very early stage, saw in Jane Seymour the means by which this might be achieved.

Jane must have given the King some indication that his advances were welcome; his courtship presented her with an opportunity that was too good to miss. With Anne Boleyn's example before her to prove that a maid of honour could successfully aspire to queenship, she does not seem to have considered that by encouraging the King she was betraying the mistress to whom she had sworn an oath of service. The Seymours belonged to the faction which despised Anne and all that she stood for, while secretly reserving their allegiance to Katherine of Aragon and her daughter; thus they abetted Jane from the beginning, urging her to encourage the King's courtship and seeing it as a means to several ends. It is likely that, as the King prepared to leave Wulfhall after a good week's hunting, some of the courtiers were already predicting the imminent downfall of the Queen. Among them was Sir Francis Bryan, the son of Lady Margaret Bryan, a member of the King's immediate entourage, and one of his friends. Bryan had paid lip-service to Queen Anne, but he privately disapproved of her, and he was perhaps the first person to see in Jane Seymour a means of toppling Anne from her throne. Certainly, he did his best to encourage Henry's affair with Jane from the beginning.

When Henry and Jane were both back at court after the progress, their affair continued, gaining in intensity. In November, the French ambassador saw them together and concluded that the King was in love again. So open was the affair that courtiers were falling over themselves to win the friendship of the new favourite, leaving the Queen to sit alone in her empty apartments. History was repeating itself.

Jane's brothers, Edward and Thomas, were both with her at court, and they prudently warned her not to yield her virginity to Henry: she must create the impression of a modest and virtuous gentlewoman who wished to preserve her virtue until she was married. Jane played her part perfectly, knowing full well that she was employing the same tactics Anne Boleyn had used years before – and, once again, Henry took the bait. A man who set much store by female virtue, he was enchanted, if frustrated, and set about laying siege to this virtuous citadel. Jane's resolve withstood this, but her virtue did not prevent her from accepting the expensive gifts that Henry gave her. Indeed, her calculated campaign to ensnare her mistress's husband shows her to have been a woman of ruthless determination. It is true that she enjoyed the vigorous support of her family, but it is impossible to believe that she was a mere tool of the imperialist party which was encouraging the affair: any woman setting out on the course Jane Seymour would follow over the next few months would have had to be possessed of both strength and resolution, as well as driving ambition and a flexible conscience. Jane had all these, hidden beneath a demure manner that deceived many. Yet, to her credit, she aimed to use her talents and her growing power to persuade the King to return to the fold of Rome and restore the Lady Mary to her rightful place in the succession. These were matters about which she felt strongly, although she knew she could only broach them once she had firmly established herself in the King's affections. Like Anne Boleyn before her, she had set her sights high.

In October 1535, Cromwell brought the King devastating news: Tunis had fallen to the Emperor, and the Turks had been crushed. Chapuys told his master that Henry and Anne looked 'like dogs falling out of a window', so dismayed were they by the news. And as if this was not enough, there were reports of a ruined harvest, due to the bad weather that year. Anne was even blamed for this by the common people: they saw it as a sign from God that He was displeased with the King for marrying her. General unrest was mounting, and there were still murmurs of disapproval about the executions that had taken place earlier in the year. It was not a happy homecoming when Henry and Anne ended their progress at Windsor on 26 October.

That same month, Katherine was writing to the Pope, begging him to find a remedy for what was happening in England; by so doing she was putting herself in grave danger, for, if intercepted, her letter could have been used as evidence that she had tried to incite a foreign power to make war upon the King, and that was treason. Henry suspected that Katherine was up to something of the sort, and in November he told his Privy Council that he would no longer remain in 'this trouble and fear and suspicion' engendered by Katherine and Mary, and insisted that proceedings be taken against them in the next session of Parliament, 'or, by God, I will not wait any longer to provide for this myself!' Seeing the dismay on the faces of his councillors, he told them it was nothing to cry or make wry faces about. 'If I am to lose my crown for it, I will do what I have set out to do,' he warned. When Chapuys reported this to Charles V, and told him that 'the Concubine has for some time conspired for the death of the Queen and her daughter,' Charles replied, 'The threats of which you speak can only be designed to frighten them, but if they really are in danger you may tell them from me that they must yield.' He did not share Katherine's professed enthusiasm for martyrdom, and he was in fact beginning to find the whole affair rather tiresome. 'I cannot believe what you tell me,' he wrote to Chapuys. 'The King cannot be so unnatural as to put to death his own wife and daughter,' even though Henry's treatment of them had been 'cruel and horrible'. But if the King would not go so far, Chapuys feared that Anne Boleyn would, for she 'is the person who manages and orders and governs everything, whom the King does not dare to oppose'. Anne believed – mistakenly, as it turned out – that while Katherine lived, her own life was in danger. 'She is my death and I am hers,' she said at this time, 'so I will take good care that she shall not laugh at me after my death.' It was a supreme irony that Katherine's existence was later shown to have guaranteed Anne's safety, rather than having threatened it, for while Katherine lived, Henry dared not set Anne aside.

Anne's influence was to some degree restored during November because she had found herself to be pregnant with a child conceived during the autumn progress. Nevertheless, she was depressed during the first months of her pregnancy because she was fearfully aware that her whole future depended on its outcome: the King would not tolerate another failure. Outwardly, he was being solicitous, but George Wyatt tells us that he 'shrank from her' in private, 'at this time when most she was to have been cherished', which did not help Anne's frame of mind. The Bishop of Tarbes, visiting the English court, noticed that 'the King's love for his wife is less than it has been, and diminishes every day because he has new amours'. Anne was well aware of his pursuit of Jane Seymour, which was another reason for her depression.

Anne Boleyn's pregnancy brought Katherine and Mary nearer than ever to being put to death by judicial process or less lawful means. Anne, with the interests of her coming child to protect, now began a campaign to eliminate them both; Chapuys heard how Henry had not only promised to disinherit Mary, but also to kill her, and Anne had also let it be known that if Henry did not make an end of the girl, she herself would. 'If I have a son, as I hope shortly, I know what will become of her,' she declared. Yet Mary stood firm.

> God [she told Chapuys] had not so blinded her as to confess for any kingdom on earth that the King her father and the Queen her mother had so long lived in adultery, nor would she contravene the order of the Church and make herself a bastard.

She had no sense of self-pity: 'Her grief is about the troubles of the Queen her mother.'

Yet Katherine's troubles would soon be mercifully at an end. She fell dangerously ill on 1 December 1535, having grown weaker and weaker during recent months, suffering pains in her chest. Unable to eat very much, she was now confined to her bed, and her physician doubted she would ever rise from it. Katherine herself realised that time was running out for her, even though she rallied after a few days and was able to get up and sit in a chair. Queen Anne, thinking she was recovering, went flying to the King and begged him once more to have the former Queen and her daughter put to death. But Henry had read the reports of Katherine's illness, and knew he need do nothing to expedite her end, although Anne, whom Chapuys called 'this she-devil', declared she would not rest 'until he is freed from these poor ladies'. From Spain, the English ambassador reported that 'people expected to hear every day of the execution of Queen Katherine, and that the Princess Mary was expected soon to follow her.'

Katherine had more mundane matters on her mind. Her funds were depleted, and on 14 December she was forced to beg the

Emperor to pay her servants: 'I am as Job, waiting for the day when I must sue for alms, for the love of God.' Three days later, she celebrated her fiftieth birthday. It would be her last. On 26 December, she suffered a relapse, and was forced, in great pain, to take to her bed again, although she could not sleep. Her doctors, Dr de la Saa and Dr Balthasar Guersye, both knew her condition was grave, and de la Saa warned Bedingfield in writing that 'if the sickness continueth in force, she cannot remain long'. As the days dragged by, the pain grew worse, but Katherine refused to let Dr de la Saa call in other doctors, saying she had 'wholly committed herself to the pleasure of God'. This dismayed him, for he privately feared that his mistress was being poisoned, and did not wish to bear the responsibility of that diagnosis alone.

By then, Chapuys had heard that Katherine had 'fallen into her last sickness'. His immediate impulse was to go to her; he had espoused her cause with a zeal beyond the requirements of his brief, and he felt it important that someone who cared for her should be there when the end came. On 30 December, he saw the King, and asked if Henry knew she was dying. 'Yes, I do not believe she has long to live; when she is gone, the Emperor will have no further excuses for interfering in English affairs,' was the reply. Chapuys, stung, retorted: 'The death of the Queen will be of no advantage! His imperial Majesty will never abandon her while she lives.' Henry shrugged. 'It does not matter, she will not live long. Go to her when you like.' He refused, however, to let Mary visit her mother.

Followed by Henry's spies, Chapuys rode off to Kimbolton that same evening; two days later, he arrived, and was duly admitted to the bedchamber of the former Queen, whom he had not seen for five years. He was profoundly shocked to see her 'so wasted that she could neither stand nor sit up in her bed'. Yet she was overjoyed to see him. 'Now I can die in your arms, not abandoned like one of the beasts,' she said. Then, remembering even now her duty as a hostess, she went on: 'You will be weary from your journey. We will speak further another time. I myself shall be glad of sleep. I have not slept two hours these past six days; perhaps I shall sleep now.'

Later that day, another visitor arrived, but this one had no permit from the King. Lady Willoughby, formerly Maria de Salinas, forced her way into the castle before Bedingfield and his men could stop her, so determined was she to be with the mistress she had served and loved for thirty-five years. Her arrival meant that Chapuys's presence was no longer necessary, and after three days he prepared to leave. 'In our last conversation,' he recorded, 'I saw the Queen smile two or three times, and after I left she was willing to be amused by one of my people whom I left to entertain her.' Before his departure on 4 January, he saw Katherine's physician and arranged with him that, if her health deteriorated further, he would make her swear before she died that she 'had never been known of Prince Arthur'. Chapuys, knowing well that his contemporaries set much store by death-bed confessions, realised that this was the last, and the only thing he could do now for the woman whose cause he had so ably championed for more than six years.

Two days later, Katherine made her will. She asked that her debts be cleared and her servants recompensed 'for the good service they have done for me'. She wished to be buried in a convent of Observant Friars, little realising that their Order had recently been suppressed in England. She asked that 500 masses be said for her soul and that someone should go to the shrine of Our Lady of Walsingham – soon to be demolished – on her behalf. To her daughter Mary she left 'the collar of gold which I brought out of Spain' and her furs. Her other bequests were to members of her household, including her tailor, laundress and goldsmith. Lastly, she asked the King, 'my good lord', if he would 'cause church garments to be made of my gowns', a request he would refuse; nor did he honour Katherine's bequests to their daughter.

On the last evening of her life, Katherine felt herself growing weaker, yet before the end came, she would make one last effort to heal the rift between herself and the man she firmly believed to be her husband. Almost at the point of death now, her thoughts turned to Henry, whom she still loved, and who had once loved her long ago. Remembering their life together, she dictated a last letter to him, even though he had expressly forbidden her to communicate with him. The words came from her heart, in that quiet bedchamber, as darkness settled upon the castle:

My lord and dear husband,
I commend me unto you. The hour of my death draweth fast on,

and my case being such, the tender love I owe you forceth me with a few words to put you in remembrance of the health and safeguard of your soul, which you ought to prefer before any consideration of the world or flesh whatsoever; for which you have cast me into many miseries and yourself into many cares. For my part, I do pardon you all, yea, I do wish and dearly pray God that He will also pardon you. For the rest, I commend unto you Mary our daughter, beseeching you to be a good father unto her, as I have hitherto desired. . . . Lastly, I vow that mine eyes desire you above all things.

Supported by her maids, the dying woman painfully traced the signature that symbolised all she had stood for and fought for during the last bitter years of her life. It was her final defiance: 'Katherine the Queen'.

Shortly afterwards, she fell asleep, with Lady Willoughby sitting beside her, who later would relate to Chapuys the details of Katherine's last hours. On the next day, 7 January 1536, she awoke at 1.0 a.m., anxious to hear mass, but not before dawn, even though her confessor was ready to allow it; he had to wait until daylight came. Katherine received her last communion 'with a fervour and devotion that it was impossible to exceed', praying God that He would pardon the King the wrong he had done her, and that divine wisdom would give him good counsel and lead him to the true road.

She was sinking fast. At ten that morning, she received extreme unction, then drifted off again into sleep, while her household gathered about her. Early in the afternoon she woke, and there were more prayers, but the end was obviously at hand. Shortly before 2.0 p.m., Katherine of Aragon, sometime Queen of England, said clearly: '*Domine, in manuas tuas commendo spiritum meum*', and rendered her spirit to God.

After Katherine's death, Sir Edmund Bedingfield informed Cromwell of her passing and arranged for the wax chandler to carry out an autopsy and then embalm the body and 'cere' it in a waxed shroud. A plumber was also engaged to seal the corpse in a leaden coffin, 'for that may not tarry'. The autopsy was carried out that evening by the chandler and his assistant; Bedingfield would not allow either of Katherine's doctors or her confessor, the Bishop of

Llandaff, to be present. The autopsy showed that most of the internal organs were normal, save for the heart, 'which had a black growth, all hideous to behold, which clung closely to the outside' and which did not change colour when washed in water; cut open, the heart was black inside. Modern medical opinion accepts this as conclusive evidence that Katherine died of a malignant tumour of the heart, yet to her contemporaries it appeared consistent with the symptoms of poisoning, and for this reason the autopsy report was suppressed. Later, Chapuys was suspicious when Dr de la Saa told him that Katherine's condition had worsened after she had drunk 'a certain Welsh beer': both men believed it had been tampered with, and Chapuys thought that if the body were properly examined 'the traces will be seen'. The bishop managed to obtain sight of the secret autopsy report, and told the ambassador about the growth on the heart. Chapuys concluded that Katherine had certainly been poisoned, and in view of the threats made by Anne Boleyn during the weeks preceding her death, this was a reasonable assumption to make. Nor was Chapuys alone in making it, for it was widely believed both in England and abroad that Anne had murdered her rival. Even King Henry had his suspicions.

The former Queen's death excited little comment in the chronicles and letters of the period, yet she was sincerely mourned by many, and it was with great sadness that Chapuys informed the Emperor of the death of his aunt, 'her, who for 27 years has been true Queen of England, whose holy soul is in eternal rest. There is little need to pray for her.' Many came to regard Katherine as a veritable saint, and an anonymous hand added a halo to one of her early portraits. Roman Catholics saw her as one of the great pillars of the old faith in England, and her death was regarded as the end of everything she had stood for. That she was in some measure responsible for what was now happening in England occurred to none of her apologists, as it had not occurred to her during her lifetime.

Katherine's devotion to the King, her single-mindedness, her strength of character, and her courage still inspire admiration, however misplaced they may seem to modern eyes. They were certainly misplaced in the view of some of her contemporaries: when Bishop Gardiner heard of Katherine's death, he announced that by taking her to Himself God had given sentence, a sentiment echoed by other reformists. Yet the people of England, who had taken Katherine to their hearts from the first, mourned her sincerely, remembering only her personal virtues, her many charities, her selflessness, and those five dead heirs to England.

It was Chapuys who broke the news of her death to the King. Henry displayed neither grief nor distress, only joyful relief – to the disgust of the ambassador – saying, 'God be praised that we are free from all suspicion of war!' Naturally, the Boleyn faction rejoiced: 'Now I am indeed a Queen,' declared Anne triumphantly, while Lord Rochford thought it a pity the Lady Mary did not keep company with her mother. The King had the Princess Elizabeth conducted to mass to the sound of trumpets, as if to underline her undoubted right to succeed him. Yet in private, the Queen showed herself troubled, perceiving with awful clarity that now only the fragile life in her womb stood between her and disaster. She had the full measure of Henry, and to her ladies expressed the fear that he might do with her as he had with Katherine, for she was perceptive enough to realise that, in the eyes of almost everyone, Henry was now a widower and free to remarry. If she were to lose this child, there was every reason to believe he would set her aside and do just that.

However, in public she showed herself confident. On 9 January, she and the King presided over a magnificent court ball held to celebrate England's liberation from the threat of war. Both Henry and Anne wore yellow, the colour of royal mourning in Spain, as a mark of respect for the woman whom Henry insisted had been his sister-in-law. The Princess Elizabeth was paraded round the room in the arms of her father, who took great pleasure in showing off the precocious child.

Henry chose Peterborough Abbey as Katherine's final resting-place, and gave orders that she was to be buried with all the honours due to a Dowager Princess of Wales, 'our dearest sister, the Lady Katherine'. He was so relieved that he spared no effort in providing her with a magnificent state funeral, at which a great train of ladies was to be present. The King himself provided black cloth for their apparel, as well as linen for the nun-like mourning veils and wimples then customary on such occasions. He also declared that it was his intention to raise to Katherine's memory a fine monument, and he kept his word, although nothing remains now of the beautiful tomb he had built over her remains: it was destroyed by parliamentary troops during the Civil War. Over the matter of a memorial service Henry was less lavish, deeming it an unnecessary expense, and he also confiscated all Katherine's remaining personal effects to meet her funeral expenses. Most of these were still in the Royal Wardrobe at Baynard's Castle, and included a clock set in a bejewelled and enamelled book of gold, a double portrait of Henry and Katherine, seven pairs of Spanish slippers, and even necessaries provided for the former Queen's confinements.

On 29 January, the body of Katherine of Aragon was conveyed to Peterborough with all the trappings of a medieval royal funeral. The chief mourners were Lady Bedingfield, the young Duchess of Suffolk and the Countess of Cumberland, Eleanor Brandon, the King's niece. Chapuys did not attend by choice, 'since they do not mean to bury her as Queen'. The funeral sermon was preached by John Hilsey, who had replaced Fisher as Bishop of Rochester; he was a staunch King's man, and alleged, against all truth, that Katherine had acknowledged at the end that she had never been the rightful Queen of England. Then the woman who had in reality stoutly maintained to the last that she had been the King's wife was buried as Dowager Princess of Wales in the abbey church, later the cathedral. Henry VIII was at Greenwich on that day, and he observed the funeral by wearing black mourning clothes and attending a solemn mass. Anne, however, donned yellow once more, and grumbled because nothing was spoken of that day but the Christian deathbed of her rival.

For more than 200 years, it was believed that Lady Willoughby was afterwards laid to rest in the same tomb as Katherine, and in 1777 an attempt was made to prove this. The grave was opened, yet only one coffin lay within. It was strongly fastened, and to open it was thought sacrilegious. Nevertheless, one curious witness bored a hole through the coffin lid and slid a wire through it, hooking out a fragment of the black and silver brocade robes in which Katherine had been buried. This smelt strongly of embalming fluid, but disintegrated upon exposure to the air. The coffin was then reinterred and has remained undisturbed ever since. Four centuries after Katherine's death, another queen, Mary of Teck, the wife of

George V, gave orders that the symbols of queenship were to be hung above Katherine's resting place, and they may be seen there still, two banners bearing the royal arms of England and Spain. Thus, Katherine has been accorded in death the honours of which she was so cruelly deprived when she was alive.

Mary's reaction to her mother's death is not recorded, but may well be imagined, for in January 1536 she again fell gravely ill, and her life was thought to be in danger. Queen Anne wasted no time in extending an olive branch, and by 21 January had thrown the first bait by inviting her to court, where she would be exempt from carrying the Queen's train and would always walk by her side – but only if she submitted to her father's laws. Mary, however, had no intention of dishonouring her mother's memory by accepting such an offer: there could never be any question of a reconciliation with Anne Boleyn. She intended to take up the cause her mother had been forced to lay down, and carry on the fight to restore herself to her rightful place in the succession. She little knew it, but fate was already on her side.

After Katherine's death, Henry VIII told Chapuys that he desired to renew his former friendship with the Emperor 'now that the cause of our enmity no longer exists', and even asked if Charles V would use his influence to have the papal sentence in Katherine's favour revoked. Charles, of course, would never accede to such an outrageous request, but he too wanted to renew the Anglo-Imperial alliance. However, there were difficulties while Anne Boleyn lived, for the Emperor was reluctant to recognise her as Queen of England, though he might soon have no choice if she were the mother of a male heir to the throne.

On 24 January 1536, during a joust at Greenwich, the King was thrown from his horse and lay for two hours without regaining consciousness. When the Duke of Norfolk broke the news to the Queen, she showed very little concern, even though the Duke told her that most people thought it a miracle that her husband had not been killed. Inwardly, however, Anne must have trembled at the thought of what would become of her if Henry died and left her to fend for herself in a hostile world in which civil war would be a near certainty.

Fortunately the King's strong constitution triumphed, and he was soon up and about again. He would never, however, be a fit man afterwards. The old wound on his leg had reopened and an abscess had formed, which would remain open and suppurating for the rest of his life, in spite of the strenuous efforts of his physicians to heal it. From now on, he would have to wear a dressing and have the leg bound up. At first he adapted well to the disability, refusing to allow it to prevent him from riding and hunting, yet in time it severely curtailed his enjoyment of the sporting activities and dancing that had hitherto meant so much to him. For an active man, it was a cruel blow, and the effect upon Henry's already uncertain temper was disastrous. As his frustration at his enforced inactivity grew, along with the pain he suffered, he would become increasingly subject to savage and unreasonable rages. He was nearly forty-five now, growing bald, and running to fat; as he grew older, he would become more and more addicted to the pleasures of the table, and more and more gross. He would also, with each passing year, become more egotistical, more sanctimonious, and more sure of his own divinity, while still seeing himself as a paragon of courtly and athletic knighthood. The discrepancy between image and reality was one he could not bring himself to face.

In January 1536, this transformation was only just beginning, and the King's self-esteem was such that he regarded himself as the epitome of masculine charm, beauty and virility. He would have been shocked to learn that that virility was shortly to be publicly called into question.

II

Shall I die without justice?

On the day of Queen Katherine's funeral, Chapuys noticed Henry paying marked attention to 'Mrs Semel [*sic*]' and giving her 'very large presents'. During the afternoon, the Queen caught her husband with Jane on his knee, and flew into a frenzy, according to the account given years later by the English Duchess of Feria, who learned of the episode from her mistress Mary Tudor, who, in turn, probably learned of it from Jane Seymour herself. Henry, seeing his wife hysterical and fearing for their child, sent Jane out of the room and hastened to placate Anne. 'Peace be, sweetheart, and all shall go well with thee,' he soothed.

But the damage had been done. That evening, Anne aborted a foetus of about fifteen weeks' growth that had all the appearance of a male. 'She has miscarried of her saviour,' wrote Chapuys. The King in disappointment and sorrow commented, 'I see that God will not give me male children.' In a cold and unforgiving mood he stalked into the Queen's bedchamber, where Anne was sobbing fearfully, and complained about 'the loss of his boy' with many harsh words. Anne burst out that the fault lay with him, because he had been unkind to her, at which Henry flung back that she 'should have no more boys by him'. Seeing him so implacable, Anne forgot all caution, and cried desperately that he had no one to blame but himself for this disappointment, which had been caused by her distress of mind about 'that wench, Jane Seymour'. Breaking down again, she told him, 'Because the love I bear you is so much greater

303

than Katherine's, my heart broke when I saw you loved others.' But she had gone too far. 'I will speak with you when you are well,' said Henry icily, and walked out of the room.

When he had gone, Anne bravely told her ladies it was all for the best: 'I shall be the sooner with child again, and the son I bear will not be doubtful like this one, which was conceived during the life of the Princess Dowager.' Yet she was being over-optimistic, for when Henry had closed the door of her room behind him, he had also closed the door on his second marriage.

There was great speculation at court as to what had caused the Queen's miscarriage. Anne herself blamed Norfolk, claiming the mishap was due to the shock she received when he told her of the King's fall from his horse. Some thought it the result of a defect in her constitution, while others, more perceptive, guessed it had been caused by fear that Henry would treat her as he had Katherine. Chapuys thought this 'not unlikely, considering his behaviour towards a damsel of the court, called Miss Seymour'; Anne's ladies knew that she was temperamentally incapable of ignoring this, as Katherine would have done.

The real reason for the miscarriage may have been that Anne was one of the small minority of people who are rhesus negative and who, during a first pregnancy which results in a healthy child, may produce in the bloodstream a substance called agglutinogen, which destroys rhesus-positive red cells in any subsequent foetus, usually with fatal results. Such a condition was of course unknown in the sixteenth century – it was not identified until 1940 – and could well account for Anne's three miscarriages after the birth of Elizabeth. If so, then she would never have borne another living child.

Cromwell had a secret interview with Chapuys on the evening of 29 January. He was anxious to promote an alliance between England and the Empire, but realised that Anne was a stumbling-block to it. However, he saw the ambassador as a necessary ally in his plan, and was eager to confide in him that the King had just said to him

that he had made this marriage seduced by her witchcraft, and for that reason he considered it null and void, and that this was evident

because God did not permit them to have male issue, and that he
believed he might take another wife.

'This is incredible!' wrote Chapuys to his master, adding that the
Queen had already repented of her hasty words and was 'in great
fear'.

Anne's chief concern was that Henry would divorce her, believing
this was the worst he could do. But the truth was that Henry did not
want any more protracted legal proceedings to end yet another
marriage, nor any more disputes about the succession. There had to
be another way of removing the Queen. That Henry was accusing
Anne of witchcraft, then a capital crime, as early as January 1536,
suggests that even then he was probably contemplating her death.
Anne's enemies had always made political capital out of her extra
fingernail and the moles on her body, calling them devil's teats, and
the people of England had long believed her guilty of using the black
arts to seduce the King. Yet there was, apart from that, no other
evidence, and Henry seems to have abandoned the idea of accusing
Anne of witchcraft almost as soon as he had conceived it. However,
the seed had been sown, both in his mind and in Cromwell's, and –
had Anne but known it – her life was already in danger.

In early February, the estrangement between the royal couple was
common knowledge, and speculation was rife. Chapuys thought
Jane would make an excellent Queen of England; she was known to
have imperialist sympathies, and had openly expressed her support
for the Lady Mary. With Jane as queen, there was every hope that
Mary might be restored to her former position and to the succession.
This was what the ambassador had been told to work towards, and
now he saw his chance. He was not without influence or friends at
court, and he knew a great many people who secretly supported
Mary and who would have been gratified to see the downfall of the
Queen. Chapuys now made it his business to form a faction with
them and to cultivate a friendship with the ambitious Seymour
brothers, who were advising their equally ambitious sister on all her
dealings with the King. And as Anne's influence waned, so did this
faction brought together by Chapuys gain in strength and confidence.

The King was no fool: he could see which way the wind was
blowing, having been told by Chapuys that the Emperor wanted

peace in order to preserve the mutually profitable trading links between his people and Henry's. He had also been made aware, by implication, that the removal of Anne would facilitate this. Were she to be sacrificed to pro-imperialist policy, few would speak out in protest, for she was almost universally disliked. The imperialists were aware of this too, and thus Jane Seymour found herself courted, not only by Henry VIII, but also by Anne's enemies and Chapuys's faction. The ambassador advised her to drop heavy hints about Anne's heretical leanings in Henry's ear, and to say that the people of England would never accept her as their true Queen. She must say these things in the presence of her supporters, who would all then swear, on their allegiance to the King, that she spoke the truth. Jane certainly acted upon this advice, and it had the desired effect upon the King, who was now receptive to criticism of his wife. Jane also followed her own instincts, and the advice of her friends, by not admitting Henry to her bed. Instead, she dropped heavy hints about marriage, which fell on fertile ground, and before long Henry began to behave towards her with great circumspection, leading others to believe that he was already considering her as a future wife. From this time on, he took care to avoid any hint of scandal attaching itself to her name; her family and adherents were quick to notice this new deference on the part of the King, and Sir Francis Bryan told Jane's parents that they would shortly see their daughter 'well bestowed' in marriage.

Henry VIII finally made up his mind to rid himself of Anne Boleyn sometime in February 1536. Apart from the fact that their marriage was in ruins, the political situation in Europe made its dissolution highly desirable. Relations between Francis and Charles were deteriorating, and Henry was anxious to secure Charles's friendship. Anne was a bar to this, and would have to go. Chapuys, who had intimated as much to Henry, sounded out Cromwell as to what might happen, and though Cromwell was noncommittal, the ambassador concluded that something was afoot.

It was indeed. Henry left Greenwich for London for the Shrovetide celebrations, taking the unprecedented step of leaving Anne behind. Jane was left behind also, for Henry wanted her out of the way while he plotted the fate of her mistress. A month after her miscarriage, Anne was still grieving over the loss of her son, realising full well that she had lost not only a child but also her husband. Her company consisted of her ladies and her female fool, whose antics did little to alleviate her wretchedness. For the first time, she could appreciate how Katherine had suffered, and she expressed the view that her fate would be the same as the former queen's. She had guessed that Henry was thinking of taking another wife.

Jane Seymour was a continual thorn in Anne's side. Presents and messages from Henry arrived regularly for her, to Anne's disgust, and jealousy made her shrewish. She kept a continual watch on Jane's activities, and on more than one occasion lashed out and slapped her rival, using her prerogative as mistress. When Jane received a locket containing the King's miniature from Henry, and made a great show of opening and shutting it in front of Anne, the Queen reacted violently, ripping the locket from Jane's neck so roughly that she cut her own finger. Anne would dearly have loved to dismiss Jane from her service, but she dared not do so.

On 29 February, Charles V formally instructed Chapuys to begin negotiating an alliance with Henry VIII, and in early March war broke out between Spain and France. The removal of Queen Anne was now a matter of urgency. Chapuys had told the Emperor much about Jane, 'the young lady whose influence increases daily', saying she was a lady of great virtue and kindness, who was known to be sympathetic towards the Lady Mary. 'I will endeavour by all means to make her continue in this vein,' he wrote, although he expressed in the same letter his concern that 'no scorpion lurks under the honey'. Chapuys, too, had sensed that Jane's meek appearance hid an inner toughness.

Henry was finding his absence from Jane unbearable, and it was at this time that an incident occurred that was to change the course of their affair. The King had sent Sir Nicholas Carew from London with a love-letter and a purse of gold for her. Until now, Jane had not scrupled to accept expensive gifts, but even she drew the line at accepting money. Instead, she seized her opportunity to drop a timely hint, hoping to provoke the King into declaring his true intentions. She kissed his letter with great reverence, then handed it back unopened to Sir Nicholas. Then, falling to her knees, she asked him to beg the King on her behalf to consider that she was a prudent gentlewoman of good and honourable family, a woman without reproach who had no greater treasure in this world than her honour, which she would not harm for a thousand deaths. If the King wished to send her a present of money, 'she prayed him to do so when God might send her a husband to marry'.

Henry was delighted with this calculated show of maidenly propriety. 'She has behaved herself in this matter very modestly,' he said, 'and in order to let it be seen that my intentions and affection are honourable, I intend in future only to speak with her in the presence of her relatives.' When he returned to Greenwich, he turfed Cromwell out of his suite of rooms that were connected to Henry's own apartments by a secret gallery and installed there Sir Edward Seymour (who had recently been made a gentleman of the privy chamber) and his wife Anne. It was arranged that Jane would share these rooms with her brother and sister-in-law, and that they would act as chaperons when the King came to pay court to her. But the secret gallery did not remain a secret for long – Chapuys already knew of it by 1 April.

The imperialists supported the idea of a royal divorce, believing that the dissolution of the King's marriage to Anne would mean recognition of the Lady Mary's right to the succession. Charles V urged Chapuys to press for Mary's restoration as her father's heiress: 'It matters not what the wrong done to her late mother may have been.' The ambassador was also to find out Anne Boleyn's views on the matter: the Emperor wanted the alliance with England so much that he was prepared to accept Elizabeth's right to a place in the succession after Mary. Above all, Chapuys was not to dissuade Henry from marrying again. Chapuys, of course, would never have dreamed of doing so. In fact, on 1 April, he learned from Cromwell that Henry was certainly contemplating taking another wife, and that it would not be a Frenchwoman. He guessed then that the King meant to marry Jane Seymour. Jane left Greenwich in April; not only was she distressed by the rumours and lewd ballads about her affair with the King then circulating in London, but Henry also wanted her away from the court while plans were laid for the elimination of the Queen. So Jane returned to Wulfhall, travelling with her brother and his wife.

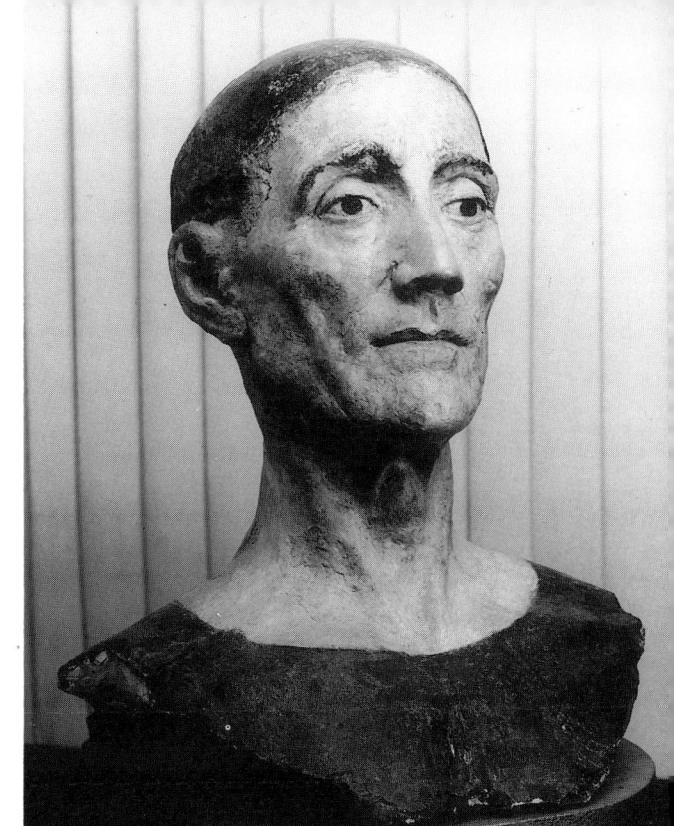

1 Henry VII: 'A dark prince, and infinitely suspicious, and his time full of secret conspiracies' (Sir Francis Bacon, *Life of Henry VII*)

2 Elizabeth of York: 'A woman of great beauty and ability' (*Venetian Calendar*)

5 *opposite page, above* Katherine of Aragon by Miguel Sittow: 'She thrilled the hearts of everyone. There is nothing wanting in her that the most beautiful girl should have' (Thomas More, 1501)

6 *opposite page, below* Katherine of Aragon (portrait in Buccleuch Collection): 'My good brother of England has no son because, although young and virile, he keeps an old and deformed wife' (Francis I of France, 1518)

3 Isabella of Castile: 'She was a very good woman, both clever and sensible' (Pulgar's *Chronicle*)

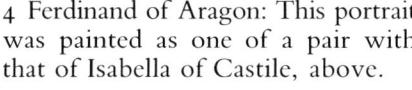

4 Ferdinand of Aragon: This portrait was painted as one of a pair with that of Isabella of Castile, above.

7 Henry VIII: 'Our natural, young, lusty and courageous king, entering into the flower of pleasant youth' (George Cavendish)

8 The Great Tournament Roll of Westminster: 'A solemn joust in honour of the Queen, the King being called "Coeur Loyal"' (Hall's *Chronicle*, 1511)

9 Thomas Wolsey: 'The Cardinal is the person who rules both the King and the kingdom'
(Sebastian Giustinian, *Venetian Calendar*)

10 Francis I of France: 'He is a Frenchman, and I cannot say how far you should trust him' (Henry VIII, *Venetian Calendar*)

11 Love letter from Henry VIII to Anne Boleyn, 1528: 'I now think the King so much in love that only God can get him out of this mess' (Letter from Jean du Bellay to Francis I)

12 *opposite page, above* Anne Boleyn (Hever Castle portrait): 'A young lady who has the soul of an angel and a spirit worthy of a crown' (Henry VIII, quoted by George Wyatt)

13 *opposite page, below* Anne Boleyn in later life: 'That thin old woman' (Eustache Chapuys, *Spanish Calendar*, 1536)

ANNA ·BOLINA   ANG ·REGINA

14 Thomas Boleyn, Earl of Wiltshire and Ormonde: 'He would sooner act from self-interest than any other motive' (Letter from the Bishop of Tarbes to the Bishop of Worcester, 1535)

15 Thomas Howard, Duke of Norfolk: 'The Duke of Norfolk, the Lady and her father have not ceased to plot against the Cardinal' (The French Ambassador, 1530)

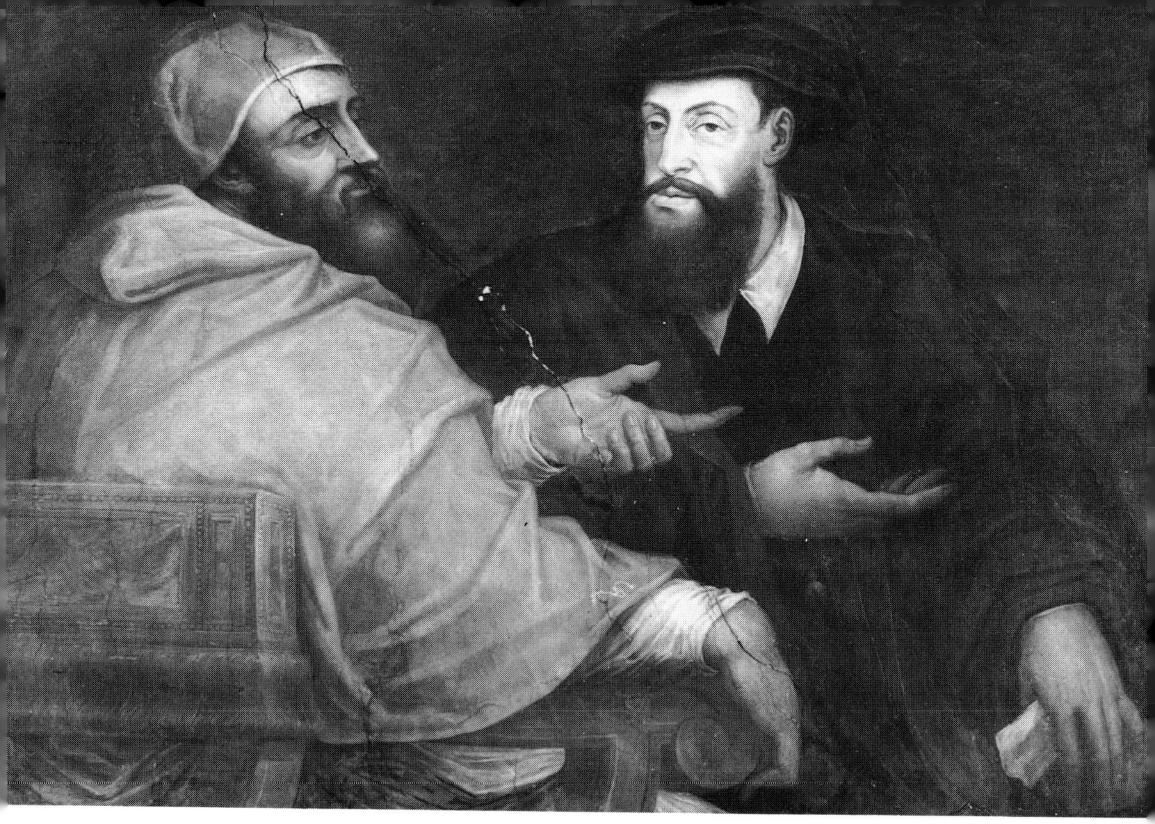

16 Pope Clement VII and the Emperor Charles V: 'The Emperor is determined to maintain the rights of his aunt, and will never consent to the divorce' (Charles V's ambassador to Pope Clement, 1527)

17 Petition from the English nobility to the Pope, 13th July 1530: 'We beg your Holiness without delay to assist these his Majesty's most just and reasonable desires'

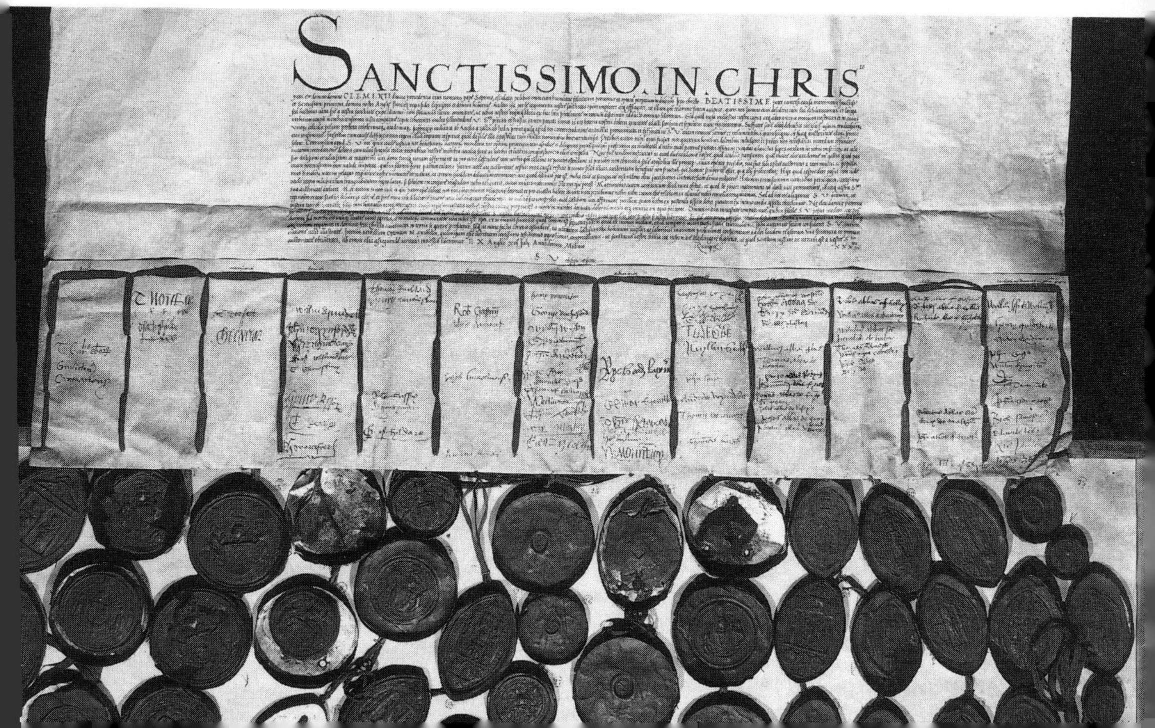

SANCTISSIMO.IN.CHRIS

18 *opposite page* Henry VIII: 'Nature, in creating such a prince, has done her utmost to present a model of manly beauty' (*Venetian Calendar*, 1531)

19 Thomas Cranmer: 'He is a servant of Anne's, and at least should be required to take a special oath not to meddle with the divorce' (Eustache Chapuys, *Spanish Calendar*)

20 Thomas Cromwell: 'Ready at all things, evil or good' (Eustache Chapuys, *Spanish Calendar*)

21 Jane Seymour: 'She is as gentle a lady as ever I knew, and as fair a queen as any in Christendom' (*The Lisle Letters*, 1536)

22 Prince Edward: 'The goodliest babe that ever I set mine eyen upon' (*The Lisle Letters*)

PARVVLE PATRISSA, PATRIÆ VIRTVTIS ET HÆRES
  ESTO, NIHIL MAIVS MAXIMVS ORBIS HABET.
GNATVM VIX POSSVNT COELVM ET NATVRA DEDISSE,
  HVIVS QVEM PATRIS, VICTVS HONORET HONOS.
ÆQVATO TANTVM, TANTI TV FACTA PARENTIS,
  VOTA HOMINVM, VIX QVO PROGREDIANTVR, HABENT
VINCITO, VICISTI, QVOT REGES PRISCVS ADORAT
  ORBIS, NEC TE QVI VINCERE POSSIT, ERIT.

23 Whitehall Palace: both Anne Boleyn and Jane Seymour were married to Henry VIII there

24 The Hampton Court dynastic group portrait. In this picture Jane Seymour appears posthumously

27 *opposite page* Henry VIII: 'The King was so fat that three of the biggest men that could be found could get inside his doublet' (*The Spanish Chronicle*, c. 1550)

25 Anne of Cleves: 'I see nothing in this woman as men report of her' (Henry VIII)

26 Katherine Howard: 'A lady of moderate beauty but superlative grace. Her countenance is delightful' (Charles de Marillac, 1540)

CATHARINE PARRE

28 *left* Katherine Parr: 'The Queen is graceful, and of cheerful countenance, and is praised for her virtue' (Eustache Chapuys, *Spanish Calendar*)

29 *below left* The Lady Elizabeth: 'Your beauty and other excellent qualities have so bewitched me that I am no longer master of myself' (Letter from Thomas Seymour to the Lady Elizabeth, 1548)

30 *below right* Thomas Seymour: 'A man of much wit, but very little judgement' (The Lady Elizabeth, 1549)

Anne had spent the early months of 1536 at Greenwich, occupying herself with charitable works, playing with her dogs, and ordering new clothes, including embroidered caps and leading reins, for her little daughter. Her accounts show that she kept the child sumptuously dressed, taking a personal interest in Elizabeth's attire. She rarely saw the King now, and no one would tell her anything while rumours of divorce and annulment abounded. Fear was closing in on her, and her inner turmoil may easily be imagined.

Henry had been pondering the problem of what to do with Anne for some weeks now. He was eager to commit himself without further delay to the proposed imperial alliance, and feared that the Emperor might think him lukewarm if he did not act soon. Then Cromwell's agile mind came up with a solution as fantastic as it was atrocious, which he presented to the King some time in April. He told Henry he had certain suspicions of the Queen as a result of information laid by his spies. His intention was to accuse Anne of a capital crime, such as high treason, and institute proceedings against her. The crime must be such as to inspire not only revulsion for Anne but also sympathy for Henry, and it must be something that would merit divorce as well as death. Given Anne's love of flirtation and her encouragement of the fashionable cult of courtly love, few would find it hard to believe that, desperate for a child, she had resorted to adultery and even to plotting the death of the King in order to save her own skin.

Adultery in a queen was not high treason at that date: according to the Statute of Treasons of 1351, 'violating the King's companion' was the treasonable act, and therefore only Anne's putative lovers would stand guilty of it. But compassing the death of the King was high treason, and it attracted the death penalty. In presenting this as a possible solution to the King, Cromwell took a risk that Henry would be angry at the suggestion that he had been cuckolded, and at the implied insults to the woman who was still, after all, his wife and the Queen of England. But Henry, spurred by his passion for Jane Seymour, his need of the Spanish alliance, and his desire for vengeance upon Anne, who had promised so much and failed to deliver, accepted the allegations at face value, merely asking Cromwell to find evidence to support them. How seriously the King took the allegations is difficult to judge; outwardly, he behaved as if he were convinced of Anne's guilt. He believed she had lied to him over her chastity before marriage, and he was well aware that she encouraged courtly flirtations with the young men in her circle. But he was also a master of the art of dissimulation, and what is more likely is that he and Cromwell, without ever acknowledging the fact to each other, both knew that they were parties to a plot to do away with an innocent woman for the sake of expediency, and that – for it to succeed – they must appear convinced of her guilt.

All that Henry asked was that the business be over and done with as soon as possible, so that he would be free to marry Jane and make peace with Charles V. Anne must be kept in the dark as much as possible until the last moment: she must not be given time to muster support. Above all, she must be prevented from appealing to Parliament, the supreme court, and accordingly Parliament was dissolved on 14 April. Two days later, Mr Secretary intimated to Chapuys that his master would soon be ready to conclude the alliance with the Emperor. Not knowing what was going on, and having heard nothing more about a divorce, the ambassador steeled himself to make friendly overtures to Queen Anne, as the Emperor had instructed, and on the Tuesday after Easter, when Anne went in procession to chapel, Chapuys bowed low to her, something he had never done before. It was a bitter moment for him, but Anne was gracious, and sank into a deep reverence. Having as a result grounds for hope that Charles V was prepared to acknowledge her title, she went about for the rest of the day loudly proclaiming that she had abandoned her friendship with King Francis and was on the side of the Emperor. But when Chapuys did not appear at a public dinner that evening she grew worried, and asked Henry why he was absent. 'It is not without good reason,' replied her husband sourly. Chapuys did not speak to Anne again: the Lady Mary and others of his faction had been astonished by his behaviour in the chapel, and he felt ashamed.

Meanwhile, Cromwell retired to his house at Stepney, ostensibly because he was ill, but in reality to give him time to compile the 'evidence' against the Queen. He returned to court on 23 April, the same day that Chapuys was telling the Emperor that Henry was 'sick and tired of that she-devil'. The King had also refused Anne's request to admit Rochford to the Order of the Garter.

Cromwell's plans were now complete, and from then on events moved swiftly. On 24 April, the Lord Chancellor appointed a commission of oyer and terminer, consisting of himself, Cromwell, Norfolk, Suffolk and others, which would hold an enquiry into every kind of treason. The King, emphasising his innocence of what was afoot, now behaved as if he meant to continue in his marriage, and on 25 April he wrote to his ambassador in Rome, saying he felt it likely that 'God will send us heirs male [by] our most dear and most entirely beloved wife the Queen'. By now several people were involved in the proceedings against that same dear and most entirely beloved wife. Norfolk had long since been alienated from his niece by her arrogance, and he was prepared to dissociate himself from her: she was too big a liability. Suffolk had never liked her, and Cromwell knew she must go. He alone knew how false the allegations were; the other commissioners were required to accept them at face value, which they did without difficulty.

Anne suspected that something was going on, and on 26 April she charged her chaplain, Matthew Parker, with the care of her daughter Elizabeth if anything happened to her. What she feared she did not say, but her plea made a profound impression upon Parker, and years later, when Elizabeth was queen, he would say he owed her allegiance, not only as her Archbishop of Canterbury, but also because 'he cannot forget what words her Grace's mother said to him not six days before her apprehension'.

Ostensibly, life went on as normal. The King was planning to go with Anne to Calais on 4 May. But before 29 April, the Privy Council had already been informed of the proceedings against the Queen, and there were rumours at court of her imminent disgrace. The Bishop of London, when asked outright if Henry meant to abandon Anne, would say nothing, but his silence was eloquent.

Cromwell's net now closed in around his victims. For some time he had been busy collating the gossip brought to him by his agents, and secretly interviewing the women in the Queen's household. One spy had heard one of the Queen's maids say that Anne 'admitted some of her court to come into her chamber at undue hours', and named Lord Rochford, Sir Henry Norris, Sir Francis Weston, William Brereton and Anne's musician Mark Smeaton in this connection. One young woman, reprimanded by the Countess of

Worcester for flirting, retorted that she was 'no worse than the Queen'. On the basis of such evidence as this Mr Secretary constructed a case. Anne was to be charged with adultery with the five men named, and also with conspiracy to murder the King. The charge of incest with her brother, which was the result of evidence maliciously laid by Lady Rochford, who was jealous of the close bond between Anne and George Boleyn, had been included to make the Queen's crimes seem all the more abominable.

We should pause here to consider Anne's so-called accomplices and ask the question: what were these men to her? Sir Henry Norris was a prominent courtier who had long enjoyed the King's favour, holding the office of Groom of the Stole, which required his attendance when Henry performed his natural functions; Norris was also Chamberlain of North Wales, a position he would not have held had he not enjoyed the King's confidence and trust. William Brereton is more obscure, but he too was a gentleman of the King's privy chamber, and may have been a witness at Anne Boleyn's wedding. Sir Francis Weston was twenty-five, and came from an honourable family whose seat was at Sutton Place in Surrey. Like Brereton, he was a gentleman of the privy chamber, and in 1533 had been one of those admitted to the Order of the Bath at Anne Boleyn's coronation. He was friendly with Henry, Anne and Rochford, played tennis with the King, and cards with Anne and Henry. He was married with a baby son.

The most remarkable inclusion in the list of Anne's supposed lovers was the musician, Mark Smeaton, whose name excited the most comment when the charges were made public. Anne's contemporaries wondered how she could ever have stooped so low. Hence we may conclude that Smeaton was not of gentle birth and had risen so far only on account of his musical talent. Of all the men accused, he would be the only one to admit his guilt, almost certainly under duress: it is possible, but not provable, that he suffered torture. Catholic writers would later make much of Anne's supposed intrigue with Smeaton, and Mary Tudor herself believed that the musician was Elizabeth's real father.

Anne certainly knew all these men except Smeaton well. Yet before April 1536, there is nothing in the records to suggest that her relations with them were anything other than circumspect. She knew her movements were watched, and she was no fool: it is inconceivable that she would have risked her crown and her life for the sake of casual sex with any man who took her fancy. The argument that she was so desperate to conceive a male heir, that she would go to any lengths to become pregnant – the implication being that the King was incapable of siring healthy children – fails when set against the fact that Anne conceived by him four times during their marriage without any difficulty, and that he expressed no doubt at any time that these children were his. As for plotting his death, Anne was well aware that, with Henry dead, her enemies would be out for her blood, and that at the very least she would suffer imprisonment or exile with her child disinherited.

Cromwell, however, felt that he had prepared a watertight case, and on 29 April he laid all the charges, with the accumulated evidence, before the King. As Henry read, he grew livid with fury – as if in fact he believed that Anne's betrayal was genuine. The evidence was enough to arouse jealous anger in any man, but Henry was also King of England and Supreme Head of the Church. He was about to be publicly proclaimed a cuckold – and it was all Anne's fault. He had suspected something of this nature, he said, and now here was proof of it, enough to convince him that he had been right all along to order an investigation. When he calmed down, he gave orders for the arrest of all those named in the charges, including Queen Anne.

Nothing is known of Jane Seymour's involvement in the plot against the Queen. She had been active for months in nurturing Henry's antagonism towards Anne, and she must have known that Henry intended to get rid of his wife before she retired from the political arena. Henry had made it clear he wanted to marry her, and she must have accepted as a necessary preliminary the removal of her rival. Yet even when it became clear that this would not be by divorce or annulment, she did not flinch. All too often Jane Seymour has been seen merely as a willing tool, yet it is clear that she was in fact quite as ambitious and ruthless as her predecessor. She was perceptive, and knew when to speak her mind, a mature woman who knew what she wanted and pursued it with steely single-mindedness. For her former mistress she had no pity whatsoever, and the most charitable thing that can be said about Jane Seymour in this context is that, given that she was ignorant of what the charges for the proceedings against Anne would be, she accepted them as justified when they were laid. Whether it occurred to her that such charges were a little too conveniently timed is another matter.

On Sunday, 30 April, the King – still smarting with anger and humiliation – spent several hours closeted with Cromwell and the Council. The Queen walked her dogs in Greenwich Park, and when she returned to the Palace in the afternoon, she saw crowds gathered outside: word had spread that the Council was meeting that evening to discuss a matter of the utmost urgency, and people had flocked to Greenwich to await news. This alarmed Anne and, sure that the matter about to be debated concerned herself and that it boded ill for her, she gathered up her daughter in her arms for maximum emotional impact and went to find her husband. Alexander Aless, a Protestant divine from Scotland, witnessed their confrontation through a window of the palace, and in 1559 recorded his memories of it in a letter to Elizabeth I:

> Alas, I shall never forget the sorrow I felt when I saw the sainted Queen, your most religious mother, carrying you, still a little baby, in her arms, and entreating the most serene King your father in Greenwich Palace, from the open window of which he was looking into the courtyard when she brought you to him. The faces and gestures of the speakers plainly showed the King was angry, though he concealed his anger wonderfully well.

Aless, unfortunately, was out of earshot of the conversation, so we do not know what was said between Henry and Anne; what is certain is that it resolved nothing. And when the Council meeting broke up that evening at eleven o'clock, it was announced that the King would not be going to Calais. No reason was given.

Cromwell was still gathering evidence against his victims. He found out that Smeaton, who only earned £100 per annum, had just spent a great deal of money on horses and liveries for his servants, and that people were wondering where he got the money, the implication being that the Queen had given it to him in return for services rendered. But Smeaton never had the opportunity to flaunt his horses and liveries, for on 30 April he was arrested and taken to Cromwell's house at Stepney for questioning.

One of the best sources for this crucial period is the account of George Constantine, the personal servant of Sir Henry Norris who would share his imprisonment in the Tower. Constantine tells us that Smeaton confessed his guilt, but only, it was thought, after he had been 'grievously racked'. There was no rack at Cromwell's house, but there was one at the Tower, even though torture was illegal. It is likely that Smeaton was racked on arrival at the Tower later that day or the next, and that this provoked his confession. The tale that he was tortured with a knotted cord round his eyes comes from the Spanish Chronicle, which is notoriously inaccurate, written as it was by a Spanish merchant living in London who relied heavily on gossip. His account probably reflects the kind of rumours that would shortly be circulating in the capital rather than what actually happened.

Anne had not noticed Smeaton's absence, and on May Day she took her seat with the King in the stands to watch a great tournament at Greenwich. Two of the contestants were Rochford and Norris, both named in the charges as the Queen's lovers. According to one late and hostile Catholic source, the account of the Jesuit Nicholas Sanders in his book on the origins of the English Reformation, Anne dropped a handkerchief to Norris to wear as a favour, which seemed to confirm the King's suspicions, but this incident is nowhere related in contemporary sources. Henry was in a thunderous mood, and hardly acknowledged Anne's presence; suddenly, without saying anything, he got up and left, leaving her to preside alone over the event, doubtless bewildered and afraid. She could not know it, but she would never see Henry again.

When the jousting ended, the King gave orders for Henry Norris to be arrested; he then departed for Whitehall, with Norris riding beside him so that Henry could question him. Norris was promised a full pardon if he would tell the truth. He had been horrified to learn he was accused of criminal intercourse with the Queen, and vowed to Henry that he would rather die a thousand deaths than be guilty of confessing to a crime he had not committed. Henry was not impressed, and Norris was sent to the Tower the following morning. The King, hearing that he had again protested his innocence to his chaplain, cried, 'Hang him up then!' On that same day, 2 May, Lord Rochford was arrested and also taken to the Tower. This took place so discreetly that few people were aware of it, and certainly not the Queen. When the blow fell, therefore, it took her almost completely by surprise.

On the morning of the 2nd she was watching a game of tennis, vexed with herself for not having laid a bet since her champion was winning, when a messenger arrived with a summons to present herself before the Privy Council. When she arrived in the council chamber, she was confronted by her uncle, Norfolk, Sir William FitzWilliam and Sir William Paulet, all grim-faced. They formally charged her, without preamble, with having committed adultery with Norris, Smeaton and one other, who was not named, and told her that both the men cited had already confessed their guilt, which was not true in the case of Norris. A stunned Anne failed to reply to the charges, and was escorted back to her apartments, there to remain under guard while the Council decided what was to be done with her. Anne did not panic at this stage: queens in the past had been found guilty of adultery, and none had suffered worse than honourable confinement. Besides, she was innocent of the charges. What did concern her was that blameless men were suffering on her account: for herself, she feared nothing worse than divorce, imprisonment or exile, but these men might face death.

Anne was still at dinner when, at two o'clock that afternoon, the door opened to admit Norfolk, Cromwell and Lord Chancellor Audley, accompanied by several lords of the Council. They all bowed. Norfolk held a scroll of parchment in his hand, the warrant for the Queen's arrest. Anne rose and asked why they had come. Her uncle replied that they came by the King's command to conduct her to the Tower, 'there to abide during his Highness's pleasure'. She answered steadily: 'If it be his Majesty's pleasure, I am ready to obey.' There was no time to change her clothes or pack anything – money would be provided for her needs while in the Tower, she was told. She committed herself to the custody of the Privy Council, and was conducted to her barge.

The conveyance of state prisoners to the Tower of London usually took place under cover of darkness, but Anne was taken in broad daylight. It was a nightmare journey. Norfolk took great pleasure in telling her with a good deal of virtuous tut-tutting that her paramours had confessed their guilt. Anne did not respond, but when, at five o'clock, the barge was rowed through the Court Gate – not the Traitors' Gate, as has traditionally been asserted – she was almost at breaking-point, and as she entered the grim fortress, her self-control gave way. At the top of the steps waited the Constable of the Tower, Sir William Kingston, and its Lieutenant, Sir Edmund Walsingham. Kingston would have charge of Anne during her sojourn; he was in his sixties, and knew her well, having often been at the court. He was not an unkind man, but he was somewhat hardened by the duties of his office, and made a point of distancing himself from the prisoners in his care. Towards Anne, he would behave with unfailing courtesy and humanity, becoming, despite his belief in her guilt, secretly impressed by her courage. He had received instructions from Cromwell that everything she said was to be recorded, in the hope that she would incriminate herself, and his reports are preserved in the Cotton MSS. in the Cottonian Library in the British Library, and are a valuable source of information about Anne's stay in the Tower.

When the Queen, in a state of near collapse, had been assisted from her barge and up the steps, she sank to her knees on the cobblestones, praying God to help her as she 'was not guilty of her accusement'. She begged the Privy Councillors, before they departed, to 'beseech the King's Grace to be good unto her'. Then she cried, 'Mr Kingston, do I go into a dungeon?' 'No, Madam,' he replied, 'you shall go into the lodging you lay in at your coronation.' 'It is too good for me!' sobbed Anne. 'Jesu, have mercy on me!' And she sank to her knees again, 'weeping a great pace, and in the same sorrow fell into a great laughing', behaviour she would exhibit many times during the early days of her imprisonment. Kingston helped her up once more, but she was distraught, repeating again and again, 'I am the King's true wedded wife! Oh, my mother, my mother!' Then, calming down, she declared: 'My God, bear witness there is no truth in these charges. I am as clear from the company of man as from sin.' She asked Kingston if she might have the Holy Sacrament placed in her bedchamber, 'that I may pray for mercy'. Already, she was beginning to suspect the worst.

Kingston now led her away. 'I was received with greater

ceremony the last time I entered here,' she remarked. The royal apartments were on the east side of the inner ward between the Lanthorn Tower, the White Tower, and the Wardrobe Tower. Very little is known about them. The Tower had been a royal palace since Norman times, but by the reign of Henry VIII it was considered old-fashioned and uncomfortable. Cromwell put in hand renovations in the early 1530s for Anne Boleyn's coronation, and the works carried out then are shown on a plan of the Tower dated 1597, by which time the old great hall would be crumbling. The royal apartments did not long survive it, which suggests that Cromwell's improvements were mainly cosmetic. The Queen's lodging comprised a presence chamber, a dining chamber, a bedchamber, and a garden. It was to these rooms that Anne was conducted on 2 May 1536.

There, she found waiting for her three ladies-in-waiting, one of whom was Margaret Wyatt, Lady Lee, the poet's sister, who had probably known Anne since childhood; her old nurse, Mrs Orchard, and a Mrs Stonor; two male servants and a boy. There were also four ladies whose duty was to inform on her: her aunt Elizabeth, wife of Sir James Boleyn; Lady Shelton, another aunt, who had formerly had charge of the Lady Mary; Mary, Lady Kingston, wife of the Constable; and Mrs Cosyn, wife of Anne's master-of-horse, William Cosyn. There was no love lost between Anne and these ladies, and she realised at once why they were there, telling Kingston she thought it 'a great unkindness in the King to set such about me as I never loved. I would fain have had mine own Privy Chamber, whom I favour most.' Kingston replied that 'the King took them to be honest and good women.' Privately, he agreed with Henry's choice, for these ladies could tell Anne nothing of her father or brother, or anything else; the King wanted her kept in ignorance of the evidence against her in the hope that she would reveal information that could be used to incriminate her.

Left alone with her attendants, Anne could not stop talking. She ate 'a great dinner', and soon afterwards called for supper. Lady Boleyn taunted her that her love of intrigue had brought her where she was, and at the end of the evening Lady Kingston and Mrs Cosyn made their report to the Constable. Anne, meanwhile, was working herself into another frenzy, saying she was 'cruelly handled at Greenwich'. She summoned Kingston, and asked him outright if he knew why she was there. He reminded her of the charges against her, saying that another name had been added to the list of her accomplices, but she answered, with spirit, 'I hear I shall be accused with four men, and I can say no more but Nay, without I should open my body!' And, with a dramatic gesture, she opened wide the overskirt of her gown: 'They can bring no witnesses.' Kingston lied that Norris had confessed his guilt. 'Oh, Norris, hast thou accused me?' she wailed. 'Thou art in the Tower with me, and thou and I shall die together! And Mark, thou art here too.' And she wept, 'Oh, my mother, thou wilt die with sorrow.' Then she turned to Kingston, and her next question showed that she understood very well how grave her situation was: 'Master Kingston, shall I die without justice?' He replied: 'The poorest subject of the King hath justice.' Anne laughed hysterically at this, knowing well that those charged with capital offences were rarely acquitted.

Anne would have been even more horrified had she known just how desperate Henry was to be rid of her. Not only was he planning to have her executed for high treason, but he had ordered Cranmer on the day of her arrest to find grounds for annulling his marriage to her. Once Anne was dead, there must be no impediment to Jane's children taking precedence in the order of succession.

News of the Queen's arrest had spread around the court by the evening of 2 May. Chapuys learned of it with relief, seeing Anne's fall as a manifestation of divine vengeance for all the wrongs she had inflicted upon Katherine and Mary. Nor did he have any difficulty at this stage in believing the charges against her, predicting that the outcome of the affair would be her execution. Indeed, there was little doubt in anyone's mind that this would be Anne's fate. When the people learned she was in the Tower, they were unmoved, believing her guilty as charged. No one spoke up in her favour. Nevertheless, Henry refrained from going out in public while Anne was in the Tower. His only sorties out of the palace were into the gardens and on evening trips by barge to visit Jane, who had just returned from Wulfhall and was temporarily staying at an unknown lodging.

By now Henry had convinced himself that Anne had been a monster of lechery. He remembered her ruthlessness in hounding Wolsey to his death, how she had more or less admitted her involvement in the plot to poison Fisher, and how she had urged him

319

to have Katherine and Mary executed or murdered. Henry had heard the rumours that Katherine had died of poison, and was now convinced that Anne had been responsible. When Henry FitzRoy, Duke of Richmond came to bid his father goodnight on the evening after Anne's arrest, Henry embraced him and wept as he told him that he and his half-sister Mary ought to thank God for escaping 'that cursed and venomous whore, who tried to poison you both'. There was no evidence for this, but Henry was prepared to believe that no crime was too monstrous to have been committed by Anne. And when Richmond died of consumption the following July, Henry and most other people would believe that Anne had administered a slow-working poison which caused his death.

The Lady Mary learned of the Queen's arrest on the following day from Chapuys, who boasted that he had been instrumental in bringing it about. Mary instructed him to join forces with Cromwell and the many other people who were working for the advancement of Jane Seymour; Chapuys had, of course, been doing this for months already.

One person who did feel sorrow on behalf of Anne was Cranmer, who wrote to the King to express his sorrow and loyalty.

> My mind is clean amazed [he wrote], for I never had better opinion of woman, but I think your Highness would not have gone so far if she had not been culpable. I loved her not a little for the love which I judged her to bear towards God and the Gospel. Next unto your Grace, I was most bound unto her of all creatures living.

He hoped and prayed she would declare her innocence. 'I am exceedingly sorry that such faults can be proved by the Queen,' ended Cranmer, 'but I am, and ever shall be, your faithful subject.' He would now go on to do exactly as the King bade him: against his sense of self-preservation, his long-standing affection for Anne counted for very little.

In the Tower, Anne learned of her brother's arrest, and declared that Norris and Rochford would vindicate her. After a night in prison she still veered from black despair to buoyant confidence and back again, as panic took her: 'One hour she is determined to die, and the next hour much contrary to that,' Kingston told Cromwell. Anne could not stop talking about the men accused with her. She told Mrs Cosyn she had made Norris swear to her almoner that she was a good woman, for she had teased him about delaying his marriage, saying he looked for dead men's shoes, 'for if aught came to the King, you would look to have me!' Norris, shocked, had denied this, but Anne had feared that her remarks had been overheard and could be misconstrued, so she made him swear to her virtue. Mrs Cosyn then deliberately let slip that Sir Francis Weston was being questioned by the Privy Council about his relationship with the Queen. Anne expressed some apprehension about what he would say, as he had told her on Whit Monday that Norris 'came more into her chamber for her sake than for Madge Shelton's [his mistress]'. Weston himself had been asked teasingly by Anne if he loved Madge, and he had replied that 'he loved one in her house better than [Madge or his wife]', which was the correct courtly answer to such a question. 'Who?' the Queen had asked. 'It is yourself,' he replied. This was all grist to Cromwell's mill, for, taken literally, it could prove very damaging indeed.

Anne's fragile confidence would have been shattered had she known that her husband was already planning his wedding to Jane Seymour. On 4 May, Jane took up temporary residence at Beddington Park, the Surrey home of Sir Nicholas Carew, a magnificent house built in 1500 and set in a large park; the great hall, on which the one at Hampton Court is said to have been modelled, still survives today. Here, Henry could visit Jane discreetly. His visits took place under cover of darkness, though nothing improper occurred; the royal swain had insisted on Jane's parents and brother Edward being present when he came courting. He was taking no chances with Jane's reputation: no one would ever be able to accuse her of light behaviour in the years to come.

Chapuys tells us that it was during one of these visits that Jane brought up the delicate subject of Mary, daring to say that when she was queen she hoped to see Mary reinstated as heir apparent. This irritated Henry, who told her she was a fool, who 'ought to solicit the advancement of the children they would have together, and not any others'. Jane replied that she did think of them, but also of Henry's peace of mind, for unless he showed justice to Mary,

Englishmen would never be content. Jane intended to have her own way over Mary, and she would not give up easily.

On the day that Jane arrived at Beddington, Sir Francis Weston and William Brereton, having failed to convince the Council of their innocence, were taken to the Tower, Brereton having previously confided to George Constantine that 'there was no way but one with any matter alleged against him', meaning that he was innocent. The next day, Friday, 5 May, saw the last arrests, those of Sir Thomas Wyatt and Sir Richard Page. Neither was ever charged, and it is probable that Cromwell had never intended that they should be: if two of those accused with the Queen were allowed to go free, it would underline the guilt of the rest. Wyatt was a natural choice, as his earlier love for Anne was well known. As for Page, nothing is known of him.

Of the prisoners in the Tower, Rochford showed the most agitation. 'When shall I come before the King's Council?' he asked Kingston. 'I think I shall not come forth till I come to my judgement.' Then he burst into tears. Anne was glad that she and her brother were under the same roof. Yet when she was told of the arrests of Weston, Brereton, Wyatt and Page, she burst out laughing uncontrollably at the absurdity of it all. She showed no compassion for Smeaton when told he was manacled in irons, saying only that he 'was a person of mean birth, and the others were all gentlemen'. Smeaton, she said, had only once been in her chamber, and that was at Winchester the previous year, when she had sent for him to play the virginals for her; nothing improper had happened then, and the only other time she could remember having spoken to the musician was the previous Saturday, when she had chided him for aspiring to a courtly flirtation with her: 'You may not look to have me speak to you as I would do to a nobleman, because you are an inferior person.' 'No, no, a look sufficeth!' Smeaton had protested, and that was the end of the matter.

Anne told Kingston that if her bishops were with the King, they would all speak for her. In fact, their silence had been deafening. Of her imprisonment she said, 'I think the King does it to prove me,' and according to Kingston, 'did laugh withal, and was very merry'. But the merriment did not last, and she was soon weeping again, saying, 'My lord my brother will die!'

Henry VIII moved to Hampton Court on Saturday, 6 May, and set in train preparations for his wedding to Jane Seymour. In a high good humour, he had his hair cropped, where hitherto he had worn it long over his ears; Anne had liked him clean-shaven, thus he was also growing a beard, which he would never again shave off.

The legal process against the Queen began on 10 May when the Grand Jury of Middlesex found a True Bill against the accused on all the charges. On the following day, the Grand Jury of Kent did likewise. The case could now proceed to trial. The indictment drawn up by Cromwell was formidable. It asserted that Queen Anne, 'despising her marriage and entertaining malice against the King, and following daily her frail and carnal lust', had procured by various base means many of the King's servants to be her adulterers. Rochford, Norris, Weston, Brereton and Smeaton were named as those who had succumbed to her 'vile provocations'. Twenty separate offences were listed, yet the indictment also mentioned other unspecified ones, 'on divers days before and after 6 October 1533', something that Anne would have found very difficult to disprove – or the Crown to prove, for that matter. Nor had Cromwell checked his facts: some of the offences could not have been committed at all, because Anne was nowhere near the man in question at the time, or, on at least five occasions, was heavily pregnant. Mark Smeaton is described as 'a person of low degree', as if to emphasise how far the Queen had stooped for her pleasure, and over her alleged incestuous affair with Rochford, said to have begun in November 1534, the indictment bristled with righteous outrage, saying that Anne had 'procured her own natural brother to violate her, alluring him with her tongue in his mouth, and his tongue in hers, against the commands of Almighty God and all laws human and divine'. The charge of incest was meant to inspire horror and revulsion, but thanks to George Boleyn's testimony at his trial, it failed; it was the alleged affair with Smeaton that captured the public's imagination, and provided endless copy for writers throughout the sixteenth century.

The indictment also alleged that, from October 1534 onwards, the Queen and her lovers, jointly and severally, had plotted the King's death, Anne having promised to marry one of them afterwards; she had also told them 'she would never love the King in her heart'.

323

Henry, it concluded, had taken the news of this treachery so badly that 'certain harms and perils have befallen his royal body'. It must be said that none of these harms and perils was at all evident.

No mention had been made in the indictment of Wyatt and Page. In fact, Cromwell had already secretly informed Wyatt's father that his son would not be harmed, for the old man wrote to him on 11 May, saying that neither he nor his son would ever forget Mr Secretary's kindness.

On Friday, 12 May, the Duke of Norfolk, as High Steward of England, presided over the trial of Norris, Weston, Brereton and Smeaton at Westminster Hall. The Queen and Lord Rochford would be tried separately by their peers, a privilege reserved for the aristocracy only; their trials were set for the following Monday.

The accused men were brought by river to Westminster. Few details survive of the proceedings. Witnesses were called, and one member of the jury, Sir John Spelman, related that some were ladies of the court who testified to such promiscuity on the part of the Queen that it was said in court that there was 'never such a whore in the realm'. One witness repeated the words of a deceased Lady Wingfield, which was hearsay. At the end of it all, the jury returned a verdict of guilty, and the four men were condemned by Lord Chancellor Audley to be drawn, hanged, castrated and quartered. Chapuys says that Brereton was 'condemned on a presumption, not by proof or valid confession, and without any witnesses'. Most courtiers reacted to the verdict with sorrow, especially on behalf of Norris and Weston, both popular and respected men. Weston's family made frantic attempts to save his life, and on 13 May it was rumoured that he might escape the death sentence. But Lord Hussey, writing to Lord Lisle on 12 May, was of the opinion that all would suffer death, even the Queen and Rochford; Anne, he said, deserved it, for her crimes had been 'so abominable' that he prayed God would give her grace to repent.

The condemnation of the four men could not but presage an unfavourable outcome of Anne's own trial and that of her brother. Her reaction to the news of their sentence is unrecorded. Equally ominous was the dissolution of her household at Greenwich, by the King's command, on Saturday, 13 May, when her servants were discharged from their allegiance. Obviously her trial would be a mere formality.

On 14 May, Cromwell wrote to all England's ambassadors abroad, informing them of the action taken against the Queen and the judgement on the men accused with her: 'She and her brother shall be arraigned tomorrow,' he wrote, 'and will undoubtedly go the same way. I write no particularities, the things be so abominable.' Abroad, it was shrewdly concluded by some that the King had invented the whole thing to get rid of Anne, though her reputation was so poor that there were also a great many people who believed Henry's actions justified.

On the same day, Henry decided he could no longer live without Jane, and recalled her to London, where he installed her in the house of Sir Francis Bryan on the Strand, one mile from Whitehall, where he himself was now in residence. Here, Jane had her first taste of what it would be like to be a queen, being housed in great splendour, attired in rich garments, and waited on by the King's officers and servants, all wearing splendid liveries. She seems to have accepted her sudden elevation with complacent calm, wasting no pity on the woman she would shortly supplant. Indeed, she was awaiting the result of Anne's trial with barely concealed impatience.

Preparations for that trial, which would be held in the great hall of the Tower, had been made over the weekend. A raised platform was erected in the centre, around which were placed rows of benches, enough to accommodate the estimated 2,000 spectators who would be present. Chairs were provided for the twenty-six peers who would act as judges, and the Duke of Norfolk, as High Steward of England, was given a throne under a cloth of estate, for he represented the King. The hall has long since been demolished, but the seating placed there for the trial was still in existence in 1778.

This was the scene that greeted Anne when she was escorted into the court by Sir Edmund Walsingham, Sir William Kingston, Lady Boleyn, and the chief executioner, with his axe turned away from her. Her entry was impressive; she presented herself at the bar with considerable dignity, curtsying to the judges and looking about her without any sign of fear, as if she had been attending some great state occasion. Gone was the hysteria, the violent mood swings; Anne was now reconciled to the inevitability of death, but she was resolved not to go down without a fight. Cromwell, knowing this, was very tense before the trial, fearing that Anne's wit and courage would undermine his case and even secure an acquittal, something he found too awful to contemplate. Far too much was at stake, including his own neck.

When Anne was seated in a chair on the platform in the centre of the court, the indictment was read in all its detail. Her face, however, betrayed no emotion, even when another charge was added, that of having poisoned the late Queen Katherine and attempting to do the same to the Lady Mary. Instead, she listened patiently, then answered clearly to each charge, refuting them all firmly, and arguing her case with such clarity and good sense that her innocence, which she protested vehemently, seemed manifest to many of those watching her.

Nevertheless, when the twenty-six peers were asked to give their judgement upon the Queen, every one pronounced her guilty. Anne stood unmoved as they each rose in turn to give their verdict, carrying herself as if she was receiving some great honour. Outside, the people in the crowds that had gathered were telling each other incorrectly that Anne had cleared herself by a wise and noble speech.

Norfolk now pronounced sentence. However poor relations between him and his niece had been in recent months, family feeling took precedence at this point, and he wept as he addressed her:

> Because thou hast offended our sovereign lord the King's Grace in committing treason against his person, the law of the realm is this: that thou shall be burnt here within the Tower of London on the Green, else to have thy head smitten off, as the King's pleasure shall be further known of the same.

There was a shriek from the gallery as Anne's old nurse, Mrs Orchard, gave way to hysterics. The Earl of Northumberland fainted, and had to be helped out – he was already mortally ill, and died some months later. But Anne received the sentence calmly, raising her eyes and saying, 'O Father, O Creator, Thou who art the Way, the Life, and the Truth, knowest whether I have deserved this death.' She said she was prepared to die, but was extremely sorry that others, innocent as she, should die through her. She believed she had been condemned for reasons other than the causes alleged, and swore she had always been faithful to the King, although

> I do not say I have always shown him that humility which his goodness to me merited. I confess I have had jealous fancies and suspicions of him, which I had not discretion enough, and wisdom, to conceal. But God knows, and is my witness, that I have not sinned against him in any other way. Think not I say this in the hope to prolong my life. God hath taught me how to die, and He will strengthen my faith. As for my brother, and those others who are unjustly condemned, I would willingly suffer many deaths to deliver them, but since I see it pleases the King, I shall willingly accompany them in death, with this assurance, that I shall lead an endless life with them in peace.

Finally, she asked for time in which to prepare her soul for death. An anonymous Frenchman who was present recorded that her speech made even her bitterest enemies pity her.

Anne was then escorted from the court by the Constable, attended by Lady Kingston and Lady Boleyn, and the executioner with his axe turned towards her, signifying that she was condemned to die. After her departure, a buzz of conversation broke out, and the Lord Mayor expressed the opinion that 'he could observe nothing in the proceedings against her but that they were resolved to make an occasion to get rid of her'. Even Chapuys felt that Anne had been condemned upon a presumption and 'without valid proof or confession', and George Constantine told Cromwell 'there was much muttering of Queen Anne's death'.

After her condemnation, Anne was not taken back to the royal apartments, but was lodged instead in rooms in the Lieutenant's house (afterwards known as the Queen's House), a half-timbered building between the Bloody Tower and the Bell Tower. It was much altered in 1540, and has been restored since, but the first floor bedroom occupied by Anne still exists, with its linenfold panelling and stone fireplace, dominated by a great four-poster bed, and overlooking Tower Green (or East Smithfield Green, as it was then known) and the Royal Chapel of St Peter ad Vincula, which had not then acquired the reputation Macaulay gave it as 'the saddest spot on earth'.

There was no longer any need for the women to inform on Anne, and Mrs Cosyn was discharged at this point. She was replaced, at Anne's request, by her own niece, Katherine Carey, who was seven years old; it was not thought unsuitable in those days to expose such a young child to the realities of suffering and death.

Jane Seymour did not show herself in public on the day of the trial. She was much agitated about its outcome, and waited with her parents for news. Chapuys, who attended, had promised to tell them about it. In the morning, Jane had received a note from the King, telling her that at three o'clock she would hear of the condemnation of the Queen from Sir Francis Bryan, and this was exactly what did happen, to Jane's intense relief.

Rochford's trial followed that of his sister. The evidence for incest rested solely upon the fact that he had once been closeted for a long time alone with Anne. Chapuys says that Rochford's 'wicked wife' supplied this information, and the French poet Lancelot de Carles, a witness at the trial, quotes Rochford as saying, 'On the evidence of only one woman, you are prepared to believe this great evil of me.' Other witnesses felt that Lady Rochford had acted more out of envy and jealousy than loyalty to the King.

Rochford was also charged with having expressed doubts that Elizabeth was the King's daughter. He made no answer to this, but to the other charges he replied so well that bets were being laid on his acquittal. And he would perhaps have escaped the death penalty, had it not been for a letter from his wife, produced in court at the last minute and containing details of the 'accursed secret' he shared with the Queen. Again he denied these allegations eloquently and sensibly, confessing to nothing. There was one tense moment when he was handed a piece of paper on which was written a statement he had allegedly made to the effect that the King was impotent. This was too sensitive to be read out in court, and Rochford sealed his fate when he declared that he would not 'create suspicion in a manner likely to prejudice the issue the King might have from a second marriage', thereby implying what had been written and creating a sensation in court. 'I did not say it!' he cried, but it was too late. The

328

twenty-six peers found him guilty by a unanimous decision, and Norfolk sentenced him to the full horrors of a traitor's death. Had he not been so proud, wrote Sir Thomas Wyatt, every man would have bemoaned his fate, if only for his great wit, but Rochford had alienated so many with his arrogance that few spoke up in his favour, although there were many who admired his courage at his trial.

The King, and most of his subjects, thought the sentences entirely justified. Told of Anne's spirited defence, Henry replied, 'She hath a stout heart, but she shall pay for it!' To celebrate the verdicts, he held a lavish river pageant, then went to supper at the house of the Bishop of Carlisle, where he produced a book he had written entitled *The Tragedy about Anne*. 'For a long time I foresaw this,' he said. Chapuys was present at that supper, and offered Henry his commiserations on the Queen's treachery. Henry answered complacently that many great men had suffered from the arts of wicked women, and he did not appear unduly upset. Then he left for the Strand, where he dined late with Jane on food prepared by his own cooks.

On 16 May, Chapuys noticed more and more courtiers going to pay their respects to Jane, while in the Strand the common people waited to catch a glimpse of her. Yet the ambassador was cynical: he thought the King 'may well divorce her when he tires of her'. Nor was Jane universally popular, for scurrilous ballads about her were circulating in London, which the King tried in vain to suppress; a letter he sent to her at this time, the only one to survive from their courtship, refers to this:

My dear friend and mistress,
The bearer of these few lines from thy entirely devoted servant will deliver into thy fair hands a token of my true affection for thee, hoping you will keep it for ever in your sincere love for me. There is a ballad made lately of great derision against us; I pray you pay no manner of regard to it. I am not at present informed who is the setter forth of this malignant writing, but if he is found out, he shall be straitly punished for it. Hoping shortly to receive you into these arms, I end for the present
Your own loving servant and sovereign,
H. R.

On the day after Anne's trial, Kingston wrote to ask Cromwell, 'What is the King's pleasure touching the Queen, as for the preparation of scaffolds and other necessaries?' Neither he nor Anne knew as yet whether she was to be burned or beheaded, or even when. In fact, Henry was waiting for Cranmer to declare his marriage to Anne null and void. The Archbishop had been studying the relevant documents, but had faced severe difficulty in finding grounds for an annulment. Northumberland had angrily reaffirmed that there had never been a precontract between him and Anne. Nor dared Cranmer imply that the King's marriage to Katherine of Aragon had not been lawfully annulled. In the end, he seems to have found a legal loophole in connection with the King's liaison with Mary Boleyn, which had placed Henry and Anne within the forbidden degrees of affinity. The Pope had issued in 1528 a dispensation permitting them to marry when Henry was free, yet the 1534 Act of Supremacy had decreed that existing papal dispensations would no longer be held as valid if they were contrary to Holy Scripture and the law of God. Cranmer probably applied this ruling to the bull dispensing with Henry's relationship with Mary Boleyn, which meant that his marriage to Anne was incestuous and invalid; and in July 1536, Parliament would declare it void because of 'certain just, true and unlawful impediments' that were not known of when it was contracted.

On 16 May, Cranmer visited the Tower to offer some spiritual consolation to Anne and administer the Holy Sacrament. He also required the Queen's consent to the annulment of her marriage; she had her daughter's rights to consider, and had she disputed it the proceedings could have been very protracted. It may be that Cranmer offered her the easier death in return for her co-operation; even more probable is the likelihood that he held out the possibility of her being reprieved and sent into exile as bait, for when he left she was much more cheerful and told her ladies that 'she was to be banished', and thought she might be sent to a nunnery at Antwerp. This in itself would have been enough to make her agree to everything Cranmer asked of her, even to abandoning her child's claim to the succession and condemning her to a lifetime marred by the stigma of bastardy.

The King had commuted the sentence on the condemned men to decapitation; the *Lisle Letters* make it clear that all of them, even

Smeaton, died by the axe on the scaffold on Tower Hill, and not at Tyburn. They were told by Kingston on the evening of 16 May that they must prepare for death on the morrow. Rochford took it well, although he was worried that his debts had not been cleared. Kingston promised to raise the matter with Cromwell. Weston spent his last evening writing a farewell letter to his parents, asking them and his wife to forgive him all the wrongs he had done them, and calling himself 'a great offender to God'. Brereton's wife certainly believed her husband to be innocent, and kept the gold bracelet he sent her as a parting gift for their son in memory of his father.

The executions of the men took place early in the morning of Wednesday 17 May before large crowds. The Queen was taken beforehand to the Bell Tower, whose windows overlooked Tower Hill, so that she might watch them die; according to Chapuys, this greatly 'aggravated her grief'. The condemned men all died 'charitably'. Rochford mounted the scaffold first, and made a long and pious speech of which there are three versions. According to the chronicler Charles Wriothesley, he said, 'Trust in God, and not in the vanities of the world, for if I had so done, I think I had been alive as ye be now.' He prayed that God would give the King a long and good life, then submitted to the axe. Weston followed: 'I thought little I would come to this,' he lamented. Then it was Norris's turn: he bravely declared that, 'in his conscience, he thought the Queen innocent of these things laid to her charge, and he would die a thousand deaths rather than ruin an innocent person.' Brereton died next. 'If any of them were innocent,' wrote George Constantine, 'it was he.' Only Smeaton was left. 'Masters,' he faltered, from a scaffold awash with blood, 'I pray you all pray for me, for I have deserved the death.' Within seconds, his head and body had joined the others in a cart standing beside the scaffold, which carried them back to St Peter ad Vincula within the Tower. Rochford was buried inside the chapel, and the rest in the adjacent churchyard, Weston and Norris in one grave, Brereton and Smeaton in the other. The heads were buried with the bodies, for the King had decided not to display them on poles above London Bridge, as was usually the case with those executed for treason.

Meanwhile, the Queen, much shaken, had returned to the Lieutenant's house. There was now no doubt in her mind that she would shortly follow the men to the scaffold, and all that concerned her now was to clear her name and prepare her soul for death. When Kingston came to tell her she must die the following morning, she asked him if any of those just executed had protested her innocence, and he told her that only Smeaton had confessed he deserved death. This upset Anne, and she cried,

> Alas! Has he not then cleared me of the public shame he has brought me to? Alas, I fear his soul suffers for his false accusations! But for my brother and those others, I doubt not but they are now in the presence of that Great King before whom I am to be tomorrow.

Kingston was now able to tell Anne that she would not die at the stake, but suffer a quicker death by decapitation, and that the King, to ensure a swift and painless end for the woman he had once loved, had sent to St Omer in France for a headsman whose expertise in cutting off heads with a sword was renowned. The man was already on his way.

During the afternoon of 17 May, Archbishop Cranmer convened a court at Lambeth for the purpose of annulling the King's marriage to Anne Boleyn. Anne was represented by her proctor, Dr Nicholas Wotton, and it was he who heard Cranmer pronounce that her union with the King was invalid and therefore null and void, and her daughter a bastard. Afterwards, it was announced publicly that Anne had never been the lawful Queen of England. She would go to the scaffold as Lady Marquess of Pembroke.

On the green outside her window she could see workmen erecting a high scaffold, for which they would be paid £23. 6s. 8d. They continued working through the night in order to have it ready by nine o'clock the next morning, the time set for Anne's execution. It was practically impossible for Anne and her ladies to sleep. At 2.0 a.m. Anne's chaplain arrived, and she spent the rest of the night praying with him. Cranmer came to the Tower soon after dawn on 18 May, as he had promised, to hear Anne's last confession and administer Holy Communion. She sent for Kingston, that he might be present when she 'received the good Lord', and also so that he could hear her declare her innocence before God. He later informed the King that, both before and after receiving the Sacrament, Anne swore on the damnation of her soul that 'she had never been unfaithful to her lord and husband'. Her ladies, who were also present, repeated this to Chapuys, who reported to the Emperor that 'the Concubine' had affirmed that she had 'never offended with her body against the King'.

Shortly before nine o'clock, Kingston received word from Cromwell that the headsman had been delayed on the Dover road and would not be at the Tower until noon. Anne, who had steeled herself to face death that morning, was 'very sorry' to hear this, 'as I thought to be dead before this time, and past my pain'. Kingston told her 'it should be no pain, it was so subtle', to which she replied, 'I have heard say the executioner was very good, and I have a little neck.' And she put her hands around it, 'laughing heartily'. Kingston told Cromwell he had seen many men and women executed who had been in great sorrow, 'but, to my knowledge, this lady hath much joy and pleasure in death'. Kingston then cleared the Tower of foreigners, since the King would allow only his own subjects to witness Anne's execution. The Constable advised Cromwell to keep the time of the event a secret in order to avoid crowds of Londoners coming to watch, for he supposed 'she will declare herself to be a good woman for all men but the King at the hour of her death'.

When noon came, the executioner had still not arrived, and Kingston had to tell Anne that her ordeal would be prolonged until nine o'clock the next morning. She was visibly shaken by the news. It was not that she desired death, she said, but she thought herself prepared to die, and feared the delay might weaken her resolve. But somehow she got through the next hours, spending most of the time at prayer and the rest in conversation with her ladies, telling them she blamed Chapuys for what had befallen her. Chapuys later said he was glad to know that 'the English Messalina' had held him accountable for her doom. 'I was flattered by the compliment, for she would have cast me to the dogs!'

Meanwhile, at Lambeth, on 18 May, Cranmer issued a dispensation permitting the King's marriage to Jane Seymour even though the parties were within the forbidden degrees of affinity, for Jane's grandmother, Elizabeth Neville, was a cousin of Henry's great grandmother Cicely Neville, Duchess of York. Henry's behaviour during the days leading up to Anne's execution astonished every-body. Displaying great *joie de vivre*, he was, Chapuys tells us, 'Out to dinner, here, there and everywhere with the ladies,' returning along the river after midnight to the sound of music and singing. The Bishop of Carlisle, who had once again hosted a dinner for his king, afterwards told Chapuys that Henry had 'behaved with almost desperate gaiety'. The ambassador thought that the King's rejuvenation sprang from 'hope of change, a thing especially agreeable to this king', and the prospect of 'getting soon a fine horse to ride'. Regarding Anne, whom Chapuys referred to as 'that thin old woman', Henry now believed that more than a hundred men had slept with her, 'but you never saw a prince or husband make greater show or wear his horns more patiently and lightly than this one does. I leave you to imagine why.'

Chapuys noted that Wyatt and Page were still in the Tower, but once Anne had been disposed of they would be freed, Wyatt upon his father's surety of his good behaviour, and Page on condition that he never again came near the King or the court.

Henry spent the evening of 18 May at the Strand with Jane Seymour, who was richly dressed and already carrying herself like a queen. Chapuys thought her behaviour 'very commendable' at this time. It is tempting to wonder how often her thoughts dwelt upon her predecessor, who was now languishing only a mile away downriver, waiting for death.

Anne could not sleep that night. She prayed, and talked with her ladies. She was quite calm, and at times almost cheerful, saying that those people who thought up nicknames for royalty would be able to call her Queen Anne Lackhead after her death, managing to laugh as she spoke. Chapuys was later gratified to hear that Anne thought her execution was a divine judgement upon her for having treated the Lady Mary so badly, and for having conspired her death. 'No person ever showed greater willingness to die,' the ambassador wrote. Robbed of everything she held dear in the world, Anne was now eager to leave it, placing her hope and trust in the deity she so firmly believed in.

Alexander Aless, the Scots reformer, was still in London. For some days, he had remained indoors, so knew nothing of the outcome of Anne's trial. On the night of 18–19 May, he had a terrible nightmare, dreaming that he beheld the severed head of Queen Anne with its vertebrae, arteries and veins exposed in all their bloody horror. Much troubled by this, he rose early in the morning and made his way to Lambeth Palace, where he encountered the Archbishop in the gardens. Cranmer looked unutterably sad, and Aless asked what was troubling him. 'Do you not know what is to happen today?' asked Cranmer, sighing. 'She who has been the Queen of England on earth will today become a queen in Heaven.' And he sat down on a bench and wept, as Aless realised with a jolt what his dream had foretold.

At nine o'clock on Friday, 19 May 1536, Kingston appeared at the door to Anne's rooms. 'Madam, the hour approaches,' he said; 'you must make ready.' Anne answered fearlessly: 'Acquit yourself of your charge, for I have been long prepared.' He gave her a purse containing £20.00, so that she could pay the headsman for his services and distribute alms for the poor, then escorted her, her ladies following, down the stairs and out into the May sunshine where a small contingent of the Yeomen of the King's Guard awaited to conduct the prisoner to the scaffold.

A crowd of two or three thousand people had gathered around the scaffold, which was now draped with black cloth and strewn with straw. Cromwell, his son Gregory (soon to marry Jane Seymour's widowed sister Elizabeth), Lord Chancellor Audley and the ailing Duke of Richmond were all present, as was the Duke of Suffolk, but Norfolk had stayed away.

A great murmur rose from the crowd as Anne Boleyn advanced on her short walk to Tower Green. She wore a robe of dark grey or black damask, trimmed with fur, with a low square neck and a crimson kirtle; from her shoulders flowed a long white cape. She looked exhausted and dazed, which was partly the result of two sleepless nights and partly from apprehension; she also kept looking behind her, as if she expected at any moment to see the King's messenger come galloping into the Tower to bring word of a reprieve. If so, it was a vain hope.

On the scaffold the headsman, black-garbed and hooded, his sword hidden in the straw, waited with his assistant and a priest beside the low wooden block. Anne mounted the steps with great

335

composure, and smiled as she gazed down on the people below her. She asked Kingston not to give the signal for her death until she had spoken 'that which she had a mind to say'. Then, with an untroubled countenance and a firm voice, she delivered a carefully prepared speech:

> Good Christian people, I am come hither to die, according to law, and therefore I will speak nothing against it. I come here only to die, and thus to yield myself humbly to the will of the King, my lord. And if, in my life, I did ever offend the King's Grace, surely with my death I do now atone. I come hither to accuse no man, nor to speak anything of that whereof I am accused, as I know full well that aught I say in my defence doth not appertain to you. I pray and beseech you all, good friends, to pray for the life of the King, my sovereign lord and yours, who is one of the best princes on the face of the earth, who has always treated me so well that better could not be, wherefore I submit to death with good will, humbly asking pardon of all the world. If any person will meddle with my cause, I require them to judge the best. Thus I take my leave of the world, and of you, and I heartily desire you all to pray for me.

She then turned to her ladies, who had ascended the scaffold with her, and told them not to be sorry to see her die, begging their pardon for any harshness towards them, praying them to take comfort for her loss, and admonishing them to 'be always faithful to her whom with happier fortune ye may have as your queen and mistress'. Anne then gave her prayer book to Lady Lee; entitled *The Hours of the Blessed Virgin Mary*, it had been made and illuminated for Anne in France around 1528, and she had inscribed it: 'Remember me when you do pray, that hope doth lead from day to day.' The prayer book still survives, and is now at Hever Castle.

Her farewell speeches done, Anne knelt with the priest for some final prayers. Then, she rose and took off her French hood, beneath which she had on a coif over her long dark hair, bound high so as not to impede the headsman, who now knelt to ask her forgiveness for what he must do. This she granted, and gave him his fee. Then she unclasped her necklace and knelt before the block. One of her maids tied a blindfold round her eyes, then withdrew to join the other ladies, who were weeping in a corner of the scaffold. The crowd also knelt, out of respect for the passing of a soul. Then, as Anne prayed aloud, saying over and over again, 'Jesu, receive my soul! O Lord God, have pity on my soul! To Christ I commend my soul!', the executioner retrieved his sword and cut off her head 'before you could say a Paternoster', according to Sir John Spelman, who was present. Then the headsman picked up the head and held it aloft, crying, in heavily accented English, 'So perish all the King's enemies!' At this moment, the onlookers saw the dead woman's eyes and lips move, a reflex action resulting from the shock of decapitation to the nervous system, yet to Tudor eyes an almost supernatural phenomenon.

'The Queen died boldly,' Kingston wrote to Cromwell later. 'God take her to His mercy.' Quickly, the crowd dispersed, and soon Tower Green was deserted, save for the broken body on the scaffold and the four weeping ladies who kept vigil beside it. No coffin had been provided, but an arrow chest lay waiting beside the steps. Reverently the ladies lifted the pathetic remains into it, and covered them with a sheet. The chest was then carried into the Royal Chapel of St Peter ad Vincula, where it was buried in the choir that afternoon, Lady Lee being chief mourner.

As Anne's head fell in the straw, the guns on the Tower wharf signalled, in a resounding report, her end to the world. Few mourned her passing, yet within two weeks of her death there were circulating in London ballads portraying her as a much wronged heroine, thus giving birth to a legend that has persisted, with gathering momentum, ever since.

Thomas Boleyn, Earl of Wiltshire, a broken man, now retired to Hever with his countess. She died in 1538 and was buried in the Howard Aisle in Lambeth Church; Wiltshire died a year later, and was laid to rest in Hever Church beneath a fine brass. Their grandson, Henry Carey, was created Viscount Hunsdon by Elizabeth I, and was much favoured by her. His sister Katherine married Sir Francis Knollys, another of Elizabeth's courtiers, and George Boleyn's son, named after his father, became Dean of Lichfield.

In the royal palaces, carpenters, masons and sempstresses were set to work removing Anne's initial wherever it occurred, and replacing it with Jane's. Portraits of Anne were taken down and hidden away. It was as if she had never existed. And not once, during the years that were left to him, would the King be heard to utter her name again.

12

Like one given by God

Henry VIII was at Whitehall Palace when the Tower guns signalled that he was once more a free man. He then appeared dressed in white mourning as a token of respect for his late queen, called for his barge, and had himself rowed at full speed to the Strand, where Jane Seymour had also heard the guns. News of Anne Boleyn's death had been formally conveyed to her by Sir Francis Bryan; it does not seem to have unduly concerned her, for she spent the greater part of the day preparing her wedding clothes, and perhaps reflecting upon the ease with which she had attained her ambition: Anne Boleyn had had to wait seven years for her crown; Jane had waited barely seven months.

It was common knowledge that Henry would marry Jane as soon as possible; the Privy Council had already petitioned him to venture once more into the perilous seas of holy wedlock, and it was a plea of the utmost urgency due to the uncertainty surrounding the succession. Both the King's daughters had been declared bastards, and his natural son Richmond was obviously dying. A speedy marriage was therefore not only desirable but necessary, and on the day Anne Boleyn died the King's imminent betrothal to Jane Seymour was announced to a relieved Privy Council. This was news as gratifying to the imperialist party, who had vigorously promoted the match, as it would soon be to the people of England at large, who would welcome the prospect of the imperial alliance with its inevitable benefits to trade.

Although the future Queen had rarely been seen in public, stories of her virtuous behaviour during the King's courtship had been circulated and applauded. Chapuys, more cynical, perceived that such virtue had had an ulterior motive, and privately thought it unlikely that Jane had reached the age of twenty-five without having lost her virginity, 'being an Englishwoman and having been so long' at a court where immorality was rife. However, he assumed that Jane's likely lack of a maidenhead would not trouble the King very much, 'since he may marry her on condition she is a maid, and when he wants a divorce there will be plenty of witnesses ready to testify that she was not'.

This apart, Chapuys and most other people considered Jane to be well endowed with all the qualities then thought becoming in a wife: meekness, docility and quiet dignity. Jane had been well groomed for her role by her family and supporters, and was in any case determined not to follow the example of her predecessor. She intended to use her influence to further the causes she held dear, as Anne Boleyn had, but, being of a less mercurial temperament, she would never use the same tactics. Jane's well-publicised sympathy for the late Queen Katherine and the Lady Mary showed her to be compassionate, and made her a popular figure with the common people and most of the courtiers. Overseas, she would be looked upon with favour because she was known to be an orthodox Catholic with no heretical tendencies whatsoever, one who favoured the old ways and who might use her influence to dissuade the King from continuing with his radical religious reforms.

Jane was of medium height, with a pale, nearly white, complexion. 'Nobody thinks she has much beauty,' commented Chapuys, and the French ambassador thought her too plain. Holbein's portrait of Jane, painted in 1536 and now in the Kunsthistorisches Museum, Vienna, bears out these statements, and shows her to have been fair with a large, resolute face, small slanting eyes and a pinched mouth. She wears a sumptuously bejewelled and embroidered gown and head-dress, the latter in the whelk-shell fashion so favoured by her; Holbein himself designed the pendant on her breast, and the lace at her wrists. This portrait was probably his first royal commission after being appointed the King's Master Painter in September 1536; a preliminary sketch for it is in the Royal Collection at Windsor, and a studio copy is in the Mauritshuis in The Hague. Holbein executed one other portrait of Jane during her lifetime. Throughout the winter of 1536–7, he was at work on a huge mural in the Presence Chamber in Whitehall Palace; it depicted the Tudor dynasty, with the figures of Henry VII and Elizabeth of York in the background, and Henry VIII and Jane Seymour in front. This magnificent work was one of the first to depict full-length likenesses of royal personages in England (although a late sixteenth-century inventory of Lord Lumley's pictures records a full-length portrait of Anne Boleyn, which has either been lost or cut down). Sadly, the Whitehall mural no longer exists, having been destroyed when the palace burned down in the late seventeenth century. Fortuitously, Charles II had before then commissioned a Dutch artist, Remigius van Leemput, to make two small copies, now in the Royal Collection and at Petworth House. His style shows little of Holbein's draughtsmanship, but his pictures at least give us a clear impression of what the original must have looked like. The figure of Jane is interesting in that we can see her long court train with her pet poodle resting on it. Her gown is of cloth of gold damask, lined with ermine, with six ropes of pearls slung across the bodice, and more pearls hanging in a girdle to the floor. Later portraits of Jane, such as those in long-gallery sets and the miniature by Nicholas Hilliard, all derive from this portrait or Holbein's original likeness now in Vienna, yet they are mostly mechanical in quality and anatomically awkward.

However, it was not Jane's face that had attracted the King so much as the fact that she was Anne Boleyn's opposite in every way. Where Anne had been bold and fond of having her own way, Jane showed herself entirely subservient to Henry's will; where Anne had, in the King's view, been a wanton, Jane had shown herself to be inviolably chaste. And where Anne had been ruthless, he believed Jane to be naturally compassionate. He would in years to come remember her as the fairest, the most discreet, and the most meritorious of all his wives.

Her contemporaries thought she had a pleasing sprightliness about her. She was pious, but not ostentatiously so. Reginald Pole, soon to be made a cardinal, described her as 'full of goodness', although Martin Luther, hearing of her reactionary religious views, feared her as 'an enemy of the Gospel'. According to Chapuys, she was not clever or witty, but 'of good understanding'. As queen, she made a point of distancing herself from her inferiors, and could be remote and arrogant, being a stickler for the observance of etiquette at her court. Chapuys feared that, once Jane had had a taste of queenship, she would forget her good intentions towards the Lady Mary, but his fears proved unfounded. Jane remained loyal to her supporters, and to Mary's cause, and in the months to come would endeavour to heal the rift between the King and his daughter.

Henry and Jane dined together in the Strand on the evening of 19 May; afterwards, the King took his barge and went straight to Hampton Court, where he would stay for a week. At six o'clock on the following morning, Jane followed him there, and at nine o'clock, they were formally betrothed in a ceremony lasting a few minutes. It is likely that Jane's family were present, for after the ceremony she returned with them to Wulfhall, there to await her marriage.

The next day, Henry wore white mourning once more, and gave orders for his daughter Elizabeth to be taken from Greenwich to Hatfield in the care of Lady Margaret Bryan, and kept out of his sight. There was an outstanding account to settle in respect of money outlayed by Sir William Kingston in respect of necessities provided for Elizabeth's mother. And there remained the problem of Mary. In spite of Jane's entreaties on the girl's behalf, Henry's attitude was unchanged: unless she acknowledged his laws and statutes, he would proceed against her. Mary was still in very grave danger.

Yet, even knowing her peril, she remained obdurate. Her father wanted her to abandon her deepest-held convictions and beliefs, and swear that her mother's marriage had been incestuous and unlawful, and that she accepted him as Supreme Head of the Church of England – something she could not bring herself to do. It seemed that coercion or force might be necessary if the King were to have his way, and several of the King's advisers thought that now would be a good time to put pressure on Mary. She was known to be weak and sickly. Seven years of insecurity and misery had made her a martyr, at twenty, to headaches, menstrual problems, and nervous depression, as well as vague, ill-defined illnesses, and she was still grieving for her mother.

The news of Anne Boleyn's death had revived Mary's spirits considerably, for she hoped the way might now be clear towards a reconciliation with her father. She knew she could count upon the support of Jane Seymour and the imperialist party, and prayed that the time had come to forget the unhappy past. She wrote to the King, begging to be taken back into his favour, humbly beseeching him to remember that she was 'but a woman, and your child'. Henry did not reply. The war of nerves had begun.

Mary, on the advice of her friend Lady Kingston, next tried approaching Henry through Cromwell, whom she had been told was secretly sympathetic towards her and might well use his very considerable influence on her behalf. On 26 May, Mary wrote to Mr Secretary, begging him to intercede for her with the King. Yet before her letter had time to arrive, Henry sent a deputation of the Privy Council to see Mary and make her submit to her father over the matter of her mother's marriage and the royal supremacy. She refused to do this, even though Norfolk told her that if his daughter had offered such 'unnatural opposition', he would have beaten and knocked her head against the wall until it was as soft as baked apples. This reduced Mary to floods of tears, but even the threat of violence was not sufficient to move her. When Henry learned of her defiance, he became more determined than ever to break her will. Nor was the Emperor inclined to interfere; Mary was not his subject, and he was more concerned about establishing the new alliance and reluctant to offend Henry VIII. Mary was on her own now.

Preparations for the royal wedding were now almost complete. Like all Henry VIII's marriages, it would be a private ceremony, although there would be public festivities to mark it. In the Queen's apartments, Anne Boleyn's falcon badge had been replaced by Jane's personal emblem, a phoenix rising from a castle amid flames and Tudor roses painted in red and white; this emblem would surmount the motto chosen by Jane, 'Bound to obey and serve'. Her initials had now replaced Anne's, although this had been done in such a hurry that at Hampton Court, the As are still visible underneath the Js. The monograms on the royal linen had been similarly altered, and at Zürich, where Coverdale's Bible with its dedication to Henry and Anne was being reprinted, the printers had to superimpose Jane's name on the frontispiece.

Both Henry and Jane returned to a transformed Whitehall Palace before 29 May. They were married there the following day in the Queen's Closet by Archbishop Cranmer. After the wedding ceremony Jane was enthroned in the Queen's chair beneath the canopy of royal estate in the great hall, where she presided over the court for the first time. Later that day, the King made her a grant of 104 manors in 4 counties, as well as a number of forests and hunting chases, for her jointure, the income that would support her during her marriage. One London estate, Paris Garden, was an unusual choice, for it was situated on the insalubrious Surrey shore of the Thames and its rents came from bear pits and brothels. Henry's personal wedding gift to his bride was a gold cup designed by Hans Holbein and engraved with the initials of the royal couple entwined with a love-knot; the Queen's motto appeared three times in the design. A drawing of this cup exists in the Ashmolean Museum in Oxford; the original was pawned by Charles I in 1625 and melted down four years later.

On 1 June, the King and Queen went by barge to Greenwich. The tradition that they spent their honeymoon at Wulfhall is based on an incorrect interpretation of a letter written by Sir John Russell in early June, in which he mentions a visit by Henry and Jane to Tottenham Parish Church. There exists today a Tottenham House not far from the site of Wulfhall, and a building called Tottenham Lodge seems in the sixteenth century to have been a dower house in the grounds of the Seymour estates; Lady Seymour lived there during her widow-hood. Nevertheless, it is not feasible to suppose that this was the Tottenham referred to in Sir John Russell's letter, for the time-scale dictates that it must have been Tottenham Church, north-east of the City of London, that was honoured by a royal visit at this time.

Within a week of his wedding, the King was optimistically speaking of 'the Prince hoped for in due season', leaving no doubt in the minds of his courtiers – who had, after all, heard of the slur on Henry's virility raised at George Boleyn's trial – that the royal marriage had been successfully consummated. Soon afterwards, prayers were being offered up in churches for the quickening of the Queen.

When Jane arrived at Greenwich, she was attended by a bevy of ladies. On that Friday, she dined in public with her husband for the first time. Sir John Russell was impressed by her demeanour on that occasion, and told Lord Lisle she was

> as gentle a lady as ever I knew, and as fair a queen as any in Christendom. I do assure you, my lord, the King hath come out of hell into heaven for the gentleness in this, and the cursedness and the unhappiness in the other. When you write to the King again, tell him that you do rejoice that he is so well matched with so gracious a woman as she is.

After dinner on that Friday, the new Queen's servants were all sworn in. There had been a great rush for places in Jane's household. In Katherine of Aragon's day the Queen's retinue had numbered 168; Anne Boleyn had increased the number, and Jane increased it further still, to 200. The King did not attend the long and tedious ceremony of oath-taking; he was busy listening to the reports of the privy councillors who had visited his daughter at Hunsdon. What they told him made him seethe with anger, and he was all for having Mary put on trial for treason, but when Queen Jane learned of his intentions, she begged him not to proceed. Her prayers fell on deaf ears, however, for the King, forgetting he was a bridegroom, told her she must be out of her senses. Thus early in her married life did Jane learn to tread warily with her husband.

Yet fate was on her side. The royal justices were reluctant to proceed against Mary, and suggested that instead of being tried for treason she be made to sign a paper of submission, recognising her father as head of the Church and her mother's marriage as incestuous and unlawful. Cromwell supported this idea, and persuaded the King to agree. He already regretted lending Mary his support, and in early June wrote her a scathing letter in which he deplored her unfilial stand against her father; with it, he enclosed the list of articles she was to sign, warning her he would not vouch for her safety if she refused. Mary, however, was still determined not to risk her immortal soul for the favour of an earthly king, however much she craved her father's love and approval. She ignored Cromwell's letter, and waited for a reply to a letter she had written to the King on 1 June, congratulating him on his marriage and begging leave to wait upon Queen Jane, 'or do her Grace such service as shall please her to command me'. Her letter had ended with the fervent hope that 'God would send your Grace shortly a prince, whereof no creature living would more rejoice than I'.

Henry did not bother to reply; and for the time being, the Queen, who had been put firmly in her place on the issue of Mary, deemed it wise to hold her peace.

Jane was proclaimed Queen of England on 4 June 1536 at Greenwich. On that day, she went in procession to mass, following the King with a great train of ladies, and in the evening she dined alone in her presence chamber under a canopy of estate before a large audience of courtiers. It appears she had clearly defined ideas of what she hoped to achieve as queen. First and foremost, she hoped to remain queen, and to this end she modelled her behaviour from the first upon that of Katherine of Aragon, whom she had greatly admired. Her other aims were threefold: to give the King a male heir, to work for the reinstatement of the Lady Mary, and to advance her family. She knew her power to be limited, and wisely concluded that it was essential not to misuse what influence she did have. Yet her quiet dignity – which endeared her to king and commons alike – hid a strong will and a determination to succeed within her chosen sphere.

Henry VIII, it must be said, was not an ideal husband, and cannot have been an easy man to live with at this stage of his life. His irritability stemmed from Mary's behaviour and from the pain of the suppurating wound on his leg. His autocracy extended to his private life, his word being law in the domestic sphere. Now that he could no longer indulge so much in the sporting pastimes he had loved in his youth, he had turned to theology for solace, and religion was now one of his chief preoccupations. He saw himself as the spiritual father of his people, appointed by God to lead them; and, as time passed, he grew increasingly pedantic and dogmatic, so that few dared argue with him. With his intimates he could be rude, intolerant, scathing and brutal; at other times, he was his old, genial self, but it was a side of him seen less and less as age and ill health encroached upon his once-splendid constitution. As he grew older, he became subject to bouts of savage temper, while at the same time a curiously sentimental streak in him became more pronounced. When he wanted to, he could exert great charm, and he was to the end of his life a man who enjoyed flirting with the ladies, much to the dismay of his successive wives and their supporters. But after his experiences with Katherine and Anne he would never again allow any woman to have it in her power to rule him. Jane Seymour, and his later wives, knew very well that to retain his favour they must adopt an attitude of adoring and respectful submission.

Henry VIII's marriage to Jane Seymour was a success, although as usual Henry's passion abated somewhat once he had secured his quarry; this had happened with Katherine, and even more dramatically with Anne. Yet it appears that he genuinely loved Jane for herself, and he accorded her the respect due to her, even though he could be very abrupt with her. In later life, he would convince himself that he had loved her the best of all his wives, and he was fond of declaring that he considered her to be his first lawful one. Jane was weighed down by jewels given to her by the King (her favourite seems to have been a fashionable IHS pendant); then there were the rich gowns with trains a statutory three yards long, the furs, and the head-dresses. There still exists an inventory of furniture provided by Henry for his wife's sojourn in the Tower prior to her coronation (which never took place), which lists such items as silk fire-screens and an elaborate inlaid box in which to keep legal documents. In all material respects, Henry was an indulgent husband.

We know very little about Jane's charitable enterprises, though fragments of information survive. For example, she offered a place in her household to Elizabeth Darrell, Sir Thomas Wyatt's destitute mistress, who had once served with her under Queen Katherine. But as for other charities, hardly anything is known of them, though had she been queen for longer, more information might have been recorded about them.

The King was now preparing for the forthcoming session of Parliament, which would confirm his marriage and settle the succession on Jane's children. He was also occupied with the advancement of the Queen's family, as he had been with the Boleyns a decade earlier. On 5 June, Sir Edward Seymour was created Viscount Beauchamp of Hache in the county of Somerset, and was appointed Chancellor of North Wales and Lord Chamberlain to the

King. His brother Thomas was made a gentleman of the privy chamber, and his other brother Henry was knighted. All three were given extensive grants of land. Edward and Thomas were now embarking on brilliant careers in public life, careers that would, in both cases, come to a tragic end on the block many years later. Sir John Seymour, the Queen's father, received no lands or titles, but he was already a sick man, and after his daughter's marriage he seems to have retired to Wulfhall with his wife.

The Seymour family certainly exercised a certain amount of patronage within the Queen's household, but mainly in the lower ranks. Some of Anne Boleyn's principal officers had been retained for their experience, and by Christmas 1536, Anne's treacherous sister-in-law, Lady Rochford, was back at court as Lady of the Bedchamber to Queen Jane. Some of the former Queen's servants had been transferred to the employ of the Lord Steward, but most had been retained, and in fact, the new Queen's household was very much as it had been in Anne's time.

On 6 June, after mass, Chapuys was personally conducted to the Queen's apartments by the King and formally presented to her. He kissed her hand, congratulated her on her marriage, and wished her prosperity, adding that, although the device of 'the lady who had preceded her on the throne' had been 'Happiest of Women', he had no doubt that she herself would realise that motto. He was certain, he said, that the Emperor would rejoice – as her husband had done – that such a 'virtuous and amiable' queen now sat upon the throne, and told her that it was impossible to comprehend the joy and pleasure which Englishmen in general had expressed on hearing of her marriage, especially as it was said that she was continually trying to persuade the King to restore Mary to favour. Jane promised Chapuys that she would continue to show favour herself to Mary, and would do her best to deserve the title of Peacemaker with which he had gallantly addressed her. The ambassador replied extravagantly by saying that, without the pain of labour and childbirth, Jane had gained in Mary a treasured daughter who would please her more than her own children by the King, to which she responded by saying again that she would do all she could to make peace between Henry and his daughter. Then she seemed at a loss as to what to say next, until the King came to her rescue and led Chapuys away, saying that he was the first ambassador Jane had received, and that she was not yet used to such audiences; he also remarked that his wife was by nature kind and amiable and 'much inclined to peace'; she would, he said, strive to prevent him from taking part in a foreign war, if only to avoid the pain and fear that separation would cause. After this Chapuys was obliged to revise his earlier, more cynical assessment of Jane, and now wrote of her virtue and her intelligence; later, he would commend her discretion, saying that she would not be drawn into discussions about religion or politics, and that she bore her royal honours with dignity.

On the following day, 7 June, Jane made her state entry into London at the King's side. They came by river, in the royal barge, from Greenwich to Westminster, and were escorted by a colourful procession of smaller boats, all gaily decked out for the occasion. Behind them sailed a great barge carrying the King's bodyguard in their scarlet and gold uniforms. As the royal procession passed along the river, the people cheered from the crowded banks, and warships and shore-guns sounded salutes. At Radcliffe Wharf, the royal barge halted so that the King and Queen could watch a pageant mounted by Chapuys in their honour: the ambassador, resplendent in purple satin, awaited them under a marquee embroidered with the imperial arms, and when they approached the quayside, gave the signal for two small boats, one carrying trumpeters, the other a consort of shawms and sackbuts, to leave their moorings and act as a musical escort for the royal barge, as it resumed its stately progress towards Westminster. The walls of the Tower had been festooned with banners and streamers, and the barges paused again to take the salute from the 400 guns lined up along its wharf, those same guns that had announced Anne Boleyn's death three weeks earlier. It is unlikely, however, that Henry and Jane allowed their triumph to be clouded by morbid thoughts; Anne was best forgotten, a conviction strongly reinforced by the loud approval voiced by the citizens of London for their new queen.

At Westminster, the royal couple came ashore and walked in procession to Westminster Abbey, where they heard high mass before returning to Whitehall Palace. In comparison to the ceremonies at the civic receptions for Katherine of Aragon and Anne Boleyn, Jane's entry into the capital was a very quiet affair. Katherine and

Anne had also been crowned within weeks of becoming queen, but Henry's Exchequer was so depleted that he could not now afford the expense of another coronation. It was his intention to have Jane crowned later in the year, when hopefully his financial situation would have improved; by then, the funds and treasures of several dissolved religious houses would have been diverted to the Crown. Indeed, Henry had already set a provisional date in late October, and had made some preliminary plans. Jane would come to the Tower by river from Greenwich in a great barge fashioned to look like the Bucentaur, the ceremonial vessel used by the Doges of Venice. She would then make a progress through London to Westminster, and be fêted with pageantry and music. Her crown would be the one worn by her two predecessors, an open coronal of heavy gold set with sapphires, rubies and pearls; sadly, it no longer exists, having been melted down on the order of Oliver Cromwell.

Next morning, on 8 June, Jane came to the gallery above the new gatehouse at Whitehall and waved goodbye to Henry as he rode in procession to open Parliament. In the House, when Lord Chancellor Audley in his opening speech praised the Queen and declared that her 'age and fine form give promise of issue', there was resounding applause, and the King departed, smiling benignly, confident that his ministers could be left to deal satisfactorily with the question of the succession. Soon afterwards, a new Act of Succession decreed that the crown should pass on Henry's death to the children of Queen Jane, 'a right noble, virtuous and excellent lady', who, 'for her convenient years, excellent beauty, and pureness of flesh and blood, is apt, God willing, to conceive issue'. The Act also acknowledged the 'great and intolerable perils' which the King had suffered as a result of two unlawful marriages, and drew attention to the 'ardent love and fervent affection' for his realm and people that had impelled him, 'of his most excellent goodness', to venture upon a third marriage, which was 'so pure and sincere, without spot, doubt or impediment, that the issue procreated out of the same, when it shall please Almighty God to send it, cannot be lawfully disturbed of the right and title in the succession'. It was also enacted that the King's first two marriages had been unlawful, and that the Ladies Mary and Elizabeth were illegitimate and unfit to inherit the throne. Failing any issue by Queen Jane, the King was granted the unprecedented power to appoint anyone he chose to be his successor, and that included the issue of 'any other lawful wife'.

The problem of Mary still had to be resolved. When she realised that Henry was not going to answer her letter, Mary also perceived, with terrible clarity, that the only way to earn his clemency was by submitting to his demands, hateful though they were to her. Both Chapuys and the Emperor were constantly urging her to do as her father required, assuring her of the Pope's absolution should she be compelled to sign against her will the articles sent by Cromwell. Yet Mary could be as stubborn as her father. She wrote to him again, begging him of his 'inestimable goodness' to pardon her offences, and saying she would never be happy until he had forgiven her. 'Most humbly prostrate' before his noble feet, she craved the favour of an audience, for she had humbly repented of her faults. Again, Henry refused to reply, and to Jane and Cromwell he expressed doubts about Mary's sincerity, which none of their reassurances could dispel. Nothing less than her signature on those articles would persuade him that she meant what she said and Cromwell, knowing his master to be implacable on this issue, privately urged her to sign at once, hinting at terrible consequences if she did not.

For the next day or so, Mary wrestled with her conscience, then she gave way. On 13 June, fortified by Chapuys's assurance that the Pope would absolve her from all responsibility for what she was about to do under duress, she finally acknowledged her father to be supreme head of the Church of England and her mother's marriage 'by God's law and man's law incestuous and unlawful'. Thus, by a few strokes of the pen, did Mary repudiate in the eyes of the world everything she had hitherto held sacred; she had capitulated for worldly reasons, where others had stood firm and suffered for their principles, and she would never, as long as she lived, forgive herself for this betrayal.

But the deed had been done, and the articles were already on their way to the King with a covering letter begging his forgiveness and stating that the writer was so conscious of having offended him that she dared not call him father. Chapuys thought she had never done a better day's work, and cheerfully assured the Emperor that he had relieved Mary of every doubt of conscience. There now remained, ostensibly, no bar to Mary's reconciliation to her father, but the King, who was certainly gratified to learn of his daughter's submission, was irritated that he had been made to wait so long for it. Instead of replying personally to her, he sent Sir Thomas Wriothesley, one of his 'new men', to Hunsdon, with orders to obtain a fuller declaration of her faults in writing. In return, Wriothesley was to ask Mary to name those ladies she would like appointed to her service should his Majesty decide to increase her household pending a return to favour. Such instructions could only have come from the King himself, and Mary was pathetically grateful; she wrote a long and abject letter to Cromwell, acknowledging her faults and thanking him for his kindness in furthering her cause with the King. When Henry read it, he allowed his long-suppressed paternal feelings to revive: it would not be long before he was ready to play once more the part of a loving father.

No one was more delighted than the Queen when Mary signed her submission. Jane had worked for months towards a reconciliation, and she now looked forward to receiving her stepdaughter at court. There were few ladies in her household with whom she could associate on virtually equal terms; in order to emphasise her rank, she had set herself apart from those with whom she might have been familiar, and the truth was that she was now feeling rather lonely. Mary would be a friend and companion to her, for she ranked high enough to enjoy the privilege of the Queen's friendship. Many other people at court welcomed the prospect of Mary's return to favour, as did the common people when news of its likelihood spread.

The King made his first friendly move towards Mary at the end of June, when he sent his officers to Hunsdon to see she had all she required and to advise her that it would not be long before he brought the Queen to visit her. In the meantime, Henry prepared to enjoy his first summer with his new wife, having just made Cromwell Lord Privy Seal in place of Anne Boleyn's father, who had retired from court, and sent to jail an Oxfordshire man called John Hill for saying that Anne had been put to death only for the King to take his pleasure with Jane Seymour. It is a fact that Master Hill was the only person on record as having spoken out against the King's new marriage, a sure indication of how popular it was.

During the long summer days there were jousts and triumphs in honour of the Queen, as well as pageants on the river. Jane was an accomplished horsewoman, and shared to some extent the King's passion for hunting, a sport in which they frequently participated. On 29 June, St Peter's Night, they visited the Mercers' Hall in Cheapside, and stood at a window to watch the annual ceremony of the setting of the marching watch of the City. It was a stirring occasion, the procession being illuminated by torchlight. Throughout that summer, Henry and Jane commuted between Whitehall and Greenwich, travelling in the royal barge, which was frequently filled with minstrels playing a variety of instruments. The royal couple watched a firework display, and went on a short progress. On 3 July, they presided over the magnificent celebrations that graced the triple wedding of the Earl of Westmorland's son and two daughters, and were guests of honour at the banquet which followed, when Henry came in procession from Whitehall wearing Turkish costume. It was, almost, like old times.

Jane, meanwhile, had sent her brother, Lord Beauchamp, to visit Mary, with instructions to obtain a list of the clothing she would need when she returned to court. Beauchamp himself, possibly at the Queen's suggestion, presented Mary with a superb horse, and told her that the King's 'gracious clemency and merciful pity' had overcome his anger at her 'unkind and unnatural behaviour'. When he had gone, Mary wrote again to the King, declaring that she would never vary from her confession and submission, and prayed that God would send him and the Queen issue. After receiving this, Henry let it be known that he would shortly be reconciled to his eldest daughter, whereupon several influential courtiers rushed to Hunsdon to ingratiate themselves with her.

Mary's health had been poor for months, and the strain of all this was almost too much for her. The King therefore decided to defer her official reception at court for a time, and visited her privately with Jane on 6 July at a house in Hackney. It was an emotional reunion, with Henry speaking affectionately to his daughter for the first time in six years. He was gentle, kind and patient with her, and told her how deeply he regretted having kept her so long from him. This much was overheard by his retinue, but the rest of the conversation took place in private. Afterwards, though, it was obvious that the meeting had been conducted with 'such love and

353

affection, and such brave promises for the future, that no father could have behaved better towards his daughter'. Jane gave her stepdaughter a diamond ring; Henry's gift was 'a thousand crowns for her little pleasures'; he did not wish her to be anxious about money and in future, he told her, she should have as much as she wished. The King and Queen left after vespers, promising to see Mary again soon.

Two days later, Chapuys was happy to report to Charles V a great improvement in Mary's circumstances: she had more freedom than ever before, and was now being served with great solemnity and honour. All she lacked was the title Princess of Wales, but that, said Chapuys, was of no consequence, because it had been announced that she was from henceforth to rank as second lady at court after Queen Jane. On 8 July, Mary wrote to thank her father for the 'perfect reconciliation' between them, and ended by once more expressing the hope that 'my very natural mother, the Queen' would shortly have children. She also wrote to Cromwell, who responded by sending her a ring inset with portrait miniatures of Henry, Jane and herself, made specially for her; the bearer of this gift was none other than the King himself, who had been so impressed with it that he insisted on presenting it in person when he and Jane next visited Mary at Richmond later in July.

So far, Jane had displayed little interest in Henry's younger daughter, who was now nearly three. The imperialist party had all along supported the restoration of the Lady Mary, but there was no political faction prepared to act in the interests of the bastard child of a convicted traitor. The King had banished Elizabeth from his sight, and wanted nothing to do with her. Yet she was an intelligent child, and highly precocious. 'Why, Governor,' she had asked Sir John Shelton, who had charge of her household, 'how hath it, yesterday Lady Princess, and today but Lady Elizabeth?' We do not know how Elizabeth found out about her mother's death, but it is likely to have been early on, as the arrival of a new stepmother on the scene would certainly have provoked awkward questions in one so forward. What is certain is that the knowledge of what had happened to Anne Boleyn had a traumatic effect on Elizabeth, and may well have crippled her emotionally for life; it is a fact that she made a point of avoiding marriage and any other serious commitment to a man. In the meantime, though, she was just a little girl who was fast outgrowing her clothes, much to the dismay of Lady Bryan, who had great trouble persuading Cromwell to replace such necessary items as nightgowns and underclothing.

Yet now, conscious of her own good fortune, Mary found time to spare a thought for her half-sister, of whom she had always been fond, for all that Elizabeth was Anne Boleyn's child. Deprived of a child of her own, Mary lavished all her frustrated maternal affection on Elizabeth, and on 21 July paid a visit to her at Hatfield. Afterwards, she wrote to their father, telling him that Elizabeth was in good health and that he would have cause to be proud of her in time to come, and ending by sending her usual felicitations to 'the Queen, my good mother'. Already, a bond of friendship had sprung up between the two women.

Late in July, the King and Queen, with the court, spent a weekend in Dover; this was the visit postponed from May, when Anne Boleyn's arrest had intervened. According to Chapuys, Henry was feeling low, not only because of his bastard son's death, but also because he was disappointed that the Queen had as yet shown no signs of being pregnant. Chapuys gained the impression that her coronation was being postponed until she had proved she could bear children, but this was not the real reason. The progress did little to restore the King's former good humour, and on 12 August he confided to Chapuys that he felt himself growing old and doubted whether he would have any children by the Queen. It would be reasonable to suppose that advancing infirmity was affecting Henry's potency, especially in view of the fact that none of his wives after Jane conceived a child by him, except, perhaps, Katherine Howard; it may even be that what had been said at George Boleyn's trial had had some basis in truth. Because Jane took so long to conceive a child, it would appear that there was a difficulty, and the likelihood is that it lay with Henry. Yet outwardly, the royal couple showed no signs of tension; indeed, they gave the impression of being harmoniously and happily married.

Henry still managed to go hunting, and on 9 August led a party out with Jane – on that day, twenty stags were brought down. Later in August the King visited Mary at Hunsdon and told her that her return to court would not be long delayed. Her health was improving steadily, and Henry was anxious to stage a public reunion. Jane had complained that she felt lonely, for there were 'none but my inferiors' with whom to make merry, and had pleaded that she might 'enjoy the company of my Lady Mary's Grace at court'. 'We will have her here, darling,' Henry had promised, 'if she will make thee merry.' Early in September, he wrote to his daughter, commanding her to prepare for a move to court in the near future, and shortly afterwards he proclaimed her his heir, in default of any issue by Queen Jane. As news of this spread, crowds gathered around the royal palaces, where apartments were being prepared for Mary, in the hope of seeing her, and Lady Salisbury, Mary's former governess, was cheered when she visited the court at the King's invitation.

Plague returned to London in September, so the court moved to Windsor. Jane was looking forward with pleasure to Mary's arrival, and was also happily involved in planning her coronation with the King and his ministers. It was due to take place on the Sunday before All Hallows' Day, and funds were now available for it, thanks to the efforts made by Cromwell and the King's commissioners to divert the wealth of dissolved monasteries into the royal coffers; the dissolution was now gaining momentum. Henry, who had read some of the reports, professed himself scandalised that the word of God was not being observed as it should have been in some houses. There were allegations of lechery, sodomy and over luxurious living, though it is hard to estimate how much corruption there actually was in the monasteries of England at that time, and how much was fabricated by the royal officials, who knew that the King meant to close them and appropriate the spoils.

The economic and social consequences of the dissolution are beyond the scope of this book, but by 1540 the wealth of the religious houses had been swallowed up by the Exchequer, and their buildings and lands had been sold at a profit to supporters of the King's reformist policies. The dissolution resulted in the secularisation of the Church, and, in many areas, notably the south, it was popular, there being a tangible resentment of the riches hitherto enjoyed by the religious houses. In addition, the heretical teachings of Luther and others had come, through closer contact with Europe, to find

356

favour with a growing number of people, while many bishops actively encouraged reform.

But gradual closure of many of the smaller monasteries meant that hordes of monks and nuns were being turned out into the world with only inadequate pensions to live on. They therefore became dependent upon the succour provided by local parishes and charitable persons. In the past, the monasteries themselves had looked after vagrants and the destitute, but those same monks and nuns who had taken in the poor were now themselves reduced in many cases to begging, a problem the government had not anticipated and did little to address.

Public outrage at the growing number of beggars whom local communities were forced to support was further exacerbated in many areas by the curtailment of ancient religious traditions occasioned by the break with Rome and the dissolution. Dissatisfaction was greatest in the northern and eastern counties where, away from the influence of London, disapproval of the King's measures was strong and religious sensibilities outraged. Conservatives were appalled to see churches and monastic buildings destroyed; they watched aghast as the King's men broke up images of the Madonna and saints, took axes to stained-glass windows, and carried away vestments and altar plate to the treasury. The King meant to purge his Church of England of all its superstitious and popish facets: holy shrines were desecrated – many being exposed as fakes – and the seeking of miracles was forbidden. Public grievance over the changes was made even more acute by the levying of heavy taxes to finance the programme of ecclesiastical reform.

Such was the social and political backdrop against which the King hoped to stage Jane's coronation. In September, carpenters were set to work in Westminster Hall, preparing it for the coronation banquet. Henry and Jane were then at Windsor. On 27 September, Sir Ralph Sadler, the Queen's secretary, arrived there with letters from Cromwell in London, and tried to see Henry before he joined the Queen in her chamber for supper; but although he said he had urgent news to impart, the King made him wait until he had eaten. Afterwards, he summoned Sadler and read the letters he had brought. The news was bad. There was plague at Westminster, even in the Abbey itself. Henry told Sir Ralph that the coronation would have to be put off for a season. As it turned out, plague was not the only delaying factor. Within days, there was worse news from London: the King now had a rebellion on his hands.

The rebellion known as the Pilgrimage of Grace began with a riot in the town of Louth in Lincolnshire, where the inhabitants felt that the King had gone too far with his religious reforms. This was no ordinary riot, however, but was organised by determined men. Others flocked to join them, and soon a contingent of the men of Norfolk had swelled their ranks; by 13 October, the rising had spread to Yorkshire, where three days later a rebel army occupied York. It was at this point that one of the burghers of York, a man named Robert Aske, set himself up as the rebels' leader. Then they were joined by the men of Hull under their leader John Constable.

Before very long this army of the people was marching south, its leaders carrying banners depicting the Five Wounds of Christ, which gave the rebellion its name; they saw their cause as nothing less than a crusade, their aim being to persuade the King to heal the breach with Rome and leave the monasteries alone.

At first, the King considered leading an army himself against them, and, acknowledging his trust in his queen, he announced that she would be regent in his absence, with Cranmer and the Privy Council acting as her advisers. But the Pilgrimage of Grace posed a personal dilemma for Jane, who was herself a religious conservative and had a certain amount of sympathy with the rebels. She ventured to voice her doubts to the King, choosing to do this in public and hoping, by her intervention, to diffuse his anger against the rebels. One day in late October, when Henry was sitting beneath his canopy of estate, surrounded by his court, she fell on her knees before him and begged him to reconsider the fate of the monasteries, asking him to restore some of the smaller ones. Henry said nothing, but his face registered his irritation; Jane ignored this, and went on, daring to suggest that perhaps God had permitted the rebellion as a punishment for the deliberate ruin of so many churches. At this, the King's patience gave way, and he exploded with anger, brutally ordering her to get up and attend to other things, and reminding her that the last queen had died as a result of meddling too much in state affairs. Jane took Henry's warning to heart, and never again interfered in politics. Those like the Prioress of Clementhorpe, who asked for her aid in saving her convent, met with disappointment, for Jane could do nothing. Her first duty, as she saw it, was obedience to her husband, and she took his advice, busying herself with domestic affairs, estate business and matters concerning her servants.

In November 1536, she was writing from Windsor to Cromwell, requesting his help in assisting a former retainer who had fallen into poverty: 'Ye could not do a better deed for the increase of your eternal reward in the world to come,' she told him. Then she was commanding her park keeper at Hampton Court to send venison to the gentlemen of the King's Chapel Royal; her warrant still survives, bearing one of only two extant examples of her signature. She also ordered a survey to be made of her lands and property, and her officers were eventually able to report to her that they found all her tenants and farmers 'as glad of her Grace as heart could be'; the year that had seen her marriage to the King was viewed by them as a year of peace in England.

Sadly, it was not to end that way. For two months, the rebellion flourished, the pilgrims being joined by more and more supporters. Henry gave up the idea of confronting them himself since he did not relish the idea of a winter campaign, and, in order to gain time in December, he sent word to Aske that he would meet his demands, promising 'with comfortable words' to send Norfolk north to ratify the agreement. He himself, he declared, would follow later. He also agreed to the rebels' demand that the Queen be crowned at York Minster. Henry was nothing if not a practised dissembler, and Aske accepted his assurances in good faith, joyfully disbanding his army in the confident belief that his sovereign would be true to his word. On 8 December, Aske was formally pardoned, and peace was restored.

The King's public rebuke to his wife caused no lasting damage to their marriage; in November, they were reported to be well and merry, and they were at Windsor in early December, planning their first Christmas together at Greenwich. The winter of 1536–7 was bitterly cold, and the roads were iced up, but this did not deter the King from summoning Mary to court for their public reconciliation. She arrived at Windsor on 17 December, richly dressed and with a train of gorgeously attired ladies, and proceeded through the ranks of courtiers in the presence chamber to where her father and Queen Jane awaited her by a roaring fire at the far end of the room. After curtsying twice, the small, spare girl with red hair and a *retroussée* nose made a sweeping obeisance to the King, fell on her knees, and asked for his blessing. He took her hand, raised and kissed her, then presented her to the Queen, who also kissed her and warmly bade her welcome. Then Henry turned to the Privy Councillors standing near by, gave them a menacing stare, and declared, with superb tactlessness, 'Some of you were desirous that I should put this jewel to death!' There was an embarrassed silence until the Queen spoke up: 'That were great pity, to have lost your chiefest jewel of England.' Henry smiled. 'Nay, nay!' he replied, patting Jane on the belly, an indication that he thought she might be pregnant, 'Edward! Edward!' Already, he had decided upon a name for the hoped-for son, though within a week or so he would know Jane was not pregnant this time.

The excitement was proving too much for Mary, and to Henry's consternation she suddenly fainted at his feet. Both he and Jane stooped to assist her, with the courtiers crowding round; when Mary regained her senses a few moments later Henry bade her be of good cheer, as nothing would go against her. When she had revived sufficiently, he took her hand and walked her up and down the room.

After this, Mary was often at court. She quickly became close to the Queen and was accorded precedence immediately after her. And it was thanks to Mary's intercession that the King invited Elizabeth to court for the Christmas season. Foreign visitors to Greenwich would have been astonished to see the royal family together; it seemed that at last the King was settling down to something resembling family life. At table, the King and Queen sat together, with Mary opposite Jane a little further along the table. Elizabeth was too young to sit at table with the adults, but those who saw Henry playing with her during the festivities observed his affection for her.

Just before Christmas, the Thames froze in London. On 22 December, Henry, Jane and Mary, warmly wrapped in furs, rode on horseback from Westminster to the City, which was gaily decorated in their honour with tapestries and cloth of gold; priests in copes with crosiers stood at every street corner waiting to bless the royal party and, in spite of the bitter cold, the people turned out in large numbers to watch the procession, cheering loudly. After a service in St Paul's to mark the beginning of the Christmas celebrations, Henry and Jane then spurred their horses across the frozen river and galloped to the Surrey shore, Mary following with the rest of their retinue. Then they rode to Greenwich Palace, where they would stay for Christmas, when Jane would preside for the first time over the glittering Yuletide court. Yet the season was marred for her by news of the death of her father on 21 December at Wulfhall. He had never lived in the public eye, so there was no observance of court mourning for him, nor did the Queen attend the funeral at Easton Priory in Wiltshire (the body was later moved to Bedwyn Magna Church). It may be that she had never been close to a father she had rarely seen in recent years; there is certainly no record that she was unduly affected by his death.

On New Year's Day, gifts were exchanged. Both Henry and Jane gave Mary costly presents, as did Cromwell, and Mary, among other gifts, gave some money to Elizabeth's chaplain because she was concerned about the child's religious education.

But this peaceful lull could not last. Robert Aske had been the King's guest at court over Christmas, and after it had ended he and his followers began to realise that the King had no intention of honouring his promises. The dissolution of the monasteries had resumed, taxes were still heavy, and there were as yet no definite plans for a royal visit to York, much less a coronation in that city. Disillusioned and bitter, the rebels regrouped, but this time, Henry was not prepared to send them fair words. Instead, he sent that redoubtable commander the Duke of Norfolk into Lincolnshire at the head of a great army, to teach those in revolt that they must not presume to question the will of their king. It was a terrible lesson. Norfolk hanged as many traitors as he could lay his hands upon, and in March 1537 presided over a Grand Assize that condemned a further thirty-six men to death. Their bodies, left rotting on gibbets for months, served as a grim warning to all those who dared contemplate further rebellion. Constable was arrested and condemned to death in June, being hanged alive in chains over the gates of Hull, where he shortly perished of exposure and starvation, and Aske was captured in July, and suffered the same fate at York. By then, the rebellion had long since been effectively crushed.

Having successfully dealt with the worst crisis of his reign, Henry VIII discovered that he had another cause for rejoicing, for in the early spring of 1537, Queen Jane discovered that she was pregnant; she had conceived around the middle of January. Shortly afterwards, Henry took her on a progress through Kent, visiting Rochester and Sittingbourne before going on to Canterbury as pilgrims and making their offerings at the shrine of St Thomas à Becket. It was characteristic of Henry that he was already planning the dissolution of the great Abbey of St Augustine there – within a year, Becket himself would have been denounced as a traitor to his king, his shrine broken up, and his bones destroyed.

From Canterbury the King and Queen rode to Dover to see the newly constructed pier. Then it was back to Hampton Court where, on 20 March, Jane granted the master of the Hospital of St Katherine-by-the-Tower, an institution serving as both church and hospice under the traditional patronage of successive queens of England, exemption from all annual tithes in consideration of the burden borne by the hospital from the increasing numbers of poor people. And, at around the same time, Jane stood sponsor at the christening of her brother Edward's child, who bore her name; Mary and Cromwell also attended the ceremony.

Jane's pregnancy was announced at the beginning of April, when the King conveyed the happy news to the Privy Council. In the minutes of this meeting, the councillors recorded that they trusted in God that the Queen's Grace would bring forth many fair children, 'to the consolation and comfort of the King's Majesty, and of his whole realm'. News of Jane's condition spread quickly, and soon there were celebrations, not only in England, but as far away as Calais, where Lady Lisle, wife of the Governor, was not only copying the gold and silk embroidered caps and nightgowns worn and popularised by Queen Jane, but was also doing her best to place one of her daughters in Jane's service. She thought the news to be 'merry tidings'.

Throughout that spring, Henry was merry himself, and cheerful, even though his leg pained him and kept him indoors for much of the time. Late in May the Queen appeared at Hampton Court in the open-laced gown of a pregnant mother, and it was announced that the child had moved in her womb. 'God send her good deliverance of a prince, to the joy of all faithful subjects,' wrote one courtier. When news that the baby – 'like one given by God' – had quickened reached London on Trinity Sunday, a special mass was celebrated in St Paul's Cathedral in thanksgiving that 'our most excellent lady and mistress, Queen Jane, hath conceived and is great with child'. On the same day a *Te Deum* was sung in churches throughout the realm, 'for joy of the Queen's quickening', and in London that evening the citizens were provided with free wine and bonfires were lit. The King abandoned plans for a summer coronation; that could wait until after October, when the child was due.

Throughout the summer, prayers were offered in churches for Jane's safe delivery. She undertook no public engagements, and led a relatively quiet life, being attended by the royal physicians and the best midwives in the kingdom. To please her, the King had her brother Edward admitted to the Privy Council on 22 May. He also made sure she lacked for nothing. Her condition had given her a craving for quails, a great delicacy at that time, but unfortunately out of season. Henry went to considerable trouble to have the birds shipped over from Calais, commanding Lord Lisle to provide 'fat quails which her Grace loveth very well, and longeth not a little for'. If none was to be found in Calais, then a search must be made in Flanders. On 24 May, a large consignment of quails arrived, a welcome sight to the Queen and her relieved husband; they ate a dozen roasted at dinner, and a further dozen for supper. Jane's craving for quails persisted right through her pregnancy; the Lady Mary sent her some in June, and Lord and Lady Lisle dispatched a constant supply from Calais, for which the Queen sent her grateful thanks.

The King was still in excellent spirits, and Sir John Russell found him behaving 'more like a good fellow than a king'; it was said he had never been merrier. Early in June, after a brief visit to Guildford, the court moved to Windsor because there was plague in London. The King hunted daily in Windsor Great Park, and the game he shot was served to the Queen along with her favourite quails. By the middle of July, Jane was very large and had unlaced her gowns to their fullest extent. As a token of appreciation to Lady Lisle, she agreed to find a place in her household for one of her two daughters, Anne and Katherine Bassett. Lady Lisle had been unsuccessful in securing places for them the previous year, and was desperate to have at least one accepted. Jane commanded her to send both girls over from Calais, so that she could decide which one she liked best. They must bring two changes of clothes, one of satin, the other of damask. The sister not chosen by the Queen would be offered a place in the household of the Duchess of Suffolk. Once the choice was made, Jane would provide wages and food only: Lady Lisle must see that her daughter was properly kitted out, and must exhort her girls to be 'sober, sad, wise and discreet, lowly above all things, obedient, and willing to be governed and ruled by my Lady Rutland and my Lady Sussex, and to serve God and be virtuous, for that is much regarded'.

It is pure speculation to suggest that, had she lived, Jane Seymour might well have been the most formidable of Henry's wives, yet this is certainly indicated by the standards she set for her household and by her warning, sent through Lord Hussey to Lady Lisle, that the court was 'full of pride, envy, indignation, mocking, scorn and derision'. She had succeeded in ridding her household of Anne Boleyn's wayward influence, and was vigorously re-establishing the virtuous precepts set by Queen Katherine. Beneath her outward show of humility, there was steel, even though it was confined to the domestic sphere only. A year on the throne had transformed Jane into a pious and godly matron who was fully conscious of her rank and dignity, and who carried the knowledge that she might well be nurturing the heir to England in her womb.

Jane's chief companions at this time were her sister Elizabeth, now the wife of Cromwell's son Gregory, and the Lady Mary. At the end of August, wagers were laid on the sex of the royal baby and the date of its birth, and the doctors and soothsayers were all confidently predicting a boy. 'I pray Jesu, an [if] it be his will, send us a prince,' prayed a courtier fervently. The birth was to take place at Hampton Court, and the court moved there early in September. On the 16th, Jane took to her chamber. Anne Boleyn had once occupied the magnificent rooms assigned to her; they were near the Silver Stick Gallery, and had linenfold panelling and gilded ceilings, much like the recently restored suite known as 'Wolsey's Rooms', except that Jane's long-vanished apartments would have been bigger.

Here Lady Lisle's daughters came. Jane picked the elder, Anne Bassett, who was sworn to her service on 17 September. Anne would become a popular figure at court during the years to come, even attracting the King's amorous attention at one time, yet she kept her good reputation. For the present, however, she was dismayed to find that her attire did not meet the Queen's exacting standards. Jane insisted her French hood would have to go, and Lady Sussex hurriedly found a suitable gown of crimson damask and a gable hood for Anne to wear when in the Queen's presence. Jane ordered the girl to obtain two new hoods with stiffened frontlets, as well as two good gowns of black velvet and black satin, and insisted that she replace her coarse linen undergarments with ones of fine lawn. Finally, to her dismay, the Queen learned that there were far too few pearls stitched to Anne's girdle, and warned her that if she did not appear at court in the proper clothes, she would not be allowed to attend the royal christening when the time came.

Jane was nevertheless a generous mistress; she gave Mary Zouche, one of Holbein's sitters whose portrait survives at Windsor, a gift of jewelled borders for a hood or gown, and after Jane's death the King granted Mary a pension of £10 per annum in consideration of her good service. The Queen also gave some jewellery to Mary, Lady Monteagle, one of her ladies-in-waiting. But she was not over-familiar with her ladies, and nor would they have expected her to be. She had the company of the Lady Mary during these last weeks of her pregnancy, and that was enough for her.

In London, the plague raged. Henry was alarmed for the safety of his wife and unborn child; as for Jane, she was horribly afraid. The King gave orders that no one who had been in London was to approach the court, but even this did not dispel her fears. 'Your ladyship would not believe how much the Queen is afraid of the sickness,' wrote Anne Bassett to her mother. To further minimise the risks, Henry moved with his household to Esher, in order to reduce the number of people staying at Hampton Court. He did not apparently consider his presence there necessary for his wife's peace of mind, but he told Norfolk that he would not travel far from her at this time,

> considering that, being a woman, upon some sudden and displeasant rumours that might by foolish or light persons be blown abroad in our absence, she might take to her stomach such

impression as might engender no little danger or displeasure to that wherewith she is now pregnant, which God forbid.

The Council had advised him not to travel more than sixty miles from Hampton Court, 'especially as she being, as it is thought, further gone by a month or more than she thought herself at the perfect quickening, remembering what dependeth upon the prosperity of that matter'.

It was obvious by early October that the birth was imminent, and the courtiers were telling each other to 'look daily for a prince'. The King was so certain that his child would be a boy that he gave orders for a Garter Stall to be made ready in St George's Chapel for 'the Prince hoped for in due season'. On 7 October, as the Queen showed no signs of going into labour, the Lady Mary went briefly back to Hunsdon to attend the christening of the child of one of her tenants; when she returned, Jane was still up and about. In Leicestershire, at Bradgate Manor, the King's niece, Frances Brandon, Marchioness of Dorset, gave birth to a baby girl and named her after the Queen; this child grew up to be the ill-fated Lady Jane Grey, who would lose her head before her seventeenth birthday. And in London, the young Duchess of Suffolk bore a healthy son.

At last, on the afternoon of 9 October, the Queen's labour pains began. As soon as they were well established, the King sent the royal heralds to London with the news. In the City, the response was overwhelming: bells were rung, masses sung in every parish church with congregations spilling out into the street in some places, and, on 11 October, a solemn procession walked from St Paul's Cathedral to Westminster Abbey, headed by the Lord Mayor and his aldermen, and including representatives of the guilds and livery companies of the City, and the clergy in their ceremonial copes. All offered prayers for the Queen's safe delivery.

Jane's ordeal lasted three days and three nights. It was rumoured in London that she would have to be cut open to facilitate her infant's safe delivery, a rumour that would in later years be embroidered by Catholic writers hostile to Henry VIII. Their lurid accounts give graphic – and entirely fictional – details of Jane's labour, alleging that her limbs were stretched to ease delivery, and that at length the King was asked who should be saved, the mother or the child. He is said to have opted for the child, as other wives could easily be found. A Caesarean operation is then said to have been performed. None of this is true. There is no evidence for a Caesarean operation being performed on a living mother before 1610 and, if it had, the result would have been a speedy and agonising death. Not until the twentieth century could this procedure be safely carried out.

Nevertheless, Jane Seymour's sufferings were great, and the labour prolonged and painful. But, finally, at two o'clock in the morning of Friday, 12 October 1537, it came to an end when she was safely delivered of a healthy, fair-haired boy. The King, after a wait lasting twenty-seven years, finally had his heir. It was, said a courtier, 'the most joyful news that has come to England these many years'.

Henry was at Esher when his son was born, but when he was informed that the Queen had been happily delivered of a prince, he rode to Hampton Court to see her and to welcome the child. The royal father was delirious with pride and joy, and named the child Edward; by a happy coincidence he had been born on St Edward's Eve. He became Duke of Cornwall at the moment of his birth, and it was confidently expected that his father would create him Prince of Wales and Earl of Chester, though this never came to pass. He was healthy, and bore resemblances to both his parents, having his father's features and his mother's fairness.

Henry wasted no time in informing the world of the glad tidings. Within minutes of his arrival at Hampton Court, his heralds had been dispatched to every part of the country with instructions to spread the news. In London, a *Te Deum* was sung in every parish church, and the bells in the City began a joyful pealing which would continue all day and all evening. There were bonfires in the streets, and the Tower guns shot off 2,000 rounds of ammunition in honour of the Prince. Banners were set up, and impromptu banquets given by prominent citizens. The messengers bearing the news were given costly gifts, and at the Steelyard the merchants of the Hanseatic League lit a hundred torches and generously provided free wine and beer for the citizens. Everywhere, housewives were hanging garlands above their doors and balconies and preparing food for the Tudor equivalent of street parties, while before the great doors of

367

St Paul's many bishops gathered to provide a feast for the people before celebrating mass. A holiday mood prevailed, and very little work was done that day; the feasting and carousing continued until the evening, when the Lord Mayor rode through the crowded streets thanking the people on the King's behalf for their demonstrations of love and loyalty. The conduits were still flowing with ale and wine, and there were many who woke with sore heads the next day, or found they had been robbed, thieves and pickpockets being certain of the King's pardon on such an occasion.

London's bells ceased their clangour at ten o'clock in the evening. At around the same time, the Queen was sitting up in bed writing to Cromwell to inform him that 'we be delivered and brought in childbed of a prince conceived in most lawful matrimony between my lord the King's Majesty and us,' and commanding him to convey the news to the Privy Council. Her letter was signed 'Jane the Queen'. Her triumph was now complete. Letters of congratulation came pouring into the palace, and the royal secretaries were kept busy announcing the royal birth to foreign princes and other dignitaries. The Prince was not the only baby born at Hampton Court on 12 October; in another suite, the Queen's sister-in-law, Lady Beauchamp, gave birth to a son who was also called Edward. In all, it was an auspicious day for the Seymours.

Overjoyed as he was with his 'fine boy', Henry was concerned for the infant's safety as there was still plague in the capital, and the first months of life were always hazardous. With these considerations in mind, he gave orders that every room, hall and courtyard in the Prince's apartments was to be washed down with soap and swept daily. Everything that came near the child – clothing, bed-linen, toys – was to be scrupulously clean. It is doubtful whether Jane saw much of her son after his birth. He had his own apartments, where he was cared for by wet-nurses, nursemaids and other servants. Unlike Anne Boleyn, Jane would not make a fuss about suckling her own child.

The Prince was christened on Monday, 15 October. Because of the risk of plague, the numbers attending were severely restricted, yet nearly 400 persons were present at the midnight ceremony in the Chapel Royal at Hampton Court, which had recently been completed and which still boasts its splendid Tudor ceiling. The guests had all gathered beforehand in the Queen's apartments, where Jane received them lying on a day bed of crimson damask lined with cloth of gold. Around her shoulders she wore a crimson mantle edged with ermine, over which flowed her loose blonde hair. Beside her sat the King in a richly upholstered chair. Her son was carried in procession through torchlit corridors just before midnight by Lady Exeter, with Norfolk holding his head steady and Suffolk supporting his feet. The King had chosen Archbishop Cranmer, Norfolk and Suffolk, and the Lady Mary as godparents. The Lady Elizabeth was in the procession too, carried in the arms of Lord Beauchamp, the Queen's brother, and holding the chrysom tightly in small fists. In the Chapel, the Prince was proclaimed heir to the King and, after he had been baptised by the Archbishop, he was conveyed back to the Queen's apartments with great pomp; this time, Elizabeth walked, holding Mary's hand. Jane took her son and gave him her blessing, then the King gathered him into his arms and, with tears of joy streaming down his face, blessed Edward in the name of God, the Virgin Mary and St George. The Prince was then carried off by the Duchess of Suffolk to his own apartments, followed by his household of 400 persons. Afterwards, refreshments were served for the guests, hippocras and wafers for the nobility, bread and sweet wine for the gentry. Then, when everyone present had kissed the hands of the King and Queen, the company dispersed. Jane had played her part to perfection; no one had noticed that anything was amiss with her.

On the afternoon of the following day, Jane suffered a bad attack of diarrhoea, which left her feeling rather ill, but by the evening she was better. During the night, however, she was sick, and early on Wednesday morning her condition was giving cause for concern. It was obvious that she was suffering from puerperal fever, a common hazard for women in childbed in those days. It is quite likely that Jane had suffered a tear in her perineum during delivery, which had become infected. Very little was known about hygiene in that period, and midwives did not understand the need for clean hands. Moreover, Jane's regime since the birth had been quite irregular, and she had been over-indulged by her attendants who were accused of having given her too rich a diet.

The Queen rapidly became so ill that it was feared she would die;

369

her confessor, the Bishop of Carlisle, was sent for, and he administered the last rites shortly before eight o'clock in the morning, before issuing a bulletin about the Queen's illness. Then, just as the Bishop was about to administer extreme unction, Jane rallied, and on Thursday she was so much restored that the King, who had been very anxious about her, felt able to continue with the celebrations in honour of the Prince's birth. On that day, he created Edward Seymour Earl of Hertford. On Friday, London was still celebrating, and the rest of the kingdom was following suit. The Bishop of Gloucester reported from the West Country that there was 'no less rejoicing in these parts than there was at the birth of John the Baptist'. Later that day, however, the Queen grew feverish again, and the King ordered a solemn intercession of the clergy; this took place in St Paul's, with the Bishop of London officiating.

For three days, she lay in delirium. On Monday night, her condition worsened, and the Bishop of Carlisle wrote to inform Cromwell that she was dying. The King had intended to return to Esher for the start of the hunting season on Tuesday, 23 October, but 'could not find it in his heart' to leave Jane in such a state. On that Tuesday, however, she seemed a little better, although she had been in great danger during the night. Her doctors told the King that, if she survived the next night, they 'were in good hope' that she would live. The Chapel Royal was full that day: 'If good prayers can save her, she is not like to die,' people were saying. 'Never was lady more popular with every man, rich or poor.'

At eight o'clock that evening, Henry was summoned urgently to his wife's bedside; she was failing fast. Norfolk wrote a hurried note to Cromwell, urging him to come to Hampton Court at once 'to comfort our good master, for as for our mistress, there is no likelihood of her life, the more pity, and I fear she shall not be alive at the time ye shall read this'. The King remained at Jane's side throughout the evening and into the night. In the early hours of Wednesday, 24 October, the Bishop of Carlisle was summoned to administer the last rites, and at about two o'clock, Jane slipped quietly from sleep into death.

Henry VIII could not bear anything to do with death. On the following morning his horror of remaining in the same house as

Jane's corpse got the better of him, and he fled to Windsor, leaving the Duke of Norfolk to look after the funeral arrangements. Once at Windsor, Henry went into seclusion for a time, refusing at first to see anyone, which was perhaps as well, for his ministers had already begun debating whether or not they should urge him to marry again for the sake of his realm. Surprisingly, when this suggestion was tentatively put to the King a few days later, he agreed that a fourth marriage might be wise, in view of the fact that his sole male heir was just an infant who might at any time succumb to a multitude of childhood ailments. 'He has framed his mind to be indifferent to the thing,' recorded one councillor. Despite his natural grief, as soon as Jane was buried he would be considering possible brides.

Jane was given a magnificent funeral. Her body was embalmed on 25 October, the entrails being removed and buried in the Chapel Royal at Hampton Court. The corpse was then dressed in a robe of gold tissue with the crown on its head and some of the Queen's jewels. It lay in state in the presence chamber for a week from 26 October, surrounded by tapers and with an altar beside it, at which masses were sung night and day for the soul of the departed. The obsequies began when Lancaster Herald charged those gathered to honour Jane's memory: 'Of your charity, pray for the soul of the Queen!' The body was then moved to a catafalque set up in the Chapel Royal, where the Queen's ladies would keep vigil beside it for a further week. The Lady Mary was chief mourner. She and the other ladies wore mourning habits of black with white head-dresses to signify that the Queen had died in childbed. Mary paid for thirteen masses to be sung for Jane's soul, and took charge of the late Queen's household, which would shortly be disbanded. It was probably Mary who carried out the King's command that Jane's beautiful diamonds and pearls were given to the wife of Sir Nicholas Carew, as Jane had wished.

Early in November, the Lord Mayor ordered 1,200 masses to be sung in the City 'for the soul of our most gracious Queen', and a solemn service was held in his presence in St Paul's. Alms were also given in the Queen's name to the poor.

On 8 November, Jane's coffin was taken to Windsor, where the King had decided she should be buried. It went in procession on a horse-drawn hearse followed by 200 poor men all wearing Jane's badge and bearing aloft lighted torches. The Lady Mary rode a horse draped in black velvet, and was attended by twenty-nine mourners, one for every year of the late Queen's life. At Colnbrook, Eton and Windsor, the poor men went ahead and lined the streets, while behind them stood the sorrowing crowds, hats in hands, watching silently as the funeral cortège wound its way past them. At the entrance to St George's Chapel, within the precincts of Windsor Castle, the coffin was received by the Dean and College, and was carried inside by six pallbearers. At the high altar, Archbishop Cranmer waited to receive it. The Lady Mary followed the coffin, her train borne by Lady Rochford. After prayers, the body was left to lie in state overnight, while the Lady Mary kept a grief-stricken vigil beside it. The next day, masses and dirges were sung, and the late Queen's ladies laid velvet palls upon the coffin, as was customary. Upon the palls was set a lifelike wooden effigy of the Queen that had been carried in the funeral procession but which has long since disappeared.

On Monday, 12 November, Queen Jane was finally laid to rest with great pomp and ceremonial 'in the presence of many pensive hearts', including those of her brothers, who would from now on enjoy enormous influence as uncles to the Prince. After the coffin had been lowered into a vault in the choir before the high altar the officers of the Queen's household broke their staves of office over it, thus symbolising the termination of their allegiance and service. On that day, the bells in London tolled for six hours, and on 14 November, a requiem mass was held in St Paul's Cathedral, thus bringing to an end the Queen's obsequies.

Etiquette precluded the presence of kings at their wives' funerals. After three weeks spent 'passing his sorrows' at Windsor while the funeral rites took place, Henry moved to Whitehall, where he once more took up the reins of government, but he was in very low spirits. The Bishop of Durham tried to alleviate his sufferings by reminding him that although God had taken from him 'that most blessed and virtuous lady', He had given him 'our most noble Prince, to whom God hath ordained your Majesty to be mother as well as father. God gave to your Grace that noble lady, and God hath taken her away as pleased Him.' Gradually, the King pulled himself together, and before very long his 'tender zeal' towards his subjects overcame his sad disposition, and he 'framed his mind' to a fourth marriage. By 3 November, he was reported to be in good health and 'merry as a widower may be'. He was now beginning to accept the tragedy that had befallen him, and to cope with his loss. He would wear full mourning, in deepest black, in Jane's memory, for three months, and court mourning would last until Easter 1538.

Jane's short, successful career and her tragic end caught the public's imagination, and she was celebrated in popular ballads long after she was dust. She had achieved nearly everything she set out to do: she had given the King the son he so desperately needed, she had helped to restore the Lady Mary to the succession and her father's affections, and she had used her influence to bring about the advancement of her family. She had provided the King with a family life for the first time in years, and had meddled hardly at all in matters of religion or politics. His grief at her death is testimony of his love for her. It was, in every respect, the most successful of his six marriages, and it was the only one to result in a surviving male heir.

In 1543, when Henry was married to Katherine Parr, he commissioned from an unknown artist a painting of himself, his wife, and his three children, which may still be seen at Hampton Court. Henry is shown seated on his throne in one of his palaces, with Mary and Elizabeth standing at either side of him. The six-year-old Edward stands at his father's knee, and sitting beside the King is not Katherine Parr, as might have been expected for she was an admirable stepmother, but Jane Seymour, wearing the gown in which Holbein had portrayed her in his Whitehall fresco. This inclusion of Jane in what was not so much a family group as a brilliant piece of Tudor propaganda is proof that Henry VIII wished to promote her image as one of the founding matriarchs of his dynasty. For Jane, this represents a considerable achievement, considering that her career, from her meetings with the King at Wulfhall in the autumn of 1535 to her death at the height of her triumph in 1537, had lasted just two short years.

When Henry VIII died, he left instructions that he was to be buried with Jane. His will gave detailed directions for the erection of a joint tomb surmounted by effigies of them both, carved 'as if sweetly sleeping'. But it was never built, and today the vault is marked only by a brass plate in the choir pavement. For a time, there was a Latin inscription to Jane's memory on the brass plate marking the grave, which, roughly translated, read as follows:

> Here lieth a Phoenix, by whose death
> Another Phoenix life gave breath:
> It is to be lamented much
> The world at once ne'er knew two such.

In 1813, the tomb of Henry and Jane was opened by order of the Prince Regent. Inside were found two coffins, one very large, of antique form, and another very small, as well as the coffin of Charles I and that of one of Queen Anne's infants. Henry's coffin was opened, revealing a skeleton 6'2" in length, with red hairs still adhering to the skull. The coffin containing the remains of Jane Seymour was left undisturbed.

Part III

How many wives will he have?

13
I like her not!

Had they ventured out of doors on New Year's Day 1540, country folk in Kent would have seen a party of horsemen, muffled to the ears in furs, galloping full tilt along the road that led to Rochester. Few would have guessed that this was the King, accompanied by eight gentlemen of his privy chamber, on his way to greet his new bride.

The visit had not been planned. After two years and two months without a wife, Henry VIII could no longer contain his eagerness to meet the lady in question, and had set out on the spur of the moment the night before, leaving behind the New Year festivities at Whitehall. His intention was to forestall the official ceremony of welcome and to meet his bride in private in order 'to nourish love'. With this in mind, the royal wooer hastened towards his destination, joyful anticipation in his heart.

The Princess whom he was contracted to marry was lodged with her retinue in the Bishop's Palace in Rochester, having disembarked at Deal some six days before. She was now awaiting a summons to London where her official reception was to take place. She was surprised, therefore, when the King was announced, and a party of men clad in coats of moire was ushered into her presence; in fact, she was trembling with nervousness.

Henry VIII had long been impatient for this moment, having a very natural desire to come face to face with the woman whose portrait he had fallen in love with. But when he entered the room

377

where she awaited him with trepidation, he took one look at her, and his face fell.

Negotiations for the marriage had dragged on for more than a year by the time of that ill-fated meeting. Nor was this the first princess upon whom Henry had set his sights since Jane Seymour's death. It has often been said that Henry paid Jane the compliment of remaining a widower for two years, but it must be remembered that he did not do this through choice. With only one son, he still needed to ensure the succession by siring others, and therefore remarriage was of paramount importance. This apart, there were advantages to be gained by an alliance with a foreign power, and this Cromwell was eager to arrange. Henry himself, although approaching forty-seven, was still one of the most eligible men in Europe, even if, in view of what had happened to his first three wives, there were few princesses who could contemplate marrying him without a shudder. He was of course unaware that any lady might have such reservations, yet it does seem that at that time there was a dearth of suitable royal brides on the marriage market, due not only to the reluctance of some of those that were available, but also to religious barriers and to the constant shifting of continental political alliances.

Fortunately, the King's son was thriving in the care of his wet-nurse, Mother Jack, who had suckled him since his birth. By the time he was a month old, he was sucking vigorously, and at this age he was also given his own separate establishment at the old royal manor house at Havering in Essex. Here, rigorous standards of hygiene were still imposed by the King: the rooms were to be swept and cleaned twice a day, and – once the child was weaned – all his food was to be tested for poison. The capable Lady Bryan was once again appointed Lady Governess, and Edward would remain in her care until he was six.

His royal father visited him frequently. In May 1538, when Edward was seven months old, Henry spent a whole day at Havering, playing with the child and making him laugh. He carried the boy around in his arms for a long time, and held him up at the window so that the assembled crowds could see their future King. That summer, Edward was brought to Hampton Court to be with his sisters; Lady Lisle saw him then, and told her husband that he was

378

'the goodliest babe that ever I set mine eyen upon. I think I should never weary of looking on him.' The Prince grew fast, and could stand alone before his first birthday, a sturdy little boy with a loving nature and an earnest expression on his face. After his birthday, Mother Jack's services were dispensed with, and in her stead Mrs Sybil Penne was appointed chief nurse under Lady Bryan. The latter was very fond of her charge, and delighted in recounting his progress in her regular reports to Cromwell. One reads:

> Would to God the King and your lordship had seen him last night, for his Grace was marvellously pleasant disposed. The minstrels played, and his Grace danced and could not stand him still, and was as full of pretty toys as ever I saw child in my life.

When Edward was summoned to court to see his father, Lady Bryan made it her business to see he was suitably dressed, and badgered Cromwell constantly for clothing and jewellery for him. Unlike his sister Elizabeth, Edward had few problems with teething, and had four teeth by the time he was one. Before he was eighteen months old, his household had been expanded and the security around him tightened. No effort or expense was spared to protect this 'most precious jewel', and it was generally agreed by all that the sooner Edward was provided with a brother the better.

Mary Tudor, of course, was next in line of succession, despite her illegitimate status. After Queen Jane's death, she returned to Hunsdon, where she settled down to a quiet and peaceful life such as any lady of rank might enjoy in the country. At Easter 1538, she visited the court, wearing white taffeta edged with velvet, for the King had already discarded mourning for Queen Jane, and had given Mary special permission to do so for her visit. Thereafter, Mary was only at court infrequently, there being no lady of sufficient rank to act as her chaperon.

As for Elizabeth, she too went to Hunsdon, where she was looked after by Mary, since Lady Bryan had been transferred to Prince Edward's household. The child was brought to court by her sister for the Easter celebrations in 1538; she was then four and a half, and even Chapuys described her as being 'certainly very pretty'. She was a sharp, precocious little girl, and under Mary's tutelage she was rigidly schooled in good behaviour. Taught at an early age to wield a needle, she was able to complete a shirt of cambric as a New Year gift for her brother Edward in 1539. Yet for all her intelligence and ability, she was still excluded from the succession, even though her father had decided to treat her as one of the family.

Henry's obsessive desire to protect his heir made him more than usually sensitive to any hint of treason. As well as crushing opposition to the Acts of Succession, he was particularly concerned about the activities of the Pole family, and at the end of August Cardinal Pole's brother Geoffrey was sent to the Tower for aiding and abetting the exile. Henry had not forgiven or forgotten Pole's shattering diatribe against him, and his hatred of his former protégé bordered sometimes upon mania. Because of this, he now viewed every member of the Pole family with suspicion, remembering that Plantagenet blood ran in their veins. Understandably, the Poles reacted with antagonism. In the autumn of 1538, Lord Montagu, Reginald's eldest brother, and the Marquess of Exeter, another Plantagenet descendant, were both executed as a result of their suspected involvement in a plot to kill the King. Exeter's son, young Edward Courtenay, was left in the Tower, where he would remain for another fifteen years. Thus, in one stroke, Henry VIII eliminated most of the remaining members of the House of York.

There remained only Margaret Pole, the Countess of Salisbury, former governess to the Princess Mary and the mother of Lord Montagu, Cardinal Pole and Geoffrey Pole. During the enquiry into the activities of her sons, the King's officers had searched the old lady's house and found a banner embroidered with the royal arms of England: it lacked any of the differences appropriate to any member of the royal house of lower rank than the sovereign. The Countess, a respectable dowager of sixty-six, denied that she had ever intended to dispute the right of the King to the throne, but her staunch protests could not save her, and she too was committed to the Tower in March 1539. Her imprisonment would be rigorous: she was put in a cold cell without adequate food or clothing. Nor was there any hope of release. The King wanted her out of the way because, obsessively, he feared that, even at her age, she might be made the focal point of a revolt against the Crown. Added to the supposed treason of her sons and herself was an old score the King meant to settle: the Countess's championship of Queen Katherine. On 12 May 1539, Parliament passed an Act of Attainder against Margaret Pole, whereby she forfeited all rights to her life, title, estates and goods. The King immediately appropriated all her property, but he did not order her execution, leaving her to languish in prison, perhaps in the hope that death would intervene before long.

With the future of his dynasty assured by only one little boy, who was subject to all the ills that carried off children in that age of high infant mortality, Henry needed to remarry, and soon. He had begun his search for a bride in November 1537, one month after Queen Jane's death. Initially, he and Cromwell had decided to opt for a marriage alliance with France in order to counterbalance the extensive power of the Emperor, and also because Henry did not want another Spanish bride. King Francis had marriageable daughters, and it was said that there were other beautiful ladies of high rank available in France. Late in November, Henry approached the French ambassador, Castillon, and confided his preference for a French marriage. The ambassador obligingly suggested a few possible brides, but Henry was being cautious, fearing that his personal requirements might be brushed aside in the interests of politics. He told Castillon he wished to see the ladies in question and get to know them a little before making a decision. Castillon, who had never heard of such a preposterous and insulting idea, replied caustically, 'Perhaps, Sire, you would like to try them one after the other, and keep the one you found the most agreeable.' Henry, he recorded, blushed at this, and did not pursue the matter any more at that time. But a few days later he saw Castillon again and, undeterred, suggested that potential French brides be brought to Calais for his inspection. When King Francis was told, he laughed, and said 'It would seem they meant to do with women there as with their geldings: collect a number and trot them out to take which goes best!' However, he was not having his daughters or the ladies of his court being taken like prize animals to market, and he refused to sanction the suggestion.

Henry VIII was not to be put off. Although he preferred the idea of a French marriage, his ambassadors abroad were instructed to report on other likely brides. John Hutton, the English envoy in Brussels, reported that the Duke of Cleves had a daughter 'but there is not great praise either of her personage or her beauty'. He then went on to say that the Duchess of Milan, who had been born Christina of Denmark, had just arrived in Brussels; she was the Emperor's niece, sixteen years old, very tall and 'of excellent beauty'. Her speech was soft, and she had a gentle face; in Hutton's opinion, she resembled Lady Shelton 'that used to wait on Queen Anne'. The young Duchess had only recently been widowed, her elderly husband having died in Italy, and she was still wearing black mourning clothes.

> There is none in these parts for beauty of person and birth to compare with the Duchess; she is not so pure white as the late Queen, whom God pardon, but when she chanceth to smile, there appeareth two pits [dimples] in her cheeks and one in her chin, the which becometh her right excellently well.

Hutton's missive was sent to a member of the Privy Council, Sir Thomas Wriothesley, who showed it to the King. When Henry read of the charms of the Duchess of Milan, he was tempted to abandon his plans to make a French marriage in order to pursue the lovely Christina. After all, she had excellent connections. Born in 1521, she was the daughter of King Christian of Denmark by Isabella of Austria, the Emperor's sister. At the age of fourteen, she had been married to Francesco Maria Sforza, Duke of Milan, who had died in November 1535. She had now come to live with her aunt, Mary of Hungary, Regent of the Netherlands, in Brussels, until another husband could be found for her.

Everyone agreed that the Duchess of Milan was beautiful, and her extreme youth was in her favour, since her character could be more easily moulded to suit her husband. But Henry had reservations; he was growing fat and preferred buxom women like Katherine and Jane had been, not slim ones like Anne Boleyn, and Christina was reported to be of slender build. 'I am big in person and have need of a big wife,' the King declared, abandoning for the present any ideas of courting her. He had heard of the charms of a French noblewoman, Mary of Guise, and was 'so amorous' at the prospect of allying himself to her that he was now disinclined to consider anyone else, even though he was bound to concede that Christina of Milan was eminently suitable in most respects.

Mary of Guise was the eldest daughter of Claude, Duke of Guise, one of the most powerful men in France, being related to the royal house of Valois. Like Christina, Mary was also a widow; she had been married to Francis, Duke of Longueville, until his death in June 1537; but unlike Christina, she was of mature age, being twenty-two, and – more importantly – had borne two sons. Rumour had it that she was as buxom as the King could desire. Henry thought she was a highly suitable candidate for the vacant consort's throne, and in January 1538, after a very quiet Christmas at Greenwich, he put out a feeler for Mary's hand. The lady, however, being given advance warning of his imminent proposal, hurriedly accepted that of her other suitor, Henry's nephew, James V of Scotland, whom she married the following May.

Henry was disappointed but undaunted, and Cromwell tried to alleviate his master's sense of rejection by suggesting that he return to his earlier intention of paying court to the Duchess of Milan. In March 1538, the King sent his court painter, Hans Holbein, to Brussels to paint Christina's portrait, and at around this time the merry widower discarded his mourning garments for Jane Seymour. Yet although his grief for her had abated, he was in constant pain from his bad leg, and in May 1538 he was forced to submit to the attentions of the barber surgeons and have his abscess lanced. This relieved the pain somewhat, but it did not cure it. The King's sporting activities were now more or less curtailed: no longer could he ride in the lists, but was forced to sit and watch the galling spectacle of younger, fitter men doing what he had once done better. And, to make matters worse, increasing immobility was making him more and more obese, and his once splendid head of red-gold hair was thinning. To mask the ravages of advancing age and ill health, Henry dressed himself more sumptuously than ever before, and set a new fashion for the men of his court of a square look with built-up shoulders and bulky sleeves: the larger the man, the better the style suited him. No longer did the King's increasing girth look conspicuous, for every man of fashion was doing his best to emulate his sovereign.

Henry's temper was less easily controlled, and constant pain and envy of others did not serve to improve it. Those that were closest to him, especially Cromwell, suffered the most from his irascibility. Henry turned on his Lord Privy Seal at least twice a week, bawling him out and calling him a knave and other derisory names, and sometimes he hit him on the head, pounding him soundly, so that Cromwell would leave the King's chamber shaking with fright and with rumpled hair, albeit with a smile on his face that acknowledged that this was the price he had to pay for his privileged position. Others, like the Poles and the Exeters, experienced the more deadly consequences of the King's anger.

By the middle of 1538, England's relations with both Spain and France had deteriorated; at the same time, Charles V and Francis I had drawn closer together. In June 1538, they signed the Treaty of Nice, which was intended to bind them in friendship for ten years, and although this was not an offensive treaty against Henry VIII, it did leave him in political isolation. Nevertheless, he had received Holbein's finished portrait of the Duchess of Milan and been enchanted with it, and in September an English embassy led by Wriothesley was sent to Brussels to convey the King's proposal of marriage. On 6 October, they saw the Regent Mary, who gave them permission on the Emperor's behalf to approach Christina, who agreed to see them the following day.

The young Duchess was very outspoken. The idea of marrying Henry VIII did not appeal to her, and she declared as much with candour. She said, reported the ambassadors,

> that the King's Majesty was in so little space rid of the queens that she dare not trust his Council, though she durst trust his Majesty; for her council suspecteth that her great-aunt was poisoned, that the second was innocently put to death, and the third lost for lack of keeping in her childbed.

If she had two heads, she said, 'one should be at his Grace's service!' She then told Sir Thomas Wriothesley that he should not labour any further 'for I mind not to fix my heart that way,' saying she thanked God she was not 'of so light sort'.

When Wriothesley asked her what her real inclination was, she would only say that she was at the Emperor's command.

Marry! [replied Wriothesley] Then I may hope to be among the Englishmen that shall be first acquainted with my new mistress, for the Emperor hath instantly desired it. Oh, Madam, how happy shall you be if it be your chance to be matched with my master! You shall be matched with the most gentle gentleman that liveth, his nature so benign and pleasant that I think to this day no man hath heard many angry words pass his lips!

These lies did not deceive Christina, who stood her ground and refused to commit herself. Later, she confided her reluctance to the Emperor, who was sympathetic, with the result that the imperial Council made it obvious to Henry VIII that his suit was hopeless.

By that time Henry was only too pleased to withdraw. For some time, Cromwell had been urging him to forget his religious scruples and ally himself to one of the Protestant German Princes, a move which he predicted would tip the balance of power in Europe in England's favour once more. The King was well aware of the cool wind blowing in his direction from France and the Empire, and also aware that the Protestant states of Germany were a permanent thorn in the Emperor's side. An alliance between England and one of these states might well divert Charles from any thought of joining with France to make war upon England. Cromwell now remembered that, back in November 1537, Sir John Hutton had mentioned that the Duke of Cleves had an unmarried daughter. In fact, he had two.

John III, Duke of Cleves, was fifty-eight, and a Protestant; his marriage to Mary of Jülich-Berg-Ravensberg had produced four children. His son, William, born in 1516, would succeed him in 1539 as Duke of Cleves. His eldest daughter, Sybilla, an auburn-haired beauty whose charm has been immortalised in a portrait by Lucas Cranach, had been married in 1526, at the age of twelve, to John Frederick, Elector of Saxony, one of the most zealous Lutheran rulers in Europe. The two younger daughters, Anne, born on 22 September 1515 in the ducal capital of Düsseldorf, and Amelia, born in 1517, were as yet unmarried. Henry VIII was now toying with the idea of taking one or other as his bride. When the Duke of Cleves learned of this, he rightly perceived that it would be a brilliant match for whichever girl was chosen, and immediately offered his elder daughter to Henry.

When, in late 1538, the Pope learned of the executions of Montagu and Exeter, and reissued the Bull of Excommunication of 1534 against Henry, the attitude of France and the Empire hardened towards England, and an alliance with Cleves seemed more attractive. Naturally, as a Protestant, the Duke of Cleves could be counted upon to remain friendly in the face of papal hostility.

On 12 January 1539, Charles V and Francis I signed a new treaty at Toledo, by the terms of which both agreed not to make any fresh alliances without the consent and knowledge of the other. This sealed the estrangement between Henry and his former allies and his resolve to make an alliance with Cleves. In February, the King told Wriothesley that his Council were urging him daily to arrange a fourth marriage in order to beget more heirs to ensure the succession. They had warned him that age was 'coming fast on, and that the time flyeth and slippeth marvellously away'. For this reason, he was not minded to waste any more time. Cromwell, whose brainchild the Cleves match had been, was appointed Lord Great Chamberlain by way of reward, and in March, Henry sent Nicholas Wotton and Robert Barnes, a well-known Protestant who would be likely to find favour with Duke John, as envoys to Cleves, to arrange a marriage with either the Lady Anne or the Lady Amelia.

The English ambassadors were well received in Düsseldorf, but not by Duke John. He had just died, and in his place was his serious-minded, Protestant son William, a young man of twenty-three. William had strong ideas about feminine modesty, and when his sisters were brought in to be introduced to Wotton and Barnes, they were so well covered with 'a monstrous habit and apparel' that the ambassadors could see very little of their faces, let alone their figures. Later, when the sisters had withdrawn, Wotton complained about this to the Duke, who retorted, 'Would you see them naked?' He had no high opinion of moral standards in England.

Wotton turned to Cromwell for help. As a result, on 23 April 1539, Cromwell dispatched Hans Holbein to Cleves, as well as another envoy, Christopher Mont, who carried instructions to the envoys to procure portraits of Anne and Amelia. Mont arrived ahead of Holbein, and in due course Wotton and Barnes appeared before Duke William and requested permission for portraits to be made. The Duke said he would consider the matter, and then kept them waiting for days. Mont intervened, and persisted in repeating the request each day, while Wotton and Barnes, in a state of great agitation, wrote to Cromwell and begged him to excuse the delay to the King, adding that by all reports the Lady Anne was the better favoured of the two princesses. At length, William said he was happy for his sisters' likenesses to be painted, but only by his own court painter, Lucas Cranach, who happened to be sick just then. When Cranach had recovered and was able to complete the portraits, William would send them on.

Cromwell reported all this to Henry, adding,

Every man praiseth the beauty of the said Lady Anne, as well for her face as for her person, above all other ladies excellent. She as far excelleth the Duchess of Saxony as the golden sun excelleth the silver moon. Every man praiseth the good virtues and honesty with shamefacedness which plainly appeareth in the gravity of her countenance.

Undoubtedly, Cromwell was exaggerating what he had been told. Few had actually seen very much of Anne of Cleves's charms, for she was always well swathed in cumbersome clothing when she appeared in public, and such occasions were rare. Her upbringing had been very strict, and anything approaching frivolity had been frowned upon. Yet Cromwell had good reason to exaggerate: this match had been his idea from the first, and it was vitally important to him that it should be successfully concluded. It would not be an exaggeration to say that his whole future depended upon that, nor is it beyond the bounds of reason to suppose that Cromwell had sent Hans Holbein off with instructions to make the lady look as attractive as possible in her portrait.

When the King read Cromwell's letter he was entranced. This princess, it seemed, was a paragon of beauty and womanly modesty, though it appeared that her brother was reluctant to let her go. He kept raising objections to the marriage: he said his sisters had been raised in a narrow environment of virtuous industry – how then would either of them fare as queen in a court known for its licentious habits? He said he was too poor to afford a dowry. He said that, in view of what had happened to the King's other wives, he felt that any woman marrying Henry VIII would only know insecurity and unhappiness. These objections were all duly conveyed to Cromwell, and a reply came back speedily. The King had decided he would take the Lady Anne without a dowry if her portrait pleased him. This was a very generous offer, and one that an impoverished ruler could not afford to turn down. The young Duke quickly capitulated, agreed to the marriage, and gave Holbein permission to paint Anne's likeness.

Holbein set to work at once, and the result was one of the most exquisite portrait miniatures ever painted, which may be seen today in the Victoria and Albert Museum in London. Anne smiles out demurely from an ivory frame carved to resemble a Tudor rose. Her complexion is clear, her gaze steady, her face delicately attractive. She wears a head-dress in the Dutch style which conceals her hair, and a gown with a heavily bejewelled bodice. Everything about Anne's portrait proclaimed her dignity, breeding and virtue, and when Henry VIII saw it, he made up his mind at once that this was the woman he wanted to marry. Cromwell breathed a sigh of relief, and the marriage negotiations went ahead.

The choice of a Protestant bride for the King of England led to avid speculation in Europe, and especially in Lutheran circles. Christopher Mont wrote to the Elector of Saxony, Anne's brother-in-law, to say that the Protestant cause would be greatly advanced once Anne became Queen, 'for the King is so uxorious that the best way of managing him is through his wives'. English Protestants believed that their new Queen might well be another Anne Boleyn, and that they would once again have a friend and champion upon the throne. Yet Mont was inaccurate in his assessment of Henry VIII, who was never uxorious, expected unquestioning obedience from all his wives, and reacted brutally when he did not get it. Henry assumed that Anne of Cleves would be happy to conform to the Catholic form of worship when she became Queen of England, and there is no evidence to show that she did otherwise from the time of her arrival. When she died, she died a professed Catholic, and it seems that the transition from one faith to another had been fairly effortless. Lutherans in England were therefore destined to be disappointed in her.

Now that his proposal had been accepted, Henry deemed it the proper time to find out more about his future bride, and wrote to Wotton, asking him to make discreet enquiries. On 11 August 1539, the ambassador reported that the Lady Anne had been brought up by her mother, 'and in a manner never far from her elbow'. The Duchess Mary was 'a wise lady', and had been very strict with her children. Anne was of a humble and gentle disposition, and the Duchess was so fond of her that she was loath to see her depart. As for her education, the future Queen of England was an expert needlewoman, could read and write her own language, and was very intelligent. However, she had no knowledge of French, Latin, English or any other tongue; nor could she sing or play a musical instrument, 'for they take it here in Germany for a rebuke and an occasion of lightness that great ladies should be learned or have any knowledge of music.' Nevertheless, Wotton believed that Anne was bright enough to learn English fairly quickly. He added that Holbein was painting full-scale portraits of Anne and Amelia: that of Amelia is now either lost or unidentified, but his masterpiece of Anne of Cleves hangs nowadays in the Louvre in Paris.

When the King read Wotton's description of Anne's accomplishments, he may well have felt a little disconcerted, especially when he learned that his wife-to-be spoke only High Dutch, a language of which he had no knowledge whatsoever. Moreover, she came from a court that scorned music, which was one of Henry's passions, and it seemed she knew nothing of dancing or fashion either, so narrow had been her upbringing. Nevertheless Henry felt that these were all minor obstacles which could be overcome by love, that supreme blessing which he felt sure would make this marriage a crowning success. Already, he was growing impatient for his bride's arrival in England.

At the end of August, however, the Duke of Cleves remembered that there might well be an impediment to the marriage. His father had once opened negotiations with the Duke of Lorraine for a marriage between the Duke's son, the Marquess of Pont-à-Mousson, and Anne, and it was just possible that a precontract had been entered into, in which case it would have to be dissolved in the ecclesiastical courts in order to facilitate the more advantageous marriage with the King of England. Enquiries were duly made both in Cleves and in Lorraine. Happily, no evidence of any precontract was unearthed, and at the end of September Wotton was able to inform the King that he found the Duke of Cleves and his Council 'willing enough to publish and manifest to the world that my Lady Anne is not bounden, but ever hath been and yet is at her free liberty to marry wherever she will'.

On 4 September 1539, the marriage treaty was signed by the Duke of Cleves at Düsseldorf, and the Lady Anne thanked her brother and the people of Cleves 'for having preferred her to such a marriage that she could wish for no better'. Duke William then sent his representatives to England where the treaty would be ratified; they arrived at Windsor on 23 September, and were entertained by the King with hunting and feasting for the next eight days, before moving to Hampton Court, where the marriage treaty was concluded on 4 October. Great preparations then commenced for the reception of the bride and the wedding to follow. Some noblemen had already ordered their wedding clothes, and there was the usual stampede for places in the new Queen's household. Katherine Bassett, whose sister Anne had gone to court to serve Jane Seymour and remained there ever since as a great favourite of the King, was now urging her mother, Lady Lisle, to 'be so good lady and mother to me as to speak that I may be one of the Queen's maids'.

The religion of the bride provoked some comment. The Lady Mary was at first dismayed to learn that her father was marrying a Lutheran heretic; yet in time she would become firm friends with Anne of Cleves, and would be partly responsible for Anne's conversion to the Catholic faith. The King saw his marriage as paving the way for a 'softening of the asperities which are now distracting Germany', and hoped to use his influence, and that of the Duke of Cleves, to 'find some honourable middle course' which would put an end to the religious problems of the German principalities. He told Marillac, the French ambassador, that, because he had but one son, he was marrying for the sake of children, and considered he could do no better than Anne of Cleves, who at twenty-four was 'of convenient age', in sound health, and of good stature, 'with many other graces which his Majesty says she possesses'.

In Cleves, discussions were taking place as to the best route for Anne to take to England. There were two ways of making the journey: one was by ship from one of the Baltic ports, and the other was overland to Calais. Duke William and his advisers were of the opinion that Anne should travel by land, as she had never before been on a ship, and might well suffer dire consequences as a result of a voyage across the Baltic during winter. There were even fears that the ordeal might 'alter her complexion' and make her unattractive to her new husband. It was decided, therefore, that Anne should travel by land along the north coast of Europe to Calais, and there take ship for England. In late October, news of her imminent departure from Cleves was sent by fast messenger to the English court, and on 5 November the eager bridegroom was informing his Council that he expected Anne's arrival in about twenty days' time, saying he intended to go to Canterbury to receive her.

Anne left Cleves early in November; she had been provided with a retinue of 263 attendants and 228 horses. Her progress was slow and, when she did not arrive at Calais on the expected date, Henry sent a courier to find out what was happening. The man returned with the news that Anne would be there on 8 December. To welcome her, Henry dispatched the Duke of Suffolk across the Channel, together with the Lord Admiral, Sir William FitzWilliam, Earl of Southampton, whose duty it would be to escort the future Queen safely to England. With them went many other lords and court officials. Norfolk and Cromwell were told to make their way to Canterbury in due course in order to greet Anne and welcome her to England on the King's behalf.

Henry planned a Christmas wedding at Greenwich, to be followed by twelve days of festivities, while Anne's official entry into London was scheduled for 1 January, to be followed by her coronation on Candlemas Day, 2 February, in Westminster Abbey. From Hampton Court, the King issued a stream of orders concerning the reception of his bride and the preparations for their wedding. Two splendid royal beds were sent to Dartford and Rochester, places where Anne was to stay en route to London, so that she would be as comfortable as possible. Plans were drawn up for the formation of the new Queen's household, since those who had served Jane Seymour had long since been discharged. The chief officers were appointed in November, as well as several ladies-in-waiting and maids of honour. Once again, Anne Basset was chosen to serve a queen of England; her mother

Lady Lisle was so grateful to the King for the appointment that she sent him some quince marmalade and damson conserve made by herself, which he so enjoyed that he asked for more. Henry had a soft spot for Anne Bassett; in 1539, he presented her with a horse and saddle. Later, when she was older, there would be rumours of an affair between them, though for the present Henry had no interest in any woman save Anne of Cleves.

He was in the best of spirits. His leg was troubling him less for the moment, he was eager to see his bride, and his gaiety was infectious. He had heard from Dr Wotton, who was part of Anne's escort, that she was tall and thin, of medium beauty, and of 'very assured and resolute countenance'; on the face of it, these were all attributes that the King admired least in women, but he was so blinded just then by what he was pleased to call love that he could only read into Wotton's description the highest praise. He was now more impatient than ever to meet the lady, and had convinced himself she would surpass his three previous wives a hundredfold.

Others were not deceived by Wotton's words. Of course, Holbein's miniature had been displayed at court, but Holbein was an artist who painted what his inner eye saw, and he had after all had his instructions from Cromwell. Several people at court were already privately expressing doubts that Anne of Cleves was as attractive as she was depicted in that portrait, and early in December, a scurrilous little rhyme was secretly circulating:

> If that be your picture, then shall we
> Soon see how you and your picture agree!

One doubts that this ever came to the King's notice; no one would venture to destroy his illusions.

Meanwhile, Anne had arrived in Antwerp, having been met four miles outside the city by a company of fifty English merchants wearing velvet coats and gold chains. She then went in procession along streets lit with torches, until she came to the English-owned house where she would spend just one night before travelling on. The house was thrown open to the public, and many came to see the future Queen of England.

Anne reached Calais on 11 December, and was given a magnificent welcome. Just past Gravelines, she was met by Lord Lisle, Governor of Calais, who greeted her on the King's behalf and escorted her towards the town. A mile from its gates, the Admiral was waiting to pay his respects, clad in a coat of purple velvet and cloth of gold, and wearing a seaman's whistle set with gems. With him were the Duke of Norfolk's brother, Lord William Howard, Sir Francis Bryan, 400 gentlemen in coats of satin damask, and 200 yeomen wearing coats of red and blue cloth, the colours of the royal arms of England. Southampton bowed low, then escorted Anne into Calais by the Lantern Gate. Here, she could see the ships in the harbour, all gaily bedecked with banners in her honour.

Anne was at last on English soil. At her entry through the gate, a salute was fired from the cannon along the harbour wall, and she was presented by the Mayor of Calais with a solid gold 'C' (for Cleves) as a compliment. On the other side of the gate, Lady Lisle and a host of ladies and gentlewomen sank into deep curtsys as Anne appeared. In front of the hall of the merchants of the Staple the town burgesses were lined up in formation, and they offered their new queen a rich purse containing 100 golden sovereigns, for which she heartily thanked them. Anne then went to view the King's ships that were in port, the *Lyon* and the *Sweepstakes*, after which she progressed through the narrow streets, while 150 rounds of ordnance were let off from those ships in her honour. Her retinue, unaccustomed to such things, were wide-eyed with astonishment at the splendour of her reception, and Anne herself took a refreshingly unaffected pleasure in it all. Finally, she passed through two lines formed by the merchants of the Staple to the entrance to the Exchequer Palace, where she was to lodge during her stay. The next morning, there was another salvo from the guns, followed by jousting in her honour.

Southampton was pleasantly impressed by Anne. On the day of her arrival, he wrote to Henry VIII to apprise him of it, saying how glad he was his Grace had decided to marry again and that he prayed that the Almighty would bless the union with children, so that 'if God failed us in my lord Prince, we might have another sprung of like descent and line to reign over us in peace'. These were very proper sentiments, but the Admiral also confessed that he had had misgivings about Anne of Cleves's suitability to be Queen. However, 'hearing great report of the notable virtues of my lady now with her excellent beauty, such as I well perceive to be no less than was reported', he had wholeheartedly revised his opinion. Lady Lisle was also impressed, and wrote to her daughter, Anne Basset, to say that her future mistress was 'so good and gentle to serve and please'. Anne thought this would be a great comfort to the Queen's servants, as well as to the King himself, who was by then 'not a little desirous to have her Grace here'.

Anne's stay in Calais was to last considerably longer than had been anticipated because bad weather prevented a Channel crossing. The King soon realised that his bride would not be with him in time for Christmas, and kept himself busy with negotiations for a proposed marriage between the Lady Mary and Duke Philip of Bavaria, another Protestant ruler, though Mary declared she would rather remain unmarried than enter into such an alliance. The King was sympathetic, but determined to press on with the negotiations, and when Philip came to London, Mary was obliged to go to court to greet him. Unwillingly, she obeyed, and the Duke afterwards told her father that he wished to proceed with the marriage. Shortly afterwards Mary fell ill – or feigned illness – and retired from court. She was away for some time, and even missed attending her father's wedding. Philip of Bavaria was therefore advised to remain in England until her return, but by then the King's enthusiasm for the German alliance would have been dramatically doused, and Philip would find that his waiting had been in vain.

The weather remained bad until Christmas Day. Anne was entertained with more banquets and jousts, and the Admiral – finding she did not play cards, which was one of the King's favourite pastimes – took it upon himself to teach her, reporting to his master that she was an apt and willing pupil, eager to please. Southampton found himself liking Anne very much, and exerted himself to make her enforced stay in Calais as enjoyable as possible. Anne obviously returned his liking: one evening, she invited him and a few other gentlemen to supper in her apartments, which was not thought by the English a seemly thing for a woman betrothed to another man to do, although Anne in her innocence was unaware of this. Southampton was worried about how the King would react when he found out, but at the same time too embarrassed to refuse the invitation. In the end he went, and was relieved to find that her 'manner, usage and semblance was such as none might be more commendable, nor more like a princess.'

On 26 December, a fair wind was blowing, and the Admiral judged it prudent to set sail for England without any further delay. He himself conducted Anne on board ship at midday; the voyage took seventeen hours, and she disembarked at Deal at five o'clock the next morning. Sir Thomas Cheyney, Lord Warden of the Cinque Ports, was waiting to receive her and escort her to Deal Castle, a fortress recently built on Henry VIII's orders as part of a chain of coastal defences. While she was resting there, the Duke and Duchess of Suffolk arrived with the Bishop of Chichester and a multitude of other notable people to pay their respects and to accompany Anne that night to Dover Castle, where she was to stay for a day or so. Then the weather turned bitterly cold, with freezing storms. Nevertheless, Anne insisted upon pressing on towards London, so 'desirous was her Grace of reaching the King's presence'. On Monday, 29 December, with hail and sleet blowing continually in her face, she journeyed with her retinue to Canterbury, where Archbishop Cranmer, accompanied by 300 gentlemen, bade her welcome, as did the Bishop of Ely. The two prelates then brought her to the great monastery of St Augustine, where she was lodged in the guesthouse. In spite of the bitter weather, crowds came out to see her, as she made her way along the streets of the ancient city. As it was evening, torches had been lit, and the Mayor had arranged for a gunfire salute to be sounded at Anne's entry. In her bedchamber, she found fifty gentlewomen in velvet hoods waiting to attend her, which especially pleased her. Suffolk told Cromwell she was 'so glad to see the King's subjects resorting to her so lovingly, that she forgot all the foul weather and was very merry at supper'.

Cromwell was relieved and gratified to hear of Anne's rapturous reception by her future subjects. She had behaved very well indeed, justifying his earlier praise of her virtues. Several people who had seen her were impressed with her looks and her manner, and she seemed eager to make up for her lack of accomplishments by learning as quickly as possible how to please the King. Cromwell now allowed himself to relax a little; all seemed set fair for a successful royal marriage, and he could look forward to the rewards he would receive from a grateful king.

Anne left Canterbury on 30 December and rode to Sittingbourne, where she stayed that night. On New Year's Eve, she went on towards Rochester; the Duke of Norfolk, accompanied by 100 horsemen in velvet coats and gold chains, met her on Reynham Down and escorted her to the Bishop's Palace in the city, where she was to stay for two nights. Here awaited Lady Browne, wife of Sir Anthony Browne, a stern matron who was to supervise the new Queen's maids of honour. When Lady Browne was presented to the Lady Anne, she could barely conceal her dismay, and later confided in a letter to her husband that Anne was wearing such dreadful clothes and was obviously the product of so gross an upbringing that everything about her was 'far discrepant from the King's Highness' appetite'. In Lady Browne's judgement, 'the King should never heartily love her.' Others perhaps shared her misgivings, but were more discreet about it, and the royal bridegroom remained blissfully unaware of such undercurrents. So eager was he to see Anne that on New Year's Eve he set out on that fateful journey to Rochester 'to nourish love'.

When Henry greeted Anne in her presence chamber in the Bishop's Palace, he gave no sign of what he was thinking. He welcomed her to England with great courtesy, while she in turn, 'with most gracious and loving countenance and behaviour', sank to her knees to receive him. Henry raised her up gently and kissed her on the mouth, as was customary in England. He stayed for the afternoon, engaging in a rather halting conversation with the aid of an interpreter, and had supper with Anne in the evening. However, inside him anger and disappointment were boiling to fever pitch. He had known, when he first looked at her, that he could never love Anne of Cleves. In fact, he now realised, she revolted him. She was so different from the image portrayed by Holbein and described by Cromwell that he felt betrayed, ill-used and deceived. He had brought with him a present of furs, but he was in such a state of agitation that he forgot to give them to Anne, and Sir Anthony Browne later presented them to her.

Someone had made a very grievous mistake, and they were going to suffer for it. Part of the fault lay with Holbein, who had so cunningly misrepresented Anne in his portrait of her. Yet Holbein

Henry could forgive: he was an artist, with an artist's conception of things, something the King understood very well. But Cromwell had suggested this marriage and manoeuvred Henry into it; Cromwell had extolled the lady's charms and her beauty. Cromwell, had he but known it, was doomed from the very moment Henry set eyes on Anne of Cleves.

When the visit was over, the King left his unsuspecting bride and found Sir Anthony Browne waiting in the corridor. Sir Anthony could see he was in a terrible temper, and was quickly enlightened when Henry told him he had been 'so struck with consternation when he was shown the Queen' that he had never been 'so much dismayed in his life as to see a lady so far unlike what had been represented'. Scowling ferociously, he said, 'I see nothing in this woman as men report of her, and I marvel that wise men would make such report as they have done!' And with that he stumped off.

As soon as Henry got back to court, he sought out the Lord Admiral, who had given him such glowing reports of Anne. 'How like you this woman?' demanded Henry aggressively. 'Do you think her personable, fair and beautiful, as report hath been made unto me? I pray you tell me true.' 'I take her not for fair,' replied the Admiral cautiously, 'but to be of a brown complexion.' 'Alas!' wailed the King, 'Whom shall men trust? I promise you I see no such thing as hath been shown me of her, by pictures and report. I am ashamed that men have praised her as they have done – and I love her not!' Years before, he had written in his book against Martin Luther of 'the fate of princes to be in marriage of far worse sort than the condition of poor men. Princes take as is brought them by others, and poor men be commonly at their own choice.' He was now for the first time experiencing the painful reality of this.

From eager anticipation, Henry had quickly descended to the depths of gloom. 'I like her not! I like her not!' he kept saying, and it was thought by his courtiers, not incorrectly, that he would do his best to extricate himself from the betrothal contract. Yet on 2 January, he departed with the court for Greenwich, as arranged, to prepare for the wedding that was supposed to take place in a few days' time. With him he took a cherished New Year's gift, the only thing that cheered him in his disappointment – a portrait by Holbein of the two-year-old Prince Edward, in a red satin gown and bonnet, and bearing a strong resemblance to his father. There was no likelihood after that of Holbein falling from the King's good graces.

Anne of Cleves was then at Dartford, where she would remain until summoned to London for her official reception. Cromwell was still receiving messages congratulating him on his sound judgement in choosing Anne as the future Queen, but the senders of these messages had not yet seen the King. However, it was not long before word of Henry's discontent spread, and it soon became apparent that he was 'very melancholy', as well as being 'nothing pleasantly disposed' towards Cromwell. As soon as Henry arrived at Greenwich, he sent for Cromwell and accused him, before the Council, of having deceived him over Anne of Cleves. For a moment or two, an alarmed Cromwell floundered, trying to think of a way to excuse himself, then he vainly tried to shift the blame on to the shoulders of the Admiral, saying that,

> When that nobleman found the Princess so different from the pictures and reports which had been made of her, he ought to have detained her at Calais till he had given the King notice that she was not so handsome as had been represented.

Southampton, who was present, reacted angrily to this, and protested that he 'was not invested with any such authority; his commission was to bring her to England, and he had obeyed his orders.' Cromwell then admitted that he had spoken of the lady's beauty 'in terms of commendation which had misled his Highness and his Council', but protested that this was not his fault, because he had received false reports. As he said this, he looked meaningfully at the Admiral, who blustered and said that 'as the Princess was generally reported for a beauty, he had only repeated the opinions of others, for which no one ought reasonably to blame him, especially as he had supposed she would be his queen'. The King agreed that the Admiral could not have acted in any other way, but he was furious with Cromwell. Cromwell had got him into this mess, he now expected Cromwell to get him out of it, and he put this to his minister in no uncertain terms.

Cromwell, still strongly convinced that the alliance with Cleves was necessary to England, stood his ground. If Henry alienated the Germans, he pointed out, he would stand alone without allies, with France and the Empire possibly poised for a joint offensive against him. Besides, Anne herself had done no wrong, and it would be most unchivalrous of the King to reject her at this late stage and send her home disgraced; no man would consider her after that. More to the point, her brother, impoverished though he was, might well retaliate by declaring war on Henry. There was no way out, in fact: the King must marry Anne of Cleves and make the best of it.

Henry stalked out of the council chamber in a rage, but even he knew that Cromwell was right, and that he must go through with the marriage. Yet he was consumed with anger against the man for having involved him with Cleves in the first place; but for Cromwell's insistence that he ally himself with these German heretics he would not now be faced with the prospect of taking a wife so repugnant to him. For all his reluctance Henry forced himself to continue with the wedding preparations. His messengers had already 'made public outcry in London that all who loved their lord the King should proceed to Greenwich to meet and make their devoir to my Lady Anne of Cleves, who would shortly be their queen,' and even now crowds were gathering around the palace and along the banks of the Thames. Many noblemen had brought their wives to court to be received by the future Queen. It was too late to back out now.

Yet Henry was not giving in gracefully. He grumbled to Cromwell that Anne was 'nothing so well as she was spoken of', declaring vehemently that 'if I had known so much before, she had no coming hither. But what remedy now?' Cromwell replied firmly that there was no remedy, and said he was sorry that his Grace was 'no better content'. Even now, Henry had not given up hope of being freed from his obligation to honour the marriage contract. When, on 3 January 1540, the Lord Chamberlain asked which day his Majesty would be pleased to name for the coronation of his queen, Henry replied tartly, 'We will talk of that when I have made her my queen!' All the same, on that same day he left Greenwich with a great train to receive his bride and her retinue at Shooter's Hill, near Blackheath, and welcome them to London.

'Blackheath hath borne some gorgeous and pleasant spectacles,' wrote the Elizabethan antiquary William Lambard many years later, 'but none so magnificent as that of King Henry VIII, when he brought in the Lady Anne of Cleves.' It was one of the last great spectacles of Henry's reign, and if the King was feeling less than enamoured of his bride he concealed it well in public. He went by barge to Greenwich on that Saturday, accompanied by all his nobles and the Lord Mayor and aldermen of London; every barge was decorated with streamers and banners. At the same time, the Lady Anne was travelling to Blackheath from Dartford. At the foot of Shooter's Hill a rich pavilion of cloth of gold had been set up; surrounding it were other, smaller pavilions. Inside them were braziers containing scented fires at which Anne and her ladies could warm themselves. Anne was accompanied by what remained of her retinue from Cleves, which now consisted of a hundred persons on horseback, as well as the Dukes of Norfolk and Suffolk, the Archbishop of Canterbury, and other bishops, lords and knights. At twelve o'clock, she led her train down Shooter's Hill, and was received in front of the pavilions by her Lord Chamberlain, the Earl of Rutland, and Sir Thomas Denny, her Chancellor, and all her other councillors and the newly appointed officers of her household. Dr Kaye, her almoner, then made a short address in Latin, and formally presented to Anne all those sworn to serve her: as she could speak no English, Duke William's secretary replied to the address on her behalf. The great ladies of her household then came forward and curtsied to her: Lady Margaret Douglas and the Marchioness of Dorset, the King's nieces, his daughter-in-law the Duchess of Richmond, the Countess of Hertford, the Countess of Rutland, and Lady Audley; sixty-five ladies of lesser rank followed them. Anne then alighted from her chariot and 'with most goodly demeanour and loving countenance' thanked everyone most heartily, and kissed the chief ladies of her household; her councillors and officers then knelt in turn to kiss her hand, after which she retired with her ladies into the main pavilion to get warm.

Word was then sent to the King, waiting at Greenwich, that Anne had arrived, and he at once set off with a great train across Greenwich Park. He had dressed himself magnificently for the occasion, in a coat embroidered with cloth of gold, diamonds, rubies and Orient pearls, with a jewelled sword and girdle and a velvet bonnet adorned with precious stones, 'so rich of jewels that few men could value them'. About his neck hung a collar of such gems and pearls 'that few men ever saw the like'. He was attended by ten footmen attired in rich liveries of goldsmiths' work. Not once did his face betray his inner feelings: his behaviour in the public eye was as usual impeccable, conveying the impression that he was an eager and satisfied bridegroom. Indeed, he would never show anything other than courtesy towards Anne of Cleves in public, and he played his part so well that it was not until weeks after their wedding that she realised she did not please him.

Yet even as Henry rode out to welcome Anne, his lawyers were examining the marriage contract to see if there were any flaws in it, and also investigating the circumstances of Anne's supposed betrothal to the son of the Duke of Lorraine. As she waited in her tent for the King to appear, Anne was happily innocent of this. She had changed into a taffeta gown embroidered with raised cloth of gold; it was in the Dutch fashion, with a round skirt, and lacked the courtly train worn by ladies of rank in England. Nevertheless, it drew flattering comments from onlookers. A caul held her hair in place, over which was 'a round bonnet or cap set full of Orient pearls', surmounted by 'a coronet of black velvet'. Around her neck she wore a parure of rich stones that glittered in the winter sunlight. In this attire, she sallied forth when word came that the King was half a mile away. At the door of the pavilion, she mounted her richly caparisoned horse, and with her footmen in liveries embroidered with the Black Lion of Cleves rode to meet her future husband. Henry, seeing her approach, reined his horse to a standstill and waited until she drew level with him. He then doffed his bonnet, 'and with most lovely countenance and princely behaviour saluted, welcomed and embraced her, to the great rejoicing of the beholders'. Whereat the Lady Anne, 'not forgetting her duty, with most amiable respect and womanly behaviour received his Grace with many sweet words and great thanks and praise'. Certainly, she was making strenuous efforts to familiarise herself with the English language.

For a while, the royal couple chatted and exchanged pleasantries; then, with Anne on the King's right hand, they rode back towards the pavilions and the vast crowds waiting to see them.

Oh! What a sight was this, to see so godly a prince and so noble a king to ride with so fair a lady of so goodly a stature and so womanly a countenance! I think that no creature could see them but his heart rejoiced!

So gushed the chronicler Hall for whom Henry VIII could do no wrong. With the trumpets going before them, King and Princess proceeded through the assembled ranks of knights and esquires, followed by the lords of the Privy Council, the gentlemen of the privy chamber, the men of Cleves in velvet coats, the Lord Mayor, the barons, bishops, earls and dukes, Archbishop Cranmer, Duke Philip of Bavaria (still waiting for an answer to his proposal to the Lady Mary), the foreign ambassadors, Lord Privy Seal Cromwell, and the Lord Chancellor. With the King rode Sir Anthony Browne, while Sir John Dudley, newly created Master of her Horse, accompanied the future queen, leading a spare palfrey for her.

For the processional journey back to Greenwich Palace, Anne rode in a carved and gilded chariot bearing the ducal arms of Cleves. With her sat 'two ancient ladies of her country', while the next chariot held six young German ladies dressed in ornate gowns, who were reckoned by the English to be very good looking. A chariot bearing Anne's chamberers followed, and then one carrying her laundresses. Behind that was drawn an empty litter of cloth of gold and crimson velvet, a gift from the King to his bride. Anne's serving men, all clad in black and riding great horses, brought up the rear of the procession. Thus they rode through the park, while the citizens of London were crowding the Thames in their boats, straining to catch a glimpse of the German princess who would soon be their queen. The guilds of London were also there in their barges, many of which had been painted with the royal arms of England and the ducal arms of Cleves, and from every barge issued the melodious sounds of minstrels and the voices of men and children singing in honour of the occasion. Henry and Anne paused on the wharf to see and hear the pageant and were lavish in their praise of it.

Soon afterwards, Anne was alighting from her chariot in the inner courtyard of Greenwich Palace. As the royal pair arrived, a great peal of guns let off a salute from one of the towers. Henry embraced and kissed his bride, and bade her welcome to her own house; then taking her by the arm, he led her through the great hall, where the King's guards were standing to attention before the hearth, and on to her privy chamber, where he left her to rest for a while.

That evening there was a sumptuous banquet in Anne's honour, after which she changed into a taffeta gown with long flowing sleeves gathered above the elbow into armlets; it was trimmed with rich sables – probably those presented to her on the King's behalf at Rochester – and the tight undersleeves were made of very costly material. On her head, she wore a lawn cap in the Dutch style, adorned with pearls and precious stones, which was judged to be of great value by those who saw it. Cleves might have been a poor duchy, but it had done its princess proud in sending her to England with such a splendid trousseau.

Later, when Anne had retired to bed, the King sought out Cromwell. 'How say you? Is it not as I told you?' he demanded. 'She is nothing fair. Her person is well and seemly, but nothing else.' Cromwell, trying to make the best of the situation, replied, 'By my faith, you say right, but me thinketh she hath a queenly manner withal.' Henry had to admit that was so, but he was not at all happy and made no secret of the fact. On the following day, Sunday, 4 January, he was complaining that he was 'not well handled', and declared that,

> If it were not that she had come so far into my realm, and the great preparations and state that my people have made for her, and for fear of making a ruffle in the world and of driving her brother into the arms of the Emperor and the French King, I would not now marry her. But now it is too far gone, wherefore I am sorry.

Cromwell was sorry too. He was filled with anxiety, for Henry was in what he recognised to be a dangerous mood. It now wanted but two days until the date set for the wedding ceremony. The King's lawyers had found no evidence at all of a precontract between Anne of Cleves and the son of the Duke of Lorraine, nor could they find any fault with the marriage contract. Every avenue of escape was closed to the King: he would have to go through with the wedding. Cromwell was staking all his hopes on Henry growing to

403

like Anne better once he had established a sexual relationship with her; should she become pregnant, then the King might well view her with very different eyes.

Henry, however, had no intention of trying to make this marriage a success. He was desperate to be free of his obligations, and on the day before the knot was to be tied, he besought a worried Cromwell to help him. 'Is there no remedy, but that I needs must put my neck into the yoke?' he cried. Once again, Cromwell patiently explained why it was too late to back out, and after a while Henry calmed down and agreed to go ahead with the wedding on the following day. In the evening, he duly informed the Privy Council that that was his intention, while his bride-to-be was making her own preparations in blissful ignorance of the controversy raging around her.

It is difficult now to pinpoint exactly what it was about Anne of Cleves that aroused so much distaste in the King. Henry was realist enough to accept that a monarch had to marry for the good of his realm, and that this might mean a union with someone with whom he might be ill matched, yet in this case he professed to feel such revulsion that he was on the brink of putting his own needs before the benefit of his kingdom. There can be no doubt that Holbein exaggerated Anne's charms, and therefore it may be concluded that looks were not her strong point. Because Anne was queen for such a short time, there was little demand for portraits of her. Apart from Holbein's work, only one other portrait type survives, being a likeness by a Flemish artist, Barthel Bruyn the Elder, which today hangs in St John's College, Oxford. This picture may well hold the clue to Anne's looks, for it depicts a more angular face than that in the Holbein portraits; it also, being a side-facing portrait, shows that Anne had a long pointed nose and heavy-lidded eyes. Figure-wise, her tall stature may well have made her seem ungainly to a man who had been married to three petite women. Furthermore, she suffered from excessive body odour, according to the King. Taken together, all these things could well account for his distaste, and he could only deplore her lack of education, wit and musical ability, three things he greatly esteemed in women. Anne's other personal qualities, and her earnest desire to please, meant little when compared with all her drawbacks. Others had been impressed by her, but then they did not have to marry her and sleep with her. Henry did, and he was so revolted at the prospect that he had even forgotten the urgent need to beget more sons.

The wedding day, Tuesday, 6 January 1540, was the Feast of the Epiphany and the last day of the Yuletide celebrations at court. The King was up early, and dressed in his wedding clothes: a gown of cloth of gold, embroidered with great flowers of silver and banded with black fur, a coat of crimson satin slashed and embroidered and fastened with huge diamonds, and a rich collar of gold about his neck. At eight o'clock, accompanied by his nobles, he paused in the gallery leading to the chapel where the marriage ceremony would take place, and declared, 'My lords, if it were not to satisfy the world and my realm, I would not do what I must do this day for any earthly thing.' And he looked pointedly at Cromwell. However, there was no time for further recriminations, as the bride was coming, escorted by the lords sent to fetch her.

Anne was wearing a gown of cloth of gold embroidered with large flowers of great Orient pearls; again, it was cut in the Dutch fashion, having a round skirt without a train. Her long fair hair was hanging loose, in token of her virginity, and she wore a coronet of gold set with precious stones, with trefoils resembling bunches of rosemary. About her neck was a costly necklace, with a matching belt around her slim waist. Walking between the Count of Overstein and the Grand Master of Cleves, with her face composed and her expression at once demure and serious, she followed the lords into the King's chamber, out the other end, and into the gallery where Henry awaited her. There, she made three deep obeisances, and together they then proceeded to the Chapel Royal, where Cranmer would marry them.

Anne was given away by the Count of Overstein. On her finger the King placed a ring engraved with the motto 'God send me well to keep.' When the ceremony was over, the King and Queen went hand in hand into Henry's closet to hear mass, and offered their tapers, Anne obediently following the rituals of the established faith to please her new husband. After mass, the bridal party was served spiced wine. The King then went to his privy chamber to change into a gown of tissue lined with embroidered crimson velvet, while Anne went with her ladies to her own chamber, escorted by the

Dukes of Norfolk and Suffolk. A little after nine, the King and Queen met in Anne's room, where a procession formed, Anne's serjeant-at-arms and all her other officers going before her, and thus in stately fashion the bridal pair passed through the palace to their wedding banquet.

Later, in the afternoon, Anne changed into a gown of rather masculine cut, with sleeves gathered above the elbow; her ladies donned gowns with the abundance of chains so popular in Germany and the Low Countries. Thus attired, they accompanied the Queen to evensong, after which she had supper with the King. A programme of masques and other entertainment followed, until it was time for the newly wedded pair to be put to bed.

Henry was in no mood by then to consummate the marriage. It was fortunate therefore that Anne's mother had not considered it appropriate to acquaint her daughter with the facts of life: the King's bride was entirely ignorant of sex, and had little idea of what to expect in the marriage bed. So she lay there, while her new husband ran his hands all over her body and then, it must be assumed, rolled over and went to sleep, leaving her undoubtedly bewildered and embarrassed.

When morning came, the King was up early. He was in a very bad mood. While he was dressing, Cromwell – who had probably not slept at all – arrived, and anxiously enquired, 'How does your Grace like the Queen?' Henry glowered at him. 'Not so pleasant as I trusted to have done,' he muttered ominously. Cromwell, with understandable apprehension, asked why his master was so dissatisfied, at which the King's temper flared, and he retorted:

Surely, my lord, I liked her before not well, but now I like her much worse! She is nothing fair, and have very evil smells about her. I took her to be no maid by reason of the looseness of her breasts and other tokens, which, when I felt them, strake me so to the heart, that I had neither will nor courage to prove the rest. I can have none appetite for displeasant airs. I have left her as good a maid as I found her.

Hearing this, Cromwell knew himself beaten, and that Henry was already smoothing the way towards having the marriage annulled.

Cromwell could not foresee how this would be done, but he knew the King, and he had little doubt as to what would be the outcome. As for himself, he could only hope that his master would not exact too terrible a revenge.

The King was in a dangerous mood. Few men would gladly admit to having failed to consummate their marriage, yet by the end of that day Henry had told most of the influential people at court of his inability to make love to the Queen, saying that 'he had found her body disordered and indisposed to excite and provoke any lust in him'. He even sought out his physician, Dr Butts, and explained that his failure to have sexual intercourse with Anne was not due to impotence on his part; indeed, he boasted that he had experienced wet dreams twice during the wedding night, and thought himself able to perform the sex act with others, but not with his wife. 'Surely,' he said mournfully, 'I will never have any more children for the comfort of the realm.' Before very long, the whole court was laughing behind closed doors at the royal-marriage farce. Fortunately, the new Queen could speak very little English, and failed to realise that she was the butt of so many cruel jokes.

It says a great deal for Anne of Cleves that she managed to settle into her position with dignity. Many people liked her and admired her courage and common sense, and the common people were impressed with what they had seen and heard of her. On 11 January, she attended a tournament held in honour of her marriage, and for the first time appeared dressed in English costume, with a French hood that everyone agreed much became her. Yet her efforts to please had little effect upon her husband. Three days later, Cromwell told the Council that the new Queen remained a virgin because the King's Highness 'liked not her body, and could not be provoked or stirred to that act, though able to do the act with other than with her'. This selective impotence posed a grave problem for the state: if there were no heirs from the marriage, its whole purpose was in vain. Yet the Privy Councillors agreed that for the moment there was no way out, for fear of reprisals from the Duke of Cleves. Anne must remain queen, and Henry must make the best of it.

Not long afterwards, the new Queen received a courteous little note from the Lady Elizabeth, her younger stepdaughter. Elizabeth was still at Hertford Castle, and was impatient to come to court and meet her father's new wife.

> Permit me to show, by this billet [she wrote in this the first of her letters to survive], the zeal with which I devote my respect to you as queen, and my entire obedience to you as my mother. I am too young and feeble to have power to do more than felicitate you with all my heart in this commencement of your marriage. I hope that your Majesty will have as much goodwill for me as I have zeal for your service.

Touched by this letter from a very accomplished and erudite six-year-old, Anne showed it to the King, and asked if Elizabeth might come to court. But Henry was in no mood to grant anyone any favours, and would not hear of it. He took the letter and gave it to Cromwell, then ordered him to write a reply. 'Tell her,' he said brutally, 'that she had a mother so different from this woman that she ought not to wish to see her.'

At this point there came about a significant change in the shifting scene of European politics. Both the Emperor and the King of France began to make friendly overtures to Henry VIII because their mutual pact was beginning to go the way of many others and deteriorate into barely concealed hostility. There were signs that both were looking for a renewal of friendship with England, and it soon became obvious to Henry that his position had strengthened immeasurably. A German alliance was now neither attractive nor necessary. In fact, in this new situation, it was positively undesirable, being not only unpopular with the Emperor and the French, but also with the strong Catholic faction at the English court headed by the Duke of Norfolk and the conservative Stephen Gardiner, Bishop of Winchester.

Henry did not hasten to rid himself of Anne of Cleves immediately, however. He realised that it was wiser to wait until the Emperor's true intentions were revealed; if Charles continued to show himself friendly, then Henry would reciprocate, in the hope that Charles would stand as a bulwark between him and Cleves when the time came for him to end his marriage. In the meantime, he got rid of

Philip of Bavaria, who left England on 27 January, much to the relief of the Lady Mary, who was now recovered from her illness. While he was about it, the King also dismissed most of Anne's German attendants and packed them off to Cleves. Before they left, he gave a sumptuous feast in their honour, and sent them away laden with gifts. As a special favour to the Queen, a few of her people were allowed to stay in England, but Henry meant to send them home too, once she had grown accustomed to English ways.

Tradition dictated that a new queen made a state entry into London prior to her coronation, but the King had abandoned his plans for a February crowning, without offering Anne any explanation as to why. Instead, he grudgingly arranged for the civic reception to take place. On 3 February, the Privy Council issued orders requiring the 'commons of London' to put on their best clothes and take to their barges on the following day in order to do honour to their queen. King and Council were united in their determination to give the Duke of Cleves no grounds for criticism.

On 4 February, the King and Queen took the royal barge from Greenwich to Westminster; with them, in other barges, sailed the nobility of England and the bishops. As they passed the Tower, a great peal of guns saluted them. The citizens of London were cheering from the riverbanks, and the guildsmen were passing in their decorated barges. The City's welcome was warm and encouraging, and Anne must have been gratified by this. At Westminster, the King helped her out of the barge, and together they walked with their attendants to Whitehall Palace, where they were to stay for a time.

It was while the court was at Whitehall that Anne Bassett, who had been appointed one of Anne's maids of honour back in December and was now reporting for duty, was informed that the Queen had brought with her so many German attendants that, even allowing for those who had been sent home, there was no place for her, or for several other English ladies, in her household. Naturally, Anne Bassett was very put out and she complained to her mother Lady Lisle, who in turn wrote expressing her grievance to Lady Rutland, wife of the Queen's Lord Chamberlain. Lady Rutland replied that the King would not allow any more maids to be appointed until there was a vacancy created by someone leaving the

Queen's household. However, she advised, it might be as well to lay her daughter's case before Mother Lowe, the strict German mistress of the Queen's maids, as she was in the best position to find a place for Anne Bassett. Lady Lisle did write to Mother Lowe and was gratified to hear from Anne, only a week later, that she was now waiting upon the Queen.

It was well known among the ladies of the Queen's household that their mistress was a wife in name only. Inhabiting a sophisticated court where intrigue and adultery were commonplace, they found it scarcely believable that Anne of Cleves should be so innocent. One day, around late February, the Queen told her senior ladies-in-waiting, Lady Rutland, Lady Rochford, and Winifred, Lady Edgecombe how kind and solicitous her husband the King was. 'Why,' she said in her guttural, halting English, 'when he comes to bed he kisseth me, and taketh me by the hand, and biddeth me "Good night, sweetheart"; and in the morning kisseth me and biddeth "Farewell, darling."' The ladies present exchanged furtive glances: was that all? After a significant pause, they told Anne they hoped she would soon be with child, to which she replied that she knew very well she was not. Lady Edgecombe asked how it was possible for her to know that: 'I know it well, I am not,' answered Anne. 'I think your Grace is a maid still,' ventured Lady Edgecombe with some daring, not to say impudence. Anne laughed at this; 'How can I be a maid, and sleep every night with the King?' she said, and repeated what she had said earlier of their nightly routine. 'Is this not enough?' she queried. It was Lady Rutland who spoke: 'Madam, there must be more than this, or it will be long ere we have a duke of York, which all this realm most desireth.' Anne's face registered dismay. 'Nay,' she said, 'I am contented I know no more.' Nevertheless, her ladies proceeded to enlighten her, and afterwards asked her if she had acquainted Mother Lowe with the King's neglect of his marital duties. By this time, Anne had had enough of being interrogated, and replied firmly that 'she received quite as much of his Majesty's attention as she wished'.

Nevertheless, the seeds of anxiety had been sown in her mind. She now knew that something was very wrong with her glittering marriage; in one stroke her illusions about the King had been effectively shattered. What was the meaning of his neglect? Did he

410

not love her? Did he intend to set her aside, as he had done Queen Katherine? Or, even worse, do away with her, as he had done with Anne Boleyn? We shall, of course, never know exactly what Anne's private feelings were at this time, but it is certain that from then on she was watchful, alert for the first signs of anything adverse, and careful to conduct herself with the utmost decorum.

In March 1540, the King's conscience reared its righteous head once more. He told his Council that it would not permit him to consummate his marriage as he felt sure he was not entitled to do so, being convinced that there had in fact been a precontract between Anne and the Duke of Lorraine's son. 'I have done as much to move the consent of my heart and mind as ever man did,' he said piously, 'but the obstacle will not out of my mind.' The Council realised they were being ordered to supply grounds for dissolving the marriage, and after some discussion they told the King it was their opinion that non-consummation was in itself grounds for annulment. There was no need to rake up the precontract with Lorraine; it was a dubious pretext at best. Nevertheless, they would have the matter investigated once more. This seemed to satisfy Henry.

The spring of 1540 saw the surrender of the abbeys of Canterbury, Christchurch, Rochester and Waltham. With this closure, the dissolution of the monasteries was complete. Henry was now wearing on his thumb the great ruby that had, since the twelfth century, adorned the shrine of Becket at Canterbury. On his orders, the saint's body had been exhumed and thrown on a dung heap, because Becket had been a traitor to his King. Not all the monastic wealth found its way into the royal coffers in the Tower. Vast tracts of abbey land were bestowed upon noblemen loyal to the crown: Woburn Abbey was given to Sir John Russell, Wilton Abbey to Lord Herbert, and so on. Many stately homes surviving today are built on the sites of monastic establishments, sometimes with stones from the abbeys themselves. This redistribution of land from church to lay ownership served the purpose of binding the aristocracy by even greater ties of loyalty and gratitude to the King: they were hardly likely to oppose radical religious reforms when they had benefited so lavishly as a result of them.

Although Henry had retained most of the old Catholic rituals when he broke with the Pope, Lutheranism had gained a foothold in

England in recent years, and was growing in popularity, even though the penalties for heresy were severe. The King's marriage to a Protestant princess had made not one whit of difference to religious practice in England; Anne of Cleves was happy anyway to conform to all the outward forms of Catholic worship. Nevertheless, she was regarded as being a figurehead for the reformist party at court, especially by the strong Catholic faction, headed by the Duke of Norfolk and Bishop Gardiner. This party was firmly opposed to any religious changes that tended towards Lutheranism, and it was very much in favour of the dissolution of the royal marriage. Thus while Cromwell was doing his best to promote the excellent qualities of the Queen, Norfolk and Gardiner were urging the King to divorce her. 'Cromwell is tottering,' reported Charles de Marillac, the French ambassador, on 10 April. It was the opposition's hope that, once rid of Anne of Cleves, Henry would marry a more orthodox bride who would represent their own interests. It must also be said that, as with Wolsey's enemies a decade before, jealousy was one of their guiding motives.

On 17 April, Henry surprised everyone by creating Cromwell Earl of Essex. This looked like a setback for the Catholic party, but in reality it was no such thing, being another example of the King's subtle cruelty. By lulling Cromwell into a sense of false security, he hoped to exact a more satisfying revenge, which would be as unexpected as it was deadly. Nor was it long before the Catholic faction suspected what would be the outcome, and realised that it was imperative to concentrate their energies on hastening the fall of the new Earl.

The King had confided to Norfolk that he meant to force Cromwell to bring about the dissolution of the marriage he had worked so hard to create before he destroyed him. Henry was still telling people that he could 'not overcome his aversion to the Queen sufficiently to consider her as his wife'; he was sure, he said mournfully, that God would never send him any more children if he continued in this marriage, and declared that 'before God, he thought she was not his lawful wife'. His councillors remembered having heard all this on another occasion, and were praying that this queen proved not so obdurate as the first had been. Everyone knew from bitter experience that a royal divorce could be a messy and fraught business that could drag on for years, and it was not surprising that the Council shrank from the prospect.

There now emerged, however, the strongest possible incentive for the King to end his marriage. In April 1540, it was noticed that he had 'crept too near another lady'. Her name was Katherine Howard, and she was the niece of the Duke of Norfolk and a first cousin to Anne Boleyn. The Catholic party had timed her entrance well. She had been deliberately placed in the Queen's household as a maid of honour with detailed instructions as to how to attract the King's attention. Norfolk had already seen one niece attain the consort's throne, and saw no reason why another should not aspire to the same dignity. Besides, this one was younger, more malleable, and much prettier than the first.

Katherine was about fifteen. She was the eldest daughter of Norfolk's younger brother, Lord Edmund Howard, who had died, aged sixty-one, in 1539. Lord Edmund had been Comptroller of Calais; being a younger son, he had very little by way of inheritance from his father, the second Duke of Norfolk, and had spent the greater part of his life shouldering heavy debts. Little is known about him; one of his few surviving letters relates how a medicine prescribed for him by Lady Lisle had caused him to 'bepiss my bed'. He had first married Joyce Culpeper, widow of Mr Ralph Legh, to whom she had borne five children. She presented Lord Edmund with another five, of whom Katherine was perhaps the fourth. There were three sons: Charles, Henry (who died young) and George, and two daughters, Katherine and Mary, who later married Thomas Arundel, who was executed for treason in 1552.

As with Anne Boleyn, Katherine Howard's date of birth may only with difficulty be determined. All contemporary writers are agreed that she was very young when she married the King. She was certainly born before 1527, as in that year, in a letter to Wolsey, her father stated he had ten children, 'my children and my wife's'. But as the date of Lord Edmund's marriage is not known, it is not possible to estimate a date of birth for their eldest son, Charles. We do know, however, that Charles, Henry and George were born before 1524, for in that year they are mentioned in the will of John Legh, their mother's former father-in-law. Katherine and her sister Mary are not mentioned in this will at all, although they are named in the will of

John Legh's wife Isabella in 1527. It may therefore be safely assumed that they were not yet born in 1524, and that the evidence contemporary to the period of Katherine's birth argues a date of *c.*1525.

   This must now be compared to later evidence dating from the time of her marriage to the King in 1540. The 1525 date is corroborated by the admittedly dubious Spanish Chronicle, which states that Katherine was fifteen when she first met Henry VIII. We have seen that this source is generally unreliable, although it has been credited with accuracy in places. Mr Richard Hilles, a London merchant, writing in 1540, referred to Katherine as 'a very little girl', and although this may refer to her diminutive stature, it could also refer to her age, as it conveys a distinct impression of extreme youth. Marillac stated in 1541 that Katherine's relationship with her admirer, Francis Dereham, lasted from the age of thirteen until she was eighteen. As their affair ended in 1539, this would place her date of birth in or around 1521, a date many historians have accepted without examining the other evidence. But if Katherine had been alive in 1524, how then do we explain the omission of her name from John Legh's will? Moreover, it must also be stressed that Marillac was frequently inaccurate in his diplomatic reports, and was not above inventing facts of his own. From other evidence, which will be examined in detail in the next chapter, it appears that Katherine's relationship with Dereham was of short duration only, much less than the five years alleged by Marillac, and probably lasting no longer than two years. Her earlier liaison with her music master, Henry Manox, was of even shorter duration. Thus, if she was born in 1525, she was twelve when she became sexually active, and we must remember that many girls were married at that age in the Tudor period.

   The date of 1519 has sometimes been given as Katherine's birthdate because of an inscription on a portrait by Holbein of a lady long identified as Katherine Howard. However, it has now been proved that the portrait in question has no connection with her, and probably represents Jane Seymour's sister Elizabeth, the wife of Gregory Cromwell. Taking all the other evidence into account, there is a strong case to be made for Katherine having been born in 1525, or thereabouts, which made her, indeed, a 'very little girl' at the time she attracted the attention of Henry VIII. And Henry, of course, was just at that susceptible age when a man likes to prove to himself and others that he is still an attractive proposition to young girls.

Katherine's mother died when she was no more than a toddler, and her father quickly remarried. Her new stepmother was Dorothy, daughter of Sir Thomas Troyes and widow of Sir William Uvedale. However, the new Lady Howard was to play very little part in Katherine's life, for she was sent at that time to live in the household of her step-grandmother, the Dowager Duchess of Norfolk, widow of the second Duke; such an arrangement was customary with daughters of the nobility. Here, she received some rudiments of education, although the Duchess was a lax guardian and allowed her charge to run wild, something that would have grave repercussions for both of them in the future. Katherine remained with the Duchess, commuting between the Dowager's town house at Lambeth and her country estate at Horsham in Sussex, until her uncle Norfolk arranged for her to go to court in the spring of 1540. Meanwhile, her father, who had lost his second wife and married yet a third time, to Mrs Margaret Jennings, had died in 1539. This left Katherine bereft of any close relatives with genuine concern for her welfare, for her uncle saw her merely as a tool with which to achieve his political ends, and her step-grandmother was not very interested in her.

Several portraits said to be of Katherine survive, but only one may be said to be authentic, and that is a miniature by Holbein, of which two versions exist, one in the Royal Collection and another in the collection of the Duke of Buccleuch. These are very similar, showing the subject seated, half-length, against a celeste-blue background. She wears a very low-cut dress of tawny brocade with furred over-sleeves and green damask false sleeves, and an ornate French hood rests on her auburn hair. The face of the sitter is faintly impudent, tilted at an angle, wearing an imperious expression, although plump and round with the rather large Howard nose. Recent research, undertaken by Dr Roy Strong, former Director of the National Portrait Gallery, has shown that the miniature's identification as Katherine Howard, dating from 1756, is probably based on sound foundations. The sumptuous costume, and the fact that the sitter was painted at all, would indicate also that here, indeed, is one of Henry VIII's unfortunate queens, and the only possible identification is with Katherine Howard. Other portraits once claimed to represent her, such as the Holbein half-length in Toledo, Ohio, copies of which are in the National Portrait Gallery, London, and Trentham Hall, a Holbein sketch of dubious authenticity in the Royal Collection, and a portrait at Hatfield House showing a lady wearing the gable hood of the 1520s, have all been shown to be spurious.

It was not long before Katherine attracted the attention of the King. By April 1540, he was said to be very enamoured of her, and before the month was out had made her substantial grants of lands confiscated from convicted criminals. Katherine's youthful charm rejuvenated Henry, and she seems to have responded warmly to his advances, having no doubt been well primed by her family. It was certainly a dazzling experience to be courted by the King, and Katherine was not without ambition – Norfolk and Gardiner had explained what their purpose was in pushing her into the spotlight. Yet she was no Anne Boleyn, being a good deal younger than Anne had been, and far more empty-headed, although she was precocious enough when it came to experience of men. It had already therefore occurred to her that she might become queen of England, and this was no doubt enough to compensate for the fact that, as a man, Henry had very little to offer a girl of her age. He was now nearing fifty, and had aged beyond his years. The abscess on his leg was slowing him down, and there were days when he could hardly walk, let alone ride. Worse still, it oozed pus continually, and had to be dressed daily, not a pleasant task for the person assigned to do it as the wound stank dreadfully. As well as being afflicted with this, the King had become exceedingly fat: a new suit of armour, made for him at this time, measured 54″ around the waist. He was frequently irascible, quick to burst out in temper, and given to bouts of black depression as the years advanced. Yet on occasion he could still exert himself to be charming, especially to the ladies, and he was doing that now for Katherine's benefit, behaving as if he were the magnificent specimen of manhood who had vanquished so many women in his youth. Katherine flattered Henry's vanity; she pretended not to notice his bad leg, and did not flinch from the smell it exuded. She was young, graceful and pretty, and Henry was entranced. The Catholic faction watched with satisfaction as their affair progressed. The Queen, not now so naïve as formerly, watched too; she bore Katherine no rancour on a personal level, for she was not in love with her husband, yet this new development made her fearful. If Henry believed she stood in the way of his future happiness, what might he not do to rid himself of her?

May Day was celebrated that year with all the usual festivities at court. The King remembered that, in the eyes of the world, he was still a married man, and appeared with his queen at the jousts that were given for five days at Westminster to mark the occasion. They also attended the banquets that were held in Durham House, which had been thrown open in order to admit the public, who were eager to view the festivities. Here, the King entertained those who had been victorious in the jousts and gave them gifts, 100 marks each and houses to live in. Cromwell, meanwhile, was watching the royal couple closely, and learned to his discomfort that they were no better acquainted than before. On 6 May, he sought out Sir Thomas Wriothesley, and told him how troubled he was. 'The King liketh not the Queen, nor ever has from the beginning; I think assuredly she is as good a maid for him as she was when she came to England.' Wriothesley said he was sorry to hear it, and urged Cromwell to 'devise how his Grace may be relieved'. Cromwell agreed that this was the only course to take. 'But how?' he asked. Wriothesley would not be drawn, or did not know, yet he too had urged the King to ally himself with Cleves, and like Cromwell, he feared for his own skin. 'For God's sake, devise relief for the King, or we shall both smart for it!' he begged. A few days later, he brought up the matter of the King's marriage in Council, lamenting 'the hard case in which the King's Highness stood, in being bound to a wife whom he could not love'. Of course, there were many men similarly afflicted, but their unwillingness to have relations with their wives did not affect the succession to the throne. The Council, to a man, agreed that something must be done to extricate his Grace from this match that was so repugnant to him.

Henry continued to complain about the Queen to Cromwell, saying she 'waxed wilful and stubborn with him'. She was probably tense with anxiety and hurt by his inexplicable neglect, but it was characteristic of Henry to shift the blame for what had happened on to her shoulders, and to take offence at her tactical withdrawal. She probably could not help herself; worry about what might happen to her resulted in her being less amiable towards her terrifying spouse

417

than she had been hitherto. Cromwell saw fit to warn her against antagonising the King, and reminded her of 'the expediency of doing her utmost to render herself more agreeable'. None knew better than he the wisdom of this advice, yet Anne was too bewildered and uneasy to heed it; in fact, she took this friendly warning to be a preamble of worse things to follow. Nor was she even aware of how she had given offence.

What with his inept minister and his difficult wife, the King was going about feeling very sorry for himself. He let it be known that he was 'in a manner weary of his life', although this was belied by his behaviour with Katherine Howard. Before very long, this assumed woefulness had given way to anger, directed chiefly against Cromwell, who was responsible for his present predicament. Once aroused, Henry's anger would not abate until he had exacted his revenge.

On 10 June 1540, Cromwell entered the council chamber as usual, in readiness for the day's business, but before he could be seated, the Duke of Norfolk stepped forward and arrested him in the King's name. Before he knew where he was, Cromwell was being transported by barge to the Tower, whither he had himself sent so many others. There were those who were sad to see him toppled, although the majority rejoiced, chief among them the members of the Catholic faction, who rightly saw in Cromwell's fall the triumph of their own ambitions. On that same day, a Bill of Attainder against Cromwell was drawn up and laid before Parliament; the charges included both treason and heresy. Such an Act, the instrument that Cromwell himself had used so often to bring others down, ironically was being employed in the same way against him. On 19 June, the Bill received the approval of the upper House, and was sent down to the Commons.

The King now laid plans for the annulment of his marriage to Anne, which would inevitably follow. He sent her to the old palace at Richmond on 24 June, on the pretext that there was plague in London and that the country air would benefit her health. Anne left without question, but with forebodings. Charles de Marillac heard 'talk of a diminution of love and a new affection for another lady'. Henry had promised to join Anne in two days, but did not do so; Marillac told his master that, had there been any truth in the story

418

that there was plague in the City, the King would not have remained for any considerations, 'for he is the most timid person that could be in such cases'. Rumours were flying fast around court and City, and people began to be aware that there was a new love in the King's life. His intention to put away the Queen was known of in the City before 24 June, as was his affection for Katherine Howard. The citizens watched the King being rowed in a small boat, in broad daylight, to visit her on many occasions at Lambeth, whither she had retired once the Queen had left court, and Bishop Gardiner entertained Henry and Katherine to banquets at his palace in Southwark. However, the cynical Londoners regarded this not so much as evidence that the Queen was about to be divorced, but as adultery. Before long, the royal barge was to be seen every night on its way to Lambeth, so that the King could pass the evening there; ostensibly, he was visiting the Dowager Duchess of Norfolk, but few were deceived by this excuse.

Far from being impotent, Henry was now laying siege in earnest to Katherine's virtue. Her family, unaware of the fact that she was already sexually experienced, had warned her to maintain her 'pure and honest condition', although she was to make it obvious that she would welcome the royal advances once a wedding ring was on her finger. Both Anne Boleyn and Jane Seymour before her had reached the consort's throne by deploying such tactics, and Katherine was wise enough to realise that her family's advice was sound. As for the King, blissfully unaware that he was being manipulated, he was, for the last time in his life, passionately in love.

It was now the end of June. As Anne of Cleves waited apprehensively at Richmond for a husband who never came, and as the King pursued Katherine Howard in London, events were moving speedily towards a climax. On 29 June, the Bill of Attainder against Cromwell passed successfully through the Commons and became law, which meant that he was adjudged a traitor and would forfeit both life and honours, as well as all his possessions. Told of this, the condemned man wrote to the King from the Tower, hoping that his master would be merciful and at least spare his life: 'To me, you have been most bountiful, more like a father than a master. I ask mercy where I have offended, but I have done my best, no one can justly accuse me of having done wrong wilfully.' His best had not been enough; even though the charges against him made no mention of his having caused the King to be bound in an unsatisfactory marriage, it was this that sealed his fate. Although Archbishop Cranmer interceded on his behalf, the King was adamant that Cromwell must die, although he was pleased to defer the execution so that he might use Cromwell to help him dissolve the Cleves marriage. When Cromwell realised that he was indeed to suffer the extreme penalty, he grew frantic, and on 3 July, sent Henry another letter of supplication, which ended with the plaintive cry: 'Most gracious Prince, I cry for mercy, mercy, mercy!' Henry was not listening.

By 5 July, some inkling of what was afoot had reached Queen Anne at Richmond; her chamberlain, the Earl of Rutland, acting on the King's orders, made a point of assuring her that Henry would 'do nothing but that should stand by the law of God, and for the discharge of his conscience and hers, and the quietness of the realm, and at the suit of all his lords and commons'. Whether this put Anne's mind at rest is debatable; what is probable is that the prospect of a divorce was not unwelcome to her. She would not be a second Katherine of Aragon.

In Parliament on 6 July the lords petitioned the King to have the legality of his marriage investigated by a convocation of the clergy, saying they were concerned about the likelihood of a disputed succession should Anne of Cleves bear children. They pointed out that if the Duke of Lorraine's son stood by his alleged precontract, the King's marriage would be null and void. However, if – as was supposed – the King and Queen were married in name only, then the Church had power to annul their union. The King readily agreed that the clergy should look into the matter; lamenting the fact that he had been 'espoused against his will', he told Parliament that he could refuse nothing to his people, and was ready to answer any questions that might be put to him, for he had no other object in view but 'the glory of God, the welfare of the realm, and the triumph of truth'. Moreover, Henry was now sure enough of the Emperor's good-will to risk angering the Duke of Cleves, though he had decided to make generous financial provision for Anne in an attempt to avert this.

That afternoon saw the Privy Council making its way to Richmond to see the Queen and obtain her consent to the institution of divorce proceedings. When they had explained the situation to her at length, Anne answered 'plainly and frankly that she was contented that the discussion of the matter be committed to the clergy as judges competent in that behalf'. The King, hearing this, was delighted that she should be so reasonable.

On 7 July, Henry made a written declaration to be laid before the clergy appointed to investigate his marriage. He assured them that he had no ulterior motive in seeking a divorce. When the Cleves marriage had been suggested, he had been anxious to proceed, 'because I heard so much both of her excellent beauty and virtuous behaviour'. But when he saw her at Rochester, he 'liked her so ill that I was woe that ever she came into England, and deliberated with myself that, if it were possible to find some means to break off, I would never enter yoke with her'. Both Admiral FitzWilliam and Sir Anthony Browne would bear this out, and Cromwell also, 'since he is a person knowing himself condemned to die, and will not damn his soul'. Cromwell, in particular, could testify that the King had gone into the marriage protesting that he did not consent to it. Moreover, went on the King, he himself had 'lack enough of the will and power' to consummate the marriage, as both his physicians could testify.

This they were glad to do. Dr Chambers confirmed what his master had said, and related how he had advised the King 'not to enforce himself', for to do so might result in an inconvenient debility of the sexual organs. He recalled that Henry had said 'he thought himself able to do the act with other, but not with her'. And Dr Butts gave evidence that the King had had nocturnal emissions of semen in his sleep during the period of his marriage to Anne of Cleves – in the good doctor's view, this was proof that intercourse had not taken place. The King himself reaffirmed later that Anne had come to him a virgin – he was perhaps mindful that remarks made by him at the time of their marriage had cast doubt on this – and said he had shared her bed every night for four months and 'never took from her by true carnal copulation'.

While the King was drafting his declaration to the clergy, his marriage was being debated in the House of Lords, where three good reasons were given for its dissolution: Anne's probable precontract with Lorraine, Henry's lack of consent to the marriage, and its non-consummation. This last was seen as most important since 'the whole nation had a great interest in the King's having more issue, which they saw he would never have by this queen'.

On 9 July 1540, the convocations of both Canterbury and York reached a decision. They announced that they found the King's marriage to Anne of Cleves to be null and void on the three grounds put forward by Parliament. Both the King and the Lady Anne were at liberty to remarry. Thus, with a minimum of fuss, was the King's fourth marriage ended.

On that day, a deputation of the Privy Council waited upon the ex-Queen at Richmond to inform her of the annulment of her marriage, and to tell her that from henceforth it was the King's pleasure that she call herself his sister. Anne must have felt considerable relief when she heard this, but her outward manner was calm. She did not faint, as some later apocryphal sources allege, but declared her consent to the annulment, and 'showed herself amenable to it'. The lords then informed her that the King had settled upon her a handsome annuity of £4,000 per annum, as well as the manors of Bletchingly and Richmond, with Hever Castle, Anne Boleyn's childhood home, which had reverted to the Crown on the death of the Earl of Wiltshire. Anne would now be a woman of means, with the added status of being the King of England's honorary sister. The world also knew she was still a virgin: Henry had made it as easy as possible for her to remarry if she so wished. There now opened before Anne such a vista of new-found freedom that she positively welcomed the dissolution of her marriage, and in this mood she declared to the lords her eagerness to co-operate in any way the King should wish.

Henry immediately despatched Dr Wotton to Cleves to break the news gently to Duke William. Wotton was also charged, on the Lady Anne's orders, with informing the Duke that she would not be returning to the land of her birth, as the grants of land made to her were only hers on condition that she remained in England. What was more, she liked it in England, and meant to stay for good. The Duke took the news mildly, merely commenting 'he was glad his sister had fared no worse'. All the same, as he explained in a letter to Henry VIII, he was sorry for what had happened, although he

would not depart from his amity for his Majesty for any such matter. He could have wished that his sister should return to

Germany, but if she was satisfied to remain, he had confidence that
the King would act uprightly towards her, and he would not press it.

Privately William thought Henry's behaviour was deplorable, and he
was fearful that Anne might be persecuted for her faith if she stayed
in England. His fears would prove unfounded.

Soon, the news was buzzing around the courts of Europe. Both
Francis I and Charles V approved of the annulment. Martin Luther
was not so charitable. 'Squire Harry wishes to be God, and do as he
pleases!' was his scornful comment, prompted no doubt by
disappointment that the Protestant cause had been deprived of a
potential champion in England.

On 11 July, at the request of the Council, the Lady Anne wrote a
tactful letter to the King, formally acknowledging the dissolution of
their marriage. In it she affirmed that, 'though this case must needs
be both hard and sorrowful for me, for the great love which I bear to
your most noble person,' she accepted and approved the decision of
the clergy, 'whereby I neither can nor will repute myself your
Grace's wife, considering this sentence and your Majesty's pure and
clean living with me.' For all this, she hoped that she would
sometimes have the pleasure 'of your most noble presence, which I
shall esteem for a great benefit'. She was comforted, she went on,
'that your Highness will take me for your sister, for the which
I most humbly thank you accordingly'. And, beseeching the
Almighty to send the King long life and good health, she signed
herself, 'Your Majesty's humble sister and servant, Anne, the
daughter of Cleves.'

It is likely that this masterpiece of diplomacy was drafted for Anne
by members of the Privy Council. While acknowledging the justness
of the clergy's decision to annul the marriage, it yet manages to
convey a poignant sense of loss, calculated to flatter the King. In
reality it seems unlikely that Anne can have felt much distress at their
separation: from a humiliating bondage she had suddenly been
translated into a life of luxurious freedom, finding herself to be, for
the first time, her own mistress. As the King's sister, she would take
precedence over most of the ladies of the kingdom, and a place at
court would always be reserved for her. There is no doubt that she
had grown to appreciate her adopted land, and she was now

fortunate enough to own three of the most charming houses it could boast. It was not such a bad bargain when all was said and done.

Anne's marriage was formally annulled by a specially introduced Act of Parliament on 12 July 1540. Immediately after it was passed, the Privy Council humbly petitioned the King to

> frame his most noble heart to the love and favour of some noble personage to be joined with him in lawful matrimony, by whom his Majesty might have more store of fruit and succession to the comfort of the realm.

Katherine Howard's name was not mentioned, yet the lords were in little doubt as to who their next queen would be. The only people at court who were dissatisfied at the prospect were those who supported the reformist cause and the ex-Queen's German attendants and their mutterings were predictably ignored.

Word that Katherine Howard might soon be Queen of England quickly spread. In Yorkshire, it came to the notice of Joan Bulmer, who had known Katherine well in her Lambeth days, prior to 1540. Joan had been a serving woman in the Duchess of Norfolk's household, and had at one time acted as Katherine's secretary since the future Queen was barely literate, her education having been largely overlooked. Then Joan married and moved to Yorkshire, where she now lived, and Katherine had doubtless assumed she would never see her again. She was wrong: Joan Bulmer was an ambitious woman, who did not enjoy being isolated in her north-country fastness. She wanted to come to court, where there was excitement to be had, and power to be gained by subtle means. So she wrote to Katherine on 12 July, begging to be accepted into her household once she was queen, 'as it is thought that the King of his goodness will put you in the same honour that [Anne of Cleves] was in which no doubt you be worthy to have.' She reminded Katherine of 'the unfeigned love that my heart hath always borne towards you', and confided that her changed circumstances had brought her 'into the utmost misery of the world and most wretched life'. There was no way out of it, either, unless Katherine, of her goodness, could find the means to invite Joan to London. If she were to command Joan's unpleasant husband, he would have to obey and send his wife. On and on the letter went, the writer pleading, cajoling, and flattering; she ended by beseeching Katherine

not to be forgetful of this my request, for if you do not help me, I am not like to have worldly joys. Desiring you, if you can, to let me have some answer of this for the satisfying of my mind; for I know the Queen of Britain will not forget her secretary, and favour you will show.

Katherine was a kind-hearted girl, and she was happy to oblige. She was too inexperienced to perceive the rather menacing undertone in the letter, the sinister reminder of things better forgotten, and the underlying threat implicit in such a reminder. Before long, Mistress Bulmer had been given a place in her growing entourage, but it was a favour Katherine would live to regret.

Meanwhile, the Lady Anne of Cleves was astonishing everyone by her exemplary conduct. To a court accustomed to redundant queens creating havoc, her behaviour was remarkable, and on 13 July the King in gratitude sent her gifts of great value and richness, as well as letters from her brother and Dr Wotton. Anne opened and read these with pleasure, and then sent Henry her humble thanks for having let her see them. Afterwards, in response to Dr Wotton's hint that the Duke of Cleves and his ministers were concerned about how she was being treated in England, Anne dutifully wrote herself, in German, to Duke William, to reassure him. Nor was that all. In the presence of Norfolk and Wriothesley, she spoke to her brother's emissary and stressed that she was 'merry and honourably treated', and so cheerful did she appear that the man could not doubt it. Afterwards, Anne dined with the lords of the Council, and promised them that she would never deviate from her acceptance of the annulment of her marriage. She had, she told them, returned her wedding ring to the King in token of this. After listening to the report of his Councillors, Henry wrote to Anne, on 14 July, to thank her for being so conformable to his 'wise and honourable proceedings'. If she continued in this way, he assured her, 'you shall find us a perfect friend content to repute you as our dearest sister.'

On 17 July, Sir Thomas Wriothesley arrived at Richmond to disband the former Queen's household, and to see her new servants, selected by the Privy Council, sworn in. Anne said farewell publicly to those who were leaving her service, and cordially welcomed the newcomers, many of whom were merely transferring, being her compatriots. Afterwards, she told Wriothesley that she knew herself to be under a great obligation to the King, and that she would never oppose him in any way, not even for her brother or her mother or anyone else. She also promised to let Henry see any letters she received from abroad, and to be bound by his advice concerning matters raised in them.

To the King, this seemed almost too good to be true, and he found himself searching for flaws in Anne's conduct. Being of a suspicious nature and devious in his own actions, he could not conceive that anyone could be so candid and straightforward. Indeed, after his nine-year battle with Katherine of Aragon over the validity of their marriage, he found it hard to believe that Anne had capitulated without any kind of fight. His suspicions were therefore aroused, and they centred upon the correspondence to which Anne had unwittingly drawn his attention, namely the letters that were to pass between her and Duke William. What Henry feared was that Anne might secretly incite her brother to make war on her behalf.

Having persuaded himself that this was a very real possibility, the King instructed his Council to visit Anne again and instruct her to write one further letter to William in German, 'to the intent that all things might more clearly appear to him'. However well Anne had behaved, she was a woman, and might choose to 'play the woman' rather than keep her promises. She was therefore to persuade her brother not to listen to 'tales and bruits', and reassure him also that she was entirely content with her lot. Unless she wrote such a letter, warned the King,

> all shall remain uncertain upon a woman's promise, viz. that she will be no woman; the accomplishment whereof, on her behalf, is as difficult in the refraining of a woman's will, as in changing her womanish nature, which is impossible.

So much for Henry's opinion of the integrity of the fair sex, though he did order the Council to say to Anne, 'for her comfort, that howsoever her brother may conduct himself, or her other friends, she (continuing in her uniformity) shall never fare the worse for their faults'. The Council dutifully returned to Richmond, where Anne was happy to comply with their request. Hopefully, the King would now be satisfied, and she deemed it the appropriate time to make a request.

Anne had by now come to know all the King's children. Mary was of an age with her, and the two had established a warm friendship. Yet, of the three, it was Elizabeth, that bright perceptive child, of whom she was most fond. Anne had a kind heart, and she undoubtedly felt sorry for this little girl who had been so cruelly deprived of her mother. Unlike Prince Edward, Elizabeth was not fussed over by an army of governesses and nurses and even Lady Bryan had been taken from her. Anne herself had no desire to remarry, and knew it was unlikely that she would ever have children of her own. Elizabeth could help to fill that empty space in her life, and she, in turn, could supply the child with something of a mother's love. She was charmed by Elizabeth's beauty, wit and demonstrative nature, and felt it would be a pleasure to have her company sometimes. So she now asked the King if she might be permitted to invite Elizabeth to visit her on occasion, saying 'that to have had [her] for her daughter would have been greater happiness to her than being queen'. The King readily granted her request, and thereafter, it may be assumed, the Lady Elizabeth was a frequent guest at Richmond.

The French ambassador, Marillac, writing on 21 July to his master, was astounded at the ease with which the King had obtained an annulment of his marriage.

> The Queen appears to make no objection [he wrote with disbelief]. The only answer her brother's ambassador can get from her is that she wishes in all things to please the King her lord, bearing testimony of his good treatment of her, and desiring to remain in this country. This, being reported to the King, makes him show her the greater respect.

The ambassador had learned how Henry had decreed that Anne was from henceforth to be regarded as a private person. No ministers were to trouble her or visit her. The people of England, went on the report, much regretted her divorce, for she had won their love, and they esteemed her as

one of the most sweet, gracious and humane queens they have had, and they greatly desire her to continue their queen. Now it is said that the King is going to marry a young lady of extraordinary beauty, a daughter of a deceased brother of the Duke of Norfolk. It is even reported that this marriage has already taken place, only it is kept secret. The Queen takes it all in good part.

Anne was, indeed, quite reconciled to the prospect of Henry's remarriage. She now thought it politic to retire for a short time from public life, and took herself off to the country, living at either Bletchingly, Richmond or Hever, and enjoying her freedom as a lady of means.

Henry had not yet married Katherine Howard, although so much secrecy surrounded his affair with her that rumours were rife at court. In late July, Marillac heard that she was with child, although this proved to be false. It was only after he had dissolved Parliament for the summer recess on 25 July that Henry began to make plans for his wedding. On 27 July, he sent for the Bishop of London to come and marry him at the palace of Oatlands, whither he had just gone with the court. The ceremony would take place in secret on the following day.

There remained just one other formality to be dispensed with and that was the execution of Cromwell. On 28 July 1540, the former minister was taken from his prison in the Tower and brought to the public scaffold on Tower Hill, where a large crowd had gathered. Among them was Cromwell's old friend, Sir Thomas Wyatt. Cromwell noticed him there, weeping, and cried out, 'Oh, Wyatt, do not weep, for if I were not more guilty than thou wert, when they took thee [i.e. to the Tower after Anne Boleyn's arrest], I should not be in this pass.' The King had commuted the sentence to decapitation, even though the condemned man was of lowly birth. But Cromwell suffered, none the less: the executioner bungled his work, and it took two strokes to sever the neck of the prisoner. The King's evil genius died in the manner of so many of his own victims, because the marriage he had arranged to bring joy to his master and profit to himself had proved his ruin.

Anne of Cleves might well have ended up as another of Cromwell's victims. It is to her credit that she did not. Her handling of a difficult and potentially dangerous situation shows that she was, perhaps, the wisest of Henry VIII's wives. She was certainly the luckiest.

14
Rose without a thorn

Today, what remains of Henry VIII's palace of Oatlands lies beneath the foundations of a council estate in Weybridge, Surrey. Much of it was pulled down in the seventeenth century, yet it was a favoured retreat of the King and his children, and Henry spent a great deal of money on it. He had acquired the manor, with its moated red-brick house, in 1537; thereafter he set about enlarging and beautifying it, adding façades, new wings, an arched bridge over the moat, and an octagonal tower. He then had the moat filled in and extended the building over it, creating a new courtyard in the process. The hunting in the nearby park was excellent, and the palace was convenient for Hampton Court. By 1540, most of the improvements had been completed, and it was because it was such a pleasant place that the King decided to take Katherine Howard there for their wedding.

The marriage ceremony, on 28 July, was conducted in private by Bishop Bonner. For ten days, absolute secrecy was maintained about it. The King was infatuated with his bride, and wished for time to spend alone with her before surrounding her with all the paraphernalia of court etiquette and the lack of privacy this entailed. At last, it seemed to him, he had found a wife who embodied all the qualities he most admired in women: beauty, charm, a pleasant disposition, obedience and, he believed, virtue. He considered himself blessed indeed. Whether Katherine was so elated with her husband is a matter for conjecture, but to all appearances the new Queen suffered

431

her wifely duties with commendable fortitude, displaying at all times a cheerful and loving manner towards her august spouse.

This marriage represented the triumph of the conservative faction at court, which meant that the Howards were once again the most powerful family in the kingdom. The changed order was to have immediate repercussions, even before the King's marriage was made public. On 30 July, Richard Fetherston, former tutor to the Lady Mary, Edward Powell, who had once championed the cause of Katherine of Aragon, and Thomas Abell, Katherine's former chaplain, were all dragged on hurdles from their prison in the Tower to Smithfield, where they were executed for high treason. On that same day, Robert Barnes, the Lutheran scholar who had helped to arrange the King's marriage to Anne of Cleves, was burnt as a heretic. The message was clear: the King would not tolerate opposition, nor was he prepared to countenance heresy. Henceforward he would be ruthless in eradicating it, and the latter years of his reign would be very dangerous times for English Protestants. Henry was to be ably assisted in his crusade against these heretics by Bishop Gardiner, an energetic opponent of Lutheranism.

While the martyrs for both faiths suffered, and the King honeymooned with his young bride, the former Queen was making the most of her new freedom. Early in August, Marillac described 'Madam of Cleves' as being 'as joyous as ever'. Far from lamenting the ending of her marriage, she was holding court at Richmond and wearing new dresses every day. The ambassador thought this either showed prudence or 'stupid forgetfulness of what should so closely touch her heart'. His report is borne out by Anne's household accounts for that month, which record payments for new gowns, among them a dress of black velvet edged with fur. Anne had not only adopted English fashions but also English food. 'There is no place like this England for feeding right well!' she declared, and her table at Richmond became renowned. Indeed, she often played hostess to guests from the court. When she was not doing that, she spent all her time at 'sports and recreation'.

The King himself was one of her visitors. After his marriage, he and Katherine left Oatlands and moved to Hampton Court. From here, Henry rode over alone to Richmond, with only a few attendants, on 6 August. Marillac reported that he and Anne were on 'the best possible terms, and they supped so pleasantly together that some thought she was to be restored to her place'. However, this was not entirely a social call. Three members of the Privy Council were present to witness Anne's signature on a document thought to have been the deed of separation. It was noticed, moreover, that Henry was treating Anne with less distinction than when she was queen. Then, she had been seated beside him at meals. Now, she sat apart, at some distance, at a corner of an adjoining table. Marillac concluded, quite rightly, that there was no likelihood of Henry taking her back.

Nevertheless, there were rumours, and on 8 August the King instructed the Privy Council to inform all his ambassadors abroad that he had remarried. On the same day, Katherine Howard appeared as queen at Hampton Court, dining publicly under a cloth of estate.

Henry's envoys were told that the King had been attracted to Katherine

> upon a notable appearance of honour, cleanness and maidenly behaviour . . . [and that] his Highness was finally contented to honour that lady with his marriage, thinking in his old days – after sundry troubles of mind which had happened to him by marriage – to have obtained such a perfect jewel of womanhood and very perfect love towards him as should have been not only to his quietness but also to have brought forth the desired fruits of marriage.

The whole realm, they were told, 'did her honour accordingly'.

The month of August was given over to banquets and hunting in honour of the King's bride. Katherine revelled in her new-found importance, for her doting husband was happy to gratify her every whim: every day, she wore new gowns, and appeared laden with the jewellery with which Henry had showered her. He had rarely been so extravagant with his previous wives. Each day, Katherine discovered some new caprice, and her greed earned her the disapproval of many of the older people at court, including the Lady Mary, who did not treat her with the same respect as she had Jane Seymour and Anne of Cleves. Mary may have found it discomfitting

433

to have a stepmother nine years her junior, for all that she came from a Catholic family, and there may well have been an element of jealousy in her attitude, for she herself was still unmarried at twenty-four. Marillac commented that the pure atmosphere that surrounded Mary was in 'marvellous contrast to the tainted air of the court'.

Whether Marillac was referring to the new Queen is not known, yet it was not long before Katherine Howard revealed herself as a frivolous, empty-headed young girl who cared for little else but dancing and pretty clothes. This seems not to have bothered the King, who looked on lovingly as his pert little wife capered through the boisterous dances of the period, dances in which he could no longer join. Instead, he encouraged the young men of the court to partner her, and watched benignly as they led her out.

Nothing in Katherine's early life had prepared her for her present position. Her youngest years had been spent in impoverished gentility, for her father had found it hard making ends meet on his limited income. She had then gone to live with the Dowager Duchess of Norfolk for the rest of her formative years; the Duchess had neglected her charge in every respect, so that she was often obliged to resort to servants and people of lowly rank for company. It was a life, moreover, devoid of luxury. But now she had the King as her husband, what seemed like unlimited riches at her disposal, power at her fingertips, and an army of servants at her beck and call. Not unnaturally, it all went to her head. However, she had a pleasing manner and a sunny personality; there is no hint that she ever displayed the arrogance shown by her cousin Anne Boleyn. Katherine had a kind heart, and was willing to use her influence on occasion to assist those in trouble. But she was also incapable of resisting the facile charm of sycophants. She had virtually no understanding of the intrigues and pitfalls surrounding her, and her obvious innocence would lay her open to compromising situations.

The King, nevertheless, found her the perfect wife in every respect. All he asked of her was that she give him more sons. She was fifteen, and ripe for this in a period when girls were married off very young. However, although Henry was visiting her bed nearly every night for the first few months of their marriage, she did not conceive, and it may be that he, with his huge bulk and advancing infirmity, was no longer capable of fathering a child.

In mid-August, the Queen's household was re-formed. The ladies appointed to serve Katherine included the Lady Margaret Douglas, the King's niece, the Duchess of Richmond, the Dowager Duchess of Norfolk, the Countess of Sussex, Lady Margaret Howard (Katherine's stepmother, now a widow), and Lady Clinton, who was not Elizabeth Blount, the King's former mistress and first wife of Lord Clinton, but his second wife, Lady Elizabeth FitzGerald whom he married after Elizabeth's death in 1539. The ladies of the Queen's Privy Chamber were the Countess of Rutland, Lady Rochford, and Lady Edgecombe, who had all served Anne of Cleves, and Lady Baynton. Other ladies and gentlewomen in attendance included Lady Arundel (Katherine's sister) and Lady Cromwell (Queen Jane's sister Elizabeth), while Mrs Stonor, who had waited upon Anne Boleyn in the Tower, was a maid of honour.

On 18 August, a new bidding prayer was said in every church in the kingdom when the new Queen's name replaced that of her predecessor. Four days later the King left Windsor to go on his usual late-summer progress, and the Queen went with him, travelling to Reading, and then through Oxfordshire. While they were away, a priest was brought before the magistrates at Windsor, accused of having 'spoken unbefitting words of the Queen's Grace', words which cast aspersions upon Katherine's moral integrity. The Privy Council was duly informed, and on their orders the priest was commanded to remain within his own diocese and admonished to be 'more temperate in the use of his tongue'.

On 29 August, Henry and Katherine arrived at the manor of Grafton in Northamptonshire, where nearly eighty years before Henry's grandparents, Edward IV and Elizabeth Woodville, had secretly married, and where, only eleven years before, Henry had parted from Wolsey for the last time. Yet there were no ghosts to trouble the happy couple on this occasion, for Marillac observed that:

> The King is so amorous of her that he cannot treat her well enough, and caresses her more than he did the others. The new Queen is a lady of moderate beauty but superlative grace. In stature she is small and slender. Her countenance is very delightful, of which the King is so greatly enamoured, and he

knows not how to make sufficient demonstrations of his affection for her.

Katherine, added Marillac, was dressed in clothes that followed the French fashion, like all the other ladies at the English court, and bore her device embroidered in gold thread around her arms: *Non aultre volonté que le sienne* ('No other will than his'). In fact Henry was so besotted with Katherine that he ordered a medal to be struck in commemoration of their marriage. It was of gold, embossed with Tudor roses and true lovers' knots entwined, and it carried the inscription: HENRICUS VIII: RUTILANS ROSA SINE SPINA, a pretty reference to the King's rose without a thorn, his perfect bride.

The royal pair remained at Grafton until 7 September before riding south into Bedfordshire, where they stayed at Ampthill for a fortnight. Katherine of Aragon had been exiled here after being banished from court. Henry, however, was more concerned about the behaviour of the Queen's vice-chamberlain, Edward Baynton, who, with others, had been drunk and disorderly in the King's presence, and Henry, fearing that their bad example might contaminate the purity of his queen, now issued stern orders 'concerning the sober and temperate order that his Highness would have them to use in his Highness' chamber of presence and the Queen's'.

The King's train left Ampthill on 1 October and travelled to Wolsey's old house, The More in Hertfordshire, before returning to Windsor on 22 October. There, Henry was astonished to learn that rumour was currently crediting him with having made Anne of Cleves pregnant while on his visit to Richmond in August. He was relieved when further investigations revealed that Anne had merely been confined to bed with a stomach upset, which some mischievous persons had whispered was morning sickness. Marillac sneered at the rumours, for the King was so openly affectionate towards Katherine Howard, and 'bestows so many caresses on her, with such singular demonstrations of affection', that it was impossible to believe he had belatedly contemplated seducing Anne of Cleves. Henry's love for his wife was further proved in October when the Queen Consort Act was passed by Parliament; this Act set out in plain terms the rights and privileges of the Queen, giving her the power to act as 'a woman sole, without the consent of the King's Highness'. Immediately after the Act was passed, Henry granted to Katherine Howard all the lands and manors that had once been in the possession of Queen Jane.

It was around this time that a crisis arose in the Queen's household. Her chief lady-in-waiting, Lady Margaret Douglas, the King's 25-year-old niece, was a young woman of strong and determined character. Some four years earlier she had clandestinely married Lord Thomas Howard, an affair that ended with his imprisonment and death in the Tower, whither he had been sent for daring to marry Margaret without the King's permission. It had taken her a long time to recover from his death, but now she was learning to enjoy life again, for, during the summer progress, she had fallen in love with the new Queen's brother, Charles Howard. So indiscreet were the lovers that, by the time the court returned to Windsor, the King had heard the gossip about them. His wrath was terrible. He packed his niece off to Syon Abbey, recently vacated by the dispossessed nuns, and forbade Howard to contact her. Katherine had wisely refused to have anything to do with the intrigue, and therefore remained in the King's good graces.

People were still expressing pious hopes that the Queen might be pregnant. In November, Richard Jones dedicated his book *The Birth of Mankind*, a treatise on reproduction and midwifery, to 'our most gracious and virtuous Queen Katherine', with a warning to all men to 'use it godly'. Although Katherine had as yet no need of such a book, being married to her had rejuvenated the King. On 4 December, Marillac reported that Henry had adopted a new daily routine: he rose between five and six, heard mass at seven, then rode out hawking until dinner, which was at 10.0 a.m. He and Katherine were staying at Woking just then, and Henry told Marillac he felt much better in the country than when he was forced to stay in London during the winter. Even his leg had temporarily improved, enabling him to ride at will.

Henry and Katherine were again at Oatlands from 7 to 18 December, and then moved on to Hampton Court for the Christmas season. The King's New Year's gifts to his wife were lavish, and included two pendant laces with 26 'fair table diamonds' and 158 'fair pearls', as well as a rope of 200 large pearls. She also received from him a square pendant containing 27 diamonds and 26 clusters of pearls, as well as a muffler of black velvet edged with sable fur into which were

437

sewn 38 rubies and 572 pearls. At least some of these gems had belonged to the King's previous wives, for the treasury was so depleted that he could not have afforded to buy them all. Indeed, Henry was so short of funds just then that he could not spare the expense of having the Queen crowned; possibly he had decided that the coronations of queen consorts were from now on conditional upon the production of an heir.

The New Year revels of 1541 brought together a family gathering. The Lady Mary had come up from Hunsdon to be present, although she had little in common with the giddy young Queen, and relations were very stilted between them. Katherine did not worry unduly about this, however, for Anne of Cleves was also at court, and she got on famously with both of them. Anne had sent the King and Queen two great horses with violet velvet trappings before arriving at Hampton Court on 3 January. That evening, the King retired early, but Anne stayed up dancing with the young Queen, and the next day dined with her and Henry. When Henry gave Katherine yet more presents, this time a ring and two small dogs, she generously passed them over to the Lady Anne.

From 7 to 10 February 1541 Henry was in London alone, attending to business with the Council while Katherine remained with the court at Hampton; this was the first time they had been apart since their marriage. On the King's return, or soon after, his leg began to pain him once more, causing him to become virtually chair-bound for a time. By Shrove Tuesday, he was sunk in apathy, and not interested in any kind of recreation, even music. Marillac described him as suffering from *mal d'esprit*, and at one point his doctors were in fear for his life. There was little they could do to alleviate his pain, or his depression, and for some weeks it was left to Queen Katherine to preside over a court that felt strangely empty. There were masques on 21 and 22 February, but the King did not attend them.

In private, the Queen was dutiful in attending to her husband's needs, yet he was not an easy person to live with at this time. He was melancholy and irascible. It was felt that his great bulk only made matters worse, and Marillac observed that the King was 'marvellously excessive in eating and drinking', adding that 'people say he is often of a different opinion in the morning than after dinner'. He could not bear people near him during those weeks, and kept to his rooms, so that it was said that the court 'resembled more a private family than a King's train'. Kings were expected to live their lives publicly, but Henry had had enough. He could not accept this latest setback to his health, or face the fact that he was now a prisoner of his ageing, sickly body. Queen Katherine could not arouse him from his depression, and he shut his door even against her.

Although Katherine was alarmed by the King's behaviour, which was contrary to all she knew of him, her fears were soon to be allayed for by 19 March Henry was much his old self again. His leg was now a little better, and this enabled him to muster his inner resources to help him face the future.

That spring saw Katherine stirred to action by the plight of three people imprisoned in the Tower. One was Margaret Pole, Countess of Salisbury, who had languished there for nearly two years with inadequate clothing and heating to protect her aged body from the bitter winter weather. When she learned of this, the Queen saw her tailor on 1 March and ordered him to make up garments which were to be sent to Lady Salisbury: a furred night-gown, a kirtle of worsted, a furred petticoat, a satin-lined night-gown, a bonnet and frontlet, four pairs of hose, four pairs of shoes and one pair of slippers. With the King's permission, Katherine paid for all these items out of her privy purse.

The second prisoner in whom the young Queen took an interest was Sir Thomas Wyatt, who was again in the Tower on a minor charge. When the King recovered from his malady, Katherine pleaded for Wyatt's release. Chapuys, who had recently returned to court, told Charles V that this was a very courageous act on her part, and that Henry had only grudgingly consented after laying down certain conditions, namely that Wyatt confessed his guilt, and undertook to resume conjugal relations with his wife, from whom he had been estranged for fifteen years. For a week, Katherine worked to persuade the King to leave out this latter condition, but Henry was in a prim and virtuous mood, and insisted upon it. Wyatt was duly released, it being given out that 'at the great and continual suit of the Queen's Majesty, the King, being of his own most godly nature inclined to pity and mercy, hath given him his pardon in large and ample sort'. Katherine also obtained the release of a third prisoner, Sir John Wallop, confined to the Tower for some petty misconduct.

The pardoning of Wyatt was a very popular move at court, and for weeks both King and Queen basked in the approval and applause of those around them. Henry was impressed by his wife's tender compassion for the prisoners, feeling it an appropriate attribute in the consort of a ruler such as himself. It was very gratifying being able to play the role of indulgent husband and merciful sovereign, and flattering to the King's vanity.

In early April 1541, Katherine thought she might be pregnant at last. This, Marillac told Francis I, 'would be a very great joy to the King, who, it seems, believes it, and intends, if it be found true, to have her crowned at Whitsuntide'. Sadly Katherine's hopes came to nothing: it may have been a false alarm, or she may even have suffered an early miscarriage. What is certain is that disappointment cast the King once more into a black mood, and in early May the Queen herself was visibly in low spirits owing to a rumour that Henry planned to get rid of her and take back Anne of Cleves. There was no foundation to this tale, as Henry hastened to reassure his wife, but his disappointment certainly affected their happy relationship for a time, and it may well have made Katherine dissatisfied with her marriage.

Life at court was mundane and quiet that spring. None of the King's children was there and there was little in the way of entertainment. The young Queen was bored. Then news arrived of an uprising against the King in Yorkshire. Headed by Sir John Neville, a fervent Catholic, its purpose was to depose Henry VIII's Lord President of the North and restore the old forms of religion in England. Henry also seems to have feared that disaffection among his subjects would lead to plots for the reinstatement of the Plantagenets. A few sprigs of that ancient royal house still lived: one was Margaret Pole, who had a valid claim to the throne, although she herself had never expressed any desire to occupy it. Indeed, for years, she had rendered loyal and devoted service to the Tudors, and it was mainly because of her sons' disaffection that she had been imprisoned in the Tower. Yet now, with a rebellion on his hands, the King behaved as if the Countess was a threat to his security, and – in spite of the Queen's protests and pleas for mercy – he ordered that the death sentence provided for in the Act of Attainder passed against Lady Salisbury be put into effect immediately.

On the morning of 28 May 1541, there occurred one of the worst atrocities of Henry's reign. The 68-year-old Countess was awakened by the Constable of the Tower with the news that she was to die that day. She was given a short while to prepare her soul for death, then led out to the scaffold on Tower Green, where Anne Boleyn had died, and where a crowd of spectators awaited her. The executioner was not the usual one employed on such occasions and was young and inexperienced. Faced with such a prisoner, he panicked, and struck out blindly, hacking at his victim's head, neck and shoulders, until he had finally butchered her to death.

The cruel end of Lady Salisbury sickened even the Tudor court, but the King was unrepentant. The northern uprising was speedily put down, and its leaders executed at the end of July. The peace of the realm had been preserved, and the security of the dynasty maintained, although Henry's reputation had suffered in the process. He was now more feared than beloved by many of his subjects.

On 30 July 1541, the King left London to go on a progress with the Queen and a great train of courtiers to the Eastern counties and the North, the centres of so much recent disaffection. He believed that his presence there might inspire loyalty and also act as a deterrent against any thought of future revolts. There were also two other matters to be accomplished. One was the collection of the huge fines levied on the cities that had supported Neville's rebellion, and the other was a meeting between Henry VIII and his nephew, James V of Scotland, who had promised to ride down to York to greet his uncle.

The royal cavalcade travelled via Dunstable, Ampthill, Grafton, Northampton, and Stamford to the city of Lincoln. Here, after formally pardoning the citizens for their part in the Pilgrimage of Grace and the recent uprising, the King went with the Queen into the cathedral, where they heard mass. During their stay, they were lodged in the adjacent Bishop's Palace. After leaving Lincoln, they journeyed to Boston, then a flourishing port, where Henry was able to indulge his passion for ships. From Boston, the progress wound its way into Yorkshire, passing into Northumberland as far as Newcastle – the furthest north Henry had ever been during his reign – and then south again to Pontefract, whose castle had been in 1400 the scene of the murder of Richard II. The court arrived there at the end of August.

Meanwhile, disturbing news from abroad had reached England. The Emperor and the King of France were on the brink of war with each other, and both wanted Henry's support. In August, Francis I proposed a marriage between the Lady Mary and his heir, the Duke of Orléans (the Dauphin had died in 1536); but Henry was reluctant to commit himself and so offend Charles. Thereafter, relations between England and France, never very good of late, deteriorated steadily. Since his excommunication in 1539, Henry VIII had been building elaborate defences along the south coast of England, in anticipation of a possible French invasion, and his castles still stand today at Deal and Walmer. He did not trust Francis, suspecting him of plotting an invasion of his kingdom, and for this reason he wanted the Emperor as a friend and ally, bearing in mind also the vital trade links between England and the Low Countries.

Henry did not let matters of state affect his enjoyment of the progress; as for the Queen, she was in high spirits, revelling in the warmth and approval emanating from the people who lined the roads and lanes to see her. Yet in Pontefract, she came face to face with her past when a young man who had once lived in the Dowager Duchess's household presented himself at court. His name was Francis Dereham, and he came with a recommendation from the Duchess, whose distant relative he is thought to have been, and who had led him to believe that the Queen would be pleased to have him in her household. But Katherine feared there was another reason that had prompted Dereham's appearance at court, the same reason that had inspired Joan Bulmer to press to be taken into her service. Dereham possessed information that could cause untold harm to Katherine's reputation, and he might well mean to exploit that knowledge, and use it to gain preferment. Hence, when he too requested employment, she dared not refuse, and on 27 August he was appointed her private secretary. 'Take heed what words you speak,' Katherine warned him. When the King asked why she had employed Dereham, she told him that the Duchess of Norfolk had asked her to be good to him – 'and so I will.'

Dereham proved to be a most unsuitable addition to her

442

household. He had a fiery temper, and was over-familiar with his royal mistress, arousing the dislike of many who felt that Katherine was giving him preferential treatment. One of the Queen's gentlemen ushers, a Mr John, fell out with Dereham when the latter remained seated at dinner or supper after the Queen's council had risen, an action that seemed deliberately disrespectful. Mr John sent a messenger one evening with orders for Dereham to rise with every-one else, but Dereham refused. 'Go to Mr John and tell him I was one of the Queen's counsel before he knew her, and shall be there after she hath forgotten him!' he said insolently. This provoked a brawl between the two men with Dereham emerging the victor. It was as well the King did not hear of it, for there were severe penalties for violent behaviour within the court, though Dereham could be discreet when he wanted to, and he kept in the background when Henry was around. Others noticed his proprietorial and somewhat familiar manner with the Queen. Katherine was always susceptible to male flattery and attention, and there were those in her household and at the court who were strongly attracted to her, and jealous of Dereham's influence. She did not know it, but she was standing on the edge of a precipice.

In the middle of September, the King's train arrived in York, where Henry was due to rendezvous with James V. James, being distrustful of his uncle, did not turn up. Relations between England and Scotland had never been very good during Henry's reign, but from now on they would be plainly antagonistic. After waiting with mounting anger for several days for the King of Scots, Henry gave up and went off to Hull, arriving there on 1 October, and staying for five days. Henry was feeling much restored and in a holiday mood, though the progress was now drawing to an end. During October, the royal cavalcade moved slowly south, passing through Kettleby and Collyweston and Ampthill, before reaching Windsor on the 26th.

Two items of bad news awaited the King on his return. One concerned the death of his sister, Queen Margaret of Scotland, on 8 October at Methven Castle, and the other was a report from Prince Edward's doctors that the four-year-old heir was ill with a fever. Marillac told Francis I that Edward was 'too fat and unhealthy' to live long, but he was clearly being malicious. Fortunately, the King's initial panic upon hearing the news of his son's illness was soon alleviated by tidings that the child was making a good recovery. Continuing reports of Edward's progress put Henry into a good mood, and he seems at this time to have become even fonder of his queen, if that were possible. He could not bear to be without her for long, calling her the jewel of his age, and continually thanking God for sending him such a wife. He was even planning a public service of thanksgiving. But his idyll was soon to be abruptly and tragically shattered.

While the King was away on progress, a Protestant called John Lascelles came and confided to Archbishop Cranmer that he knew things about the Queen's past that would reflect upon her marriage with the King. He vowed he would rather die declaring the truth, since it so nearly touched the King, than live with the concealment of the same. Cranmer asked why he had not come forward before, to which he replied that he had been wrestling with his conscience.

Cranmer was not an unkind man, but he preferred to do whatever was expedient, and he was, it must be remembered, a secret Protestant himself, as well as an advocate of reform. He had never approved of the King's marriage to Katherine Howard, although he held nothing personal against her: it was what she represented that he privately and passionately opposed. He therefore saw in John Lascelles a catalyst for change: if anything could be proved against the Queen, it might be possible to remove her from the political scene and discredit her supporters, the powerful Catholic faction. The way would then be clear for the King to marry a bride put forward by Cranmer and his partisans who would be as energetic as Anne Boleyn in the reformist cause.

Cranmer therefore listened patiently and courteously to what John Lascelles had to say. He heard that Lascelles's sister Mary had, before her marriage to a Mr Hall, lived with Katherine in the ladies' dormitory in the Duchess of Norfolk's house at Lambeth, and had known her well. Later, when it was announced that Katherine was to become Queen of England, Mrs Hall had been prompted by her brother to seek service with her. 'I will not,' she answered, 'but I am very sorry for her.' Lascelles had asked why. 'Marry, for she is light,

444

both in living and in conditions [i.e. behaviour],' was the answer. Lascelles did not elaborate on this, but told the Archbishop that his sister could supply more details if she was required to.

When Lascelles had gone, Cranmer pondered for a long time. Anne Boleyn had been found guilty of misconduct after marriage; was it possible that the same thing might be proved against Katherine Howard? Fornication before marriage was not a crime, but it argued a lightness of morals that might lead a young and impressionable girl into an adulterous relationship after the knot was tied. The possibility was there. Yet Cranmer knew he was treading on very dangerous ground. Anne Boleyn's fall had come about because the King was desperate to be rid of her: he was deeply in love with Katherine, and likely to react violently to any inference that she was not as virtuous as he believed her to be. It would not be wise to act until a solid case of incontrovertible fact had been established. Indeed, it might be wiser not to do anything at all.

There was much at stake. Cranmer knew Henry well enough to predict that he would sacrifice his personal needs in the interests of the state; adultery in a queen jeopardised the succession and was insulting to the King. Henry's vast pride would not permit him to retain a wife who had cuckolded him, or made a fool of him. He would be devastated, but he would not be stupid. It was essential, however, for Cranmer to get his facts right beforehand, for it would be death to incur the King's displeasure over such a matter.

He summoned Mary Hall. Her information was far more precise than her brother's. She told Cranmer that some years before, when she was living in the household of the Dowager Duchess of Norfolk, it was common gossip that the Queen, then a very young girl, had been encouraging the attentions of her music master, Henry Manox. One of the ladies of the household, Dorothy Barwike, had told Mary that Manox was troth-plight to Katherine Howard, 'with whom he was much in love'. Manox, of course, had no business to be affiancing himself to a daughter of the Howards, and Mary Hall took it upon herself to reprove him for his behaviour.

Man [she had said sharply], what mean thou to play the fool of this fashion? Know not that if my lady of Norfolk knew of the love betwixt thee and Mistress Howard, she will undo thee? She is come of a noble house, and if thou should marry her, some of her blood would kill thee!

Manox had sneered and replied,

Hold thy peace, woman! I know her well enough. My designs are of a dishonest kind, and from the liberties the young lady has allowed me, I doubt not of being able to effect my purpose. She hath said to me that I shall have her maidenhead, though it be painful to her, not doubting but I will be good to her hereafter.

Mary had been appalled by his cynicism, and the fact that he was leading Katherine on with empty offers of marriage, but she was a charitable woman and excused him on the grounds that he 'was so far in love with her that he wist not what he said'. Which says far more about Mary Lascelles's ignorance of the ploys of the male sex than it does about Manox's true intentions.

But Katherine could also be fickle. Shortly afterwards she transferred her affection to Francis Dereham, without having granted Manox the ultimate favour. Their affair progressed quickly and soon, according to Mrs Hall, they became lovers. For a hundred nights and more, Dereham had crept into the ladies' dormitory and climbed, dressed in doublet and hose, into Katherine's bed. The other women and girls in the room were left in little ignorance of what was going on by the noises that issued from beyond the drawn bed-hangings, and one maid refused to sleep nearby because Katherine 'knew not what matrimony was'. At the same time, Manox, full of spite, was going about boasting that he knew of a private mark on Katherine's body. He told Mary Hall that he would speak to Katherine about her behaviour with Dereham, but Mary told him to keep quiet. 'Let her alone,' she said, unable to contain her disgust at Katherine's behaviour 'for if she holds on as she begins, we shall hear she will be naught within a while.'

Cranmer listened to all this with interest, giving due attention to his informant. He could find nothing amiss in her character, and later reported to the Council that 'she did from the first opening of the matter to her brother seem to be sorry, and to lament that the King's Majesty had married the Queen'. Now he dismissed her after taking a written statement, and retired to think about what she had told him.

On 30 October, the King and Queen came to Hampton Court. Henry now gave orders for the special service of thanksgiving for his marriage to take place on 1 November. On that day he publicly thanked God in the Chapel Royal for blessing him with so perfect a companion: 'I render thanks to Thee, O Lord, that after so many strange accidents that have befallen my marriages, Thou hast been pleased to give me a wife so entirely conformed to my inclinations as her I now have.' At the same time, in churches throughout the land, every good subject paid similar honour to the Queen's virtues.

While Henry was giving thanks, Cranmer softly entered the Chapel, not without apprehension. He had decided, after much deliberation, that he ought to lay what information he had before the King now, although he had agonised for hours over how best to do it. In the end, he had decided to summarise the facts in a letter, which he now laid by the King's side before retiring from the service.

Back in his chamber, Henry read what Cranmer had written: that his cherished Katherine was accused of 'dissolute living before her marriage with Francis Dereham, and that was not secret, but many knew it'. His first reaction was one of astonished disbelief. He summoned Cranmer at once and demanded an explanation. Cranmer repeated all that had gone before, and ended by saying he had been forced to convey the news by letter 'as he had not the heart to tell him by mouth'. Henry was stunned, but he kept his composure. He told the Archbishop he did not think there was any foundation in these malicious accusations; nevertheless, Cranmer was to investigate the matter more thoroughly. 'You are not to desist until you have got to the bottom of the pot,' said Henry. At the same time, he gave orders that the Queen was to be confined to her apartments with just Lady Rochford in attendance until her name was cleared, as he was confident it would be. He himself would stay away from her until then. In fact, he never saw her again.

Katherine and her ladies were practising dance steps when the King's guards arrived and said it was 'no more the time to dance'. When they dismissed most of her servants, Katherine – who had more on her conscience than pre-marital romps with Manox and Dereham – became extremely agitated, and demanded to know the reason for her confinement, but the guards could not enlighten her. She thought she knew already, and in the days to come the knowledge prevented her from eating and sleeping. In fact, she was not, as yet, in such a bad case as she feared, for the King was inclined to believe in her innocence because, in his view, the evidence provided by John Lascelles and Mary Hall was a malicious fabrication. On 2 November, he told Sir Thomas Wriothesley and Sir Anthony Browne that:

> He could not believe it to be true, and yet, the accusation having once been made, he could not be satisfied till the certainty hereof was known; but he would not, in any wise, that in the inquisition any spark of scandal should arise against the Queen.

On the following day, Cranmer questioned John Lascelles again, but the man only repeated and confirmed what he had said earlier, affirming it to be the truth. Cranmer sat on this knowledge for two days before passing it on to the King. In the meantime, he discovered that the Queen had taken Francis Dereham into her service. On 5 November, he and the Council informed the King that they believed the allegations against Queen Katherine had a sound basis in fact: that she now employed one of her former lovers was seen as very sinister indeed. 'She has betrayed you in thought,' Cranmer told his master, 'and if she had an opportunity would have betrayed you in deed.'

It should be remembered that at this stage Cranmer had not one jot of evidence beyond what he saw as his own logical conclusions that Katherine had ever committed adultery. But Henry's suspicious mind had also jumped to that same logical conclusion. He slumped in his chair, pierced to the heart; for some time he could not speak. Finally, he broke down in tears in front of the Council, weeping copiously and pouring out his heartbreak. They marvelled at this, thinking it 'strange in one of his courage' to show such emotion. 'The King has wonderfully felt the case of the Queen,' reported Chapuys. Indeed, from that moment onwards, Henry was an old man. The semblance of youth had gone for ever. On the same day, he left Hampton Court with a few attendants and galloped to Oatlands, even though the house was full of poignant memories. He

448

remained there for some days, away from the public gaze and the court gossip, his pride broken, and his heart. He did not want to air his shame.

Chapuys thought the King might well be more merciful towards Katherine than her relatives, who had already abandoned her in an attempt to save their own skins. Only Norfolk, who perhaps felt to a degree responsible for what had happened, showed some compassion towards his niece. He was present when Katherine was informed of the charges of misconduct laid against her, and witnessed her hysterical reaction. He told Marillac that she was refusing to eat or drink anything, and that she did not cease from weeping and crying 'like a madwoman, so that they must take away things by which she might hasten her death'. Norfolk had already assumed that his niece would end on the block as her cousin had done, and it is obvious that Katherine herself expected it.

The Queen was not the only person affected by what had happened. Lady Rochford, who was guilty of aiding and abetting crimes the Council did not yet know about, suddenly realised the danger she was in and 'was seized with raving madness'. Since the two women were confined together, it was thought by many that the same fate would befall the Queen. Earlier on, before Henry left Hampton Court, Katherine had dashed past her guards and tried to reach him while he was at prayer in the Chapel Royal, but she had been intercepted by her pursuers and dragged screaming back to her rooms. She knew, as well as everyone else, that if she could see Henry she stood a good chance of being forgiven. But Henry knew his own weakness in this respect, and kings must not be seen to be weak. He had removed himself, and Katherine knew her case was hopeless.

At Lambeth, the Dowager Duchess of Norfolk heard reports of the Queen's misconduct, and realised that it was under her roof that that misconduct had taken place. She also recalled certain incidents that tended to confirm what was being said. Nevertheless, she took a more rational view of what was happening than most of her clan. 'If there be none offence sithence the marriage, she cannot die for that was done before,' she reasoned. Yet she began searching the house for incriminating evidence, knowing that, if Katherine fell, the Howards would topple with her.

449

Cranmer was now certain that he could uncover evidence of adultery after marriage. When he visited the Queen in her apartments on 6 and 7 November, it was in the hope of wringing a confession of this from her. Without it, no one could proceed against her, for pre-marital fornication was neither a crime nor acceptable grounds for annulling a marriage. Knowing that much depended upon the outcome of the interview, Cranmer assumed his most paternal and solicitous manner. Afterwards, he wrote an account of what had happened for the King.

He found the Queen 'in such lamentation and heaviness as I never saw no creature, so that it would have pitied any man's heart in the world to have looked upon'. It was impossible to speak rationally with her in this state, and therefore he did not stay long. Katherine remained in 'a vehement rage' all night, and was still quite frenzied when he returned the next morning. Even Cranmer was shaken by her behaviour, and feared for her sanity. Yet he brought her hope, in the form of a letter from her husband, promising her mercy if she would confess her faults. When this letter was read to her, she calmed down a little, although Cranmer feared it was only a temporary lull. But at least they were able to converse sensibly for a while, Katherine telling him she was willing to do all he asked of her and that she would reply to his questions 'as truly and faithfully as she would answer at the Day of Judgement and by the Sacrament which she received on All Hallows Day last past'. Cranmer himself admitted later that he meant to frighten her by exaggerating the grievous nature of her offences as well as 'declaring to her the justness of your Grace's laws, and what she ought to suffer by the same'. Only then did he intend to extend the offer of mercy to her.

Yet Katherine was so distraught that he felt constrained instead to stress the 'benignity and mercy' of the King in an attempt to comfort her, sensing that any mention of the law might drive her 'into some dangerous ecstasy, or else into a very frenzy, so that the words of comfort, coming last, might have come too late'. When Katherine at last understood that Henry really did mean to deal gently with her, 'She held up her hands and gave most humble thanks to your Majesty, who had showed her more grace and mercy than she herself could have hoped for.' After that, she became 'more temperate and moderate', even though she did not cease sobbing and weeping, and

450

at one point, when panic hit her once more, she started screaming. The Archbishop was becoming familiar with this pattern, and tried hard to reason out the cause, doing his best to allay her fears while at the same time trying to glean more information. If she had 'some new fantasy come into her head', he said gently, she could confide it to him.

Gradually, Katherine pulled herself together. When she could speak coherently, she cried,

> Alas, my Lord, that I am alive! The fear of death did not grieve me so much before as doth now the remembrance of the King's goodness, for when I remember how gracious and loving a Prince I had, I cannot but sorrow. But this sudden mercy, more than I could have looked for, maketh mine offences to appear before mine eyes much more heinous than they did before. And the more I consider the greatness of his mercy, the more I do sorrow in my heart that I should so misorder myself against his Majesty.

And she wept so bitterly that nothing Cranmer could say would comfort her. Eventually, she calmed down, and he left her to rest until the evening.

When he returned, she was still relatively calm, and they talked awhile, he giving her words of comfort, but at six o'clock she again grew hysterical, remembering that at that hour Master Heneage usually brought her news of the King and a loving message from him.

Cranmer did not obtain a great deal of information from Katherine about her liaison with Dereham before her marriage, but he did learn enough to conclude that there had probably been some kind of precontract between them that would invalidate Katherine's marriage to the King, even though Katherine herself 'thinks it to have been no contract'. The Archbishop obtained a written declaration or confession from her, describing what had passed between her and Dereham, but, after he had left, she sent word to say that she wished to change it. On Cranmer's return, she insisted that Dereham had in fact raped her with 'importunate force', and that she had not at any time freely consented to intercourse with him. Cranmer knew, of course, that she was lying, and suspected she might well have lied about other things, such as whether or not she had betrayed the King after her marriage. He warned her that her life was forfeit – although there was no legal basis for this statement – and reminded her again that the King was prepared to be merciful. Her written confession of her fault and her plea for her husband's forgiveness might soften Henry's heart. It was her only hope.

The Queen's confession did not satisfy Cranmer. In it, Katherine declared that Dereham had 'many times moved me unto the question of matrimony', but she had never accepted any of his proposals. She had neither willingly indulged in illicit intercourse with him, nor had she said the words alleged by Mary Hall to have been spoken by her to Dereham, 'I promise you I do love you with all my heart.' She was also sure she had never promised by her faith and troth that she would have no other husband but him. She was too naïve to realise that by admitting to a precontract she could have saved her life, for if she had never been the King's legal wife, she could not be accused of adultery, which she now realised they were trying to prove. Instead she seems to have felt that confessing to the existence of a precontract would somehow prejudice her case. She had certainly been affectionate towards her lover, for she had given him a collar and sleeves for a shirt, which had been made by 'Clinton's wife of Lambeth', as well as a silver bracelet, although she accused him of snatching the latter from her and keeping it in spite of her protests. A ruby ring found by the King's men in Dereham's possession was 'none of hers'.

The news that Dereham, Manox and other members of the Duchess of Norfolk's household had been arrested a day or so previously and imprisoned in the Tower was enough to send her into another paroxysm of hysterical panic, yet it also constrained her to be more truthful. Dereham, she continued, had given her presents, mainly lovers' tokens. 'He knew of a little woman in London with a crooked back, who was skilled in making flowers of silk,' who made him a French fennel to give to Katherine, and later a heart's-ease for a New Year's present, although the Dowager Duchess returned it to him, considering it a most improper gift. Yet Dereham was not put off. He bought some sarcenet, which Katherine had had made up into a quilted cap by the Duchess's embroiderer, a man surnamed Rose. Although Katherine had not specified any particular pattern, Mr Rose decorated the cap with friars' knots, which were a symbol of true love. When Dereham saw it, he exclaimed, 'What, wife, here be friars' knots for Francis!' The fact that he was used to addressing her as 'wife' was taken to be strongly indicative of a precontract between them.

These, then, were the only gifts that passed between the lovers, except for £10.00 that Dereham gave to the Queen during the recent progress – for what purpose is not specified. There was also the matter of £100 he left with her when he went away from the household at Lambeth to seek his fortune in Ireland, where he is thought to have turned to piracy. This money was the bulk of his savings, and he entrusted it to Katherine, saying that, if he did not return, 'I was to consider it as my own.' To Cranmer and others, this argued an established relationship based on a firm understanding that the young couple would marry some day.

When Katherine was asked whether she had called Dereham husband and he had called her wife, she answered that it was common gossip in the household that they would marry; some of Dereham's rivals – a reference to Manox, perhaps – were very jealous of him, and it pleased him to flaunt his conquest in their faces. He had asked Katherine if he might have leave to refer to her as his wife; she agreed, and promised to call him husband. Thus they fell into the habit of using these terms.

Dereham seems to have been quite a ladies' man: he kissed Katherine openly and often, and did the same to many other women in the house. On one occasion, he kissed Katherine so passionately that those watching them observed 'that he would never have kissed me enough'. Dereham retorted, 'Who shall let [prevent] me to kiss my own wife?' Then the others teased him, saying the day would surely come when 'Mr Dereham will have Mrs Katherine Howard.' 'By St John!' said Dereham, 'You may guess twice and guess worse!' Katherine inwardly cringed at such talk, and asked Dereham what would happen 'an [if] this should come to my lady's ear?' But it never did. The Duchess was a neglectful guardian, and was either deaf to the rumours or deliberately ignored them. If she was confronted with something not to her liking, then she dealt with it, but otherwise she seems to have cared little for the moral welfare of those in her charge.

Katherine's confession next dealt with the delicate matter known as 'carnal knowledge', and dealt with it honestly and frankly. She confessed that on many occasions Dereham

> hath lain with me, sometimes in his doublet and hose, and two or three times naked, but not so naked that he had nothing upon him, for he had always at the least his doublet, and as I do think his hose also; but I mean naked, when his hose was put down.

On the nights he visited her bed, he would bring with him wine, strawberries, apples, 'and other things to make good cheer, after my lady was gone to bed'. He never attempted to steal the Duchess's keys, and nor did Katherine; the door to the ladies' dormitory was frequently left unlocked at night for a variety of reasons, so they had no need. Sometimes, he would arrive at Katherine's bedside early in the morning, and behave 'very lewdly', but never, she insisted, was this at her request or with her consent.

There was always the fear of discovery. 'What shift should we make if my lady should come in suddenly?' asked Wilks and Baskerville, two of the women sharing the dormitory. Katherine told them she would send her lover into a nearby gallery, and on one occasion was obliged to do this. When Dereham learned that Katherine might be going to court, he said he would not remain for long in the Duchess's household, to which she replied that he might do as he liked. She had felt little grief at the prospect of being parted from him, and had not shed a tear over it; nor had she told him – as alleged by Mary Hall – he would never live to say, 'Thou hast swerved.' Everyone that knew her was aware how glad she was to be going to court, and once she had left the Duchess's household and Dereham had gone to Ireland, she had not written to him. As far as she remembered, the last conversation between them prior to their parting had concerned Katherine's distant cousin, Thomas Culpeper. Dereham had heard a rumour that she was going to marry Culpeper, and asked if it were true, but she denied it, saying, 'What should you trouble me thereabouts, for you know I will not have you; and if you heard such report, you know more than I.'

In mentioning Thomas Culpeper in her statement, Katherine unwittingly played into Cranmer's hands, for Culpeper was now at court, one of the most highly favoured gentlemen of the King's privy chamber. He was a cousin of the Queen on her mother's side, and Katherine had been fond of him since childhood. In fact, in recent months, that fondness had developed into something far deeper and more dangerous. Cranmer did not know this, but his suspicions were now aroused – he was, it must be remembered, searching for evidence of adultery – and he persuaded the Council to order Culpeper's arrest and detention for questioning.

Thus the evidence against the Queen built up. Cranmer sent her confession to the King on 7 November, along with the further statement alleging that Dereham had raped her by force. In the meantime, Katherine received a visit from some of the lords of the Council, who helped her to draft a plea for forgiveness to send to the King. It read:

I, your Grace's most sorrowful subject and vile wretch in the world, not worthy to make any recommendations unto your Majesty, do only make my most humble submission and confession of my faults. And where no cause of mercy is given on my part, yet of your most accustomed mercy extended to all other men undeserved, most humbly on my hands and knees do desire one particle thereof to be extended unto me, although of all other creatures most unworthy either to be called your wife or subject. My sorrow I can by no writing express, nevertheless I trust your most benign nature will have some respect unto my youth, my ignorance, my frailness, my humble confession of my faults and plain declaration of the same, referring me wholly unto your Grace's pity and mercy. First at the flattering and fair persuasions of Manox, being but a young girl [I] suffered him at sundry times to handle and touch the secret parts of my body, which neither became me with honesty to permit, nor him to require. Also Francis Dereham by many persuasions procured me to his vicious purpose, and obtained first to lie upon my bed with his doublet and hose, and after within the bed, and finally he lay with me naked, and used me in such sort as a man doth his wife, many and sundry times, and our company ended almost a year before the King's Majesty was married to my Lady Anne of Cleves, and continued not past one quarter of a year, or a little above.

455

This dates the liaison with Dereham to the autumn and winter of 1538–9, when Katherine was about thirteen; her affair with Manox belongs to the period immediately prior to that.

Now that she had declared the whole truth to the King, she humbly besought him to consider

the subtle persuasions of young men and the ignorance and frailness of young women. I was so desirous to be taken unto your Grace's favour, and so blinded with the desire of worldly glory, that I could not, nor had grace, to consider how great a fault it was to conceal my former faults from your Majesty, considering that I intended ever during my life to be faithful and true unto your Majesty after; nevertheless, the sorrow of mine offences was ever before mine eyes, considering the infinite goodness of your Majesty towards me from time to time ever increasing and not diminishing. Now I refer the judgement of all my offences with my life and death wholly unto your most benign and merciful Grace to be considered by no justice of your Majesty's laws but only by your infinite goodness, pity, compassion and mercy, without the which I acknowledge myself worthy of extreme punishment.

When Henry read this abject plea, he was somewhat cheered. His beloved wife had not been unfaithful to him after all. Then Cranmer arrived, to inform him that, in his opinion, the Queen had in fact been precontracted to Dereham, and that her marriage to the King was therefore invalid. An annulment now seemed inevitable, but at least it would spare Henry from having to execute another of his wives.

In more buoyant mood, Henry returned to Hampton Court, where he 'socialised with the ladies, as gay as ever I saw him', wrote Marillac. He did not, however, see his wife. Then, on 10 November, on the pretext that he was going hunting, he returned to London, picnicking in a field on the way. At Whitehall, he sat in council from midnight until 4.0 or 5.0 a.m., and again the following day, remaining closeted for some time and only breaking for meals. Obviously a matter of great importance was under discussion, as the

King did not often attend Council meetings, nor stay so long when he did. When they emerged, the councillors seemed troubled, especially Norfolk, who was not normally a man to show in his face what he was feeling. The court, which had now arrived from Hampton, was seething with rumours, not least of which was that Henry wanted to change his queen yet again. Marillac's master, Francis I, was anxious for Henry to take back Anne of Cleves, as he had already allied himself with the German princes and hoped that by such a connection Henry would see fit to join forces with him against the Emperor. Marillac was therefore working for a reconciliation between Henry and Anne, a sure indication that it was being taken for granted by most people that the King would soon be a free man. Marillac also reported a rumour that the Queen's physicians had told the King she would never bear children. This is unlikely to have been true, and was probably one of the wilder rumours current at that time. Not so wild was his supposition that Katherine would follow Anne Boleyn, her cousin, to the block.

She, meanwhile, was still confined to her chamber, and was permitted no entertainment; there she would remain until the Council had determined what to do with her. Cranmer was playing for time. He was still trying to uncover evidence of adultery, although as yet there was none. He was also worried that Henry would break his resolve and see Katherine: the chances that a reconciliation would then take place were high. Cranmer therefore suggested that the Queen be sent to a private house until her fate was decided. He had yet, he said, to question Dereham, Culpeper and others who had been involved in the affair. Henry agreed. On 11 November, the Archbishop went to Hampton Court and informed Queen Katherine that she was to be sent to the former Abbey of Syon at Brentford in Middlesex, where she would be under house arrest but 'yet served as queen'. In two days' time she would be taken by river to her new lodging. Lady Rochford, who was believed to know more than she would divulge about her mistress's behaviour, was sent to the Tower to await questioning.

While he was at Hampton, Cranmer learned from the Council that the King had decided to lay before Parliament, as the supreme court, the matter of the Queen's 'abominable behaviour'; Henry meant to arouse Parliament's indignation and disgust at her conduct and

457

therefore her precontract with Dereham would not be referred to, as it constituted her only defence.

> No man would think it reasonable that the King's Highness (although his Majesty doth not yet take the degree of estate utterly from her) should entertain her so tenderly in the high degree and estate of a queen, who for her demerits is so unworthy of the same.

It seems that what Henry wanted from Parliament at this stage was a divorce.

On 13 November, while Katherine prepared to leave Hampton Court, Sir Thomas Wriothesley arrived, paid his respects, then summoned her household into the great chamber, where he 'openly declared certain offences she had done', urging those in possession of useful information to divulge it. Then he discharged everyone present except those few ladies who were to accompany Katherine to Syon Abbey. These were given clothes for their mistress: six French hoods with edges of goldsmiths' work, six pairs of sleeves, six gowns, and six kirtles of satin damask and velvet. On the King's orders, all were of sober design, and unadorned with precious stones or pearls, such as a queen would usually wear. Katherine was obliged to leave all her other clothes, her gorgeous court dresses and jewelled hoods, at Hampton Court, as well as her jewellery, which was delivered into the keeping of Sir Thomas Seymour, who took it, with other valuables, back to the King. Katherine was then taken by barge to Syon Abbey, which had recently been vacated by Lady Margaret Douglas, who had been sent to Kenninghall in Norfolk.

15
Worthy and just punishment

At Syon, Katherine was treated with respect. She lacked neither food nor warmth, and was served by her own ladies. Yet, from her point of view, she had been deprived of all the trappings of queenship that mattered to her and consigned to a seclusion that did little to alleviate her depression or allay her fears. She had no idea of what was to happen to her, nor was she informed of what was being said about her by those under questioning. She was certainly not aware that the interrogation of all the suspects had begun that very day, nor that letters had already gone out to all English ambassadors at foreign courts, relating her offences – her name would soon be a byword in Europe for immorality.

She was left to wander around the three chambers assigned to her. They were furnished in moderate comfort, but the hangings were of 'mean stuff'. There was no cloth of estate. Edward Baynton, her chamberlain, dined in one room with the rest of the staff, while Katherine kept to the other two. She had four gentlewomen and two chamberers in attendance, as well as her confessor. Lady Baynton was chief lady-in-waiting. Katherine had certainly fared better than Anne Boleyn. There were no spies listening to her every word, and she was not yet in the Tower. There was, perhaps, still hope.

Archbishop Cranmer was not a cruel man, but he was determined that the Queen should be sacrificed in the cause of reform. If she was allowed to live, there was always the possibility that the King might relent and take her back. It was therefore imperative that a charge of

459

adultery be brought against Katherine, even though there was as yet no evidence for it. It was hoped by the Archbishop and his supporters that the interrogations of the prisoners in the Tower would yield enough information to send the Queen to the block.

The musician, Henry Manox – said by Mrs Hall to have taken sexual liberties with Katherine – was the first to be questioned. He said that he had been engaged by the Dowager Duchess of Norfolk to teach Katherine music and singing. He admitted having tried to seduce her, and divulged how the Duchess had unexpectedly come upon them both one day while they were indulging in intimate foreplay. She had beaten them both for it, and commanded them never to be alone together again. This had not deterred Manox, and he had continued to lay siege to Katherine until she had agreed he might caress her private parts – in his own words, he had 'felt more than was convenient'. However, he swore on the damnation of his soul that he had never enjoyed full intercourse with her. Eventually, he said, Katherine had tired of him, and transferred her affections to Dereham. He, Manox, had been extremely jealous, and had waylaid her one day, saying, 'Let me perceive by some token that you love me.' 'What token shall I show you?' Katherine had retorted, 'I will never be naught with you, and able to marry me you be not.' Manox had then sought to be revenged on his former sweetheart, and had gone straight to the Duchess with a friend surnamed Barnes and warned her that, if she were to rise again half an hour after retiring to bed, and go to the ladies' dormitory, 'you shall see that which shall displease you'. He did not know whether she had acted upon his advice. The Council, seeing that he had committed no crime and could help them no further, then released him.

They next called Katherine Tylney, one of the Queen's chamberers, as it was believed that she might help to prove adultery against the Queen. Knowing that Katherine had engaged Dereham as her secretary during the recent progress – an action that now seemed damning in the light of what had been discovered about her past – Sir Thomas Wriothesley questioned Mrs Tylney about the Queen's behaviour on that progress. Had she left her chamber any night at Lincoln or elsewhere? Tylney recalled that at Lincoln Katherine left her room late at night on two occasions and went to Lady Rochford's chamber, which was up two short flights of stairs. On the first occasion, Mrs Tylney and Margaret Morton had accompanied their mistress, but Katherine had sent them both downstairs again. Tylney went to bed, but Morton had later returned upstairs, and did not come to bed until around two o'clock. Tylney woke then, and said, 'Jesus, is not the Queen abed yet?', to which Margaret replied, 'Yes, even now.' On the second night, Katherine made all her other ladies go to bed, and took only Tylney upstairs with her. She remained in Lady Rochford's chamber as long as before, and Tylney was obliged to wait outside with Lady Rochford's waiting woman, so she never saw 'who came unto the Queen and my Lady Rochford, nor heard what was said between them'. Tylney was certain that Katherine had gone to Lady Rochford's room to meet someone. She also remembered taking 'sundry strange messages' from her mistress to Lady Rochford, so strange that she 'could not tell how to utter them'. This had gone on after the court returned to Hampton. There, one day, Katherine had told Tylney to go to Lady Rochford and ask her 'when she should have the thing she promised her'. Lady Rochford had answered that 'she sat up for it, and she would the next day bring her word herself.'

Wriothesley was pleased with Tylney's evidence, and told Sir Ralph Sadler that she 'hath done us worthy service' and that he was 'picking out anything that is likely to serve the purpose of our business'. Certainly Tylney's evidence pointed at something very odd going on, and the Council had little difficulty in concluding that the Queen had gone to meet a lover – possibly Dereham – in the room of Lady Rochford, who had acted as her bawd. If this were true, then Tylney's evidence would be damning.

In a mood of grim anticipation, the Council summoned Margaret Morton, Tylney's companion on the nights in question. She deposed that Lady Rochford had definitely been a party to some intrigue being carried on by the Queen, not only at Lincoln, but also at Pontefract and York. At Pontefract, the Queen had had angry words with herself and another chamberer, Mrs Luffkyn, and had forbidden them to enter her bedchamber. Morton was implying here that Katherine had an ulterior motive for keeping them out. Lady Rochford had also conveyed letters between the Queen and a third party, whom Morton supposed to have been Thomas Culpeper. One night, while the court was at Pontefract, Katherine was in her bedchamber with no attendant other than Lady Rochford – which, in itself, was unusual; Lady Rochford had not only locked the chamber door, but also bolted it on the inside. Consequently, when the King came unexpectedly to spend the night with his wife, he found the door fastened, and there was some delay before Lady Rochford opened it to admit him.

The Council now questioned Morton closely about Thomas Culpeper. Hitherto, they had suspected Katherine of intriguing with Dereham, but it now appeared that she might have been even more profligate with her favours. Morton confirmed their suspicions when she declared that she 'never mistrusted the Queen until at Hatfield I saw her look out of her chamber window on Master Culpeper, after such sort that I thought there was love between them'. Once, Katherine had been alone in her closet with Culpeper for five or six hours, and Morton thought 'for certain they had passed out' (a Tudor euphemism for orgasm). All the while, she remembered, Katherine had 'been in fear that somebody should come in'.

Katherine had not only been playing with fire, but she had also been indiscreet about it, and incredibly stupid. The Council now wasted no time in searching through Culpeper's effects, and found a letter, signed by the Queen (and appallingly spelt, for she was barely literate), which confirmed what everyone had begun to suspect, that she had, indeed, been conducting a love affair with her cousin. It read:

Master Culpepper,
I heartily recommend me unto you, praying you to send me word how that you do. I did hear that ye were sick, and I never longed for anything so much as to see you. It maketh my heart to die when I do think that I cannot always be in your company. Come to me when Lady Rochford be here, for then I shall be best at leisure to be at your commandment. . . . And thus I take my leave of you, trusting to see you shortly again. And I would you were with me now, that you might see what pain I take in writing to you.
Yours as long as life endures,
Katherine

Katherine's letter, although undated, was the most telling evidence against her, supported as it was by a weight of incriminating allegations by Tylney and Morton.

The Council continued its relentless quest for evidence: it was now hot on the trail. Alice Restwold, one of the inmates of the Duchess's household at Lambeth, gave an account of the time Dereham came into Katherine's bed when she herself was sharing it. She had got out 'for shame' and refused to sleep there again, for she was a married woman, and knew 'what belonged to that puffing and blowing'. This might have brought a touch of humour into the otherwise grave enquiry, but it did not assist a charge of adultery. Joan Bulmer also gave evidence, but her statement is no longer extant. It appears that she had at some stage abetted the Queen's intrigues.

The Council decided to call Lady Rochford next. Jane Rochford, who was later described as 'the principal occasion of the Queen's folly', had by now calmed down a little, and was lucid enough to be questioned. Thinking only of saving her own skin – for she, more than anyone, had cause to know the penalties for adultery in a queen – she abandoned Katherine to the wolves and admitted that Culpeper had had sexual intercourse with her mistress – she could not think it otherwise, 'considering all things that she hath heard and seen between them'. She testified that their intrigue had begun back in the spring, probably at the time when the King was suffering from depression and had left his wife to her own devices. Apparently, Culpeper had always cherished an affection for his pretty cousin, and it was he who had made the first advances. At first, they had not been welcome. 'Will this never end?' Katherine had sighed irritably to Lady Rochford, and had asked her to 'bid him desire no more to trouble me, or send to me.' But Culpeper had been persistent, and eventually the Queen had admitted him into her chamber in private. Before very long, they were meeting in Lady Rochford's rooms, with Lady Rochford standing guard in case the King came. It is likely that Culpeper had been there on the occasion described by Morton when Henry had come to sleep with his wife.

According to Lady Rochford, Katherine was well aware of the risks she was taking. 'This will be spied one day, and then we will all be undone,' she had said. Marillac later told Francis I that Katherine had used Dereham to incite Culpeper's jealousy, telling Lady

463

Rochford to say to Culpeper that, if he would not listen to Katherine's side in the petty arguments they frequently engaged in, 'there was behind the door another'. Lady Rochford, however, said nothing of this, but her evidence was of vital importance, because it was that of an eyewitness and a participant. She was also guilty of aiding and abetting acts of treason, and the King was not known to be merciful to such offenders. Thus, for all her willingness to co-operate, she found herself back in the Tower after her examination. It was then that madness took its final hold on her.

Thomas Culpeper was the next to be interrogated. He was 'a beautiful youth', and had stood high in the King's favour. He confessed to having fallen in love with the Queen some months before, and admitted that she would at first have nothing to do with him. Later, she had grown warmer towards him. He was aware of her past, for she told him that, had she remained in the maidens' chamber at Lambeth, she would have 'tried' him. But her high rank had, he said, precluded any intimacy between them. Nevertheless, according to Culpeper, she was before very long 'languishing and dying of love for him', and would call him her 'little sweet fool'. He admitted that he had visited her in private, saying that Lady Rochford had contrived the interviews. Yet it was Katherine who, at every house she visited on the progress, would 'seek for the back door and back stairs'. At Pontefract, she was fearful that the King had set a watch on the back door, so Lady Rochford made her servant watch the courtyard to see if this was so.

As the affair progressed, so the Queen's fear of discovery deepened, although it was not sufficiently acute for her to abandon her lover. She warned him to

> beware if he went to confession, lest he should shrive him of any such things as should pass betwixt her and him; for if he did, surely the King, being Supreme Head of the Church, should have knowledge of it.

Culpeper had promised not to say anything compromising.

At this stage, the Council wanted to know if Culpeper had committed adultery with the Queen. He answered that, although Lady Rochford had 'provoked him much to love the Queen, and he intended to do ill with her and likewise the Queen so minded to do with him, he had not passed beyond words'. This, of course, was not what the assembled lords had been expecting to hear. Lord Hertford spoke for them all, therefore, when he told Culpeper that his intentions towards Queen Katherine were 'so loathsome and dishonest' that in themselves they could be said to constitute high treason. By this, it became apparent to Culpeper that he was doomed, and Katherine with him, and, the interrogation being at an end, he was taken back to prison.

The privy councillors deliberated. At length, they concluded that they 'vehemently suspected' the Queen of adultery with Thomas Culpeper, especially in view of his having been brought by Lady Rochford to her chamber at Lincoln during August, and having stayed there alone with Katherine from eleven o'clock at night until four o'clock in the morning. It was also considered significant that the Queen had, around this time, given him a gold chain and a 'rich cap'. 'You may see what was done before marriage,' reasoned Cranmer; 'God knoweth what has been done since!' The Council thought it might be expedient for the Archbishop to examine the Queen again, 'for she hath not, as appeareth by her confession, so fully declared the circumstances of such communications as were betwixt her and Culpeper'. It was felt that Cranmer, by careful questioning, 'might get of her more information'. A signed confession of adultery was what was really required, and the councillors had few doubts that the young Queen could be bullied or coerced into making one. Accordingly, Cranmer and Wriothesley went to visit Katherine at Syon to question her 'with respect to her intimacy with Culpeper'. They promised her mercy if she would make full confession of her faults, but Katherine, under their interrogation, strenuously denied intimacy with Culpeper, and persisted in her denial, even though she was probably lying to save her own skin and her lover's.

Meanwhile, the rumourmongers were once again busy. Two London housewives had been hauled before the Council and reprimanded for their unthinking *lèse-majesté*. One, Elizabeth Bassett, had wondered if 'God is working His own work to make the Lady Anne of Cleves queen again'. Her friend, Jane Ratsey, had replied that 'it was impossible that so sweet a queen as the Lady Anne could be utterly put down', and Mrs Bassett had exclaimed, 'What a man the King is! How many wives will he have?' Speculation that Henry might take back Anne of Cleves was widespread, since it was understood by many that the reformist party was working to bring down the Queen and the conservative Howard faction. But such an idea had never crossed the King's mind, and the Bishop of Winchester was obliged to be quite blunt with an eager German diplomat, saying that Henry 'would never take back the said lady'.

The Queen's fall was now common knowledge. Instinctively, her Howard relations banded together, fearful in case her disgrace should reflect upon them. They guessed that Cranmer would bring down the whole clan if he could. The Dowager Duchess's servant, Pewson, had broken the news to her that the Queen had played the King false (he said, incorrectly, that it was with Dereham), and that Katherine Tylney, the Duchess's relative, was privy to her guilt. This rather inaccurate version of the truth so frightened the Duchess that she ordered the immediate burning of all Dereham's papers and effects remaining at Lambeth House. At the same time she made it known that she did not believe the tales about the Queen to be true; however, if they were, then Katherine and her lovers 'deserved to be hanged'.

The Duchess also took it upon herself to question William Damport, a friend of Dereham's who still remained in her household. She told him she had heard that Dereham and Queen Katherine had been arrested, and asked if he knew why. Damport said he thought the evidence was based upon 'some words spoken by a gentleman usher'. The Duchess confided to him that she was greatly alarmed 'lest any harm should befall the Queen in consequence of evil report'. She was also worried that the King would point the finger of blame at her for having neglected her duties in respect of Katherine's moral welfare. She realised now that she had been very remiss, and it was far too late to do anything about it.

Contrary to what the Duchess had heard, Katherine was as yet suspected of adultery with Culpeper only, and not with Dereham, though rumour was doing its best to magnify her crimes. The Duke of Norfolk, having washed his hands of his niece, told Marillac that she had 'prostituted herself to seven or eight persons'. Norfolk was in fact making sure that his own neck was safe by publicly slandering

Katherine at every opportunity, in case people remembered who it was that had first brought her to the King's notice, and his voice spoke louder than any in denouncing her.

Henry now knew the worst, that Katherine had cuckolded him with Culpeper, whom he had favoured. He took the news relatively calmly, yet it must have been a dreadful blow to him. On 16 November, Chapuys told the Emperor that the King would be more likely to show mercy to Katherine than her own relatives, especially Norfolk, who said, 'God knows why, that he wished the Queen was burned.' Yet whether the King wished to show mercy or not, the law would take its course. Nor could he permit someone so unsuitable to enjoy the rank of Queen of England. On 22 November, a proclamation made at Hampton Court announced that Katherine had forfeited her honour and should be proceeded against by law; henceforth, she would no longer be called Queen, just plain Katherine Howard.

The Council was still collecting evidence. Norfolk was sent to search his stepmother's household at Lambeth and to interrogate its occupants. William Ashby, one of the Duchess's servants, revealed how his mistress had searched Dereham's coffers and removed all his papers, saying she would 'peruse them at her leisure, without suffering any person to be present'. She had declared, in the presence of her comptroller, that 'she meant not any of these things to come to revelation'. The Duchess, he added, had been 'in the greatest fear' lest her servants tell her son, Lord William Howard, about the 'familiarity' between the Queen and Dereham. She had wondered whether the King's promised pardon would extend to 'other persons who knew of their naughty life before the marriage'. Finally, Ashby told Norfolk that the Duchess had rifled through the papers of Damport, who by now was also a prisoner in the Tower, suspected of misprision of treason. The picture Ashby presented was one of a very frightened woman with an overburdened conscience, who was almost certainly guilty of that same crime. Her failure to disclose what she knew of Katherine's early life, and her attempts to destroy all evidence of it, pointed convincingly to this.

After the Duke had left, the Duchess began to realise what a nasty predicament she was in. Feigning illness, she took to her bed, but this did not prevent the lords of the Council, among them

Wriothesley and Southampton, from coming to Lambeth to arrest her. She sent word down to them that she was 'not well enough to be moved', yet they insisted on seeing her, 'the better to perceive whether she were indeed as sick as she pretended'. They quickly perceived she was not, and informed her that the Lord Chancellor wished to question her. At this, the old lady pretended to suffer a relapse, but the lords, 'with much ado, got her to condescend to her going'. The Duchess's fears were not unfounded. By nightfall on the day of her arrest, she too was a prisoner in the Tower, after a most unsatisfactory session of interrogation by Lord Chancellor Audley, in which she said enough to incriminate the whole Howard family.

Towards the end of November, the Council decided to question the Dowager Duchess again. Wriothesley and Southampton visited her in the Tower, where they found her in bed, and genuinely ill this time. They assured her 'on his Majesty's behalf of her own life if she would in some sort make us her ghostly confessors'. She replied that 'she would take her death of it, that she never suspected anything wrong between them'. She had indeed 'perceived a sort of light love and favour between them more than between indifferent persons, and had heard that Dereham would at sundry times give [Katherine] money', but she had thought this all 'proceeded from the affection that groweth of kindred, the same Dereham being her kinsman'. She begged the King's forgiveness for not having disclosed what she knew before his marriage to Katherine, and the lords were able to assure Henry that she appeared 'wondrous sorrowful, repentant and sickly'.

They then asked her a long list of questions: How did she educate and bring up Mistress Katherine? What changes of clothing had she given her? When had she first realised that the King favoured her? Had they discussed the King's courtship? What advice had she given the girl? The Duchess's answers revealed nothing that could point to the continuation of the liaison between Katherine and Dereham after the former's marriage to the King. In fact, she said Katherine herself had admitted later that she had no idea where Dereham was. It was obvious that the Duchess could help no further with the enquiry, so she was left alone to brood upon her shortcomings as a guardian.

Living with the knowledge of Katherine's infidelity was no easy task for the King. On 26 November, Sir John Dudley told the Earl of

Rutland that Henry was 'not a little troubled with this great affair'. To spare him further pain, therefore, the Council was carrying out the investigation on its own, while he sanctioned further action as necessary. It was all too obvious that the King was a broken man: this tragedy touched him too closely.

Thus the arraignment of Culpeper and Dereham on 1 December in Westminster Hall was arranged entirely by the Privy Council. Dereham was to be tried for 'presumptive treason', according to the indictment, which accused both the Queen and her accomplices of having led 'an abominable, base, carnal, voluptuous and licentious life'; Katherine, who was not being tried, was described as 'a common harlot'. While 'maintaining an appearance of chastity and honesty', she had led the King on to fall in love with her 'by word and gesture', he believing her to be 'pure', and had 'arrogantly contracted and coupled herself in marriage' in spite of being a harlot before and an adultress after.

A separate indictment was brought against Culpeper, who was charged with having had criminal intercourse with the Queen on 29 August 1541 at Pontefract, and at other times, before and after that date. Katherine was accused in the indictment of having insinuated to Culpeper 'that she loved him above the King and all the others', and Culpeper was accused of inciting her to adultery. Jane Rochford was named as their go-between, who contrived meetings in the Queen's lavatory and 'other suspect places' and 'falsely and traitorously aided and abetted them'.

The two men were tried together. Dereham was accused of joining the Queen's service with 'ill intent', traitorously imagining that he and she might continue their wicked behaviour. He was further accused of having concealed the precontract between them to facilitate Katherine's marriage to the King; her acquiescence to this was taken as proof of her intention to continue in her abominable life. Of course, Dereham pleaded not guilty to all these accusations, although there was little he could say in his defence. Likewise Culpeper, although realising that the evidence was heavily weighted against him, changed his plea to guilty during the course of the trial and thus sealed his fate. A verdict of guilty was given against both prisoners, and the Duke of Norfolk, grim faced, sentenced them to be drawn on hurdles to Tyburn 'and there hanged, cut down alive, disembowelled, and, they still living, their bowels burnt; the bodies then to be beheaded and quartered'. Such was the terrible penalty meted out to those who had dared to be intimate with the Queen of England.

Marillac quickly scribbled down news of the outcome of the trial to send to Francis I, saying he felt that Culpeper especially deserved to die, even though he would not admit to having full intercourse with Katherine, 'for he confessed his intention to do so, and his confessed conversations, being held by a subject to a queen, deserved death'. Many people had been disgusted by the unsavoury details of the Queen's intrigues that had been made public at the trial, and some felt that they should not have been divulged, but, as Marillac said, 'the intention is to prevent it being said afterwards that they were unjustly condemned'. As for the fate of the Queen, the ambassador held out little hope, predicting that 'the end of these tragedies will be no less scandalous than pitiful'. Pitiful indeed, for Katherine was not yet seventeen years old. Nor did it seem that the King would be merciful, for he had 'changed his love for the Queen into hatred, and taken such grief at being deceived, that of late it was thought he had gone mad'. On one occasion, he had

> called for a sword to slay her he had loved so much. Sitting in Council, he suddenly called for horses without saying where he would go. Sometimes he will say irrelevantly that the wicked woman had never such delight in her incontinence as she should have torture in her death.

On one occasion, Henry was so distressed that be burst into tears, 'regretting his ill-luck in meeting such ill-conditioned wives, and blaming the Council for the last mischief'. A few days later, Marillac recorded that the King had gone 'twenty-five miles from here with no company but musicians and ministers of pastime, and spent most of his time hunting, seeking to forget his grief'. Yet for all his anger, all his sport, and all his efforts to cheer himself up, Henry had never been so miserable in his life. Apart from the wound to his heart, there was the wound to his pride – he had been made to look a fool.

Not everyone sympathised. Chapuys, who had had long experience of the King's ways, told Charles V on 3 December that Henry had shown more sorrow at Katherine Howard's misdemeanours than he had at the treason, loss or divorce of any of his previous wives. As Chapuys put it,

It is like the case of the woman who cried most bitterly at the loss of her tenth husband than at the death of all the others together. Though he had been a good man, it was because she had never buried one of them before without being sure of the next; and as yet this King has formed neither a plan nor a preference.

The Council was still trying to wring a confession of adultery from Dereham, or at least uncover evidence of it. They tortured his friend, William Damport, but although they used the brakes to force out his teeth, he would not or could not say anything to incriminate Dereham. All he would say was that, just prior to Katherine's marriage to the King, Dereham had boasted that, if Henry were dead, he would marry her. And, some months later, he had seen the Duchess of Norfolk point out Dereham to a gentleman in the Queen's chamber, saying, 'This is he, who fled away to Ireland for the Queen's sake.'

On 6 December, Dereham himself was tortured. Asked if he had said he was sure he might marry the Queen if the King were dead – it was treason to predict the death of the King – he denied it, until told that Damport had confessed it. Then he admitted it, although, as Wriothesley later told Sadler, 'no torture could make him confess this before.' Afterwards, the condemned man was made to sign a written confession, which set forth all the circumstances of his affair with Katherine. In it, he admitted that they had exchanged 'a promise of marriage', that they had lived together as man and wife while he was in the service of her grandmother, and that they were regarded as betrothed by their friends in that household. He had been accustomed to call her wife, and she had often called him husband before witnesses; they had exchanged gifts and love-tokens frequently in those days, and he had given her money whenever he had it. At Lambeth, he had haunted her chamber nightly, and they were then so far in love that they would 'kiss and hang by their bellies together as they were two sparrows'. Onlookers would joke, 'Hark to Dereham, broken winded!' to which he would reply, 'Who should hinder him from kissing his own wife?' He recalled that the Duchess had once caught him kissing her granddaughter, for which she beat him, also giving Joan Bulmer a blow for having allowed it. Dereham stated that he had been brought into the royal household by the Queen's desire, 'who told the Duchess of Norfolk to bring him'. It seems unlikely, however, that Katherine would have suggested such a thing: she was at the time involved with Culpeper, of whom Dereham was very jealous. It is more likely that it was Dereham, anxious for preferment, who wormed his way into the Queen's household, by means of the good offices of the Dowager Duchess, knowing Katherine dared not refuse him. He knew too much about her past, and her long-standing affection for Culpeper, for her to risk offending him.

In his confession, Dereham vehemently denied committing adultery with Katherine. Nevertheless, the Council felt that his applying to join the Queen's household, and her acceptance of him into it, was proof in itself of evil intent; it was said by some that 'they were worthy to be hanged one against the other'.

Later that day, the King was asked if he would remit the sentence against Dereham. He read the confession, and was angered that the prisoner had not admitted adultery with the Queen, declaring that he thought Dereham 'hath deserved no such mercy at his hand, and therefore hath determined that he shall suffer the whole execution'. On the following day, the Council, having also read Dereham's confession, wrote to Sir John Gage, the new Constable of the Tower, and Richard Rich, who had supervised the torturing, with instructions to proceed to the execution of the prisoners, if they felt that no more was to be gained from them by further interrogation. The condemned men must of course be allowed time to prepare to meet their God for the salvation of their souls, but unless the King decreed otherwise, the executions would take place on 9 December.

In the meantime, the families of both Dereham and Culpeper had been making frantic pleas to the Council to have the sentences commuted to beheading only. On 9 December, Gage was advised, early in the morning, that, though Culpeper's offence was considered 'heinous', he was to be drawn to Tyburn on a hurdle, but would be spared the full rigours of a traitor's death, and suffer only

decapitation, 'according to his Highness's most gracious determination'. Culpeper was, after all, a gentleman born, unlike Dereham,
and those of gentle birth were usually spared the full sentence.

The executions, however, did not take place on the 9th, as the
Council was too busy with another urgent matter to issue the final
order authorising them. This other matter concerned Anne of
Cleves: the Council's attention had been drawn to a rumour,
probably spread by Protestants, that she was expecting the King's
child, and had also had a son by him, born at one of her country
houses during the summer of 1541. The matter was debated all day
by the lords, who felt they had quite enough on their hands with one
immoral queen and that they could well do without another. After
deliberating, they consulted the King, who thought it expedient to
order a full enquiry into the matter. Members of the Privy Council
were immediately despatched to Richmond to question the members
of the Lady Anne's household, and the Lady Anne herself if needs be.
The questioning was to take some time, but eventually, two
members of Anne's household, Frances Lilgrave and Richard
Taverner, admitted having slandered the Lady Anne, and were
committed to the Tower for their impudence.

Dereham and Culpeper were put to death at Tyburn on 10
December. Culpeper died first, after exhorting the crowd to pray for
him. No block had been provided: he knelt on the ground by the
gallows, and was decapitated with one stroke of the axe. Dereham
then suffered the full horror of being hanged, disembowelled,
beheaded and quartered, after which both heads were set up on pikes
above London Bridge.

There was no hope now for the Queen, although it was the King's
wish that she should not stand open trial. Instead, an Act of
Attainder was to be brought against her when Parliament reassembled
in January. This would allow her a few weeks in which to prepare for
death.

Even now, the reformist party was doing its best to bring further
evidence against her and her family; it was imperative to them that
the whole Howard faction be neutralised, thus paving the way for
Cranmer and his partisans to gain ascendancy over the King. The
Duchess of Norfolk was already in custody, 'so enmeshed and
tangled up' in the affair that 'it will be hard for her to wind out

473

again'. She was questioned again by Wriothesley on the day Katherine's lovers died, when she admitted having pushed Katherine into the King's way even though she knew of her previous affairs, and confessed to having persuaded the Queen to take Dereham back into her service. She also admitted to having destroyed all his letters.

In the middle of December, other members of the Howard clan were arrested by Wriothesley in the King's name. Lord William Howard and his wife, and Anne Howard, the Dowager Duchess's daughter, were committed to the Tower; Lord William had had hardly anything to do with Katherine Howard, and 'stood as stiff as his mother and made himself most clear from all mistrust and suspicion'. His arrest was absurd anyway, as he had been acting as Governor of Calais for the past year or so, and could not have been a party to Katherine's adultery. But the lords of the Council were determined to bring him down with the rest of his family, and had summoned him home in foul weather, so foul that some of his staff had been swept overboard during the voyage from France. Lord William's sister, another Katherine Howard, the Countess of Bridgewater, was also put in the Tower, and her children sent with Lord William's to be cared for by Archbishop Cranmer and others. When, on 14 December, the Duke of Norfolk learned of these arrests, he was fearful for his own safety – he had, after all, more cause than they to fear the King's justice – and wrote at once to Henry, excusing himself from all guilt and abandoning his family. He was sure, he said, that the arrests were justified. After the

> abominable deeds done by my two nieces, I fear your Majesty will abhor to hear speak of me or my kin again. Prostrate at your Majesty's feet, I remind your Majesty that much of this has come to light through my own report of my mother-in-law's [*sic*] words to me when I was sent to Lambeth to search Dereham's coffers. My own truth, and the small love my mother-in-law and my two false traitorous nieces bare me, make me hope, and I pray your Majesty for some comfortable assurance of your royal favour, without which I will never desire to live.

But no comfortable assurance came. Henry was displeased with all the Howards, including the Duke. He was no fool, and remembered vividly how Norfolk had furthered his intrigue with Katherine in the first place. He had placed a viper in his sovereign's bosom, and he should pay for it. He did not reply to the letter, and hearing nothing, the Duke deemed it politic to maintain a low profile, hoping that the King's displeasure would not last. After a time, he was received back, but Henry never fully trusted him again.

As for the rest of the Howard family and their servants, King and Council had decided on a highly profitable solution. Lord William and his wife, Katherine Tylney, Joan Bulmer, Alice Restwold, William Ashby, William Damport, and Elizabeth Tylney and Margaret Bennet, the two other witnesses to the Queen's misconduct, were all, on 22 December 1541, arraigned for misprision of treason 'for concealing the evil demeanour of the Queen, to the slander of the King and his succession'. All pleaded guilty, and were sentenced to perpetual imprisonment and loss of goods and lands; however, not long afterwards, the King pardoned most of them and had them freed. The old Duchess of Norfolk was also included in the indictment, but she was not brought to trial as she was 'old and testy' and 'may die out of perversity to defraud the King's Highness of the confiscation of her goods'. She too was sentenced to loss of liberty and lands, and the King ended up somewhat richer as a result.

This did not, however, provide a panacea for his misery. He knew now that the illusion of youth he had enjoyed with Katherine had gone for ever; all he had to look forward to were encroaching illness, old age and death. To begin with, he had meant to be merciful towards Katherine, but now he found he had no desire to save her from the headsman, and wished her to suffer as he was suffering. The law would take its course and he would not lift a finger to stop it. Then the world would see how he dealt with those who made a fool of him.

Francis I had reacted to the news of Katherine's fall with sympathy. 'She hath done wondrous naughty!' he exclaimed, when Sir William Paget informed him of the Queen's misconduct. And to Henry he wrote:

I am sorry to hear of the displeasure and trouble which has been caused by the lewd and naughty behaviour of the Queen. Albeit,

475

knowing my good brother to be a prince of prudence, virtue and honour, I do require him to shift off the said displeasure and wisely, temperately, like myself, not reputing his honour to rest in the lightness of a woman, but to thank God of all, comforting himself in God's goodness. The lightness of women cannot bend the honour of men.

Comforting words indeed from Henry's greatest rival and Europe's most debauched monarch. Henry must have squirmed when he read them.

The festive season passed gloomily that year, with the King making no effort to join in the half-hearted revels staged by his courtiers. Marillac described him as 'sad, and disinclined to feasting and ladies'. He was putting on even more weight, and looked very old and grey. His ministers, however, were begging him to marry again, reminding him that he had only one son, but there was not one among the court ladies that he fancied: the wound left by Katherine Howard's infidelities was too raw as yet. The Council could only hope that time would heal it. With 'such an exceptional prince', all things were possible.

Parliament reconvened on 16 January 1542, and the Lords and Commons combined to urge the King 'not to vex himself with the Queen's offence, and that she and the Lady Rochford might be attainted'. To make this easier for him, it was suggested that he give his royal assent to the proceedings under the Great Seal, which could then be done by the Lord Chancellor. The King agreed to this, and the Lords at once began debating the fate of the Queen. The Lord Chancellor, recounting her 'vicious and abominable' deeds, urged that a Bill of Attainder be drawn up without delay, which was done that same afternoon. It was in the form of a petition, from the Lords and Commons, requesting the King to consent to the conviction of 'Mistress Katherine Howard, late Queen of England' and Lady Rochford for high treason, the penalty being death and confiscation of goods. The Act received its first reading that evening. Shortly afterwards, another Act would be passed, ruling that 'an unchaste woman marrying the King shall be guilty of high treason'. Anyone concealing any flaw in the character of a putative queen of England would likewise be guilty of high treason. And if any woman

476

presumed to marry the King without admitting she had been unchaste, she would merit death.

Henry seems to have been concerned that Katherine had as yet had no chance to defend herself in public. 'Wishing to proceed more humanely', he sent some members of his Council to see her on 25 January; they invited her, in the King's name, to 'come to the Parliament chamber to defend herself'. She declined, however, saying she submitted herself to the King's mercy and good pleasure, and confessed she had deserved to die. Her humility did much to soften the hearts of the privy councillors, and three days later the Lord Chancellor reminded the peers in the House of Lords

> how much it concerned them not to proceed too hastily with the Bill of Attainder for the Queen, that she was no mean or private person, but a public and illustrious one. Therefore her cause ought to be judged in a manner that should leave no room for suspicion of some latent quarrel.

He proposed that a second deputation, comprising members of both Houses, should go to see her, 'partly in order to help her womanish fears', and partly to advise her 'to say anything that makes her cause the better'. It was only just, he concluded, that such a princess should be 'tried by equal laws with themselves', and he assured his listeners that 'her most loving consort' would find it acceptable if she cleared herself in this way, even now.

Katherine, however, knew she had no plausible defence, and was resigned outwardly to her fate. She told the second deputation that her only care was to make a good death and 'to leave a good opinion in people's minds now at parting'. Gone was the hysterical girl of a few weeks past, and in her place was one who even found the courage to be gay. Chapuys reported on 29 January that she was

> very cheerful, and more plump and pretty than ever; she is as careful about her dress and as imperious and wilful as at the time she was with the King, notwithstanding that she expects to be put to death, that she confesses she has deserved it, and asks for no favour except that the execution shall be secret and not under the eyes of the world.

Chapuys thought that if the King did not intend to marry again he might show mercy to her, or even divorce her on a plea of adultery. Learned theologians had debated the possibility of a divorce, but had as yet not made public their conclusions. But Chapuys was still pessimistic, and even as he was writing his letter news came to him that the Commons had debated the Queen's fate and had come to the same conclusion as the Lords, and the Queen, he feared, 'will soon be sent to the Tower'.

The Council, however, felt that Parliament was being too humane towards Katherine; the reforming faction felt there had been no need to give her any opportunity to defend herself, as the case against her had already been proved. Accordingly, the privy councillors petitioned the King that the Bill of Attainder be put through its second and third readings without delay so that the case could be concluded and judgement given. Henry gave his assent, and Parliament was urged to speed up the passing of the Bill. Its second reading took place on 6 February and, on the following day, after its third and final reading, it became law, which meant that the Queen and Lady Rochford were both sentenced to death and loss of goods and lands. All that was needed now was the royal assent. On that same day, the King went into the House of Commons and thanked them 'for that they took his sorrow to be theirs'.

Henry was feeling a little better now, more himself. Since November, he had hunted daily to divert his 'ill humour' and would not attend to much business. Now, however, he was again seeking the company of the ladies of his court. After the Act of Attainder against the Queen was passed, Chapuys told Charles V that Henry had 'never been so merry since first hearing of the Queen's misconduct'. On 29 January, he had given a banquet attended by sixty-one ladies, and was particularly attentive to the estranged wife of the poet Wyatt, 'a pretty young creature with wit enough to do as badly as the others if she were to try'. Yet Elizabeth Brooke was a notorious adultress, and the King did not pursue the matter. He also showed a marked preference for Anne Bassett, for whom he had long cherished a soft spot. 'The common voice,' went on Chapuys, 'is that this King will not be long without a wife, because of the great desire he has to have further issue.'

The passing of the Act of Attainder seemed to satisfy Henry, although he complained that there was as much reason to convict the Duchess of Norfolk of treason as there had been to convict Dereham. In her case the Council urged the King to leniency, and he relented, agreeing that the old lady might live. She was eventually released on 5 May 1542, and died three years later. But he was not so merciful towards his wife or Lady Rochford, and on 9 February sent the Duke of Norfolk to Syon Abbey with his fellow deputies to inform Katherine of her sentence. The only comfort the Duke brought was the promise that it would be carried out in private, as she had wished: she would die on Tower Green, as Anne Boleyn had.

Katherine took the news bravely. She again confessed to and acknowledged 'the great crime of which she had been guilty against the most high God and a kind prince and lastly the whole English nation', and begged Norfolk 'to implore his Majesty not to impute her crime to her whole kindred and family', asking instead that Henry extend his 'unbounded mercy and benevolence to all her brothers, that they might not suffer for her faults'. Lastly she asked if the King would kindly bestow her clothing upon her maidservants after her death, as she had no other means of rewarding them for their loyalty. Norfolk promised to convey her requests to the King, and then left without having been able to tell her the date set for her execution.

Her suspense did not last long, however. On Friday, 10 February, the lords of the Council returned to Syon with orders to convey the Queen to the Tower of London. As soon as she learned what they had come for, Katherine knew a moment of blind panic, finally realising in that instant that Henry did mean to have her executed. All her calm deserted her, and she refused to go. The lords tried persuasion and then bullying, but to no avail. Eventually, they bundled her, shrinking with fear, into the waiting barge, which was then escorted along the river by a barge containing the Lord Privy Seal, other members of the Council, and those servants who were to look after the Queen in the Tower. The barge carrying Katherine was enclosed; this was as well, for the rotting heads of Culpeper and Dereham were still to be seen above London Bridge. The Queen, wearing a black velvet dress, sat with four of her ladies and three or four members of the Privy Council. Behind came the Duke of Suffolk's barge, crowded with his retinue. At the Tower stairs, the lords disembarked first and the Queen followed. The same forms of respect were shown to her as in happier days. She was greeted by the Constable of the Tower, Sir John Gage, who 'paid her as much honour as when she was reigning', but he was concerned to find that his prisoner was in a state of such abject distress that she seemed on the verge of collapse. 'She weeps, cries and torments herself miserably without ceasing,' he wrote to the Privy Council, after having conducted Katherine to her lodging. It is uncertain where this was, but likely that it was the rooms in the Lieutenant's house once occupied by Anne Boleyn.

In the evening, John Longland, Bishop of Lincoln, came to hear the Queen's confession and to offer her spiritual comfort. She swore to him, 'in the name of God and His Holy angels, and on the salvation of my soul', that she was innocent of the crimes for which she stood condemned. She had never 'so abused my sovereign's bed'. She did not seek to excuse the faults and follies of her youth; God would be her judge, and she looked for His pardon. She asked the Bishop to pray with her for divine mercy, and fell to her knees beside him, beseeching the Almighty for strength to cope with her coming ordeal.

The Act of Attainder against Katherine still lacked the King's signature, and the execution could not go ahead without it. To spare Henry any further distress, the Council arranged for the royal assent to be signified by attaching the Great Seal; and at the top of the Act was written the time-honoured phrase: '*Le Roy le veut*' – 'The King wills it.' On Saturday, 11 February, the Act was read in Parliament to the assembled members of both Houses, and the royal assent proclaimed.

The Queen's execution could now take place, but not on a Sunday, so Katherine had a day's reprieve. On the evening of that Sunday, she was visited by Sir John Gage and instructed to 'disburden her conscience' to her confessor, for she was to die the following day. Calmer now, she spoke of her anxiety about making a good impression on the scaffold, and asked if the block might be brought to her room, so that she might learn how to place herself. Gage thought this a strange request, but he did not refuse it. The block was brought and Katherine spent the evening coming to terms with her fate.

The Tower was a hive of activity that weekend, for the Constable's staff were busy caring for the illustrious prisoners then lodged within the fortress. But at least Katherine's last night on earth was not disturbed, as Anne Boleyn's had been, by the noise of workmen erecting the scaffold.

Monday, 13 February 1542 was cold and dull, with a ground frost. At seven o'clock, every member of the King's Council except Norfolk, who had been excused this final duty, and Suffolk, who was ill, presented themselves at the Tower with a number of other lords and gentlemen, among them the Earl of Surrey, who was Norfolk's son and the Queen's cousin. All were conducted to Tower Green, where the scaffold had once again been hung with black cloth and strewn with straw. When Katherine was led out of her lodgings by Sir John Gage and a detachment of yeomen warders, she appeared so weak that she could hardly stand or speak. Nevertheless, she made what one onlooker, Otwell Johnson, in a letter written to his brother the next day, described as a 'godly and Christian end'. She asked

> all Christian people to take regard unto her worthy and just punishment with death, for her offences against God heinously from her youth upward in breaking of all His commandments, and also against the King's Royal Majesty very dangerously.

She admitted she had been justly condemned and that she merited a hundred deaths, and required the people to look to her as an example and amend their 'ungodly lives', urging them to obey the King in all things. She prayed for her husband, and willed everyone present to do the same, before commending her soul to God and 'earnestly calling for mercy upon Him'. Not for Katherine the elegant sword that had beheaded her cousin, but – as the chronicler Hall confirms – an axe, that severed her pretty auburn head in a single stroke just moments after she had made her last speech.

Lady Rochford followed her to the block. She was still 'in a frenzy', according to Chapuys, and the King had had to order the passing of a special Act enabling him to have insane persons executed before he could dispose of her. Yet, at the last, faced with the axe and the spectacle of the Queen's blood-soaked remains being wrapped in a black blanket by her sobbing ladies, she recovered her reason

481

sufficiently to enable her to make an edifying speech before submitting to the executioner.

Katherine's attendants laid her remains in a waiting coffin and carried it into the nearby Chapel of St Peter ad Vincula. There, later that day, she was buried near Anne Boleyn. Then her name was tactfully forgotten by all until, in 1553, the Act of Attainder against her was among those reversed by Queen Mary; because they did not bear the royal signature, such Acts were no longer recognised as legal.

16

Never a wife
more agreeable
to his heart

The marriage of Henry VIII and Katherine Howard was never formally annulled, even though there were good grounds for so doing, and consequently the King became a widower on her death. For a time, though, he was anything but a merry one, and it was eighteen months before he found the woman he wanted to make his sixth wife and before he recovered fully from the blow dealt by Katherine's adultery.

On 25 February 1542, a fortnight after Katherine's execution, Chapuys reported him to be in better spirits; he had presided over three court banquets prior to the onset of Lent, and was now following a new rule of life: 'Sunday was devoted to the lords of his Council, Monday to the men of law, and Tuesday to the ladies.' On the previous Tuesday he had gone from room to room ordering and arranging the lodgings prepared for those ladies still remaining at the court, and had 'made them great and hearty cheer, without showing special affection to any particular one'. It soothed his hurt vanity to be once more the centre of female attention, yet he was in no hurry to remarry, and Chapuys thought he would not do so unless Parliament pressed him to it. Anyway, there were few ladies at court who would aspire to such an honour, the ambassador added wryly, because of the new Act requiring 'any lady the King may marry, on pain of death, to declare any charge of misconduct that can be brought against her'. This rather narrowed down the field, since the ladies of Henry's court were not known for their virtue.

There remained, as ever, the problem of the succession. Prince Edward was still thriving, but in May 1542, there were fears – fortunately unfounded – that he was once more ailing, and this prompted both Privy Council and Parliament to remind the King of the need for more sons for the future peace of the realm. But Henry was not ready to face marriage again, though his health had improved. The physician and scholar, Andrew Boorde, who saw the King at this time, noted that his hair was still plentiful and red, if a bit thin on top, and his pulse strong and regular. His digestive system was in perfect working order, and he was better able to curb his temper than in former years. A huge man in height and girth, he sweated a lot, and overate, but Boorde ignored this last fact. The King's leg was still troubling him, but it was better than it had been. His contemporaries thought him fit enough to remarry and sire children, and ignored his mental state. Chapuys sagely concluded that the next queen would be one of Henry's own choosing – 'When he takes a fancy for a person or a thing he goes the whole way.'

The Duke of Cleves, however, hearing the news of Katherine Howard's fate, had other ideas. He was hoping that Henry would take back his sister, and in the spring of 1542 instructed his ambassadors to use their influence to promote a reconciliation. One German envoy visited Cranmer at Lambeth and asked him outright to bring this about. Cranmer replied that he thought it 'not a little strange' that the Duke of Cleves should ask him, of all people, as he was the one person who knew all the 'just causes' for the annulment of the Lady Anne's marriage. The King, hearing of this from his Archbishop, instructed Cranmer to inform the Duke of Cleves most firmly that there could never be a reconciliation between Anne and himself.

It could not be denied, however, that there was a significant dearth of likely candidates to fill the empty consort's throne. Most ladies saw queenship as fraught with insecurity, for the King 'either putteth away or killeth his wives', and it was generally conceded among them that the woman he eventually married would need nerves of steel and sharp wits, not to mention virtue beyond question.

For the present Henry concentrated on possible matches for his children. Elizabeth had been deeply affected by Katherine Howard's end, and stated there and then that she would never marry, a resolution she never broke. Marriage, for her, had too close an association with death to ever seem safe. As for Mary, her opinion of Katherine Howard had never been particularly high, so she was not as shocked as her young sister when she heard the news. That spring, the King reopened negotiations with France for a marriage between Mary and the heir to the French throne, the Duke of Orléans, though these came to nothing as neither side could agree on the dowry, and the already fragile relationship between England and France suffered a further buffeting. The King now made it a priority to reinforce his country's defences against a possible attack by the French, and continued with his programme of coastal fortifications.

The other thorn in his side was Scotland. There had been an alliance between the French and the Scots for centuries, both nations being hereditary enemies of England, and James V of Scotland had consistently frustrated Henry's hopes of arranging a treaty of friendship advantageous to England. Understandably, the King did not want the Scots pouring over his northern border – as they had done in 1513 – while he was occupied with repulsing a French attack in the south. He was furious with James, and had retaliated by sending a military force against him; on 24 November 1542, James V's army was utterly defeated by the English at the Battle of Solway Moss. When Henry received news of the victory, he showed some of his old jubilation, and Chapuys remarked that the habitual sadness he had displayed since learning of the conduct of Queen Katherine had gone. He now confidently expected his nephew of Scotland to treat with him in more deferential terms, terms that would give Henry some control over Scottish affairs. But King James was in no position to treat with his uncle. When he learned of the defeat of his army, he took to his bed at Falkland Palace and died on 14 December, the day he learned his wife had just presented him with a daughter, Mary, who was now Queen of Scots in her own right.

Nothing could have suited Henry VIII better. With its monarch dead and a baby occupying the throne, Scotland no longer posed a threat to England's security. The nobles would be too busy fighting among themselves for power to concern themselves with England, and the Queen Regent, Mary of Guise, would have her hands full controlling them. It was the infant Queen of Scots who interested the

King most, though: he wanted her as a bride for Prince Edward. Such a union would necessarily unite the two countries under Tudor rule, a very attractive prospect to Henry, who wasted no time in sending envoys to the Queen Regent to lay his proposal before her. And on New Year's Day, 1543, Prince Edward, now five, performed his first public duty, entertaining at Enfield a party of noble Scotsmen captured at Solway Moss. They ended up warmly praising the little boy, calling him 'so proper and towardly an imp'. Already, he had beautiful manners and was well behaved. He was fair like his mother, and had something of her retiring, unexuberant manner, but facially he resembled his father, and he had inherited Henry's formidable intellectual powers. Already the child was learning the rudiments of theology and other disciplines, and his father was excessively proud of him.

After Solway Moss, Henry livened up considerably. He spent a good deal of time 'feasting ladies', and began eyeing one or two as prospective wives. He seemed to have forgotten Katherine Howard, and the court recovered some of its gaiety. His good mood was further enhanced by his satisfaction at having concluded a new alliance with the Emperor Charles, whereby both sovereigns had pledged themselves to invade France within two years and to assist each other when called upon to do so. Now, with his new fortifications and his new alliance, Henry could rest assured that he had done all that was needful for the defence of his kingdom.

There was, however, another reason for his new-found contentment: he had at last, to the relief of his advisers, found a lady he could both love and respect. But this was no grand passion – he was done with that. Besides, the lady was married, although her husband was very ill and not expected to live long. She was virtuous and attractive, and Henry wanted her: even as her husband lay on his sick-bed, the King was sending her gifts to signify his esteem. He was certain that in the fullness of time his suit would be accepted, and that the object of his affection would be honoured and delighted to join with him in holy wedlock. He was wrong. She was dismayed at the prospect.

Katherine Parr had been born around the year 1512, the eldest child of Sir Thomas Parr, a descendant of Edward III, by Maud, daughter of Sir Thomas Green of Green's Norton, Northants. She was born either in her father's castle at Kendal in the county of Westmorland, where she spent her childhood, or in his London house at Blackfriars. Kendal castle dated from Norman times, and Katherine's ancestors had lived in it since the fourteenth century. The fabric of the building was much decayed in 1586, according to the antiquarian William Camden, although some rebuilding had taken place in early Tudor times. The Parrs were respected gentry, not very rich but connected to all the noble families of the north, such as Vaux, Throckmorton, Neville, FitzHugh and Dacre.

Lady Parr was only seventeen when she gave birth to Katherine. Shortly afterwards she presented her husband with a son, William, and later on a second daughter, Anne. But on 11 November 1517, when Katherine was five, her father died, and was buried in the monastery of the Black Friars in London, leaving Lady Parr to bring up her three children single-handed. This was a task she undertook conscientiously and with commendable ability, disdaining all offers for her hand in order to devote her full attention to their education. She was a very religious woman and she inspired in them from the first a simple yet reverent love of God, whose word permeated every aspect of her teaching. She was something of a disciplinarian, and expected her daughters to learn proficiency in the traditional feminine skills. There is a tale, probably apocryphal, that Katherine Parr did not take kindly to her mother's strictures and protested that her hands were destined to touch crowns and sceptres, not needles and spindles. Yet she grew up with a great respect for learning and an appreciation of the more sober pleasures in life; of all the wives of Henry VIII, she was the most erudite and the most intellectual.

When Katherine was nearly twelve, her mother entered into negotiations with Lord Dacre for her marriage to Henry Scrope, Lord Scrope's son and heir. Lord Scrope was Lord Dacre's son-in-law, and the marriage had been proposed by Lord Dacre himself, who was a cousin of Sir Thomas Parr, and felt that the young Katherine would be a good match for his grandson. Lady Parr was agreeable, but later ran into difficulties with Lord Scrope over the amount of dowry and jointure to be settled upon her daughter. A series of letters survives which shows that not only was Lord Scrope offering a paltry sum, but he was also unwilling to return Katherine's

487

dowry if she died before the marriage could be consummated, or if it was not consummated for any other reason. Lord Dacre was sympathetic to Lady Parr, and tried to persuade Scrope to change his mind, reminding him that he could save money by sending young Henry to live with Lady Parr until such time as the young couple were of an age to live together, when they would both return to Lord Scrope's house. He reminded his son-in-law that Lady Parr was of the 'good wise stock of the Greens', and warned him that his demands were so 'far asunder that it is impossible ye can ever agree'. If Henry went to stay with Lady Parr he would not only be kept by her but would 'learn with her as well as in any place that I know, as well nurture as French and other languages'. Even after this, however, Lord Scrope persisted in his demands, and early in 1525 Lady Parr informed Lord Dacre that she had decided to abandon the project. This was as well, for young Henry Scrope died on 25 March that year.

Katherine was by then nearing thirteen and growing into a comely girl with auburn hair and a *retroussée* nose; her family background ensured that she did not lack for suitors, yet when it came to choosing her a husband, Lady Parr opted for a man old enough to be Katherine's grandfather. Around 1526 she married her daughter to the Lord Borough. Some confusion exists as to the identification of this gentleman, some sources naming him as Sir Edward de Burgh, who died before April 1533. He was, in fact, Sir Edward's grandfather, another Edward de Burgh, second Baron Borough of Gainsborough in the county of Lincolnshire. He was a member of a distinguished family, and had been born in 1463 or thereabouts, making him sixty-three in 1526, old even by modern standards to marry a girl of fourteen. Such matches, however, were not uncommon in Tudor times, particularly among the aristocracy. Lord Borough had been married before, in 1477, to the daughter and heiress of Lord Cobham, and by her he had had three children. Anne Cobham died early in 1526 and Lord Borough lost no time in seeking a replacement.

After her marriage, Katherine was taken by her new husband to live in the house he had inherited around 1496, the charming Old Hall in Gainsborough, with its magnificent timbered great hall with a stone oriel window, which had been erected by his father on the site of an earlier dwelling in 1484. Lord Borough himself had added to the house, and two kings had visited it, Richard III in 1485 and Henry VIII in 1509. A year after Henry's visit, Lord Borough had been described as being 'distracted of memory'; it is not clear whether or not he ever recovered, nor was mental disturbance considered in the sixteenth century to be an impediment to marriage. Nevertheless, there are indications that the Borough household was a happy one.

Like many girls in her position, Katherine found herself a stepmother to children older than herself. Lord Borough had two sons: his heir, Thomas, was a man of thirty-eight, who was married to Agnes Tyrwhitt, whose brother Sir Robert was married to Lord Borough's daughter. This lady, whose first name is unknown, quickly became firm friends with her young stepmother, a friendship that would endure throughout their lives. Completing the family was Henry de Burgh, whose wife, Katherine Neville, was – at twenty-seven – the member of it nearest to Katherine Parr in age. Then there were Thomas's children, Edward, Thomas and William, who of a certainty would have commanded much of Katherine's attention, for she was fond of children.

Katherine's marriage to her ageing husband did not last long. He died in 1528, leaving her a widow at sixteen. Whether she stayed on at the Old Hall is not known. All that is certain is that her mother died the following year leaving Katherine virtually independent and her own mistress. Around the year 1530 she received an offer of marriage from Lord Latimer of Snape Castle in the north riding of Yorkshire, which she accepted. A woman on her own could not live comfortably without a male protector in those days, when marriage or the conventual life were the only acceptable options open to her if she wished to guard her reputation – only old women ruled their estates alone. And Lord Latimer was, after all, a good matrimonial catch. He was in his late thirties, a more suitable age for marriage to a young woman of eighteen. Born John Neville, he was a member of the great medieval house of Neville that had been so closely related to the Plantagenets. Like Lord Borough, he had been married before, twice in fact: firstly to Dorothy de Vere, daughter of the Earl of Oxford – she had borne him one daughter and his heir, John. Lady Dorothy died on 7 February 1527 and was buried at Wells in

Yorkshire. After her death, Lord Latimer took as his second wife, on 20 July 1528, Elizabeth Musgrave, but she bore him no children and died soon afterwards. Lord Latimer and Katherine Parr were married before 1533: the date of their wedding is not recorded.

Thus Katherine came to live in Snape Castle, described by the antiquarian John Leland as 'a goodly castle in a valley with two or three good parks well-wooded about it'. It was Lord Latimer's chief residence, and was sited two miles from the village of Great Tanfield, near Bedale. Today, it is a ruin, only the perpendicular chapel with its Dutch carvings of the life of Christ surviving intact. Here Katherine Parr, the new Lady Latimer, settled down to her first experience of mature married life, ordering her household and accompanying her husband on his occasional trips to London, where he also had a house conveniently situated for attending the court.

Little of note marked the early years of this marriage and there were no children. In 1534, Katherine's sister Anne married Sir William Herbert. Then, in 1536–7 occurred the Pilgrimage of Grace, in which Lord Latimer, coming from a Catholic family, fought on the side of the rebels, for which he later received the King's pardon. It may have been around this time that Katherine first became interested in Protestantism, a leaning she would be forced to conceal for many years; it was not until much later that she would be able to embrace openly the Lutheran faith. At this date she could merely sympathise in private with the reformist cause. Being intelligent, forthright and having sound common sense, it was perhaps natural that she should favour the tenets of the new religion above the mysteries and intricacies and, it must be said, contemporary abuses of Catholicism. Yet, for the duration of her marriage to Lord Latimer and for some time afterwards, she would be obliged to conceal her true religious inclinations beneath a facade of conventional observance.

In the late 1530s, Lord and Lady Latimer were often at court, where they were on good terms with Henry VIII, who had fortunately decided to overlook Latimer's part in the Pilgrimage of Grace. In 1540, Katherine interceded with the King for the release of her cousin, Sir George Throckmorton, who had been imprisoned in the Tower by Cromwell because of his open criticism of the royal supremacy. Spurred on by the pleas of Throckmorton's wife, Katherine Vaux, another of her cousins, who was very distressed at the plight of her husband, Katherine sought out the King when he was in a good mood and humbly asked him to free Sir George. This was a good moment to appeal to Henry, for he was just then plotting the downfall of Cromwell, and was happy to agree to Lady Latimer's request, being doubtless impressed by her integrity and sincerity. However, there was no question of his feelings for her at that time being anything other than affectionate, for he was deeply in love with Katherine Howard and planning to marry her.

A year after Katherine's execution, however, Henry was looking at Lady Latimer through different eyes, and very much liking what he saw. She was then thirty-one, and still attractive, and on 16 February 1543, Henry made her a gift of 'pleats and sleeves'; his exchequer accounts also record that he ordered gowns in the Italian style for her. It was known by then that Lord Latimer was failing in health and would not live long; he had been ill since the previous autumn, having made his will on 12 September. It was highly unusual for the King to give rich gifts to a married woman, and Katherine, doubtless concerned about her husband's state of health, was disconcerted at receiving them, although she did not dare return them. Then, on 2 March 1543, Lord Latimer died, and the King was obliged to bide his time out of respect for the widow. After the funeral in St Paul's Cathedral, Lord Latimer's will was proved, and Katherine inherited the manors of Nunmonkton and Hamerton with an annuity for four years to finance the upbringing of her step-daughter, Margaret Neville. Thus Katherine became an independent woman of substance.

She seems to have remained at court after her husband's death. What kept her there was not so much having to finalise the details of her husband's estate, nor the interest of the King, but the very obvious admiration of Sir Thomas Seymour, brother of the late Queen Jane. Sir Thomas was about six years older than Katherine Parr, and very handsome. He was also impetuous and extremely ambitious, and he saw in the rich and attractive widow a means of increasing his fortune. He had been working on her emotional susceptibilities since January, when he had returned to court after a diplomatic mission to Nuremberg in Germany, and after Lord Latimer's death, Katherine began to encourage this dashing and unscrupulous adventurer as a suitor. She was both physically and emotionally attracted to him, and it was not long before the two were discussing marriage.

At the same time, a scandal erupted in the Parr family. Just as the King was also beginning to nurture an amorous interest in the widowed Lady Latimer, her brother William, Lord Parr, applied to Parliament for a divorce from his wife, on the grounds of her adultery with an unidentified lover with whom she had eloped in 1542. She was Anne Bourchier, daughter and heiress of the last Earl of Essex of the Bourchier line, whom he had married in February 1526. Furthermore, Lord Parr was so incensed at his wife's infidelity that he was pressing the King to authorise the highest penalty for her offence, which in those days was death.

Her brother's action shocked Katherine Parr, who refused to stand by and allow her sister-in-law to suffer execution. According to the chronicler Hall, she went straight to the King and threw herself at his feet, nor would she rise until he had promised to spare Lady Parr from the headsman's axe. At first, Henry remonstrated with her: 'Madam, you know that the law enacts that a woman of rank who so forgets herself shall die unless her husband pardon her.' Katherine answered, 'Your Majesty is above the law, and I will try to get my brother to pardon.' Eventually, Henry agreed that 'if your brother can be content, I will pardon her'. At this, Katherine went to William and told him that the circumstances of the case were not as he had been given to believe by false witnesses; she would use her influence with the King to have them tortured, she said, 'and then by God's help we shall know the truth'. Parr was already, it seems, aware of the King's interest in his sister, and he knew himself defeated. He forgave his wife, and was rewarded for his clemency when, on 17 April, Parliament granted him a divorce. Lady Parr's adultery was established in law, and an Act passed at the same time declared her children bastards and unfit to inherit. Her Essex estates were then entailed upon her husband, who was created Earl of Essex the following December.

The King, it appears, was following his time-honoured custom of advancing the relatives of the woman he meant to marry. Although there is no evidence that Henry had as yet declared himself to Katherine Parr, he admitted Lord Parr to the Privy Council in March 1543, and made him a Knight of the Garter on 23 April following.

This alone should have warned Katherine that the King's intentions were serious, but she either did not notice or affected to ignore the fact, being too involved emotionally with Seymour. Henry saw this and was jealous: Seymour was a younger man who epitomised many of the things Henry had been in his youth, and this in itself did not exactly endear him to his sovereign. His courtship of the comely widow was not to be borne. Henry wanted her, and Henry meant to have her.

Until this time, around late April or early May 1543, Katherine had been unaware of the King's true feelings and intentions towards her. Yet now it began to dawn on her that he too was a suitor, not in an aggressive way, but by appearing 'sad, pensive and sighing' whenever she was around. He was lonely and feeling sorry for himself, and only Lady Latimer's presence could ease him. Katherine responded correctly and respectfully, but she had no desire to be Queen of England or wife to a man who had already gone through five spouses. Her heart was given to Thomas Seymour; as she was to write to him, referring to this time, five years later, 'As truly as God is God, my mind was fully bent the other time I was at liberty to marry you before any man I know.' Henry sensed that this might be the case, and – seeing that Katherine showed no sign of becoming anything more than friendly towards him – decided on a course of rather more drastic action. In May, he dealt with the problem of Thomas Seymour by simply removing him from the scene and sending him on a permanent embassy to the court of the Regent of the Netherlands in Brussels. This must have been a blow, for different reasons, to both Katherine and Sir Thomas, yet Katherine was obliged to hide her true feelings because the King now began to pursue her in earnest, and she had no alternative but to let him think his advances were welcome.

On 1 July 1543, negotiations for the future marriage between Prince Edward and Mary, Queen of Scots were concluded with the signing of the Treaty of Greenwich. With the marriage of his heir so satisfactorily provided for, Henry felt that he might now marry for his own comfort, and it was at this time that he proposed to Katherine Parr. Her initial reaction was one of dismay. The King was not Katherine's idea of a desirable bridegroom, being, according to an eyewitness, the author of the Spanish Chronicle, 'so fat that such a man had never been seen. Three of the biggest men that could be found could get inside his doublet.' At fifty-two, he was already an old man, with an old man's set ways and uncertain temper. His bad leg sometimes rendered him immobile and needed constantly redressing; on occasions it stank. There was grey in his red hair and beard. All the same, he presented himself as a prospective bridegroom with all the assurance he had displayed to Anne Boleyn nearly twenty years before, and it was obvious that he would not brook any refusals. Katherine knew she had little choice in the matter, and when Henry, sensing her reluctance, became insistent, she capitulated.

Katherine was no giddy girl, and she was more suited than most for the task facing her, having been once before married to an old man, and having nursed Lord Latimer through his final illness. She was steady and she was sensible, and, having had the care of grown stepchildren before, all of whom seem to have got on well with her, she was uniquely fitted for the role of stepmother to the King's three children, whose interests she would protect with her customary efficiency.

She was not a pretty woman, or a beauty, but rather comely with red-gold hair and hazel eyes. For many years, portraits of various widely differing ladies were identified as Katherine Parr: these include one at Lambeth Palace, one by Ambrosius Benson in the collection of the Earl of Ashburnham, and a miniature at Sudeley Castle. There is only one portrait that can be said with certainty to depict Katherine, and that is the half-length painted by William Scrots in 1545, which is now in the National Portrait Gallery. The sitter wears a rich costume of scarlet damask banded with cloth of gold; the gown is loose fitting and has the upturned collar that became popular in the 1540s. She is past the first flush of youth, and appears rather plain. On her head is a jaunty cap atop her pearly hood, from which hangs a feather. William Scrots replaced Hans Holbein as Henry's court painter after Holbein's death, but his work lacks the draughtsmanship of Holbein's, and is somewhat mechanical in quality.

There is also, in the Royal Collection, a Holbein drawing that may well portray Katherine Parr. Inscribed 'The Lady Borough', it is a very faint sketch of a face, but enough remains to show a striking resemblance to the lady in Scrots's portrait. Holbein painted most of his English portraits after his return from Germany in 1532, yet some had been executed earlier, during the years 1526 to 1528, when Katherine Parr was married to Lord Borough. It could be argued that the drawing represents Katherine Neville, who married Lord Borough's son Henry in 1528, but comparison with the Scrots portrait, especially in the line of the nose and the slant of the eyes, lends credence to the likelihood that this is in fact an early portrait by Hans Holbein of Katherine Parr.

Katherine's looks, however, were not her chief attraction. People were drawn more to her warm and amiable personality and her intellectual qualities; she exuded goodwill. She was a good conversationalist, and loved a friendly argument, especially on matters of religious doctrine. She found favour with Cranmer and his reformist party because she was known to be 'very zealous towards the Gospel', according to the Elizabethan author of *The Book of Martyrs*, John Foxe, and they perceived that, like themselves, she might secretly nurture Protestant views. Foxe also remarked of Katherine that she was 'but a woman accompanied with all the imperfections natural to the weakness of her sex', yet in spite of this prejudiced masculine view, typical of that period, Katherine was seen by the reformers to be the perfect instrument whereby they could influence the King. They put heart and soul into encouraging the marriage, grateful that the King's inclinations at last coincided with their hopes.

Katherine proved to be popular with most people, mainly because she had a pleasant manner with both nobility and servants alike. Her chaplain, John Parkhurst, who later became Bishop of Norwich, remembered in his latter years that she was 'a most gentle mistress'. Perhaps the most outstanding thing about her was her formidable intellect, which had been cultivated to an unusual extent by her mother and by the people with whom she had associated in later life. She was perceptive, articulate, thirsty for knowledge, both general and religious, and industrious. Her virtue, a female quality always suspect in an age that believed that teaching women to write would encourage them to pen love-letters, was beyond question. After her marriage to the King, she made a point of 'avoiding all occasions of idleness and condemning vain pastimes'. No one would have cause to believe that she had ever been loose like Katherine Howard.

495

In many ways Katherine was a rather austere woman, who may be cited as the perfect example of the Renaissance ideal of the godly matron. However, far from being an early feminist, she used her intellectual powers to promote her own strong views, which were strictly conventional, on the conduct of the female sex. She believed, she wrote in her treatise *The Lamentations of a Sinner*, published in 1547, that women should 'learn of St Paul to be obedient to their husbands, and to keep silence in the congregation, and to learn of their husbands at home'. She herself, however, did not always practise what she preached, for she was to grow fond of disputing with her royal husband – who liked to think himself far superior to her on such topics – and was not above telling him what he ought to think, especially on religious matters. Naturally the King resented this, and there would be clashes. For all this, though, Henry admired her learning, and still more her virtue. She was, in every way, a woman he could respect, and she made the perfect companion for his later years. She was quieter and more staid than most of his previous wives, nor did she display the caprices of Anne Boleyn and Katherine Howard.

Katherine's chief interest was theology; 'godly matters' fascinated her. Like a true subject of Henry VIII, she detested the Pope, and once compared him to Pharaoh, saying 'He hath been, and is, the greater persecutor of all true Christians than ever was Pharaoh of the Children of Israel.' She was so anxious to promote her religious views that she wrote and published two books, proof indeed of her intellectual ability. This was the first time a queen of England ever aired her personal views to her subjects, and we are fortunate in having these works as testimony to the workings of the mind of this remarkable queen. Of course, much of what she wrote reflected the political ideology of the day. Of Henry VIII, Katherine was, naturally, lavish with praise:

> Thanks be to the Lord that He hath sent us such a godly and learned King in these latter days to reign over us, King Henry VIII, my most sovereign, favourable lord and husband: one, if Moses had figured any more than Christ, through the excellent grace of God, meet to be another expressed verity of Moses' conquest over Pharaoh.

She wholeheartedly approved of the King's reforms within the Church, and loved to discuss them with him, putting forth her own views without reserve. Fortunately, they usually coincided with his.

Katherine could also speak and write fluent French, which her mother had taught her. There exists today in the Cecil Papers at Hatfield House a poem said to have been written by her in that language. There is good reason to believe that, had Katherine lived in an age when women were encouraged to develop their intellectual powers, and had she not been hampered by the conventions of her time, she would have turned out to be a very successful and formidable lady in her own right.

With all her excellent qualities, there can be little doubt that the King 'deigned to marry' her for the companionship she could give him rather than for sensual pleasure or assuring the succession. It may well be that Henry was now impotent, and had been since he was married to Katherine Howard, which would account for the fact that neither union produced any children. It is true that Katherine's previous marriages had been childless, yet she did later conceive and bear a child by her fourth husband, so it is unlikely that the fault was hers.

On 10 July 1543, Archbishop Cranmer issued a special licence for the marriage of his sovereign lord King Henry with Katherine Latimer, late the wife of Lord Latimer, 'in whatever church, chapel or oratory he may please, without publication of banns, and dispensing with all ordinances to the contrary for reasons concerning the honour and advancement of the whole realm'. Henry was not minded to wait, and wanted to be married with as little fuss as possible. Accordingly, two days later, on 12 July, the wedding took place privately in the Queen's closet at Hampton Court. The Lady Margaret Douglas, lately returned to court after being pardoned for her illicit love affair, was chief bridesmaid. When the King was asked if he would take Katherine Parr to be his lawful wife, he answered 'Yea', with a 'joyful countenance', and the ghost of Katherine Howard was laid to rest at last.

One of the witnesses to the marriage was the Lady Anne of Cleves, who showed not the slightest annoyance at her former husband uniting himself to another lady; indeed, she seemed very

497

pleased about it. She knew, more than anyone else, what Katherine was letting herself in for: 'A fine burden Madam Katherine has taken upon herself!' she later remarked, though Chapuys understood her dismissive attitude to mean that she was bitter because the King had not returned to her. He reported that she wanted to return to Cleves, but that was because her mother was ill, and not because she had 'taken great grief and despair at the King's espousal of his new wife, who is not nearly so good looking as she is'. Moreover, after the Duchess of Cleves died later that year, there was no more talk of Anne returning home.

Nearly everyone approved of the new Queen. Wriothesley, writing to inform the Duke of Norfolk of the marriage, described her as

> a woman, in my judgement, for certain virtue, wisdom and gentleness, most meet for his Highness. And sure I am that his Majesty had never a wife more agreeable to his heart than she is. The Lord grant them long life and much joy together.

Chapuys told the Emperor that Katherine was 'praised for her virtue'; he added that she was 'of small stature, graceful, and of cheerful countenance'. The King, it was said presently, was very satisfied with her. The people of England, too, rejoiced when news of the marriage was made public. Sir Ralph Sadler sent a letter of congratulations to Lord Parr, saying it had

> revived my troubled spirits and turned all my cares to rejoicing. I do not only rejoice for your lordship's sake, but also for the real and inestimable benefit and comfort which thereby shall ensue to the whole realm, which now with the grace of God shall be stored with many precious jewels.

One of Katherine's first acts as queen was to write to her brother, that same Lord Parr, informing him of her advancement, 'it having pleased God to incline the King to take me as his wife, which was the greatest comfort that could happen to me'. Thoughts of Sir Thomas Seymour had been resolutely banished out of her head. She went on:

498

I desire to inform my brother of it as the person who has most cause to rejoice thereat. I pray you to let me know of your health, as friendly as if I had not been called to this honour.

For Lord Parr, as for other members of Katherine's family, there was now the heady prospect of continual advancement and the acquisition of wealth and status. The Queen's sister and her husband, Sir William Herbert, came to court, as did members of the Throckmorton family, one of whom, Clement, became Katherine's cupbearer. And her former stepdaughter, Lady Tyrwhitt, was taken into her household, as was the Queen's cousin Maud, the widow of Sir Ralph Lane.

Once the Queen's household had been organised, the King took his bride to Windsor, where he celebrated his marriage by having three Protestant heretics burned to death in the Great Park. Conservatives such as Bishop Gardiner, who already suspected the Queen of having Lutheran sympathies, were watching her closely at this time to see how she reacted to the burnings, but she made no attempt to intercede for the victims and settled down afterwards to enjoy her honeymoon.

The court stayed at Windsor throughout August. Katherine had already resolved to be a loving stepmother to the King's three children, and she was determined to provide for them a happy and stable domestic life. It concerned her that all three lived away from the court and rarely saw their father, so, in August, with the King's approval, she wrote to them all, expressing the wish that they should come and visit her at court, as it was the King's pleasure and hers. The Lady Elizabeth responded promptly, and expressed – in very eloquent terms – her appreciation of Katherine's kindness, which she was sure she did not deserve. She promised that she would so conduct herself that Katherine would never have cause for complaint, and that she would be diligent in showing obedience and respect: 'I await with much impatience the orders of the King my father for the accomplishment of the happiness for which I sigh, and I remain with much submission, Your Majesty's very dear Elizabeth.'

Before long, both Elizabeth and her sister Mary arrived at court. Their new stepmother must have been a very welcome presence in their lives, especially to Elizabeth, who had for most of her young life lacked a mother's love and guidance. The King had never felt comfortable in the company of Anne Boleyn's precocious daughter, but now, under Katherine Parr's benign influence, he softened and unbent towards her.

Elizabeth was nearly ten. Her early promise had been fulfilled, and she was now as intelligent and sharp-witted as many an adult. Already she showed signs of having inherited her mother's love of flattery and her coquettish manner, as well as her courage. But, although she was temperamental, Elizabeth was not as volatile as Anne Boleyn had been, and her insecure childhood had taught her the value of discretion and dissimulation. Already she spoke several languages and was well grounded in the classics. This impressed Queen Katherine, and she immediately took upon herself the duty of supervising Elizabeth's education; indeed, she was to make such a good job of it that the King would later ask her advice when it came to appointing a suitable tutor for Prince Edward.

Henry's eldest child, the Lady Mary, was again finding it a pleasure to visit the court. She and Katherine Parr soon became great friends, and it is certain that Katherine did much to ease Mary's frustration by according her all the respect due to a princess. She became her confidante in everything except matters of religion, and – being near in age – they shared similar interests.

That left Edward. His visits to court would be less frequent than his sisters', for the King feared he might catch some mortal disease from too great a contact with the world beyond the rigorous standards of hygiene in his nursery. However, this did not prevent Katherine from overseeing his progress or being watchful of those who looked after him. In time, Edward would come to love his stepmother as much as his cold nature allowed him to love anybody; she was perhaps the most gentle influence he knew in his short life. At last there was a degree of harmony in the King's family.

On 12 October 1543, Edward celebrated his sixth birthday, and his royal father decided it was time to begin his formal education. Prior to this date, Edward had been 'brought up among the women', as he later recorded in his journal. Now he was to be handed over to male tutors and governors, chief of whom was a man with reformist views, Dr Richard Cox, a fellow of King's College, Cambridge, and the future Bishop of Ely. On the King's orders, the child was to be taught the usual curriculum of the period: classics, theology, languages, mathematics, grammar, and the known sciences, as well as sports and gentlemanly pursuits. Barnaby FitzPatrick, the son of an Irish nobleman, was shortly afterwards appointed Edward's whipping-boy, for it was unthinkable that the heir to the throne be chastised by lesser mortals. Fortunately, the boys became firm friends.

So absorbed was the King in plans for his heir's education and for an invasion of France scheduled for the following summer, that he did not notice fresh trouble brewing in Scotland. Thus the revocation of the Treaty of Greenwich by the Scottish Parliament in December 1543 came as an unpleasant shock to him, as did news that the 'auld alliance' between Scotland and France had been renewed. Henry's rage was terrible indeed. Gone were his hopes of a united Britain, gone his ambition to rule Scotland. Worse still, it had been intimated that his precious son was not good enough for the Scottish Queen. Such insults were not to be borne.

In retaliation, Henry sent an army to Scotland under Lord Hertford with the intention of subduing his rebellious neighbour. He could not afford to leave his northern border open when he took the offensive against the French the following year, and he wished, above all, to teach the Scots a lesson they would never forget. The English army set off just before Christmas to begin its 'rough wooing' of the Queen of Scots, and Hertford executed his master's orders with devastating thoroughness. Leith, Edinburgh and Holyrood were burned, and then he blazed on to Berwick, leaving a trail of destruction and misery along the borders; even today, in such towns as Jedburgh and Melrose, the results of his depredations may still be seen.

The campaign wore on throughout the spring and summer of 1544, while the young Queen Mary was hidden by her mother in a remote abbey. Nor did reports of the destruction appease Henry; in 1545, Hertford was again commanded to attack the Scots, and this time he wrought havoc by sacking, among others, the great abbeys of Dryburgh and Coldingham. At this point, any Scottish nobles who might have been sympathetic to an alliance with England had been alienated, and the Scots had been driven further into the arms of the French. All internal struggles ceased as the aristocratic factions united against England. English raids persisted until Henry's death, and eventually the Scots were obliged to send Queen Mary to France, for fear she might be abducted by the English. There, she would be brought up by the French royal family, and marry into it.

Katherine Parr's first Christmas season as queen was overshadowed by events in Scotland, yet the festivities at Hampton Court were much as usual. On the Sunday before Christmas Lord Parr was created Earl of Essex and the Queen's uncle, another Sir William Parr, was created Lord Parr of Horton and appointed chamberlain to the Queen. After Christmas, however, Henry's leg began to give him trouble, and in January 1544 he suffered several agonising attacks of pain. Chapuys, who was by now himself a virtual invalid and hoped to be going home to Savoy soon, thought that Henry's 'chronic disease' and 'great obesity' were endangering his life and needed careful attention. The King, he reported, was so weak on his legs he could hardly stand. Yet no one dared remonstrate with him about the amount he was eating, nor did they try to prevent him from going about his daily duties as if nothing were wrong with him. His one comfort was the kindness of his wife, who proved as devoted a nurse as she was a companion. He could not praise her enough: evidently the first six months of their marriage had been a success.

On 7 February 1544, as a mark of his esteem, the King passed a new Act of Succession. 'Forasmuch as his Majesty, sithence the death of the late Queen Jane' – Queen Anne and Queen Katherine are not mentioned, for as far as the King was concerned they did not count – 'hath taken to wife Katherine, late wife to Lord Latimer, by whom as yet his Majesty hath no issue, but may full well, when it shall please God,' it was provided that, 'if their union might be blessed with offspring', such offspring would be placed after Prince Edward in the order of succession. Failing any issue of the King's present marriage, the Act optimistically – and alarmingly, as far as Katherine was concerned – invested the succession in 'the children [the King] might have by other queens'. After them, would come the Lady Mary and then the Lady Elizabeth. The new Act was generally approved of by the King's subjects, and many hoped that the Queen might yet have a child, although she had now been married for seven months with no sign of pregnancy. As Sir William Paget wrote, 'We

502

trust in God, which hath hitherto preserved his Majesty to his glory and honour and our comfort, to preserve him longer and send him time enough to proceed' to the siring of heirs. It was to prove a vain prayer.

That February, the Queen entertained the Spanish Duke of Najera, who arrived at court on the 17th, and the Lady Mary, who could speak Spanish, was there to assist her. When Eustache Chapuys, the Spanish ambassador, escorted the Duke into the Queen's presence, both royal ladies asked courteously for news of the Emperor. Unfortunately, Katherine was not feeling very well, but she put on a brave face and danced 'for the honour of the company'. Chapuys was impressed by her manner towards Mary, and he told the Emperor that she had constantly urged the King to keep Mary as second in line to the throne after Edward in the new Act of Succession.

Also present on that occasion was the Duke of Najera's secretary, Pedro de Gant, who left an account describing how the Duke kissed the Queen's hand on being presented, and of her leading him to another room where he was entertained with music and 'much beautiful dancing'. Katherine danced first with her brother, 'very gracefully', and then the Lady Mary partnered Lady Margaret Douglas and then some of the gentlemen of the court. A Venetian from the King's household danced galliards 'with such extraordinary activity that he seemed to have wings upon his feet – never was a man seen so agile!' The dancing went on for several hours, after which the Queen signalled to a nobleman who spoke Spanish to present some gifts to her guest. Najera again kissed her hand and she retired to her chamber. Pedro de Gant thought her 'graceful', and said she had a 'cheerful countenance; she is praised for her virtue'. On this occasion, she wore an underskirt of cloth of gold beneath a sleeved overdress of brocade lined with crimson satin, the sleeves being lined with crimson velvet, and the train being two yards long. Hanging around her neck were two crosses and a jewel of very magnificent diamonds; there were 'a great number of splendid diamonds in her head-dress' also.

After Najera had left the court, Mary stayed on. She had been occupying her time lately with translating Erasmus's *Paraphrases of the Gospel of St John*, an exercise of which the Queen heartily approved, for she felt that it became a woman of rank to undertake intellectual pursuits. Also, around this time, Mary sat for her portrait by a certain Master John, who charged her £4.00 for it. This same artist was also commissioned by Katherine Parr to paint another portrait, now in the National Portrait Gallery, and said to be of the King's great-niece, Lady Jane Grey, who in 1548 lived in the Queen's household. For a long time this second portrait was thought to be of Katherine herself, but the identification with Jane is said to be proved by the similarity of a brooch worn by the sitter to a brooch on an authenticated engraving of Jane. It is probable that Katherine gave Jane this piece of jewellery, and that the portrait is after all one of the Queen. The lady in the portrait looks more than ten years old, as her figure is quite developed and her jowls sag slightly; facially, she bears a striking resemblance to the Scrots portrait of Katherine Parr and she also wears an identical pendant.

On 22 April 1544, Lord Chancellor Audley died, and the indefatigable Wriothesley replaced him on 3 May. Wriothesley, for all his flattery, did not like Katherine Parr, and later did his best to bring about her downfall. He was not a man of great religious bias, but one who adapted his views to suit the times. His antipathy may have been purely personal. He had helped to bring down both Anne of Cleves and Katherine Howard, and seems to have enjoyed political intrigue for its own sake. For the present, he was the political ally of the staunchly conservative Stephen Gardiner, Bishop of Winchester, who suspected the Queen of heresy and was awaiting his opportunity to unseat her. Together, Wriothesley and Gardiner posed a potential threat to Katherine's future as Queen, although fortunately she was aware of their suspicions and careful to give them no cause for complaint.

One of the chief pleasures of queenship, Katherine found, was the ability to help others. To her mind, it was the chief duty of a queen to assist those who came to her in need. Thus, when Lady Hertford grew anxious about her husband, who was absent in Scotland and engaged on a very dangerous mission, Katherine spoke to the King on her behalf, and was able to inform Lady Hertford, in a letter written on 3 June 1544, that her husband would be recalled before Henry set sail for his planned invasion of France. The King's children and some of his other relatives had good reason to be grateful to her also, as did her servants and the humble people who benefited from her charity.

At the end of June, the King and Queen were present at the wedding of the Lady Margaret Douglas to the Earl of Lennox, one of the few remaining Scottish nobles with Anglophile sympathies. This took place in the chapel of Henry's new London palace, which had been built on the site of the old leper hospital of St James, not far from Whitehall. It had been intended as a residence for Anne Boleyn, but she had not lived to see its completion, and it was Katherine Parr who stood by Henry's side when St James's Palace was first used for a state occasion.

Preparations for the invasion of France were now so far advanced that the King decided to set out in early July. Before then, however, he accorded his wife the highest honour of all, in token of his trust in her and his respect for her integrity. On 7 July, it was announced in Council that she was to be regent in his absence, and Archbishop Cranmer, Lord Chancellor Wriothesley, Lord Hertford, Dr Thomas Thirlby and Sir William Petre were designated her advisers.

Prior to his departure, Henry also gave instructions about the education of his son. Dr John Cheke, a fellow of St John's College, Cambridge, and a famous academic with secret Lutheran tendencies, was appointed to supplement Dr Cox 'for the better instruction of the Prince'. Sir Anthony Cooke was also engaged to teach sports and recreational activities. Henry's choice of Cheke was applauded by all the great minds of his day and we may be certain that Katherine Parr had either urged or approved of it. Roger Ascham, who later became tutor to the Lady Elizabeth, called Cheke 'an excellent man, full of learning'.

When Cheke arrived upon the scene, he and Cox drew up a new curriculum of study for the Prince, to include languages, philosophy and 'all liberal sciences' in addition to his usual studies. Already, Edward was an extremely precocious and solemn child; so serious was he that he is known to have laughed out loud in public only once during his life. No doubt this was due to the fact that he was very early on made aware of the great destiny awaiting him, and whose shoes he must one day fill. From birth, he was isolated from the hubbub of court life and over-protected by an anxious father; he had never known the security of a mother's love, and hence grew into a self-contained child. His father was an affectionate yet distant, glittering figure, who must have inspired awe in his son whenever they met. It was left to Katherine Parr to alleviate the little boy's loneliness; it was slow progress, but she eventually won his affection, although it was too late to repair all the damage that had been caused by his early upbringing.

With Elizabeth, Katherine had initially had more success, for this child was eager and able to reciprocate the warmth emanating from her stepmother, even though she was inclined to use it as a stepping-stone to the King's favour. Through Katherine's good offices, she too had a new tutor at this time, William Grindal. Yet, early in 1544, a rift occurred between Elizabeth and her father. The cause is not known, yet it was enough to make Henry banish his younger daughter from the court. Queen Katherine did all she could to effect a reconciliation between father and daughter, but the King proved obstinate, and her efforts were in vain. Now he was going abroad with the rift unhealed, and there was nothing that Katherine could do about it.

By the second week in July, the English fleet was ready to sail, and the royal army was mustered at Dover. The Queen accompanied her husband to the port and kissed him farewell on 14 July, when he embarked for France. She then led the whole country in a prayer of intercession for his safety and success which she had composed herself to be read in churches:

> O Almighty King and Lord of Hosts, which by Thy angels thereunto appointed dost minister both war and peace . . . our cause now being just, and being enforced to enter the war and battle, we most humbly beseech Thee, O Lord God of Hosts, so to turn the hearts of our enemies to the desire of peace that no Christian blood be spilt. Or else grant, O Lord, that with small effusion of blood and little damage of innocents, we may to Thy glory obtain victory; and that, the wars being ended, we may all with one heart and mind knit together in concord and amity, laud and praise Thee, who livest and reignest, world without end, Amen.

After the King's departure, Katherine returned to Greenwich, there to attend to her duties as regent and await news of her husband

and his campaign. She wrote to him regularly throughout their time apart, gentle, touching letters that testify plainly to the lively affection that had grown between them. In the first, she spoke of how much she was missing him:

Although the distance and time and account of days neither is long nor many of your Majesty's absence, yet the want of your presence, so much desired and beloved by me, maketh me that I cannot quietly pleasure in anything until I hear from your Majesty. The time seemeth to me very long, with a great desire to know how your Highness hath done since your departing hence, whose prosperity and health I prefer and desire more than mine own. And whereas I know your Majesty's absence is never without great need, yet love and affection compel me to desire your presence. Again, the same zeal and affection forceth me to be best content with that which is your will and pleasure. Thus love maketh me in all things set apart mine own convenience and pleasure and to embrace most joyfully his will and pleasure whom I love.

She acknowledged herself greatly indebted to God for His benefits bestowed upon her:

even such confidence have I in your Majesty's gentleness, knowing myself never to have done my duty as were requisite and meet for such a noble prince [is this, one wonders, a reference to her seeming inability to conceive a child?], at whose hands I have found and received so much love and goodness that with words I cannot express it.

This said, the Queen concluded, 'lest I should be too tedious to your Majesty,' committing Henry to God's care and governance.

Shortly afterwards, she received a letter from the Lady Elizabeth, bewailing her exile from the court and thanking Katherine for her hitherto fruitless intercession with the King. She had not dared to write to her father, she confessed, and begged her stepmother to send a letter on her behalf, 'praying ever for his sweet benediction' and

507

beseeching God to send him victory over his enemies, 'so that your Highness and I may as soon as possible rejoice in his happy return'.

Absence from his wife had made Henry all the fonder, and when Katherine wrote again, begging him to forgive Elizabeth for her unknown offence and receive the child again at court, he relented, and gave his permission for her to go to Greenwich to keep Katherine company. Mary was already there, which meant that the Queen could extend her own special brand of kindness to both of Henry's daughters at once.

Meanwhile, the King had arrived in France and had laid siege to the city of Boulogne. The campaign had worked wonders for his health, as Chapuys noted in August, saying that he 'works better and more than I would have thought'. In fact, Henry was in his element, and was enjoying himself as much as he had on his earlier campaign in France, more than thirty years before. It was a relief to find that, despite encroaching age and infirmity, he could still mount a horse and bully the French. If he could not recapture his youth, he could at least enjoy this Indian summer.

On 9 August, the Queen wrote to Henry to tell him that she had dispatched the Earl of Lennox to Scotland in the hope that he would be able to seize the reins of government there, and she imputed the enthusiasm and speed with which he was carrying out his mission to serve a 'master whom God aids'. God, unfortunately, was not disposed to aid this particular venture, which was doomed to end in failure since Lennox's feeble efforts to grasp power were ineffectual. Not knowing this as yet, Katherine set out on a short progress in order to avoid the plague which was raging in London just then. News of her coming sent local gentry into hasty flurries of preparation; the Countess of Rutland, learning that Katherine was at Enfield and would be staying with her two nights hence, wrote to her father, Sir William Paston, asking him to send her some fresh fish, as 'here is small store, and the court is merry!'

Katherine was still worrying about the King, and she had not had news of him for some time. Even her enemy, Lord Chancellor Wriothesley, was moved by her concern.

God is able to strengthen His own against the devil [he told her] and therefore let not the Queen's Majesty in any wise trouble herself, for God shall turn all to the best; and sure we be that the King's Majesty's person is out of all danger.

Feeling somewhat cheered at his words, Katherine wrote yet another letter, which is now lost, to her husband, and sent him some venison, which he loved. At last, on 8 September, he wrote to her in response to her enquiries about certain domestic matters:

Most dearly and most entirely beloved wife,
We recommend us heartily unto you, and thank you as well for your letter as for the venison which you sent, for the which we give unto you our hearty thanks, and would have written unto you again a letter with our own hand, but that we be so occupied, and have so much to do in foreseeing and caring for everything ourself, as we have almost no manner rest or leisure to do any other thing. And whereas you desired to know our pleasure for the accepting into your chamber of certain ladies in places of others that cannot give their attendance by reason of sickness, albeit we think those whom you have named unto us as unable almost to attend by reason of weakness as the others be, yet we remit the accepting of them to your own choice, thinking nevertheless that though they shall not be meet to serve, yet you may, if you think so good, take them into your chamber to pass the time sometime with you at play, or otherwise to accompany you for your recreation. . . . No more to you at this time, sweetheart, both for lack of time and great occupation of business, saving we pray you to give in our name our hearty blessings to all our children, and recommendations to our cousin Margaret [Douglas] and the rest of the ladies and gentlewomen, and to our Council also.
Written with the hand of your loving husband,
Henry R.

Three days after this letter was written, the King realised that the inhabitants of Boulogne would not withstand the siege for very much longer. Wrote Chapuys: 'I never in my life saw the King so joyful and in such good spirits and so elated.' Henry told one of the Emperor's generals that he had vowed to bring France to submission and was now fulfilling that promise. 'I have been all my life a Prince of honour and virtue,' he said sanctimoniously, 'who never contravened my word, and am too old to begin now, as the white hairs in my beard testify.' His elation was justified, at least for the time being. On 14 September 1544, Boulogne fell to him; four days later he entered it in triumph, riding through the streets at the head of his army. On the same day, the King of France was forced to sign a peace treaty with the Emperor at Crêpy.

In the meantime, Katherine Parr had been staying with the Countess of Rutland at her medieval castle at Oakham; the Queen had brought with her all three of her stepchildren, to keep them safe from the plague. From Oakham, she issued strict orders to the Council, commanding them to make a proclamation that no person who had been in contact with a plague victim was to come near the court nor was anyone to allow any courtier into a house where there had been infection, 'under the Queen's indignation and further punishment at her pleasure'. These sensible measures effectively eliminated any threat of danger to the Prince and his sisters, and to Katherine herself. Fortunately, by late August the epidemic was on the wane, and the Queen deemed it safe to return to Greenwich, where she was when she heard news of the fall of Boulogne.

Katherine was well aware of the importance of her husband's victory, and she immediately ordered that a general thanksgiving be offered up in all the towns and villages throughout England, in gratitude for the taking of the city. These special services were held on 19 September. And to her husband, Katherine wrote: 'I thank God for a prosperous beginning of your affairs, and I rejoice at the joyful news of your good health.'

Late in September, the Queen went to Hanworth for a short break from state duties. There, she read the Lady Mary's translation of Erasmus's *Paraphrases*, and was very impressed with it; at the end of the month she returned the manuscript with a letter full of warm praise, suggesting that Mary have it published, as it was a 'fair and useful work'. Mary declined to do so, but Katherine replied that she did not see 'why you should reject the praise which all deservedly would give you; yet I leave all to your own prudence, and will approve of that which seems best to you.' Mary responded by saying she was willing to have the work published, but only under a pseudonym, to which Katherine answered that in her opinion Mary would 'do a real injury if you refuse to let it go down to posterity under the auspices of your own name'. Her words made Mary relent. The translation was printed and widely read, receiving high praise from scholars such as Nicholas Udall, Provost of Eton College.

After leaving Hanworth, the Queen returned to Greenwich, there to await the King's homecoming. On 30 September, a triumphant Henry disembarked at Dover, and travelled as fast as possible to see the wife from whom he had been parted for three months. It was a happy reunion, the King and Queen openly showing their affection for each other, and their pride in each other's achievements during the past weeks. Katherine may well have reflected at this time that, if she had given up the chance of a marriage more to her liking with Thomas Seymour, she had at least achieved a measure of contentment with the King, who had been consistently loving and kind to her.

For the remainder of the autumn, Henry diverted himself with his favourite pastime, hunting. His recent burst of energy had not yet spent itself. This was, however, the last time he would ever engage in such pursuits.

In October that year, Sir Thomas Seymour's embassy to the Low Countries came to an end and he returned to court. The King knew very well how things had once stood between Seymour and Katherine, and once again appointed Seymour to an office that would necessitate his being away from court for long periods, that of Lord High Admiral of England. Evidently Henry was still suspicious of Seymour's intentions towards the Queen, although no breath of scandal or hint of impending infidelity tainted her good name. Whatever her private feelings were, she hid them well, and paid no more attention to Seymour than to anyone else, while he, following her lead, betrayed by no sign that there had ever been anything more than friendship between them.

At Christmas, Chapuys took the opportunity to thank the Queen, on behalf of the Emperor, for all that she had done for the Lady Mary, to which she 'replied very graciously that she did not deserve so much courtesy. What she did for the Lady Mary was less than she would like to do, and was only her duty in every respect.' As to maintaining the friendship between England and Spain, Katherine told the ambassador that she 'had done and would do nothing to prevent its growing still further, and she hoped that God would avert the slightest dissension, as the friendship was so necessary and both sovereigns were so good'. Chapuys could not help admiring her. She was, in his opinion, a very pleasant and well-meaning person, whose goodwill could be used to advantage when it came to preserving the alliance between his master and Henry VIII. Yet Chapuys feared he would not be there to use this advantage: he was growing old and nearing retirement, and was so infirm that he was now confined to a kind of wheelchair on occasions. He had already applied for his recall, and was awaiting the Emperor's assent.

New Year arrived, the beginning of 1545. The Lady Elizabeth sent her stepmother her own translation, neatly written in fine italic script, of Margaret of Navarre's book, *Le Miroir de l'Ame Pécheresse*, a devout meditation on the love of a Christian soul towards God and His Christ. Elizabeth hoped that there was nothing in it 'worthy of reprehension', and begged that no other person than Katherine be allowed to see it, 'lest my faults be known of many' as 'it is all imperfect and incorrect' and 'in many places rude', with 'nothing done as it should be'. This was the kind of gift Katherine liked best, and she was deeply touched that her young stepdaughter should have gone to such trouble. And when she turned to the first page of the work, she read the dedication: 'To the most noble and virtuous Queen Katherine, Elizabeth, her humble daughter, wisheth perpetual felicity and everlasting joy.'

In March, the King's health took a turn for the worse, and he was down with 'a burning fever' for several days; this seems to have affected his leg, and he suffered more bouts of agonising pain. His illness did not improve his temper, which was further aroused by reports of heresy within his realm, which was spreading at an alarming rate. Henry himself had never approved of Lutheranism. In spite of all he had done to reform the Church in England, he was still Catholic in his ways and determined for the present to keep England that way. Protestant heresies would not be tolerated, and he would make that very clear to his subjects. As a result of his enquiries, twenty-three people were arrested and examined at this time, among them a woman called Anne Askew. This Anne was twenty-three, and had not long since applied to the King for a legal separation from her husband, Thomas Kyme, who had quite literally thrown her out of doors and kept her from seeing her two children. It has often been alleged that at some time in her life Anne was acquainted with Katherine Parr, but there is no evidence to substantiate this, though Katherine was certainly sympathetic towards Anne Askew for she secretly shared the same Protestant views. Under questioning, Anne Askew admitted to being a Protestant, whereupon she was put in prison to wait further examination and lay there for many months. Queen Katherine would one day have reason to regret ever having heard of her.

The summer of 1545 was a sad one for several reasons. Katherine's ward and former stepdaughter, Margaret Neville, died, having appointed her 'dear sovereign mistress, the Queen's Highness' as her heir, since she was 'never able to render to her Grace sufficient thanks for the godly education and tender love and bountiful goodness which I have evermore found in her Highness'. Then, in May, Eustache Chapuys, who had been the Emperor's ambassador to the court of Henry VIII since 1529, informed the King that he was at last being recalled to Spain. Henry, saddened at the prospect of losing an old sparring partner, went immediately to the Queen and warned her of the envoy's imminent departure. The next morning, as Chapuys sat sunning himself in the palace gardens, he saw Katherine approaching, accompanied only by a few attendants. She told him that the King had told her he was coming to say goodbye, and said she was

> very sorry, on the one hand for my departure, as she had been told that I had always performed my duties well, and the King trusted me; but on the other hand she doubted not that my health would be better on the other side of the sea.

Chapuys could, she added, do more there to maintain the friendship between England and the Empire, which he had done so much to promote, and for this reason she was glad he was going. After more pleasantries, the Queen begged Chapuys to 'present to your Majesty [i.e. the Emperor] her humble service' and 'to express explicitly to you all that I had learned here of the good wishes of the King'. She then took leave of him. Chapuys left England shortly afterwards and died a few months later. In his place, the Emperor appointed a new ambassador, a Dutchman, Francis van der Delft.

Death also claimed, on 22 August, Charles Brandon, Duke of Suffolk, one of the King's oldest and closest friends, who left a widow with two young sons. The elder, Henry, aged ten, succeeded his father as duke, and was sent to join the household of Prince Edward. Here, the régime was tough. In fact, both the King's younger children were subject to a rigorously strict education, which – as Edward later recalled in his journal – was to 'satisfy the good expectation of the King's Majesty, my father'. This was having the effect of turning both Edward and Elizabeth into intellectual prodigies, who devoted almost every waking hour to books and religious exercises. When Edward was called out of the schoolroom for martial exercises, Elizabeth would practise the lute or viol, or occupy herself with needlework. It was the King's wish that Queen Katherine personally supervise the education of his children, a task for which she was eminently suited. Nor did she neglect her own intellectual pursuits. On 6 November 1545, she published – with the King's approval – a collection of prayers and meditations she had collated, under the excessively wordy title *Prayers and Meditations wherein the mind is stirred patiently to suffer all afflictions here, to set at naught the vain prosperity of this world, and always to long for the everlasting felicity: Collected out of holy works by the most virtuous and gracious Princess Katherine, Queen of England.*

The book was widely acclaimed. The universities of Oxford and Cambridge begged the Queen to become their patroness, an honour she gratefully accepted. In reply to her letter, Roger Ascham, then fellow of St John's College, Cambridge, wrote:

Write to us oftener, erudite Queen, and do not despise the term erudition, most noble lady: it is the praise of your industry, and a greater one to your talents than all the ornaments of your fortune. We rejoice vehemently in your happiness, most happy Princess, because you are learning more amidst the occupations of your dignity than many of us do in all our leisure and quiet.

The Queen's book represented a real breakthrough in an age when only the most privileged women were fortunate enough to receive an

514

education. Not even the Lady Margaret Beaufort had achieved as much, nor Katherine of Aragon. Two of the finest female minds of the century were fortunate enough to be moulded under Katherine Parr's influence – the future Elizabeth I and, later on, the Lady Jane Grey. Katherine's court was already a centre of feminine learning, and competition for places in her household was fierce. Even male scholars sought her patronage. One, Francis Goldsmith, could not find words enough to praise her, save to say that 'Her rare goodness has made every day a Sunday, a thing hitherto unheard of, especially in a royal palace.' Nor had her high rank affected Katherine's essential humanity and warmth. She was sympathetic towards poor scholars, and did her best to assist them whenever she could. Sometimes she sent them to Stoke College, of which she was patroness. Matthew Parker, who had once been chaplain to Anne Boleyn, was put in charge of them, and it was his duty to ensure also that the children of the Queen's tenants and farmers received an education 'meet for their ages and capacities'. Not surprisingly, Parker was moved to point out that all this could be done 'at no small cost and charge', but the Queen felt that no outlay was too much to pay for something she held dear. The money to fund her scholars and educational projects came entirely from her privy purse, nor would she turn away any poor scholar who came to her seeking assistance.

In the late autumn of 1545, while staying at Windsor, the King suffered some kind of attack, which laid him low for a time. On Christmas Eve, he was reported by the new Spanish ambassador to be 'so unwell that, considering his age and corpulence, fears are entertained that he will be unable to survive further attacks'. Henry was suffering terrible pain from what seems to have been venous thrombosis in his leg, and there was nothing his doctors could do to alleviate it. The Queen did her best to cheer him, and would sit by his bed and try to involve him in what he loved best, a lively dispute, preferably on some theological matter, in order to take his mind off the pain. Yet these seemingly innocent domestic interludes caused concern to the conservative faction at court, who believed that the Queen's sympathies were with the Protestant heretics and that she was being urged by the reformists to convert the King. The Seymour brothers, the widowed Duchess of Suffolk, Lady Hertford, and Lady Dudley – the last three being members of the Queen's own household – were strongly suspected of having infected Katherine with their private views, and as the King showed favour to them all, there was little anyone could do about it. Yet staunch Catholics such as Gardiner and Wriothesley believed that if the King knew the true beliefs of these people then he would deal with them as he had dealt with other Protestants. This might be one way of bringing down the Queen and removing the dangerous influence she had upon Henry VIII.

It is hardly likely that Katherine was unaware of the danger in which she stood, yet she refused to be intimidated. She knew very well that several persons in her inner circle were Protestant converts, and she also knew that heretics risked a dreadful penalty. She realised, therefore, that she should proceed with the utmost care. She had seen that the King's love could easily turn to hatred, and she did not imagine that he would react kindly to the news that his wife was a secret Protestant.

Katherine was occupied just then with a second book, *The Lamentations of a Sinner*, which was a theological discourse on faith and the proper behaviour of Christians. Its author protested, in her introduction, that she had 'but a simple zeal and earnest love to the truth, inspired of God, who promised to pour His spirit upon all flesh, which I have by the Grace of God felt in myself to be true'. The book was largely an attack on popery, and its central theme was the comparison between Moses leading the people of Israel out of Egypt and Henry VIII freeing his subjects from the iniquity of Rome. In it Katherine also put forth her views on the conduct of her own sex:

> If they be women married, they learn of St Paul to be obedient to their husbands and to keep silence in the congregation, and to learn of their husbands at home. Also, that they wear such apparel as becometh holiness and comely usage with soberness, not being accusers or detractors, nor given to much eating of delicate meats or drinking of wine; but that they touch honest things, to make the young women sober-minded, to love their husbands, to love their children, to be discreet, housewifely and good, that the Word of God may not be evil spoken of.

Such views reflected exactly the King's own opinions on the role of women within the natural order of things; he was greatly impressed by the book, and even a little jealous, taking as he did great pride in his own learning, and finding it disconcerting to wonder if a mere woman could possibly be as clever as he was.

Trouble was already brewing for Katherine. In February 1546, the King was informed that the heretic Anne Askew had implicated the Queen in a new confession. Further questioning showed that she had not even mentioned Katherine Parr, but the incident was enough to prove to Katherine that her enemies were poised to attack. There is no contemporary evidence to prove that the Queen had anything to do with Anne Askew, and the only authorities for it date from the Elizabethan era. Robert Parsons, in his *Treatise of Three Conversions of England*, published in 1603, says that Katherine received heretical books sent by Anne, and that her ladies-in-waiting, Lady Herbert, Lady Lane, Lady Tyrwhitt and others, were party to this. John Foxe, in his *Acts and Monuments*, published in 1563, tells another story, giving his source as one or more of these ladies.

Foxe gives no date for the events he describes, but if they happened at all, it must have been during the summer of 1546, probably in July. In June, the King gave his permission for Anne Askew to be examined again for heresy in the Tower. Lord Chancellor Wriothesley was in charge of the interrogation, and he saw this chance as another to incriminate the Queen. When Anne Askew proved obdurate, he ordered her to be put on the rack, and, with Sir Richard Rich, personally conducted the examination. Anne Askew later dictated an account of the proceedings, in which she testified to being questioned as to whether she knew anything about the beliefs of the ladies of the Queen's household. She replied that she knew nothing. It was put to her that she had received gifts from these ladies, but she denied it. For her obstinacy, she was racked for a long time, but bravely refused to cry out, and when she swooned with the pain, the Lord Chancellor himself brought her round, and with his own hands turned the wheels of the machine, Rich assisting. Afterwards, Anne's broken body was laid on the bare floor, and Wriothesley sat there for two hours longer, questioning her about her heresy and her suspected involvement with the royal household. All in vain. Anne refused to deny her Protestant faith, and would not or could not implicate anyone near the Queen. On 18 June, she was arraigned at the Guildhall in London, and sentenced to death. She was burned at the stake on 16 July at Smithfield, along with John Lascelles, another Protestant, he who had first alerted Cranmer to Katherine Howard's pre-marital activities. Anne died bravely and quickly: the bag of gunpowder hung about her neck by a humane executioner to facilitate a quick end exploded almost immediately.

If Katherine Parr was grieved by Anne Askew's death, she dared not show it. Like everyone else, she had been horrified to learn that the heretic had been carried to her execution on a chair as her legs were useless after the racking. Yet she kept her thoughts to herself, knowing that if it were to be discovered by her enemies that she shared Anne's views, then she too might face the flames. Foxe tells us that at this time Henry was feeling a little jaded with his marriage because the Queen had not conceived in three years; he had also heard complaints from his councillors about her interference in matters of religion. Hitherto, he had heartily approved of the strong religious bias in his wife's household. He was pleased to see Katherine spending so much time studying the Scriptures and discussing them with learned divines, and he enjoyed their debates on the subject. Now, it seemed that Katherine was going a little too far, becoming over-zealous and exhorting her husband 'that as he had to his eternal fame begun a good work in banishing the monstrous idol of Rome, so he would finish the same, purging his Church of England clean from the dregs thereof'. Where else could this lead, some were wondering, but to a Protestant state? Even Henry did not like it, and grew very stern and opinionated whenever the subject was raised. Foxe says his affection for Katherine cooled, though this is nowhere borne out by contemporary sources. Be that as it may, the Catholic party smelled a Protestant rat that was heralding the destruction of everything they held dear; until now, they had not dared to broach the matter with the King, because of his obvious love and esteem for the Queen, but now they saw their chance, and were looking daily for an opportunity to discredit her in Henry's eyes. Gardiner knew, better than most, that Henry hated being contradicted in any argument. In the past it had galled the Bishop to see the King being corrected by his wife, but now he perceived that Henry himself was becoming irritated with her arguments. Encroaching infirmity made him peevish and impatient; he ceased making his daily visits to his wife's apartments, and it was left to Katherine to decide whether or not to brave his black moods and go and sit with him after dinner or supper. At these times, her enthusiasm more often than not got the better of her, and she persisted in urging the King to carry his reforms still further.

The day came when Henry had had enough and rudely cut short what the Queen was saying and changed the subject, which left Katherine somewhat amazed. However, once the conversation had been steered to less contentious matters, Henry was his old self again 'with gentle words and loving countenance'. When it was time for the Queen to leave, he said, 'Farewell, Sweetheart', and Katherine left the room, little knowing that her enemies were about to pounce.

Bishop Gardiner had been within earshot of that conversation, and he seized his chance when the King began to grumble about her behaviour. 'A good hearing it is, when women become such clerks, and much to my comfort to come in mine old age to be taught by my wife!' he fumed. The Bishop soothed his sovereign's vanity by replying that 'his Majesty excelled the princes of that and every other age, as well as all the professed doctors of divinity', and then poured oil on troubled waters by saying that

it was unseemly for any of his subjects to argue with him so malapertly as the Queen had just done; that it was grievous for any of his Councillors to hear it done, since those who were so bold in words would not scruple to proceed to acts of disobedience.

He added significantly that he

could make great discoveries if he were not deterred by the Queen's powerful faction. Besides this, the religion by the Queen maintained did not only dissolve the politic government of princes, but also taught the people that all things ought to be in common.

In fact, according to Foxe, Gardiner spared no efforts in persuading the King 'that his Majesty should easily perceive how perilous a matter it is to cherish a serpent within his own bosom', and reminded him that 'the greatest subjects in the land, defending those arguments that she did defend, had by law deserved death. For his part, he would not speak his knowledge in the Queen's case,' because to do so might bring about his own destruction 'through her and her faction', unless the King agreed to give him his protection.

Henry was incredulous at the Bishop's words, but his suspicious nature allowed him to believe that the matter was indeed a serious one, otherwise Gardiner would never have dared to be outspoken. In one clever stroke, the Bishop had managed to convince him that his wife was at the centre of a heretical conspiracy to bring down traditional forms of government, and that she was supported by many influential people at court. This was enough to set all the alarm bells ringing in the King's head, and he questioned Gardiner closely on the matter, remaining closeted with him for some time. When they parted, the triumphant Bishop came away with the knowledge that Henry had consented to articles being drawn up against the Queen, with a view to putting her on trial for her life, 'which the King pretended to be fully resolved to spare'. Gardiner was to provide the proof that was needed to support his accusations.

Foxe seems to be saying here that Henry was playing a double game, and it does seem that he was reserving his judgement until all was made clear. Yet the peril in which the Queen and her ladies now stood was very real, and this was made obvious to them when the Council ordered the arrests of Lady Herbert, Katherine's sister, Lady Lane and Lady Tyrwhitt, her three favourite ladies-in-waiting. They were interrogated about the books they had, and whether the Queen kept forbidden reading matter in her closet, and their coffers were searched in the hope that proof of the Queen's heresy might be discovered. Then they were released. The King knew all this, and seemed content for it to be done.

Henry was then at Whitehall Palace with the court. Because of his health, he did not often leave his rooms, and only a few privileged members of the Privy Council were allowed access to him. Through them, he let it be known that he was agreeable to a warrant being drawn up for the Queen's arrest, should there be any suspicion of heresy. Katherine guessed nothing of this, and heedlessly continued to engage the King in religious debates. He allowed her to do this, for he was now on the alert for a sinister meaning to her arguments, and was carefully weighing every word she said. It appears he was not yet completely convinced of her guilt, and late one night, when Katherine had gone, he confided all his suspicions to his physician, Dr Thomas Wendy, who had replaced Dr Butts on the latter's death in November 1545. Henry pretended 'he intended no longer to be troubled with such a doctress as she was,' and told the Doctor what was afoot, swearing him to secrecy.

When a warrant for Katherine Parr's arrest was drawn up, the King signed it, and it was entrusted to an unnamed member of the Privy Council who fortuitously dropped it. A servant loyal to the Queen found it and brought it straight to her, and Katherine found herself confronting her doom. There was the King's signature: there could be no mistake. Her reaction was instantaneous and dramatic, her agony of mind manifesting itself in tears and hysterical screaming, which was 'lamentable to see', as her ladies remembered many years later. She was distraught with terror, recalling the fate of Anne Boleyn and Katherine Howard and realising that, on a charge of heresy, her death would be much more horrible than theirs. In her grief and fear, she took to her bed, shaking and wailing. Her cries could be heard throughout the palace, and even penetrated the King's apartments. Henry, little realising what was the matter, sent Dr Wendy and other physicians to her to try and calm her down. Wendy guessed that the Queen had somehow found out what was afoot, and sent the other doctors away. He then told her what he knew and warned her that Gardiner and Wriothesley were plotting her downfall; she should 'conform herself to the King's mind', he advised, then she might find him 'favourable unto her'.

Wendy's words afforded the Queen little comfort. Still she lay, weeping and crying, her self-control shattered. Eventually, the King, learning of her 'dangerous state', went to her himself. At the sight of him, Katherine calmed down a little, and managed to say that she feared he had grown displeased with her and utterly forsaken her. She was so obviously sincere in her grief that Henry was deeply touched and, 'like a loving husband, with comfortable words so refreshed her careful mind that she began somewhat to recover'. Henry stayed with her an hour, and when he had gone, Katherine made up her mind to cease interfering in matters of religion and to forbid her ladies to dabble in heresy. She ordered them to get rid of any forbidden books in their possession, and made it clear that from now on her chief priority was to conform to her husband's wishes.

That night, accompanied only by her sister and Lady Lane, who carried a candle before her, she made her way to the King's bedchamber, where she found Henry chatting with his gentlemen. When he saw Katherine, he welcomed her courteously, and after a while he brought up the subject of religion, 'seeming desirous to be resolved by the Queen of certain doubts'. Katherine, guessing what game he was playing, gave meek and dutiful answers, saying, 'So God hath appointed you, as Supreme Head of us all, and of you, next unto God, will I ever learn.' But Henry was not that easily mollified. 'Not so, by St Mary!' he cried. 'Ye are become a doctor, Kate, to instruct us, as oftentime we have seen, and not to be instructed or directed by us.' Katherine protested her meaning had been mistaken, 'for I have always held it preposterous for a woman to instruct her lord'. If she had ever differed with him on religion, she went on, it was only for her own information, and also because she realised that talking helped to

> pass away the pain and weariness of your present infirmity, which encouraged me in this boldness, in the hope of profiting withal by your Majesty's learned discourse. I am but a woman, with all the imperfections natural to the weakness of my sex; therefore in all matters of doubt and difficulty I must refer myself to your Majesty's better judgement, as to my lord and head.

This was a masterful speech, and a triumph of diplomacy, and the King was deeply impressed – if not a little relieved – by it. 'Is it so, sweetheart?' he replied. 'And tended your arguments to no worse end? Then we are perfect friends, as ever at any time heretofore.' Katherine's sense of relief may be imagined: a crisis had been averted and the King was once more her loving husband. Again she sat beside him as he took her in his arms and kissed her before everyone present; then he told her it did him more good to hear those words from her own mouth than if he had heard news of £100,000 coming his way. Never again, he promised, would he doubt her. It was late in the night when he finally gave her leave to depart, and when she had gone he praised her highly to his gentlemen.

Henry was shrewd enough to guess why Gardiner and his party wanted the Queen out of the way, and had known all along what game the Bishop was playing. Now that he had ample proof of the Queen's loyalty, he was very much looking forward to discountenancing them. Katherine's servant had been careful to replace the warrant for the Queen's arrest where she had found it; it was quickly retrieved by the councillor, and on the afternoon following the royal couple's reconciliation, Lord Chancellor Wriothesley prepared to use it, knowing nothing of the events of the previous night.

On that afternoon, the King made sure that the Queen joined him to take the air in the palace gardens, where he was 'as pleasant as ever he was in all his life'. Suddenly, in the midst of their laughter, the Lord Chancellor arrived, with forty of the King's guards at his heels, intending to escort the Queen to the Tower with her three ladies, who were also present. Wriothesley was nonplussed at finding his master and mistress so happily engaged, then the King, looking very stern, got up and walked off a little way, calling his Chancellor after him. Wriothesley fell to his knees and began to explain why he was there, but he was brutally cut short by Henry, who shouted 'Knave! Arrant knave! Beast! Fool!', and ordered him out of his presence. Everyone stared at the discomfited Chancellor as he and his men scuttled away. Henry strode back to the Queen; she could see he was in a fury, although he was struggling to 'put on a merry countenance', and innocently enquired what was wrong, saying charitably that she would be a suitor for the Lord Chancellor, 'as she deemed his fault was occasioned by some mistake'. To which her husband replied, 'Ah, poor soul, thou little knoweth Kate how little he deserveth this grace at thy hands. On my word, sweetheart, he hath been to thee a very knave, so let him go.' Katherine wisely held her peace. She knew very well what Wriothesley had come for, and that she had had a lucky escape.

She had learned her lesson and would from then on act the meek and dutiful wife. There would be no breath of heresy in her household, and she would comport herself with greater circumspection than ever, giving her enemies no room for criticism. She would confine herself to corresponding with men of letters such as Roger Ascham, pursuing her intellectual interests and charities, and overseeing the education of her stepchildren. Prince Edward wrote to her that August, saying that her letters and the 'excellence of your genius' made him sick of his own writing: 'But then I think how kind your nature is, and that whatever proceeds from a good mind will be acceptable, and so I write you this letter.' It seemed an age since he had seen her, he added.

August was a busy month for Katherine. On the 24th, Claude d'Annebaut, Admiral of France, visited the court as a consequence of a new treaty of peace between Henry VIII and Francis I. He was entertained with the usual banquets and hunting forays; in the evenings, rich masques were staged for his pleasure and that of Queen Katherine and her ladies, after which there was dancing in two new banqueting houses hung with rich tapestries and furnished with court cupboards containing gold plate set with precious stones.

After the Admiral had returned to France, the King and Queen went on a short progress, even though the King's health was now noticeably failing. His leg was paining him more than ever and, although he preferred to make light of his suffering, it showed in his face. He could no longer walk up or down stairs, and a mechanical hoist was needed to assist him. Norfolk told van der Delft that the King 'could not long endure'. Soon, he could barely walk at all, and an order was given for two chairs (called trams), covered in tawny velvet, 'for the King's Majesty to sit in to be carried to and from in his galleries and chambers'. His councillors believed his illness was incurable and would soon kill him, and were already plotting, each and every one, to gain control of the Prince.

Henry himself was aware that his end could not be far off, and he now made plans for the inevitable regency that would follow his death, since his heir was only nine years old. He was determined to exclude all foreign influence from the regency Council, retaining to the end his mistrust of aliens. At the same time, he was perceptive enough to realise that the general trend was towards a radical reform of the Church, and he showed himself inclined to favour those lords who supported it. As for the Prince, there was little doubt in anyone's mind that he would come to embrace the Protestant faith, and Henry wisely accepted that there was little he could do to stem the tide in this respect. Perhaps some of Katherine's arguments had taken root in his mind. He may well have sensed that his own era was dying and with it the last vestiges of medievalism: a new age was dawning, and it was his duty to lay a solid foundation for it.

But he was not dead yet; there still remained some life in that diseased body. The King's thoughts turned to his son, who had always been the chief delight in his life; now he sent the boy some presents, chains, rings, jewelled buttons, and other valuables, which prompted a stiff little note of thanks from the child.

> You grant me all these [wrote Edward], not that I should be proud and think too much of myself, but that you might urge me to the pursuit of all true virtues and piety, and adorn and furnish me with all the accomplishments which are fitting a Prince.

December arrived. Despite the King's illness, a plot to get rid of the Queen and replace her with the King's daughter-in-law, the Duchess of Richmond (daughter of the impeccably Catholic Duke of Norfolk) was uncovered. It seems to have originated with her brother, the Earl of Surrey, who had instructed her on how to win the King's favour, 'that she might rule as others had done'. On being questioned, the Duchess managed to incriminate not only her brother but also her father the Duke. On 12 December, both men were arrested on a charge of high treason and taken to the Tower. The King was in no mood to listen to pleas for mercy; since the fall of Katherine Howard he had distrusted Norfolk, and welcomed this opportunity to rid himself of him: he had suffered enough at the hands of the Howards. They could stew in the Tower until after Christmas, then he would deal with them as they deserved.

On Christmas Eve, Henry prorogued Parliament for the last time, and harangued both Houses on their attitude to religion:

> Charity and concord is not amongst you, but discord and dissension beareth rule in every place. I am very sorry to hear how unreverently that most precious jewel, the Word of God, is disputed, rhymed, sung and jangled in every ale-house and tavern. And yet I am even as much sorry that the readers of the same follow it so faintly and so coldly!

Sir John Mason said afterwards that the King had spoken 'so kingly, so rather fatherly, that many of his hearers were overcome and shed tears'. It was obvious to everyone present that this would be the King's last public speech. A Greek visitor to England in the train of the Spanish ambassador reported that the English were 'wonderfully well affected' towards their monarch; they would hear nothing disrespectful about him, and the most binding oaths were sworn on his life. He was already a legend in his own lifetime.

The court was closed to all but the Privy Council and some gentlemen of the privy chamber that Christmas, a sure indication that the King was now in a critical condition. The Queen and the Lady Mary were the only members of his family in attendance. Two days after Christmas the Spanish ambassador told the Emperor that Henry's physicians were despairing of doing anything to help their royal patient, who was 'in great danger' and 'very ill'. His leg was agony, and he was running a high temperature. Reports that he had died already were circulating in the capital.

On 30 December, Henry dictated his will. He left his kingdom and his crown to Prince Edward, and after him to any posthumous heirs that 'our entirely beloved wife Queen Katherine' might bear him. Failing those, the succession should pass to the Lady Mary and her heirs, then to the Lady Elizabeth and hers, and finally to the heirs of the King's late sister Mary, Duchess of Suffolk. His antagonism towards the Scots had ensured that he pass over the heirs of his elder sister Margaret Tudor. The King was adamant: Mary of Scotland should never rule England unless it was as Edward's consort.

With the succession provided for, Henry now made provision for his widow. As token of his appreciation of 'the great love, obedience, chastity of life and wisdom being in our wife and Queen', he bequeathed to her £3,000 in plate, jewels and household goods for the term of her life. She could also help herself to as many of the King's clothes as she pleased, and they were worth a considerable sum. She would, in addition, receive £1,000 in cash and her dower and jointure, as decided by Parliament. Katherine would find herself a very rich widow indeed when the time came.

Henry then expressed his desire to be buried beside the body of 'our true and loving wife, Queen Jane' in the choir of St George's Chapel, Windsor, and left instructions for the raising of an 'honourable tomb' which would be surmounted by effigies of Henry and Jane, fashioned 'as if sweetly sleeping'.

He rallied a little after making his will, and was well enough to leave Greenwich and travel with the Queen to London on 3 January 1547. When they were settled in Whitehall Palace, Katherine did her best to carry on as normally as possible, and tried to counteract rumours that the King was dead or dying. At New Year, she had sent her stepson portraits of Henry and herself, and on 10 January he wrote to thank her, addressing the letter to his most 'illustrious Queen and dearest mother'. He had no idea that his father was so ill, and the King and Queen were anxious to spare him the heavy knowledge that the burden of kingship would soon be his.

On 7 January 1547, an Act of Attainder against Norfolk and Surrey was passed by Parliament. Surrey was tried at the Guildhall six days later, and condemned to death. He was executed on 19 January on Tower Hill, his being the last blood to be shed on the scaffold in Henry VIII's reign. Norfolk remained in the Tower, his fate hanging in the balance, while the King fought his last struggle with mortality. On 23 January, he announced the names of those men he had appointed to serve on the regency Council: Hertford was to be Lord Protector during Edward's minority, assisted by Cranmer, John Dudley, now Lord Lisle, Lord Chancellor Wriothesley, and others including the Queen's brother, the Earl of Essex, all of whom were known to be favourable to the cause of reform. When, however, someone suggested that Sir Thomas Seymour be one of their number, Henry cried out, 'No! No!', even though his breath was failing him. He knew Sir Thomas to be a self-seeker and a scoundrel, seeing clearly through the easy charm that so deceived others, and, of course, he had other, more personal reasons for resenting the man.

What killed Henry VIII was probably a clot detaching itself from the thrombosed vein in his leg, and causing a pulmonary embolism. On 26 January, he realised he was failing fast, and summoned his wife to his bedside. Then (according to William Thomas, who wrote *The Pilgrim: A Dialogue on the Life and Actions of King Henry the Eighth* that same month) he thanked God that, 'amongst all the happy successes of his reign' and 'after so many changes, his glorious chance hath brought him to die in the arms of so faithful a spouse'. Katherine was understandably overcome with emotion, for she had become attached to this complex man who was her husband, and whom she had so unwillingly married. In spite of his appalling matrimonial history, he had on the whole been very kind and generous to her, and she had no reason to doubt the sincerity of his affection for her. Now it was time to say farewell, and she began to weep. Henry spoke gently to her, saying, 'It is God's will that we should part,' then he gestured in the direction of the lords of the Council who were waiting near his bed and said:

> I order all these gentlemen to treat you as if I were living still, and if it should be your pleasure to marry again, I order that you shall have £7,000 for your service as long as you live, and all your jewels and ornaments.

At this, Katherine broke down completely, and could not answer. Henry ordered her out of the room, not wishing to witness or prolong her distress.

On the following morning, the King saw his confessor, received Holy Communion, and commended his soul to God. He saw his daughter Mary and made her promise to be a kind and loving mother to her brother, whom he would leave as 'a little helpless child'. Mary, in floods of tears, begged him not to leave her an orphan so soon, but the King said farewell and dismissed her. On that same day, a warrant was drawn up for the execution of the Duke of Norfolk, but Henry was still incapable of signing it. Norfolk would, as a result, languish for six years in the Tower, before being released to serve yet another Tudor sovereign.

Old rivalries died hard. The King sent a message to Francis I, rumoured to be dying of syphilis – he died a month later – bidding him remember that he too was mortal. Yet Henry himself was loath to hear any mention of death, and as it was high treason to mention the death of the King, those about him were reluctant to advise him to prepare his soul for its last journey. At length, Sir Anthony Denny, one of the King's most trusted advisers, ventured to tell him that 'in man's judgement, he was not like to live', and urged him to make ready his soul for death: 'All human aid was now vain, and it was meet for him to review his past life and seek for God's mercy through Christ.' The King listened meekly, then replied, 'After the judges have passed sentence on a criminal, there is no more need to trouble him. Therefore begone.' At this, the physicians withdrew from the room. Henry spoke again: 'The mercy of Christ could pardon all my sins, though they were greater than they be.' His advisers and attendants said they doubted that so great a man could have any sins on his conscience, but Henry shook his head feebly. He refused Sir Anthony Denny's offer to send for someone to hear his final confession and administer extreme unction, saying he would have 'only Cranmer, but he not yet'. Presently, he dozed off.

Shortly after midnight, the King woke and asked for his Archbishop, and a messenger was dispatched to Lambeth. Meanwhile Henry grew weaker, before heaving a sigh and whispering, 'All is lost.' But then, just in time, Cranmer arrived. Henry was now beyond speech, and the Archbishop, speaking gently, 'desired him to give him some token that he put his trust in God, through Jesus Christ'. The King's hand lay in his, and Cranmer felt him wring it hard, proof that his master 'trusted in the Lord'.

The minutes ticked by as everyone in the room silently knelt in prayer. At two o'clock in the morning, on 28 January 1547, King Henry VIII 'yielded his spirit to Almighty God and departed this world'. He was fifty-five.

It was the end of an era. England was now to be ruled by King Edward VI, a child of nine, although few as yet knew it. The old King's death was not announced for three days, although Queen Katherine, now Queen Dowager, was told of it immediately. She seems to have gone into seclusion for a while to mourn her husband, for there is no mention of her activities at this time in contemporary sources, nor did she attend the King's funeral, but that was for reasons of etiquette – women did not attend the funerals of kings. The new King was at Hertford Castle when his uncle, the Lord Protector, arrived on 30 January to take him to Enfield, where he found his sister Elizabeth waiting for him. The two children were then informed of their father's death, at which news they wept bitterly and could not be consoled. However, when Edward had calmed down, Hertford paid homage to him as his new sovereign lord, the other lords of the Council following suit. Then the little boy was brought to London, where, on 31 January, he was proclaimed king, while the Lord

Chancellor, with tears in his eyes, informed both Houses of Parliament of the death of Henry VIII. Early in February, the Lord Protector ordered the Council to send a messenger to Anne of Cleves to break the news to her.

On 14 February, the body of the late King began its last journey, conveyed in a coffin on a rich chariot covered with a pall of cloth of gold. Resting on the coffin was a wax effigy of the King dressed in velvet adorned with precious stones. The cortège was escorted by the lords of the Council, followed by a contingent of the King's guard. Behind the hearse trotted the King's riderless charger. Banners were carried aloft in the procession, but only two of the King's six wives were represented: Jane Seymour and Katherine Parr. Henry had not considered his other marriages worthy of commemoration.

That night, the King's body rested in the ruined chapel of Syon Abbey. There the lead coffin, weakened by the motion of the carriage, burst open, and liquid matter from the body seeped on to the church pavement. A dog was with the plumbers who came the next morning to repair the coffin, and it was seen to lick up the blood from the floor, just as Friar Peto had predicted back in 1532: that if the King cast off Katherine of Aragon and married Anne Boleyn, he should be as Ahab, and the dogs would lick his blood. Those who were witnesses to this macabre scene were understandably shaken by it, for the prophecy was well known and it was a superstitious age.

Two days later, Henry VIII's coffin was carried into St George's Chapel, Windsor, where a vast concourse of black-clad mourners awaited it. There in the choir lay the open vault containing the coffin of Queen Jane. Her husband's body was laid beside her amid 'heavy and dolorous lamentation'. Gardiner preached the funeral sermon, taking as his text 'Blessed are the dead who die in the Lord'; he spoke at length on the 'loss which both high and low have sustained in the death of so good and gracious a King'. As Sir Anthony Browne said afterwards, 'there was no need to pray for him, since he was surely in Heaven.'

At the end of the service, the officers of the late King's household broke their staves over their heads and cast them after the coffin into the vault 'with exceeding sorrow and heaviness, and not without grievous sighs or tears'. Thus did they signify the termination of their allegiance and service. Then the herald cried, '*Le roi est mort! Vive le roi!*'

Far away, the young King shed bitter tears. 'This, however, consoles us,' he wrote, 'that he is now in Heaven, and that he hath gone out of this miserable world into happy and everlasting blessedness.'

It would be true to say that Henry's contemporaries saw him as something more than human. One called him 'the greatest man in the world', another 'the rarest man that lived in his time'. He certainly possessed exceptional qualities of leadership and a charismatic personality. No king of England has enjoyed such posthumous publicity as he, and no king before him or after him ever held such absolute power, nor commanded such respect and obedience. This is the measure of the man.

In his capacity as a husband Henry's worst failings were glaringly obvious. The deepest, most abiding passion in his life was for Anne Boleyn, yet it was a destructive one, souring with the familiarity of marriage and leaving the King embittered. Her death was contrived for political reasons rather than emotional ones, and Henry did not scruple to get rid of her for the sake of expediency. It is possible to feel sympathy for him after his discovery of Katherine Howard's promiscuity, yet we must remember that his sorrow did not prevent him from executing an ignorant seventeen-year-old girl as a traitor. His marriages to Katherine of Aragon and Anne of Cleves were both annulled, and Katherine was treated with appalling cruelty.

The guiding motive behind his treatment, or ill-treatment, of these four of his wives was the King's very real need for a male heir, something that was always at the forefront of his mind. It should be remembered, in his favour, that Katherine Parr showed a very genuine grief at his death, and that – apart from one occasion, when it appears that Henry kept an open mind about Katherine's activities until proof was available – they were extremely contented together, as their letters prove. Nor did Jane Seymour find Henry less than a loving, if overbearing, husband. What turned the King into the ruthless tyrant of latter years was to some extent Katherine of Aragon's stubbornness and Anne Boleyn's ambition. Taking into account the ever-present problem of the succession, it is impossible to dismiss Henry VIII as the cruel lecher of popular legend who changed wives whenever it pleased him.

His subjects certainly did not view him in that light. He never lost their affection, even during his worst excesses, nor did he ever cease to exercise that charm and common touch that came so easily to his dynasty. Out of the ruins of his marriages and the monasteries, he founded a new church and corrected abuses within it, a policy which certainly found favour with the English in the long run. Although he was a Catholic to the last and rigorous in stamping out heresy, he had the foresight to realise that religious developments in England would lead eventually to a Protestant state – there is proof of this in his choice of the men who were to sit on the regency Council. When he died, he was regarded by his subjects as 'King, Emperor and Pope in his own dominions' and as the 'father and nurse' of his people. For all his faults, he would be remembered with love by them.

17
Under the planets at Chelsea

Katherine Parr was not given a place on the regency Council by Henry VIII. He had foreseen that, being a very rich, attractive, royal widow, the chances were that she would marry again within a short while, and that the advent of a new husband upon the scene might well create discord, especially if – as Henry suspected – he was called Thomas Seymour. Added to this, she was a woman, and Henry had never approved of female rulers. Indeed, Katherine had never sought power, and she had very little to complain about. She was well provided for and, at nearly thirty-five, free to order her life as she pleased. If she remarried, she could now choose for herself, and there was, perhaps, still the possibility of her having children of her own, something she had always desired.

The only thing that pained her was that the Council quickly made it very clear that the young King was under its exclusive control; this meant that Edward was not allowed to see either his stepmother or his stepsisters, his guardians being jealous of any outside influences upon him. The boy missed their company, and consoled himself by corresponding with them, yet he was upset when he learned in early February that the Queen Dowager was planning to leave the court and retire to the Old Manor at Chelsea, one of his father's properties. 'Farewell, venerated Queen,' he wrote, knowing he would rarely see his stepmother in the future.

Very early on in the new reign, it was made clear that the sympathies of the Lord Protector and the Council were with the

533

Protestants, which meant that people like Katherine Parr could now practise the reformed faith openly, without fear of persecution from the government. The King, who had been educated by scholars such as John Cheke and others, who were committed if secret Lutherans, had himself already embraced the Protestant religion, and would in time become one of its most fervent exponents. Moreover, Archbishop Cranmer – who as long ago as the 1530s had been a closet Lutheran – was still Primate of the Church of England. It would only be a matter of time before the heresy laws were repealed; in fact, during Edward's reign, it would be the English Catholics who suffered persecution, the reformist party having finally gained ascendancy.

On the day of the late King's funeral, the Lord Protector conferred patents of nobility upon himself and his fellow councillors. He himself became Duke of Somerset, a title once borne by the King's Beaufort forbears, and lastly by Henry VIII's infant brother Edmund. William Parr was created Marquess of Northampton, and Wriothesley was made Earl of Southampton. Sir Thomas Seymour was back in England and able to appear at court without fear of banishment on yet another diplomatic mission. Perhaps to compensate for his exclusion from the regency Council, his brother had him elevated to the peerage as Baron Seymour of Sudeley Castle in the county of Gloucestershire, and on the next day confirmed him in his post as Lord High Admiral for life, at the same time admitting him to the Order of the Garter.

Lord Sudeley was then about forty years old, good looking, charming, and very popular. Katherine Parr had fallen victim to his looks and dashing personality before her marriage to the King, and she and Seymour had even discussed marriage at that time. During her years as queen Katherine had resolutely put Seymour out of her mind and the Admiral had played his part, though it seems that he quickly forgot about Katherine, being a rather shallow man. His contemporary and Edward VI's biographer, Sir John Hayward, described him as 'fierce in courage, courtly in fashion, in personage stately and in voice magnificent', but, he added, he was 'somewhat empty in matter'.

Lord Sudeley found it galling to be denied what he considered to be his rightful place on the regency Council; after all, he was the

King's uncle, and his brother was Lord Protector. He had also served his country both as a diplomat and on the high seas, and he was determined to get on the Council, and perhaps even supplant his brother, of whom he was very jealous. To do that, he needed power and he needed money, and the best way to gain both was by an influential marriage. With this in mind, Seymour went straight to the top. He did not at first renew his suit to Katherine Parr: she was, after all, only the late King's widow, and completely lacking in influence in a court from which she was about to depart. Real power would come with a marriage to one of the King's sisters, who were next in line of succession, a move which might, in time, bring Lord Sudeley a crown.

The Lady Mary was a staunch Catholic, so he passed her over. That left the Lady Elizabeth. She had a proud and disdainful manner which sometimes eclipsed the beauty of her red-gold hair and the flashing eyes she had inherited from her mother, yet she also had her mother's capacity for flirtation and her attraction for men, and even at thirteen, the Admiral thought her eminently desirable. In February, he began to court her, declaring his affection in flattering letters, and begging to know 'whether I am to be the most happy or the most miserable of men'.

Elizabeth did not reply at once, having a shrewd idea of what lay behind the Admiral's letters. All the same, it was flattering for a young girl to be the object of attention from such a handsome and sought-after man. Yet Elizabeth was not any young girl, and she had to have the Council's permission if she wished to marry; it was unlikely to be granted in this case. Consequently, she turned down Seymour's proposal, saying 'neither my age nor my inclination allows me to think of marriage', and that she needed at least two years to get over the loss of her father before contemplating it. She went on:

Permit me, my Lord Admiral, to tell you frankly that, though I decline the happiness of becoming your wife, I shall never cease to interest myself in all that can crown your merit with glory, and shall ever feel the greatest pleasure in being your servant and good friend.

The Admiral was crestfallen at her refusal, which had the effect of making her seem all the more desirable, but he had to recognise the fact that she was not his for the taking. It was at this point that he turned his attentions once more to Katherine Parr.

At the beginning of March the Dowager Queen was about to leave the court for Chelsea when she realised that her former lover was eager to renew their relationship. This knowledge was more than welcome to her, for she was still strongly attracted to Seymour and eager to share what remained of her youth with him. Thus their courtship proceeded, although it had, of necessity, to be conducted in secret in case the Council found out and forbade its continuance. Katherine was officially mourning Henry VIII, and could not with honour contemplate remarriage in the near future, yet so happy was she at this latest turn of events that, just before she left court, she could not resist confiding her feelings for the Admiral to her friend, Lady Paget, who replied, 'All I wish you, Madam, is that he should become your husband.' Katherine answered that she wished 'it had been her fate to have him for a husband, but God hath so placed her that any lowering of her condition would be a reproach to her'. These doubts soon receded, however, under the force of Seymour's charm, and when, that March, he proposed marriage, Katherine gladly accepted, for she was now, for the first time in her life, deeply in love. She stipulated that a suitable period of mourning must elapse before the wedding could take place, but the Admiral overruled her, urging her to marry him in secret at once. And at that, sensible, virtuous, but all-too-human Katherine Parr seized what she saw as her last chance of happiness with a man she loved; she was not, after all, so young that she could afford to waste time, and she could battle no longer with the strong emotions that were overwhelming her. Lord Sudeley was delighted; if he could not aspire to a crown, he would at least be rich, and the husband of the first lady at court accorded precedence over nearly everyone else. He would have money, prestige and a devoted wife. What more could a man want?

There were, however, obstacles: it was unlikely that the Council would approve of his marriage to the Dowager Queen, and more than probable that it would withhold its consent, if only because there might be reason to dispute the paternity of any child born to the Queen so soon after her late husband's death, which would put the succession in jeopardy. Henry VIII had, after all, only been dead for six weeks. The Admiral did not care about technicalities, and he decided to bypass the Council and go straight to the young King for permission to marry. Edward was fond of his colourful Uncle Thomas, and might well agree, and the Admiral considered it unlikely that the Council would gainsay him. In this, he showed considerable lack of judgement.

Edward, unfortunately, was kept well guarded, and not allowed to see anyone unless the Council had first sanctioned it. Sudeley therefore bribed one of the royal servants, John Fowler – a man known to be an admirer of the Queen, and trustworthy – to sound Edward out on 'whom he would have to be my wife'. Fowler saw the King later that night, and said he marvelled that the Lord Admiral was not yet married; was the King content that he should marry? 'Yea, very well,' replied Edward. Then said Fowler, 'Whom would your Grace like him to marry?' The boy considered for a minute. 'My Lady Anne of Cleves!' he piped up, but then he thought again. 'I would he married my sister Mary, to turn her opinions.' (Edward deplored Mary's adherence to Catholicism.) That was not, of course, the answer that Fowler had been hoping for, or the Admiral. But the Admiral was well aware that the Council kept the young King chronically short of money, and so he sent Fowler back the next night, well supplied with gold coins, to ask Edward 'if he should be contented I should marry the Queen'. To the Admiral's delight, Edward did not hesitate to signify his approval and consent: he was fond of his stepmother and his uncle, and did not understand the political motive behind Sudeley's proposal.

It was at this time that the Queen moved to the Old Manor House at Chelsea, which occupied an extensive site at the eastern end of what is now Cheyne Walk. It had been built by Henry VIII in 1536–7 for Jane Seymour, although she never lived there. Of red brick, it bore some resemblance to St James's Palace, which was built around the same time, although it was only two storeys in height and was built around two quadrangles. It was quite a large house, more than adequate for a queen dowager, with its three halls, three parlours, three kitchens, three drawing-rooms, seventeen chambers, four closets, three cellars, a larder, a large staircase, summer rooms (presumably without fireplaces or open on one side), and nine other

537

rooms. It had casement windows and a water supply brought by a conduit from Kensington, and its most attractive feature was its five acres of beautiful gardens intersected by privet hedges and containing a fishpond and a variety of trees: cherry, peach, damson and nut. There were also 200 damask rose bushes.

Katherine was at Chelsea when the Admiral called to inform her of the King's consent to their marriage. Now that she was away from the public arena of the court, it would be easier to make secret preparations for her wedding, which she hoped would take place as soon as possible. Yet, while Katherine was thus happily preoccupied Sudeley's mind was on more contentious issues. He had already proved to himself that it was better to bypass the Council and go direct to the young King to get what he wanted, and he saw no reason why he should not capitalise further on Edward's admiration and affection for him. He even foresaw the day when he might ultimately rule through the King, and planned to achieve this by providing Edward with a consort who had been trained to be sympathetic to the Admiral's interests. It did not matter that the Council was already contemplating a marriage between Edward and Elisabeth of France, daughter of the new French King, Henry II; the Admiral thought he had a better candidate, one to whom Edward was close, and of whom he would thoroughly approve, for, whereas the Princess Elisabeth was a Roman Catholic, this girl was already a committed Protestant. Her name was the Lady Jane Grey, and she was the eldest daughter of the Marquess of Dorset by Henry VIII's niece, Frances Brandon, daughter of Mary Tudor and the Duke of Suffolk. Jane was almost the same age as Edward, having been born in the same month; she had been named after his mother, Jane Seymour. Her parents had arranged for her to receive a very thorough academic education from Protestant tutors, which had already developed her formidable intellect far beyond what was normal for a child of her years. As a result, she was precocious, strong willed and an intellectual snob, as well as being completely dedicated to Protestantism. Notwithstanding this, her parents demanded still more of her, and beat her when she did not come up to their expectations. As a result, her home life was desperately unhappy, and the only solace she knew was in the hours she spent with her tutors.

538

It was the Admiral's plan to make Jane his ward and have her join the household at Chelsea after his marriage so that the Queen could supervise her education. Sudeley saw no reason why Lord Dorset should refuse such an offer; indeed, any father with ambitions for his child would be glad of it, with its advantage of an education under the auspices of one of the most erudite women of the age, and its prospects of a good marriage for Jane when the time came – a royal one, if the Admiral had his way. Yet when Lord Sudeley's man, William Harrington, broached the matter with Lord Dorset at the latter's house at Bradgate in Leicestershire, the Marquess was unimpressed, even when informed that the Admiral hoped to match his daughter with the King. He wanted to know who would look after the child, since he had not been let into the secret of the Admiral's impending marriage, and could not see how Lord Sudeley was placed to arrange a match between the King and Jane when he was not even on the regency Council. To Dorset, it seemed a futile plan at best, and he privately doubted whether the Admiral's intentions were honourable, so he withheld his permission, and Jane stayed at home.

The Admiral was disappointed, but not unduly so, foreseeing that in time to come fathers would be queuing up to place their daughters in the household of the Queen Dowager, especially when it was known that her husband enjoyed the special favour of the King. He could afford to wait.

The Queen, meanwhile, was wondering how the news of her marriage would be received at court, and by her stepchildren. Edward would be glad for her, she knew, and perhaps Elizabeth, but in all likelihood Mary would disapprove, thinking it accomplished in indecent haste and disrespectful to her father's memory. Mary kept away from the court nowadays; there was no place for her there, and she preferred to live in the country where there was no one to censure her for following what she believed to be the true faith. At this time, she was arranging with the Duchess of Somerset, who had once served Katherine of Aragon, to reward those servants of her mother who were still living, thus fulfilling a desire she had cherished for eleven years.

Katherine Parr was still officially in mourning for the late King when she married the Lord Admiral some time before the end of

April, probably at Chelsea. Very few knew of it, for it was conducted with such secrecy that it is impossible to determine a date. Sir Nicholas Throckmorton, the Queen's cousin, may have been a witness. The King learned of the marriage in May, for he recorded it then in his journal, but the world at large did not hear of it until it was already several weeks old. Thus Katherine Parr was married for the fourth time, making her England's most married Queen. Yet, unlike her previous marriages, this was her own choice, and for a time at least she knew great happiness, unworried by the prospect of inevitable censure from the outside world. 'If the Duke [of Somerset] and the Duchess do not like the marriage, it will be of no consequence,' she told her husband, knowing that her sister-in-law would be jealous, and that it would anger the proud Duchess to have the wife of her husband's younger brother taking precedence over her, especially when the Duchess's husband was Lord Protector of England. Somerset himself was a mild and rational man and, although he would be much displeased to learn of his brother's marriage, he would in time have come to accept it with good grace had it not been for his wife, who never ceased urging him to punish the couple for their temerity. The Duchess Anne was an intolerable woman whose pride was monstrous, a termagant who exercised much influence over her weaker husband by the lash of her tongue.

Knowing that they would make a bitter enemy of the Duchess did not unduly concern the Admiral and his bride. They had flouted the authorities, defied convention, and even jeopardised the succession, but this meant little in comparison to the joy they found in each other. Initially, this was a passion that had to be indulged in secret (which undoubtedly gave it added spice), at least until Katherine invited the Lord Protector to come to Chelsea on 18 May to break the news to him. Until then, there were secret meetings at Chelsea, and love-letters between husband and wife, who had decided that the safer course was to live apart for the present. Katherine states in one letter that she had promised to restrict herself to writing once a fortnight; however, she could not restrain herself from writing more frequently, although she was happily busy and found that 'weeks be shorter at Chelsea than in other places'. Referring to her feelings for the Admiral, she went on to say:

I would not have you think that this, mine honest goodwill towards you, proceeds from any sudden motion of passion; for, as truly as God is God, my mind was fully bent the other time I was at liberty to marry you before any man I know. Howbeit, God withstood my will therein most vehemently for a time, and through His grace and goodness made that seem possible which seemed to me most impossible: that was, made me renounce utterly mine own will, and follow His most willingly. It were long to write all the process of this matter. If I live, I shall declare it to you myself. I can say nothing, but – as my Lady of Suffolk saith – God is a marvellous man. By her that is yours to serve and obey during life, Katherine the Queen, K.P.

On 17 May, Sudeley replied to his wife's letter. He was staying with her sister and Lord Herbert in London and had suffered some anxious moments there, as Lady Herbert seemed to know that he had been visiting Chelsea Old Manor at night. He denied it, yet Lady Herbert pressed the point and made it obvious that she knew very well there was something going on between the Admiral and her sister. Sudeley, blushing with embarrassment, asked her where she had heard such things, and she confessed that Katherine had confided the truth to her. The Admiral related all this in his letter to his wife, thanking her for asking her sister to invite him, 'For, by her company, in default of yours, I shall shorten the weeks in these parts, which heretofore were three days longer than they were under the planets at Chelsea.' He ended by saying he was going to take Lady Herbert's advice about how to obtain the goodwill of the Council and, more importantly, his brother. He begged the Queen to write to him every three days, and to send him one of a series of miniatures she had of herself, and signed himself as 'him whom ye have bound to honour, love and in all lawful things obey'. The letter is deferential, as to the Queen, and very formal, and shows that the Admiral was well aware of the difference between his station and Katherine's.

The Lord Protector did not turn up at Chelsea on 18 May, and sent word he would not be able to come until the end of the month. The Admiral was by now concerned about his brother's reaction to his marriage, and wrote again to Katherine, telling her that, when she saw Somerset, she must press for a public announcement of their union within two months; previously, he had thought it wise to conceal it for as long as two years, with the Protector's consent, but now, after weeks of living apart from his bride, he was reluctant to play the role of secret husband for that length of time. He confessed also to Katherine that he was worried about how to win over his brother's support. To this she replied sensibly that to deny his request to announce the marriage soon would be an act of folly on the part of the Protector, since news of it might well leak out, or the couple's clandestine meetings would be noticed. Either would cause a scandal which would touch the entire Seymour clan and discredit the family, the last thing the Protector would want.

Katherine emphasised that she did not want the Admiral to beg for his brother's goodwill if it was not given freely from the first. It would be better if he obtained letters from the King in his favour, and also the support of certain members of the Privy Council, if possible, 'which thing shall be no small shame to your brother and loving sister if they do not the like'. Next time he visited her, she said, he must come early in the morning and be gone by seven o'clock, having warned her beforehand of the time of his arrival, so that she could 'wait at the gate of the field for you'.

This state of affairs could not and did not last very much longer. At the end of May, when Somerset fulfilled his promise and came to dine with the Queen at Chelsea, she informed him of her marriage. He, in turn, broke the news to the Council. 'The Lord Protector was much offended,' noted the King in his journal, mainly because of the threat to the succession but also because he had not been consulted. The matter was debated at great length by the Privy Council, it being argued that, if the Queen was already pregnant, 'a great doubt' would exist as to 'whether the child born should have been accounted the late King's or [the Admiral's], whereby a marvellous danger might have ensued to the quiet of the realm'. Lord Sudeley was summoned to account for his actions, but at the end of the day there was little anyone could do. The marriage had been lawfully solemnised before witnesses and consummated. It was, anyway, late May: King Henry had been dead for four months, and his widow showed no signs of pregnancy, which was fortunate for the Admiral and for Katherine, for it meant that the Protector was prepared to overlook the small risk to the succession occasioned by their marriage. All the same, Somerset made his displeasure clear, and his wife was mortified at the news. The only person who remained calm was the young King, who, on 30 May, in defiance of the advice of his Council, took it upon himself to write and congratulate Queen Katherine upon her marriage, and to thank her for the many letters she had sent him since she left court. In his letter, he spoke affectionately of 'the great love' she had borne his father, her goodwill towards himself, and lastly her 'godliness and knowledge in learning and the scriptures'. If there was 'anything wherein I may do you a kindness, either in word or deed,' he ended, 'I will do it willingly.'

Katherine responded by begging the King to plead her case with the Council, which he did at the beginning of June, saying that he had known for some time that the Admiral intended marrying the Queen, and that he had sent a letter signifying his approval to Katherine. He did not divulge that the Admiral, knowing he was kept short of funds, had paid him well to do so, nor did he say that he had so phrased his letter as to request his stepmother to accept the Admiral in marriage, thus leaving her – as a loyal subject – no alternative. Against the authority of the King, Somerset was powerless; he was also a peace-loving man who loathed dissension, and he was glad enough to be reconciled with his brother and new sister-in-law. Thus he and the Council grudgingly sanctioned the marriage, giving the Admiral leave to take up residence at Chelsea with his wife.

Naturally, many people were scandalised when news of the marriage leaked out at court, and none more so than the Lady Mary, whose respect for Katherine Parr was shattered in a single blow.

Mary received a letter from the Admiral asking for her to use her influence to gain him favour with the Council, and also begging her to persuade the Queen to agree to the immediate public proclamation of their marriage. Mary was horrified at his impertinence, and dispatched a frigid reply, saying:

> It standeth least with my poor honour to be a meddler in this matter, considering whose wife her Grace was of late. If the remembrance of the King's Majesty will not suffer her to grant

543

your suit, I am nothing able to persuade her to forget the loss of him who is yet very ripe in mine own remembrance.

Where matters of the heart were concerned, she said, 'being a maid, I am nothing cunning'. By the time the Admiral received Mary's reply, he no longer needed her help and could afford to ignore her as Katherine had come round to his way of thinking and agreed that their marriage should be made public. She grieved, nevertheless, for the loss of Mary's friendship, fearing that her marriage and the widening religious gulf between them would ensure that it was never likely to be regained.

It then occurred to Mary that her sister Elizabeth might put herself morally at risk by contact with their stepmother; Mary was determined to protect her innocence and prevent her from associating with Katherine, and she wrote at once to Elizabeth, warning her against contact with such wickedness and begging her to think of her own reputation. But Elizabeth, who was fond of her stepmother and had good reason to know why she had fallen prey to the Admiral's charm, would only write a non-committal reply saying she shared Mary's 'just grief' in seeing the 'scarcely cold body of the King our father so shamefully dishonoured by the Queen our stepmother', and that she could not express 'how much affliction I suffered when I was first informed of this marriage'. However, she rationalised, neither she nor Mary were 'in such condition as to offer any obstacle thereto', and the Seymours were all powerful, having 'got all the authority into their hands'. In her opinion, the best course to take was one of dissimulation and 'making the best of what we cannot remedy'. With regard to visiting the Queen, 'the position in which I stand' and 'the Queen having shown me so much affection' obliged her to 'use much tact in manoeuvring with her, for fear of appearing ungrateful for her benefits. I shall not, however, be in any hurry to visit her, lest I should be charged with approving what I ought to censure.' In other words, she would bide her time until the furore had died down, and then do as she pleased.

Although she had married a mere baron, Katherine was yet entitled to retain and enjoy all the privileges of queenship, and now that she was known to be respectably married, she saw no reason why she should not go to court with her new husband from time to time and take her rightful place there. Accordingly, she moved the Admiral to request his brother the Protector to deliver to her the jewels traditionally worn by the queens of England, which were at that time in safe keeping in the Treasury. It was Katherine's legal right to wear them until such time as King Edward had a consort of his own, but the Duchess of Somerset had already decided that, as wife of the Lord Protector, the jewels would adorn her own person and not that of her sister-in-law. When she heard of the Queen's request, she saw the perfect opportunity to have her revenge, and wasted no time in putting pressure on her husband to make him refuse the Admiral's request.

Somerset dithered. The Admiral, impatient now, complained to the Council, saying the Protector should 'let me have mine own'. Of course, he knew very well – as did Katherine – who was causing the trouble, and when it came to a deadlock he did not hesitate to name her. From that time onwards, it was open warfare between the Duchess and the Queen. According to the Elizabethan historian William Camden, Anne Stanhope bore Katherine Parr 'such invincible hatred', and had done since the days they had sparred over 'light causes and women's quarrels'. Now the root cause of her enmity was jealousy because Katherine had precedence over her. She was to prove, in every respect, a formidable enemy.

When Katherine Parr returned to court for a visit in June, the Duchess was waiting for her. The Queen had still not been given her jewels, and was feeling annoyed. Nevertheless, she insisted on being shown every deference due to her rank, and commanded the Duchess to carry her train for her. This was a duty to which great honour was attached, but the Duchess only understood that she was being put very firmly in her place. Livid, she refused, saying 'It was unsuitable for her to submit to perform that service for the wife of her husband's younger brother.' Katherine bore the insult in silence, but she did not forget it. After that the Duchess made no secret of her animosity and did all she could to undermine the respect in which many people at court still held the Queen and to blacken her reputation. She would recall how the late King had married Katherine Parr 'in his doting days, when he had brought himself so low by his lust and cruelty that no lady who stood on her honour would venture on him.' Why, therefore, should she herself give place 'to her who in her former estate was but Latimer's widow, and is now fain to cast herself for support upon a younger brother? If Master Admiral teach his brother no better manners, I am she that will!'

While her husband was away at court, Katherine received a letter from the Lord Protector telling her she could not have the jewels. The Queen knew very well why not, and flew into a fury, only calming down to write and tell her husband the news.

> My lord your brother hath this afternoon made me a little warm! [she fumed] It was fortunate we were so much distant, for I suppose else I should have bitten him! What cause have they to fear, having such a wife? It is requisite for them to pray continually for a short despatch of that hell. Tomorrow, or else upon Saturday, I will see the King, when I intend to utter all my choler to my lord your brother, if you shall not give me advice to the contrary.

It seems, however, that either the Admiral advised his wife against such a course, or she changed her mind about going, perhaps fearing another public snub by the Duchess of Somerset.

After that supreme insult, Katherine refused to return to the court, remaining at Chelsea until she and her husband moved to the country a year later. Her reign was effectively over – that much had been made clear to her. Happy in her marriage and with time to pursue her intellectual interests, she was in fact content enough now to play the role of private gentlewoman.

On 25 June, Katherine received a letter from the King, telling her she need not fear any further recriminations regarding her marriage to Sudeley, and assuring her that 'I will so provide for you both that if hereafter any grief befall, I shall be a sufficient succour in your godly and praisable enterprises.' It gave the young King great pleasure to think of himself as the instigator of a marriage that had brought his stepmother and his favourite uncle such happiness and, although in reality he was powerless to help them further – for example, he was unable to arrange for Katherine's jewels to be restored to her – the knowledge of his goodwill was a comfort to the Queen. He wrote whenever he could, which was not often for he was rarely 'half an hour alone', and when he could not write, he sent a message of goodwill. In return, the Admiral supplied him secretly with pocket money, of which the Protector kept him very short. This only increased Edward's gratitude, and the Admiral was hopeful that, when the day came for him to propose a marriage between the King and the Lady Jane Grey, Edward would be more than amenable. The Admiral had not abandoned his master plan; he had only to wait, and in time Lord Dorset would come running.

Somerset realised he had acted unfairly, yet he dared not risk offending his wife, who was so jubilant now that victory was hers. Instead, as compensation for the loss of the jewels, he conferred upon his brother the office of Captain General and Protector's Lieutenant in the South of England, and in that same month of August made a grant to him of the manor of Sudeley, with the castle. The Admiral was delighted; situated just south of the village of Winchcombe in Gloucestershire, and set in a beautiful park, the main fabric of the castle dated from the late fifteenth century, and had been grafted on to an earlier manor house by Richard III. It had a chapel, and was in every way a residence fit for a queen with an ambitious husband. Today, much of what can be seen at Sudeley is a Victorian reconstruction, though the ruins of part of the old castle remain to give some idea of what it must have been like in Katherine's day.

The Admiral gave orders immediately for the castle to be renovated and made ready for occupation; he and the Queen hoped it would be habitable within a year, then they could escape from the hostile climate of London and the court for a while to lead the lives of wealthy country gentry. For the present, Katherine spent her time reading, writing or at her devotions. Her second book, *The Lamentations of a Sinner*, was now completed, and both her brother, Lord Northampton, and her friend, the Duchess of Suffolk, urged her to have it printed. She agreed to do so, and in November the first copies went on sale with an introduction by a young lawyer called William Cecil, who would later become Queen Elizabeth's councillor Lord Burleigh. Cecil wrote that he joined all 'ladies of estate' in following 'our Queen in virtue as in honour' in order to taste 'everlasting bliss'. The book was an even greater success than *Prayers and Meditations* had been, and was highly praised by scholars everywhere, thus sustaining Katherine's reputation as a woman of learning.

It was at this time that she invited her stepdaughter Elizabeth to join her household at Chelsea. Elizabeth had been at court, but she had not been very happy there. The introduction of rigid ceremonial required her to drop on one knee five times in front of her brother before seating herself on a mean bench far from his side. The Queen was probably aware of Elizabeth's situation, and sought to rescue her, and Elizabeth responded with enthusiasm, arriving at Chelsea early in the new year of 1548. The scandal surrounding the Queen's remarriage had long since died down, and her stepdaughter saw no reason why she should not move in with her. Katherine thought it an ideal arrangement: she could oversee Elizabeth's education once more, chaperon her through her development to womanhood, and enjoy the stimulating company of her excellent mind.

Katherine's decision to invite Elizabeth into her household was to precipitate a tragedy. She had no idea, of course, that her husband had once tried to marry Elizabeth, still less that he had seen her as an infinitely more desirable catch than a dowager queen. It never occurred to her that this slight young girl of fourteen would hold any attraction for the Admiral. From the first, the situation was fraught. In spite of herself, Elizabeth was fascinated by the handsome 'stepfather' – as the Admiral was pleased to call himself – who welcomed her with undisguised affection to her new home, and wasted no time in making it clear to her that he found her both stimulating and desirable.

He took care to conceal this from his wife, who so implicitly trusted him that she suspected nothing. She regarded Elizabeth as a child still, the orphan she had taken under her wing, an innocent whom she could guide and nurture and who would be a cherished daughter to both Katherine and her husband. The Admiral had other ideas. So did Elizabeth. As the short winter days lengthened, so did their mutual attraction develop, under the guise of an affectionate relationship between stepfather and daughter. There was no outward hint of the sexual tension between them. Both knew that if they acknowledged it they risked wounding the woman who meant a great deal to both of them.

Cocooned in her marriage, Katherine settled into her new life, a stepmother once more. On 15 January 1548, she and the Admiral attended her brother's wedding to Elizabeth Brooke, the daughter of Lord Cobham. Then, in February, the Admiral again approached Lord Dorset about the wardship of the Lady Jane Grey. To sweeten Dorset, he had installed in the Old Manor his aged mother, Lady Seymour, who would treat Jane 'as if she were her own daughter'. As for Queen Katherine, she would be only too happy to order Jane's education, and the Lady Elizabeth would provide eminently suitable companionship. It all looked very respectable, and this time Dorset leaped at the chance, as the Admiral had known he would.

Thus Jane came to join the household at Chelsea. It was a welcome change for her. She was at last out of the clutches of the parents who had made her life a misery, and of whom she strongly disapproved. There were no beatings at Chelsea, no harsh words. The Queen, the Admiral, and the Lady Elizabeth all seemed intent on enjoying their peaceful existence there, and Lady Seymour was like an affectionate grandmother. Jane could freely follow the Protestant faith to which she was devoted, and there was also freedom to study without the ever-present fear of parental criticism.

Jane was a small, thin child, yet graceful. She had small features and a well-shaped nose, with arched eyebrows darker than her hair, which was of a reddish colour. She had sparkling eyes and freckles, and to some extent resembled her cousin Elizabeth, with whom she took her lessons. The Queen herself supervised the girls' studies, and was careful to appoint tutors who would cultivate the proper attitudes to religion and learning in their minds. Katherine won so much praise for her endeavours in this respect that other ladies of noble birth did their best to emulate her, and not long afterwards Nicholas Udall, the Provost of Eton College, was writing to the Queen with the highest praise for what she had achieved through her influence.

When I consider, most gracious Queen Katherine [he wrote], the great number of noble women in this our time and country of England, not only given to the study of human sciences and of strange tongues, but also so thoroughly expert in Holy Scriptures, that they are able to compare with the best writers, as well in penning of godly and fruitful treatises to the instruction and edifying of the whole realm in the knowledge of God, as also in translating good books out of Latin or Greek into English for the use of such as are rude and ignorant of the said tongues, it is now no news at all to see queens and ladies of most high estate and progeny, instead of courtly dalliance, embrace virtuous exercises, reading and writing, and with most earnest study, apply themselves to the acquiring of knowledge.

Katherine's own household, he went on, was famous as the place 'where it is now a common thing to see young virgins so trained in the study of good letters that they willingly set all other vain pastimes at naught for learning's sake.' This much had Katherine accomplished for her own sex, whose education had by now been freed from many of the taboos formerly attached to it. Thanks to the Queen's influence, the learned female had become fashionable, and a pattern had been set for the future.

In February, Elizabeth asked her stepmother if she might have the renowned Roger Ascham as her tutor instead of Mr Grindal. Katherine, who had long corresponded with Ascham on scholarly matters, warmly approved of the change and Ascham arrived at Chelsea later that month, after Katherine and her husband had gone to stay at the London house of Lord and Lady Herbert. There was a family scandal brewing, and the Parrs were taking counsel together. It was only a month since William Parr, the Marquess of Northampton, had married Elizabeth Brooke, yet already it was being alleged by the Privy Council that his divorce from Anne Bourchier had not been legal. When this was confirmed, Northampton was ordered to put away his new wife, and never speak to her again on pain of death, as his true wife was still living. This was a blow for Parr, and a grievous disappointment for Katherine, since it was she, along with the Duchess of Suffolk, who had suggested and promoted the union with Elizabeth Brooke. Yet there was nothing that she or anyone else could do about this new situation, and before very long the Admiral took her back to Chelsea.

Then, early in March 1548, after more than twenty years of married life with four husbands, Katherine Parr discovered that she was at long last to have a child. Both she and the Admiral were delighted. Good wishes came pouring in, as well as plenty of advice and warnings to take care of herself, for she was, by the standards of her time, well into middle age and rather old to be having a first child. Nevertheless, she seems to have enjoyed good health throughout most of her pregnancy.

So wrapped up was the Queen in her personal happiness, that she failed to notice what was going on under her nose. For her husband, considering his wife to be suitably occupied with approaching motherhood, had now renewed his pursuit of the Lady Elizabeth. The Queen did not realise that while she was at her daily prayers, which took place regularly each morning and afternoon, her husband would always be elsewhere, nor did she suspect anything when Elizabeth began making excuses to be absent. The Admiral would openly romp with Elizabeth in front of members of the household, so that no one would think anything of it, and when he and the Queen stayed with Elizabeth at Seymour Place in London that spring, he went up to Elizabeth's bedroom every morning, wearing only his night-gown and slippers, and burst in, regardless of whether or not she was in bed. Her lady-in-waiting, Mrs Katherine Ashley, was present, and was immediately suspicious, thinking it 'an unseemly sight to see a man so little dressed in a maiden's chamber'. She made her feelings very clear to the Admiral, which angered him, but he did at least go away on that occasion. What really disturbed Mrs Ashley, according to her later deposition to the Privy Council, was that he only stayed if Elizabeth was in bed; if he found her up and dressed, he would just look in at the gallery door, then leave.

Lord Sudeley was irritated by Mrs Ashley's attitude, but he was undeterred by it, and it only served to make him all the more determined to have what he wanted. Elizabeth was ripe for seduction and probably willing enough; she was at a highly impressionable age, and very flattered that the dashing Admiral's attentions were focused upon her. Not for nothing was she Anne Boleyn's daughter, and male admiration was already the breath of life to her, while her budding sexuality was aroused. It is likely that she was rather frightened at the prospect of the sex act itself, and yet equally likely that her passion for the Admiral would have overcome her fear and her good sense, given time.

The morning visits continued, to Mrs Ashley's dismay. The Admiral would go into Elizabeth's bedchamber and tickle her as she lay in her bed, clad only in her night-gown. Once he tried to kiss her, but Mrs Ashley was there and ordered him out 'for shame'. However, he was back the next morning, and most mornings thereafter. What was more, Elizabeth did not rebuff him; she was thoroughly enjoying it. Soon, matters had reached the stage where the Admiral would bid her good morning, ask how she did, and smack her on the back or buttocks with great familiarity. Then he would go back to his rooms, or go to the maids' room and flirt with them.

The Queen saw nothing wrong in all this. Her husband had told her about it, knowing full well that she still regarded her stepdaughter as a child. She raised no protest when she heard that the Admiral would pull apart Elizabeth's bed-curtains and 'make as though he would come at her', causing her to shrink back giggling into the bed to avoid being tickled. The Admiral said it was harmless, and the Queen believed him. Mrs Ashley, however, was not so sure; and she was concerned about her charge's reputation. One day, when the Admiral chased Elizabeth out from behind the bed-curtains where she had hidden with her maids, the lady-in-waiting spoke to him, and said there had been complaints about his behaviour and that 'my lady was evil spoken of', presumably among the servants. The Admiral answered that he would report to the Protector 'how I am slandered,' but Mrs Ashley insisted she herself must always be present whenever he entered Elizabeth's bedchamber, and made certain from then on that she was.

But the romps continued. Sometimes, even the Queen joined in. When they were at Anne Boleyn's old manor of Hanworth in the spring, Katherine accompanied her husband to Elizabeth's room on two mornings, and joined in the tickling, amid peals of laughter. While still at Hanworth, the Admiral chased Elizabeth through the gardens; when he caught her, they wrestled together, then Seymour called for shears and cut her black gown into strips, while the Queen, in fits of laughter, held her still. Afterwards, Elizabeth fled indoors where Mrs Ashley asked in horror what had happened to her. Elizabeth told her, and received a telling off, but would only reply that 'it could not be helped'.

Elizabeth's infatuation with the Admiral was becoming quite obvious, and she was too young to have the guile to conceal it. This concerned Seymour, for obvious reasons, so, in order to divert any suspicion from himself, he told Katherine he had recently seen Elizabeth, through a gallery window, 'with her arms round a man's neck'. The Queen was shocked, and sent for Mrs Ashley, who divulged nothing of what she suspected but advised Katherine to speak to the girl herself. She did so, but Elizabeth burst into tears and denied that such a thing had ever happened, begging her stepmother to ask all her women if it were true. She had little opportunity for such things, as she was hardly ever alone, and the only men who came into contact with her, apart from servants, were her school-masters and the Admiral.

At once, the Queen's suspicions were aroused. If Elizabeth was telling the truth, her husband must be lying, and why should he do this but to protect himself? Suddenly, like pieces in a jigsaw, the truth dawned upon Katherine with terrible clarity. Everything now made sense, the morning romps, Elizabeth's behaviour, Mrs Ashley's tight-lipped disapproval. She had no proof that the affair had proceeded beyond a mere romp, but there was no doubt in her mind that her husband was after Elizabeth, and that he was the kind of man who would seduce her if the opportunity presented itself. It was therefore imperative that she take some action to protect the girl, who was, after all, under her roof and in her care.

The Queen now sent for Mrs Ashley, and confided her suspicions to her, telling her to 'take more heed, and be as it were in watch betwixt the Lady Elizabeth and the Admiral'. Mrs Ashley was relieved that Katherine was now in command of the situation, and also to know she did not suspect it to have progressed very far. Later that day she told Sir Thomas Parry, who was in charge of Elizabeth's financial affairs, that 'the Admiral had loved the Princess [*sic*] too well, and had done so a good while', but his bluff was about to be called. Parry, too, promised to be watchful.

Katherine's happiness was shattered. Whether or not the Admiral had actually been unfaithful to her did not matter: it was his intention that had hurt her. Yet she hid her feelings well, hoping against hope that she had been wrong. It was not long, however, before she had her worst suspicions confirmed. One day in April at Chelsea, she realised that both her husband and stepdaughter were missing. She went in search of them, throughout that vast house, until at last she came upon them, without warning, alone together, Elizabeth in the Admiral's arms. At the sight of Katherine, they fell apart at once, guilt all over their faces. But it was too late, the Queen had seen enough to tell her that her husband and the girl she had sheltered and mothered had betrayed her. She did not wait to hear their apologies, but left the room and ordered Mrs Ashley to attend her. When the woman came, the Queen told her she was displeased with Elizabeth, and why, and warned her that she would not have the girl in her house any longer than was necessary. When Mrs Ashley had gone, Katherine did not vent her sorrow in tears, nor did she indulge in a tirade of useless recriminations when once again she came face to face with her husband. Withdrawn and cold, she was sustained by her innate dignity and never betrayed by word or gesture her inner turmoil.

In May, Elizabeth left Chelsea for her manor of Cheston. Her guilt lay heavily upon her conscience, and far outweighed any attraction she had felt for the Admiral. Their affair was over, that much was obvious. He had made no attempt to see her, and she welcomed this, for it made things much easier. She told Mrs Ashley that she had 'loved the Admiral too well', and that the Queen was jealous of them both.

Before her departure, she had one last painful interview with Katherine. Her stepmother was aloof and cool, and made no reference to the reason for her going. She merely said, 'God has given you great qualities. Cultivate them always, and labour to improve them, for I believe you are destined by Heaven to be Queen of England.' Elizabeth kissed her, and was gone, unable to bear Katherine's coldness.

When she arrived at Cheston, Elizabeth was told by Mrs Ashley that the Admiral would have married her, if he had had the chance, rather than the Queen. Elizabeth asked how she knew that, whereupon Mrs Ashley told her 'she knew it well, both by herself and others'. Before very long, it was common knowledge, and caused further grief to Queen Katherine; what was worse, however, were the rumours that had suddenly sprung up regarding Elizabeth's relationship with the Admiral. There were tales of illicit meetings, criminal intercourse, even of a child born in great secrecy. Such tales, most of them fabrications, probably originated with the servants' gossip at Chelsea, yet they captured the imagination of the public. It would be another year, however, before the government took them seriously and the storm broke.

Not long after her arrival at Cheston, Elizabeth fell sick and took to her bed, which gave the rumourmongers further food for thought; however, she was up and about by July. In the meantime, she had received a letter from the Admiral, taking the blame for what had happened upon himself, and swearing to testify to her innocence if necessary. No words of love adorned his letter or her reply, in which she wrote, 'You need not to send an excuse to me', and ended 'I pray you to make my humble commendations to the Queen's Highness.' By telling the Admiral she was committing 'you and your affairs into God's hand', she was in effect telling him that all familiarity between them must cease; and while his wife lived, the Admiral took her at her word. Elizabeth saw now that she had not only caused terrible hurt to the Queen, but had also risked her reputation and her place in the succession. Never again would she be so stupid.

After Elizabeth's departure, Katherine made an effort to forget what had happened and rebuild her shaken marriage. Thanks to her determination, relations between her and her husband improved, assisted by the Queen's advancing pregnancy and the shared pleasure of anticipating the birth of their child. Early in June, the Admiral's duties called him to court, so Katherine went away to Hanworth for a few days, and while she was there, she felt her child move inside her for the first time. It was a joyful moment, and did much to erase her unhappy memories of the spring. With renewed affection, she wrote to her husband:

Sweetheart and loving husband,
I gave your little knave your blessing, who like an honest man stirred apace after and before; for Mary Odell [the midwife, who was already in attendance], being abed with me, laid her hand on my belly to feel it stir. It has stirred these three days every morning and evening, so that I trust when you come it will make you some pastime. And thus I end, bidding my sweetheart and loving husband better to fare than myself.

The Admiral replied on 9 June that Katherine's letter had 'revived my spirits'. He was still trying, with little success, to get Somerset to agree to restoring her jewels to her. Hearing that 'my little man doth shake his poll', he trusted that 'If God should give him a life as long as his father's, he will revenge such wrongs as neither you nor I can at present.' He had spoken to Somerset, he said, and had 'so well handled him' that the Duke was no longer so sure of his ground, and had said that 'At the finishing of the matter, you shall either have your own again, or else some recompense as ye shall be content withal.' He ended his letter with instructions to Katherine

> to keep the little knave [i.e. the baby] so lean and gaunt with your good diet and walking that he may be so small that he may creep out of a mouse-hole! And I bid my most dear and well-beloved wife most heartily well to fare. Your Highness' most faithful, loving husband, T. Seymour.

It is obvious from this letter that the Admiral was doing his best to regain the love and respect of his wife, especially now she was about to bear him, he hoped, an heir. And it is obvious from Katherine's letter, too, that she was happy to pretend that all was well between them. An uneasy peace had been achieved. But underneath, her wound was still raw.

Chelsea held too many painful memories, and so the Admiral had decided to take the Queen to Sudeley Castle, where their child would be born. He returned from court on 11 June, and on Wednesday, 13 June they set off for Gloucestershire. When they reached their new home, a letter from John Fowler awaited them, enclosing one from the King. Edward sent his commendations to his stepmother and to the Admiral, and informed them that the Duchess of Somerset had just given birth to 'a fine boy', to be named after the King and after her elder son, born eleven years before, who had died in childhood. This was encouraging news for Katherine, whose own confinement was now not many weeks off.

The Queen soon settled into the peaceful routine of life in the country. Then a letter arrived from Elizabeth, who wrote 'giving thanks for the manifold kindnesses received at your Highness's hand at my departure' and saying how 'truly I was replete with sorrow to depart from your Highness' and that

> I weighed it deeply when you said you would warn me of all evilnesses that you should hear of me; for if your Grace had not a good opinion of me, you would not have offered friendship to me that way at all, meaning the contrary.

There was more, in the same appealing and penitential vein, and the letter was signed 'Your Highness's humble daughter, Elizabeth'. It was undoubtedly a plea for forgiveness, and Katherine sensibly realised that Elizabeth had never intended her any real harm; she had lost her head over a handsome man who should have known better. With this in mind, Katherine could not remain angry any longer, and even though she had hurt her wrist, which was so weak that she could hardly hold the pen, she wrote a warm reply, assuring her stepdaughter of her friendship. The Admiral wrote also, at his wife's request.

Elizabeth replied on 31 July, saying Katherine's letter was 'most joyful to me', although she was concerned to hear 'what pain it is to you to write', and would have been happy to receive her 'commendations' in the Admiral's letter. She rejoiced, she said, to learn of Katherine's otherwise excellent health and enjoyment of life in the country, and was grateful to the Admiral for undertaking to let her know from time to time 'how his busy child doth; if I were at his birth, no doubt I would see him beaten, for the trouble he hath put you to!' And with the passing on of good wishes for 'a lucky deliverance' from Mrs Ashley and others, Elizabeth ended her letter, 'giving your Highness most humble thanks for your commendations'.

There was no question, of course, of Elizabeth rejoining Katherine's household. Yet the Queen did not lack for company in these final weeks of her pregnancy. Lady Jane Grey was still with her and like a daughter, and many of her old friends and acquaintances made the long journey from London to visit her; in fact, Sudeley Castle quickly became renowned as the second court in the realm because it was so well populated with the nobility and because the Admiral spared no expense in providing hospitality or in maintaining his wife's royal estate. They had, after all, more than £8,000 a year to live on, a princely sum in those days. Most welcome of all were Katherine's old friends, Sir Robert and Lady Tyrwhitt, and it was to Sir Robert that the Queen mentioned one day, when they were walking in the gardens, and Sir Robert was admiring the scenery and the castle, that when the King came of age he would ask for the return of Sudeley Castle. Sir Robert was dismayed to learn that the Queen might have to leave her beautiful home, and asked, 'Then will Sudeley Castle be gone from my Lord Admiral?' Katherine smiled, and told him that she had the King's promise that, if he recalled all the lands deeded away by the regency Council he would freely return Sudeley when that time came.

It was now August, and the Queen's child was due within the month. Most of her visitors tactfully departed, leaving only the Tyrwhitts and a few other faithful friends in attendance. Katherine spent much of her time with Lady Jane Grey, of whom she was very fond, and there had been, of late, a reconciliation with the Lady Mary, whose disapproval of Katherine's remarriage had melted as soon as she heard that her stepmother was to bear a child. Again, the two women had begun to correspond, and in the middle of August William Parr arrived at Sudeley with another letter from Mary, who was going to Norfolk and would not return until Michaelmas, 'at which time, or shortly after, I trust to hear good success of your Grace's great belly, and in the meantime shall desire much to hear of your health.' And with commendations to the Admiral, she signed herself 'Your Highness's humble and assured loving daughter.'

Katherine was therefore seemingly at peace with the world when, on 30 August 1548, her child was born at Sudeley Castle. It turned out to be no 'little knave', but a daughter, who was afterwards christened Mary, in honour of her stepsister, the Lady Mary. It was a difficult birth, and Katherine was very weak afterwards, although her physicians and the midwife, Mary Odell, were optimistic about her recovery.

The Admiral was naturally disappointed that the child was a girl, but it was not long before he was doting upon the baby, and sending the news of her birth by fast courier to the Protector. Somerset was right glad to understand by your letters that the Queen, your bedfellow, hath a happy hour, and, escaping all danger, hath made you the father of so pretty a daughter; and although (if it had pleased God) it would have been both to us and (we suppose) also to you more joy and comfort if it had, this first-born, been a son, yet the escape of the danger, and the prophecy of this to a great sort of happy sons is no small joy and comfort to us, as we are sure it is to you and her Grace also, to whom you shall make again our hearty commendations, with no less congratulation of such good success. From Syon, the 1st of Sept., 1548. Your loving brother, E. Somerset.

Of course, the Duchess of Somerset was delighted that Katherine Parr had borne a daughter; had not she herself presented her husband with a fine son, triumphing where Katherine had failed?

There was no thought of failure, or even of success, in the mind of the Queen by then. Hours after the birth, she was laid low with puerperal fever, that scourge of medieval and Tudor childbeds, and remained delirious for almost a week. With each passing day, it became more obvious that she was not going to recover. In her delirium, she spoke of her anguish over her husband's faithlessness and betrayal, which was to trouble her to the end, and which she no longer had the strength or wit to conceal. On 5 September, Lady Tyrwhitt went into the Queen's bedchamber to bid her good morning and see if there was any improvement in her condition. Katherine was half lucid, and asked Lady Tyrwhitt where she had been for so long, saying 'that she did fear such things in herself that she was sure she could not live'. Lady Tyrwhitt replied, with feigned confidence, 'that I saw no likelihood of death in her.' But Katherine was not listening; she was back at Chelsea, reliving the moment when she had found her husband and Elizabeth in an embrace. The Admiral was by the bed, and she grasped his hand, saying, 'My Lady Tyrwhitt, I am not well handled, for those that are about me care not for me, but stand laughing at my grief, and the more good I will to them, the less good they will to me.'

There was shocked silence, then the Admiral hastened to reassure her, saying, 'Why, sweetheart! I would you no hurt!' To which

Katherine replied, with heavy irony, 'No, my lord, I think so.' Then, as he leaned over her, she whispered, 'But, my lord, you have given me many shrewd taunts.' Lady Tyrwhitt remembered afterwards that she said these words 'with good memory, and very sharply and earnestly, for her mind was sore disquieted'. The Admiral pretended not to hear, and, taking Lady Tyrwhitt aside, asked her what his wife had said; 'I declared plainly to him,' she recalled. He asked if she thought he should lie down on the bed with the Queen 'and pacify her unhappiness with gentle communication'. Lady Tyrwhitt agreed this might be a good thing, whereupon the Admiral lay down and put his arms around his wife, soothing her with words of love, without regard to the presence of her ladies. He had not, however, said more than three or four words when Katherine burst out, 'My lord, I would have given a thousand marks to have had my full talk with [Dr Robert] Huicke [her physician] the first day I was delivered, but I durst not, for displeasing you.' What she actually wanted to discuss with Huicke we shall never know, but Lady Tyrwhitt guessed that it was something of a very personal nature, possibly about the resumption or otherwise of sexual relations after the difficult confinement, and because of this, and her realisation that Katherine's agony of mind was very great, Lady Tyrwhitt tactfully withdrew out of earshot: 'My heart would serve me to hear no more.' The Queen's tirade against the Admiral continued for more than an hour, and was heard by the ladies about her bedside, though they did not leave accounts of it for posterity.

Later that day, Katherine's fever subsided, leaving her with no recollection of what she had said. She was very weak, and realised, with her usual common sense, that she was dying, and that it would be best to make her will now, while she was in possession of her senses. Writing materials were brought by her secretary, and the Queen dictated:

I, Katherine Parr, etc., lying on my death-bed, sick of body but of good mind and perfect memory and discretion, being persuaded and perceiving the extremity of death to approach me, give all to my married spouse and husband, wishing them to be a thousand times more in value than they are or been.

560

The will was then signed by the Queen and witnessed by Dr Huicke and her chaplain, John Parkhurst, who gave her the last rites soon afterwards. We do not know if the Queen asked to see her baby daughter before the end, nor are her last words recorded, nor any details of her death, which occurred the following day, 7 September 1548, between two and three in the morning.

The Admiral was genuinely grieved at her passing, and gave orders for her body to be buried in the castle chapel. The corpse was embalmed, dressed in rich clothes, and wrapped in cerecloth, then placed in a lead coffin and left in the Queen's privy chamber until arrangements for the funeral had been completed. Young Jane Grey shed bitter tears over it, not only for the woman who had been a better mother to her than her own, but also because Katherine's death meant she would have to return home, a prospect that appalled her.

On the morning of 8 September, Katherine Parr was laid to rest. The chapel was hung with black cloth embroidered with the Queen's escutcheons; the altar rails were covered in black cloth, and stools and cushions provided for the mourners. The coffin was preceded into the chapel by two conductors in black carrying black staves, gentlemen, squires, knights, officers of the household carrying white staves, gentlemen ushers, and Somerset Herald in a tabard. Six gentlemen in black gowns and hoods bore the body, with torchbearers at either side, hooded knights walking at each corner. The Lady Jane Grey, acting as chief mourner, came next, her train borne by a young lady, then six other ladies, and other ladies and gentlemen, walking in pairs, then yeomen and lesser folk. Etiquette prevented the bereaved husband from attending.

When the coffin had been set down between the altar rails, psalms were sung in English and three lessons read; after the third, the mourners placed their offerings in the almsbox. Then Dr Miles Coverdale, the Queen's confessor, preached the sermon and led the prayers. When he was finished, the coffin was lowered into a vault beneath the altar pavement while the choir sang the *Te Deum*. After the service, the mourners went back to the castle for dinner, and then departed, leaving the Admiral to his memories in the great house that now seemed so empty. His servant Edward informed the Lady Elizabeth that 'my lord is a heavy man for the loss of the Queen his wife', but if the Admiral had hoped to find her willing to console him, he was quickly to be disappointed for there was no reply from her. For all this, his thoughts were very much with the woman who lay not far from him in her tomb, and he was heard to vow that 'no one should speak ill of the Queen, or if he knew it, he would take his fist to the ears of those who did, from the highest to the lowest.' At length, he returned to the world of men and affairs, and early in 1549 joined the English army at Musselburgh to do battle against the Scots. Yet not even his valorous performance in combat could dispel the whispers about his lack of scruples, nor the rumour, spread by Thomas Parry, 'that he had treated the late Queen cruelly, dishonestly, and jealously'.

As time passed his grief – which was undoubtedly sincere – faded. Memories grew dim. The Duchess of Somerset told him that

> if any grudge were borne by her to him, it was all for the late Queen's sake, and now she was taken by death, it would undoubtedly follow that she, the Duchess, would bear as good will to him as ever before.

With Katherine's memory daily receding, the Admiral patched up the feud and returned again to court, taking the first of many ill-considered steps that would, in 1549, lead him to the block for having schemed to gain control of the young King. When news was brought to her of his death, the Lady Elizabeth merely commented, 'This day died a man of much wit, and very little judgement.'

Lady Jane Grey mourned her benefactress most sincerely, and when she had returned to her parents' house, she wrote to thank the Admiral for 'all such good behaviour as she learned by the Queen's most virtuous instruction'. She, too, was fated to die violently, at only sixteen years of age, and her months with Katherine Parr were undoubtedly the happiest time in her short life.

Mary and Elizabeth grieved also for the loss of a stepmother who had been unfailingly kind and protective towards them. Mary could never forget what her father owed to Katherine Parr, and often spoke of 'the great love and affection that [he] did bear unto her Grace'. Her death would herald the beginning of a great divide between the sisters, who had once been close but would now gradually grow ever

562

more suspicious of each other and end as formidable rivals in the dangerous arena of politics and religion.

When, on 20 March 1549, the Lord Admiral was executed for high treason, his seven-month-old daughter, Lady Mary Seymour, was left an orphan. Nor was this the only calamity that befell her, for later that month Parliament passed an Act disinheriting the child. The dispossessed baby was taken in by her late mother's friend, the Duchess of Suffolk, to be brought up with twelve other orphans in her care at her house at Grimsthorpe. Mary's uncle, Lord Northampton, hinted that he would be willing to have the child, but only if the Duchess of Somerset paid him the allowance she and the Duke had promised him for the infant's upkeep. The tight-fisted Duchess, however, would not pay up, and thus the burden of Lady Mary's keep fell upon the Duchess of Suffolk. Within a month, the good woman was finding it too onerous a burden, as, being the daughter of a queen, the child had to be provided with all the trappings suitable to her rank, and these were expensive. The Duchess of Suffolk wrote to William Cecil, who had been a great admirer of Katherine Parr, and asked him to use his influence with the Duchess of Somerset in persuading her to agree to paying the allowance she had promised for the Lady Mary; Lady Suffolk knew that Northampton would never take her without it, for he 'hath as weak a back for such a burden as I have'.

Despite Cecil's pleas, the allowance was not forthcoming. Anne Somerset did send her servant, Richard Bertie (who later married the Duchess of Suffolk) with a message to say that she would be forwarding some nursery plate for her niece; in turn, she wished to see an inventory of all the valuables in use in the child's nursery, so that she could decide for herself what pension was needful. Lady Suffolk was furious when she received this message, and in exasperation wrote to Cecil to say:

> The Queen's child hath lain, and doth lie, at my house, with her company [i.e. servants] about her, wholly at my charge. I have written to my Lady Somerset at large; there may be some pension allotted to her, according to my lord's Grace's [Somerset's] promise. Now, good Cecil, help at a pinch all that you may help.

563

Enclosed was a parcel containing the requested inventory of all the valuables that had been set aside for the Lady Mary's use when she left Sudeley Castle, as well as a letter from the child's nurse, Mistress Eglonby, demanding wages for herself and her maids, 'so that ye may the better understand that I cry not before I am pricked', wrote the Duchess, whose coffers were emptying fast.

The inventory of Lady Mary Seymour's effects survives, and provides us with a fascinating account of what a well-born baby was provided with in those days. There were silver pots and goblets in her nursery, a silver salt cellar, eleven silver spoons, a porringer banded in silver, a quilt for the cradle, three pillows and one pair of sheets, three feather beds, three more quilts and sets of sheets, a tester of scarlet, embroidered, with a counterpane of silk serge, and bed-curtains of crimson taffeta, two counterpanes with embroidered pictures for the nurse's bed, six wall-hangings, four carpets to hang over the windows in cold weather, ten more hangings depicting the months of the year, two cushions of cloth of gold and a chair of the same, two stools and a gilded bedstead with tester, counterpanes and curtains (presumably for when the child was too big for a cradle), two 'milk beasts' – probably pewter jugs fashioned like animals – which were earmarked as gifts for the two maids looking after the child as and when they married, and a lute. This last may once have belonged to Katherine Parr, and was perhaps used to lull her little daughter to sleep.

The inventory was forwarded by Cecil to the Duchess of Somerset in the summer of 1549. However, not long afterwards her husband the Lord Protector was overthrown by the Duke of Northumberland – formerly John Dudley, Earl of Warwick – and she was no longer able to fulfil any of her promises, even had she wished to, for the Seymours were now in disgrace. Somerset would end his days as his brother had done, on the block, accused of high treason, in 1552. However, a few months after Somerset's fall, Parliament passed an Act restoring to Mary all her father's lands and property, though not his titles. After that, Lady Suffolk's financial troubles were at an end.

Nothing more is recorded in contemporary sources of Katherine Parr's daughter, and it is likely that she died young while still at Grimsthorpe. In the eighteenth century, most of the papers relating to Katherine Parr were destroyed in a fire at Wilton House, where they were stored, a sad loss for historians since they may have held clues to the fate of Katherine's daughter. In the nineteenth century, the historian Agnes Strickland was shown a genealogy belonging to the Lawson family of north-west England, showing that they were descended from a Lady Mary Seymour, who had grown up and married a knight called Sir Edward Bushel, who is known to have been in the household of Anne of Denmark, wife of James I. The evidence for this marriage, however, was based only on a family legend and is unsubstantiated by sixteenth-century sources; it may therefore be discounted. The sad reality was probably that Lady Mary followed her mother to the grave within a few years.

In time, a beautiful tomb was raised by the Admiral over Katherine Parr's remains within the chapel at Sudeley Castle. A marble effigy resembling the Queen was placed on it, and around the sepulchre was written an epitaph composed by her chaplain, Dr Parkhurst, who described her as 'the flower of her sex, renowned, great and wise, a wife by every nuptial virtue known'. Within a hundred years of Katherine's death, the chapel fell into decay, and the tomb was broken up by vandals. In 1782, her coffin was found amid the ruins, and opened. The body was seen to be in a good state of preservation, being clothed in costly burial garments – not a shroud, but a dress. There were shoes on the feet, which were very small. The Queen, it was noted, had been tall – the coffin measured 5′10″ in length – but of delicate build, with long auburn hair. There were traces of beauty in the dead face, the features being perfect on first exposure to the air; however, the process of decomposition began almost immediately, and the vicar insisted that the body be reinterred. This was done, but inebriated workmen buried it upside down. However, two years later, the body was to be seen outside the chapel, in the remains of the original coffin, and another vicar, Mr Tredway Nash, lamented that he wished 'more respect was paid to the remains of this amiable queen'. He wanted them put into a new coffin and buried elsewhere, so that 'at last her body might rest in peace'. The chapel was by then used for the keeping of rabbits, and was not a suitable place, as the rabbits 'scratch very irreverently about the royal corpse'. It seems, however, that the vicar's plans came to nothing, and that the coffin was merely covered with rubble.

By 1817, when the chapel was being restored, local opinion favoured a search being made for the Queen's remains, and the owner of the castle, Lord Chandos, gave his permission. Eventually, the coffin was found: it was badly damaged and found to contain only a skeleton. It was repaired, however, and finally reburied in the Chandos vault within the Chapel. During the reign of Queen Victoria the restoration of the chapel was completed, and Sir George Gilbert Scott was commissioned to design a fine new tomb in the medieval style for Katherine Parr. He made a marble effigy, copied from lost engravings of the original, which was placed on the finished monument in 1862, and this is the tomb we see there today, along with some vivid Victorian stained-glass windows, depicting Katherine Parr with her last two husbands, Henry VIII and Thomas Seymour. It is a fitting memorial to this most charming of queens.

After the death of Katherine, only one of Henry VIII's wives still lived, Anne of Cleves, who was perhaps the most fortunate, for after her divorce she had lived on in England in peace and contentment, enjoying the respect and affection of her former husband's family. Until the King died in 1547, she knew prosperity also, for her annual allowance of £3,000 was paid regularly, though after Henry's death the payments fell into arrears, and in 1550 so much was owed that Anne was driven to petitioning Edward VI about it; she was curtly informed, however, that 'the King's Highness, being on his progress, could not be troubled at that time about payments.' Nevertheless, he did authorise some of the debt to be paid soon afterwards, although Anne never received the full balance due to her for those years. In 1552 she complained again, and was granted various lands and manors, the rent from these being intended to supplement her income. Yet, as Anne pointed out, in a letter to her close friend, the Lady Mary, 'I was well contented to have continued without exchange,' to which end she had 'travailed to my great cost and charge almost this twelve months'.

This letter was written at Bletchingly in Surrey, one of the houses granted to Anne of Cleves after the annulment of her marriage. The others were Richmond and Hever, and she seems to have divided her time among all three. Richmond had once been the favourite home of Henry VII, and was by far the largest; after Anne's death,

Elizabeth I would come to love this mellow, red-brick palace on the banks of the Thames, and would die there in 1603. Bletchingly Place was also built of red brick; it had once been in the hands of that Duke of Buckingham who had been executed by Henry VIII in 1521, after which it had come into the possession of the Crown. All that remains of it today is a Tudor gatehouse at Place Farm. Hever Castle, of course, had been the home of Anne Boleyn from childhood until her marriage to the King; it had fallen to the Crown on the death of Anne's father, the Earl of Wiltshire, without heirs, in 1539. Anne of Cleves seems to have favoured it least among her houses, probably because it held too many memories of her unfortunate predecessor. Yet she did go there from time to time; in 1547, Katherine Bassett, who had entered Anne's household after the latter's divorce, was married to Mr Henry Ashley of Hever, whom she no doubt met when accompanying her mistress on a visit to the castle.

Anne was always welcome at court and therefore able to enjoy the best of both worlds, as an honourary member of the King's family and as a country gentlewoman. She was therefore a witness to the shifting vicissitudes of power and the changing fortunes of the monarchy that characterised the middle years of the sixteenth century. She saw Edward VI decline in health and learned of his death from consumption at the age of fifteen in July 1553. She heard, not long afterwards, how Northumberland had plotted to set the Lady Jane Grey – whom he had married to his son, Lord Guildford Dudley – upon the throne, that he might conserve power for himself and thus preserve the Protestant religion in England. And she learned, with sincere gladness, how the country had rallied to Mary Tudor's cause, and how Mary had overthrown Queen Jane and been herself proclaimed Queen of England. In October 1553, Anne was present at Mary I's coronation in Westminster Abbey, and occupied the same litter as the Lady Elizabeth in the procession to and from the Abbey.

Some months later, Anne was writing from Hever to congratulate Mary on her marriage to the Catholic Philip of Spain, son and heir of the Emperor Charles V, and to ask 'when and where I shall wait on your Majesty and his'. She sent also a wish that they should both enjoy 'much joy and felicity, with increase of children to God's glory and the preservation of your prosperous estates'. Sadly, Mary –

567

whose first legislation in Parliament had been an Act declaring her parents' marriage lawful – was never to bear a child. What was at first thought to be a pregnancy later turned out to be a malignant growth within the womb.

Mary had originally been responsible for Anne of Cleves's conversion to Roman Catholicism, and by the 1550s Anne had long since repudiated Protestantism. She would have heard, no doubt, of the coming of the Inquisition to England, and also of the burning of more than 300 heretics, among them Archbishop Cranmer, on the Queen's orders. It had been Mary's intention from the first to eradicate the Protestant heresy from her realm, and to return her kingdom to the fold of the Roman Church. This she had done, but at a price, and when she died she would be remembered, not as the saviour of the English Church, but as 'Bloody Mary', a monster of cruelty.

It appears that during these years Anne of Cleves rarely went to court, preferring to lead the life of a private gentlewoman, attending to domestic affairs and managing her estates. She seems to have become quite efficient at this, and to have converted her property into a thriving asset. The rents she received from her manors now enabled her to live in comfort, and her steward, Sir Thomas Cawarden (who had formerly been Henry VIII's Master of the Revels), assisted her so ably that when she died she bequeathed to him her manor of Bletchingly as a reward. It was Cawarden who in 1556 made her a generous loan with which to buy furniture for a small house she had recently purchased at Dartford in Kent; indeed, she seems to have relied on him implicitly in financial matters.

Anne never married again, nor did she ever leave England; her parents were dead, and her brother, a strict Protestant, did not approve of her conversion to the old faith. Thus a return to Cleves, even had she wished it, was out of the question. In fact she had grown fond of England and its people, and intended to die in her adoptive land. In her latter years, when her health began to fail, she was allowed by Queen Mary to live at Chelsea Old Manor, where Katherine Parr had once lived with Admiral Seymour, and it was here, in mid-July 1557, that she dictated her will, a document that bears witness to her kindness and compassion for others. To her brother she left a diamond ring, and to his wife a ruby ring; to her

568

sister, the Lady Amelia, went another diamond ring, as also to the Duchess of Norfolk and the Countess of Arundel. The Lady Elizabeth was to have Anne's second-best jewel, and there was a request for her to find employment in her household for 'one of our poor maids named Dorothy Curzon'. To Mother Lovell, 'for her care and attendance upon us in the time of our sickness', there was a bequest of £10.00, likewise to 'our poor servant, James Powell'; Elya Turpin, Anne's laundress, was to receive £4.00 'to pray for us'. Each of the executors was remembered 'for their pains': the Lord Chancellor was to have a standing cup and cover of gold or a crystal glass set with precious stones; Sir Richard Preston would get 'our best gilt bowl with a cover', and Edmund Peckham a jug of gold.

The Queen, 'our most dearest and entirely beloved sovereign lady', was asked to be overseer of the will, 'with most humble request to see the same performed as shall to her Highness seem best for the health of our soul'. In token of 'the special trust and affection which we have in her Grace', Anne bequeathed to Mary Tudor her best jewel, begging her to see that her servants were well provided for, in consideration of their long service; many had been with her since 1540, and Anne reminded the Queen how her father King Henry had 'said then unto us that he would account our servants his own; therefore we beseech the Queen's Majesty to accept them in this time of their extreme need.'

Anne knew she was dying when she dictated her will, and she ended it with the requests that all those benefiting from it should pray for her soul and see her body buried 'according to the Queen's will and pleasure', and that she might be given the last rites of 'Holy Church, according to the Catholic faith, wherein we end our life in this transitory world'.

Anne of Cleves died on 16 July 1557, at Chelsea, a few weeks short of her forty-second birthday. The illness that caused her death is not named. She was buried, on 3 August, by order of the Queen, in Westminster Abbey with great ceremony. The coffin was borne from Chelsea on a hearse, and was covered with seven rich palls. Many priests and clergy walked in the procession, as well as the Bishop of London and some of the monks who had not long before been allowed to return to Westminster Abbey. With them was their Abbot, John Feckenham, with the dead woman's executors, followed by several representatives of the nobility and gentry. The late Queen's banners were carried aloft by members of her household, who also walked in the procession. At Charing Cross, the cortège was met by a hundred more of Anne's servants, all bearing torches, who joined the throng of mourners, together with her ladies, clad in black, mounted on horses, as well as twelve 'beadsmen' of Westminster and eight heralds bearing white banners of arms, who ringed the corpse.

At the Abbey door, everyone dismounted, and the Bishop of London, with the Abbot of Westminster, received the body, swinging censers of incense over it. Then the coffin was borne into the great church, covered with a canopy of black velvet, and put in position before the altar, where it remained all night while the monks sang dirges. The next morning, a requiem mass was sung, and the Abbot preached a sermon. Bishop Bonner, wearing his mitre, said mass, then the coffin was laid in its tomb in the south transept of the Abbey. The chief officers of Anne's household then came forward and broke their staves of office, casting them after the coffin. Jane Seymour's sister Elizabeth, Marchioness of Winchester, was chief mourner, and she led the ladies in making their offerings afterwards. When the obsequies were concluded, her husband, John Paulet, Marquess of Winchester, entertained all the mourners to a funeral banquet at his London home. Within a month, the monks of Westminster had despoiled the hearse left over Anne's tomb, removing all the palls and banners adorning it, and Queen Mary gave orders for Anne's countryman, the stonemason Theodore Haveus, to come over from Cleves and fashion a proper monument. In 1606, a bare marble slab decorated with the earliest example of a skull and crossbones to appear in England was placed above Haveus's tomb. Today, Anne's final resting place is obscured by two monuments dating from the late seventeenth century.

Mary I did not long survive Anne of Cleves. She died, embittered and unloved, on 17 November 1558, and was succeeded by her sister, who became Queen Elizabeth I. Mary was buried not far from Anne of Cleves, in one of the side-chapels to the great Henry VII Chapel in Westminster Abbey.

Half a century after Anne's death, the chronicler Raphael Holinshed remembered her as 'a lady of right commendable regard, courteous, gentle, a good housekeeper, and very bountiful to her servants'. There had never been, he wrote, 'any quarrels, tale-bearings or mischievous intrigues in her court, and she was tenderly loved by her domestics.'

It was an apt and well-deserved tribute.

Bibliography

General

The major sources for this book have been the monumental *Calendar of Letters and Papers, Foreign and Domestic, of the Reign of Henry VIII* (21 vols in 33 parts, eds J. S. Brewer, James Gairdner and R. Brodie, HMSO, 1862–1932), which is said to include at least one million separate facts about Henry; *State Papers of the Reign of Henry VIII*, published under the Authority of Her Majesty's Commission (11 vols, Records Commissioners, 1831–52); and, for the latter part of the reign in particular, the *Acts of the Privy Council of England* (32 vols, ed. John Roche Dasent, HMSO, 1890–1918).

Of the diplomatic sources, by far the most useful and informative, if necessarily biased, is the *Calendar of Letters, Despatches and State Papers relating to negotiations between England and Spain, preserved in the Archives at Simancas and Elsewhere* (17 vols, ed. G. A. Bergenroth, P. de Goyangos, G. Mattingley, R. Tyler et al., HMSO, 1862–1965). This incorporates ambassadors' dispatches and a large volume of the correspondence of Katherine of Aragon and the Spanish monarchs. Also very useful, especially for descriptions of pageantry and ceremonial, is the *Calendar of State Papers and Manuscripts relating to English Affairs preserved in the Archives of Venice and in the other Libraries of Northern Italy* (7 vols, eds L. Rawdon-Brown, Cavendish Bentinck et al., HMSO, 1864–1947). Other diplomatic sources for

573

the period are the *Calendar of State Papers and Manuscripts existing in the Archives and Collections of Milan: vol. 1, 1385–1618* (ed. A. B. Hinds, 1912); the *Mémoires* of Martin and Guillaume du Bellay, French ambassadors to the court of Henry VIII (4 vols, eds V. L. Bourrilly and F. Vindry, Paris, 1908–19); *Correspondance du Cardinal Jean du Bellay* (ed. R. Scheurer, Paris, 1969); *Correspondance Politique de MM. de Castillon et de Marillac, Ambassadeurs de France en Angeleterre, 1537–1542* (ed. J. Kaulek, Paris, 1885); *Correspondance Politique de Odet de Selve, Ambassadeur de France en Angleterre, 1546–1549* (ed. G. Lefèvre-Pontalis, Paris, 1888); *Négociations Diplomatiques entre la France et l'Autriche, 1491–1530* (2 vols, ed. A. J. G. Le Glay, Paris, 1845–47); and *Papiers d'État du Cardinal Granvelle, 1500–1565* (9 vols, ed. C. Weiss, 1841–52).

Official records for the period are contained in the Rolls of Parliament, *Rotuli Parliamentorum* (7 vols, ed. J. Strachey et al., Records Commissioners, 1767–1832), in which are detailed all the Acts and Statutes, as well as parliamentary proceedings; *Household Ordinances: A Collection of Ordinances and Regulations for the Government of the Royal Household* (Society of Antiquaries, 1790); *Journals of Parliament for the Reign of Henry VIII, 1509–1536* (*c.* 1742); *Privy Purse Expenses of Henry VIII from November 1529 to December 1532* (ed. H. Nicolas, 1827); *Proceedings and Ordinances of the Privy Council of England* (ed. H. Nicolas, Records Commissioners, 1834–7); *The Statutes, AD 1235–1770* (HMSO, 1950); *Statutes of the Realm* (11 vols, Records Commissioners, 1810–28); *State Trials vol. 1, 1163–1600* (ed. D. Thomas, W. Cobbett and T. B. Rowell, Routledge & Kegan Paul, 1972); *English Historical Documents, 1485–1558* (eds C. H. Williams and D. C. Douglas, 1967); and, for documentary sources for the latter period of the book, the *Calendar of State Papers, Domestic Series, of the Reigns of Edward VI, Mary and Elizabeth, 1547–1580* (2 vols, ed. R. Lemon, Longman, Brown, Green, 1856) and the *Calendar of State Papers, Foreign Series, Elizabeth I* (ed. J. Stevenson et al., 1863–1950).

There are also several invaluable chronicle and narrative sources dealing with the reign of Henry VIII in general. Three are contemporary, or written by contemporaries. The first is Edward Hall's Chronicle, published in two versions: *The Union of the Noble and Illustrious Families of Lancaster and York* (first published 1542; ed.

H. Nicolas; G. Woodfall, Printer 1809) and *The Triumphant Reign of King Henry the Eighth* (first published 1547; ed. C. Whibley and T. C. and E. C. Jack, 2 vols, 1904). Hall was a lawyer; his chronicles have a strong patriotic bias in favour of Henry VIII, and he tends to gloss over compromising issues. His descriptions of state occasions have not been surpassed, and his true value is as an annalist. The second contemporary source is George Cavendish's *The Life and Death of Cardinal Wolsey* (first published 1557; ed. R. Sylvester, Early English Texts Society, 1959), which is particularly useful for the early career of Anne Boleyn. Cavendish was Wolsey's secretary and well placed to record contemporary events, yet his admiration for his master makes him a biased observer. The third, and most controversial, source is the *Cronico del Rey Enrico Otavo de Inglaterra*, written before 1552 and sometimes attributed to Antonio de Guaras, who came to England in the train of Eustache Chapuys, the Spanish ambassador. It was printed as *The Chronicle of King Henry VIII* (ed. M. A. S. Hume, George Bell and Sons, 1889), but is commonly referred to by historians as the 'Spanish Chronicle'. Much of the information in it is based on hearsay and rumour, although many writers have been fooled by a seeming authenticity of detail which is not always corroborated by other sources. This source should therefore be treated with caution.

There are several later narrative sources for the reign of Henry VIII; these may be divided into Protestant or Catholic sources, and most are accordingly biased. The Protestant sources are all English. John Foxe, in his popular *History of the Acts and Monuments of the Church* (better known as Foxe's Book of Martyrs) (published in 1563; ed. G. Townshend and S. R. Cattley, 8 vols, Seeley and Burnside, 1837–41), gives interesting details about Anne Boleyn and Katherine Parr, both of whom he represented as Reformation heroines. Raphael Holinshed's *Chronicles of England, Scotland and Ireland* (first published 1577; ed. H. Ellis, 6 vols, G. Woodfall, Printer, 1807–8) draws mainly upon Hall's chronicle. Charles Wriothesley, Windsor Herald, wrote before 1562 his *Chronicle of England in the Reigns of the Tudors from 1485 to 1559* (ed. W. D. Hamilton, 2 vols, Camden Society, 2nd series, X and XX, 1875, 1877). Wriothesley was the first cousin of Thomas, Earl of Southampton and Lord Chancellor of England, and may therefore be considered a reliable primary source, especially for

575

the 1540s, although his work was not published until 1581. The antiquarian John Stow wrote two useful books, *The Annals of England* (1592; ed. E. Howes, London, 1631) and his celebrated *Survey of London* (1598; ed. C. L. Kingsford, 2 vols, Oxford University Press, 1908). Another valuable later work is Lord Herbert of Cherbury's *The Life and Reign of King Henry the Eighth* (published a year after his death in 1649; ed. White Kennett, 1870), which may be considered to be the first 'modern' biography of the King. Herbert used original source material, some of which has since been lost or destroyed, and he was less subjective in his approach to his subject than earlier Protestant writers.

The later Catholic sources for Henry VIII's reign, most of which were printed abroad, are all biased against the King. Nicholas Harpsfield's *A Treatise on the Pretended Divorce between King Henry VIII and Katherine of Aragon* (ed. N. Pococke, Camden Society, 2nd series, XXI, 1878) was published in 1556 when Katherine's daughter Mary I was reigning and is consequently imbued with the spirit of the Counter-Reformation. Like most later Catholic sources, Harpsfield's work contains much that is apocryphal. One of the most damaging works ever printed was Nicholas Sanders' *De Origine ac Progressu Schismatis Anglicani* (first published in 1585 in Rome; printed as *The Rise and Growth of the Anglican Schism*, ed. D. Lewis, 1877). Sanders was an English Jesuit, exiled to Rome in the reign of Elizabeth I. He had nothing but contempt for Henry VIII, but the chief object of his venom was Anne Boleyn, whom he portrayed as evil personified, the cause of the English Reformation, and the English Jezebel. Sanders is responsible for many apocryphal anecdotes about Anne – such as the tale that she was the result of an affair between Henry VIII and Elizabeth Howard, or the tale that she was raped at the age of seven – and his treatise was received with scornful scepticism in England, prompting a reply by George Wyatt (see below, under chapter 7). Another Catholic writer working at the end of the sixteenth century was Gregorio Leti, who wrote a life of Elizabeth I which was suppressed by the Catholic authorities in Italy, probably because it was too favourable to its subjects. Nearly all the original copies were destroyed, and the work only survives in a French translation of 1694, *La Vie d'Elisabeth, Reine d'Angleterre*, from which some of the original material is certainly missing. It is thought that Leti made use of contemporary sources now lost to us, and for this reason his narrative may be of some value, although parts have been shown to be apocryphal. Girolamo Pollino, another Italian Catholic, wrote his *Istoria dell' Ecclesiastica della Rivoluzion d'Inghilterra* in 1594. Although he was biased against Henry VIII, there is evidence that much of his information was drawn from reliable sources, as many of his statements are corroborated by more contemporary sources. Unfortunately, there is much that has also been shown to be fanciful. The best Catholic source is Henry Clifford's *Life of Jane Dormer, Duchess of Feria* (published 1643; ed. E. E. Estcourt and J. Stevenson, Burns and Oates, 1887). Jane Dormer was one of Mary I's maids of honour and confidantes. When the Duke of Feria came to England in 1554 in the train of Philip of Spain, he fell in love with Jane and took her back to Spain as his wife. Many years later she dictated her memoirs to her English secretary, Henry Clifford, who published them after her death. They remain one of the better late sources, although one must allow for a certain bias and lapses in an old lady's memory.

There are several collections of primary source material for the period: *Archaeologia, or Miscellaneous Tracts relating to Antiquity* (102 vols, Society of Antiquaries, 1773–1969); *The Antiquarian Repertory: A Miscellany intended to Preserve and illustrate several valuable Remains of Old Times* (4 vols, London, 1775–84, and a later edition by F. Grose and T. Astle, 1808); Thomas Fuller's *The Church History of Britain* (1655) preserves details from sources now lost to us; *Records of the Reformation: The Divorce, 1527–1533* (2 vols, ed. N. Pococke, Oxford, 1870); Thomas Rymer's *Feodera* (ed. T. Hardy, Records Commissioners, 1816–69); John Strype's *Ecclesiastical Memorials* (3 vols, 1721–33; Oxford edn, 1822); John Weever's *Ancient Funeral Monuments within the United Monarchy of Great Britain, Ireland and the Islands adjacent . . . and what Eminent Persons have been in the Same interred* (Thomas Harper, 1631); and *Excerpta Historica* (eds S. Bentley and H. Nicolas, 1831).

Of primary importance to the historian are the printed collections of correspondence. The letters of Henry VIII appear in four compilations: M. St Clair Byrne's *The Letters of King Henry VIII* (Cassell, 1936); *Lettres de Henri VIII* (ed. G. A. Crapelet, 1826); and *Love Letters of Henry VIII* (two edns: H. Savage, 1949 and Jasper Ridley,

1988). Letters written by Henry's wives appear in *Letters of Royal and Illustrious Ladies* (ed. M.A.E. Wood, 1846) and Margaret Sanders's *Intimate Letters of England's Queens* (1957). Also worth consulting are: *Lettres de Rois, Reines et autres Personages des Cours de France et d'Angleterre* (ed. J. J. Champollion-Figeac, Paris, 1845–7, vol. 2); *Original Letters illustrative of English History* (11 vols, ed. H. Ellis Richard Bentley, 1824–46); *Original Letters relative to the English Reformation* (ed. H. Robinson, Parker Society, 1846–7); *The Lisle Letters* (ed. M. St Clair Byrne, 1981), which is particularly useful for the period 1533 to 1540; *Miscellaneous Writings and Letters of Thomas Cranmer* (ed. J.E. Fox, Parker Society, 1846); *The Correspondence of Matthew Parker, 1535–1575* (ed. J. Bruce and T. Perowne, Parker Society, 1853; and the *Epistles* of Desiderius Erasmus (3 vols, trans. F. M. Nichols Russell and Russell, 1962).

The chief secondary sources for the period in general are as follows: *Handbook of British Chronology* (ed. F. M. Powicke and E. B. Fryde, Royal Historical Society, 1961), which is invaluable for details of officers of state and the peerage; the *Dictionary of National Biography* (63 vols, eds L. Stephen and S. Lee, Oxford University Press, 1885–1900) gives biographical details of the lives of most of the people in this book; *The Complete Peerage* (ed. G. H. White et al., St Catherine's Press, 1910–59) gives a wealth of genealogical data on the aristocracy; *Burke's Guide to the Royal Family* (Burke's Peerage, 1973) gives details of royal genealogy and institutions; Alison Weir's *Britain's Royal Families: The Complete Genealogy* (The Bodley Head, 1989); and C. R. N. Routh's *They Saw it Happen, 1485–1688* (Blackwell, 1956), *They Saw it Happen in Europe, 1540–1660* (Blackwell, 1965), and *Who's Who in History, 1485–1603* (Blackwell, 1964).

For general history of the Tudor period, see J. D. Mackie: *The Earlier Tudors, 1485–1588* (Oxford, Clarendon Press, 1952); G. R. Elton's *England under the Tudors* (Methuen, 1955) and *The Tudor Constitution* (Methuen, 1960); David Harrison's delightfully illustrated study, *Tudor England* (2 vols, 1953); Christopher Morris's interesting series of character portraits, *The Tudors* (Batsford, 1955); M. Roulstone's lavish *The Royal House of Tudor* (Balfour, 1974); Godfrey E. Turton's *The Dragon's Breed* (1969); G. W. O. Woodward's *Reformation and Resurgence, 1485–1603* (Blandford, 1963); and P. Williamson's *Life in Tudor England* (Batsford, 1964).

There are several books on the Reformation. J. H. Merle d'Aubigny's *The Reformation in England* (1853) is outdated and inaccurate, but there are several more modern works that are well worth consulting: Sir F. Maurice Powicke's *The Reformation in England* (Oxford University Press, 1951); Philip Hughes's *The Reformation in England* (Macmillan, 1950) – vol. 1 covers Henry VIII's reign; H. Maynard-Smith's *Henry VIII and the Reformation* (Macmillan, 1962); and, for related subjects, see Erwin Doernberg's *Henry VIII and Luther* (Stanford University Press, 1961), William A. Clebsch's *England's Earliest Protestants, 1520–1535* (Yale University Press, 1964), and James Kelsey McConica's *English Humanists and Reformation Politics under Henry VIII and Edward VI* (Oxford University Press, 1965).

Henry VIII has been the subject of many biographies. The most recent and best ones have been Jasper Ridley's *Henry VIII* (Constable, 1984), J. J. Scarisbrick's *Henry VIII* (Constable, 1968) and Carolly Erickson's brilliantly detailed *Great Harry* (Dent, 1980). Previous biographies consulted include J. J. Bagley's *Henry VIII* (Batsford, 1962), Lacey Baldwin-Smith's *Henry VIII: The Mask of Royalty* (Jonathan Cape, 1971), John Bowle's *Henry VIII* (Allen and Unwin, 1964), N. Brysson-Morrison's *The Private Life of Henry VIII* (Robert Hale, 1964), Francis Hackett's *Henry the Eighth* (1929; Chivers Edition, 1973); Robert Lacey's *The Life and Times of Henry VIII* (Weidenfeld & Nicolson, 1972), Philip Lindsay's *The Secret of Henry VIII* (Howard Baker, 1953), Kenneth Pickthorn's *Early Tudor Government: Henry VIII* (1951); A. F. Pollard's *Henry VIII* (Longmans Green and Co., 1902) and Beatrice Saunders's rather subjective study, *Henry the Eighth* (Alvin Redman, 1963). For Henry's youth, see Frank Arthur Mumby's *The Youth of Henry VIII* (Constable, 1913), which draws heavily on the Spanish Calendar, and Marie Louise Bruce's enjoyable *The Making of Henry VIII* (Collins, 1977).

All six of Henry VIII's wives are dealt with in the following works: Agnes Strickland's *Lives of the Queens of England* (8 vols, Henry Colburn, 1851, and the Portway Reprint by Cedric Civers of Bath, 1972), much outdated now but a milestone of historical research in its time; Heather Jenner's *Royal Wives* (1967); and Norah Lofts's *Queens of Britain* (Hodder and Stoughton, 1977). The last serious collective biography of the six wives was Martin A. S.

Hume's *The Wives of Henry the Eighth* (Eveleigh Nash, 1905), long out of print and out of date. Paul Rival's *The Six Wives of Henry VIII* (Heinemann, 1937) is nearer to fiction than fact, and gives no details of sources.

There have been several individual biographies of Henry VIII's wives. For Katherine of Aragon, see Garrett Mattingley's excellent *Catherine of Aragon* (Jonathan Cape, 1942), Mary M. Luke's *Catherine the Queen* (Muller, 1967), Francesca Claremont's *Catherine of Aragon* (Robert Hale, 1939) and John E. Paul's *Catherine of Aragon and her Friends* (Burns and Oates, 1966), a very useful study. (It should be noted that Katherine herself signed her name with a 'K', not a 'C'.) Anne Boleyn has attracted more biographers than any of Henry's wives: Paul Friedmann's *Anne Boleyn: A Chapter of English History, 1527–1536* (2 vols, Macmillan, 1884) was for years the standard biography, but has since been replaced by more recent works: Philip Sergeant's *The Life of Anne Boleyn* (Hutchinson, 1923); Marie Louise Bruce's *Anne Boleyn* (Collins, 1972); Hester W. Chapman's *Anne Boleyn* (Jonathan Cape, 1974); Norah Lofts's *Anne Boleyn* (Orbis Books, 1979), very much popular history, drawing on Strickland; Carolly Erickson's *Anne Boleyn* (Dent, 1984); E. W. Ives's compelling academic study, *Anne Boleyn* (Blackwell, 1986), to which this author is greatly indebted; and Retha Warnicke's controversial *The Rise and Fall of Anne Boleyn: Family Politics at the Court of Henry VIII* (Cambridge University Press, 1989). There is no separate biography of Jane Seymour, but there is a good account of her life and the fortunes of her family in William Seymour's *Ordeal by Ambition: An English Family in the Shadow of the Tudors* (Sidgwick and Jackson, 1972). Anne of Cleves also lacks a biographer, and the major account of her life is still the chapter in Strickland's *Lives of the Queens of England*. Lacey Baldwin-Smith has written a superb study of the life of Katherine Howard in *A Tudor Tragedy* (Jonathan Cape, 1961). Anthony Martiensson's *Queen Katherine Parr* (Secker and Warburg, 1973) is another excellent work.

For Henry VIII's 'great matter', see Geoffrey de C. Parmiter's *The King's Great Matter* (Longmans, 1967) and Marvin H. Albert's *The Divorce* (Harrap, 1965). William Hepworth Dixon's *History of Two Queens* (4 vols, Bickers and Son, 1873) is now greatly outdated.

There are several good biographies of Henry VIII's children, all of which have proved useful for research purposes. Mary I's early life is related by Milton Waldman in *The Lady Mary* (Collins, 1972), and there is an excellent full biography by Carolly Erickson, *Bloody Mary* (Dent, 1978). The early life of Elizabeth I is described in several books, viz.: Alison Plowden's *The Young Elizabeth* (Macmillan, 1971), Mary M. Luke's *A Crown for Elizabeth* (Muller, 1971), Edith Sitwell's *Fanfare for Elizabeth* (Macmillan, 1949), and in full biograhies by B. W. Beckinsale, *Elizabeth I* (Batsford, 1963), John E. Neale, *Queen Elizabeth I* (Jonathan Cape, 1934), Jasper Ridley, *Elizabeth I* (Constable, 1987) and Neville Williams, *Elizabeth, Queen of England* (Weidenfeld & Nicolson, 1967). For the early life of Edward VI see Hester W. Chapman's *The Last Tudor King* (Jonathan Cape, 1958) and W. K. Jordan's *Edward VI: The Young King* (Allen and Unwin, 1968).

For the royal palaces of the Tudors see James Dowsing's fascinating *Forgotten Tudor Palaces in the London Area* (Sunrise Press, no date, 1980s); Janet Dunbar's *A Prospect of Richmond* (Harrap, 1966); Ian Dunlop's *Palaces and Progresses of Elizabeth I* (Jonathan Cape, 1962); Benton Fletcher's *Royal Homes near London* (1930); Bruce Graeme's *The Story of St James's Palace* (Hutchinson, 1929); and Philip Howard's *The Royal Palaces* (Hamish Hamilton, 1960).

For the Tower of London and its history see J. Bayley's *History and Antiquities of the Tower of London* (Jennings and Chaplin, 1830); D. C. Bell's *Notices of Historic Persons Buried in the Tower* (1877), an account of the bones found in St Peter ad Vincula; *The Tower of London: its Buildings and Institutions* (ed. John Charlton, HMSO, 1978), a book that throws new light upon Anne Boleyn's imprisonment in the Tower; John E. N. Hearsey's *The Tower* (John Murray, 1960); R. J. Minney's *The Tower of London* (Cassell, 1970); and A. L. Rowse's *The Tower of London in the History of the Nation* (Weidenfeld & Nicolson, 1974).

For details of coronations and burials in Westminster Abbey, see the highly detailed *Official Guide*, Arthur Penrhyn Stanley's *Historical Memorials of Westminster Abbey* (1886) and Edward Carpenter's *A House of Kings* (Baker, 1966). For the Archbishops of Canterbury of the period, see Edward Carpenter's *Cantuar: The Archbishops in their Office* (Baker, 1971). For Scottish affairs, see Caroline Bingham's *James V, King of Scots* (Collins, 1971).

Bibliography

For pageantry and ceremonial in the Tudor period, see Sydney Anglo's *Spectacle, Pageantry and Early Tudor Policy* (Oxford, Clarendon Press, 1969) and Robert Withington's *English Pageantry: An Historical Outline* (1918). For the Tudor court, see Neville Williams's fascinating *Henry VIII and his Court* (Weidenfeld & Nicolson, 1971), Christopher Hibbert's *The Court at Windsor* (Longmans, 1964) and Ralph Dutton's *English Court Life from Henry VII to George II* (Batsford, 1963). Henry VIII's courtiers are the subject of an excellent book by David Mathew, *The Courtiers of Henry VIII* (Eyre and Spottiswoode, 1970). William Edward Mead's *The English Mediaeval Feast* (Allen and Unwin, 1931) gives interesting information about court banquets. The cultural background to the period is described in Elizabeth M. Nugent's *The Thought and Culture of the English Renaissance* (Cambridge University Press, 1966). For Tudor drama, see Frederick Boas's *An Introduction to Tudor Drama* (Oxford University Press, 1933). For poetry, see Maurice Evans's *English Poetry in the Sixteenth Century* (Hutchinson, 1967) and Philip Henderson's *The Complete Poems of John Skelton, Laureate* (1931; 2nd rev. edn, Dent, 1948). Sir Thomas Wyatt's poems are dealt with under the heading to chapter 7. Sir Roy Strong's *Tudor and Jacobean Portraits* (2 vols, HMSO, 1969) is the most exhaustive study of Tudor royal portraits so far, but Christopher Lloyd's and Simon Thurley's *Images of a Tudor King* (Phaidon Press, 1990) is useful for its descriptions of Henry VIII's iconography. Hans Holbein, the greatest painter of the early Tudor period, painted Henry VIII and at least two of his wives; the greatest authority on Holbein is Paul Ganz: *The Paintings of Hans Holbein* (Phaidon Press, 1956). For Tudor costume, the best authority is Herbert Norris's *Costume and Fashion, vol 111, The Tudors, book 1, 1485–1547* (Dent, 1928); see also Norman Hartnell's *Royal Courts of Fashion* (Cassell, 1971).

Introduction

Contemporary views of the role of women in sixteenth-century society are to be found in the following works: John Colet's *A Right*

Fruitful Monition (1515); Colet was a friend of Sir Thomas More, Dean of St Paul's and founder of St Paul's School, and his views were those of a traditional churchman; Miles Coverdale's *The Christian State of Matrimony* (1543); Desiderius Erasmus's *The Institution of Christian Marriage* (1526); Henry VIII's own view on matrimony in his *Assertio Septem Sacramentorum adversus Martinus Lutherus* (published 1521; ed. O'Donovan, New York, 1908); the Scots reformer John Knox's *First Blast of the Trumpet against the Monstrous Regiment of Women* (ed. E. Arber, The English Scholar's Library of Old and Modern Works, 1878), for an extreme view; Sir Thomas More's *Utopia* (1516) for an idealistic view; two tracts by Queen Katherine Parr, *The Lamentations of a Sinner* (1547) and *Prayers and Meditations* (1545); and William Tyndale's *The Obedience of a Christian Man* (1528). See also Doris Mary Stenton's *The English Woman in History* (Allen and Unwin, 1957).

For enlightened views on education, see Roger Ascham's *The Schoolmaster* (1570), Ascham having been tutor to Queen Elizabeth I and the Lady Jane Grey. Juan Luis Vives's rigorous plan for the education of the Princess Mary is encapsulated in *De Institutione Foeminae Christianae* (Basle, 1538; trans. R. Hyrd, and printed in London by Thomas Berthelet, 1540).

1 *The princess from Spain*

The negotiations for the marriage of Katherine of Aragon to Arthur, Prince of Wales, during the period 1488 to 1501 are detailed extensively in the Spanish Calendar. Katherine's presentation to the English ambassadors at the age of two is described by the herald Ruy Machado in *Memorials of King Henry VII* (ed. J. Gairdner, Rolls Series, Longman, Brown, Green and Roberts, 1858). Accounts of the reigns of Ferdinand and Isabella are given by two Spanish chroniclers, Hernando del Pulgar, in his *Crónica de los Señoras Reyes Católicas* (published 1567; to be found in the *Biblioteca de Autores Española*, vol. LXX, Madrid, 1878) and Andres Bernaldes, in his *Historia de los Réyes Católicos D. Fernando y Doña Isabel* (Seville, 1870, and a later edition by M. Gomez-Moreno and J. de M. Carriazo, Madrid, 1962). The descriptions of Ferdinand and Isabella are based on those given by Pulgar, who was Queen Isabella's secretary. An excellent secondary authority on the history of Spain in the late-fifteenth and early-sixteenth century is *The Castles and the Crown: Spain, 1451–1555* by the English historian Townshend Miller (Gollancz, 1953). The only primary source to mention Katherine of Aragon and her sisters during their childhood is Vives.

Henry VII's instructions to the City of London for the state reception of Katherine of Aragon are in the Corporation of London Records Office and also in the Harleian MS. and Cotton MS. Vitellius in the British Library. Katherine of Aragon's departure from Spain and journey to England is described by Bernaldes.

2 A true and loving husband

The Spanish Calendar gives details of the dispute over Katherine's dowry and Henry VII's prevarication over her accompanying Arthur to Ludlow. It also describes Katherine's reception in England, as does Leland in *Collectanea*. Henry VII's insistence on seeing Katherine at Dogmersfield is described in *Proceedings and Ordinances of the Privy Council of England* and *Collectanea*; *Collectanea* is the source for Katherine's first meeting and evening with Prince Arthur.

The description of Henry VII derives from that given by the King's official historian, Polydore Vergil, in his *Anglica Historia* (Basle, 1534; ed. D. Hay, Camden Society, 3rd series, LXXIV, 1950). Vergil is the chief primary authority for the reign of Henry VII. The first 'modern' biography of the King was Sir Francis Bacon's *History of the Reign of King Henry the Seventh* (ed. J. R. Lumby, Cambridge, 1875); today, the definitive life is S. B. Chrimes's *Henry VII* (Eyre Methuen, 1972); Eric N. Simons's *Henry VII: The First Tudor King* (Barnes and Noble, 1968) is also useful. There is a good biography of Elizabeth of York by N. Lenz-Harvey, *Elizabeth of York, Tudor Queen* (Arthur Barker, 1973), which replaces the memoir by Strickland. Both Vergil, and John Foxe, in his *Acts and Monuments*, credit Henry and Elizabeth with four sons, as does Dean Stanley. However, the contemporary Windsor altarpiece shows only three, Arthur, Henry and Edmund. Dean Stanley says that an Edward Tudor (1495?–9) was buried in Westminster Abbey; he has perhaps confused him with his brother Edmund. Details of the youth of Henry VIII are to be found in *Letters and Papers of the Reign of Henry VIII* (detailed above), hereafter to be referred to as *L & P*; for his education see Bernard André's *Vita Henrici VII* (1500–8; in *Memorials of King Henry VII*, detailed above) – André was tutor to Henry VII's two elder sons.

    The major events and state occasions of the reign of Henry VII are chronicled by Polydore Vergil, Pietro Carmelianus of Brescia, in his '*Solomnes Ceremoniae et Triumphi*' (1508; ed. H. Ellis, Roxburgh Club, 1818), the London merchant Robert Fabyan in *The Concordance of Histories: The New Chronicles of England and France* (1512; ed. H. Ellis, Rivington, 1811), *The Great Chronicle of London* (eds A. H. Thomas and I. D. Thornley, Alan Sutton, 1938), *Memorials of King Henry VII*, and *The Reign of Henry VII from Contemporary Sources* (3 vols, ed. A. F. Pollard, Longmans, 1913–14). The description of Prince Arthur's manor at Bewdley comes from John Leland's *Itinerary* (5 vols, ed. L. T. Smith, London, 1906–8). Leland was an antiquary who toured England in the early sixteenth century. His other important work was *De Rebus Brittanicis Collectanea* (published 1612; ed. T. Hearne, Chetham Society, 6 vols, Oxford, 1715), an important source for the period. The best account of Katherine's state entry into London is in Hall's Chronicle, and the *Great Chronicle of London* records details of the pageants and verses performed on that occasion. For the wedding of Katherine and Arthur, see Hall's Chronicle and also William Longman's *A History of the Three Cathedrals dedicated to St Paul in London* (Longmans, Green & Co., 1973) and W. S. Simpson's *St Paul's Cathedral and Old City Life* (Elliot Stock, 1894). The wedding banquet is described in Hall's Chronicle and *Collectanea*, and the pageants to celebrate the marriage are detailed in *The Great Chronicle of London*.

    Next to nothing is known of Katherine of Aragon's daily life as Princess of Wales. Accounts of her brief marriage to Prince Arthur appear in Dulcie M. Ashdown's *Princess of Wales* (John Murray,

1979), *Lives of the Princesses of Wales* by M. B. Fryer, A. Bousfield and G. Toffoli (Dundurn Press, 1983) and Francis Jones's *The Princes and Principality of Wales* (University of Wales, Cardiff, 1969). Prince Arthur's death is described by Bernaldes, and the breaking of the news of it to Henry VII by Leland in *Collectanea*.

3 Our daughter remains as she was here

The major source for this chapter is the Spanish Calendar, which recounts the enquiries into Katherine's virginal status, negotiations for her marriage to Prince Henry, events leading up to the signing of the marriage treaty, negotiations with the Vatican for a dispensation, the text of the dispensations obtained, Queen Isabella's doubts as to its validity, negotiations for the payment of Katherine's dowry, her finances, her ill health and depression, her chafing at the restrictions imposed on her by etiquette, and Henry VII's treatment of her. Pope Julius's prevarication over the granting of a dispensation is mentioned in *L & P*. Hall is the source for Prince Henry's creation as Prince of Wales. The Prince's repudiation of his betrothal to Katherine is described by Lord Herbert.

4 Pain and annoyance

The Spanish Calendar continues to be the major source for this period of Katherine's life: it describes the secret negotiations to find another bride for Prince Henry, Katherine's problems with her household and finances, the course of her illness and depression, the dispute over her dowry, her status at court, the visit of King Philip and Queen Juana to England, Henry VII's plans to marry Juana, Katherine's appointment as her father's ambassador to the English court, her relations with Henry VII, with various Spanish diplomats, and with her confessor Fray Diego Fernandez, her correspondence, her reconciliation with Fuensalida who replaced her as ambassador, and the reopening of negotiations for her marriage with Henry VIII after his father's death.

Another account of the visit of Philip and Juana is given in the Cotton MSS. in the British Library. Prince Henry's letter is quoted by Byrne. The account of Henry VII's death, and the summary of his reign and achievements is based on those given by Bacon and Carmelianus. His wealth is referred to in the Venetian Calendar. Henry VIII's love for Katherine of Aragon, his desire to marry her, and his constant reiteration of this desire before their marriage is vouched for by his cousin, Reginald Pole, in *Pro Ecclesiasticae Unitatis Defensione*, 1536, (Rome, 1698).

5 Sir Loyal Heart and the Tudor court

Hall's Chronicle mentions the doubts felt by some about the validity of Henry VIII's proposed marriage to Katherine of Aragon. The wedding ceremony, and the date on which it took place, are recorded by Bernaldes.

Descriptions of Henry VIII's appearance appear in the Spanish Calendar, the Venetian Calendar, Cavendish's *Life of Cardinal Wolsey* and the dispatches of the Venetian ambassador Sebastian Giustinian, ed. L. Rawdon Brown in *Four Years at the Court of Henry VIII* (2 vols, Smith Elder and Co., 1854). The King's sporting and musical talents are described in the Spanish and Venetian Calendars, *L & P*, Hall's Chronicle, and the Milanese Calendar; his linguistic abilities are related in the Venetian Calendar and in *L & P*; his other accomplishments in the Venetian Calendar, which also mentions his piety, his genial informality, his popularity, his hatred of the French and the clothes he wore. His reluctance to attend, and boredom at, Council meetings, and his pursuit of frivolous pleasures in his early years are attested to by the Spanish and Milanese Calendars, and John Stow in his *Annals*.

Pageants, tournaments and court festivities are described in detail in Hall's Chronicle, the Venetian Calendar and *Four Years at the*

Court of Henry VIII. The royal visit to Coventry is mentioned in the Harleian MSS. in the British Library. Henry and Katherine's inscriptions on her missal appear in the Kings' MSS. in the British Library. The plague of 1517 is mentioned by Hall. For Katherine of Aragon's visit to Merton College, Oxford, see *Registum Annalium Collegii Mertonensis* in the Library of Merton College, Oxford, and for her Chapel of Calvary see Stow's *London*. Surviving examples of Katherine's needlework were described by John Taylor in *The Praise of the Needle* (1634). The Spanish Calendar records Henry's correspondence with King Ferdinand, and Katherine's relations with Maria de Salinas, Fray Diego, and other members of her household.

6 A chaste and concordant wedlock

The description of Henry VIII's coronation and the succeeding celebrations is derived from Hall's Chronicle. The Spanish Calendar records Henry and Katherine's early love for each other, details of Katherine's first pregnancy, the birth of a stillborn daughter in 1510, the conduct of Fray Diego and his dismissal, the FitzWalter affair, and the Queen's fall from favour in 1514. The ordinances for royal confinements are to be found in the State Papers. The Queen's taking to her chamber in December 1510 and the Christmas festivities at Richmond are described by Hall, who also recounts the birth and death of Prince Henry in 1511, the celebrations to mark the birth, and the grief of the King and Queen at their loss. The funeral of Prince Henry is mentioned in a manuscript in the Chapter House, Westminster Abbey.

Henry's farewell to Katherine and his departure for his campaign in France in 1513 are described by Hall. Details of the Flodden campaign are given in a letter from Sir Bryan Tuke to Richard Pace in *L & P*; Katherine's speech to her troops is reported in Peter Martyr: *Opus Epistolarum Petri Martyris* (published in Alcala de Henares, Spain, 1530); the losses at Flodden are recorded in the State Papers, and the events immediately following the battle are described by Hall. Henry's conduct on the French campaign is mentioned in the Milanese Calendar, and his return to England and reunion with Katherine is related by Hall.

Hall's Chronicle also gives details of Henry's anger at the perfidy of Ferdinand and Maximilian and the collapse of their triple alliance in 1514. The betrothal of the King's sister Mary Tudor to Louis XII is related in the Spanish and Venetian Calendars and in Hall's Chronicle. Hall also tells of the early death of Katherine's son, born in 1514. Henry VIII's distrust and jealousy of the new French King, Francis I, is recounted in the Venetian Calendar. For Francis I, see Desmond Seward's *Prince of the Renaissance* (Constable, 1973) and R. J. Knecht's *Francis I* (Cambridge University Press, 1982). For Mary Tudor's marriage to Suffolk and her later life see Walter C. Richardson's *Mary Tudor, the White Queen* (Peter Owen, 1970) and Hester W. Chapman's *The Sisters of Henry VIII* (Jonathan Cape, 1969). Margaret Tudor's visit to London is recounted by Hall.

There are numerous references to Wolsey's growing power in the Venetian Calendar. For modern lives of the Cardinal, see A. F. Pollard's *Wolsey* (Longmans, Green and Co., 1929), Charles Ferguson's *Naked to mine Enemies: The Life of Cardinal Wolsey* (Little, Brown, 1958), Neville Williams's *The Cardinal and the Secretary* (Weidenfeld and Nicolson, 1975) and Jasper Ridley's *The Statesman and the Fanatic* (Constable, 1982). The birth and christening of the Princess Mary are described in Hall's Chronicle. There are several references to Henry's growing egotism in the Venetian Calendar. Sir Thomas More's friendship with the King and Queen and his rise to favour are detailed in the biography written by his son-in-law, William Roper, *The Life of Sir Thomas More, Knight* (published *c.* 1556; ed. E. V. Hitchcock, Early English Texts Society, vol. CXCVII, 1935). More's uprightness is attested to in the Spanish Calendar. Contemporary with Roper's *Life* is that by the Catholic historian Nicholas Harpsfield, *The Life and Death of Sir Thomas More* (published *c.* 1557; ed. E. V. Hitchcock and R. W. Chambers, Early English Texts Society, 1932). Selected letters of Sir Thomas More were edited by Elizabeth Frances Rogers (1961). More has attracted several biographers this century: Algernon Cecil, *A Portrait of Thomas More, Scholar, Statesman, Saint* (John Murray, 1937), Leslie Paul, *Sir Thomas More* (1953), E. E. Reynolds, *The Field is Won* (Burns and Oates, 1968), and, for revised and less sympathetic assessments, Jasper Ridley, *The*

Statesman and the Fanatic (Constable, 1982) and Richard Marius, *Thomas More* (Dent, 1984).

Katherine of Aragon's last pregnancy is detailed in *L & P* and the Venetian Calendar, the latter relating the birth of a daughter who died soon afterwards. Descriptions of the Princess Mary in childhood are to be found in the Spanish Calendar, the Venetian Calendar, Pollino, and the *Diarii* of Marino Sanuto (ed. R. Fulin, F. Stefani et al., 59 vols, Venice, 1879–1903). Hall relates the Princess's betrothal to the Dauphin, 1518. The birth of Henry FitzRoy is recorded by Hall, and public outrage at the marriage arranged by Wolsey for Elizabeth Blount is attested to in *L & P*.

For descriptions of the Field of Cloth of Gold, see Hall, Holinshed and the Venetian Calendar. A good modern account is given by J. G. Russell in *The Field of Cloth of Gold* (1969). Katherine's objections are recorded in the Spanish Calendar. Charles V's visit to England in 1520 is described by Hall, Holinshed and the Venetian Calendar. For Charles V, see *Charles the Fifth, Father of Europe* by Gertrude von Schwarzenfeld (1957). The visit of Henry and Katherine to Charles V is noted by Hall. For Thomas Cromwell's life and career, see Neville Williams's *The Cardinal and the Secretary* (Weidenfeld and Nicolson, 1975), A. G. Dickens's *Thomas Cromwell and the English Reformation* (1959), and B. W. Beckingsale's *Thomas Cromwell, Tudor Minister* (Macmillan, 1978). Henry VIII's defence of the seven sacraments, published in 1521, *Assertio septem Sacramentorum adversus Martinus Lutherus*, was edited by O'Donovan (New York, 1908). For his being awarded the title *Fidei Defensor*, see Hall. Charles V's visit to England in 1522 and his betrothal to the Princess Mary is recorded in Hall's Chronicle and the Spanish Calendar. Mary's education at Ludlow is described in the Cotton MS., Vitellius in the British Library and by Vives. The Duke of Norfolk's qualities and abilities are mentioned by Vergil and in the Venetian Calendar; the cruelty of his mistress is described in *L & P*.

The outward appearance of the marriage of Henry and Katherine is attested to by Erasmus in *The Institution of Christian Marriage* (1526). The Spanish Calendar and *L & P* both testify to Katherine's being past the age for childbearing. Henry's reluctance to send Mary to Spain is noted in Hall's Chronicle and the Venetian Calendar. Henry FitzRoy's elevation to the peerage is described in Hall's

Chronicle, *L & P*, and Stow's *Annals*. The Venetian Calendar records how Katherine took offence at it. Both *L & P* and Pollino describe Mary taking up residence at Ludlow in 1525.

Henry VIII's presence at Mary Boleyn's wedding is recorded in *L & P*. The arrival of the Spanish ambassador Mendoza is recorded in the Spanish Calendar and by Hall. The Spanish Calendar also records that he found it difficult to see Katherine, and that Katherine was against a new French alliance. The Bishop of Tarbes's doubts are explained by Hall. For the sack of Rome, see the Spanish Calendar. The King's doubts of conscience over the validity of his marriage are attested to by many sources, chiefly Hall, Cavendish, Roper, Harpsfield, various ambassadors and William Tynedale in *The Practice of Prelates* (1530).

7 Mistress Anne

One of the chief primary sources for Anne Boleyn's life is the biography written by George Wyatt in the late sixteenth century, *Extracts from the life of the Virtuous, Christian and Renowned Queen Anne Boleyn* (published London, 1817). Wyatt was the grandson of the poet Sir Thomas Wyatt, Anne's Kentish neighbour and admirer, and he drew his information from anecdotes handed down within his own family and the reminiscences of Anne Gainsford, who had been Anne Boleyn's maid of honour. This is a work strongly biased in favour of its subject, written as it was in answer to Nicholas Sanders's crushing attack on Anne, published in 1585. See also George Wyatt, *Memorial of Queen Anne Boleyn* (reproduced in *The Life of Cardinal Wolsey* by George Cavendish, ed. S. W. Singer, 1827) and *Papers of George Wyatt* (ed. D. M. Loades, Camden Society, 4th series, V, 1968). For hostile opinions of Anne Boleyn, see the Spanish Calendar, Reginald Pole's *Pro Ecclesiasticae Unitatis Defensione* (1536) and Sanders.

The early Boleyns are mentioned several times in the Paston Letters (ed. N. Davis, Oxford University Press, 1971), Stow's *London*, and the *Calendar of Inquisitions Post Mortem for the Reign of*

Henry VII. For Hever Castle, see the current Official Guide, also the pamphlet by Gavin Astor, *The Boleyns of Hever* (1971). For the character of Sir Thomas Boleyn, his children and early income, see *L & P.* Anne Boleyn's birthdate has been arrived at after considering evidence in William Camden's *Annales rerum Anglicarum et Hibernicarum, regnanto Elizabetha, ad annum salutis MDLXXXIX* (London, 1615), *The Life of Jane Dormer*, Lord Herbert's life of Henry VIII, Leti's suppressed life of Elizabeth I, William Rastell's *Life of Sir Thomas More* (fragment in the Arundel MSS. in the British Library) and the Patent of Creation of Anne Boleyn as Marquess of Pembroke (MS. in the Chapter House, Westminster Abbey); see also Ives's *Anne Boleyn.* For George Boleyn's date of birth, see George Cavendish's 'Metrical Visions' (included in *The Life of Cardinal Wolsey*, ed. S. W. Singer, 1827).

   Anne Boleyn's virtues and accomplishments are described by Lord Herbert. For the duration of her stay in France, see Herbert, and also Emmanuel von Meteren's *Histoire des Pays Bas: Crispin, Lord of Milherve's Metrical History* (1618); *Epistre contenant le proces criminel fait à lencontre de la Royne Boullant d'Angleterre* by Lancelot de Carles, Clement Marot, and Crispin de Milherve (1545; included in *La Grande Bretagne devant l'Opinion Française* by G. Ascoli, Paris, 1927); *Histoire de la Royne Anne de Boullant* (MS. in the Bibliothèque Nationale, Paris; before 1550); and Charles de Bourgueville's *Les Recherches et Antiquités de la Province de Neustrie* (1583). Carles, Marot and Milherve were three great French men of letters and a valuable source of information on Anne Boleyn. Milherve was an eyewitness at her trial, and the other two, Marot in particular, knew her in France. Milherve wrote a separate metrical history. For Anne's stay in France, see the above, and also, for her accomplishments, Pierre de Bourdeille, Seigneur de Brantôme, *Lives of Gallant Ladies* (trans. R. Gibbings, 1924). For Anne's erotic experiences in France, see *L & P* and Brantôme.

   Cromwell's denial of the King's having been Lady Boleyn's lover is recorded in *L & P.* For the Butler marriage negotiations, see *L & P* and the *Calendar of Ormonde Deeds, 1172–1603* (vols 3 and 4, ed. E. Curtis, 1942–3); *L & P* mentions Francis I's regret at Anne's leaving France. George Wyatt describes Anne's arrival at the English court and her success there. For her affair with Percy, see Cavendish,

L & P and the Percy MSS. at Alnwick Castle. Anne Boleyn's appearance is described by Wyatt, Sanders (a surprisingly unbiased account), Carles etc., and *L & P*. For the poet Wyatt's interest in her, see George Wyatt. The accounts by Harpsfield and Sanders are far-fetched and malicious, owing nothing to contemporary sources. For Sir Thomas Wyatt, see his *Collected Poems* (ed. J. Daalder, Oxford, 1975), Kenneth Muir's *Life and Letters of Sir Thomas Wyatt* (Liverpool University Press, 1963) and Patricia Thomson's *Sir Thomas Wyatt and his Background* (Routledge and Kegan Paul, 1964). The rise of the Boleyns is charted in *L & P*. For Anne Boleyn's early life, see J. H. Round's *The Early Life of Anne Boleyn* (pamphlet published 1885).

There are two good primary sources for Henry VIII's courtship of Anne Boleyn, those of George Wyatt and Cavendish. Henry's love letters, now in the Vatican Library, are in the collections edited by Byrne and Ridley. None of Anne's letters to Henry survives: that quoted by Leti is spurious. A letter headed 'To the King from the Lady in the Tower', purported to have been written by Anne Boleyn in 1536, is of dubious authenticity. Cavendish refers to the patience of Queen Katherine with regard to her husband's affair with Anne, and is also the chief source of evidence for Anne's deadly hostility towards Wolsey. Her cordial outward relations with the Cardinal are described in *L & P*.

8   A thousand Wolseys for one Anne Boleyn

The King's passion for Anne Boleyn is described in George Wyatt's Memorial, Cavendish, the Spanish Calendar and *Ambassades en Angleterre de Jean du Bellay, 1527–1529* (ed. V. L. Bourilly and P. de Vassière, Paris, 1905). Jean du Bellay was the French ambassador to the court of Henry VIII and a friend of Anne Boleyn. His dispatches are therefore a good source to balance against the hostile reports in the Spanish Calendar. Jewels given to Anne by Henry in August 1527 are listed in a document in the Public Record Office. For the course of their affair, and the first rumours of a divorce and of the King having found a new mistress, see Cavendish, George Wyatt and Hall. The secret hearing at Westminster is described by Cavendish, Hall and Holinshed. The Spanish Calendar describes Mendoza's activities, the Queen's apprehension and Henry's confrontation with her. It also contains details of diplomatic relations between Charles V, his ambassadors, and the Vatican, and correspondence between the Emperor, his ministers, Katherine of Aragon, Mendoza and his successor Eustache Chapuys, and the Vatican.

Bishop Fisher's opinion on the King's case is given in *L & P.* Roper is the source for the decision to refer the case to Rome; doubts about the wisdom of this are referred to in *L & P.* Wolsey's mission to France is described in *L & P,* Cavendish and Harpsfield. The Venetian Calendar includes several references to Katherine's popularity. The Felipez affair is recorded in *L & P.* Rumours of Henry's intention of marrying Anne are first mentioned in the Spanish Calendar. George Wyatt alone speaks of Anne's reluctance to marry Henry. Wolsey's resistance to the match is referred to by Cavendish and Holinshed. The embassies to Rome are described in *L & P* and in Foxe's Book of Martyrs; the Spanish Calendar includes Henry's dispensation to marry Anne. Anne's enmity towards Wolsey is attested to by Cavendish, du Bellay, the Spanish Calendar and Harpsfield. Hall is, as usual, the source for festivities at court.

The Pope's appointment of Cardinal Campeggio as legate to try the case with Wolsey in England is recorded by Hall, Cavendish, Roper and Foxe. Wolsey's solution to the Boleyn/Butler feud is found in the Ormonde Deeds. Hall and du Bellay describe Henry's treatment of Katherine. Du Bellay is the chief source for the sweating sickness epidemic of 1528; he mentions Henry's fear of catching the disease and constant moves to escape it, as does Hall's Chronicle and *L & P.* Du Bellay was the first to record that Anne Boleyn was stricken with the sweat. The Spanish Calendar reports public outrage at the King's nullity suit. Du Bellay speaks of Henry's growing disillusionment with Wolsey. William Carey's death is noted in the Spanish Calendar, and the wardship of his heir in *L & P.* The Spanish Calendar is also the source for the view that Wolsey was doing his best to prevent an annulment. Anne's letter to the Cardinal of July 1528 is in Corpus Christi College, Cambridge. Henry's staunch belief that his case was righteous is attested to in the Spanish

Calendar. Katherine's retort to Anne while playing cards comes from George Wyatt.

Campeggio's delayed arrival, and his coming to London are related by Hall and Cavendish, who both describe the legate's discussions with Henry, Wolsey and Katherine. The brief produced by Queen Katherine is discussed in *L & P*, the Spanish Calendar and the State Papers, and the Council's advice to her is contained in a document in the Public Record Office. William Tynedale, in *The Practice of Prelates* (1530), avers that Katherine's women were made to spy on her. Henry's address to the Londoners at Bridewell Palace is recorded by Hall, du Bellay and Foxe. Du Bellay refers to Anne Boleyn's unpopularity. For the Nun of Kent, see *Rotuli Parliamentorum*, *L & P*, and Alan Neame's *The Holy Maid of Kent* (Hodder and Stoughton, 1971). Anne's growing power is documented by du Bellay, Cavendish and the Venetian Calendar. Her reformist sympathies, and her reading of forbidden books are described by George Wyatt and Foxe. For Henry's piety see *L & P*.

Both Hall and du Bellay describe the preparations for the legatine hearing. Henry's gifts to Anne Boleyn are listed in *L & P*. The account of the proceedings of the legatine court is drawn from those given by Cavendish, Hall, du Bellay, Foxe, Stow's *London*, Holinshed and Herbert. Du Bellay reports rumours of Anne Boleyn's pregnancy. Wolsey's fall from favour is related by Cavendish, Hall and Roper. Campeggio's return to Rome is recorded by Foxe. Roper records Henry's sounding out of Sir Thomas More's views. For the arrival of Chapuys and his early dispatches, see the Spanish Calendar. For Thomas Cranmer, see Foxe, Cranmer's Miscellaneous Writings (see above), and the following modern works: A. F. Pollard, *Thomas Cranmer and the English Reformation, 1489–1556* (2nd edn, Cassell, 1965), Jasper Ridley, *Thomas Cranmer* (Oxford University Press, 1962) and Edward Carpenter, *Cantuar: The Archbishops in their Office* (Baker, 1971).

9 It is my affair!

The Spanish Calendar is a major source as before for relations between England and the Emperor, the fortunes of Queen Katherine, and correspondence with the Vatican. The dispatches of Eustache Chapuys are one of the major sources for this period of Henry VIII's reign. For the fall and death of Wolsey, see Cavendish, Hall, *L & P*, the Milanese Calendar, du Bellay and Holinshed. Anne Boleyn's growing power is charted in the dispatches of du Bellay, the Milanese Calendar and *L & P*; for York Place see the Spanish Calendar and Stow's *London*. For the Reformation Parliament, see *Rotuli Parliamentorum*, Hall, and Stow's *Annals*. The Venetian Calendar describes relations between Henry and Katherine and Katherine's appearance and demeanour. The ennoblement of the Boleyns is noted by Hall, who is again the chief source for court festivities for this period.

The English embassy to Bologna is related by Hall and Foxe. For the Vatican's stand on the nullity suit, see *Acta Curiae Romana in cause matrimoniale Regis cum Katherina Regina* (1531). In the same year John Stokesley, Bishop of London, Edward Foxe and Nicholas de Burgo published *The Determination of the most Famous and most Excellent Universities of Italy and France that it is unlawful for a man to marry his brother's wife, that the Pope hath no power to dispense therewith*; Hall gives details of each individual determination. For the petition of the nobility of England to the Pope, see Cavendish; Lord Herbert provides the transcript. Foxe describes Cromwell's role in the origins of the English Reformation. For Anne Boleyn's books, see William Latimer's *Treatise on Anne Boleyn* (MS. in the Bodleian Library, Oxford), a contemporary reformist source of great value.

For Katherine's confrontation with the lords of the Council in 1531, see the Spanish Calendar, Hall and *L & P*. The Princess Mary's appearance and accomplishments are described in the Venetian Calendar. Thomas Abell's book, *Invicta Veritas: an answer that by no manner of law it may be lawful for King Henry the Eight to be divorced* (Luneberg, 1532) is referred to by Hall and Foxe. Katherine's life in exile from the court is described by Hall and the Venetian Calendar.

The Venetian Calendar gives details of the banquet at Ely Place, as does Stow's *London*. The near lynching of Anne Boleyn is recorded only in the Venetian Calendar, which, with *L & P*, gives details of opposition to the King. The resignation of More from the office of Lord Chancellor is related by Roper. For the Calais trip, see Hall, the *Mémoires* of Guillaume du Bellay (see above), and the Milanese Calendar. Descriptions of Anne Boleyn's appearance are to be found in the Venetian Calendar and Marino Sanuto's *Diarii*. Her creation as Marquess of Pembroke is described by Hall and Milles's *Catalogue of Honour* (1610); the Patent of Creation is now in the Chapter House, Westminster Abbey. George Wyatt tells of Anne finding the book of prophecies. For Cranmer's request to examine the King's case, see *L & P*.

10 Happiest of Women

The dispatches of Chapuys are again one of the chief sources consulted. The Spanish Calendar records Anne Boleyn's first appearance as queen, as does Hall. Anne's coronation is described by several authorities, viz. the Spanish Calendar, Hall, *L & P*, Holinshed, Stow's *London* and *Annals*, Wriothesley's Chronicle, and Wynkyn de Worde's *The Noble Triumphant Coronation of Queen Anne, wife upon the most noble King Henry the VIII* (printed 1533). Evidence of Anne's unpopularity manifested on the day is given only in the Spanish Chronicle, but is hinted at by Chapuys. For Norfolk's row with Anne, see the Spanish Calendar. For Katherine of Aragon's effects, see *Inventories of the Wardrobes of Henry FitzRoy, Duke of Richmond, and of the Wardrobe Stuff at Baynard's Castle of Katherine, Princess Dowager* (ed. J. G. Nichols, Camden Society, old series, LXI, 1854). See also W. Loke's *An Account of Materials furnished for the use of Queen Anne Boleyn* (Miscellanies of the Philibiblon Society, vol. VII, 1862–3). Public opposition to the King's second marriage is detailed in *L & P*.

Cranmer's ecclesiastical court and its proceedings are described in *L & P*, Hall's Chronicle, Harpsfield's *Pretended Divorce*, and

Holinshed's Chronicle. See also *Articles devised by the whole consent of the King's most honourable Council, His Grace's license obtained thereto, not only to exhort, but also to inform his loving subjects of the Truth* (1533). The Lady Mary's obstinacy is described in the State Papers. Anne's befriending of Protestants and her reformist literature are detailed by William Latimer and Foxe. The help she gave Thomas Winter is mentioned in *L & P*; Nicholas de Bourbon records his debt to her in *Nugarum Libri Octo* (Lyons, 1538).

For Katherine's confrontation with the Council, July 1533, see the report of her chamberlain, Lord Mountjoy, in the State Papers. The King's progress is recounted by Hall; the Lisle Letters refer to the good health and high spirits of the King and Queen. Henry's adultery with an unknown mistress, with Margaret Shelton, and later his affair with Jane Seymour, are all mentioned in the Spanish Calendar. Harpsfield records that Katherine pitied Anne. Letters announcing the birth of a prince, and their alteration, are referred to in *L & P*. The birth of Elizabeth is recorded in the Spanish Calendar and Hall's Chronicle. The comment of John Erley and other disparaging remarks about Anne's child are in *L & P*. The Milanese Calendar records foreign reaction to the birth. For Elizabeth's christening, see *L & P*, Hall and Holinshed. The Spanish Chronicle mentions Anne's intense love for her child. The dispatches of Jean de Dinteville, the French ambassador, give details of Anne's unpopularity and her diminishing power. Elizabeth's household at Hatfield is described in the State Papers.

Katherine's defiance of Suffolk is recounted in the Spanish Calendar, *L & P* and Hall. Henry's New Year's gifts to Anne's ladies, including Jane Seymour, are listed in *L & P*. The order to Hugh Latimer to keep his sermons short also appears in *L & P*; for Hugh Latimer, see Harold S. Darby's *Hugh Latimer* (1953). The Lisle Letters record Lady Lisle's gifts to Anne Boleyn, details of Katherine's jointure conferred upon Anne, the execution of the Nun of Kent, and Little Purkoy's death. The involvement of Fisher and Katherine with the Nun is referred to in *L & P*. For Katherine's life at Kimbolton, see *The Kimbolton Papers in the Collection of the Duke of Manchester* (1864).

The text of the Act of Succession 1534 is given in *The Statutes* and *Rotuli Parliamentorum*. Anne's second pregnancy is documented in the Spanish Calendar and *L & P*. The oath of succession is printed in Wriothesley's Chronicle, and Fisher's and More's refusal to take it is related by Hall, Roper, and Chapuys in the Spanish Calendar. For Reginald Pole's views on the King's marriages, see *Pro Ecclesiasticae Unitatis Defensione* (1536). Katherine's defiance of Tunstall is recorded in the State Papers and the Spanish Calendar. The gifts of a peacock and a pelican are noted in *L & P*.

The Spanish Caendar, the Venetian Calendar, George Wyatt and William Roper all describe Henry's growing disillusionment with Anne. His stable of girls at Farnham and Webbe's tale are noted in *L & P*. Lancelot de Carles et al. mention Anne being blamed for the executions of 1535. Roper is the best source for More's sojourn in the Tower. Hall records the executions of the monks of the Charterhouse and Bishop Fisher. The bad harvest is mentioned in *L & P*, where there is also the sole reference to Anne's third pregnancy. Katherine's letter to Forrest, and the search of her house for incriminating evidence are related by Pollino; Hall gives a grim description of Forrest's ultimate fate. The allegation (unauthenticated) that Henry blamed Anne for More's death comes from *The Life of Jane Dormer*.

Anne's visit to Syon Abbey is described by William Latimer. Her charities, needlework, and interest in education are recorded by George Wyatt and Foxe. Her fear of being cast off as Katherine had been is noted in *L & P*. The Spanish Calendar is the chief source for Katherine's death. Pollino records Anne's jealousy of public interest in Katherine's 'good end'.

11 Shall I die without justice?

The tale of Anne catching Henry with Jane Seymour on his knee comes from *The Life of Jane Dormer* and Sanders, and may well have some basis in fact. Wriothesley's Chronical says that Anne's fright at the King's fall caused her to miscarry of a son. Anne's miscarriage is documented by the Spanish Calendar, Hall, George Wyatt, *The Life of Jane Dormer* and Sanders, and her comment to her ladies afterwards comes from *L & P*. The Spanish Calendar, in particular the dispatches of Chapuys, is a major source for the fall of Anne Boleyn. Jane Seymour's rise to prominence is noted in the Bodleian MSS. Jesus College, Oxford. Henry's courtship and the jealousy between Anne Boleyn and Jane Seymour is recorded in the Spanish Calendar and *The Life of Jane Dormer*. For Sir Nicholas Carew, see R. Michell's *The Carews of Beddington* (London Borough of Sutton Libraries and Arts Services, 1981), which also gives details of Beddington Park, where Jane stayed before her marriage. The plot against Anne Boleyn is described by Lancelot de Carles et al. and by Milherve in his Metrical History. Coverdale's Bible, with its inscription to Anne, is in the British Library. *L & P* mentions Cromwell sounding out the Bishop of London on the subject of a royal divorce. Henry's letter to Pace on the likelihood of his having male heirs is in the State Papers. The proposed trip to Calais is mentioned in the State Papers and the Lisle Letters. For Matthew Parker, see his Correspondence (mentioned above) and V. J. K. Brook's *A Life of Archbishop Parker* (1962). The Spanish Chronicle refers to Smeaton's newly acquired wealth. The torturing of Smeaton is hinted at by George Constantine, body servant to Sir Henry Norris in the Tower, in his *Memorial* (in *Archaeologia*), and the Spanish Chronicle gives unauthenticated details. For the May Day jousts, see Hall and Wriothesley.

Anne Boleyn's committal to the Tower is described in Sir John Hayward's *Life of King Edward the Sixth* (1630), but the best contemporary source for this and her imprisonment are the dispatches of Sir William Kingston, Constable of the Tower, to Thomas Cromwell, which give a day-by-day account of Anne's stay there. They are to be found in the Cotton MSS. in the British Library. Henry's nocturnal jaunts are described in the Lisle Letters. The arrests and imprisonment in the Tower of Rochford, Weston, Brereton, Norris, Wyatt and Page are described in the *Histoire de la Royne Anne de Boullant*, an almost contemporary French manuscript (Bibliothèque Nationale, Paris; before 1550). Wyatt's spurious confession is related by the Spanish Chronicle and Sanders. The information given by the Spanish Chronicle about these events is notoriously untrustworthy. George Boleyn's distress is noted in *L & P*. George Constantine avers Brereton's innocence. The King's new hairstyle is recorded in Stow's *Annals*.

The trial of Anne's so-called lovers is described by Hall and Wriothesley, and the Lisle Letters record public speculation as to the fate of the accused. Wriothesley records the breaking up of Anne's household. Anne's trial is documented by the Spanish Calendar, George Wyatt, Wriothesley, the Harleian MSS. in the British Library, the *Baga de Secretis* in the Public Record Office (in which are preserved all the surviving documents relating to the trials of Anne and her brother), Cobbett's *State Trials*, and the *Reports of Sir John Spelman* (ed. J. A. Baker, Selden Society, 93, 94, 1977–8) – Spelman attended Anne's trial. The belief of the people in Anne's innocence is attested to by Chapuys in the Spanish Calendar, George Wyatt, George Constantine, William Camden and Sir John Spelman, all of whom refer to the unfairness of the trial. For Rochford's trial, see Spelman, Wriothesley, the Spanish Calendar, George Wyatt, George Constantine, *Excerpta Historica*, Lancelot de Carles et al., Cobbett, and the *Baga de Secretis*. The sentence on Rochford is recorded in *L & P*. Thomas Fuller names Lady Rochford as a principal witness for the Crown.

Henry's announcement that he foresaw Anne's downfall is quoted in *L & P*. The execution of the male prisoners is described by Hall, Wriothesley, the Spanish Calendar, George Constantine, the *Histoire de la Royne Anne de Boullant*, the Lisle Letters, and Milherve's Metrical History. Rochford's scaffold speech appears in three versions: quoted variously by George Constantine, Wriothesley, and the Spanish Chronicle. Anne's reaction to Smeaton's confession is related by Lancelot de Carles et al. and Milherve. The case papers for the annulment of Anne's marriage to Henry have disappeared, but see Wriothesley's Chronicle and Ives's *Anne Boleyn*. The cost of erecting the scaffold and Anne's expenses in the Tower are listed in *L & P*. For Anne's execution, see the Spanish Calendar, the Lisle Letters, *L & P*, the *Histoire de la Royne Anne de Boullant*, Lancelot de Carles et al., Milherve, George Wyatt, Sir John Spelman, Hall, the Harleian MSS. in the British Library, Wriothesley, the Spanish Chronicle, Foxe. and *The Chronicle of Calais in the Reigns of Henry VII and Henry VIII, to the year 1540* (attributed to Richard Turpin; ed. J. G. Nichols, Camden Society, XXXV, 1846).

For the tomb of Thomas Boleyn, Earl of Wiltshire, see the

guidebook to St Peter's Church, Hever, Kent. For Elizabeth Howard's tomb in the Howard Aisle of Lambeth Church, see *The History of the Parish of Lambeth* by J. Nichols (1786).

12 Like one given by God

The Spanish Calendar, chiefly the dispatches of Chapuys, is a major source for this chapter. Jane Seymour's former service as maid of honour to both Katherine of Aragon and Anne Boleyn is recorded by Chapuys and Wriothesley. Hall notes that Henry wore mourning for Anne Boleyn. For the marriage of Henry VIII and Jane Seymour, see Wriothesley's Chronicle and the Lisle Letters. Wriothesley incorrectly gives the date as 20 May and the place as Chelsea; the Lisle Letters have the correct date and place. Wriothesley describes Jane's first appearance as queen. Chapuys and Lord Herbert describe how she looked and dressed. The Act of Succession 1536 is reproduced in *The Statutes* and *Rotuli Parliamentorum*. For John Hill see *L & P*. Stow's *London* describes the King and Queen attending the marching-watch ceremony. Henry's reconciliation with Mary is documented by the Spanish Calendar, *L & P* and Wriothesley; Wriothesley describes their meeting at Hackney. For Holbein's portraits of Jane Seymour, see *Holbein and the Court of Henry VIII* (Exhibition Catalogue, The Queen's Gallery, Buckingham Palace, 1978). Hall describes the King and Queen's trip on the ice. Mary's reception at court is recounted in the Belvoir MSS. (Historical MSS. Commission, report XII, appendix IV, vol. I, the Duke of Rutland's Papers). For Jane's patronage of the Royal Hospital of St Katherine-by-the-Tower, see Hall, and Catherine Jamison, *The History of the Royal Hospital of St Katherine by the Tower of London* (1952).

Confirmation of the Queen's pregnancy is recorded in the State Papers, and the thanksgiving services for it in *L & P*. The Lisle Letters give details of the pregnancy, Jane's fancy for quails, and details of her household and the dress of her maids of honour. The prayers for Jane when in labour are mentioned by Wriothesley. For the birth of Prince Edward, see Hall, *The Chronicle and Political Papers*

of King Edward VI (ed. W. K. Jordan, Allen and Unwin, 1966), and
Jack Dewhurst's *Royal Confinements* (Weidenfeld and Nicolson,
1980), which explodes once and for all the theory – quoted by
Harpsfield and Sanders – that Edward was born by Caesarean section.
Wriothesley describes the celebrations in London in honour of the
birth, and Hall describes the christening. Both chroniclers mention
the ennoblement of Jane's brothers. Prayers of intercession for the
Queen's life are referred to by Wriothesley. Her death is recorded in
L & P, Wriothesley, Hall, the journal of Edward VI, and Foxe, and
her obsequies are described in the State Papers and Hall's Chronicle.

13 *I like her not!*

For Henry VIII's search for a fourth wife and abortive negotiations in
this connection, see *L & P*. From 1537 onwards, the dispatches of the
French ambassador, Marillac, are a rich source of information on the
period, especially with regard to Henry's wives, but Marillac is not
always a reliable source. There are few dispatches from Chapuys
relating to this period: he had been recalled to Spain when relations
between England and the Empire deteriorated after the Pilgrimage of
Grace. The Lisle Letters offer some fascinating information about the
domestic life of the court at this time: Henry's piety, his friendship
with Anne Bassett, courtly festivities, Prince Edward, and the
selection of ladies for the new Queen's household. For further details
of the childhood of Prince Edward, see *L & P* and the Cotton MS.
Vitellius in the British Library. For the Exeter conspiracy, see
Horatia Durant's *Sorrowful Captives* (Griffin Press, 1960).

   For the embassy to Cleves, see Hall, Foxe and the Cotton MS.
Vitellius in the British Library. The *Allgemeine Deutsche Biography
vols 1 and 14* (Duncker and Humbolt, Berlin, 1967–71) provides
good genealogical details of the family of Anne of Cleves. Anne's
journey to England is described in the State Papers, the dispatches of
Marillac, and the Lisle Letters. Thomas Wriothesley's opinion of
Anne is in *L & P*. Anne's reception in Calais is described in Hall's
Chronicle and the Lisle Letters, and her arrival in Dover by Hall and

William Lambard in *A Perambulation of Kent* (1576); her progress through Kent is described by Hall. Henry's visit to Rochester is related in *L & P*, the State Papers, and Hall's Chronicle, and his displeasure and attempts to get out of his marriage contract are chronicled in the State Papers. Marillac describes the preparations for Anne's reception on Shooter's Hill, which event is detailed by Hall, the Lisle Letters, Lambard, and the Cotton MS. Vespasian in the British Library. For the banquet afterwards, see Hall.

Henry's decision to go through with the marriage is recorded in the State Papers. Hall describes the marriage ceremony and the events immediately afterwards. Henry's inability to consummate the marriage is attested to in the State Papers. For Anne's secretary, see *Proceedings and Ordinances of the Privy Council*. Anne's presence at the jousts is recorded by Hall, who also tells of the return of the foreign nobles to Cleves and Anne's reception in London. For Lord Edmund Howard's letter, see the Lisle Letters. Cromwell's fall is chronicled by Marillac and Hall. The May jousts are referred to in Hall and Stow's *London*. Anne's banishment to Richmond is mentioned by Hall and Marillac.

Henry's affair with Katherine Howard is detailed by Marillac and Foxe. For her date of birth, see Marillac's dispatches, the Spanish Chronicle, and *A Tudor Tragedy* by Lacey Baldwin-Smith. The petition for the examination of the validity of the King's marriage to Anne of Cleves is in the *Journals of Parliament for the Reign of Henry VIII* (published *c.* 1742), and the decision to refer the matter to the clergy is recorded in the State Papers. The debate in the Lords is described in the *Journals of Parliament*, as is the annulment of the marriage; for this, see also Hall and Foxe. The reaction of the Duke of Cleves is recorded by Lord Herbert, and his doubts over Henry's treatment of Anne are mentioned in the State Papers. Anne's request to see Elizabeth is referred to by Leti. Anne's contentment is vouched for by Marillac. The execution of Cromwell is described by Hall.

14 *Rose without a thorn*

Henry VIII's marriage to Katherine Howard is mentioned by Hall and Foxe. Hall also describes the executions of Fetherston, Powell and Abell. Henry's armour in the Tower measures 54″ around the girth. Anne of Cleves's merriment and Henry's visit to her are described by Marillac. Katherine's first appearance as Queen is recorded by Hall; her new clothes and caprices are referred to in the Spanish Chronicle. For a description of the Lady Mary, see Marillac's dispatches and the Venetian Calendar. Katherine Howard's household is detailed in the State Papers. The priest's slander is reported in Acts of the Privy Council. Henry's amorous behaviour is attested to by Marillac. Richard Jonas's *The Birth of Mankind* (1540), a treatise on birth and midwifery, is dedicated to Katherine Howard. The private life of Henry and Katherine is recorded by Marillac, who also gives details of Anne of Cleves's visits to court. Henry's gifts to Katherine are referred to in *L & P*.

Henry and Katherine's separation in the spring of 1541 is deduced from information in Acts of the Privy Council; Marillac describes the King's depression and illness. The release of Wyatt is mentioned in the Spanish Calendar and the State Papers (note that Chapuys was now back in England). Rumours of a reconciliation between Henry and Anne of Cleves are reported in *L & P*. Margaret Pole's execution is described by Chapuys. Dereham's appointment as Katherine's secretary, and his row with Mr John are reported in *L & P*, as are details of the progress of autumn 1541. Marillac mentions Prince Edward's illness. For the testimonies of Lascelles and Hall, see the State Papers. Henry and Katherine's return to Hampton Court is mentioned by Hall, and the thanksgiving service for the King's marriage is referred to in the Acts of the Privy Council. Hall tells of Cranmer's letter to Henry. Henry's initiation of an enquiry into the conduct of the Queen is recorded in Acts of the Privy Council, and the investigations arising from this are recorded in the Spanish Calendar, the Acts of the Privy Council, the State Papers, and *L & P*.

15 *Worthy and just punishment*

Hall, the Acts of the Privy Council, and the State Papers describe
Katherine's banishment to Syon and her life there. The discharge of
her household is related in Wriothesley's Chronicle. For the Council
being informed of the proceedings against the Queen, and the
debates over the action to be taken, see the State Papers and Proceedings of the Privy Council. The interrogations and testimonies of the
suspects and witnesses are recorded in the State Papers, *L & P*, and
Hall's Chronicle. Pollino mentions Culpeper's beauty. *L & P* refers
to Katherine being deprived of the trappings of queenship and
degraded. The arraignment of her lovers is described in Marillac's
dispatches, *L & P* and the State Papers. Marillac and Chapuys both
testify to Henry's grief. His refusal to commute Dereham's sentence
is recorded in the State Papers and Acts of the Privy Council.
Dereham's confession, obtained under torture, is in the State Papers.
Harpsfield says people were saying that Katherine and Dereham
were worthy to be hanged one against the other. The State Papers
report the rumours of Anne of Cleves's pregnancy. For the execution
of Katherine's lovers, see Hall and Wriothesley. The account of
Nikander Nucius in the Spanish Calendar (1546) is the authority for
the heads of the Queen's lovers being displayed on spikes on London
Bridge.

The committal of members of the Howard family to the Tower,
their arraignments and their ultimate fates are all described in the
State Papers, the Acts of the Privy Council, the Journals of
Parliament and Hall's Chronicle. For Henry's advancing stoutness,
see Marillac. Hall records the passing of the Act of Attainder for
treason against the Queen and Lady Rochford; the Act is in the
House of Lords Record Office. Chapuys and the Journals of
Parliament report Katherine's refusal to plead before the Lords. The
Spanish Calendar describes Katherine's last days at Syon and
speculation as to her fate. Hall and the Journals of Parliament
confirm that Henry's assent to the Attainder was given under Letters
Patent. His recovery from his grief and flirtation with ladies of the
court is documented by Chapuys. The Journals of Parliament record

Katherine being informed of the sentence of death passed on her. Her removal to the Tower is described by Chapuys and *L & P*; Chapuys tells how she sent for the block. For Otwell Johnson's letters, and Katherine's last days in the Tower, see Barbara Winchester's *Tudor Family Portrait* (1955), also the Lisle Letters. Katherine's execution is described by Chapuys, Marillac, Hall and Foxe; spurious details are given by the Spanish Chronicle and Leti.

16 Never a wife more agreeable to his heart

The dispatches of Chapuys are one of the chief sources for Henry VIII's domestic life during this period. Henry's health is described by Andrew Boorde in *A Breviary of Health* (1542; ed. F. J. Furnivall, Early English Texts Society, London, 1870), and his happier frame of mind by Chapuys. For Scottish affairs, see Hall and Byrne. For the affairs of the Lady Mary, see the dispatches of Marillac, the Venetian Calendar and the Spanish Calendar. Negotiations for the marriage of Katherine Parr to Henry Scrope are described by Strickland. For Katherine Parr's Throckmorton relations, see A. L. Rowse's *Raleigh and the Throckmortons* (Macmillan, 1962), and for Anne Parr, see Sir Tresham Lever's *The Herberts of Wilton* (1967). Snape Hall is described in *Collectanea*. For William Parr's matrimonial entanglements, see Hall, the Spanish Calendar and the Complete Peerage. Chapuys records that Henry used emotional blackmail to win Katherine's sympathy. His corpulence is described by Sir John Spelman.

Katherine Parr's religious zeal is mentioned by Foxe, and there is ample evidence for it in the two tracts published by her: *Prayers and Meditations* (1545) and *The Lamentations of a Sinner* (1547). Her character is discussed in the Spanish Calendar, the Spanish Chronicle and Foxe's Book of Martyrs. A poem by her in French is in the Cecil Papers at Hatfield House, and corroborates contemporary references to her ability to speak French. The special licence for her marriage is in the State Papers, and the ceremony itself is described by Hall.

Anne of Cleves's reaction is mentioned in the Spanish Calendar and the Spanish Chronicle.

The education of Prince Edward is described in the journal of Edward VI, Sir John Hayward's Life, and Roger Ascham's *Toxophilus* (1545). Hall refers to the ennoblement of William Parr. Chapuys mentions Henry's obesity and growing infirmity. For Najera's visit, see the Spanish Calendar, which also mentions Margaret Douglas's marriage. Henry's appointment of Katherine as Regent during his absence in France is recorded in *L & P* and the State Papers. The Spanish Calendar describes the Siege of Boulogne. Katherine's injunctions against the plague are in the Harleian MSS. in the British Library. Her farewell to Chapuys is recorded by him in the Spanish Calendar, which also refers to her reputed reformist tendencies. For her owning heretical books, see Robert Parsons's *A Treatise of Three Conversions of England* (1603); for Anne Askew, see John Bale's *The First Examination of Anne Askew* (1546) and *The Latter Examination of Anne Askew* (1547); and for the Duchess of Suffolk see Evelyn Read's *Catherine, Duchess of Suffolk* (Jonathan Cape, 1962). For Gardiner's plot against Katherine and the events that allegedly occurred in *c.* July, 1546, see Foxe. Hall records the fate of Anne Askew. The visit of the Admiral of France is described by Wriothesley.

The Spanish Calendar mentions Henry's popularity at the end of his life. His death is recorded in the Spanish Calendar, the dispatches of George de Selve, the French ambassador, Hall's Chronicle, Foxe's Book of Martyrs, and William Thomas's *The Pilgrim: A Dialogue on the Life and Actions of King Henry the Eighth* (*c.* 1547; ed. J. A. Froude, Parker, Son and Bourn, 1861). Harpsfield gives an apocryphal account. Edward VI's journal and Hayward give accounts of how the news was broken to the King's children. Hall relates the proclaiming of Edward VI as King. Henry's funeral is described by Hall and Foxe, and the summary of his life and achievements is based on those given in the Spanish Calendar, Foxe's Book of Martyrs, and William Thomas's *The Pilgrim*.

17 Under the planets at Chelsea

For the character of Sir Thomas Seymour, see Hayward. The character of the Lady Elizabeth is described in the *Life of Jane Dormer*. Hall records Katherine's wish to marry Seymour. For Katherine's house at Chelsea, see Mary Cathcart Borer's *Two Villages: The Story of Chelsea and Kensington* (W. H. Allen, 1973) and Thea Holme's *Chelsea* (Hamish Hamilton, 1972). Katherine's marriage to Seymour is mentioned by Edward VI in his journal, which also refers to the offence taken by Lord Protector Somerset and the Council; see also the indictment of Lord Sudeley, 1549, in the State Papers. William Camden relates the feud between Katherine and the Duchess of Suffolk. For a description of Lady Jane Grey, see the letter of Baptist Spinola, 10 July 1553, in the Genoese Archives. There are two excellent modern biographies of Jane: Hester W. Chapman's *Lady Jane Grey* (Jonathan Cape, 1962) and Alison Plowden's *Lady Jane Grey and the House of Suffolk* (Sidgwick and Jackson, 1985). Udall's praise is recorded in his *The First Tome or Volume of the Paraphrase of Erasmus upon the New Testament* (1548).

Details of the affair between Seymour and Elizabeth are to be found in the State Papers (Deposition of Katherine Ashley, January 1549, Deposition of Thomas Parry, January, 1549, and Deposition of the Lady Elizabeth, January, 1549). The rumours that Elizabeth bore the Admiral a child are referred to in *The Life of Jane Dormer*. Elizabeth's illness is recorded in the State Papers. Sudeley Castle is described by Leland in *Collectanea*; for Throckmorton's description of it as a second court see Rowse. Katherine's death and funeral are recorded in *A Breviate of the Interment of the Lady Katherine Parr, Queen Dowager, late wife to King Henry VIII etc.*, a manuscript in the Royal College of Arms.

For the later life of Anne of Cleves, the best sources are the State Papers and Strickland, who quotes most of the relevant documents relating to Anne. See also Fuller's *Church History*. For Anne's funeral, see the Cotton MS. Vitellius in the British Library.

The inventory of effects belonging to Katherine Parr's daughter is in the Lansdowne MSS. and is reproduced by Strickland, who also quotes all the evidence for and against the child growing to maturity. The fortunes of Katherine Parr's tomb and corpse are recounted by Treadway Russell Nash in *On the Time of Death and Place of Burial of Queen Katherine Parr* (1876), and also by Martiensson and Strickland.

Genealogical Tables

Table I. Rival Dynasties: Lancaster, York and Tudor

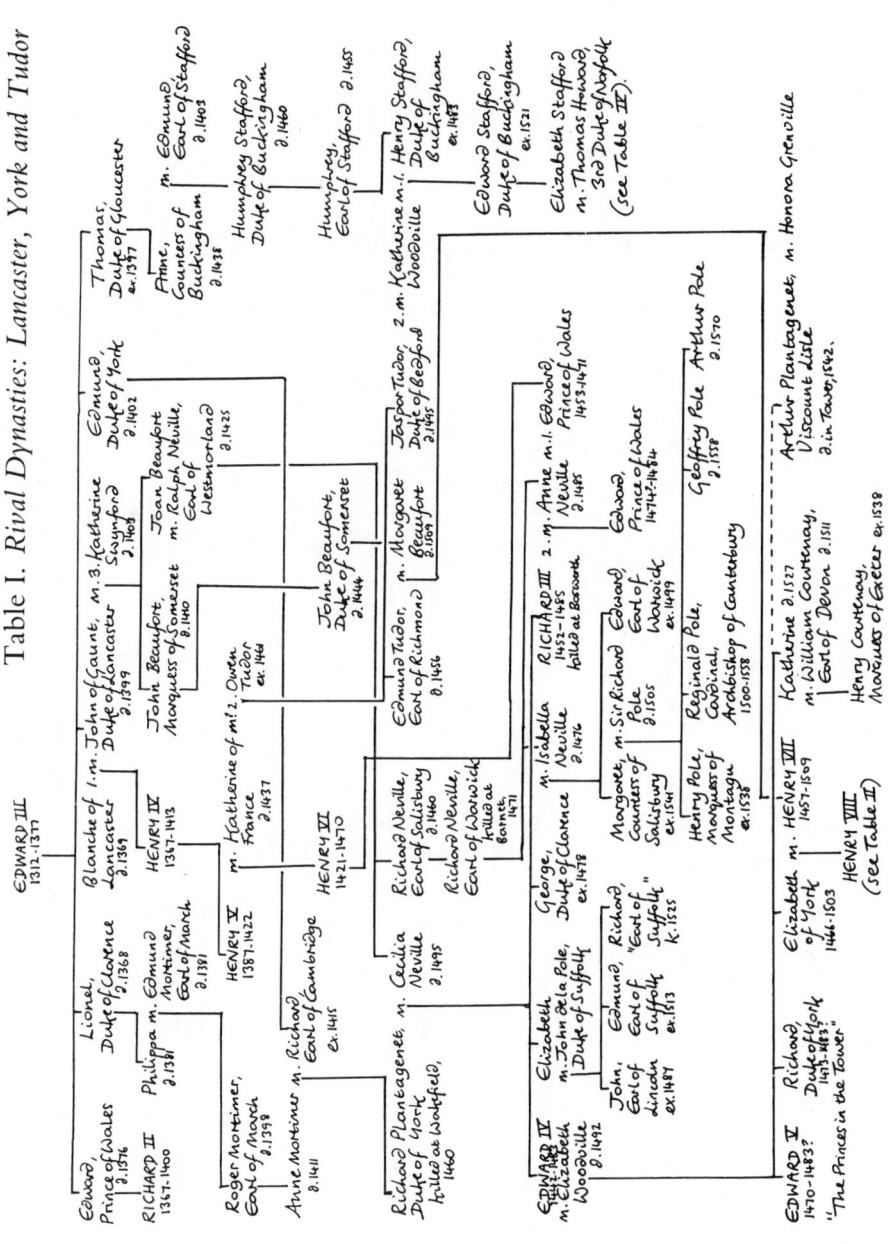

Table II. The Tudors

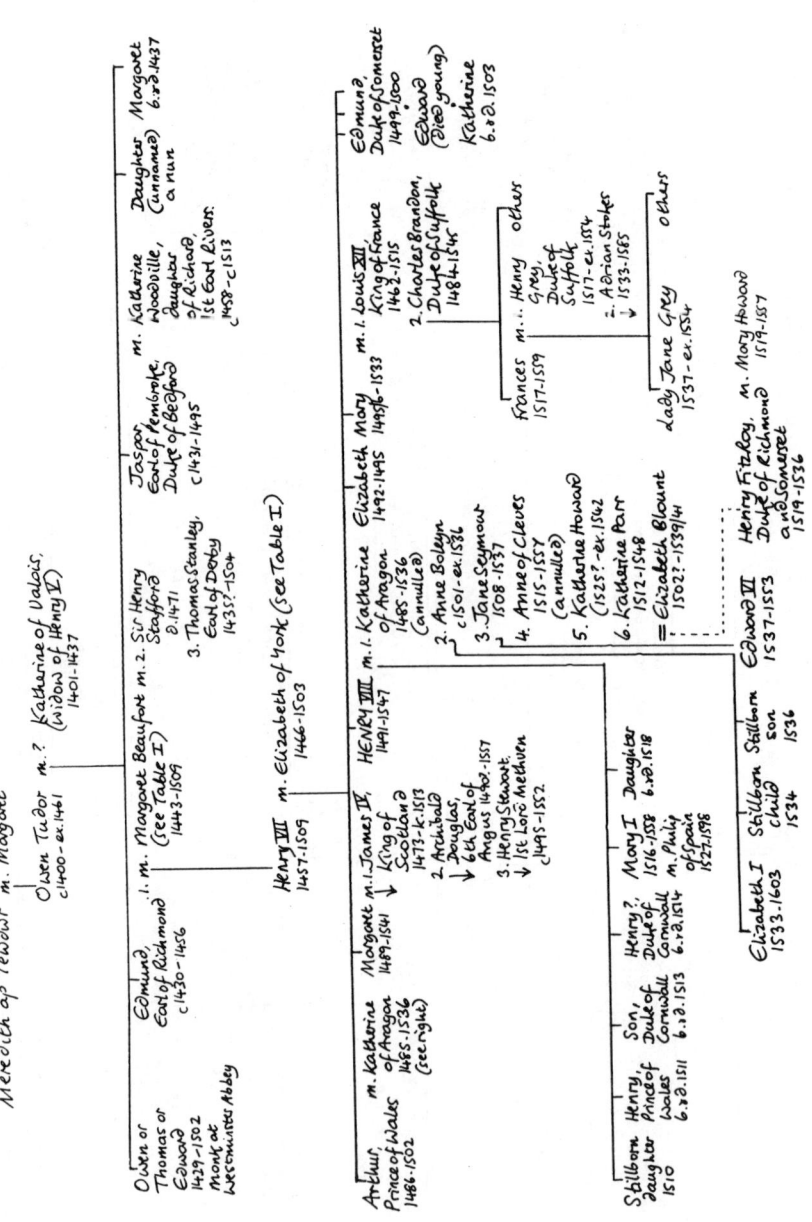

Table III. The European Royal Dynasties

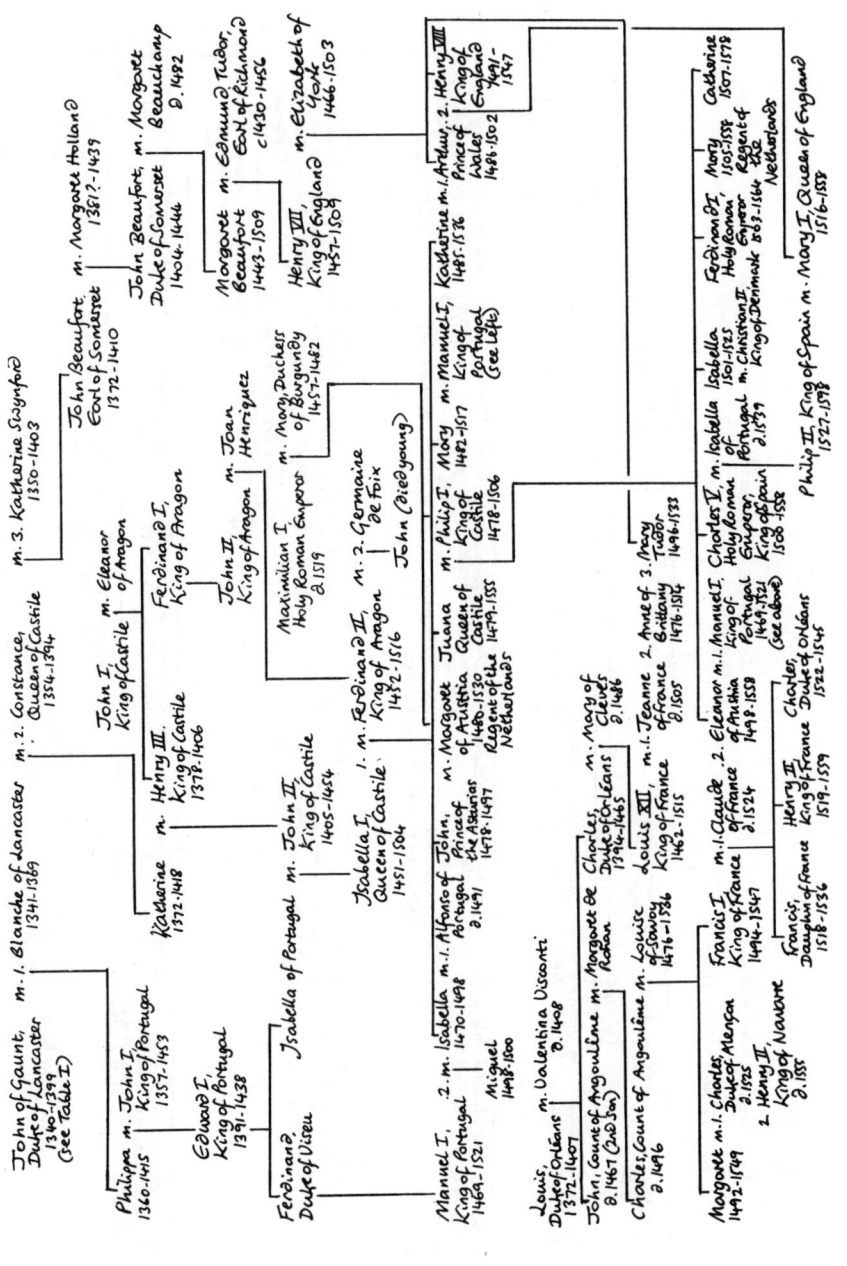

Table IV. The Boleyn Family

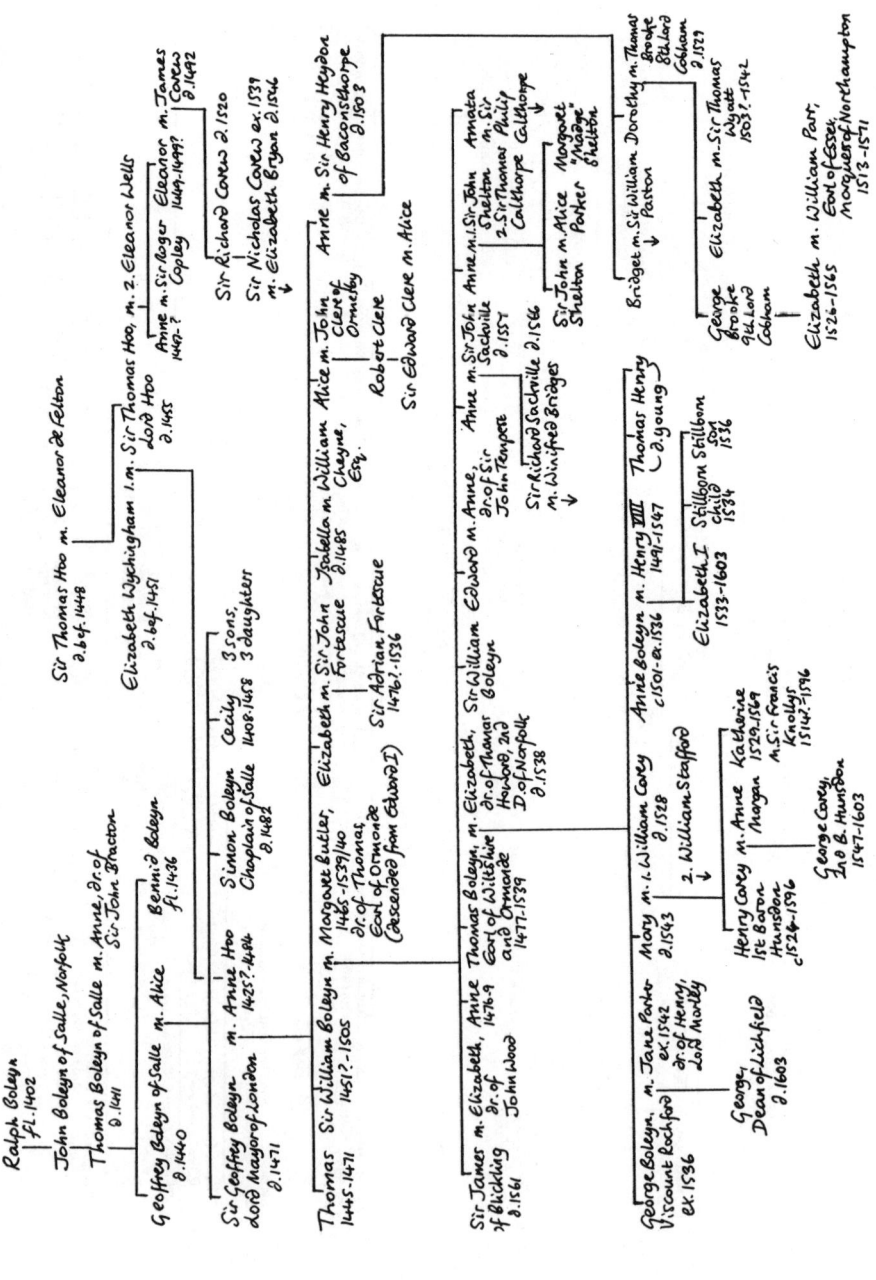

Table V. *The Seymour Family*

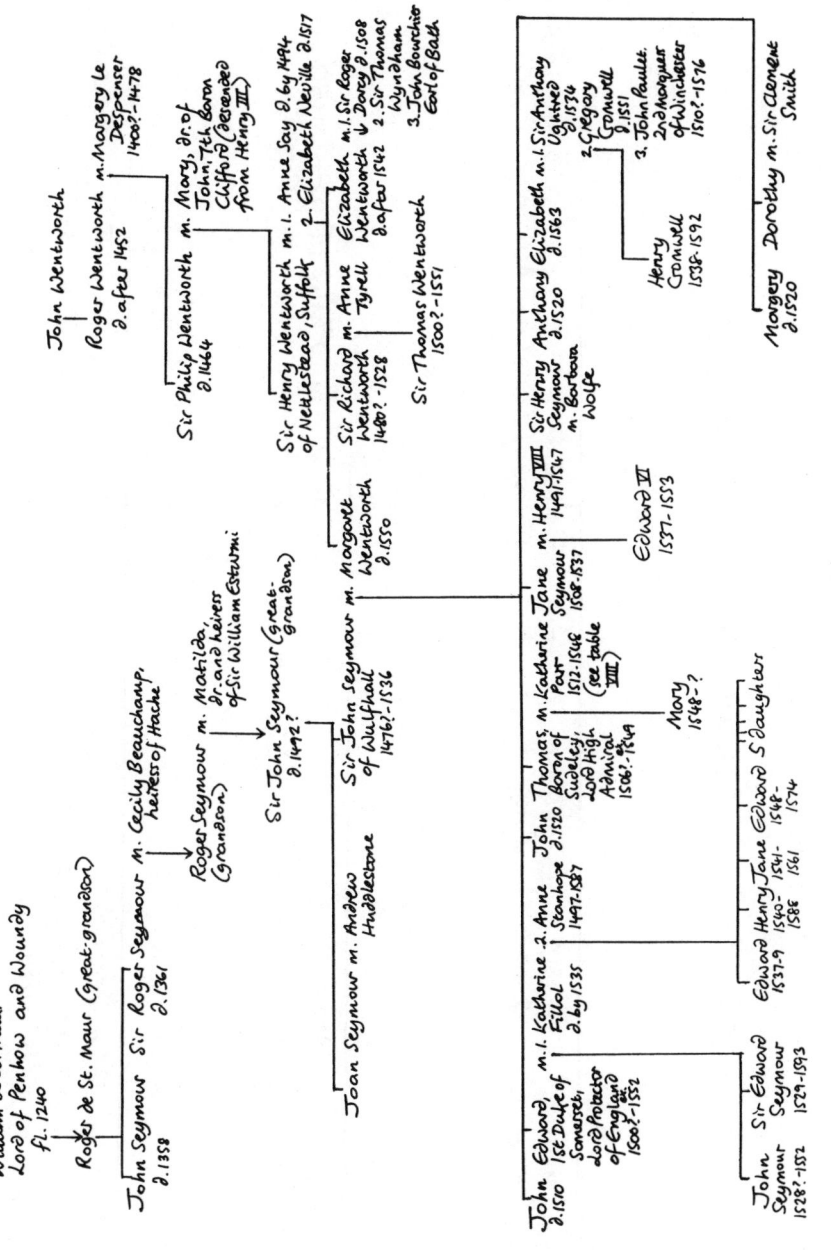

Table VI. The Ducal House of Cleves

John I,
Duke of Cleves
1419-1481
m. Elizabeth of Burgundy-Nevers
∂.1483

John II,
Duke of Cleves
1458-1521
m. Matilda
of Hesse

Adolf
∂.1498

Engelbert
∂.1506

Dietrich

Philip,
Bishop of Rivers and Autun
∂.1505

Mary m. Adolf of Jülich-Berg
∂.1473

John III,
Duke of Cleves
1490-1539
m. Mary of
Jülich-Berg-Ravensburg
∂.1543

Adolf
1498-1505

Anne
∂.1567

m. Philip II of Waldeck-Eisenberg
∂.1539

Sybilla
1514-1554
m. John Frederick,
Elector of Saxony
1503-1554

Anne of Cleves
1515-1557
m. Henry VIII
1491-1547

William III,
Duke of Cleves
1516-1592

Amelia
1517-1586

Table VII. *The Howards*

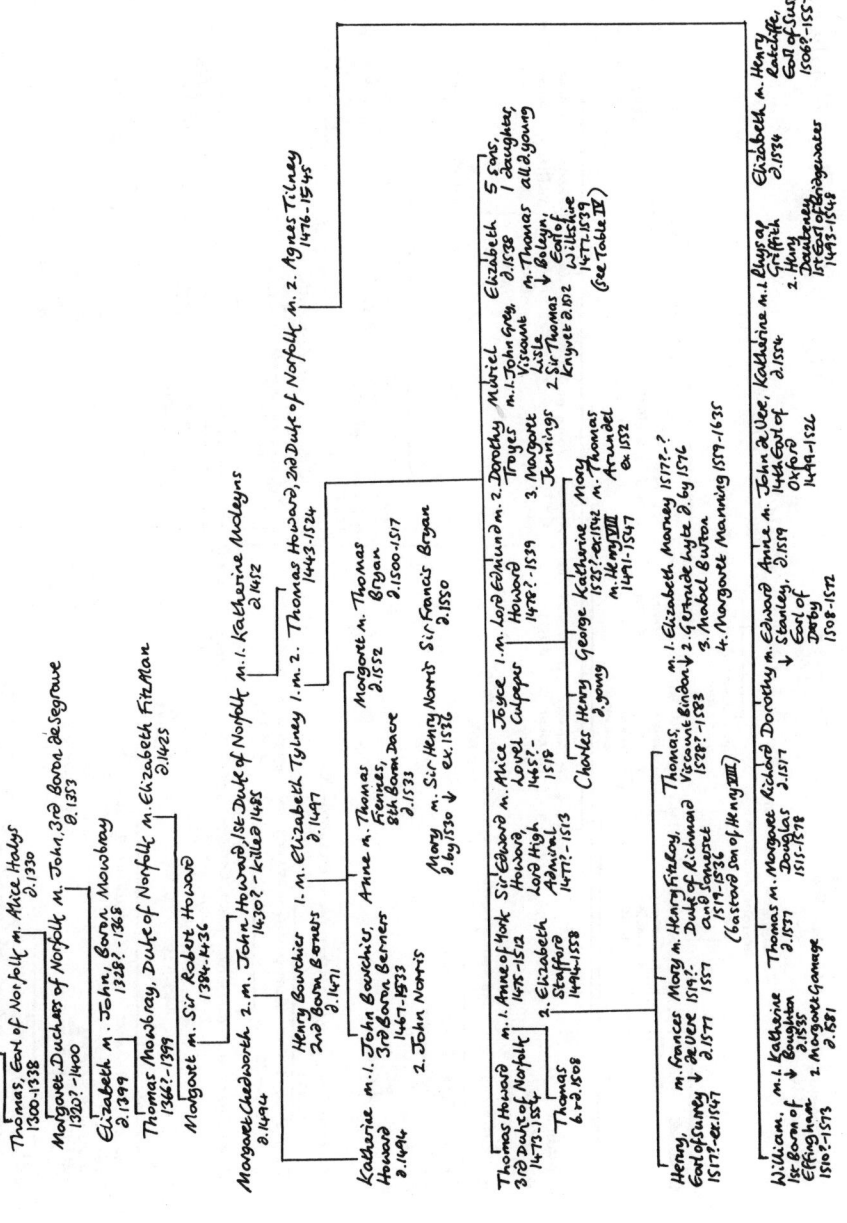

Table VIII. The Parr Family

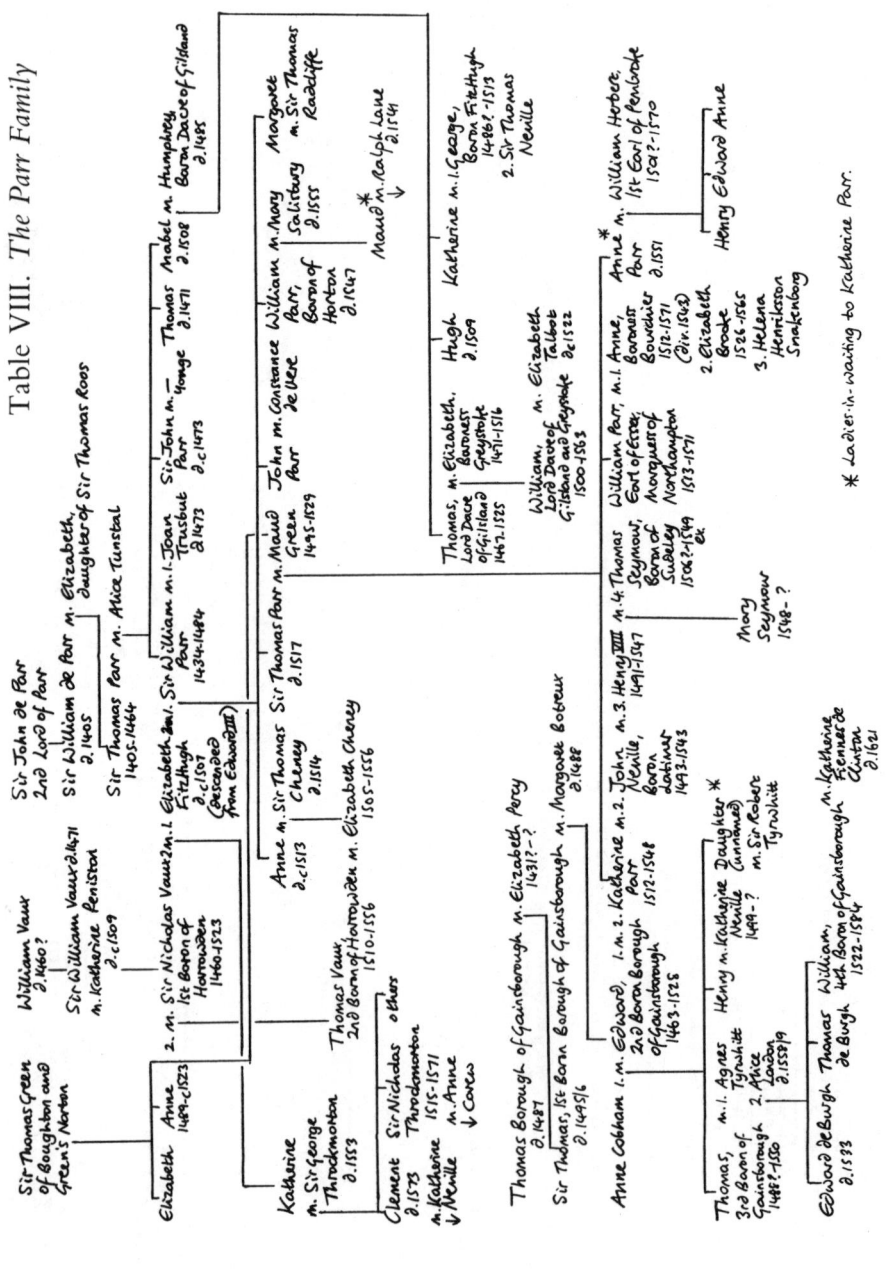

Index

Index

Index

The illustrations appearing between pages 308 and 309 are reproduced by kind permission of the following:

1. Wax death-mask of Henry VII, 1509, Norman Undercroft Museum, Westminster Abbey (by courtesy of the Dean and Chapter of Westminster). **2.** *Elizabeth of York*, date and artist unknown, the Hamilton Collection at Lennoxlove. **3.** *Isabella of Castile, c.* 1501, artist unknown, Royal Collection (by gracious permission of Her Majesty the Queen). **4.** *Ferdinand of Aragon, c.* 1501, artist unknown, Royal Collection (by gracious permission of Her Majesty the Queen). **5.** *Katherine of Aragon,* 1505, by Miguel Sittow, Kunsthistorisches Museum, Vienna. **6.** *Katherine of Aragon, c.* 1525–6, by Lucas Hornebolte, miniature in the collection of the Duke of Buccleuch and Queensberry KT (by courtesy of the Trustees of the Victoria and Albert Museum). **7.** *Henry VIII, c.* 1509–20, painted terracotta bust, probably by Pietro Torrigiano, the Metropolitan Museum of Art, New York (Fletcher Fund 1944, All Rights Reserved). **8.** Henry VIII jousting before Katherine of Aragon in 1511, from *The Great Tournament Roll of Westminster* (© the College of Arms). **9.** *Thomas Wolsey, Cardinal of York,* date unknown, by Jacques le Boucq, Bibliothèque d'Arras (photo Giraudon). **10.** *Francis I, c.* 1525–8, by Jean Clouet, Louvre Museum, Paris (photo Giraudon). **11.** Letter from Henry VIII to Anne Boleyn, *c.* September 1528, Vatican Library. **12.** *Anne Boleyn,* date and artist unknown, Hever Castle, Kent (photo Woodmansterne). **13.** *Anne Boleyn,* late sixteenth century, artist unknown, private collection. **14.** *Thomas Boleyn, Earl of Wiltshire and Ormond, c.* 1532, drawing by Holbein, Windsor Castle Library (© 1990 Her Majesty the Queen). **15.** *Thomas Howard, Duke of Norfolk, c.* 1538, by Holbein, Royal Collection (by gracious permission of Her Majesty the Queen). **16.** *Pope Clement VII with the Emperor Charles V,* 1530, by Giorgio Vasari, Palazzo Vecchio, Florence (photo Scala). **17.** Petition from the English nobility to the Pope, 13 July 1530, Vatican Library (photo Scala). **18.** *Henry VIII,* 1536–7, by Holbein, Thyssen-Bornemisza Collection, Lugano (photo Bridgeman Art Library). **19.** *Thomas Cranmer,* 1546, by Gerlach Flicke, National Portrait Gallery, London. **20.** *Thomas Cromwell,* date unknown, after Holbein's lost original *c.* 1533–4 (© Frick Collection, New York). **21.** *Jane Seymour,* 1536–7, by or after Holbein, Mauritshuis Museum, The Hague (photo Scala). **22.** *Edward VI as a Child,* 1539, by Holbein, National Gallery of Art, Washington, D.C., Andrew W. Mellon Collection. **23.** Drawing of Whitehall Palace, *c.* 1555, by Anthony van Wyngaerde, Ashmolean Museum, Oxford. **24.** *The Family of Henry VIII, c.* 1543, artist unknown, Hampton Court Palace, Royal Collection (by gracious permission of Her Majesty the Queen). **25.** *Anne of Cleves, c.* 1540, attributed to B. Bruyn the Elder (by courtesy of the President and Fellows of St John Baptist College, Oxford). **26.** *Katherine Howard, c.* 1540–41, miniature by Holbein, Royal Collection (by gracious permission of Her Majesty the Queen). **27.** *Henry VIII,* date unknown, after Holbein, Hever Castle (photo Woodmansterne). **28.** *Katherine Parr,* 1545, by William Scrots, National Portrait Gallery, London. **29.** *Elizabeth I as a girl, c.* 1546, artist unknown, Royal Collection (by gracious permission of Her Majesty the Queen). **30.** *Thomas Seymour,* late sixteenth century, possibly after William Scrots, National Portrait Gallery, London.